UNION COUNTY PENNSYLVANIA

A Celebration of History

BY

Charles M. Snyder

AND

John W. Downie   *Lois S. Kalp*   *Jeannette Lasansky*

SPONSORED BY

Bucknell University President's Office
Buffalo Valley Telephone Company, Division of CEI
Paul E. Crow and Geneva Sanders Crow Trust
Judith and Raymond Goehring Jr.
John D. and Sue A. Griffith
JPM Company
Mary Ruhl Maher
Mifflinburg Bank & Trust
New Berlin Heritage Association
Playworld Systems, Inc.
Lois Reichenbauch
Thomas R. Rippon
Ethel Dieffenderfer Ruhl
Helen P. Strunk and Robert K. Strunk II
Union County Historical Society's Board of Directors
and A Friend

PUBLISHED BY THE UNION COUNTY HISTORICAL SOCIETY, LEWISBURG, PENNSYLVANIA

Editor: Jean M. Ruhl
Design: Jeannette Lasansky and Adrienne Beaver
Printer: Paulhamus Litho, Montoursville, PA

Library of Congress Cataloging-in-Publication-Data

Snyder, Charles McCool.
    Union County, Pennsylvania : a celebration of history /
    by Charles M. Snyder and John W. Downie, Lois S. Kalp
        p.cm.
    Revised and updated version of 1976 ed.
    Includes bibliographical references and index.
    ISBN 0-917127-13-7
    1. Union County (Pa.) -- History. I. Downie, John W.
    II. Kalp, Lois. III. Title.

F157.U5 S57 2000
974.8'48--dc21   00-038187

PAGE 3: Historian and author Charles McCool Snyder alights from a Mifflinburg buggy in 1984. Photo by the Terry Wild Studio, courtesy of the Oral Traditions Project.

PAGE 4: The driver with his horse and buggy is headed into Lewisburg on River Road, East Buffalo Township c. 1910. In the background is the Halfpenny/Gundy house called "Lan Avon." From the collection of the Union County Historical Society, #82.4.3.23.

ACKNOWLEDGMENTS

Union County, Pennsylvania was originally sponsored by the Union County Bicentennial Commission. Quickly sold out but still in demand, it was revised by the Union County Historical Society in 1999. As Charles M. Snyder, the primary author, noted in 1976, "The research has been done in the courthouses, historical societies, archives, and libraries as well as in offices, homes, schools, and churches of the area. It has also included conversations with hundreds of residents — an experience which has been both inspirational and joyful to the writer. There are so many people to thank that it is difficult to single them out individually."

Assistance was acknowledged by neighborhoods. In Gregg, White Deer, and Kelly Townships: Marion and Harold Danowsky, B.B. Huntington, Delia Meckly Sanders, Arna Mae Dersham, Janet Soars Platt, Earl Koch, Martha Ranck Farley, and Heather Clewell; in Lewisburg: Elizabeth Hitchcock, Elizabeth Bates Hoffman, Ethel and George Ruhl, Baker Kohler, Bessie Deans, Edith Cummings Wilson, Barbara Winslow, Mrs. W.G. Painter, Maria Spyker, Merrill W. Linn, D. Paul Souders, Ruth Mohn Baker, Thomas R. Deans, Warren Stapleton, and Abbott Bucher; in East Buffalo and Buffalo Townships: Peggy Gundy Ulmer, Mrs. C.B. Comstock, Mary Ruhl Maher, Dorothy Johnson, Mary Alice Dietrich, Pauline Poggi, Millard Boyer, and Mrs. Elmer Lohr; in Mifflinburg: Cloyd Frederick, James Brawn, Nevin Barnitz, Doris Earnest, Carol Bohn, Sandra Doebler Haire, Robert Linke, Harry Stuck, C. Marlyn Steese, Julia Steadman Francis, Katherine Roush, Marie and Harold M. Musser, Mary Koons, Jessie Sankey, Dorothy and Earnest Ruhl, R.R. Finkel, Joseph Foster, W. Earl Thomas, Mrs. Frank P. Boyer, Robert J. Smith, and Flora and Reuel Mitchell; in New Berlin, and Limestone and Union Townships: Ray and Roy Sauers, Randall Chambers, Charles Beaver, Helen Eberhart, Joan Maurer, Stewart Oldt, Louis A. Eaton, Harry Nagle, Murray Kline and Elizabeth Vance Hull; in Hartley and Lewis Townships: the August K. Bauers, George Dersham, the Francis Keisters, Lewis Dorman, Jeanne Sampsell, Asher J. Harter, and Charles M. Showalter; in West Buffalo Township: Luther B. Grove, Mary and Warren Dieffenderfer, and Homer J. Foust; and from other sources: Raymond B. Winter, Earnest Geiswite, Hilda Zimmerman Jeffries, and Charles F. Snyder.

Snyder said of Nada Gray, chairperson of the Union County Bicentennial Commission, "Without her decision

Kemmerer, Robert Linke, Mary Belle Lontz, Bob Lynch, Marie Purnell Musser, Tom Musser, Mary Ruhl Maher, Clyde Peeling, Ethel D. Ruhl, Jeanne Sampsell, Joannah Skucek, Gary W. Slear, Gary Sojka, Jim Walter, Hertha Wehr, William B. Weist, John and Martha Zeller, and Ruth Wehr Zimmerman. Jean M. Ruhl was the copy editor. Jim Walter checked all endnote references, entered in Jean Ruhl's editorial changes, and did extensive new photography for the project. The chapter on architecture written by Elizabeth Hitchcock has not been reprinted here, as the Union County Historical Society is currently planning on a book that will focus solely on that subject. The chapter on James Aiken also was eliminated in this reprint to avoid focusing on any one individual when so many distinguished county residents are equally worthy of such singular attention. An extensive history of the county's role in World War I, also written by Charles M. Snyder but published elsewhere, has been added to the volume. Also, Ted Strosser compiled an appendix on county architecture, while Jim Walter updated the other appendices. To bring the text up to date, Jeannette Lasansky wrote a new last chapter, aided by Carol Manbeck, research assistant, and Bill Deitrick, Pat Longley, David Goehring, Gloria Maize, and Tony Shively.

The new edition of *Union County, Pennsylvania* was underwritten with major financial support by the New Berlin Heritage Association, Mifflinburg Bank & Trust Company, Ethel D. Ruhl, Mary R. Maher, Thomas R. Rippon, JPM Company, Judith and Raymond Goehring Jr., Playworld, Inc., Bucknell University/President's Office, John D. and Sue A. Griffith, the Paul E. and Geneva Sanders Crow Trust, Lois Reichenbauch, Helen and Robert K. Strunk II, the current Union County Historical Society Board of Directors, Buffalo Valley Telephone Company, and an anonymous friend. Citizens' Electric Company underwrote the printing of an advertising flyer, and an anonymous giver provided support for the new photography. The book was designed by Jeannette Lasansky with technical support from Adrienne Beaver.

This has been a real team effort.

three years ago [1973] to make the Bicentennial a meaningful and pleasurable experience for the county, and her boundless enthusiasm and perseverance in moving the project through the months which followed, this history would not have materialized." Indeed, in a basement room in the Union County courthouse, about three dozen individuals of all ages and backgrounds — some new to the county, some from multi-generation families — came together in November 1973 to learn that through Gray's efforts funding had been secured from the Union County commissioners to embark upon a number of projects of significance in celebration of the nation's bicentennial in 1976. The audience rose to the challenge; and within short order, projects such as school programming, the Oral Traditions Project, and research for a new and up-to-date history book were begun.

Union County, Pennsylvania, the basic text on the county's history after John Blair Linn's *Annals of Buffalo Valley* (1877), has been out of print for two decades, and its original printer's plates destroyed. The Union County Historical Society decided to reprint the bicentennial effort, bring its last chapter up to 2000, and make any necessary corrections or additions to the text. Enrolled in this effort under the direction of Jeannette Lasansky were readers Bronwen Anderson, Vincent Barsch, Carl R. Catherman, Betty Cook, Paul Ernst, Sally Farmer, Thomas Finsterbush, Karin Fullam, Nada R. Gray, Lois Huffines, Harvey W. Ilgen, Clara Ellen and Larry

FOREWORD

Union is one of Pennsylvania's smallest counties, encompassing a bare 258 square miles and containing a population of 36,176, according to the 1990 federal census. This includes 3,550 college students and 5,706 inmates at the federal penitentiary complexes at Lewisburg and Allenwood. Few of its residents have held high political office, and few of its names have appeared in the columns of *Who's Who in America.*

Yet the historical significance of this beautiful valley and its rim of mountains is worthy of documentation. Situated athwart the frontier during the bloody struggles for the interior of the American continent during the French and Indian as well as the Revolutionary Wars, it was the homeland of intrepid Scots-Irish and German frontiersmen and a pathway for others moving northward and westward.

Its fertile land, surely deserving William Penn's evaluation that "the country itself, its soil, air, water, seasons and produce, both natural and artificial, is not to be despised," provided surpluses for the agriculturist, and its extensive forests yielded enormous harvests of timber. Together, the farms and forests opened opportunities for the craftsmen and shopkeepers, and, in time, for manufacturers of boats, farm implements, buggies, sleighs, and furniture. Transportation kept pace with these developments—the sturdy wagons and primitive arks of the earlier years yielding successively to canals, railroads, and trucking systems on interstate expressways.

The county was a microcosm of the political and social currents which swept the nation. A hotbed of Jeffersonian Republicanism at the outset and of Antimasonry in the Jacksonian era, the county saw the "Free Soil" issue give rise to Republicanism prior to the Civil War, the impact of which endured for more than a century.

Union County mirrored the great changes in American education. Reluctant to accept the principle of public education at first, it later maintained more than 70 one-room schools, several private academies, and two collegiate institutions. Its churches reflected the heritage of its settlers, and the enthusiastic response of its German-speaking element to the ministry of Jacob Albrecht (Albright) was instrumental in transforming a small band of disciples into the Evangelical Church.

Lacking deposits of coal and oil in its subsoil, the county's growth was gradual, permitting new buildings to mingle with the old. Thus the physical heritage of generations gone by endures in wood and masonry, preserving more than a century-old charm seldom equaled elsewhere.

TABLE OF CONTENTS

CHAPTER 1

A LAND OF PROMISE

The region of Pennsylvania which would be designated as Union County was shaped in geologic ages by the alternating lifting and sinking of the Appalachian land mass. In the course of time the mountains rose and the surface was eventually covered with vegetation. In the Pleistocene period variations in temperature subjected the area to massive run-offs from melting glaciers blanketing New York and northern Pennsylvania. These meltwaters gouged out sluice ways for the Susquehanna River and its tributaries. During these hectic periods of alternating freezing and thawing, the hills were eroded and the bottom lands covered with alluvial deposits. Migrating animals moved in and out of the region according to variations in temperature.

When the first humans arrived as well as where they came from and how they got here are subjects of considerable debate. When William Penn departed from England in 1682, the domain that had been granted to him was already populated by American Indians. The Indians' ancestors had crossed the land bridge from Asia to North America some 11,200 years earlier, populated the western part of the continent, and begun moving eastward as the glaciers retreated toward the Arctic Circle.

Nevertheless, evidence found recently near Penns Creek strongly suggests human presence at least 13,000 years ago.[1] Archaeological excavations elsewhere in Pennsylvania also indicate human activity before the aboriginal inhabitants of the West arrived here. Thus, a new theory proposes that the first inhabitants of the region came from Europe, traveling by boat along a frozen sub-Arctic shoreline during a period of extensive glaciation.[2] Perhaps these earliest arrivals were conquered or assimilated by the western invaders. Perhaps they existed only in relatively small bands who died out as a result of natural causes.

In any case, the original inhabitants were supplanted by the American Indians, who acquired the science of agriculture, settled down, and made the region their home. Although there was plenty of game, the human population remained sparse, the rigors of climate and disease limiting growth.

When Europeans penetrated the area they encountered the Delaware Indians, a branch of the Algonkian nation. The Delawares were friendly and eager to exchange furs for trading goods, and their relations with William Penn and his deputies remained cordial for a half century — a record unequaled among the other North American colonies.

In the eighteenth century Pennsylvania's Indians were no match for the aggressive Iroquois of New York, especially once the latter were armed with the deadly weapons of the Europeans. The Delawares were reduced to a tributary relationship and labeled a nation of women. The Iroquois further humiliated the Delawares by trading away their lands to the Proprietors of Pennsylvania and by foisting an overlord upon them to guarantee good behavior. The Iroquois' emissary was the famous Shikellamy, an Oneida chief, who set up headquarters on the Susquehanna below Milton, presumably on the west side of the river, about 1728.[3] A few years later he moved to the forks of the Susquehanna, where he remained until his death in 1749. By mid-century the Delawares and Shawnees, a sub-division of the former, were withdrawing to western Pennsylvania and Ohio, and, resentful of their shabby treatment, they cast their lot with the French.

Meanwhile, Buffalo Valley [hereinafter used interchangeably with Union County] was on the fringe of a population explosion in the Berks/ Lancaster area, where some thousands of Scots-Irish and Germans had settled after their passage from their homelands to the New World via the port of Philadelphia. By 1750 they were seeking lebensraum in the Schuylkill and lower Susquehanna valleys — beneficiaries of the liberal land policy of the colony's founder. Five pounds and an annual land tax (quitrent) of one shilling was sufficient to acquire and retain 100 acres. Many who lacked the purchase price simply staked out a "settlement" or "tomahawk right" without the formality of a deed. They were seldom disturbed by the law, nor were they distressed at the thought of crossing a treaty line and trespassing upon Indian land.

In 1754 the Proprietors bargained with the Iroquois for a huge tract on the west side of the Susquehanna extending northwestward from the mouth of Penns Creek and crossing Dry Valley east of New Berlin and the Mifflinburg/Hartleton road near Ray's Church, thus opening all of present-day Snyder County and the southwestern corner of Union

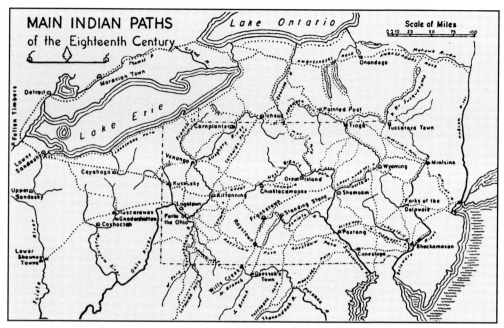

The map traces the major Indian paths in Pennsylvania in the 18th century. From Philip S. Klein and Ari Hoogenboom, *A History of Pennsylvania*, 2nd. ed. (State College: Penn State University Press, 1980), 200.

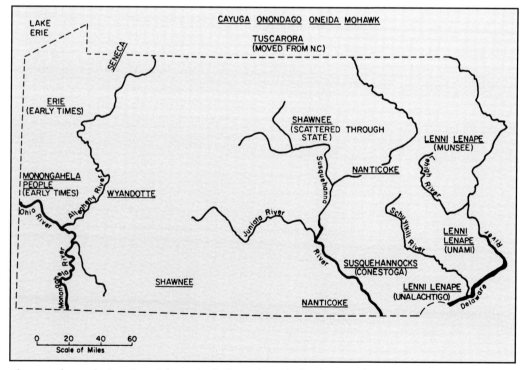

The map shows the location of the major Indian tribes which inhabited the Pennsylvania region prior to the "Walking Purchase" of 1737. From Philip S. Klein and Ari Hoogenboom, *A History of Pennsylvania*, 2nd. ed. (State College: Penn State University Press, 1980), 7.

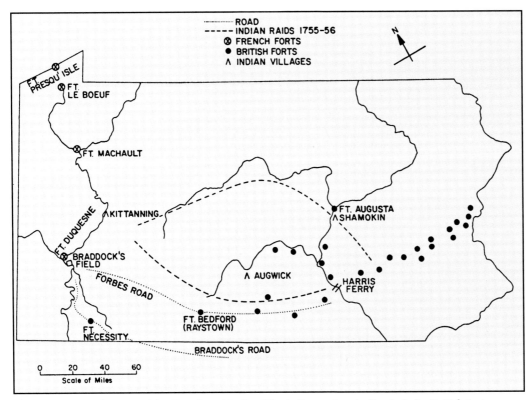

The map depicts the sites of the French and Indian War in Pennsylvania. Symbols for British forts between the Delaware River and Fort Bedford show the major Pennsylvania defense posts after the Indian raids of 1755-1756. From Philip S. Klein and Ari Hoogenboom, *A History of Pennsylvania*, 2nd. ed. (State College: Penn State University Press, 1980), 71.

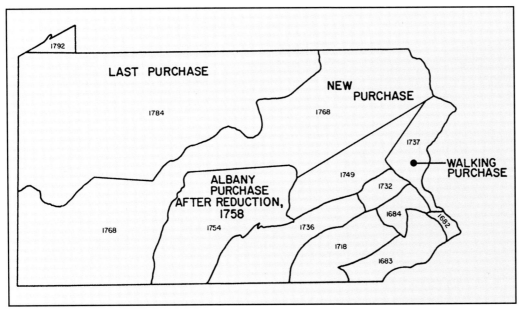

The map outlines the major purchases of land by the Pennsylvania Proprietors from the Indians. From Philip S. Klein and Ari Hoogenboom, *A History of Pennsylvania*, 2nd. ed. (State College: Penn State University Press, 1980), 60.

County. Pioneers were soon streaming into this region and beyond it as well, to the north side of Penns Creek.

By the summer of 1755 there were about 25 families in this region. On July 9 of that year General Edward Braddock, commanding a combined British and American army against the French at Fort Duquesne, marched into an ambush a short distance from his objective. His army was routed and he was mortally wounded. Ignited by the victory, the disgruntled Indians came out of the wilderness to assault the settlements along the exposed frontier.

They struck first in Buffalo Valley. Emerging from the forest at the clearing of Jean Jacques LeRoy (Jacob King) near the head of Switzer Run, they tomahawked LeRoy, shot a neighbor who happened to be there, and took young Marie and her brother into captivity. The LeRoys had emigrated from the Canton Berne in Switzerland three years earlier, arriving in Philadelphia aboard the Phoenix after a passage from Rotterdam. They were members of the plain sect called Amish.[4]

Proceeding down Buffalo Valley, the Indians stopped at the cabin of Sebastian Leininger, where they killed Leininger and his son, and carried off his daughters Barbara, age twelve, and Regina, about ten. Mrs. Leininger was on an errand and thus was spared. Halting at other clearings, the Indians continued their bloody work and killed or captured the families of Jacob Brylinger and Peter Lick. Then turning about, they reentered the forest and began the long march westward.

A plaintive post-mortem from survivors provides a graphic resume of the tragedy — remembered to this day as the Penns Creek massacre:

We, the subscribers, living near the mouth of Penns Creek, on the west side of the Susquehanna, humbly show that, on or about 16th October, the enemy came down upon said creek, killed and scalped, and carried away all the men, women and children, amounting to twenty-five in number, and wounded one man, who, fortunately, made his escape, and brought us the news. Whereupon the subscribers went out and buried the dead. We found thirteen, who were men and elderly women, and one child, two weeks old; the rest being young women and children, we suppose to be carried away. The house (where we supposed they finished their murder) we found burned up, the man of it, named Jacob King, a Swisser, lying just by it. He lay on his back, barbarously burned, and two tomahawks sticking in his forehead; one of them newly marked W. D. . . . The terror of which has drove away all the inhabitants except us. We are willing to stay, and defend the land, but need arms, ammunition, and assistance. Without them, we must flee, and leave the country to the mercy of the enemy.[5]

There were seventeen signers.

John Harris at Harrisburg learned of the massacre a few days later and recruited a posse to investigate. On the return trip the posse was attacked as they forded Penns Creek near the site of Selinsgrove, sustaining several casualties in dead and wounded.

The Indians, traveling in small war parties, subsequently moved eastward from the Susquehanna and were soon attacking settlements along Swatara Creek in the Berks/Lebanon area. During the panic the remaining settlers at the mouth of Penns Creek abandoned their cabins while the Indians in their village of Shamokin (Sunbury), fearful of reprisals from both their tribesmen and the whites, burned their houses, and sought safety farther up the river. The frontier was now deserted.

In fact, the first settlement and its removal had occurred so quickly that the people who entered Buffalo Valley a few years later were almost unaware of its existence. When John Blair Linn began his research for *The Annals of Buffalo Valley*, he had expected to begin his narrative with the land grants to the officers in General Bouquet's expedition against the Indians in the Ohio country in 1768; instead, he came upon a reference to Barbara Leininger and Marie LeRoy in the *Pennsylvania Archives* in the form of a deposition given by the girls after their escape from their captors and safe return to Philadelphia in 1769. With this account of their hardships as a start, Linn reconstructed the Penns Creek massacre but was unaware of its equally interesting sequel — the return from captivity of Barbara's younger sister, Regina, which was to become a cherished part of the folklore of southeastern and central Pennsylvania.

THE
NARRATIVE
OF
MARIE LEROY
AND
BARBARA LEININGER
WHO SPENT
THREE AND ONE-HALF YEARS
AS PRISONERS AMONG THE INDIANS
AND ARRIVED SAFELY IN THIS CITY ON
THE SIXTH OF MAY
WRITTEN AND PRINTED AS DICTATED
BY THEM
PHILADELPHIA
PRINTED AND FOR SALE IN THE
GERMAN PRINTING OFFICE
SIX PENCE PER COPY
MDCCLIX[6]

The depositions and a substantially enlarged version of the three-and-a-half-year captivity, published as a pamphlet later the same year, was a tale of hardship and fortitude.

After two days of killing and pillaging, the Indians gathered to divide the spoils consisting of fifteen scalps, fourteen horses, and ten prisoners — namely one man, one woman, five girls, and three boys. Barbara and Marie were given to the same master, Regina to another. Regina is not mentioned again in the account. They lived at Kittanning in western Pennsylvania for a year.

We had to tan leather, to make shoes (moccasins), to clear land, to plant corn, to cut down trees, and build huts, to wash and cook. The want of provisions, however caused us the greatest sufferings . . . We had neither lard nor salt, and sometimes we were forced to live on acorns, roots, grass and bark. There was nothing in the world to make this new sort of food palatable excepting hunger itself. [7]

The group was forced to flee from Kittanning in September of 1756 by the advance of Colonel John Armstrong's Corps upon the Indian settlement, when they returned they found it burned to the ground. An Englishman and an Englishwoman who had attempted to escape during the retreat were tortured and executed in the girls' sight. They were taken to Fort Duquesne for two months, where "we could again eat bread,"[8] and were then moved to Kaskaskunk near the Ohio border. When the English defeated the French and Indians at Ligonier in the summer of 1758, the group was moved farther west to Muskingum in Ohio.

Here in February of 1759 Barbara and Marie decided to make a break for freedom in the company of two English captives, Owen Gibson and David Breckenreach. They found a raft to navigate the Muskingum River and built another to cross the Ohio; but having lost flint and steel, they spent the last four nights of their month-long ordeal without fire amidst rain and snow. Finally they reached Fort Pitt (Duquesne), now in the hands of the English, wet, cold, and hungry but at last free and among friends. The girls were taken in wagons to Harris' Ferry and went from there on foot to Philadelphia. Neither girl seems to have ever returned to Buffalo Valley, and the deposition and pamphlet appear to have attracted only momentary attention.

In February 1765 the Reverend Heinrich Melchoir Muhlenberg, patriarch of the Evangelical Lutheran Church in America, learned of the restoration of a mother and daughter at Carlisle on December 31, 1764, after the latter had returned almost miraculously from a nine-years captivity among the Indians. Seeing divine intervention in the reunion, he reported the story to the church fathers in Halle, Germany. According to Muhlenberg, a widow and her adult daughter, then living a few miles west of Reading, came to see him with the following revelation.

The widow was born in Reutlingen in the Duchy of Wuertemburg, and her husband near Tuebingen. They migrated to America and settled in the interior of Pennsylvania about 100 miles from Philadelphia. On October 16, 1755, shortly after Braddock's defeat, Indians invaded their remote settlement, killed her husband and son, and carried off their two daughters, Barbara, age twelve, and Regina, going on ten. The mother and another son were saved because they were at a mill some distance from home. Returning to find everything in ruins, they fled to Berks County.

Meanwhile, the two daughters were taken 400 miles into the wilderness and separated one from the other. Regina traveled much of the way on foot with a small child (a captive also) strapped to her back. She was placed in the custody of an old Indian squaw who worked her unsparingly through nine years of servitude. Through terrible calamity, the exhausting journey, and the years of privation, however, "the passages of Scripture and the sacred hymns, which she had learned from her parents, became her chief delight."[9] She had prayed numberless times under the trees with the child by her side.

During 1763 the Indians had been put to flight by General Bouquet and compelled to sue for peace. General Bouquet had assembled the captives and taken them to Fort Pitt and thence to Carlisle; notices had appeared in the papers that relatives should be on hand to claim their own:

Accordingly, the above-mentioned poor widow with her only yet remaining son journeyed thither. She asked the Commissioners for her little daughter Regina, describing her as she was when but nine or ten years of age. But she could find no one resembling her among the crowd. For Regina was now more than eighteen years of age, fully grown to womanhood, stout, with the bearing of an Indian, and speaking the language of the savages. The Commissioners asked the mother whether she could not designate some characteristic by which her daughter might be known. The mother replied in German that her daughter frequently sang the hymns, "Jesus I Love Evermore," and "Alone, and yet not Alone am I in my Dread Solitude." Hardly had the widow said this when Regina sprang from among the others and repeated the Creed, the Lord's Prayer, and the hymns named. Finally, the mother and daughter fell upon each other's neck shedding tears of joy.

The tombstone of George Etzweiler on Brouse Road, Limestone Township, notes that he was killed on May 26, 1780, by Indians and features carved crossed tomahawks above his name. Photo by Jim Walter.

After they had finished their story, the widow asked Muhlenberg whether he could provide them with a German Bible and hymn book, and he was able to gratify her, a shipment having only recently arrived from Germany. Opening the former, he found that Regina could still read from it, even though she could no longer express herself in the language. Closing his letter, Muhlenberg observed that Regina's experience proved the necessity of implanting true Christian doctrine in the hearts of the young. Were Martin Luther alive, he added, he would rejoice that a Reutlinger girl (a free city which had supported Luther) had maintained its spiritual life in this far distant wilderness. It should be noted that while Muhlenberg identified the family with Reutlingen, he never mentioned the family name. Thus, when his letter was published 75 years later, it became the source of both a mystery and a controversy.

As the touching story was passed around by word of mouth in the Swatara and Tulpehocken country — the old 1754 frontier — it became even more dramatic. In this version the mother not only mentioned the titles of the old hymns, she sang one or more of the verses and thereby elicited the tender and stirring response from the daughter:

Allein und doch nicht ganz alleine,
Bin ich in meiner Einsamkeit,
Dann wenn ich ganz verlassen scheine,
Vertreibt mir Jesus selbst die 'zeit,
Ich bin bey ihm, und er bey mir,
So kommt mirs gar nicht einsam vor.

Komm ich zur Welt, man redt von sachen,
So nur auf Eitelkeit gericht,
Da muss sich lassen der verlachen,
Der etwas von dem Himmel spricht,
Drum wunsch ich lieber ganz allein,
Als bey der Welt ohn Gott zu seyn.

Alone, and yet not all alone,
Am I, in solitude though drear,
For when no one seems me to own,
My Jesus will himself be near,
I am with Him and He with me,
I therefore cannot lonely be.

Seek I the world? Of things they speak,
Which are on vanity intent,
Here he is scorned and spurned as weak,
Where mind on heavenly things is bent,
I rather would my lone way plod,
Than share the world without my God.

The commemorative LeRoy Massacre marker was erected by the Union County Historical Society in 1919 during one of its annual pilgrimages. It is located across the road from the massacre site on Ridge Road, Limestone Township. Photo by Jim Walter.

Regional historians were soon identifying Regina with their respective locales and providing her with a surname. In Lebanon, for example, she was identified as Regina Hartman. A biography, *Regina, the German Captive*, by the Reverend Reuben Weiser and a chapter, "The Indian Forts of the Blue Mountains," by H.M.M. Richards of Reading, in the *Frontier Forts of Pennsylvania* published by the Commonwealth of Pennsylvania in 1895, both accept Regina Hartman as the heroine. But the resurfacing of the Barbara Leininger-Marie LeRoy pamphlet several years later solved the mystery and ended the controversy. Regina was unmistakably the sister of Barbara Leininger, and by general consent,

the setting of the story shifted to Penns Creek and the Leininger cabin there.

Little is known about either the LeRoys (Kings) or Leiningers after their resettlement in Berks County beyond several crumbling grave stones there. On an old deed there is a recital indicating that John James LeRoy of Prince Georges County, Maryland, the brother of Marie, sold the LeRoy tract in Limestone Township, Union County, to Andrew Pontius of Tulpehocken, Berks County. Thus it is known that he — like Marie and the Leininger sisters — survived the ordeal of captivity. A Pontius anecdote, recorded by Linn, relates that while clearing up the Hoy farm adjacent to the LeRoy property, several gold eagles were found — dropped, it was assumed, by the Indians or their captives. A number of diggings were made at night for additional treasure, but presumably nothing was ever found.

In 1756, with the frontier suffering grievously from Indian incursions, the Provincial Government overcame the traditional Quaker opposition to military expenditures and agreed to construct a line of forts along the gaps of the Blue Mountains from Bethlehem to Fort Hunter on the Susquehanna north of Harrisburg, with another at the forks of the Susquehanna upon the ruins of the deserted Indian town there. In March Lieutenant Governor Robert Hunter Morris commissioned Colonel William Clapham to recruit a regiment and erect the fort at Shamokin (Sunbury). He arrived there on July 6 with the troops, a gang of artisans, and a set of plans, whereupon they set to work. Indians were observed from time to time, but they made no serious attempt to stop the operation. An ambush at the edge of a clearing resulted in the shooting and scalping of a guardsman and gave Bloody Spring its name. By fall Clapham reported that the fort was substantially completed and that he was prepared to defend it to the last extremity. He was probably exaggerating the progress of the work since other reports indicated delays, shortages, and insubordinations.

When completed the fort was a four-pronged, star-shaped structure faced with a stout palisade along the river and horizontally laid logs on the other three exposures. It was the most extensive defense among the aforesaid fortifications. The Proprietors named the post Fort Augusta for the widow of Frederick, Prince of Wales, whose son would soon reign as King George III.

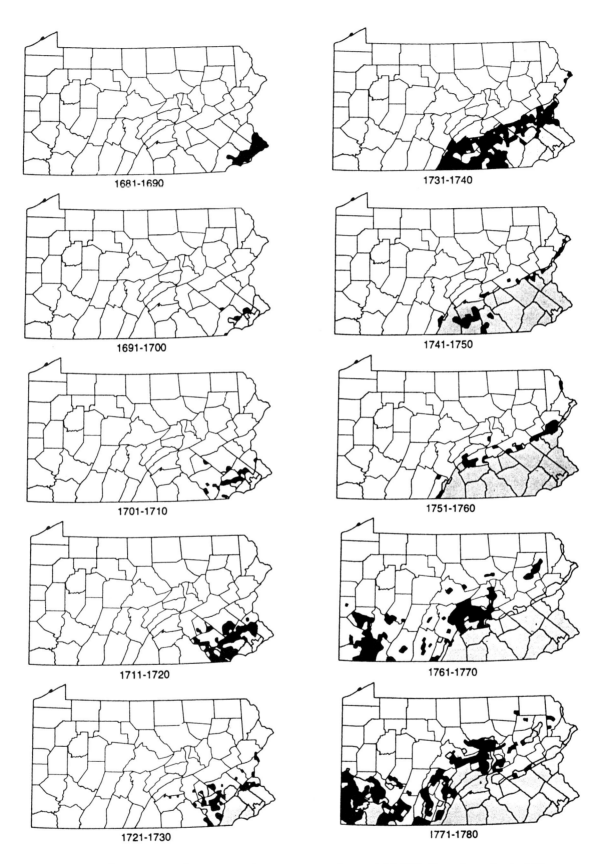

Maps illustrate the advance of the European frontier in Pennsylvania, 1690-1780. From *Pennsylvania 1776*, Robert Secor, ed. (State College: Penn State University Press, 1975), 91.

Whatever its condition, the fort was not tested during the French and Indian War. Its stout walls and garrison, however, helped restore confidence along the frontier, and good news on other battle fronts dispelled the prevailing gloom. General John Forbes' reduction of Fort Duquesne in 1758 seemed to reverse the tide of war; the official restoration of peace in 1763, followed by Colonel Henry Bouquet's campaign against the Indians in Ohio and his culminating victory at Bushy Run, seemed to eliminate the Indian menace. In 1768 the Proprietors signed a treaty with the Iroquois at Fort Stanwix; this treaty provided for the purchase of all of Buffalo Valley as well as the North Branch and West Branch of the Susquehanna as far as Lycoming Creek. The "New Purchase" cleared the way for the legal occupation of the entire region — or so it seemed at the time.

The occupation of Buffalo Valley received an additional impetus when the officers of the First and Second Battalions, who served with Colonel Bouquet, decided to choose this area for settlement. During their return from the Ohio country in 1764 they met at Bedford and at the instigation of Colonel Turbutt Francis formed an association with both patriotic and personal overtones. They agreed "to apply to the Proprietors for a tract of land, sufficiently extensive and conveniently situated, whereon to erect a compact and defensible town," which would serve as a "powerful barrier to the Province," and provide each of its members with a plantation. They chose the West Branch of the Susquehanna River for their ambitious plan and applied for 40,000 acres.

In subsequent negotiations, the last of which was held at Fort Augusta in February 1769, the acreage was reduced to 24,000 acres in three tracts: the first on the east side of the river between Northumberland and Watsontown; the second in the heart of Buffalo Valley; and the third on Bald Eagle Creek west of Lock Haven — thus nullifying the notion that it would serve as a buffer against hostile Indians on the frontier. The plots were surveyed in blocks of approximately 300 acres, and each officer received two of them except Colonel Francis, who obtained a princely estate of 2,775 acres on the east side of the Susquehanna between Milton and Chillisquaque Creek.

The surveying of the Buffalo Valley portion was assigned to William Maclay, who employed his brother Samuel to execute it. Upon the completion of the surveys, the officers assembled at Harris' Ferry, where they drew lots. Captain James Handricks received the first choice in Buffalo Valley and selected the "Hendricks Sale Tract," the easternmost portion of the survey near Lochiel. Captain William Plunkett obtained the Dreisbach Church area and Captain Jacob Kern the site of Vicksburg. Ensign William Piper received the tract "Piper's Parade" just west of Kern's, and the Reverend Captain Conrad Bucher the Cedar Run area, once the site of the Pontius farms and later of the Fairchild, Grove, Brungard, and Wehr properties. Captain Timothy Green secured the Fought or Rockey Mill site; Lieutenant Thomas Askey, the location of Mifflinburg; Captain James Irvine, the tract west of Mifflinburg long owned by the Kleckners; Lieutenant Charles Stewart, the "Joyful Cabbin Tract," encompassing the farms near the Church of the Brethren. Captain Kern also received the Chamberlain-Hoffa Mill tract; Lieutenant McAlister, the land west of it; and Captain Sems, the land adjacent to Mazeppa. The eventual disposition of the land is difficult to follow in that some of the officers immediately traded with one another while others sold or subdivided their holdings.

As the officers were "wheeling and dealing," the land office in Philadelphia was preparing to dispose of thousands of additional acres. It informed the public on February 23, 1769, that it would receive applications for lands in the New Purchase on April 3, a date which would permit "the back inhabitants time to repair to the office." Applicants might apply for as much as 300 acres and were charged five pounds sterling for each 100 acres plus a one penny per acre per year quit-rent. As might be expected, a great crowd attended the opening with their applications or "locations," consisting of short descriptions of the plots they had in mind. The slips were dropped into a trunk, mixed well, and drawn out by an "indifferent" person. They were numbered as withdrawn, a lower number taking priority over a subsequent application for the same location — of which there were many. Michael Weyland's application for land on the so-called Shikellamy town site in Kelly Township was the 32nd slip drawn.

It was a "land office" time for surveyors, and the Maclay brothers profited from the often perplexing and frustrating experience. By year's end they had laid out most of the arable land in the Valley. It scarcely needs mention that litigation over titles was the bread and butter of the first generation of lawyers

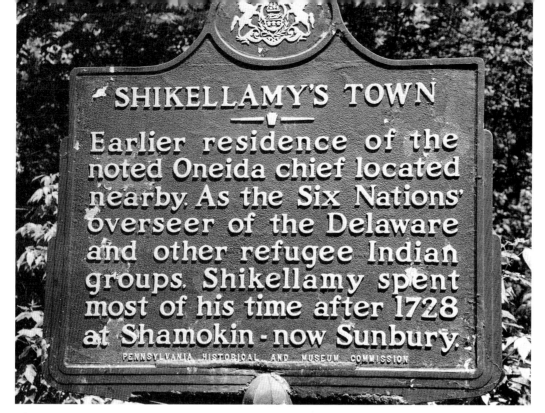

Photo by Jim Walter.

Native American artifacts. Counterclockwise (from top) are: 1. Penns Creek Archaic Corner Notch, c. 6500-3000 B.C.; 2. Lavanna, Early Woodland c. 700 B.C.- 1350 A.D.; 3. Lecroy Bifurcate, Early Archaic c. 6300 B.C.; 4. Fox Creek, Mid-Woodland c. 400-300 B.C.; 5. Susquehanna form, Drill, Terminal Archaic c. 1600-750 B.C.; 6. Cruciform Drill/Perforator, Archaic 4000 B.C.; 7. Trade Beads, c. 1700-1800; 8. Piney Island, Mid-Archaic c. 4000-2000 B.C.; 9. Oriental Fishtail, Terminal Archaic c. 1200-750 B.C. Artifacts identified by Kim Mattern. From the collection of the Union County Historical Society, gift of Robert and Lucy Donehower.

NEXT PAGE: Early tax assessments for Buffalo Township, Northumberland County (now Union), from 1780 have personal and land assessments entered in English pounds, shillings, and pence. From the archives of the Union County Courthouse.

Acres land	Number		Valuation	Total Valuation	State Tax £ S D			County levy £ S D		
5	30/	Black Thomas senr:	7-10							
		2 horses	12							
		2 Cows	6	25-10		1	0			6
265	30/	Black Thos Junr	397-10							
		2 horses	8							
		1 Cow	3	408-10		14	10		8	6
		Black James								
		1 horse	4							
		1 Cow	3	7			6			3
200	25/	Baldy Christopher	250							
		2 horses	10							
		3 cows	9	269		9	10		5	7
300	30/	Brundage Joseph	450							
		2 horses	8							
		2 cows	6	164		16	11		9	8
200	35/	Billmire Andrew	350							
		4 horses	24							
		3 cows	9	383		14	0		7	2
500 89 41 225 186	25/	Brady John	228							
		2 horses	8				8	10		5	0
		2 cows	6	242 639		3	3		13	4
00	15/	Barnhart Matthias	150							
		2 horses	8							
	16	2 Cows	6	164		6	0		3	5

in the area.

By the fall of 1769, John Lee had settled at Winfield — Linn believed that this may have been the first clearing in lower Dry Valley. John Beatty was at New Berlin; Jacob Grozean at the Chamberlain-Hoffa-Grove Mill site; John Wilson at the mouth of Turtle Creek; Barney Parsons near Spruce Run; Adams Haines, William Blythe, and Joseph McLaughlin at White Deer; William Armstrong and James Parr at New Columbia; and Michael Weyland below West Milton.

By 1772 the sounds of the ax could be heard at hundreds of clearings along the West Branch, and the need was felt for governmental controls nearer the frontier. The long travel required to reach the county seats: Reading, Carlisle, Lancaster, Bedford or Northampton — depending upon the place of residence — was a recurring difficulty. The General Assembly responded to this need on March 21 by creating Northumberland County, named for its counterpart in the North Country of England. To implement the act, Governor Richard Penn ordered that Surveyor General John Lukens "with all convenient speed, repair to Fort Augusta on the Susquehanna, and with the assistance of Mr. William Maclay lay out a town for the County of Northumberland to be called by the name of Sunbury at the most commodious place between the Fort and the mouth of Shamokin Creek." Thus, as Northumberland County historian Charles F. Snyder has noted, the town was named before it came into existence either by survey or settlement. Penn seems to have selected the name of his childhood home in Middlesex Shire for the new county seat.

Pieced together from the northern parts of Northampton, Berks, Lancaster, Cumberland, and Bedford counties, the new county of Northumberland sprawled across north-central Pennsylvania from the head of Little Juniata River on the northwest, to the New York border on the north, to the head of the Lehigh River (Pike County) on the east, and to the two Mahantongo creeks (the one on the east and the other on the west side of the Susquehanna River) on the south. The original Northumberland County included more than ten percent of the land in the province and encompassed all of present-day Northumberland, Snyder, and Union counties in addition to all or parts of eleven other counties. One of the first actions taken at the initial session of the court on April 9, 1772, was the division of the county into seven townships, four of which remain in Northumberland, Snyder and Union counties today: Augusta and Turbot in Northumberland, Penns in Snyder, and Buffalo in Union.

Buffalo Township at the outset commenced at the mouth of Penns Creek at the head of the Isle of Que, ran up the same to its forks (Coburn), and thence north to the West Branch of the Susquehanna at the mouth of Bald Eagle Creek below Lock Haven. It then followed the river to the place of beginning. It thus included all of Union and a large part of Snyder, Centre, and Lycoming counties. Like Northumberland County, it would be repeatedly whittled down during the century to follow.

Buffalo Township was named for Buffalo Creek; the same might be said for Buffalo Valley and Buffalo Mountain; but the origin of the creek's name remains an enigma. A cartographer has noted that buffalo was used as a place-name for at least eight sites in Pennsylvania in the eighteenth century, when the buffalo seems to have no longer existed there with the exception of the Ohio border. Anthropologists also note the absence of buffalo in the cultures of the Pennsylvania Indians and the absence of buffalo bones in the excavations of Indian burials and refuse heaps. This, of course, conflicts with the folklore of the Buffalo Valley, which indicates that there were large herds of wood bison, which were eventually exterminated by the avaricious pioneers, whose removal of the forests prevented their migration and left them to starve in the mountain recesses.

It should be noted, however, that tales such as the "Last Buffalo Hunt" were not recorded until the late nineteenth or early twentieth centuries, long after possible eyewitnesses were gone. Colonel Henry Shoemaker, the noted folklorist and naturalist, attributed the most frequently repeated tale of the last buffalo hunt to one Flavel Bergstresser, an aging, bibulous hostler, who had related the story to Shoemaker on the steps of the Kleckner Hotel in New Berlin about 1914.[10]

The alleged incident involved Bergstresser's grandfather and his neighbors near Troxelville at the foot of Jack's Mountain in Snyder County; the date given was January 1801. The winter was severe and "the last herd" of buffalo, near the point of starvation, was huddled in deep snow in a "basin" in the mountains. The leader, "Old Logan,. . . a coal black bull of immense size. . . his spacious sides scarred with bullet marks and wounds left by attacks from wolves," decided to make a last, desperate charge for survival. As the herd entered the valley, one following the other in single file, a witness counted them. There were 345. As they passed the farm of Mr. McClellan, the young pioneer fired a "Fusillade," laying low one, two, three, and four. He would have dropped more,

The Bucknell Bison at the football stadium; and the Bucknell marching band c. 1940. The student playing cymbals is John Zeller, who served as the university's vice president from 1955 to 1988. Courtesy of Bucknell University Archives.

PAGE 19: Buffalo images abound in Union County, only a few of which were photographed in 1999. TOP TO BOTTOM ON LEFT: Bucknell University football helmets; stone Bison on Moore Avenue at the entrance to Davis Gym, which is seen in the background with its own bison; the real thing at Don and Jo Ritzenthaler's farm east of Mifflinburg on the south side of Route 45; East Buffalo Township building sign. TOP TO BOTTOM ON RIGHT: Campus Theater on Market Street, Lewisburg, built by the four Stiefel brothers in 1941; Buffalo Valley Telephone Company logo; side of New Berlin police car; East Buffalo Township home recycling container. Other images include East Buffalo Township police patches, cars, and main recyling bins; and Bucknell entrance marker. Photos by Jim Walter.

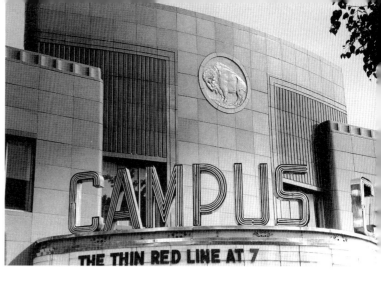

THE THIN RED LINE AT 7

BUFFALO VALLEY TELEPHONE COMPANY

NEW BERLIN

POLICE

EAST BUFFALO TWP.

POLICE

Property of

EAST BUFFALO

TOWNSHIP

but he wasted many volleys at Old Logan, "his impenetrable hide rolling off the bullets, and permitting him to amble away grunting amicably." A little farther on the bison came to the farm of Martin Bergstresser where the hungry herd sighted a haystack in his barn yard. They broke through the rail fence, "crushing the farm animals beneath their mighty rush (six cows, four calves and 35 sheep)." Bergstresser picked up his gun and fired at Old Logan, but again the bullets bounced away. He and McClellan, who came to his assistance, dispatched several others. When the animals saw their companions kicking convulsively, they revealed a strong communal feeling and set up "the most pitiful groaning imaginable." At length, Old Logan led the herd away.

When McClellan returned to his home, he saw the herd snorting and tramping around his house. Squeezing his way between them, he found Old Logan guarding the front door. Terrified — his wife and three children were inside — he fired at close range, tearing a hole in the big bull's throat. Maddened, the monster plunged through the door with the other bison following him one by one until the cabin was jammed "as tightly as wooden animals in a toy Noah's Ark." Hearing the animals a mile away, neighbors gathered with battering rams and pounded the back of the stout-walled cabin until they made a large opening. Headed by the bloody Old Logan, the animals now came out. Seizing his gun again, McClellan shot the bull squarely through the head, but Old Logan continued to move, bellowing hideously for several hundred yards before falling dead. The air now resounded with the herd's moans "as they battled with one another to lick his wounds." Inside the cabin, the bodies of McClellan's wife and children were found crushed on the ground floor.

When McClellan recovered from his shock, he called upon the settlers to accompany him into the mountains to exterminate the surviving bison. About 50 persons assembled, and, after combing the mountains for several days, they found the buffalo in the great "Sink" in the White Mountains south of Weikert. The animals were numb from cold and "crushed" in the deep snow, unable to move so much as a foot. Going through the herd the men slit the animals' throats, pausing only long enough to remove some of the tongues. When the job had been finished, "the ice about them resembled a sheet of crimson glass." Triumphant, the huntsmen returned to their homes, "singing German hymns" as they marched. "In the spring and summer travelers crossing distant ridges could notice one portion of the sky black with the pinions of huge birds. They were the carrion-seekers, bald eagles, golden eagles, a half dozen kind of hawks, buzzards, ravens, crows, which picked clean the bones of Pennsylvania's last herd of bison."

How much of this stirring story is Bergstresser's tale and how much is Colonel Shoemaker's art remains undetermined. It might be added that the killing of the very last buffalo in Buffalo Valley has been reserved for the famous Colonel John Kelly. Shoemaker added a second bison to the Kelly story; this one eluded the Colonel and made its way to Weikert where it was hunted without success for several years. Shoemaker attributed his sequel to Jonas Barnet, a great nephew of Jacob Weiker — the founder of Weikert. Barnet was born in Weikert in 1838, about the same time that Weiker moved to the West. If Barnet heard the story during his youth, the time would have been 50 years after the events which he related at the age of 77 to Shoemaker in 1915. Barnet told Shoemaker that Weiker went after the buffalo repeatedly, "at last driving it out of the valley in the direction of Lewistown."[11] As an afterthought on Jacob Weiker, Shoemaker wrote that "he probably killed over one thousand panthers, wolves and bears, as well as countless deer and other game." One tale, it seems, spawns another.

No contemporary record of buffaloes in Union County seems to exist, and the County's first historians make no mention of them, yet the unwritten testimony endures. Residents of Cowan will show the visitor "buffalo wallows" — depressions along the north bank of Buffalo Creek below the village, and foresters along the White Deer mountains will point out the old buffalo trails there. Images of buffalo abound locally. A more definitive answer may have to await future anthropological studies.

The pioneers who settled in Buffalo Valley during the early years unwittingly became a part of an inter-colonial quarrel which became so heated that it produced the armed conflict called "the Pennamite War." King Charles II disposed of the royal holdings in North America with commendable largess; after granting a charter to Connecticut for the land between the 41st and 42nd parallels of latitude to the Pacific Ocean, he disposed of a sizable part of the same land to William Penn to satisfy a personal debt. Surveys revealed that Connecticut's claim stretched southward to a line just south of Milton. Yielding to such a claim would have reduced Pennsylvania by more than a third. In the seventeenth century, when land was plentiful, the conflicting claims could be ignored; but by the middle of the eighteenth century, land was becoming scarce and costly in Connecticut. Hundreds of its families were looking westward for greener pastures.

Like the Israelites of old, Connecticut dispatched observers to evaluate the land and found that the Wyoming Valley in Pennsylvania was rich in soil and timber — a welcome change from the rocks and hills of New England. In 1753 inhabitants of Windham, Connecticut, met on the village green and organized the Susquehanna Company to facilitate settlements in the Wyoming Valley. They made little headway during the French and Indian War, but in 1769 they moved a band of settlers with their livestock and tools, and erected forts at Forty Fort and Wilkes-Barre. To counter this move, the Proprietors built Fort Wyoming but soon lost it to the "Yankees." Alternating successes and failures followed with sieges, arrests, and occasional bloodshed. Most of the Pennsylvania offensives were launched from Northampton County, but on one occasion 60 armed frontiersmen from Fort Augusta, marching behind Colonel Turbutt Francis, invaded Wyoming. Finding Yankees barricaded behind their fortifications, Francis had to be satisfied with a verbal blast at his adversaries. It went unheeded. The military activity at this time has been termed the first Yankee-Pennamite War.

Meanwhile, the Susquehanna Company was granting land in the Muncy area to its colonizers. To "play it safe," at least several of Buffalo Valley's pioneers negotiated for land with both the Pennsylvania land office and the Susquehanna Company. Marcus Huling, for example, received "one quarter of a right or shair of land in ye Susquehanna purchase," and also "a tract of land lying on ye River and up Limestone Run (Milton) . . . said tract contains 374 acres and 87 perches." William Speddy of Buffalo Township (later East Buffalo) paid six pounds for one-half a share of land in the Susquehanna Purchase.

The need to take the pretensions of the Yankees seriously was demonstrated in June 1773, when they unexpectedly appeared at the clearing at Muncy and destroyed several settlements, charging them with trespassing. Colonel William Plunkett, who had shared in the officers' grant and was then a judge of the Northumberland County Court, headed an invasion of the Wyoming Country in retaliation, but he fared no better than Colonel Francis. In this, the so-called second Yankee-Pennamite War, the Connecticut colonizers became more aggressive. They laid out the county of Westmoreland, founded the town of Wilkes-Barre, and by the outbreak of the Revolutionary War, settled about 2,600 people in the area. During the war the Connecticut and Pennsylvania frontiersmen fought side by side against a common enemy, but the controversy was renewed near its close. The con-

The first Barber house at White Springs still has its original springhouse, constructed over the spring for which the town was named. Photo by Jim Walter.

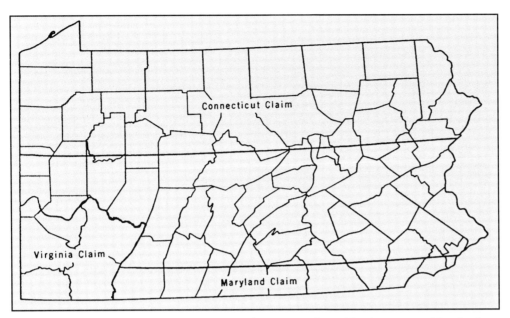

A map of contested boundaries of Pennsylvania shows areas claimed by Connecticut, Maryland, and Virginia. From Philip S. Klein and Ari Hoogenboom, *A History of Pennsylvania*, 2nd. ed. (State College: Penn State University Press, 1980),189.

flicting claims were finally resolved in 1782 by a Commission appointed by the Continental Congress which ruled in favor of Pennsylvania.

The creation of Buffalo Township in 1772 was a boon to the area. In the initial year of its existence Ludwig Derr bought the tract where Lewisburg now stands and constructed a mill; John Aurand built another mill near the mouth of Turtle Creek; Robert Barber built the first house in White Springs; and Captain John Lowdon, one of the founders of Northumberland, moved to "Silver Spring," his farm north of Mifflinburg. In December the first marriage in Buffalo Valley, joining Magdalena, widow of Michael Weyland, to Peter Swartz, was consummated. William Gray served on the first Board of County Commissioners as well as on the first grand jury where he was joined by Captain John Brady, foreman. Other grand jurors were George Overmeier, John Rearick, Peter Leonard, Ludwig Derr, Andrew Hafer, Hawkins Boone, James Park, and John Walker. Robert Clark and Robert Fruit sat on the first petit jury.

A year later James Boveard was serving as constable in Buffalo Township; Joseph Green and Martin Trester as its supervisors; and William Irwin and John Lee its overseers of the poor. Arrivals in the township included Abel Reese (East Buffalo), Joseph Sips (Buffalo), Philip Hoy (Limestone), and James Fleming (Kelly). Christian Van Gundy obtained a license to keep a tavern at Strohecker's landing below Lewisburg, and a road was authorized from "the fording between

Ludwig Derr's and John Aurand's mill through Buffalo Valley to the Narrows." The Buffalo Cross Roads Presbyterian Church was organized this year with James McClenahan and Samuel Allen as its first ruling elders.

In 1774 James Young was the constable. The office could scarcely be written off as a sinecure since loosely worded titles to real estate prompted no less than 140 suits in the August court term. During 1775 the turbulence in Wyoming Valley elicited a petition from inhabitants of Northumberland County to the Provincial Assembly calling its attention to the great body of intruders from the Colony of Connecticut who refused to accept the laws of Pennsylvania, and the inability to enforce the laws through the want of a proper gaol (jail). The Assembly responded with an appropriation.

The focus of Buffalo Valley's citizenry at this time was more and more upon the ominous cloud hanging over all the colonies. The power assumed by the English Parliament to bind the people of the American colonies "by statutes in all cases whatsoever" became more than a play upon words. When England's so-called "Intolerable Acts" of that year were passed to punish Massachusetts for the "Boston Tea Party," the colonists felt that the ideals of home rule and personal liberties were being attacked.

A letter from the Committee of Correspondence of Philadelphia dated June 28, 1774, asking for the sense of the citizenry in the present crisis and for their participation in the appointment of delegates to a proposed congress, was received by William Maclay, William Plunkett, and Samuel Hunter. The response was a call for action. In the words of Joseph Green, who served as secretary for the gathering, "At a meeting of a number of the principal inhabitants of the Township of Buffalo at Loudowick [sic] Derr's, of Saturday, the ninth of July, John Lowden, Esquire, and Samuel Maclay were chosen as committeemen to meet the other committeemen from the other townships, on Monday the 11th instant, at Richard Malone's, in order to choose proper persons out of the township committees to go to Philadelphia to the general meeting of the committees chosen by the respective counties of this Province, and likewise to fix upon some proper way and means to correspond with the other committees of this Province."[12]

At Richard Malone's home, William Scull of Turbot Township and Samuel Hunter of Sunbury were chosen to represent the county at the Provincial Congress in Philadelphia, and Scull was to serve on the committee to prepare instructions to the Provincial Assembly. Thus, Buffalo Township and Northumberland County had a hand in declaring that the inhabitants of the colonies were entitled to the same rights and liberties as were those subjects born in England; that they would support a suspension of trade with Great Britain if their petition were rejected; and that it was absolutely necessary that a congress of representatives of the several colonies be immediately assembled (the First Continental Congress).

Though acknowledging themselves to be "liege subjects of His Majesty King George III" to whom they owed "true and faithful allegiance," these men dared to assert that his government had acted illegally and that they were awaiting satisfaction. William Plunkett and Casper Weitzel represented Northum-

Ludwig Derr's original mill in Lewisburg was photographed by James M. Houghton in 1860, nearly a century after it was built. The mill stood near the mouth of Spring Run (later called Limestone or Wilson Run, and more recently Bull Run). The photograph was reissued as a real photo postcard by Edwin S. Heiser prior to 1907. From the collection of the Union County Historical Society, #89.5.6.7.

berland County at the Pennsylvania Provincial Convention on January 23, 1775, which declared its earnest wish to see harmony restored between England and the Colonies but warned of "our indispensable duty" to resist the late arbitrary acts of Parliament.

Failing to obtain redress, a mass meeting was held on May 1 at Constable Henry Van Dyke's near Beaver Run (presumably Buffalo Cross Roads) in Buffalo Valley "to form a plan, in conjunction with our countrymen, to give every opposition to impending tyranny and oppression either by force or otherwise."[13] Noting that there could not be much accommodation at the meeting place, the committee recommended that every man should provide for himself. Unbeknownst to the assemblage, patriots resisting a redcoat incursion at Lexington and Concord, Massachusetts, had already turned the dispute into an armed conflict.

When this startling news reached the area several days later, it was accompanied by a request for enlistments. Buffalo Valley men began to fall into line in a company organized by Captain John Lowdon. At the invitation of the Continental Congress, residents of the West Branch joined their fellow Americans across the Thirteen Colonies in a "Fast Day" on Thursday, July 20. Those living close enough to Sunbury put their work aside to attend religious services, where they heard a sermon by the Reverend Philip Fithian, itinerant missionary of the Presbyterian Church. He spoke in an unfinished house without partitions to a crowd which overflowed into the cellar and the street outside.

Assessments for Buffalo Township in 1775 provide a partial view of Buffalo Valley's manpower and economic resources as it was caught in the maelstrom: 249 names on the roll, 215 of whom were landholders. The average farm contained nineteen cultivated acres. They were planting 4,323 acres and owned 340 horses, 414 cows, and 141 sheep. Obviously, with crops and livestock so limited, Buffalo Valley's greatest contribution to the cause of American independence would be its human resources. John Blair Linn in *The Annals of Buffalo Valley* gave the names of the settlers in Buffalo Valley in 1775. There were about 248 families of which at least 90 were men who stayed in Union County and fought in the America Revolution.

ENDNOTES

[1] Erica L. Shames, "Documenting Prehistoric Native American Life," *Susquehanna Life*, Fall 1998.

[2] Sharon Begley and Andrew Murr, "The First Americans," *Newsweek*, April 26, 1999.

[3] John Blair Linn, *Annals of Buffalo Valley, Pennsylvania, 1755-1855*, Harrisburg, 1877. He locates Shikellamy's original headquarters on the west side of the river about one half mile south of West Milton on the old James Moore farm. However, evidence based on the early visitations by Conrad Weiser in 1737, John Bartram in 1743 and Bishop Joseph Spangenberg in 1745 indicate that they reached the town on the east side of the river. See Charles F. Snyder, "Where Was Shikellamy's Old Town?" *Proceedings of the Northumberland County Historical Society XXV* (1967), 38-51.

[4] Donald Carpenter in a presentation to the November 9, 1995 John B. Deans Annual Banquet of the Union County Historical Society.

[5] Quoted in Linn, 10.

[6] Published by Peter Miller in Philadelphia, 1759.

[7] The captive girls quoted in Miller's publication.

[8] The captive girls quoted in Miller's publication.

[9] *Publications of the Pennsylvania German Society*, XV, 82-91.

[10] Henry W. Shoemaker, *A Pennsylvania Bison Hunt*, Middleburg Post Press, 1915, 254-267.

[11] Shoemaker, 41.

[12] Quoted in Linn, 56.

[13] Quoted in Linn, 76.

Continental Congress currency. From the collection of Jeannette Lasansky.

CHAPTER 2

IN THE SPIRIT OF 1776

by John W. Downie

Even before 1775 the people of Buffalo Valley had shown their determination to resist what they considered to be British oppression. In the course of the Revolution, there were changes in governmental structure, but the transition does not seem to have occasioned any particular difficulties in the area, nor is there any real basis for suspicions of disloyalty to the American cause among the people of the later Union County.

In 1775 Buffalo Valley was growing in population and was not without signs of prosperity. New settlers continued to arrive, even after the first ominous signs of local shortages in arms had begun to appear. In early 1778 it was apparent that people were conscious of vulnerability to attack since less than half the militia could be armed and emigration to safer areas started. The "Runaways" of 1778 and 1779 resulted in the abandonment of significant stretches of territory. One cannot say that the Redcoats would have been welcome, but they would certainly have been preferred to their Iroquois allies.

The story of Union County in the Revolution is one of limited resources in arms, of a greatly reduced population, and, perhaps, of too great a contribution of the best qualified men to the main army in the East.[1] Nevertheless, Union County was never completely abandoned. The Iroquois incursions of 1778 and 1779 were devastating to the settlers along the West Branch north of Buffalo Valley, but there was little penetration into Union County at that time. Families continued to reside here, and as early as 1780 there were signs of renewed confidence. Even so, from 1780 to 1782 there were no less than fifteen incursions which resulted in 31 known deaths and seventeen people being taken captive. When the "runaways" and the veterans returned, they found the hardy and the tenacious who had remained throughout the war, who had defended themselves against almost impossible odds, and who had saved the frontiers for the new arrivals. With the end of the war there was no place to go but forward.

The transition from royal to revolutionary government in Union County was gradual and not marked by difficulty. As early as July 9, 1774, John Lowdon and Samuel Maclay had been chosen members of the Committee of Correspondence in Buffalo Township.[2] The area had joined in selecting representatives from Northumberland County to the Convention of Deputies, which met in Philadelphia in January 1775. The Convention had expressed an "earnest wish to see harmony restored" between England and the colonies but it had also resolved to resist "at every hazard" any attempt by Britain to force submission to the Intolerable Acts.[3] Even before news of Lexington, it was known that England did intend to use force. The County Committee of Correspondence, on April 20, 1775, met to effect a plan "to give every opposition" to Parliament.[4]

So great was the consensus among Pennsylvanians for opposition to Parliament that the existing Proprietarial government continued to function until after the Declaration of Independence. Indeed, White Deer Township, formed in February 1776, was established under the authority of the Proprietarial government. It was the Proprietarial Assembly which appointed a Committee of Safety on June 30, 1775, charged with taking measures for the defense of Pennsylvania.[5] It was this Committee which requested the counties to form their own Committees of Safety. In Northumberland County the Committee of Safety was composed of three representatives from each township, elected for a six month term. The first meeting was held February 8, 1776. At various times, Buffalo Township was represented by William Clark, William Irwin, Joseph Green, Martin Treaster, William Speddy, Philip Cole, John Aurand, Thomas Sutherland, and George Overmeier. The members for White Deer were Walter Clark, Matthew Brown, Marcus Huling, James M'Clanahan. Robert Frite, William Gray, William Blythe, James McCormak, and William Reed. The County Committee of Safety was both administrative and military, and occasionally judicial.[6]

The Pennsylvania Constitutional Convention, which first met in Philadelphia July 15, 1776, took upon itself the government of the State and appointed a Council of Safety to replace the Provincial Committee of Safety. The minutes of the Assembly's Committee terminate on July 22, 1776 and those of the Convention's Council begin on July 24, 1776.[7]

The change from Committee to Council in Philadelphia seems to have had no effect in Buffalo and White Deer Townships. The relationship between the County Committee of Safety and the Pennsylvania Council of Safety continued as it had with the Assembly's Committee. The extant minutes of the Northumberland County Committee of Safety end with a meeting in early 1777.[8] This was probably the last meeting of the County Committee because its purpose had been served and it was no longer needed. The Council of Safety had been left by the adjourning Constitution Convention as an interim executive until the new government, established by the Constitution, could become effective. The Supreme Executive Committee under the new Constitution met on March 4, 1777. On March 13 it established a Board of War and a Navy Board. The Council of Safety's functions were absorbed, and the minutes of the last meeting of the Council are dated March 13, 1777.[9]

Appointments of county officials responsive to the new government began in March 1777. Samuel Hunter was appointed County Lieutenant on March 21, 1777. His duties included the general direction of the militia of the county.[10] The administrative, military, and judicial functions formerly performed by the Committees of Safety were integrated into the formal Constitutional government.

Surviving records show the County Lieutenant to have been the executive in the county responsible for responding to the Supreme Executive Committee of Pennsylvania. This does not mean that the citizens did not, on occasion, address the new government directly. A "Memorandum from the Inhabitants" was not unusual. The Memoranda show quite clearly the uneasiness and even misery of those who remained after the "Runaways," but they do not justify any suspicion of mass disloyalty, as suggested by Van Doren.[11]

The population in the area which later became Union County continued to grow throughout the first part of 1778; thereafter it declined sharply until 1781 or 1782 when it again experienced a steady increase as some "Runaway" victims returned and as veterans and their families settled after the war. A visitor to Northumberland in the summer of 1775 reported seeing families from New Jersey passing through in wagons en route to the West Branch. The same visitor, a traveling minister, was impressed by the dress of the ladies at Sunday services at Buffalo Crossroads. He called them the "silk gown congregation."[12] The separation of White Deer Township from Buffalo Township in February 1776 is testimony to the growing population of the area. Meginness says that large numbers of immigrants came to Buffalo Valley in 1776, mostly from New Jersey.[13] A contemporary letter, quoted by Linn and dated May 31, 1778, speaks of the "Jersey people who came in the winter and

spring." Unfortunately, the same letter says that they were going home and that older settlers in Buffalo Valley were leaving too.[14]

While the population was still growing, signs of shortages of arms and material for war were evident. The original Resolution of Congress for the establishment of a militia, repeated by the Pennsylvania Committee of Safety, had required each militiaman to furnish his own weapon.[15] In July 1775 State authorities supplied a quantity of powder and lead for distribution to the Northumberland County militia.[16] In September, 3,000 pounds was voted to John Weitzel for "making arms in Northumberland County,"[17] and Colonel James Potter was allowed to contract for 50 rifles for his battalion.[18]

Whether arms were made and rifles bought in the area of Union County has not really been established. The Widow Smith did not have a rifle-boring mill at White Deer active until July 1779.[19] T. Kenneth Wood, in an article published in the *Northumberland County Historical Society Proceedings*,[20] doubts that the mill was used for the manufacture of new rifles. Wood explains that the rifle tended to foul its barrel with use and had to be periodically rebored. In his opinion, the function of the mill was the reboring of used rifles.

In any case, the shortage of arms in the entire county was aggravated as time went on. On August 30, 1776, a policy had been adopted which would contribute to the shortage. The needs of the main army came first, and it had been ordered that militiamen who completed service with the main army would turn in all arms and accouterments before leaving so that these could be furnished for their replacements.[21] Beginning in December 1776, Northumberland County provided a steady flow of two-month servicemen to the main army. On November 1, 1777, the County Lieutenant reported to the Executive Committee of Pennsylvania that the third and fourth classes of militia would march to join the main army but that they had no arms.[22] On November 11 he reported: "The militia that now marches is badly off for blankets, several go without any, and but thinly clothed."[23] A return of May 1, 1778, shows four Northumberland County militia battalions with a total strength of 1,582 men.[24] On May 31, though, there were not enough arms for more than three classes of militia.[25] The 1,582 men represent eight classes of militia.

The greatest contribution of Union County to American independence, it was said earlier, was in human resources. Men from Union County served in regular Continental units throughout the war.

Associators and militia from the county served with the main army while militiamen from Union County fought on the frontier. To make the story as coherent as possible, it is best to separate regulars from militia. It has been suggested earlier that the absence of these men in Continental units may have contributed to the weakness of the defense of Union County.

On June 14, 1775, the Continental Congress resolved to provide the New England army before Boston with ten companies to come from Pennsylvania.[26] The regular Army of the United States celebrates June 14 as its birthdate.[27] One of the Pennsylvania companies was formed on the West Branch of the Susquehanna with men from Union County as prominent members. Captain John Lowdon, whose home was near Mifflinburg, commanded; First Lieutenant James Parr came from near New Columbia. The Company was integrated into Thompson's Pennsylvania Rifle Battalion at Boston. Indicative of the organizational problems of the new army is the fact that before the year ended, Thompson's Battalion would be known successively as the 2d Foot, United Provinces Army, and as the 1st Continental Infantry. Although our Company's service ended on July 1, 1776, James Parr remained with the army, taking command of the Company, and about half the original membership remained with him. In January 1777 the regiment was redesignated the 1st Pennsylvania. The affiliation with the frontier remained until the old regiment disappeared in the reorganization of the Pennsylvania Line, following the mutiny of 1781. Many of its former members remained in Continental service until the end of the Revolution. Since the unit never served in Union County, relating its distinguished military record with the main army would be a digression beyond the purpose of this history.[28]

Congress had specified, when the riflemen were first raised, that they "find their own clothes and arms."[29] Thus they would have carried their personal shot bags, powder horns, knives, hatchets, and rifles, but their clothing was surprisingly uniform. A witness noted in his journal that they arrived at Boston wearing round hats [similar to those of our Amish neighbors] and white linen hunting shirts.[30] Authorities agree that riflemen customarily wore Indian leggings and moccasins.[31] After 1776 rifles were taken into store and muskets were issued.[32] Uniforms were issued after 1777 as they were available, and there are descriptions of brown coats with green facings, blue with red, brown with red, and

Pennsylvania colonial currency.
From the collection of Jeannette Lasansky.

even one of blue coats faced with white and red flannel overalls.[33] Washington favored the hunting shirt, however,[34] and it was probably worn more often than any other uniform.

By March 1776 the 1st Continentals had their own flag, and the same design was used when they became the 1st Pennsylvania. It was green, enclosing a red quadrangle. On the quadrangle, in white was a hunter threatening a netted lion. Below the device was the motto "Domari Nolo."[35]

By March of 1776 Pennsylvania had raised six battalions for Continental service in addition to Thompson's.[36] In that month the Northumberland County Committee of Safety expressed concern about the activities of recruiting parties in the County.[37] The recruiting was not stopped, however; recruiting officers of the 1st, 9th, and 12th Pennsylvania were in Buffalo Valley seeking enlistments as late as February 1777.[38]

In March of 1776 Casper Weitzel's company was raised in Northumberland County for service with Miles' Pennsylvania Rifle Regiment. Although certainly not dominated by Union County representation, it did contain members from Union County. Miles' was raised for State service but soon found itself with the main army. After very heavy casualties at Long Island, Miles' Pennsylvania Rifle Regiment was combined with Atlee's Pennsylvania Musket Battalion, another state-service unit, to form the

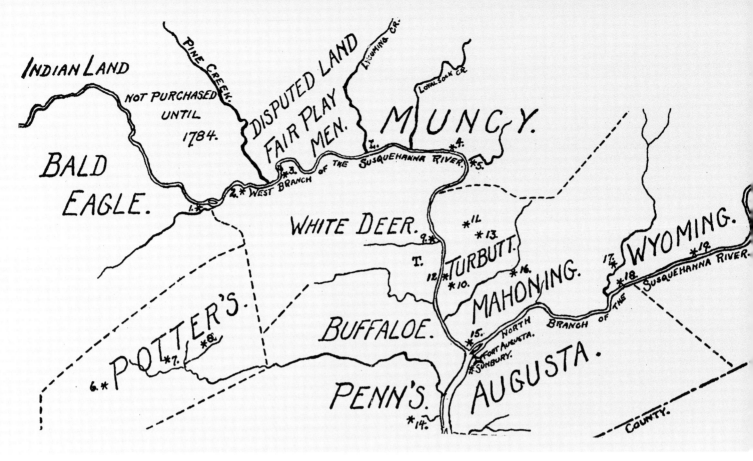

The map of Northumberland County during the Revolutionary War was drawn by Charles Fisher Snyder in 1949. From the *Proceedings of the Northumberland County Historical Society, Vol. XVIII* (Sunbury, PA, 1950), 64.

Pennsylvania State Regiment. In 1778 the State Regiment went into Continental service as the 13th Pennsylvania and was combined with the 2nd Pennsylvania on July 1, 1778.[39] A deserter from Weitzel's company was described in the *Pennsylvania Gazette*, July 3, 1776, as wearing a "rifleman's uniform of a lead color."[40] The Pennsylvania State Regiment wore blue coats faced with red, and blue coats with white facings.[41]

In October 1776 the 12th Pennsylvania was raised in Northumberland and Northampton Counties. Captain Hawkins Boone, a Union County man, raised one of the Northumberland companies. The Regiment suffered heavily at Germantown and after wintering at Valley Forge was nearly destroyed at Monmouth. On July 1, 1778, the remnants of the Regiment were incorporated into the 3rd Pennsylvania.[42] If the 12th was ever provided with a uniform, no description is known to survive. Deserter notices for other Pennsylvania units in 1777 frequently refer to "new regimentals," a blue coat with red facings. The 3rd Pennsylvania is known to have had coats of this description in 1779.[43] It is not likely that the Regiment ever had a flag.

It took a Virginian to unite the Union County

elements of the 1st and 12th Pennsylvania. In March 1777 Washington ordered Colonel Daniel Z. Morgan, 11th Virginia Regiment, to raise a provisional "Partisan Corps" from "chosen men" of Washington's Army in order to reinforce the Northern Army opposing Burgoyne. Although there were Virginians in the new unit, 193 of the 508 men in the new command were Pennsylvanians; others were from Maryland. The Partisan Corps wore the round hat and the hunting shirt.[44] Captain James Parr, 1st Pennsylvania, commanded the Sixth Company and Hawkins Boone the Seventh in the Partisan Corps. The Corps was present at all the actions in the Saratoga Campaign where Burgoyne was captured. In 1778 the officers and men were returned to their parent units.[45] Parr, as a major, commanded his own provisional rifle corps in 1779 and 1780, composed of men drawn from the 1st and 3d Pennsylvania.[46] Without question, this unit represented another reunion of men from Union County.

Even as John Lowdon's men were settling in to life in the Continental Army before Boston in 1775, measures were being taken for defense at home. In Pennsylvania, the term "Associators" had meant volunteer militia since 1747;[47] but in 1775 the title was in general use throughout the colonies to describe

1. Fort Reed
2. Fort Horn
3. Fort Antes
4. Fort Muncy
5. Fort Brady
6. Potter's Fort
7. Watson's Fort
8. Lower Fort in Penn's Valley
9. Fort Menninger (Widow Smith's mill)
10. Boone's Fort
11. Fort Freeland

By the summer of 1780, the forts above had been either abandoned or destroyed.

12. Fort Swartz
13. Fort Montgomery called "Fort Rice"
14. Hendrick's Fort (the Schoch Block-house)
15. Fort at Northumberland
16. Fort Bosley
17. Fort Wheeler
18. McClure's Fort
19. Fort Jenkins

L – Assembly Point at mouth of Lycoming Creek in October 1777

T – Titzel's Mill garrisoned in November 1779

those who had "associated" for defense against the British, in distinction to those who were neutral or who supported the crown.[48] On July 18, 1775, the Committee of Safety had begun issuing regulations for the guidance of Pennsylvania's Associators.[49] Shortly thereafter, the Continental Congress had resolved on the formation of the able-bodied men of all the colonies into militia, and this resolve was repeated by the Pennsylvania Committee on July 28.[50] From that time there was a growing tendency in Pennsylvania to use the terms "Associators" and "militia" interchangeably in correspondence. Nevertheless, the first organizations were, properly, Associators. On March 17, 1777 the new Pennsylvania constitutional government passed a militia law, making service compulsory for able-bodied men.[51] The appearance of new colonels and the apparent renumbering of battalions in 1777 are indicative of the application of the new law and the end of the Associators.

Northumberland County had three Associator Battalions in 1775[52] and the area later known as Union County was represented in all three. These units were Hunter's 1st, Potter's 2nd, and Plunkett's 3rd battalions. Elections for officers for Potter's Battalion had been held at Derr's Mill on September

12,[53] but Northumberland County historian Charles F. Snyder found Union County members likely, in early 1776, to have predominated in the Second Company of the 1st Battalion, the 2nd and 4th Companies of the 2nd Battalion, and in the 5th and 6th Companies of the 3rd Battalion.[54] In March 1776 the Committee of Safety for Northumberland County complained that some Associators had to travel two days from their homes to reach their place of assembly,[55] and later in that year changes were made. Two White Deer companies — the 2nd and the 4th — remained in Potter's 2nd Battalion but a 4th Battalion was formed with predominantly Buffalo Township elements under the command of Philip Cole.[56]

The frontier counties of Bedford, Westmoreland, and Northumberland did not furnish Associators to the "Flying Camp" formed to support the main army between July and December 1776.[57] In December Northumberland County did furnish a battalion to the main army. Buffalo and White Deer Township men were part of this unit. They were not well equipped. John Weitzel, writing from Sunbury to the Council of Safety on December 2, 1776, reported, "Blankets and woolen cloth are not to be had here. Linens are very scarce . . ."[58]

The men who composed this battalion were drawn from the Associators. The original rule for Associators, adopted September 12, 1775, specified that companies were to be numbered by lot so that each could be sent on alarms in turn.[59] Apparently this rule was not followed. The companies may have volunteered *en masse* or the men may have volunteered individually. The Pennsylvania Council of Safety referred to them as "volunteers."[60]

Colonel James Potter was the senior officer from Northumberland County with the volunteers but he functioned as a militia brigadier until April 1777, when he was, in fact, promoted to Brigadier of Militia.[61] Lieutenant Colonel James Murray was in actual command of the Northumberland County Battalion.

Some elements of the battalion served at Princeton on January 3, 1777, but the entire unit had not been assembled. Samuel Stelle Smith, who is meticulous in his order of battle, described those who represented Northumberland County at the battle as "detachments."[62] Clarke's Company (Clarke was from Buffalo Township) was at Reading on the day of the battle.[63] Linn writes of a skirmish at Piscataway, New Jersey, in February 1777 in which Clarke's Company was engaged.[64] This was probably the last action in which our Associators were involved.

It is probable that our Associators wore no uniform other than home-made varieties of hunting shirts. In the summer of 1775 the four battalions of Associators in Philadelphia did have uniforms, but when they served in the Princeton campaign, only the light infantry companies were still uniformed.[65]

The Northumberland County Associator Battalions probably had a flag. The original organization of the Associators included a "Standard-bearer" for each battalion.[66] Colonel Cole, of our own 4th Battalion, was authorized to spend 100 pounds for "drums, colours, etc., for the use of his Battalion."[67] Two Associator flags are known, those of the Hanover Associators and of Proctor's Battalion of Westmoreland County.[68] None from Northumberland County are known to have survived.

On March 17, 1777, the new Constitutional government of Pennsylvania passed a compulsory militia law. All able-bodied men, eighteen to 53 years old, constituted the militia of the state. Officers up to and including colonels were elected and, on election, commissioned for three years. A County Lieutenant commissioned by the state government was in general charge of the organization and operation of the militia in each county.

In every company the men were divided by lot into eight classes. In case of need the first class of each company was to be called to duty first. If the need were greater, the first two or three classes were to be called simultaneously. A class was liable for two months of service after which it was to be succeeded in numerical rotation by classes which had not served.

Officers were arranged for service in an elaborate scheme. The first draft of militia was to be commanded by the captain of the first company, the first lieutenant of the second company, the second lieutenant of the third company, and the ensign of the fourth company. The plan was carried through to the eighth class in which the captain of the eighth company, the first lieutenant of the seventh, the second lieutenant of the sixth, and the ensign of the fifth company were to command. Field officers of the battalions were also to be divided for service in turn.[69]

In effect, militia battalions were administrative and training organizations which furnished appropriately proportioned shares of members to ad hoc organizations for two months of operational service. Northumberland County had four battalions of militia under the new law. Kelly's 1st Battalion, with the exception of one company, was composed of men from Buffalo and White Deer Townships. Murray's 2nd Battalion was from Turbot and Mahoning Townships; Hosterman's 3rd were residents of Penn

and Augusta Townships; and Cookson Long's 4th were men from Bald Eagle and Muncy Townships.[70]

The new militia system seems to have been in effect by the summer of 1777 although the battalion commanders appear to have been forced by circumstances to remain in duty stations without relief. Kelly, of the 1st Battalion, had the first class of militia on the frontiers in the summer of 1777.[71] One authority says that he was at Fort Reed (Lock Haven) for six months.[72] Murray, of the 2nd Battalion, seems to have had the second class with the main army; and later the third and fourth classes of three battalions.[73] The third and fourth classes of Cookson Long's 4th Battalion went to relieve Kelly.[74] Linn says that Murray's Battalion was at Brandywine on September 11, 1777.[75] They must have made a hairbreadth arrival, for the returns of the Deputy Adjutant General show no Northumberland County battalion with the Pennsylvania militia on September 6, 1777.[76] The third and fourth classes of the 1st, 2nd, and 3rd Battalions of Northumberland County were ordered to join the main army on October 23. It was these men who had no weapons and were so "badly off for blankets. . . and but thinly clad."[77] They were in an engagement at Guelph's Mill on December 11, 1777,[78] and in camp near Philadelphia on December 22.[79]

In January 1778 orders for the fifth class of militia to join the main army were rescinded because of the threat of attack by Indians.[80] There would be no further need to go to Philadelphia to find the war. The war was coming to Union County.

We have already seen the uneasiness of the early inhabitants as well as the new immigrants who had begun to leave the area in May 1778. Samuel Hunter noted that Cookson Long's Battalion, reporting at strength of 265 in May, 1778, was "now less than it was last fall by sixty men on account of them leaving the frontiers for fear of the Indians."[81] The County Lieutenant had weapons for only three of the eight classes of militia on May 31, 1778, and he could not deploy some classes "for want of provisions, as for meat there is little to be had in this County, and that very dear."[82]

The land between Pine Creek and the West Branch of the Susquehanna was still Indian territory before and during the Revolution, and it gave ready access to the Indians for attack on the settlers. In 1777 there had been a series of attacks by Indians on settlers in what are now Clinton and Lycoming Counties. An arrow drawn on a map to represent the thrust of Indian pressure would aim east from Pine Creek towards Muncy and then turn south between the North and West Branches of the Susquehanna River. In 1778 there were rumors of an intended Tory and Indian assault on the North Branch with Northumberland itself thought to be their objective.[83]

Colonel John Kelly was on duty in Penn's Valley in May 1778 when there were further Indian attacks near the mouth of Bald Eagle Creek, near Lycoming Creek, and at Loyalsock. In June a massacre occurred in what is now downtown Williamsport.[84] The people of "White Deer and Buffalo Valleys fled to the river and forted themselves at various points."[85] About June 12th Colonel Hunter ordered the evacuation of all settlers on the West Branch above Fort Muncy, since he had no means to defend them.[86] The "Big Runaway" had begun.

On July 3 Walter Butler, leading a contingent of Tories and Indians, totally defeated and almost annihilated the militia of the Wyoming Valley in the vicinity of modern Wilkes-Barre. The news precipitated a panic, and even some of the militia were affected. John Allen, serving in McMahon's Company on the east bank of the West Branch near Chillisquaque, said: ". . . everybody, officers, privates, women, and children," went down the river.[87] Samuel Wallis, in a letter written July 24, says that Samuel Hunter had ordered all troops off the West Branch when he heard of the Wyoming Massacre, and that this order precipitated the Runaway.[88] Hunter may have given such an order, but the Runaway had already started in May. Hunter's order, given in June, aggravated an already tense situation. John Allen made no bones about it as he offered no excuse for running because of orders. The men of McMahon's Company, at least, had needed no order to leave their station.

By July 24 Brodhead's 8th Pennsylvania — the Continentals — had reached Sunbury.[89] Taking station at Muncy, Brodhead sent a captain and 25 men to Penns Valley.[90] One cannot escape the suspicion that, in the Buffalo Valley at least, the Runaway had not lasted long. Brodhead would not have sent troops into Penns Valley if there were no one to protect. He could not have supported that small detachment at that distance. Kelly's men must have been available to support and to cover the interval between Muncy and the detachment. General Potter, returning from military duty to Penns Valley, wrote on July 25 that the farmers had generally returned.[91]

The men of the 8th Pennsylvania were soon replaced by Hartley's Additional Continental Regiment, which sent Carberry's mounted troop across the West Branch. In the fall of 1778 Kelly, commanding

Clarke's, Forster's, and Thompson's Companies of militia, was active scouting Bald Eagle, Pine, Lycoming, and Fishing Creeks.[92] The Runaway had encouraged the Indians, and there were Indian attacks at White Deer and at Dry Valley in 1778.[93]

The inhabitants, in a Memorial of November 25, 1778, addressed to the House of Representatives of Pennsylvania, asked for exemption from taxes. They described their situation: "Scarce a single family remained in their habitations; the women and children were most generally removed; great loss of property was sustained by almost every individual; and what was still more distressing, the harvest in most places was lost."[94] Linn[95] and Meginnes[96] agree that most people had left the Buffalo Valley and the West Branch by 1779.

Nicholas Pontius loyalty oath of 1777. From the collection of Glenn and Ruth Wehr Zimmerman.

Most had gone, perhaps, but not all. In May 1779 John Sample and his wife were killed at White Deer.[97] Indian attacks had continued between the North and West Branches throughout the autumn of 1778 and had gained intensity in the spring and summer of 1779. "Several families were taken prisoner."[98] The fact that nearly 60 men, woman, and children were either killed or taken captive after 1779 strongly suggests that many had remained.

Hartley's Continentals were withdrawn to march in the Sullivan Expedition but Kelly's Battalion along with Clark's, Forster's, and Thompson's companies were called to duty in the spring.[99] Kelly's Battalion moved its station in 1778 and 1779, always southward and closer to the Susquehanna; by mid-1779 the Battalion had its headquarters at Derr's Mill, in present-day Lewisburg.[100] Fort Menninger, built in 1778 near the Widow Smith's Mill at White Deer,[101] was abandoned and on July 8, 1779, was burned by the Indians.[102] Forts Menninger and Muncy had been evacuated in early July in the face of an impending Tory and Indian attack, and the ensuing flight of women and children has been called the "Second Runaway." The fall of Fort Freeland has sometimes been given as the reason for this Runaway, but Freeland with its garrison was captured later, on July 28, 1779. [103]

In 1779, as in 1778, some inhabitants stayed in their clearings while others soon returned to theirs. One family, former residents of the east bank, moved back in October 1779; this was Mary Brady, widow of Captain John Brady (killed by Indians near Muncy in 1778), who with her children moved to Smoketown in Buffalo Township.[104]

The German Regiment, another Continental unit, was assigned to Northumberland County in 1779. Very small detachments of this Regiment were stationed in the Buffalo Valley until mid-1780 at Smith's Mill, Titzell's Mill, and French Jacob's Mill. Kemplen's very small Northumberland County Ranger Company garrisoned Fort Menninger in November 1779.[105] They were in place to protect settlers, evidence that the area of White Deer and Buffalo Townships had not been completely abandoned. Additional evidence that the area was not totally deserted is provided by the victims of Indian attack in 1780; between April and July thirteen people, five of them children, were killed in an area extending from White Deer to West Buffalo Township. In April 1780 Hunter wrote, "We could turn out one hundred of good woodsmen, but the country is quite drained."[106] In August the inhabitants, protesting the removal of the German Regiment, told the State Executive Council that the County was "now so much reduced as to be unable of itself to support a war with the Indians."[107]

The militia system was, in fact, inadequate to the needs of the area. In 1777 Kelly was in command of the first class of Northumberland militia on the frontiers, Murray had the second class with the main army, and the third and fourth classes were called to the frontiers in their turn. This was the system prescribed by the militia law, but by 1778 and 1779, the system had failed. In both years Kelly was in command of three companies of his own Battalion. It was almost as though the west bank of the West Branch was on its own. Scouting and patrolling in anticipa-

tion of raids by small Indian war parties was required from April to October. Even if it had been possible to arm the entire militia, it was economically impossible to maintain the entire male labor force of the county on duty for any two months of that period, the most important farming months. Similarly, no significant proportion of the militia could be expected to be off the farm during those months.

Several solutions to the problem were attempted. On May 26, 1780, the State authorized the formation of "Pennsylvania Volunteers," who were to undertake the active duty normally performed by the militia. Each company was to provide or hire two men to be "Volunteers." Small detachments and parties of militia were active for short periods in the years that followed and were probably "Pennsylvania Volunteers." Unfortunately, there are no records extant to confirm that hypothesis.[108]

Another solution was the formation of long-service "Ranging Companies." In early 1776 the Northumberland County Committee of Safety had recommended such a solution.[109] In 1779 a company was raised in Northumberland County for seven months of service and did serve at Fort Menninger in 1779. It was again raised in 1780, but it did not relieve the need for militia completely. In 1780 Kelly had called Thompson's Company to duty following an Indian attack near the mouth of Buffalo Creek,[110] and McCay's Cumberland County Militia Company was on duty in the Buffalo Valley in November.[111]

Thomas Robinson's Ranging Company, enlisted for seven months but continued through reenlistment and recruiting, was raised in 1780.[112] Linn says some members were from the Buffalo Valley.[113] Detachments of the Company, Lieutenant Peter Grove's and Lieutenant Samuel McCrady's, operated independently and often in the Buffalo and White Deer Township areas. It is not surprising that the Detachments were separated from the company. On April 8, 1781, Captain Robinson had 40 men enrolled, "but many . . . naked, not a blanket among them."[114]

Grove's and McCrady's Detachments were active that summer on the frontier, but nineteen people, men, women, and children, were killed or captured at Buffalo Creek, Kelly's Crossroads, Mifflinburg, and Dry Valley. There is no record of militia activity. In December the inhabitants protested to the Executive Council about the transfer of Robinson's Company to Lancaster and said it was impractical to draw from the militia for defense.[115]

Mary Brady and her children, working their farm at Smoketown by day, spent their nights during the

ABOVE: Colonel John Kelly's marker is located in the Lewisburg Cemetery, while a Pennsylvania Historical and Museum Commission marker can be seen near his home in Kelly Township. Photo by Jim Walter.

MIDDLE RIGHT: Colonel John Kelly's house stands a short distance off the road on Colonel Kelly and Red Ridge Roads, Kelly Township. Photo by Jim Walter.

Colonel Kelly's Revolutionary War payroll for the First Battalion of Northumberland County Militia covered the period from July 16, 1780 to August 15, 1780. On the payroll were Colonel John Kelly; Captain James Thomson; Lieutenant Joseph Poak; Ensign Alex Ewing; Joseph Glen; John Young; Peter Wilson; John, Thomas, and James Smith Poak; John Wilson; Joseph Brindage; Hance Fleeman; William and Thomas Black; James Hamerly; Hugh Rodman; and Jonathan Iddings. From the collection of the Union County Historical Society, #91.38.1, a gift of Robert B. Webster.

dangerous months of the year in the company of ten or twelve families at Jenkin's Mill.[116] Despite the danger, signs of optimism had begun to appear A mill was built at New Berlin in 1780 and the first mill in Lewis Township was built in 1781.[117]

Robinson's Company returned to the West Branch in March 1782.[118] In mid-April Lieutenant Moses VanCampen and twenty men of the Company were defeated by Indians at Bald Eagle Creek, and the entire group either killed or captured.[119] Meginess says that Robinson's was at Fort Muncy; but Thomas Black, serving with McCrady's, was stationed at Fort Menninger for six months beginning in the spring, and he says that Robinson's and possibly Grove's Detachment as well were there.[120]

On May 6 Indians ambushed a party of George Overmeier's Company in Limestone Township and killed two men.[121] Winfield was the site of the next Indian attack. On August 13 John Lee's home was struck. Six persons died or were captured; among the prisoners were two children. The cessation of hostilities was proclaimed on April 6, 1783, but hostilities had practically ceased when American independence was recognized on November 30, 1782. There was a general return to the area of those who had left. A certain sign of better times is a receipt signed in Wyoming and dated July 8, 1783. The receipt shows that Robinson's Company had finally received new

The John Lee stone springhouse in Winfield was at or near the site of the last Indian massacre in Union County in 1782. The structure still stands on the south side of Main Street, Winfield, and appears in real photo postcards c. 1906. From the collection of Gary W. and Donna M. Slear.

BELOW: The marker for the Overmyer Fort on Smith Road was erected by descendants in 1976. Photo by Jim Walter.

clothing.[122] Times had been bad; "blankets and woolen cloth are not to be had . . . as for meat there is little to be had . . . great loss of property was sustained by almost every individual . . . so much reduced as to be unable . . . to support a war with the Indians . . . many are naked and not a blanket among them."

The toll of casualties from Indian attacks and the location of the attacks are grim proof that not all inhabitants had abandoned Buffalo Valley. The efforts of Kelly's militia are proof not only of service but of continued residence. There would have been no reason for defense and no militia to offer defense had the area been uninhabited.

The West Branch had contributed men to the main army: Thompson's Pennsylvania Rifle Battalion; Morgan's Partisan Corps; Parr's Rifle Corps; the 1st, the 12th, and the 13th Pennsylvania. These are proud names, distinguished regular Continental units to which Union County made the gift of more fighting men than could be afforded. More men from Union County had served in the Northumberland County battalions, both Associator and Militia, of 1777. The significant contribution of Union County to American independence had been in human resources, not only the men who fought in the main army, but also the men and women who had the courage to stay and fight when their homes became the battlefield. The story of the trying days of the Revolution were finished. A solid foundation for building in the future had been laid.

THE OVERMYER FORT

NEAR THIS MARKER STOOD THE HOME OF JOHN GEORGE OVERMYER WHO CLEARED THIS LAND IN 1775 AS ONE OF ITS FIRST SETTLERS. HIS TWO STORY HOUSE WAS BUILT OF WHITE PINE LOGS UP TO 2 FEET THICK WITH A SPRING RUNNING THROUGH ITS PARTIAL CELLER. IT SERVED AS A PLACE FOR NEIGHBORS TO RALLY DURING TIMES OF INDIAN ATTACK. WHEN THEIR NUMBERS INCREASED, THE SETTLERS ERECTED THE OVERMYER FORT NEAR THIS HOUSE. CAPTAIN OVERMYER SERVED IN THE REVOLUTIONARY WAR AND FROM 1776 TO 1777 LED A COMPANY OF VOLUNTEERS AGAINST THE INDIANS AND LATER THE BRITISH. HE ALSO ORGANIZED AND LED SQUADS OF MEN TO PROTECT THE FRONTIER SETTLEMENTS DURING THE DIFFICULT YEARS FROM 1779 TO 1783. BORN IN BLANKENLOCH, BADEN GERMANY IN 1727 AND IMMIGRATING TO AMERICA IN 1751, HE DIED ON HIS FARM IN 1805. HIS GRAVE IS IN DRY RUN CEMETERY.

ERECTED IN THE BICENTENNIAL YEAR OF 1976 BY HIS DESCENDANTS

ENDNOTES

[1] A list of Revolutionary War soldiers was compiled by the D.A.R. and Dr. MaryBelle Lontz and is the library of the Union County Historical Society. It is very informative and lists the place of burial of each soldier.

[2] John Blair Linn, *Annals of Buffalo Valley, Pennsylvania, 1755-1855*, Harrisburg, 1877, 56.

[3] Linn, 65.

[4] Linn, 76.

[5] *Colonial Records of Pennsylvania X*, Harrisburg, 1852, 279.

[6] John Carter, "The Committee of Safety of Northumberland County," *Northumberland County Historical Society Proceedings XVIII*.

[7] *Colonial Records X*, 652-653.

[8] Carter.

[9] *Colonial Records XI*, 146.

[10] *Colonial Records XI*, 187, 194, 197; Heber G. Gearhardt, "Col. Samuel Hunter," *Northumberland County Historical Society Proceedings IV*.

[11] Van Doren provides details of correspondence to General Clinton from William Rankin, Colonel of militia in York County, and one "Martin" Weaver, said to have been a Captain of Northumberland County militia, in which they offered to furnish an entire battalion for British service in 1778. By 1780 Rankin claimed to have 7,000 secret recruits willing to serve the British. Samuel Wallis of Muncy, in correspondence with Clinton and with Howe, never offered such rosy prospects to the British, although he was instrumental in effecting Arnold's defection. The Memoranda of the inhabitants to various State authorities never hint at changing sides if requests are not met. The letters of Samuel Hunter, reporting attitudes to the central government of Pennsylvania, contain no hint of suspected disloyalty. The experience of the British during the War of the Revolution was disillusioning to them. Tory promises of numerous recruits were very seldom kept. The conspiracy, if there was one, could not have been widespread. Not enough people knew of it.

[12] John F. Meginness, *Otzinachson: A History of the West Branch Valley of the Susquehanna*, Williamsport, 1889, 432-458, quoting the journal of the Reverend Philip Vickers Fithian.

[13] Meginness, 475.

[14] Linn, 154, quoting Samuel Hunter.

[15] *Colonial Records X*, 310-313.

[16] *Colonial Records X*, 662.

[17] *Colonial Records X*, 715.

[18] *Colonial Records X*, 730.

[19] Frederick A. Godcharles, *Chronicles of Pennsylvania III*, New York, 1944, 381; Linn, 175; Meginness, 472.

[20] T. Kenneth Wood, "The Kentucky Rifle and The Rifle Boring Mill of 'Widow Smith,' " *Northumberland County Historical Society Proceedings VII*.

[21] *Colonial Records X*, 706.

[22] Linn, 143, quoting letter by Samuel Hunter, written Nov. 1, 1777.

[23] Linn, 144, quoting letter by Samuel Hunter written Nov. 11, 1777.

[24] *Pennsylvania Archives 2nd series XIV*, 332; and *5th series VIII*, 637.

[25] *Pennsylvania Archives 1st series VI*, 570.

[26] *Journals of the Continental Congress II*, 104.

[27] "History of the Organization of the United States Infantry," *The Army Lineage Book*, Washington, D.C., 1953.

[28] Francis B. Heitman, *Historical Register of the Officers of the Continental Army During the War of the Revolution*, Washington, D.C., 1914, 47; John Blair Linn and William H. Egle, *Pennsylvania in the War of the Revolution, Battalions and Line*, Harrisburg, Pa. 1880, I, 1-42, 303-309; "Notes on Troop Units in the Cambridge Army," *Journal of the Company of Military Historians 23:3*, Washington, D.C.

[29] *Journals of the Continental Congress*, 1775.

[30] Linn and Egle, I, 5 quotation from James Thacher's *Military Journal of the Revolution*, Hartford, CT, 1862.

[31] Alan Kemp, *American Soldiers of the Revolution*, London, 1972, 12; Robert L. Klinger and Richard A. Wilder, *Sketch Book 76*, Arlington, VA, 1967, 16; Harold L. Peterson, *The Book of the Continental Soldier*, Harrisburg, 1968, 219, 221-223, 229; C. Keith Wilbur, *Picture Book of the Continental Soldier*, Harrisburg, 1969, 30; Brigadier Peter Young, *George Washington's Army*, New York, 1972, Plate G.

[32] Fritz Kredel and Frederick P. Todd, *Soldier of the American Army*, Chicago, 1941, text accompanying Plate 2; Colonel John Womack Wright, "Some Notes on the Continental Army," *William and Mary College Quarterly Historical Magazine*, reprinted by Hope Farm Press, Cornwallville, NY., 1963.

[33] Lefferts, *Uniforms of the American, British, French and German Armies of the War of the Revolution*, New York Historical Society, 1928, Reprinted WE, Inc., Old Greenwich, CT (undated), 73, 122-126, quoting contemporary news items describing the dress of deserters; "The Thompson Wescott Description of Military Dress during the American Revolution," *Journal of the Company of Military Historians, 12:1*.

[34] Kemp, 12, quoting Washington's General Order of July 24, 1776.

[35] Linn and Egle, illustration at frontispiece, details, 12.

[36] Heitman, 48-50.

[37] Linn, 106; *Pennsylvania Archives 2d series XIV*, 358.

[38] Heitman, 114, 256-599.

[39] Heitman, 47-48, 52; Linn and Egle, I, 193-234, 256-286, 767-774.

[40] Lefferts, 122.

[41] John R. Elting, *Military Uniforms in America: The Era of the American Revolution*, San Rafael, CA, 1974, 86-87; Lefferts, 125, 131; "Thompson Wescott Descriptions," *Journal of the Company of Military Historians 12:1*.

[42] Heitman, 52; Linn and Egle, I, 757-764.

[43] Elting; Lefferts; Young; "Thompson Wescott Description," *Journal of the Company of Military Historians, 12:1*.

[44] Peterson, 222, copied after illustration by Trumball.

[45] Linn and Egle, I, 311-315; Gearhardt; Wright, 57.

[46] Wright, 57.

[47] William P. Clarke, *Official History of the Militia and of the National Guard of the State of Pennsylvania I*, 1909, 65.

[48] *Colonial Records, X*, 279, 282, 310-313; Pauline Maier, *From Resistance to Revolution*, New York, 1972.

[49] *Colonial Records, X*, 316-319.

[50] *Colonial Records, X*, 292.

[51] Clarke, I, 19.

[52] *Pennsylvania Archives 2d series XIII*, 258.

[53] Linn, 90, points out that the report of election, dated February 24, 1776, in its full text confirms the date and place of election as stated; *Pennsylvania Archives 5th series VIII.*

[54] Charles F. Snyder, "The Militia of Northumberland County During the Revolution," *Northumberland County Historical Society Proceedings XVIII.*

[55] *Pennsylvania Archives 2d series XIV*, 334-367.

[56] *Colonial Records X*, 746; Snyder; *Pennsylvania Archives 2d series XIV*, 325; and *5th series VIII*, 657-661.

[57] "Notes on Troop Units in the Flying Camp," *Journal of the Company of Military Historians* 26:1.

[58] *Pennsylvania Archives 1st series V*, 85.

[59] *Colonial Records X*, 319-320.

[60] *Colonial Records, X*, 28.

[61] Linn, 139, 143-144; Gearhardt.

[62] Samuel S. Smith, *The Battle of Princeton,* Monmouth Beach, NJ., 1967, 35.

[63] Linn, 121.

[64] Linn, 141.

[65] "Associators of the City and Liberties of Philadelphia, 1775," *Journal of the Company of Military Historians II:1*; "Dover Light Infantry Company, Delaware Militia, 1776 1777," *Journal of the Company of Military Historians, 8:2.*

[66] *Colonial Records X*, 319-320.

[67] *Colonial Records X*, 744; *Pennsylvania Archives 2d series I*, 578-579 provides an unsigned and undated regulation which must have applied to either the Associators or the militia of Pennsylvania. It could not have applied to the Continental or the State troops, since they were promised uniforms as inducements to enlist. The regulation: "Each Battalion to have a Grand regimental Colour (if they chose to put themselves in Uniform) their facings to be of this colour, & four Grand Division Colour Flags of Colours from each other. The Grand Regimental Colour to be more Showy than the others & to be bourne by the Ensign in Chief whose rank shall be that of the Eldest Lieutenant."

[68] *National Geographic Magazine*, Sept. 1934, 268, 365, 370.

[69] Clarke, 19-22.

[70] Snyder; *Pennsylvania Archives 2d series XIV.*

[71] Linn, 141, 143.

[72] Thomas L. Montgomery, *Report of the Commission Forts of Pennsylvania*, Harrisburg, 1916, 359, 417.

[73] Linn, 143.

[74] Linn, 143.

[75] Linn, 143.

[76] Clarke, 92.

[77] Gearhardt; *Pennsylvania Archives, 1st series, V*, 610, 762. The 1st class of Militia had left for Bristol on June 23, but had been brought back. They were again requested for duty on September 10. The 2d class was requested on September 12. The 3d and 4th classes were asked for on October 23, but did not leave until November 11. The presence of Buffalo and White Deer members of the militia at Brandywine should be considered with some reservation. Linn, 143, confirms the departure of Kelly's 3d and 4th classes on November 11, but the 1st class had been on the frontier for two months.

[78] Linn, 146.

[79] Clarke, 93; Linn, 146.

[80] Linn, 151.

[81] *Pennsylvania Archives 5th series VIII*, 663.

[82] Meginness, 490; *Pennsylvania Archives 1st series VI*, 570.

[83] Meginness, 494, 516.

[84] Meginness, 489-495.

[85] Meginness, 506.

[86] Meginness, 506.

[87] *Archives of Bucknell University*, John Allen.

[88] Meginness, 510, quoting letter from Wallis to Timothy Matlack.

[89] L. E. Theiss, "The Hartley Expedition," *Susquehanna Tales,* Sunbury, PA. 1955.

[90] Theiss; Meginness, 510.

[91] Meginness, 511; Linn, 163; Theiss.

[92] *Archives of Bucknell University*, Thomas Black; John Blair Linn, *History of Centre and Clinton Counties*, Philadelphia, 1883, 20, quoting letter written by General Potter, May 19, 1779.

[93] Linn, *Annals*, 158.

[94] *Pennsylvania Archives 2d series III*, 250.

[95] Linn, *Annals*, 163.

[96] Meginness, 511.

[97] Linn, *Annals*, 171.

[98] Meginness, 591.

[99] Linn, *Annals*, 163.

[100] *Archives of Bucknell University*, Thomas Black.

[101] Dewey S. Herrold, "Frontier Forts in the Revolution," *Susquehanna Tales*; Montgomery, 393.

[102] Herrold, 393; Linn, *Annals*, 175; Meginness, 472.

[103] Theiss, "The Battle of Fort Freeland and the Second Runaway," *Susquehanna Tales*, Sunbury, PA, 1955.

[104] Linn, *Annals*, 221; Meginness, 583-584.

[105] Godcharles, 383; Linn, *Annals*, 179; Montgomery, 393.

[106] Linn, *Annals*, 104.

[107] *Pennsylvania Archives 2d series III*, 428.

[108] Clarke, I, 25; *Pennsylvania Archives 5th series VIII*, 672-682.

[109] Linn, *Annals*, 106, citing a letter from the Northumberland County Committee of Safety; *Pennsylvania Archives 2d series XIV*, 358.

[110] Godcharles, 384; Linn, *Annals*, 188; *Pennsylvania Archives 2d series XV*, 672-673, to locate the sites of frontier.

[111] Godcharles, 428.

[112] *Pennsylvania Archives 2d series XV*, 673; and *5th series VIII*, 682.

[113] Linn, *Annals*, 207.

[114] Linn, *Annals*, 200, citing a letter from General Potter; Meginness, 624, cites a letter from Robinson, dated June 15, 1781, in which he claims that 52 men enlisted, but utterly destitute of clothing and supplies.

[115] *Pennsylvania Archives 2d series II*, 540.

[116] Linn, *Annals*, 221; Meginness, 581-584.

[117] Godcharles, 392.

[118] Meginness, 647.

[119] Meginness, 648.

[120] Meginness, 647; *Archives of Bucknell University*, Thomas Black.

[121] Linn, *Annals*, 210.

CHAPTER 3

THE FRONTIER GENERATION

Like rural people elsewhere, the first generations in Union County were sometimes hard-pressed to provide the necessities through the changing seasons. A bumper crop filled the pots to overflowing during the late summer and fall, but the long winter and late spring might exhaust even well-stocked larders. For townsmen and villagers dependent upon wages for their daily bread, the scarcity of money was ever a problem. Cash inevitably flowed toward Pennsylvania's older communities to the south and east; three generations would come and go before a local bank appeared on the scene. The country store, where eggs and other country produce were exchanged for sugar and tea, tin-, iron-, copper-, and glass-ware, is, of course, proverbial. Bartering went far beyond this stereotype and was an essential part of almost every household.

The relative self-sufficiency of the region and the interdependency of neighborhoods is suggested by accounts kept by David and Jane Clarke Watson, prosperous farmers of West Buffalo Township. Scattered across 150 yellowed pages of a muster book for a company in which David had served during the Revolution are hundreds of entries relating to their sales and purchases between 1815 and 1830. Even incomplete, these records reveal many insights into their economy and into the daily lives of the persons with whom they dealt. The Watsons marketed a sizable list of farm products spread across the four seasons. In the spring, there were butter, bacon, eggs, oats, buckwheat, flax, and clover seed; in the summer wool, cheese, vinegar, soap fat, and meats; in the fall water, cider, apples, rye, oats, corn, wheat, beef, pork, and cordwood; and during the winter soap, lump fat and tallow, grains they threshed on the barn floor, smoked meats, and "strong" cider helped to take up the slack.

Meanwhile, neighbors of the Watsons, with less land and produce, exchanged either their services or money for the above-mentioned surpluses. In July 1817, for example, twelve persons were employed for periods ranging from one to three days mowing, pitching, and making hay; such temporary employees also did cradling, raking, and binding wheat. Two were women, each of whom raked hay for three days. The employment of women as field hands, however, seems to have been exceptional and limited to the peak of the harvest season. Mrs. Adam Miznor, one of the rakers mentioned above, was also employed by

Mrs. Watson to spin and sew for her in 1817 and 1818. She spun two dozen and three cuts of flax yarn at one shilling and six pence per dozen (a total of forty and one-half cents in the currency at that time), as well as three and one-half dozen of tow (flax) at one shilling and six pence per dozen; she also sewed two shirts for four shillings. In lieu of cash Mrs. Miznor accepted seven and one-half pounds of bacon, two quarts of vinegar, three bushels of buckwheat, and, presumably on her husband's account, twelve bundles of rye straw and one-half bushel of flax seed. In December Mrs. Miznor remained one shilling and six pence in debt; in June Mrs. Watson was the debtor by one pound, nineteen shillings and eight pence; but by July the account was "almost squared."

During the years covered by the accounts, Mrs. Watson engaged additional women to spin flax or wool in return for country produce; she also employed them to knit gloves and stockings, wash clothes, pick geese, hatchel flax, and help with butchering. A day's wage was usually equated to 25 cents. Mrs. Watson also had hired girls and provided them with boarding and lodging as well as goods equivalent to 50 cents per week. One was employed for several years, others for shorter periods. Such a relationship appears to have been an opportunity for a hired girl to acquire a wardrobe which she could not otherwise afford. In return for their services, Mrs. Watson supplied such items as cloth for a coat, flannel, ticking, combs, shirting, check, linen, and wool by the pound; she also provided credit at Mr. Cummings' store in Mifflinburg for the purchase of calfskin shoes and a bonnet and silk ribbon to decorate it. Mrs. Watson also extended credit to an employee to hire a seamstress for dressmaking and paid a debt of 87 cents owed by a girl's mother. On one occasion she paid tuition for schooling and 25 cents for a spelling book. The expenditure of cash was exceptional.

Meanwhile, David Watson was also exchanging goods for services with a variety of people: a local blacksmith; a painter, exchanging cider and apples for a coat of red paint on a wagon and feed trough; Elias Youngman, a hatter and founder of Mifflinburg, trading fresh beef and smoked pork for two neck collars and two pairs of "brich bands"; Withington, a clock maker; Dr. VanValzah, a physician; and Henry Moore, bartering apples and cider for hay-making.[1]

Had the Watson accounts been recorded through the decade of the 1830s, they might have reflected the

A working man's portrait by the Millmont amateur photographer, Urs H. Eisenhauer, was most likely purchased in a small, limited quantity by the sitter. "Twelve for a dollar" is what Eisenhauer charged for postcards that were often not sent but rather presented to people. From the collection of Delphia Shirk.

Buttermaking was documented on September 6, 1897, at the Slifer family farm on the grounds of the present-day federal penitentiary in Kelly Township. Clara (Long) Slifer and her mother-in-law, Charity V. Slifer, are pictured. From the collection of the Slifer House Museum.

Oliver Catherman and his daughter, Matilda, stand beside their bushel measures c. 1915 at his farm in Lewis Township. Red Astricans, Gravenstines, Sweet Boughs, and Starks are some of the apple varieties grown in that era. From the collection of Harold T. Catherman.

Butchering is the subject of a rural portrait c. 1902 at a farm on Cannon Road between Mazeppa and Cowan. The picture was taken by a photographer who was staying at the Great Western Hotel in Vicksburg. Left to right are: Bessie Rute Snyder, Elias B. Rute, Emma Rute Dieffenderfer, Sarah Elizabeth Stover Rute, Maize Rute Moyer, Charles Rute, and Aaron Nogle. Courtesy of Ethel D. Ruhl.

Boiling apple butter at the Jodon home at Forest Hill, West Buffalo Township c. 1922. From left to right: Mrs. Susan Jodon Heiser, Miss Flora Jodon, Mrs. Eva Jodon Cromley, Mrs. Mader, and Mr. Edgar Cromley. From the collection of Cherry Reigle Will.

advent of greater specialization on the farm resulting from the opening of the Pennsylvania Canal with outlets to it at Lewisburg, West Milton, and White Deer. Farmers might now carry grain to Frick and Slifer at Lewisburg or Datesman at West Milton for delivery to markets as distant as Philadelphia and Baltimore. Later dealings would have indicated a substitution of iron tools and implements for wooden ones. The pioneers had used wooden rakes and forks, flails and drags, and wooden plows tipped with iron; but as blacksmiths arrived upon the scene, metal tools and implements replaced wood in the fields and in the homes as well as in the barns and shops.

Specialization and the increasing use of labor-saving devices on the farm were promoted through the years by area farm organizations. As early as 1810, a handful of progressive farmers of Union County gathered at Milton with farmers of Lycoming, Columbia, and Northumberland Counties to organize an agriculture association. Seven years later the Union County Agricultural Society was awarding premiums for the best specimens of wheat and corn, the finest breed of hogs, the largest yields of potatoes, beets and cabbage, and butter judged to be superior in color and taste.[2]

Farmers who could afford to take advantage of horse-powered mowers and reapers eagerly awaited the inventions of Obed Hussey and Cyrus H. McCormick as they appeared on the market. Forty-seven years after an exciting demonstration of a reaper at East Lewisburg by Joseph M. Nesbit, an eyewitness recalled "the great crowds, composed of both farmers and townspeople, who came to witness the trial of the Hussey reaping machine, introduced by him for the harvest of 1853, the first machine of its kind ever seen in this section."[3] The firm of Geddes, Marsh and Company in Lewisburg hastily obtained use of the patent to build Hussey's reaper and were soon in operation.

Meanwhile, S.D. Bates, a young Yankee mechanic in the employ of Slifer, Walls and Shriner, a foundry at Sixth and Market Streets in Lewisburg, designed a reaper which the company considered superior to Hussey's. Whatever the merits of the two reapers, Slifer, Walls and Shriner turned out one hundred of their "Buckeye" reapers and mowers in 1860; spurred by Civil War demand, they doubled the output in 1862, only to see that doubled again in 1863. On a day in late May of 1863, headed by a banner identifying the maker, thirteen farmers from Columbia County drove their new Buckeye reapers down Market Street

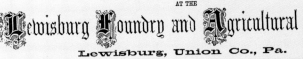

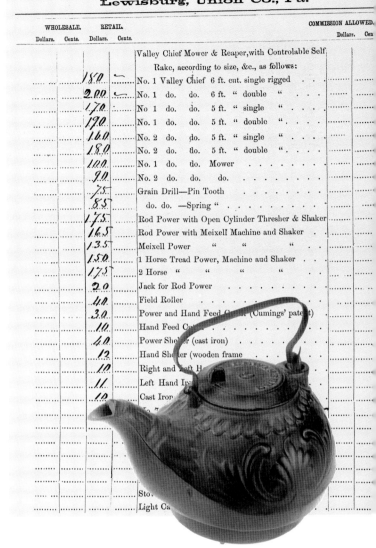

Price list for the Lewisburg Foundry and Agricultural Works. From the collection of the Union County Historical Society, #92.9.3.

Castiron teakettle marked LEWISBURG on its lid is 14 inches across and 12 inches high. From the collection of the Union County Historical Society, #98.20.1. Photo by the Terry Wild Studio.

PAGE 41 TOP: Clarence Zeller was photographed along with John Gower, brakeman, at the Union County Fair in 1915 with the county's first gas tractor. It had been purchased from Francis T. Baker, who ran a farming implement store at 217 Market Street, Lewisburg, for $585 in 1913. From the collection of Michael McWilliams.

PAGE 41 MIDDLE: Jacob Gundy (b. 1807, d. 1892).

PAGE 41 BOTTOM: Union County Fair booklet. From the collection of Gary W. and Donna M. Slear.

in a procession, halting other traffic along the way. After a short display of their shining implements, they crossed the river bridge enroute for home. Sixty-three other reapers were driven from the plant the same week. Unable to keep up with orders, the company built a new factory on the river bank, described as an "ornament to the town," where with a work force of 55 they manufactured more than 1,000 machines per year.

The phenomenal success of Slifer, Walls and Shriner did not destroy their competitor. Geddes, Marsh and Company was also turning out hundreds of their "Valley Chief," which they styled "The King of Harvesters," a "self-raking reaper and mower combined." For several decades the two implement makers were the largest employers in Lewisburg.

After slumbering for a few years, the Union County Agricultural Society was revived in 1853 through the efforts of Jacob Gundy of East Buffalo Township. Conversant on scientific farming in Europe and America, Gundy briefed his associates on new developments year after year at the Agricultural Society's annual meeting. On October 13 and 14, the first fair was held at New Berlin, where spectators viewed 275 articles which had been entered into competition and witnessed a stirring plowing match. Four years later, a committee headed by Gundy purchased a ten-acre tract at Brook Park on the turnpike west of Lewisburg for $150 per acre. They justified the high price with the convenience of the location and the fine stream of water (Bull Run), where they could water their stock. The Union County Fair caught on and was a fixture on the calendar for both farmers and townsfolk each September or October for a century.

PREMIUM BOOK

Union County Fair
BROOK PARK
Lewisburg, Penna.

Tuesday, Wednesday, Thursday, Friday

September 4 to 7, 1923

DAY AND NIGHT

Midway Attractions by the Corey Carnival Co.

THERE will be excursions on all railroads to and from UNION COUNTY FAIR to be held at Lewisburg, September 4 to 7, 1923. Special trains will be run from Brook Park through to Bellefonte. Look for Posters. For further information inquire of Sec'y

Local barn raisings — phenomenal sights — were photographed in the early twentieth century, as well as later in the 1970s when only plain sect Union Countians were still doing them the old way. TOP: From left to right in front of a barn frame are: Willard Klingman, George Bottiger, William Klingman, George Dietrich, William Rehrer, and David J. Boyer. From the collection of the Union County Historical Society, #89.5.9.6C. BOTTOM: Area Groffdale Conference Old Order Mennonites, assisted by others from Lancaster County, replace Miller's barn near Dice a week after the barn burned in the early 1970s. From the collection of the Union County Historical Society, #89.5.9.6 c.

Changes in farm production stemming from changing markets and the application of more scientific methods can be followed in the census returns. Wool production began to fall as early as 1850 as factory goods made inroads upon homespun. Rye acreage declined also at this time as most of the local distilleries succumbed to competition from larger population centers. By contrast, corn and wheat production increased each decade until 1890 when hard times and more intensive competition from the Midwest began to curtail plantings. Oats peaked a decade later, as did butter-making in the face of national brands and oleomargarine. Milk production and grass crops, on the other hand, expanded through the twentieth century despite a decline in the number of milk cows. Hogs increased in number until about 1920 when competition from western packers began to close local slaughter houses.

The number of horses on Union County farms averaged about 4,700 during the last twenty years of the nineteenth century, equaling one for each four persons in the county. In many respects it was also the apogee of horsemanship. Local breeds were rated below those of Indiana, Illinois, and Iowa, and farmers eagerly awaited the spirited auctions of western horses each spring at the Great Western Hotel in Vicksburg or at the stables of hotels in Lewisburg and Mifflinburg. A well-matched team for the plow or the carriage was a source of pride to the owner, and the loss of a horse from an accident or disease was a tragedy. The local newspapers frequently mentioned the purchase or sale of a horse and occasionally recorded one's death. For the unfortunate town dwellers who owned no horses, they were always available at local liveries.

Both field and carriage horses fell victim to the horseless carriage and tractor during the first quarter of the twentieth century, and with their demise an epoch in American life ended. It was evident in the late 1960s that horses were returning to Buffalo Valley, the property of Amish and Mennonite farmers who were leaving suburban Lancaster County and resettling upon Union County's prime farm lands. The momentum continued throughout the 1980s, making the sleek trotters and box-shaped buggies familiar sights on the area's highways as they are still at the close of the century.

Scientific farming and costly horse-drawn implements were beyond the reach of many of the smaller husbandmen. A typical farm in 1860 had less than 100 acres, and a sizable portion of a farm was apt to be unsuited for agriculture. Furthermore, many farmers were "croppers" or tenant farmers, who received a half or smaller portion of the crops in return for their labor; the details of the agreement depended upon the ownership of the stock and machinery. Farm labor for these families was penurious and back-breaking during planting and harvesting. Leisure was limited to Sundays, winter, rainy days, and special events such as weddings, butcherings, and barn-raisings.

Recreation for young and old stemmed largely from their work and their intra-family relationships. Children spent much of their play time in the out-of-doors. In the spring there were woods and meadow flowers to entice them and young tea leaves and birch bark to titillate their taste buds; in the summer there was berry picking, fishing, wading, or bathing though many remained unable to swim; in the fall there were hickory nuts, walnuts, and chestnuts awaiting the gatherers; and in the winter there was sledding and skating.

There were also pets to enjoy, dogs and cats, of course, and it was not unusual for the family to make a pet of a horse, lamb, or cow and maybe even a squirrel, crow, chicken, or goose. When J.R. Follmer's goose died at the unusual age of 21, its obituary was reported in Lewisburg's *Chronicle*. It had been hatched in Centre County and had also lived in Clinton County before accompanying the family to Gregg Township. For twelve years it had hatched and reared about twelve goslings annually, and it died "full of honors, if not full of eggs."[4] In Lewisburg, John Reamer's goose was known to every resident of the town as it was seen daily from 1913 to the early 1920s, a few feet from his master and as attentive as a dog, as they trudged back and forth from the railroad depots to the post office with the mail sack.

For the children, there was also the barn with huge mows of hay and straw stacks to explore. There were the daily walks to school, Sunday school and church. For all of the family a drab day might be brightened by a buggy or wagon ride to the store or a call by a huckster or peddler.

Children were assets and were assigned duties appropriate to their ages: turning out or bringing in the cattle or ducks, gathering eggs and feeding livestock, or churning and other household chores. School terms, arranged to fit into the work calendar, were suspended during harvests and reopened when children could be spared. Unmarried daughters remained at home and shared the work with their mothers. Their responsibilities varied but sewing, knitting, spinning, gardening, berrying, and training younger brothers and sisters as well as the nieces and nephews as they came along were typical responsibilities.

Providing a farm for one's children was a goal close to the hearts of farm parents, but it was frequently beyond their means. Tillable land in the county was taken up rapidly. A second generation White Deer or Union Township family might find land suited to agriculture in more remote Hartley Township while lumbering occasionally opened farm-size tracts along the mountains, but there were more seekers than finders. By the 1840s the countryside was filled to overflowing, and for many years thereafter hundreds of the region's sons and daughters migrated to the west in search of homes. Some found them in western Pennsylvania and Ohio, others in Illinois, and a generation later in Iowa and Kansas.

In 1837 Dr. Thomas Van Valzah led an emigrant group from Union and Centre Counties to Freeport, Stephenson County, Illinois, and built the first gristmill there. No stone in that section was suitable for milling, so Van Valzah imported millstones from Union County. These same stones were used later in another mill owned by Union County native Reuben Cotherman.[5] The stones disappeared after Cotherman closed his mill around 1900, and their whereabouts is the subject of much speculation in Stephenson County 100 years later. Eight years later the Barber brothers of Limestone Township headed a party of 63 from the White Springs area to the prairies of northwestern Illinois, traveling by horse and wagon in the covered wagon tradition. A Mifflinburg colony settled in Bellevue, Ohio, in 1856; in 1878, 84 residents of Buffalo Township, representing almost 50 families, removed by rail to Severance, Kansas; in time place names such as Tiffin and Bellevue in Ohio, Monroe in Wisconsin, Freeport and Piper City in Illinois, Des Moines in Iowa, Kansas City in Missouri, as well as Winona, Minnesota, became familiar to those who remained behind. The advent of trunk line railroads, facilitating visitations back and forth, perpetuated and renewed the ties with the region's émigrés.

Meanwhile, it was not unusual for three generations to live under the same roof on Union County farms, the roles of each adjusting to the passage of time. Additional parts were added to houses so that the youngest child with his or her family could live in the larger part while the parents (now grandparents as well) could live in the smaller part, often called a *gross dawdi* or *gross mudda* house. Grandparents sometimes moved to town, however, leaving the farm to a daughter or son or to a tenant on shares. Lewisburg, Mifflinburg, and New Berlin had sizable numbers of such "retirees"; and hamlets such as Mazeppa, Winfield, Vicksburg, and New Columbia owed their growths in considerable part to such senior citizens. Removal to town, however, was apt to be a reprieve rather than a termination of farm labor; the need for additional hands brought them back during harvests, butchering, threshing, and other labor-demanding situations.

The Mensch farmstead on Mensch Road in Limestone Township is a good example of a local *grossdawdy* (grandfather) house. Photo by Jim Walter.

PAGE 45: 1867 plot drawing for the John Pontius farm. From the collection of Glenn and Ruth Wehr Zimmerman.

Assuring the inheritance of a farm by a son or daughter while providing fairly for other children in the family could become a knotty problem. Old deeds in the local courthouses offer documentation. In one instance a son agreed to take over his parents' farm of 150 acres for $3,000. One thousand dollars was to be divided equally among his brothers and sisters six months after the death of the surviving parent. The $2,000 was paid earlier as follows: "twenty bushels of wheat, twenty bushels of rye, ten bushels of buckwheat, ten bushels of corn, one bushel of salt, 150 pounds of hog meat, 50 pounds of beef, one-half acre of flax sowed, one-half acre of potatoes, leather for shoes, as much as needed, to be delivered yearly to the father and mother as long as they live whenever they call for them, delivered at market price and deducted from $2,000. Also, as many apples from the orchard as needed and fodder for two milk cows." In the event that the sum should be exhausted, the son was required to continue to provide the above-mentioned materials as needed as long as the parents lived, as

Farm families were usually photographed together, often with animals such as the cat and chicken seen here with the John Hoy family c. 1910. From left to right are: Gertrude Hoy, Thomas Shively, Mary Belle Hoy (wife of William Hoy, a missionary, not present), Mary Shively (daughter of Thomas and Ella), Ella Hoy Shively (sister of William and wife of Thomas), Mabel Hoy, and Charles Hoy. The Hoys lived a short distance south of Mifflinburg on what is now Brouse Road. Tom and David Brouse are the fifth generation living there. From the collection of the Union County Historical Society.

well as goods, money, or property to siblings who had not left home.[6] The latter is the concept of *aussteier* or "a good start" that is practiced in the same manner by our contemporary plain sect farmers, the Mennonites and Amish.[7]

A similar arrangement between parents and son provided that the son supply, during their natural lives, food and drink, clothes and washing, as they had need for them ". . . also a horse with saddle and bridle when he will ride out and if sick to find a good doctor, and if they cannot live peacefully together, to build a sufficient and good warm house with an iron stove in it close to the old house for them to live in."[8] Given the time and place, better insurance against adversity in old age can scarcely be imagined.

Of course, many farm sons, either from choice or necessity, left home to find employment elsewhere. The transition was eased by finding a master crafts-man who was in need of an apprentice. If both parties were satisfied, the arrangement was formalized in a contract. Master-apprentice contracts or indentures covered a host of occupations from carpentry to blacksmithing, and from pump making to practicing medicine.

One such agreement illustrative of the conditions prescribed in such situations was entered into by Michael Schoch with John Bubb and his father in 1797; in the agreement Schoch agreed to teach "the said apprentice the art and mastery of a joiner and also provide sufficient meat and drink, washing, and lodging fitting for said apprentice. At said term, the said master will give said apprentice a new freedom dues of woolen cloth or ten pounds speatie (cash) in lou thereof — said apprentice to take his choice." John Bubb, in turn, bound himself to serve for a term of two years and eight months. During this period "said apprentice his master faithfully shall serve, his secrets keep, his lawful commands everywhere gladly obey. He shall not do damage to his master . . . nor waste his goods nor lend them unlawfully. He shall not commit fornication, nor contract matrimony within said term. He shall not play at cards, dice or any other unlawful game whereby his said master may have damage with his own goods nor the goods of others. During the said term without license from his said master, he shall neither buy nor sell. He shall not absent himself day nor night from his said master's service without leave, nor haunt ale houses, taverns and play houses. But in all things as a faithful apprentice he shall behave himself toward his said master and all his during the said term." Both master and apprentice agreed to live in "true harmonae."[9] Thus the master

took over the responsibilities of a parent, taught the apprentice his trade, and provided him with a "nest egg" at the end of his term of service, receiving in return the apprentice's labor.

Obviously, spelling out the terms of the indenture in such detail did not always produce "harmonae." Samuel Frey, an eleven-year-old Cowan boy, whose father bound him out to work for a farmer during September and October of 1847 for three dollars per month and "board and keep," completed the inden-ture despite what must have been a heavy load for a boy of his age: morning barn chores by lantern before breakfast, field work throughout the daylight hours, and evening barn chores after dark. On the last day the farmer asked him to remain for several additional months and work for his board, explaining that he would expect him to "help with threshing, cutting wood, feeding stock, currying stock, etc., and go to school in between times." Samuel replied that he preferred to go to school regularly since the term lasted only four months. The farmer was displeased and said that the younger generation was being pampered. When he settled with Samuel's father, he complained that Samuel's work had not been satisfactory and that he would pay five dollars instead of six. Samuel never forgot his disappointment. Fifty years later, while looking through an old account book of his father, he found the following entry made with a quill pen: "Two months work by Samuel at $2.50 = $5.00, paid with beef and cider."[10]

By and large, farmers were a conservative people. They were distrustful of taxes levied in Washington, Harrisburg, or the county seat; and they preferred to do work days on the road in lieu of money payments. They at first opposed the public school law because it would require local taxes, and the promise of state subsidies did not sweeten the prospect. They tightened their belts through periods of depression when crops glutted the markets or when late spring frosts or inclement weather spoiled their harvests, pinning their hopes upon the next year's harvest rather than political nostrums. Some of them enjoyed the social activities of the Grange but most shunned its politics, and in the hard times of the 1890s they rejected Populism despite its appeal to western farmers. William Jennings Bryan with his panacea of "Free Silver" was no hero on Union County farms.

If farmers were rugged individualists in the management of their businesses, they were quick to respond to adversity. If a fire destroyed a neighbor's house or barn, they were ever ready to provide clothes, food, and shelter. Barn raisings frequently brought out 50 to 80 helpers, and sometimes as many as 100. In preparation for one, neighbors volunteered their teams and services to transport the timber from the sawmill to the barn site and to prepare it for the raising under the direction of a "master barn builder." Arriving at the scene just after daybreak, they ordinarily completed the framing before noon, in time to celebrate around a table "groaning" with food.

A raising in 1904 at the West Buffalo farm of Levi Shoemaker to replace a barn destroyed by sparks from a steam-driven threshing machine was typical of many others. Jacob Strickler selected the trees from the Shoemaker wood lot a mile from Pleasant Grove. John Burkey and William Roadarmel drew the logs to James K. Reish's mill and helped to saw them. Several parties hauled the timber to the foundation, which had been restored by local masons. "Uncle" Mike Noll, "the master builder," arranged the beams and planking, and mortised and tenoned the bracing, and had it all laid out with the floor in place for the designated November morning. The neighbors, including some wives who helped with the cooking and serving, arrived before the frost had melted, and the barn was raised with dispatch. One unpleasant incident marred the proceedings when a wind-blown board dropped upon Noll's back leaving him bruised and sore.[11] Barns are still raised in this manner by members of the plain sects. Daniel Zimmerman, a harness maker who lived and worked in the 1960s to 1980s behind

Buffalo Crossroads Grange in 1999. Photo by Jim Walter.

Ray's Church in Lewis Township, was such a master barn builder.

Whether Shoemaker's barn raising was celebrated with or without liquor was not recorded, but barn-raising and liquor were obviously congenial. However, the helpers respected the wishes of an owner who refused to condone alcohol. The danger involved in handling heavy timbers from perilous heights is suggested by a routine observed in the press where an account typically closed with the observation that the last timber had been put into place without incident. Having finished their work at Shoemaker's, the participants were reminded that the tenant had no straw, hay, fodder or grain, and that they would be needed through the winter. Presumably his plight did not need repeating, and the tenant survived to return the favors as they were needed.

Accidents and illnesses were common concerns at a time when there were few physicians and no rapid means of travel. Farms as well as saw and gristmills were dangerous places to work, and accidental deaths and injuries were reported in gruesome detail as they are now among the plain sects in their monthly paper, *The Diary*. Burns, scaldings, and drownings were relatively common, especially among children. Adults and children alike on farms were prone to serious injury or death from unruly animals and falls in the barn. Advances in farm machinery introduced new hazards to rural life. The train track with its fast-moving trains was another site of not-infrequent deaths for farmer or town dweller alike.

Home remedies were the usual means of treatment, and it was generally the mother who acted as the family doctor. Catherine Frederick, who married Daniel Catherman and bore seventeen children between 1818 and 1844, managed to raise all of them to adulthood with virtually no assistance from medical practitioners.[12] However, such successes were relatively rare. Complications arising from childbirth resulted in the death of many mothers. Epidemics of typhoid and other diseases took many lives. Tombstones and newspaper accounts reveal many cases where three or more members of a family succumbed to disease in a matter of days. Just across the county line in Centreville (Penns Creek), five members of the Daniel Weirick family died in a five-month period in 1860.

The artifices of pow-wow healers were in frequent demand, especially among the Pennsylvania Germans, and remarkable tales of healing abound. It was a skill passed down through generations from male to

A number of families in Union County have been living and working continuously on their farms for over a century. Among these families are TOP: Dwayne Reed, who is pictured with his favorite Arabian mare on his Furnace Road farm east of Mifflinburg, in West Buffalo Township. Reed raises salmon in the barn, taking advantage of the fine spring water supply on his farm. BOTTOM: Gerald and Kathy Boop are pictured in the new barn they recently built to hold 40 head of Holstein cows. Their farm, which has been in the family since 1780, is located on the south side of Penns Creek, southwest of Millmont. Photos by Jim Walter.

female and from female to male practitioner. Even after trained physicians became easily accessible, many area families continued to consult pow-wowers in the neighborhood and sometimes traveled a distance to go to an especially skilled one. This preference persisted well into the twentieth century, and as late as the mid-1970s there were some who still removed warts, cured headaches, and more. The area's practice of pow wow was the subject of a doctoral thesis at the University of Pennsylvania's Department of Folklore by Barbara Reimensnyder, originally a resident of Milton. Reimensnyder began her research as a graduate student working with the Union County Bicentennial's Oral Traditions Project in 1976.[13]

Other cooperative enterprises among neighboring farm families included butchering, which was too laborious for a family to undertake single-handedly. Thus, farmers pooled their resources and repeated the operation until all were served. November was butchering time; the hogs were then in prime condition, the autumn temperatures were low enough to preserve fresh cuts for some time, and the pressures of harvest were behind them. "The butchering campaign is well on now," one observer noted, " 'How much did your hog weigh?' is heard daily."[14] Newspapers reported hogs of exceptional size and congratulated their owners: "Daniel Rengler of West Buffalo Township has a living mass of pork and 'sassengers' which weighs 778 pounds."[15] Townspeople found it to be a good time to call on their friends in the country; "W.B. Mussina of Cowan butchered his porkers last week," one wag observed, "and the preacher visited him next day."[16]

Woodfires were kindled under the giant iron cauldrons, and the men moved to the pig pen with long knives for the throat cutting. They strung up the carcasses, still bleeding, to a tripod and applied scalding water to facilitate the scraping of the bristles. Once the principal butcher had carved out the loins, shoulders, and sides, the women took over the finer cutting, extracting head meat and cleaning the intestines. Later, they also participated in the grinding and stuffing of the sausage. By the time dinner was served (much of the preparation having been readied the day before), the heavier work was done, and there was time for relaxation and jollification. The pickling and smoking were completed during the days which followed.

A similar cooperative approach was used for threshings at the turn of the twentieth century. Threshing machines, powered and towed by steam engines belching sparks from their wood-burning fire pits, were halted a few yards from the great barn doors, and the entire crop of wheat and oats was threshed at a single sitting. It was a hot, strenuous, and occasionally frightening experience, but again the dinner assuaged the aches and pains.

Winters also created situations calling for cooperative labor. A blizzard might completely block a road and leave isolated families in peril. February of 1895 was the most severe in the memory of 89-year-old Henry Gast, Mifflinburg's venerable storekeeper. The temperature dropped to 26° below zero, and fierce winds lashed the snow into drifts of fifteen feet. Traffic on the roads and railroads halted. Ordinarily a farmer might "break" his road with a heavy team and box-sled, but such efforts were now ineffectual. For several days farmers could do little more than reach their barns and take care of necessities at home. On the fourth evening, Sunday, February 10, a gang of "twenty-three staunch hay seeds" from the Rand area of Lewis and West Buffalo Townships, with only horses and shovels to assist them, reached Mifflinburg. Residents greeted them like explorers returning from the Arctic. Peter Grove opened his oyster house and prepared a dinner for them while Augustus Heiter, the town's barber, invited them to his shop for a clean shave.[17] Other gangs spent several days breaking a track on the turnpike, starting from Lewisburg. The first evening found the group at Lochiel and second at Vicksburg; on the third day the 30 shovelers and mule team entered Mifflinburg just before noon. Several groups who had gone on sleighing parties to Milton and Lewisburg on Thursday, and whose safety had been a matter of concern, followed the triumphant shovelers into town. "The icy dignity" of Horace Glover, a member of one of the sleighing parties and a former member of the state House of Representatives, was said to have melted amidst the revelry of homecoming.[18]

Working cooperatively upon projects beyond the scope of his household, yet valuing his self-sufficiency, the attitude of the farmer toward public welfare is easily understood. When word circulated that families along the mountain in West Buffalo Township were suffering from unusually severe winter weather, generous donations of food and clothing were forthcoming; but when proposals were made to erect tax-supported county or township poor houses, the farmers gave them an almost unqualified rejection.

Yet, when oleo-margarine seemed to threaten their livelihood, these same farmers reversed their anti-government attitude. In the first decade of the twentieth century this laboratory concoction of hydrogenated vegetable oils and artificial coloring seemed to threaten the dairy industry, and farmers turned to the government for protection. A committee from Lewisburg, made up of Mr. and Mrs. John Wingert and C. Dale Wolfe, went incognito to the "oleo belt" in Pittsburgh where they purchased pound packages of "butter" at more than 100 stores. An analysis indicated that 75 of the samples were oleo and 35 were the genuine dairy product.[19] They submitted their evidence in court, and it became a part of the drive to prohibit the coloring of oleo by the manufacturer. These laws remained in effect in the state until the exigencies of World War II led to their repeal. Farmers backed the regulation of oleo to the hilt. They were also advocates of better roads and found a champion in Gifford Pinchot in the 1920s. Their bolt from the Republican Party machine in his behalf helped to undermine "boss" politics in the state and region.

ENDNOTES

[1] Papers of J. Clarence Watson.

[2] John Blair Linn, *Annals of Buffalo Valley, Pennsylvania, 1755-1855*, Harrisburg, 1877, 528-529.

[3] *Mifflinburg Telegraph*, July 6, 1900.

[4] May 28, 1875.

[5] *History of Stephenson County*, Freeport, IL, 1970, 175.

[6] Northumberland County Courthouse, Deed: D 223 (1820).

[7] Jeannette Lasansky, *A Good Start: The Aussteier or Dowry*, Oral Traditions Project of Union County Historical Society, Lewisburg, PA, 1990.

[8] Northumberland County Courthouse, Deed: M 359 (1803).

[9] Archives, Union County Historical Society.

[10] S.F. Frey's reminiscences, *Lewisburg Saturday News*, August 14, 1907.

[11] *Mifflinburg Telegraph*, November 25, 1904.

[12] *Lewisburg Saturday News*, November 16, 1895.

[13] *Powwowing in Union County: A Study of Pennsylvania Folk Medicine in Context*. Ph.D. thesis by Barbara L. Reimensnyder at the University of Pennsylvania, 1982.

[14] *Mifflinburg Telegraph*, November 26, 1897.

[15] *Mifflinburg Telegraph*, November 28, 1883.

[16] *Lewisburg Chronicle*, January 13, 1871.

[17] *Mifflinburg Telegraph*, February 15, 1895.

[18] *Mifflinburg Telegraph*, February 15, 1895.

[19] *Mifflinburg Telegraph*, July 30, 1909.

TOP: Edgar and Dorothy Schnure's farm stand on the Old Turnpike (a few yards east of Smeltz' gas station on Route 45) in the 1970s. School groups enjoyed coming to his pumpkin patch each fall. From the collection of the Union County Historical Society, #89.5.9.16.

BOTTOM: The farmers' market, also called "the auction," (recalling its beginning as a produce auction), has been a busy site each Wednesday since the 1950s. From the collection of the Union County Historical Society, #89.5.9.15.

CHAPTER 4

TRANSITIONS IN TRAVEL AND TRANSPORTATION

The Tulpehocken Road was as familiar to first-generation residents of Union County as the Pennsylvania Turnpike or Interstate Routes 80 or 81 are to their descendants seven generations later. Following older Indian trails, the Tulpehocken Road connected the Schuylkill Valley in the Reading area with Fort Augusta at the forks of the Susquehanna. When opened for wagons in 1769, it approached Sunbury by way of Herndon and the river, but a few years later an alternate was cut across Mahanoy Mountain, shortening the distance but increasing the perils of the traveler.

The Tulpehocken Road was the shortest route between the heavily populated southeast and the unoccupied frontier, and hundreds of pioneers followed it to Union County as well as the eastern townships of Centre County and the northern panhandle of Northumberland County. "Born in Berks County" appears over and over again in the obituaries of the first two generations to settle in Union County. It was the Tulpehocken Road which drew the attention of Philadelphia land speculators to the region and made many of the townships and villages "little Germanies."

Few contemporary accounts of the migration to Union County along this highway remain, but Samuel G. Frey of Cowan, who made the trip as a child in 1839 on a road roughly paralleling the older Tulpehocken trail, recalled the journey 57 years later: "Our folks chartered two Conestoga wagons, with two horses to each wagon, and packed them full with such goods as they wished to take with them, consisting in part of bureaus, chests, bedsteads, bedding and one ten-plate heating stove." Friends and neighbors gathered to wish them a successful journey, and *Viel Glick un en seef Reis* (We wish you good fortune and a safe journey) was heard on all sides as they took their departure from their old Berks County home to better their condition in the new country further west.

"We traveled on slowly, but sure. Sometimes they would use double teams from a valley to the top of the mountain; then go back and bring up the other wagon." Frey recalled that Ashland and Mount Carmel were only taverns and water-troughs while Sunbury was a village around a courthouse, where "cattle and sheep were roaming around the streets at large, unmolested from either citizen or pound master." Though there were bridges at Sunbury and

Lewisburg, Samuel Frey distinctly remembered driving their wagons onto a flat, perhaps at Northumberland or Winfield from which they were ferried across the Susquehanna. After six days on the road they reached Cowan, where a house, rented from a Berks County acquaintance, awaited them.[1]

From Sunbury the earliest arrivals followed trails left by the Indians which gave them access to Middle, Penns, and Buffalo Valleys. Recognition for the first improved road running the length of Buffalo Valley belongs to a Philadelphia brewer, Reuben Haines. A land speculator in the area, he helped to lay out Northumberland and purchased hundreds of acres in Penns Valley in what would become the eastern townships of Centre County. In 1766 Haines opened this region for purchasers by building a road from Blue Hill westward along the present-day Snyder/Union County line through or near the future sites of New Berlin, White Springs, Swengel, and Hartleton, and then across the Seven Mile Narrows by way of "Four Mile Tree" (Hairy John's Park) to Woodward. By the outbreak of the Revolutionary War, settlers were living along this track as far west as Hartleton.

In 1775 two public roads were laid out by the Court of Quarter Sessions at Sunbury. The first began on the Susquehanna just south of Lewisburg, crossed present-day Route 15 at the Lewisburg cemetery, angled into what would later be the route of the turnpike to Mifflinburg, and connected with the Haines Road just below Hartleton. The second, known as the Bridle Road, ran from the mouth of Bald Eagle Creek near Lock Haven to Sunbury by way of the Nippenose Valley and the West Branch of the Susquehanna River from the mouth of White Deer Hole Creek. The original sketch of this route in the Northumberland County Courthouse includes the principal clearings along the way — in Gregg, the homes of Hugh Colwell and Matthew Brown; in White Deer, the Smith Mill at White Deer Mills and the William Blythe Mill dam a mile below that; near West Milton, the Jacob Baker, John Fisher, and Peter Swartz tracts; in Kelly, the William Clark, Robert Fruit, and William Gray sites; and across Buffalo Creek, the Derr Mill dam and mill. At the mouth of Turtle Creek John Aurand's barn is identified, and at Winfield the home of John Lee — later the scene of an Indian massacre — is shown. At the foot of Blue Hill it intersected the Reuben Haines Road a short distance from the Northumberland Ferry.

The Watsontown/White Deer ferry was operating as early as 1822. At first it was poled, but the c. 1850 addition of a wire rope across the Susquehanna allowed it to be pulled across the river by Captain John Bly. The Blys operated the ferry for approximately 60 years. From the collection of the Union County Historical Society, #82.2.32.

In 1792 the Brush Valley Narrows Road was laid out, connecting at Cowan with the road to Lewisburg by way of Buffalo Cross Roads. Two years later a public highway "of the breadth of thirty-three feet forever" was ordered to be opened, cleared, and maintained from Watson's Ferry (White Deer) to Renegar's Mill on Little Buffalo Creek.

In 1802 Boal's Ferry, one mile south of West Milton, was linked to Buffalo Cross Roads by way of Kelly Point. Meanwhile, lateral roads between the military grants were opened, connecting with the main roads running east and west, and in a surprisingly short time the roadways familiar to twentieth-century residents were already in use. The roads ameliorated the isolation of the frontier and helped to create a community relationship. Residents with business at the county seat might reach Sunbury on horseback by fording the river or resorting to the ferry in high water. After 1814 New Berlin, the county seat of the newly formed Union County, became the hub of a network of roads serving all parts of the county.

Roads enabled the politically-minded to play politics and church-goers to make their way to Sunday services. They were obviously a boon to nascent villages. Their facilitation of travel is indicated by Linn, who listed the owners of six hotels in 1802: John Metzgar and Andrew Albright at the Lewisburg Ferry, Isaac Latshaw in Lewisburg, Christopher Baldy at Buffalo Cross Roads, Richard Van Buskirk in Mifflinburg, and Adam Wilt at the entrance of the Seven Mile Narrows.

Obviously there were serious limitations. Road maintenance, which was performed by the residents living on a particular thoroughfare, stopped when the track was passable; travel, particularly to more distant places, was reserved for winter when sleds could pass smoothly over the snow-flattened ruts, and horses could cross streams on the ice. Occasionally, hardy wagoners set out for markets in Easton or Philadelphia with produce. On February 18, 1803, diarist Flavel Roan noted that Shearer, McClure, and Fruit had returned with their wagons from Philadelphia after a three-week trip; and in February of 1809 he added that George and Davy Reznor went to Easton with grain in sleds, returning on the seventh day. Unfortunately, he offered no evaluation of either expedition, but few others seem to have been as venturesome.

Where traffic on a particular highway warranted the expenditure of substantial sums for construction and maintenance, the turnpike offered at least a partial solution to the road problem. Borrowing a procedure used widely in the Old World, businessmen in Philadelphia and Lancaster obtained a charter from the state in 1792 permitting them to build and operate a graveled road between these two municipalities. In return for their investment the company was permitted to collect tolls from the users, depending upon the size of the vehicle and the distance traveled.

Linking the port of Philadelphia with the fertile Lancaster Valley, the turnpike was an immediate success, and state legislatures from New Hampshire to Georgia were soon voting such franchises. Main roads thus became turnpikes and unimproved tracks — paralleling the turnpikes and usable without tolls — "shunpikes." Bridges across the principal streams were soon provided in the same manner.

A charter for a river bridge in Lewisburg was granted in 1814, and two years later the Burr-style bridge was open for business. Theodore Burr, the famous bridge builder, went to court, seeking damages from the Lewisburg Bridge Company for infringing upon his patents. The architect admitted to using Burr's plans but insisted that they had been used only after consulting him and obtaining his consent. Burr failed to collect.

By the 1820s local capital was available to build a turnpike between Lewisburg and Youngmanstown, and in 1828 a committee of Lewisburg businessmen obtained a charter and engaged James F. Linn to survey it. The contract was let, and by the close of 1829 the turnpike was in operation with toll gates at the west end of Lewisburg and eastern edge of Youngmanstown. The mailing address for the section closest to Lewisburg remains to this day "The Old Turnpike."

Meanwhile, a more ambitious project, to link Youngmanstown with Bellefonte (the Bellefonte, Aaronsburg and Youngmanstown Turnpike Company) by way of Penns Valley, was initiated in Aaronsburg. A charter was obtained in 1825, and the following year contracts were awarded to build it in four sections. Its completion put Buffalo Valley on a main line of travel from Lewisburg to Bellefonte and Pittsburgh. Additional turnpikes were immediately projected from Lewisburg to Brush Valley and from New Berlin to

1830 stock certificate of John Dunkle's for the Derrstown and Youngmanstown Turnpike, signed #17 by Treasurer R. Hayes. From the collection of Gary M. and Donna W. Slear. Photo by Terry Wild Studio.

Lewistown, but they failed for the lack of subscriptions. In 1851, however, Sugar Valley in Centre County was linked to White Deer by a turnpike after the state subscribed for a block of the stock.

Turnpikes did not take the farmer out of the mud, but they accommodated heavier and faster traffic. Centre County farmers found outlets for their grain and flour at Datesman's in West Milton, at White Deer, and at Lewisburg where connections were made with the Pennsylvania Canal. Travelers found the turnpikes a vast improvement over township roads; and as turnpikes were linked together, a passenger might board stage coaches at Lewisburg, Hartleton, or Youngmanstown bound for Pittsburgh or Philadelphia on a weekly schedule.

Water transportation, when available, had many advantages, but there were obvious limitations. The local creeks, Middle, Penns, White Deer, and Buffalo, were ordinarily too shallow for boating while the West Branch of the Susquehanna River, despite its grandeur, was a boatman's nightmare — alternating rock-filled rifts and shallows followed one upon the other in seemingly endless succession. The river was navigable for a brief season in the early spring, and unpredictable shorter periods in other seasons, when melting snow and heavy rains swelled the run-off, and a one-way passage was opened from Penns Creek to Havre de Grace and the markets of Baltimore and Philadelphia. Products such as whiskey, potash, flax and clover seed, flour, and pork could be loaded upon arks — box-like, flat-bottomed, planked rafts measuring about 50 feet by thirteen feet and four feet high, with a capacity of about 400 barrels.

A successful passage usually yielded a fair return, but the risks were great. The maelstrom at Conewago Falls took its toll; and if a freshet on Penns Creek did not raise the level of the broader Susquehanna sufficiently, the ark would have to be beached or, worse, end its passage hard upon a rock. There was the possibility also that the market at Baltimore would be glutted and the prices depressed. Such was the experience of a Lewisburg merchant in 1828 who obtained but 65 cents a bushel for a cargo of wheat at Baltimore. He finally pacified his suppliers with a promise of 72 cents, payable in installments.[2] Despite failure, water-borne merchandising continued for more than a quarter century, to be superseded by the Pennsylvania Canal system after 1830.

No valid estimate of the volume of river trade can be made. However, the *New Berlin Times* in 1825 esti-

The turnpike between Lewisburg and Mifflinburg had a number of toll houses at which travelers had to stop and pay. Those still standing at the end of the twentieth century are at 237/239 North Water Street (moved there from Market Street) and at 2039 West Market Street, Lewisburg; as well as at 101 East Chestnut Street and 1200 Chestnut Street, Mifflinburg. Photos by Jim Walter.

mated that Union (including Snyder) County sent to market about 150,000 bushels of wheat, 2,600 barrels of whiskey, 600 bushels of clover seed, and 200 tons of pork; a Lewisburg committee in 1831 estimated annual exports and imports of Buffalo Valley at 6,000 tons valued at $150,000.[3] Thomas Cooper, compatriot of Joseph Priestly at Northumberland, noted in 1794 that a boat with 1,600 bushels of wheat had gone down Penns Creek to Baltimore; this would have been one of the earliest ventures. Linn described the launching of an ark by Thomas Treaster in Penns Creek at the mouth of Sinking Creek in Centre County in 1807, as well as the crowd that gathered to see it off.[4] Treaster apparently succeeded despite the tortuous course of the creek through the Seven Mountains where the stream drops 423 feet in twenty miles. Linn reported also that John Motz, a pioneer of Woodward, shipped flour and pork from the Forks (Coburn). Farther downstream at Laurel Park, Henry Kiester constructed, turned, and launched arks while Henry Roush stored Baltimore-bound produce in his warehouse, awaiting the proper stage of the water. At least eight pilots can also be identified.

It is recorded that arks and rafts were sometimes launched at White Deer, New Columbia, Lewisburg, Turtle Creek, and Selinsgrove. The significance of the trade was not overlooked in Harrisburg. It is a matter of record that the Pennsylvania legislature declared Penns Creek to be a public highway and voted funds to clear obstacles to navigation from it. An act of 1807 authorized a lottery to raise $4,000 to remove barriers to navigation as far upstream as Green's Mill (Weikert), but the tickets did not sell. Later, residents on Penns Creek west of Selinsgrove went to court to prevent Simon Snyder from erecting a dam, which, they alleged, would block navigation on the stream. If such scattered references leave many gaps in the story, they nevertheless attest to the significance of the natural waterways in the early years.

The volume of water-transported goods increased after 1830 with the advent of the canal system, even though its pace slowed to that of a horse's walk. The canals of nineteenth-century America involved few inventions; virtually similar ones served the Low Countries of Western Europe for several centuries, having had their origin in the era of the "Benevolent Despots." Canals had a new birth when New York State completed the famous Erie Canal in 1825. Overnight, it seemed, New York City swallowed the Atlantic trade with the West, leaving Philadelphia, its perennial rival, little more than a regional market.

Philadelphia merchants and residents along the state's principal waterways soon joined in a chorus to call for a statewide system of public canals to offset New York's advantage and to make a Pennsylvania route linking Philadelphia with Pittsburgh, the "Gateway to the West" at the forks of the Ohio and the springboard to the Mississippi Valley. The cost would be tremendous and before its completion would necessitate political "log rolling" on a scale perhaps unequaled before or since — the state financially prostrate on one occasion as it was unable to meet the interest on its bonded indebtedness.

As the system evolved, it consisted of a main line, beginning at Columbia on the Susquehanna below Harrisburg and extending westward from Clark's Ferry along the Juniata River to Hollidaysburg, where the barges were drawn from the water and lifted over three ridges of the Allegheny Mountains by a stationary steam engine. Near Johnstown the boats were returned to the canal, which followed Conemaugh Creek and the Allegheny River into Pittsburgh. Columbia, in turn, was linked to Philadelphia by an 83-mile horse-drawn railroad at the outset.

As the plan developed, the canal was extended northward from Clark's Ferry along the west bank of the Susquehanna. It was taken across the West Branch at Northumberland where it divided into two divisions: the North Branch continuing to the New York State line, and the West Branch going as far as Lock Haven. With an eighteen-mile frontage on the river, Union County had a big stake in the proposition, and its initial objective was to have the West Branch Canal follow the west side of the river from Shamokin Dam to Williamsport. People voiced their position at public rallies and dispatched delegations to Harrisburg to bolster the county's assemblymen, but the engineers reported that a location on the east side of the river would be more economical.

Swallowing their disappointment, local citizens next lobbied for a side-cut or extension of the canal from the present site of Montandon to the river bank opposite Lewisburg. Combined with a dam in the Susquehanna to provide slack water and a passage on the river bridge for two horses, the canal could be brought to the docks of Lewisburg. This time Union County was not denied. Its Assemblymen, Ner Middleswarth and Philip Ruhl, found a place for it in the "Improvement Bill" despite the spirited opposition of Henry Frick, the Milton legislator who feared that Lewisburg's gain would be Milton's loss.

The return of William Cameron, Dr. William Joyce, and Thomas Van Valzah from the capital with the good news triggered a town-wide illumination con-

TOP: A glass-plate negative of the Lewisburg/Montandon crosscut canal (active 1833-1869) was reissued as a real photo postcard by Stephen B. Horton c. 1911, while ACROSS: another card shows the remnants of the crosscut canal. From the collections of Helen Hopp, and Dorothy G. Reish.

sisting of lamps and candles burning brightly in the windows, cannon fire, an impromptu parade, and the inevitable speeches and toasts. When the first canal boat, *The Merchant's Choice*, appeared at Montandon on May 11, 1831, with a cargo of merchandise out of Philadelphia at one-third the usual transportation cost, Lewisburg had visual proof of the prize which would soon reach their port. The victory was especially satisfying to Cameron, who picked up the contract for the construction of the cross-cut and added it to a sizable list of other public works contracts.

After a number of delays and the expenditure of just over $30,000, the cross-cut canal, consisting of a ditch two-thirds of a mile in length, three locks changing elevation 21 feet, and a culvert of four and one-half feet to carry the canal over the Montandon wetlands, was officially opened in October of 1833. On the appointed day a crowd gathered at Montandon and followed the flow of the water to its outlet at the river. Public celebration toasts were offered to "internal improvements"; "the cross-cut"; Canal Commissioner John Mitchell; Robert Faris, the engineer; Canal Superintendent William Parsons; William Packer, Superintendent of the West Branch Division; Samuel J. Packer, who had led the battle for the cross-cut as a state legislator; and Governor George Wolf, who had reluctantly signed the swollen Improvement Bill. Before winter closed, several barges had been drawn into the port of Lewisburg via the completed canal.

The cross-cut stimulated a land boom along its banks. Churchville, a "town" of 100 lots was surveyed and offered for sale. It died on the vine, but this was not the case in Lewisburg, where the canal stimulated mercantile activity long dormant: "Business is becoming quite lively . . . produce is departing daily . . . houses

are going up," an editorial observed.[5] In 1830 Lewisburg's population was 924; only twenty years later it had passed 2,000, with a foundry, machine shop, and boat yards demonstrating its new-found industrial activity. Only the moving of the county seat to Lewisburg in 1855 was as catalytic.

A pocket diary of Eli Slifer written during the canal season of 1845 helps to personalize the role of the canal boatman. At 27, Slifer was the junior partner of William Frick and business manager of one of the canal barges operated by the firm. On March 15 he was caulking and fitting out the *Coquet* for the coming season. After waiting several days for buffeting March winds to calm, he and his helpers towed the barge across the river and loaded it with lumber for I. Candor of Baltimore. On March 24, with three hands and a stock of provisions aboard, he started for Northumberland and at day's end tied up at Herald's, a few miles below Selinsgrove (17 miles). Second day the Junction (Clark's Ferry, 22 miles). Third day High Spire (below Harrisburg), "day, fine and warm." Fourth day Marietta (20 miles), "had ruder [sic.] torn off by tow line." Fifth day at Peach Bottom, "no meeting (church service) near; consequently staid about the boat all day." Seventh day "run to Havre de Grace, till noon (18 miles). Started out with *Fredericksburg* [as one of a number of barges towed in tandem]. It was windy; had to run into harbor at 11 o'clock at night." Eighth day "got to Baltimore about noon. Pushed into the falls and commenced unloading." Ninth day "finished unloading." Tenth day "settled accounts: the lumber totaled 51,195 feet." Eleventh day "Got to Havre de Grace early in the morning with the *Fredericksburg*. Run to McCall's, distance 26 miles." Twelfth day "Run to Columbia;

left the boat in the afternoon to come home and take charge of the *Philadelphia*; left boat with James McFaddin." Fourteenth day "Got home horseback."

Enroute, Slifer paid tolls on the Pennsylvania and Tidewater Canals as well as the towing fee to Baltimore. He also expended sums for unloading and dockage, rental for a small boat, wages, and boat keeping; and he collected from Candor. He also assembled small quantities of merchandise at Baltimore for delivery at Lewisburg, possibly as a favor for friends, including "a bill of grocery for Rhoads ($14.42) and sugar for Mrs. Wilson ($2.40)."

On April 9, two days after his return to Lewisburg, Slifer began to load wheat. The following day he set out at noon and ran to Fisher's (below Selinsgrove), seventeen miles. Second day New Buffalo, 26 miles. Third day Middletown, 29 miles. Fourth day (Sunday) Columbia. Fifth day Havre de Grace, 45 miles. Sixth day "Started for Philadelphia, toll towage-$28.75." Eighth day "unloaded part of load." Ninth day "finished unloading, and took some goods." Tenth day "Started out with tow." Eleventh day "Towed from Delaware City to Chesapeake [through the Chesapeake and Delaware Canal]." Twelfth day "from Havre de Grace to Kelys [?], 38 miles." Thirteenth day "To Highspire, 29 miles." Fourteenth day "To Liverpool, 36 miles." Fifteenth day (April 24) "Home, 35 miles."

On his next trip Slifer went first to Montoursville (April 28), where he loaded lumber which he delivered to Baltimore. He spent Sunday, May 11, in Baltimore, where he attended three services. Enroute home, he picked up an unspecified cargo near Columbia and, turning around, delivered it to Baltimore. This time he was one of sixteen barges towed by the *Boston*. He repeated the procedure at Columbia and made a third

return to Baltimore from Middletown. Meanwhile, he supervised the unloading of a second barge belonging to his firm [*Lucretia*]. He finally returned to Lewisburg on June 11, after spending forty-five days on the canal.

Later in June he loaded an unnamed cargo, presumably lumber, at the railroad basin in Williamsport and conveyed it to Philadelphia. Enroute back, he again picked up cargo where it seemed to be advantageous; and after three additional loadings, he made his way back to Lewisburg, arriving on July 31.[6] This canal journey, which had consumed 51 days, was his last, as he had decided to supervise the work in the boat yard. Slifer's future would be in managerial positions.

Frick and Slifer subsequently specialized in the construction of barges, and under their successor, Philip Billmeyer, the business became one of the most extensive in the area. Some of his crafts, designed as colliers for use on the Delaware and Hudson Canal in New York, were too large to fit into the locks of the Pennsylvania canal system and so were floated down the river to Havre de Grace during high water to reach their destination by way of the Chesapeake Bay and the Delaware River. A press release of January 1880 indicated that 39 boats were under contract at Billmeyer, Dill and Company, and that they were eagerly awaiting the breakage of the ice and the spring flood to speed rafts of heavy oak to them from the headwaters of the river — wagoners having been unable to furnish them enough local timber.

The canals, of course, also provided service for passengers. Travel was slow, but in contrast to jolting stagecoaches, the greater comfort and relaxation afforded by the packet was usually preferred. Canal travel had scarcely become established, however, before the railroad offered a faster and more exciting alternative.

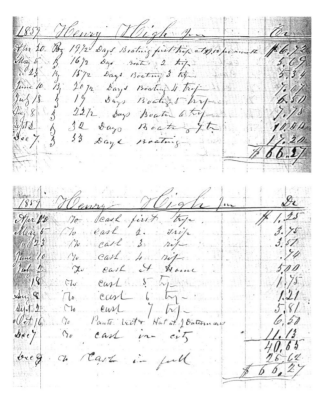

Two pages from the store ledger of R. Datesman of West Milton illustrate the nature of the barter system still in effect in 1859 as evidenced by the debit and credit entries. Henry High apparently took a boat downriver for Datesman at $9.00/month, and in exchange received primarily cash but also a pair of pants. From the collection of the Union County Historical Society, #84.49.1.

Meanwhile, at mid-century Union County people became involved in still another transient mode of water transportation — the rafting of logs from the great boom at Williamsport to points on the lower Susquehanna. Following its construction in 1850 by Maine capitalists, thousands of rafts were floated down the West Branch during the periods of high water, stopping enroute as the situation dictated. New Columbia owed its growth in part to servicing the rafts which tied up at its bank; Lewisburg and the river bank below Winfield were also stops, where raftsmen waited for passage through the chutes in the dams situated there.

During the season, rafts were seldom out of sight. In the spring of 1858 an observer standing on Blue Hill made a tally of rafts going by during the daylight hours of April 18 to 20. He reported 780 rafts and arks with 2,311 hands.[7] Rafting declined after 1880 as the "inexhaustible" forests of north central Pennsylvania were expended. Residents still remember the ceremonial "last raft" in 1938 conducted by veterans of the

old rafting days. Those rafters failed to estimate the difficult cross currents near Muncy, and the raft crashed into the river bridge with the tragic loss of seven lives. The romance had now gone out of rafting, and the survivors of the last raft beached the archaic craft at old Fort Hunter north of Harrisburg.

Like canals, railroads were operating in Western Europe before they were introduced in the United States; but unlike the canals, the railroads were built and managed by private enterprise. Railroad promoters, it is true, exerted great pressure upon the states and later upon the Federal Government for land and monetary assistance; but the states were already staggering under a burden of debt to finance canals, and none more so than Pennsylvania. The state was unable to finance the railroads. Hence many Pennsylvania railroads began as short lines, financed by the sale of stocks and bonds, and later consolidated into larger systems.

In Pennsylvania much of the early railroad activity originated in the coal regions where "stone coal" [anthracite] was finding users in the eastern cities for heating and industry. Union County people thus witnessed this exciting and revolutionary development in transportation in adjacent counties but could only bide their time until they might be drawn into the network. During the 1830s mines in the Schuylkill County area were linked to Reading and Philadelphia, and by 1835 horse-drawn cars were transporting coal from the newly opened mines at Shamokin to Sunbury upon wooden stringers covered with strips of iron. Locomotives soon replaced the horses, but their weight destroyed the track, and it was not until 1852 that they were operative there when iron rails replaced the wood.

By the 1840s the consolidation of smaller lines was underway; local capital was becoming available for investment, and Union County's promoters were impatiently waiting to embrace the "iron monster." In 1846 a railroad meeting in Mifflinburg explored the possibility of joining Union County to a prospective route between Philadelphia and Pittsburgh. A year later, using an older canal survey of the Valley of Penns Creek as a guide, a public meeting in New Berlin recommended this route for a railroad and sent delegates including James Moore II, the renowned bridge builder of Kelly Township, to a railroad convention in Philadelphia.

A decade later Lewisburg bonded itself for $75,000 to purchase stock in the Susquehanna Railroad — organized to build a line along the west bank of the Susquehanna River — hoping thereby to extend it northward to the town limits. Caught up in the enthusiasm, the Union County Commissioners subscribed to a block of the stock, to be paid through a bond issue of $200,000. Except for some grading near Winfield, the railroad did not get beyond the drawing board in Union County, but the repercussions were to be deafening.

In 1853 Lewisburg investors headed by William Cameron obtained a charter for the Lewisburg, Centre and Spruce Creek Railroad, a system which would join Lewisburg on the east with projected trunk lines in the Susquehanna and Juniata Valleys. The sponsors held public meetings in Mifflinburg and Hartleton which attracted delegations from Centre County. Lewisburg leaders put pledges of money on the line: George F. Miller, John Walls, Peter Beaver, John Chamberlin, and Thomas Hayes risked $4,000 each; William Frick and Eli Slifer, as well as Geddes, Marsh and Company, pledged $2,000 each. Lewisburg's *Chronicle* advised that a Brush Valley route was impractical and that the public would do well to settle for a Penns Creek plan. Lewisburg, it insisted, had done her share; what about other benefactors? Stock sales lagged, and the project slumbered for a decade.

During the lull between railroad promotions, an invention revolutionizing communication approached Lewisburg mile by mile and pole by pole along the right-of-way of the Pennsylvania and Erie Railroad. Just seven years earlier Samuel F.B. Morse had demonstrated the feasibility of sending electrical impulses over a wire which he had stretched from Washington to Baltimore. Overnight his telegraph became a success. The wire reached town on May 26, 1851 and Washington, New York, and Philadelphia never seemed as far from Union County again.

Meanwhile, in 1856, two railroads almost touched the borders of the county: the Catawissa and Danville at Milton, as well as the Pennsylvania and Erie at Montandon. The latter provided service from Sunbury to Lock Haven and gave many county residents their first opportunity to feel the awesome surge of a locomotive. One early rider, who boarded the northbound train at Montandon, noted that "McGinley" had built a shanty near the track and that he lighted a fire in it at train time and flagged the train for the passengers. He was impressed by the speed — in an hour and a half he was dining in the United States Hotel in Williamsport — and he found the cars "comfortable and easy."[8] In 1858 Sunbury was linked to Harrisburg, giving county residents a convenient connection to Philadelphia.

The Civil War emphasized the need for railroads, but it increased their cost and curtailed the availability of railroad iron. The post-war boom set off an era of railroad construction unparalleled in the nation's history. The first local project in this period was designed to connect Lewisburg to the Pennsylvania and Erie Railroad at Montandon and, hopefully, to reinvigorate the Lewisburg, Centre and Spruce Creek line. The former was complicated by the destruction of the Lewisburg river bridge, which had been swept away by the St. Patrick's Day flood of 1865. The Pennsylvania and Erie agreed to build the track to Lewisburg provided that Lewisburg would contribute the bridge and depot. Accepting the challenge, Lewisburg leaders reorganized the defunct bridge company and raised funds to purchase a lot and erect a depot. A highlight of the campaign was a railroad/bridge rally which filled the courtroom. Attorney Van Gezer and Judge Bucher extolled the project while James Aiken, the region's homespun orator and poet, read a poem he had written for the occasion. The latter, it was said, received a "tumultous applause," and purses seemed to open.

The promotion struck but one sour note. Mifflinburg residents assumed that once Lewisburg had its spur from Montandon, it would heed the claim of the "West End" for a line to Centre County. Disgusted by delays, its railroad men agreed to seek a connection with the Pennsylvania and Erie at Milton, a move calculated to inspire enthusiasm at Farmersville (Cowan), Buffalo Cross Roads, and Boyertown (Mazeppa), as well as rebuke Lewisburg. To remove any doubt as to their displeasure with the latter, the Mifflinburg men admonished Eli Slifer and John Walls for their failure to satisfy Buffalo Valley. Lewisburg's *Chronicle* had an immediate rejoinder. No two men, it insisted, had done more to promote railroad building in Union County than Slifer and Walls, and the *Chronicle* attributed the hostility at Mifflinburg to a faction seeking to make political capital out of the issue. It advocated that the railroad be extended toward Mifflinburg mile by mile as money became available, presumably from stock purchases by residents along the proposed route.

Lewisburg raised the needed funds, built a bridge designed to serve the railroad and the canal as well as vehicular and pedestrian traffic, and provided a depot at North Second and St. John's Streets. At seven o'clock on the morning of July 23, 1869, Congressman George F. Miller, President of the incipient Lewisburg, Centre and Spruce Creek Railroad, accompanied by five guests in car #1047 behind engine #1008, rode across the new bridge to the empty depot. Unwilling to let the moment pass unheralded, Miller and his friends returned to Montandon until the stage was set. Then, with the crowd filling the depot lot and the streets adjacent to it, and the simultaneous ringing of the church bells, "the sweet-toned new Baptist bell mingling with the others," the locomotive, its hissing and panting dulled by the clanging and cheering, made its formal entry.[9] Thereafter, for 25 cents a trip, county residents could meet any of the Pennsylvania and Erie trains.

It was a day to remember for the Bridge Company. A toll from the railroad for each train added to the more customary revenues, and the profits soon warranted dividends; but twenty years later there was a day of reckoning in the guise of the Johnstown flood.

The fruition of the Montandon spur induced the directors of the Lewisburg, Centre and Spruce Creek to reopen the company's books for the push toward Centre County. The *Mifflinburg Telegraph*, reflecting the local response, termed the decision "of transcending importance" and added, "Let there be no such word as fail."[10] Two Mifflinburg committees were soon at work: the first, to obtain a right-of-way from land owners; the second, to promote stock subscriptions. Enthusiasm was high, though admittedly tempered by rumors that special taxes would be involved and that the company was expecting the town to donate a lot and depot. The project hung in the balance through the spring and summer of 1871 awaiting the stock sales. A stockholder's group in Philadelphia, meanwhile, recommended a narrow gauge track to cut costs, but meetings of local stockholders held at the Old Fort in Centre County and at Mifflinburg protested against it, arguing that it would be contrary to the basic understanding between stockholders and management.

By September, after local guarantors had given notes to provide the funds demanded by the management, the controversy was resolved, and Mifflinburg was assured that the railroad would be built with a gauge of 4 feet, 8-1/2 inches, a width which would soon be designated as "standard." Track laying moved rapidly, and late in October both freight and passenger trains were entering and backing out of town. Awaiting a depot, a turn-about, and sidings, the residents do not appear to have held a celebration. The *Lewisburg Chronicle* offered its congratulations and urged both Lewisburg and Mifflinburg to take advantage of the railroad and work to attain their industrial and commercial potential.[11] The *Mifflinburg Telegraph* expressed the sentiment of the community: misgivings had not been completely dispelled, for the small station and the single, crowded coach, it charged, indicated "an indifference to the trade and travel here, which is highly dissatisfactory."[12]

While Mifflinburg agonized over its railroad problems, farmers in Buffalo Township adjacent to the turnpike reacted more positively. Donating a 400 foot by 150 foot plot for a depot and siding, they founded the hamlet of Vicksburg, which would soon attract stores and a gristmill.

Meanwhile, the controversy was shifted to the western section of the county where the company had delayed a determination of the exact route to await response to stock sales. The principal bid came from Hartleton, the only village of any size at this time, but its pathway westward, though the shortest to Penns Valley, led to the uninviting slopes of Stitzer Mountain. The engineers' final decision in favor of the valley of Penns Creek meant that the track bypassed Hartleton by about a mile. The decision was probably the village's greatest disappointment in its long history.

During 1872 and 1873 the railroad inched westward. At a point about four miles west of Mifflinburg, where the track crossed the old Haines Road, the builders added a siding, thereby creating the hamlet of Swengel or Swengelville. A mile farther along they made a similar gesture toward Hartleton and designated it Hartleton Station. The name did not catch on, however, and it was soon changed to Millmont. At Weidensaul's Mill, two miles beyond Millmont, they provided a whistle stop for Laurelton, first called Laurelton Station, then renamed Rutherton, only to revert in time to an older cognomen, Laurel Park. One mile west of it, the Berlin Furnace merited a siding; it was named, quite appropriately, Glen Iron.

Stirrings along the newly built track were soon apparent. Donations of land at Swengel and Millmont facilitated the erection of depots, and the handful of farmers there dreamed of a transformation into thriving cities. A newspaper correspondent at Swengel noted a post office and several buildings under construction, but a jaundiced Hartletonian ridiculed the post office, labeling it a small wheel with several cigar boxes. The writer alleged that a typical delivery consisted of a mail bag, dropped from a passing train into the snow, containing two papers and a post card.[13] Ridicule, however, did not hide the gristmill, steam sawmill, blacksmith shop, and a lengthening street lined with new houses and a church, or a siding with ten cars of coal. Other correspondents reported a brick depot, three new dwellings, and a solicitation for funds for a Lutheran Church at Millmont. Glen Iron, meanwhile, obtained a depot, two stores, and a less circuitous roadway to Laurelton. Like Hartleton, the latter was incensed to see the railroad pass it by and somewhat illogically placed a share of the blame upon upstart Glen Iron.

The panic of 1873, which dragged on for a number of years, halted plans to continue the line into Centre County, and Glen Iron remained the railhead for several years. Finally, in 1876, the Pennsylvania Railroad leased the line and resumed construction. The convolutions of Penns Creek, where it cuts its way around the end of Paddy Mountain, induced the engineers to straighten the road bed by boring two tunnels: at Paddy Mountain, and between Cherry Run and the Forks (Coburn). Awaiting their completion, the track moved forward toward Spring Mills. By the following summer, the tunnels were finished, and the track was in place to Spring Mills. It was time to celebrate.

The grand opening into Centre County took the form of an excursion from Lewisburg to Spring Mills on July 4, 1877. For one dollar per couple, and children at half-price, Union County participants boarded coaches at Lewisburg, Mifflinburg, Swengel, Millmont, and Glen Iron — at least 1,200 persons, loaded with baskets of food and accompanied by the Lewisburg and Freeburg cornet bands. For many it was the first train ride, and for almost all it was an initial opportunity to explore the mountains and feel the darkness of a tunnel. At the picnic grove near Spring Mills they were welcomed by several thousand hosts who had followed the Haines Road into Penns Valley. After dinner there was croquet, music, and dancing, as well as a wedding, speeches, and fireworks. A misguided rocket fell into a wagon filled with explosives, but the resulting fusillade produced no fatalities. Before four o'clock the train whistles beckoned the picnickers back to the cars, but not before Eli Slifer, former State Secretary of the Commonwealth and President of the railroad company, had invited the Centre County residents to a harvest home picnic at Lewisburg on August 15.[14]

Six weeks later Penns Valley made its pilgrimage to Union County, with an estimated 3,300 passengers filling 44 coaches, divided into four sections. The trains discharged their passengers at Derr's Woods west of Lewisburg where they were met by several thousand Union County friends. Again, there was merrymaking as railroad director James P. Coburn

supplied 60 barrels of lemonade. A platform provided the setting for the waltz, the Scottish, and the polka, and there was dancing "Till their heads swam." The Cameron Fire Company, renowned as a model of precision, put on a demonstration, and elsewhere hundreds were finding recreation in quoits, "ring tag," "Copenhagen," and "flying horses."

Through the day trains shuttled local citizens back and forth from Lewisburg. There was "a little rowdyism," blamed upon a few who indulged too freely in "tanglefoot." Centre County visitors boarded the cars for the return trip shortly after four o'clock in the best of spirits.[15] Tales of the two excursions lived through the years to become a part of the folklore of the region: the cat that was placed in John Young's picnic basket; the kiss revealed by the burst of light at the end of the tunnel; and the tobacco juice which plastered a curious rider's face when he leaned his head out of the window.

After a pause of several years another reorganization, in which the Pennsylvania Railroad took title to the line and redirected the western terminal to Bellefonte, permitted the resumption of the work. In July of 1885, the last rail was in place and traffic moved from Montandon to Bellefonte.

The first run, however, was not made without a bit of fanfare, somewhat embarrassing to the engineer and crew and possibly to the management as well. As the day of the initial departure from Lewisburg approached, John Hess, who, with his brother Charley, operated a stage and mail line along the route, boasted that his "pale face" horses could negotiate the run as quickly as the locomotive. His friends at the bar of the Revere House (later the Cameron or Lewisburger Hotel) found his assertion ridiculous and spread the story around the town. Hess was prepared to prove his point. He placed relay teams at Mifflinburg, Woodward, and Centre Hall. On the morning of the train's departure, he was poised in a light rig behind two of his matched "pale faces" in front of the hotel, awaiting the opening of the locomotive's valve on the track a block away.

When it sounded, Hess and his stage coach took off amidst the cheers of supporters. His steeds surged westward on Market Street and entered the turnpike beyond. By the time he reached Lochiel, the train was already pulling out from the station, and at Mifflinburg Hess lost a few moments while his second team was being hitched, but the train's "whistle stops" west of Mifflinburg enabled the stage to stay abreast. Beyond Hartleton the stage coach entered the mountains while the train remained in Buffalo Valley, and Hess could hear only an occasional whistle of the locomotive to judge its speed. The mountain and the hills of Penns Valley reduced his speed, but he reached Centre Hall just after the train had pulled out. Hess could now cross Nittany Mountain on a direct line toward Bellefonte while the train followed the arc around it through Lemont and past the site of the future Rockview Penitentiary. Using his long experience as a driver and his knowledge of the terrain to the fullest advantage, Hess pressed on — never using the whip but offering the horses encouragement with his words and reins — and flew into Bellefonte as fast as the curving road would allow. He came to a stop at the Bush House just as the locomotive hissed into the station a few yards away. It was a thrilling moment for the driver and the "pale faces." Hess rested for a few days, enjoying the accolades of his admirers and then returned more leisurely, presumably stopping to be refreshed and to display his fine horses at the taverns enroute. A welcoming committee was on hand to toast the driver and his steeds when they reached the hitching post at the Revere House.[16]

With the completion of the line to Bellefonte, Union County residents might reach the main line of the Pennsylvania system by way of Tyrone and Altoona. They might also go to Buffalo and Niagara Falls by way of Williamsport, or to Philadelphia or Baltimore by way of Harrisburg. As early as 1876 hundreds went by rail to the glamorous Centennial Exposition. Meanwhile, the more affluent enjoyed summer vacations on the Atlantic beaches of New Jersey and the less affluent took advantage of special excursions to Watkins Glen, Niagara Falls, New York City, and Washington. The railroad was also a boon to special events in Buffalo Valley. On the Fourth of July in 1901, 271 people purchased tickets at the Mifflinburg depot for Lewisburg where they witnessed the dedication of its Civil War Monument at Third and St. George Streets,[17] and year after year crowds boarded excursion trains for the Union County Fair at Brook Park.

A second railroad entered the county at West Milton in 1871 when the Catawissa, Danville and Milton Railroad bridged the Susquehanna. The line put West Milton on the map and stimulated activity in the older villages of New Columbia, White Deer, and Allenwood as it pushed northward to Williamsport. A decade later, the Reading System, which had taken it over, built the Shamokin, Sunbury and Lewisburg Railroad as an alternate route between Mahanoy Junction and West Milton. The Reading Railroad crossed the Susquehanna River at Sunbury and proceeded northward through Winfield and Lewisburg. At the latter, a protracted battle with the Lewisburg and Tyrone over the crossing of its tracks at Fifth and St. John's Streets was at length resolved in June of 1883, and a junction was consummated at West Milton. Thereafter, heavily laden coal and freight trains took the Catawissa route southward, avoiding the steep grades on the Shamokin road, whereas traffic moving northward used the alternate to bypass the forbidding slopes on the Catawissa.

The Reading provided Union County with direct service to Williamsport, with connections there to Elmira, Buffalo, and Erie, in addition to a short route to Philadelphia by way of Reading and the Schuylkill Valley. At Philadelphia passengers might transfer to the Central Railroad of New Jersey and in a few hours scan the skyline of New York from the wharves of Jersey City. Many did so.

As the momentum of railroad building slowed, residents of White Deer and Dry Valleys salvaged a share of its coveted services. With financial and managerial assistance from I.C. Burd of Shamokin and his brother, Samuel F. Burd of New Berlin, the New Berlin and Winfield Railroad was organized in 1904 to link New Berlin with the Reading Railroad at Winfield, fulfilling a long but elusive dream. Capitalized at $25,000, the company laid a narrow gauge track along the nine mile right-of-way; it purchased several secondhand locomotives, a string of passenger, freight, and coal cars as well as providing depots and storage sheds at the terminals.

A successful trial run was made to New Berlin on June 10, 1905, and within a few days passenger and freight trains were running. On July the Fourth, the citizenry gathered for a more formal opening; the throng, it was said, was the largest ever assembled in picturesque New Berlin. Professor M.W. Whitmer of Union Seminary expressed the community's gratitude to the management, and President I.C. Burd extolled his hearers for their interest and liberality.

The hopes of the promoters, however, were not realized. While it was a convenience to salesmen, housewives, and students at Union Seminary as well as a stimulant to business generally, the New Berlin/Winfield line did not pay its way; and when a freshet in Dry Valley in 1912 undermined the track, capital was lacking to restore it. A Mitchell automobile or "auto train" with flanged wheels kept passenger traffic alive for a time, but the company closed opera-

ABOVE: The Philadelphia and Reading Railroad stations at New Columbia and West Milton are subjects for real photo postcards c. 1907. From the collections of the Union County Historical Society, #86.3.17, and Gary W. and Donna M. Slear.

The exterior and interior of the Philadelphia & Reading Railroad (later the Reading) station in Lewisburg. The station had a telegraph office on the second floor as well as a separate baggage room and two waiting rooms. From the collections of Gary W. and Donna M. Slear, and Paul and Catherine Ernst.

A Mitchell automobile or "auto train" with flanged wheels kept passenger traffic alive on the New Berlin railroad between 1912 and 1916 when the company ceased operations. From the collection of the Union County Historical Society, #89.5.11.21.

tions in 1916, leaving only a few scars on the ground to mark its path.

One tale, reminiscent of the frail little railway or "Jerk Water Line," as it was affectionately referred to, was repeated in the *Mifflinburg Telegraph*. "Brain (Brainard) Schoch of New Berlin, a man broad-of-beam, was the only passenger on a trip to Winfield one day. When the conductor strolled down the car for his ticket he noticed that the car was leaning dangerously to one side—Schoch's side to be sure. He at once commanded "Brain" to kindly sit nearer to the center of the car. He complied, and was credited with avoiding a train wreck.[18]

In White Deer Valley, lumberman John F. Duncan constructed a narrow gauge railway in 1900 to draw logs from the mountains bordering Union and Clinton Counties. The line extended from a junction with the Reading Railroad about a mile north of White Deer Mills to Duncan's Station or Tea Springs with laterals reaching into the mountains north and south. Following Duncan's death in 1904 the Whitmer, Steel, Lumber Company purchased Duncan's tract including the railway and continued the lumbering operation until 1916. Meanwhile, the White Deer and Loganton Railway Company, organized in 1906, extended the track and provided a daily service between Loganton and White Deer, a distance of 24 miles. The train, ordinarily consisting of a small Climax engine and a second-hand passen-

ger and freight car, left White Deer at 9:20 A.M., and twelve stops and two-and-one-half hours later pulled into Loganton. The slope was gradual and required no switchbacks. The return trip was made at 2:00 P.M. with an expected arrival at White Deer at 4:20 P.M.

The morning train might deliver coal for a lime kiln at Eastville, fertilizer for Loganton or mail and passengers for Carroll and Loganton. It sometimes supplied lumber camps with foodstuffs from the stores of White Deer, Watsontown, and Milton. On the return trip it might carry produce from eastern Sugar Valley; a Tea Springs resident recalls that hundreds of bushels of apples were shipped out on the railroad and that a telegraph line along the right-of-way facilitated communications.

Without doubt, the best-remembered trips were the family excursions from White Deer to Tea Springs, where a pavilion and picnic tables added a convenience to a beautiful setting, a clearing surrounded with forest land. Members of the Farley and Bucher families, among others, remember the forest-lined ride and the festivities on the grounds. Never a money-maker, however, the railroad had to suspend operations the moment Whitmer, Steel, and Company wildcatted their last truck of logs in 1916.

The contributions of the railroads to travel in the county have been noted, but their impact upon the region's economy is more difficult to evaluate. While a number of local craftsmen such as the butchers, bakers, cigar makers, tailors, hatters, milliners, seamstresses, tinners, and blacksmiths continued to ply their trades through the balance of the nineteenth century, the bulk of the merchandise on the shelves of the general stores, once railroads were available as carriers, came from the factories and wholesalers of Philadelphia, Baltimore, New England, and elsewhere. The railroads facilitated the marketing of Lewisburg's mowers and reapers, Mifflinburg's buggies, Winfield's and Glen Iron's pig iron, and Pardee's timber, thus putting cash in the pockets of area businesses as well as West Milton's roundhouse and yard workers, but perhaps their greatest value to the economy was the marketing of the produce of the area's farms. In the wake of the railroads, the sidings in the villages and towns became transfer centers for country produce, much of it destined for the populous coal mining regions.

Week after week, and year after year, for example, J.D.S. Gast and Son of Mifflinburg loaded a boxcar with eggs, live poultry, flour, bran, and seasonal crops each Monday, dispatching it to Hazleton. At Thanksgiving or Christmas, turkeys and chickens, which they slaughtered and dressed on the premises, were added. During the Christmas season of 1898, the *Telegraph* noted the "great slaughter" at Gast's mill: "We are told it consisted of 1,600 turkeys, 400 ducks and a corresponding number of chickens, which were dressed and shipped to eastern markets. It was a very fowl proceeding."

A block away on another siding, James Beaver, who specialized in vegetables and fruits, followed a similar routine. On Mondays his agent, Perry Hassinger, took the passenger train to Hazleton to await the freight. He spent Tuesday morning vending the produce to dealers there; and if the market was brisk, he finished the job by noon. Hassinger then hiked across the mountain with the receipts in his pocket; and catching the west bound train on the Catawissa and Milton branch of the Reading Railroad, he reached Mifflinburg the same evening on the trolley. Hassinger's daughter recalls that he was never beset by thieves on the lonely mountain road. Agents for the other shippers appear to have followed a similar routine.

At Rutherton and Vicksburg local millers shipped flour and grain; at Linntown Francis Brown freighted livestock; at Lewisburg the Buffalo Milling Company was the major shipper with its flour; at Allenwood the Reading Railroad picked up fresh cream from the Dewart Creamery and sped it in unrefrigerated baggage cars to Catawissa, Mahanoy City, and Mt. Carmel.

The railroads brought the region within reach of the daily newspapers of Philadelphia and Harrisburg, and they supplied villages as small as White Deer, Glen Iron, and West Milton with a telegraphic service. "Waiting for the train" became a daily pastime for many who gathered at the depot to hear the news.

Late in the golden age of the railroad, the electric trolley added another dimension to local transportation. Projections for lines appeared in the local newspapers as early as 1893; but the high cost of trackage and rolling stock delayed construction until 1897, when Philadelphia capitalists headed by Henry V. Massey and Edward A. Tennis organized the Lewisburg, Milton and Watsontown Passenger Company. In a few months the dirt was flying from the picks and shovels of a work-gang of Italian and Hungarian laborers recruited in Philadelphia, whose hustle was described as an object lesson for the American workmen. On February 9, 1898, a trial run was made from Milton to the east end of the river bridge at Lewisburg, with the first car carrying

managers and directors of the company and invited guests including William H. Follmer of Lewisburg, and the second car, the wives.

The track paralleled the east bank of the river and had its southern terminal at East Lewisburg, a few yards away from the railroad bridge. Passengers paid five cents for a ticket to Milton and reached their destination in twenty minutes. From Broadway in Milton another nickel and another twenty minutes were required to take the traveler to Watsontown. The trolley provided a convenience for shoppers, workmen, and students at Bucknell University. Members of the class of 1902 recall the innovation and the brisk hike across the bridge and along University Avenue to college hill beyond.

In 1912, a new railroad bridge at Lewisburg opened the way for the trolleys to deliver their passengers to the railroad depot. The grade from the river bank to the railroad bridge at East Lewisburg was steep and difficult to negotiate. Before crossing the bridge, the conductor called the Pennsylvania Railroad station agent at Lewisburg on the telephone for a clear track. He would then open the switch, cross the bridge, and pull onto a siding at the station at North Second and St. John's Streets.[19]

Also in 1912 a service between Montandon and Mifflinburg was opened, utilizing trolleys powered by storage batteries. The trolley offered five trips daily in both directions and thereby brought Mifflinburg into

The trolley which operated from Milton to Lewisburg to Mifflinburg was photographed some time prior to its demise in 1928. Starting in 1898, this electric-powered trolley ran between Watsontown, Milton, and Lewisburg. In 1912 service was added to Mifflinburg. From the collection of the Union County Historical Society, #85.55.1.

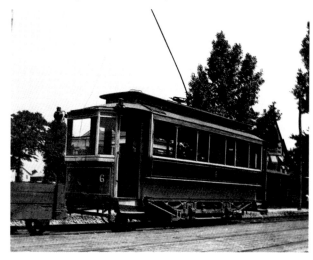

the trolley orbit and supplied a service to the principal trains at Montandon. There were also special runs from Mifflinburg and Lewisburg to Riverside Park, a trolley-owned amusement center between Milton and Watsontown. In the 1920s the battery car was replaced by a railbus manufactured by the Mack Truck Company.

The coming of the automobile gradually reduced the traffic on the trolleys; and profits, which appear to have been elusive from the beginning, turned into deficits. In 1928 the company gave up the struggle, and the last trolley stopped at the Lewisburg bridge on August 1, unwilling even to pay the cost of crossing the bridge. The rusting rolling stock remained in the barn at Milton and on the siding at Lewisburg for a few years before it was finally cut into scrap metal. However, the service stimulated a plethora of schemes for additional lines — from New Berlin to Winfield, from Mifflinburg to New Berlin, and from Lewisburg to Mifflinburg along the turnpike, with branch lines in each. In their enthusiasm, few Mifflinburgers seem to have questioned the feasibility of fitting street cars into their narrow streets. Survey followed survey, but no tracks materialized.

If Colonel Kelly or any of his contemporaries could have returned to Buffalo Valley a century after they had traveled upon its roads, they would have seen much that was familiar. Excepting the oft-neglected turnpikes, most of the highways remained dirt tracks — muddy and dusty by turns and barely passable during the spring thaw; but the coming of the automobile inevitably changed the situation.

Autos were first driven on country roads at the turn of the century, a feat requiring both fortitude and patience. The first registration of motor vehicles between 1903 and 1905 revealed that twelve were owned by residents of the county. Dr. O.K. Pellman, a Mifflinburg dentist, broke the ice on June 13, 1904, when he became the owner of a one-cylinder Cadillac. (His life and that of Franklin S. Frederick, one of the region's first auto mechanics, would end tragically nineteen years later when his car was struck by a train at a Mifflinburg crossing.) In 1905 there were eleven additional registrations: John Anderson, Lewisburg, Mobile Co. of America; Rev. John Blood, Lewisburg, a Cadillac; A.C. Stahl, Lewisburg, a Cadillac; George M. Wolfe, Lewisburg, a Ford; Wesley B. Stark, Brooklyn, NY, a Franklin; Ira M. Higbee, Lewisburg, an Autocar; Robert A. Hoffa, Kelly Township, an Oldsmobile; Harry W. Fauver, Laurelton, a Rambler; Ira M. Higbee,

Mr. and Mrs. Bowersox were photographed in their new car by Millmont amatuer photographer Urs H. Eisenhauer c. 1909-1911. From the collection of Delphia Shirk.

Lewisburg, a Winton; A.C. Stahl, Lewisburg, a Queen; and Charles L. Braucher, Millmont, an Oldsmobile.

Ford's economical Model "T" in 1907 proved to be a boon to purchasers, and a stretch of paved road between Lewisburg and Mifflinburg (Route 45), built cooperatively by the Commonwealth, Union County, and Buffalo Township in 1910, attracted cars as well as bicycles. The Sproul Act of 1911 and Governor Gifford Pinchot's program to "get the farmer out of the mud" in the 1920s and early 1930s brought about the so-called Pinchot roads, while the Works Progress Administration's projects during the Great Depression made Pennsylvania's highways the envy of the nation. Thus by the 1920s hundreds of Union County's families enjoyed the pleasures of motoring, rode to work in cars, and were served by an ever-growing fleet of motor trucks.

Meanwhile, Lewisburg initiated the paving of Market Street — bricks over concrete — in the fall of 1915 while Mifflinburg paved Chestnut Street in 1920, with both boroughs sharing the cost with the property owners facing the streets. Amidst the enthusiasm there were also a few negatives. Auto accidents crowded lesser news from the front pages of the local newspapers while punctures and speed traps were frustrating motorists. As early as 1915 disgruntled Mifflinburgers were warning tourists that the constable had two special officers, on duty with stop watches, to fine speedsters for sums of $12 to $23 for driving in excess of the legal fifteen miles per hour.

TOP LEFT: The construction of the new turnpike from Lewisburg to Mifflinburg was photographed in a series of at least nine shots by Millmont amateur photographer Urs H. Eisenhauer c. 1919. From the collection of Gary W. and Donna M. Slear. TOP: The grading for US Route 15 as it appeared east of Winfield in 1930. From the collection of the Union County Historical Society, #2000.2.1.

BOTTOM: The Bailey Tire Company with its Sunoco gas pumps was located on the former site of the Lewisburg Opera House on South Third Street near Market Street (the east end of the current municipal parking lot). From the collection of the Union County Historical Society, #89.5.15.30.

In a much more limited way, local people also became acquainted with the air age during and just after World War I, and the drone of an aircraft was sufficient incentive to bring householders to the streets to see the strange and marvelous sight. In World War I local youths had opportunities to qualify as pilots, and the forced landing of an Army plane near Barber's Station west of Mifflinburg drew a huge crowd. In the 1920s Buffalo Valley was on the main line of the early air mail route from New York to the West. Beacons were mounted on Woodward and New Berlin Mountains, and an emergency landing field was constructed at Hartleton. Air buffs gathered along the landing strip in the evening hours, sometimes remaining far into the night, seeking no disaster yet hoping that a "small" emergency might bring a plane to a landing. Pilots sometimes supplemented their income by landing in over-sized fields to take up passengers — two at a time in a tiny, open cockpit, at five dollars a head. Along the side lines, youths might be seen imploring their parents for permission to fly, and they frequently got it, despite the forebodings of their elders. In World War II dozens of Union County's sons served in the United States Air Corps, and following the war residents accepted air travel as a way of life.

ENDNOTES

[1] *Lewisburg Saturday News*, August 14, 1907.

[2] John Blair Linn, *Annals of Buffalo Valley, Pennsylvania, 1755-1855*, Harrisburg, 1877, 495.

[3] March 26, 1825.

[4] *History of Centre and Clinton Counties*, 167.

[5] *Lewisburg Journal*, April 3, 1833.

[6] Slifer Papers, Bucknell University Archives.

[7] *Lewisburg Chronicle*, May 7, 1858.

[8] *Lewisburg Union Argus*, January 2S, 1856.

[9] *Lewisburg Chronicle*, July 30, 1869.

[10] *Lewisburg Chronicle*, January 21, 1870.

[11] November 3, 1871.

[12] November 17, 1871.

[13] *Mifflinburg Telegraph*, February 25, 1875.

[14] *Mifflinburg Telegraph*, June 21 and July 12, 1877.

[15] *Mifflinburg Telegraph*, August 23, 1877.

[16] Reminiscence of W.F. Brown, *Lewisburg Saturday News*, March 4, 1916.

[17] *Mifflinburg Telegraph*, July 12, 1901.

[18] *Mifflinburg Telegraph*, July 7, 1905.

[19] Gene D. Gordon, *Toonerville's of the Susquehanna* n.d.

The first air mail delivery to and from Lewisburg occurred on May 19, 1938 in this plane photographed before take off at the Brown farm on Stein Lane. One of the letters sent that day was from the parents and grandparents of Nora Jean Berge. The letter made the round trip flight to Williamsport during National Air Mail Week. Courtesy of Norma J. Berge.

CHAPTER 5

LOCAL GOVERNANCE AND POLITICS
ACROSS TWO CENTURIES

Union County pioneers brought with them the political principles and biases which they had acquired when youths in their homes in Berks County and elsewhere. A tax receipt or an occupation ordinarily qualified males 21 or over to vote and hold office, and most of them exercised the privilege. Those who grew up before 1776 were apt to dislike the so-called "Quaker Oligarchy," which had dominated the Provincial Assembly and manipulated apportionment to the advantage of the Quaker-controlled "Three Lower Counties" at the expense of the German and Scots-Irish districts along their borders. They were also apt to be defenders of home rule and critics of dictation from either King or Parliament; and when the test came, they cast their lot with the Revolution.

After the Revolutionary War most area people, attracted by Jefferson's dream of a nation of self-governing landholders, became ardent Jeffersonians rather than followers of Hamilton and his goal of cities and workshops, with commercial and social classes suggestive of the Old World. As political parties evolved, most voters identified themselves with the Democratic Republican Party and helped to bury the Federalist minority on election days.

Political activities at first centered at Sunbury, the county seat. The legal profession lived or gathered there during the quarterly session of the court, and the citizenry from the farms and scattered settlements looked to it for guidance. Political organization at the outset was somewhat informal and loose-knit, for a name was apt to carry more weight than a party label, but controversial issues radiating from the national capital in Philadelphia in the 1790s fostered the growth of political parties.

The most exciting issue during Washington's Presidency was the whiskey tax. Like pioneers elsewhere, local citizens regarded the tax as a levy on the farmer's grain. Threats of violence were made; and when protesters seized the arsenal at Sunbury, troops from Lancaster marched to the scene and made arrests. Learning that a liberty pole had been unfurled, in defiance of the law, at Billmyer's Tavern near Lewisburg, the troops crossed the river to investigate; but when they arrived, the pole was gone. At the ensuing election in 1794, the Democratic Republicans defeated the Federalist incumbent in the legislature and elected Samuel Maclay to Congress.

A short time later the Jay Treaty with England split the Presbyterian congregation at Buffalo Church. The Reverend Hugh Morrison, an outspoken Federalist, weathered the storm, but pew rents remained unpaid as Maclay and others left the church. When President Washington proclaimed the first Thanksgiving Day for February 19, 1795, Republican Henry Spyker of Lewisburg noted in his diary, "Good George, take care you do not fall."[1]

The mounting opposition to Federalist policies is indicated by the elections for sheriff in 1794 and 1797. In the former, Robert Irwin, a leading Republican, who was also a distiller, was elected over his Federalist opponent, John Brady. Thomas Mifflin, the Federalist Governor, however, using a discretionary power to name either of the two candidates having the highest votes, chose Brady. Three years later Irwin's vote almost doubled that of Brady, and Mifflin, not daring to thwart public opinion again, reluctantly accepted Irwin. The "infamous" Sedition Act of 1798 precipitated public protests, and in the gubernatorial election of 1799 Northumberland County gave 2,997 votes to Thomas McKean, the Republican candidate, and only 637 to James Ross, his Federalist opponent.

Failing to obtain a revenue from the Whiskey Tax, Federalists levied a tax on window glass. It too was extremely unpopular, and Kimber Barton, the Youngmanstown assessor, was quickly made aware of this. As he moved from house to house, he discovered that glass had been replaced by paper, and he found few windows to assess.

As might be expected, the Democratic Republicans hastened to the polls on election day in 1800 to cast their votes for electors committed to Jefferson, and his subsequent inaugural on March 4, 1801, was a day of rejoicing. Among the few surviving details is the toast of Colonel John Kelly, delivered at a victory celebration at Milton: "May this be the happy day to unite the hearts of all true Americans to their duty to God and our illustrious President, Thomas Jefferson."[2] There appear to have been few Federalists in the region to mourn President Adams' downfall.

The demise of the Alien and Sedition Acts and Jefferson's insistence upon governmental economy solidified his popularity and his partisans rejoiced over his second election. In Linn's words, "Maclay's boys went to Derrstown, where they had large bonfires, fired cannon, and burned up their hats. Old Judge Wilson and Nathan Stockton took the back road home by Baldy's at the Crossroads. Their Dearborn was loaded with China and crockery. Getting a little too much cider oil on, they upset at the little bridge, a few rods east of the hotel. The broken China and crockery laid there for years after."[3]

The region's outstanding political figure in the 1790s was William Maclay. A native of Chester County, he had fought with Forbes and Bouquet in the French and Indian War and qualified for a land grant on the West Branch of the Susquehanna River. He practiced law in York County and combined his practice with surveying and land speculation — not an unusual combination in those days. Removing to Northumberland County, he became an early resident of Sunbury and a land owner in Buffalo Valley.

A born leader, Maclay became a spokesman for the Scots-Irish along the frontier, and represented Northumberland County in the state legislature from 1781 to 1785. In 1789 he was elected as a United States Senator in the first Congress of the United States. Unfortunately for his political future, he drew a two-year term, whereas his colleague, Robert Morris of Philadelphia, remembered as the financier of the American Revolution, drew a full six-year tenure. The two soon became antagonists, Morris, representing the commercial interests, joined Alexander Hamilton to stretch the newly established Constitution to encompass the assumption of the debts owed by the states, whereas Maclay, as spokesman of the frontier, supported strict economy. He rejected the Hamilton-Morris scheme to obtain Virginia's consent for the assumption of state debts by removing the national capital to the banks of the Potomac and urged instead that it be placed on the Susquehanna River. Obviously he failed.

William Maclay disapproved of President Washington for yielding to the views of Hamilton and others who, in his judgment, were seeking to reproduce an aristocracy in America comparable to the ruling classes in Europe. For his leadership in the Senate, Maclay was lauded by the distinguished historian Charles A. Beard as "the original Jefferson Democrat — that is, the Democratic Republican Party of Jefferson."[4] On the other hand, the writer of a biography of Morris castigated him as "an utterly unyielding individual, to whom the interests of the country were secondary to those of his section of Pennsylvania."[5]

During his brief tenure in the Senate Maclay kept a journal, in which he crowded his thoughts and frustrations. His simple manners and democratic philosophy made him increasingly critical of Washington for countenancing extravagance and display. His description of the first President's discomfiture and embarrassment when he appeared in person to seek the advice and consent of the Senate, where he faced unsolicited questions and dissenting opinions, is regarded as one of the most revealing contemporary pictures of Washington's personality. In fact, Beard evaluated the journal as "one of the most precious human documents for the study of American manners, morals, and intelligence, political and general."[6]

It is not difficult to see why Maclay made political enemies and why they would have blocked his reelection in 1791. Unable to agree on a successor, the legislature postponed the election for a year; and when at last it was consummated, the office went to Albert Gallatin, who would become one of the Nation's outstanding statesmen.

Maclay's rebuff in the legislature did not discredit him at home. He was a county judge and served again as a legislator. In 1796 he was chosen as a Presidential Elector in a statewide election and cast his vote for Thomas Jefferson. Adams defeated Jefferson by three votes in the Electoral College, but four years later Maclay had the satisfaction of seeing Jefferson reverse the decision. Late in life he moved to Harrisburg and served a final term in the legislature where he agitated for the transfer of the state capital from Lancaster, a Federalist stronghold, to Harrisburg. The county's great democratic spokesman died in 1804 at 70.

Meanwhile, Maclay's younger brother Samuel, who settled on a farm near the site of the Dreisbach Church, was following in William's footsteps. He too was a woodsman and surveyor as well as an enthusiastic Jeffersonian and like his brother avoided ostentation. It was reported that he bought a handsome coach, but after using it once to attend the old Buffalo Church he returned it to the stable and never used it again.

Samuel Maclay's public life began in 1790, when he was named to a state commission to survey the streams of northwestern Pennsylvania to ascertain their use for transportation. The work required months in the wilderness and included about one-third of the Commonwealth, taking him as far as the borders of New York and Ohio. Samuel served successively in the legislature, Congress, and the State Senate, where he became its Speaker. In 1802 he was elected to the United States Senate. His popularity among his

Maclay marker on Dreisbach Church Road. Photo by
Jim Walter.

A monument honoring Samuel Maclay was dedicated in
October 1906 at the Dreisbach Church (right) quite near his
eighteenth-century stone farmhouse (bottom). Both the
monument and house, still standing today, are subjects of
real photo postcards from the early twentieth century. The
Dreisbach Church shown here was razed in 1963 because its
foundation had been undermined. Maclay's eighteenth-century home is across the road. Both from the collection of the
Union County Historical Society, #89.5.2.7 and #92.9.89.44.

colleagues in the legislature is suggested by the vote sending him to the Senate, when he received 66 votes and his opponent 39 on the first ballot. In the Senate he replaced James Ross, the last Federalist in the state to hold the office.

Senator Maclay spoke infrequently, but he was active behind the scenes. In 1805 he was frequently mentioned as his party's candidate for Governor, but the choice went instead to Simon Snyder. In 1808 he backed George Clinton, a seven-term Governor of New York, for President, despite Jefferson's support of James Madison, regarding the latter as a late convert to the cause of Republicanism. When a Congressional Caucus endorsed Madison, Maclay joined a minority protesting the action. Returning to Northumberland County, he obtained the backing of his party for Clinton, but Madison ultimately secured Pennsylvania's support, leaving Maclay in an untenable position.

In addition to his ill-fated opposition to Madison, Samuel Maclay opposed Jefferson's controversial embargo upon the importation of European goods to force the warring nations there to respect American neutral rights on the high seas. By then Maclay was so far out of step with party policies that he saw no hope of reelection and resigned his seat on January 12, 1809. The Embargo Act was soon an admitted failure and was repealed, but it came too late to help Maclay. Returning to his stout stone farm house in Buffalo Township, he died two years later and was buried in the family plot there. One hundred years later, a granite monolith was raised in his memory in the Dreisbach Church cemetery a short distance away.

While the Maclay brothers were in the Senate of the United States representing Pennsylvania, a younger contemporary was shaping a political career which would eventually take him to the governorship. Born at Lancaster in 1759, the son of German immigrants, Simon Snyder's boyhood was a struggle against poverty. He was apprenticed to a tanner and currier while acquiring the rudiments of a formal education at night school. He followed the trade for a few years then moved to Selinsgrove where an older brother was a storekeeper. In a few years Simon opened a store of his own and went into milling in partnership with Anthony Selin, his brother-in-law, who had founded the village.

Simon Snyder became active in local politics and was appointed a justice of the peace. In 1789 he was elected as a delegate to the State Constitutional Convention, where he became acquainted with some of the outstanding legalists of the Commonwealth. In 1797 he was elected to the Assembly and reelected each year thereafter until he was chosen as Governor in 1808. Meanwhile, Snyder became a leader of the Democratic Republican Party and was thrice elected as Speaker.

After the passage of so many years, it is difficult to pinpoint the qualities which permitted Simon Snyder to attain the state's highest office; he never studied law; he lacked eloquence as a speaker; and, reversing the practice of his predecessors, he dispatched his annual messages to the legislature for delivery by the clerk rather than present them in person. But his open, friendly manner, his preference for simplicity in his daily life, and his reputation for integrity perhaps appealed to the voters and his German name was also an asset at the outset. Though Scots-Irish were far more active in politics than the Germans, it was no secret that the latter were preferred at the polls. In Snyder's dealings with fellow politicians, he was conciliatory and seldom dictatorial and always willing to listen.

His political rise paralleled the decline of the Federalist Party. Politics in this period were largely a matter of reconciling factions within the Democratic Republican ranks — factions which lacked stability and seemed to change with the weather. Here Snyder had an obvious advantage. He left the in-fighting to others and remained available to all combinations. With strong grass roots support up-state to commend him, he could not be overlooked.

In 1805 opportunity knocked almost unexpectedly when the Democratic Republican legislative caucus nominated Simon Snyder for Governor. Ordinarily, this would have been tantamount to election, but dissident groups combined with traditional Federalists to give the incumbent, Thomas McKean, a belated nomination also. In the ensuing contest McKean's experience prevailed over Snyder's lack of it. Even so, Snyder lost by just 4,700 votes to an opponent who had been prominent in both state and national affairs in his first state-wide contest. A year later Snyder was elected Speaker of the Assembly by one vote and he won the following year by two — during the absence of two members of the opposition.

In 1808 with McKean completing a third and final term under the constitution, Snyder's right to the gubernatorial nomination was not seriously challenged. The party's caucus gave him a unanimous endorsement, and in the election he defeated James Ross, the candidate of the Federalists and Quids (dissident Democratic Republicans), by a vote of 67,975 to 39,575. Three years later he was triumphantly reelected with only scattered opposition, and in 1814 he won a third term by a margin of almost two to one.

Snyder's nine years in office were years of controversy. Intra-party quarrels produced a barrage of charges and countercharges. Federal and state troops almost clashed in Philadelphia during the Olmstead controversy, and the War of 1812 threatened to make the state a battlefield.[7] But in retrospect his administration was marked by solid achievement. His years in the Assembly helped to smooth his relations with the legislative branch, and his messages were consistently forthright and down-to-earth. Executive privilege was not in his vocabulary.

In the early nineteenth century, a governor would recommend legislation to the lawmakers, but the legislature showed a great deal of independence and vetoes were exceptional. In 1814, a gubernatorial election year, the legislature adopted an omnibus bill providing for the chartering of some 40 banks. The bill blatantly violated the principles of the party, but it gained the support of a majority of legislators by extensive logrolling and was sent to the Executive Office at the same time the legislative nominating caucus was postponed to await the Governor's response. He vetoed it, and his action was sustained. Having failed to intimidate him, the caucus voted him a renomination. Ironically, a year later the legislature passed a similar bill and found support to carry it over his veto. In the panic of 1819, two years after Snyder's retirement, bank failures intensified and prolonged the economic depression in the state.

Like William Maclay, Snyder was in favor of the removal of the state capital from Lancaster to Harrisburg, and in January of 1811 he had the satisfaction of issuing the official proclamation accepting the offers of land made by John Harris and the late William Maclay. A year later governmental offices were opened at the new location, awaiting the completion of a more fitting capitol structure.

Snyder was less fortunate in his advocacy of public education and the amelioration of the criminal code. The School Act of 1809 was designed to provide for the poor, who could not afford the tuition required in the subscription schools. Since the names of the families accepting its benefits were made a part of the public record, parents frequently ignored it rather than accept the stigma of pauperism. Snyder made no further headway toward a comprehensive public education system. Also, the state's criminal code at this time was considered enlightened, but Snyder believed that juries permitted murderers to go free rather than find them guilty, knowing that a conviction would result in a death sentence. He also found that setting dates for the execution of the convicted was one of his most difficult responsibilities. Of all of his duties, he noted, "that of announcing to a fellow-being, the day, the hour, on which he shall cease to exist, is the most painful and distressing." Again, the legislature had no satisfactory solution to offer.

In his annual message of 1811, Governor Snyder urged the legislature to look into the possibility of a system of canals; in another passage he protested against slavery. Neither recommendation was implemented, however. While no "War Hawk," Snyder offered the full cooperation of the state to President Madison upon the declaration of war against Great Britain in 1812. Unlike New England, where the war destroyed the shipping economy, the manufacturers of Pennsylvania expanded to meet the emergency. When the British invaded the Chesapeake Bay and burned the capitol in Washington in 1814, Snyder hurriedly established his headquarters in Philadelphia to meet a possible invasion. Fortunately none occurred, and he returned to Harrisburg in a few months.

Back in Selinsgrove after the expiration of his three terms, the maximum tenure permitted by the constitution he had helped to draft, Snyder gave no consideration to retirement. Instead, he accepted election to the State Senate. After he had served the first year of a four-year term, Snyder died of typhoid fever at 60 on November 9, 1819. His fine stone residence on Selinsgrove's main thoroughfare remains an historic landmark.

It was during Snyder's tenure as Governor that Union County separated from Northumberland County. A glance at a map of Central Pennsylvania would suggest that a county centering at the forks of the Susquehanna River and including present-day Northumberland, Union, Snyder, Montour, and Columbia Counties would be geographically compact and that its county seat at Sunbury would be central with water communications radiating in three directions. However, logic had little to do with county lines whereas politics was all-important. That any growing town might aspire to be a county seat scarcely requires an explanation. The convenience of county offices and the business and legal talent it would attract would contribute substantially to the fledgling community's growth. If the borough of Northumber-

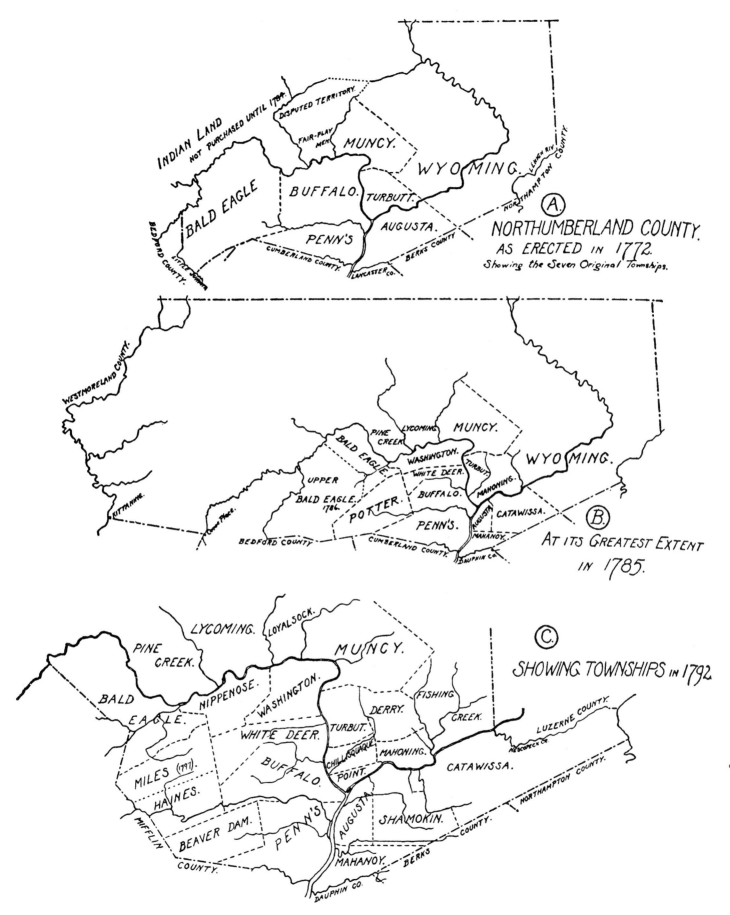

Series of maps of Northumberland County from 1772 through 1813, compiled and drawn by Charles Fisher Snyder in 1936. From the *Proceedings of the Northumberland County Historical Society, Vol. VIII* (Sunbury, PA, 1936), 195.

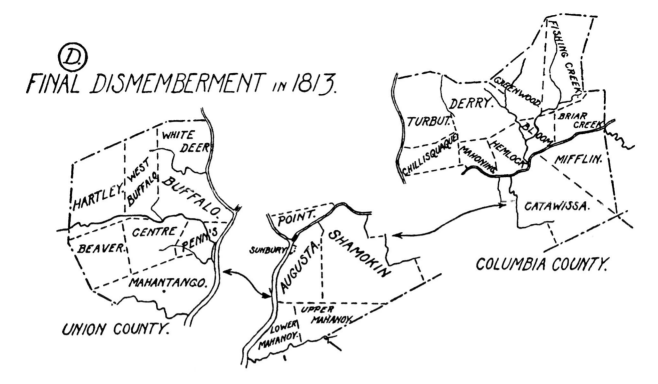

D. FINAL DISMEMBERMENT IN 1813.

UNION COUNTY.

COLUMBIA COUNTY.

land wished to wrest the county seat from Sunbury, its aspirations might be written off as covetousness; but if two or three potential county seats could act in concert and elect legislators sympathetic to their collective ambitions, the battle might be won.

In the struggle for fragmentation or "disintegration" as a Northumberland County historian terms it, an unwritten rule observed in the state capitol was that the local legislator should have the last word in the matter.[8] If he opposed the plan, the legislators closed ranks to reject it. Between 1772 and 1810 parts of Luzerne, Lycoming, and Centre Counties were cut away from over-sized Northumberland. At this point Sunbury area residents were convinced that the process had gone far enough; but they were to be overruled by movements in the hinterland: one in Derry Township, and the other in the townships west of the river including Penns, Center, Buffalo, West Buffalo, White Deer, Washington (Gregg), and Hartley in what would become Union County.

Early in 1811 an article appeared in Lewisburg's *Argus* favoring division. It emphasized the great distance to the county seat, the cost of taking a ferry over the river, and the expense of ornamenting the town — presumably a reference to expenditures for a fire engine and a fireproof building for records. Subsequent articles stressed the likelihood of increased property values in the new county, the convenience of a nearby county seat, and the savings in money spent upon court trials. Linn termed these

articles the "entering wedge" for the erection of Union County.[9] In the fall of 1811 Frederick Evans, a "divisionite," was elected to the Assembly, and in February he wrote to George Kremer in Lewisburg that the plan was progressing. He urged more petitions and longer lists of names to offset those presented by the people of the "Forks" in opposition. "If five hundred more signatures can not be obtained, send on as many as can be got. Four hundred and fifty-one would be a majority of the taxables," he added.[10]

Division was not forthcoming at this session, but the next year advocates renewed the pressure. The local legislator was now George Kremer, a Lewisburg storekeeper and political spellbinder; a tall, rawboned, and coarse-featured man with a head seemingly too large for his body, he had a wit and vivacity which made him an attraction at political rallies or social gatherings. A nephew of Governor Snyder, he had been reared in Snyder's home, and his close ties with the Governor abetted the chances of the divisionists. Even so, it might not have been decisive had not a movement in Derry Township, designed to combine the townships in the eastern part of the county to create Columbia County, coincided with the drive to detach the western townships.

Attacked on both flanks, Northumberland was beaten, the divisions cutting away more than two-thirds of its land and population and leaving but 450 square miles and 10,000 people. Columbia County received 700 square miles and a population of 20,000,

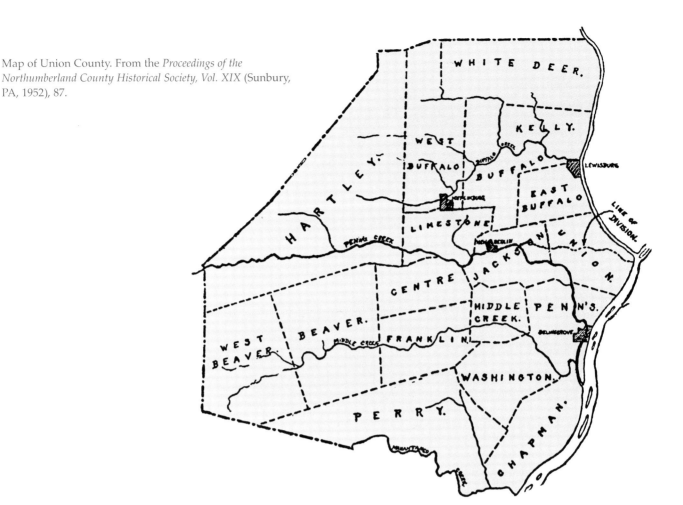

Map of Union County. From the *Proceedings of the Northumberland County Historical Society, Vol. XIX* (Sunbury, PA, 1952), 87.

and Union (including Snyder) 647 square miles and 15,000 residents. There was no hint at this time that the southeastern townships of Northumberland would become a populous coal mining area. If Northumberland mourned, Union County rejoiced. Yet one extremely divisive issue remained. The enabling bill, passed on March 22, 1813, did not designate a county seat, and its omission was not accidental.

To forestall a battle royal between claimants for the coveted honor, the bill provided that commissioners would locate near the county's center. After signing the bill Governor Snyder appointed "three discreet and disinterested persons not resident in the county of Northumberland or Union" to carry out the delicate assignment. They settled upon New Berlin, at that time a hamlet of 59 taxables residing in one frame and 44 log buildings. Time would prove, however, that Selinsgrove, Lewisburg, and Mifflinburg simply deferred their ambitions and would be heard from again. While the location of the county seat was being determined, the first county court was held in Mifflinburg in February of 1814. In May of 1815 the county government was transferred to New Berlin, where a courthouse was nearing completion.

The Democratic Republican Party retained an inharmonious hegemony through Monroe's Presidency, remembered inaccurately as the "Era of Good Feelings"; but it was torn by factionalism in the 1820s when conventions "fresh from the people" replaced legislative caucuses, and a host of "favorite sons" challenged the older leadership. When John Quincy Adams bested General Andrew Jackson, the nation's first folk-hero, for President in 1824, despite the latter's larger popular vote, Jackson's partisans charged that Henry Clay had turned over his electoral votes to Adams in return for an appointment as Secretary of State. The accusation had been made in the Washington press by Union County's Congressman, George Kremer, and "bargain and sale" became the catchwords of the Jackson (Democratic) Party. Four years later Jackson was swept into the Presidency by a popular fervor hitherto unseen in American politics.

On the strength of his charge, George Kremer became a hero in his own right. Returning to Lewisburg, he was met by a delegation of citizens and invited to a public dinner at the house of Thomas R. Lewis. After a sumptuous meal, the cloth was removed and "toasts were drunk with much hilarity and good glee." "Honorable George Kremer," one of the toasts boasted, "the intrepid and watchful guardian of the people's rights. When corruption reared its hydra head, he cried aloud, and spared not."[11] When Clay called for proof, however, Kremer could produce nothing more substantial than rumor and his fame was short-lived; but in Union County, among Jackson men, to be sure, he remained a prophet and, in old age, the seer of the party.

The Adams-Jackson controversy recreated the two-party system: the National Republicans were the party of Adams, Clay, and Webster; the Democrats, the party of Jackson, Calhoun, and Van Buren. Local politicians had to make their choice. This orientation had scarcely crystallized when another issue, Anti-masonry, threw politics and politicians into another maelstrom.

Masonry in the 1820s was a nation-wide fraternal organization, drawing its membership in large part from the business and professional classes. It was a prestigious body, including in its membership some of the highest-ranking political leaders such as President Washington, but it was not without critics. Some people, in particular Quakers as well as German pietistic sects which disapproved oath-taking, believed that a secret society was inimical to American principles. The pardoning of a convict was sometimes sufficient to create rumors that it had been effected by Masonic influence, and it was alleged that prisoners in the dock had given signals of distress to Masons in the jury box. Such allegations were usually dismissed as inspired by jealousy and for a time had little effect upon the reputation of the order.

Then suddenly, in 1826, the disappearance of William Morgan of Batavia, New York, who had threatened to publish the secrets of Masonry, created a sensation. Accusations that he had been kidnapped and murdered by Masons were broadcast in the press, and the air was soon charged with denuncia-tions. Hostility toward Masonry was so virulent that it forced the closing of dozens of its chapters, including the Lafayette Lodge in New Berlin, which surren-dered its warrant and remained dormant for twelve years. It also gave birth to the Antimasonic Party, which was committed to the exposure and elimina-tion of the society. Beginning in Western New York, the Antimasonic Party spread into Pennsylvania, virtually eliminating the National Republican Party in rural areas; and, in coalition with the National Republicans in urban districts, it defeated the Democrats in several state-wide elections. In 1835 the Antimasonic Party elected Joseph Ritner as Governor, and it was the springboard for the political career of Thaddeus Stevens.

The movement spread across Pennsylvania in 1828 to 1829 and took root in Union County, particularly in the German townships in the southern part of the county, and for a decade it won most of the elections. In 1835 Union County voters cast 2,185 votes for Ritner and 1,231 for his two Democratic opponents: incumbent Governor George Wolf and Henry A. Muhlenberg. They gave Ritner a majority again in 1838 in his unsuccessful bid for a reelection.

In the welter of Antimasonic politics locally, the outstanding figure was Ner Middleswarth. Born in Scotland in 1783, he spent his early childhood in New Jersey and at ten moved with his family to Beaver Township, Northumberland County (now Snyder). Growing up on the frontier, he had a scanty school-ing, but he became so fluent in Pennsylvania Dutch that his contemporaries assumed that he was Pennsylvania German. He was successful in farming and business, having accumulated property. In the War of 1812 Middleswarth organized two companies and saw duty in Canada. This act of patriotism was a stepping stone into politics, and shortly thereafter he won election on the Democratic Republican ticket to the Pennsylvania State Assembly. Middleswarth subsequently served for fifteen terms and was twice elected as Speaker. He was a Jacksonian Democrat for a few years but switched to the Antimasonic Party and became one of its leaders in the state. When Antimasonry receded, he joined the Whig Party, and under this new banner he served terms in the State Senate and the Congress of the United States.

A newspaper editor who saw Ner Middleswarth in action many times described him as a plump man of about medium height, who appeared very common and even "slouchy in both dress and manners."[12] He could manage a meeting with tact and skill, however, and he was eloquent on the stump. In his later years "Old Ner" joined the Republican Party, and at 75 he began a five-year term as Associate Judge of Snyder County, which he lived to complete, dying just one year later at 81.

Antimasonry soon lost its momentum. A Joint Committee of the two houses of the legislature, headed by the redoubtable Thaddeus Stevens, launched an investigation of Masonry and went so far as to call former Governor George Wolf and other high state officials before it. Wolf heeded the summons but

The masthead for the *Anti-Masonic Star* as published in New Berlin on April 16, 1836. From the collection of the New Berlin Heritage Association, #91.445.1

refused to testify; and when Stevens attempted to cite him for contempt, the legislature would not support him. The investigation went no further. In 1838 the Antimasons renominated Ritner, but he was defeated by 5,000 votes in one of the most scurrilous elections in the history of the Commonwealth. With the vote in several Philadelphia districts in dispute, passions ran so high that the Antimasons refused to yield gracefully, claiming fraud; and the word was given that Ritner and his administration would remain in office until the issue was resolved. In December, as members of the legislature assembled in Harrisburg, hundreds of Protestants, many from the Philadelphia area, descended upon Harrisburg to make their wishes heard. For the moment focus was on the lower house where several disputed elections left its organization in doubt. Unable to agree upon a procedure, members of the two parties met separately, each claiming to be the legal body. The government was paralyzed; and, fearing mob violence, Ritner called the militia from Philadelphia and armed them with thirteen rounds of buckshot cartridges. A break in the impasse came when three members of the "Cunningham House" (Antimasonic) withdrew from it and took seats in the "Hopkins House" (Democratic), giving it an indisputable majority. No shots were fired, and the so-called "Buckshot War" was over.

Union County's citizenry had a personal interest in that affair in that John Montelius of Mifflinburg had been one of the pivotal figures involved. An Antimasonic member of the Assembly, he had entered the Cunningham House reluctantly. After sitting through the stalemate for several days, he found that two representatives from Luzerne had similar doubts. The three decided to break the impasse despite the anger and derision of their Antimasonic colleagues. Montelius was not returned to the legislature but later served as a county commissioner and associate judge. He was respected through the remaining years of his life for his courage in the crisis.

By 1840 most Antimasons had gravitated to the Whig Party. The move was timely. The Democratic administration of Martin Van Buren had been identified with the Panic of 1837, thereby leaving it discredited. Seeing an opportunity to elect their first President, the Whigs found a hero of the Jackson image in General William Henry Harrison; and heralding him as the hero of Tippecanoe, they made "Tippecanoe and Tyler too" the slogan of the famous "log cabin and hard cider" campaign which followed. The election of 1840 provides insights into politics as it was played in Union County more than a century ago. Excitement pervaded all of the communities, but descriptions will be confined to three celebrations: the first at Beavertown, the second at New Berlin, and the third at Lewisburg. Beavertown led off on April 20:

> Rising of the People.
> 1000 F R E E M E N!!

A meeting in favor of Harrison and Tyler was held on the premises of Mr. Ulsh in Beaver Township on the 20th inst., not in the house, but in a field. It was large and enthusiastic, yet peaceable, but determined . . .

The day was fair. At Beavertown a Log Cabin was built for the occasion, about 45 feet long, sufficiently large to carry sixty persons. About 9 o'clock a splendid team drawn by four, and a coach by two horses arrived from New Berlin to join the Log Cabin boys on their way to the meeting. A large concourse of people had assembled at that place, and hopes of better times appeared to dawn in the sparkling eyes of the collected yeomanry. A procession was then formed with riders in front — next to the Log Cabin, filled with patriotic farmers and mechanicks, drawn by eight splendid grey horses, bearing a large flag with the following appropriate inscription,

> HARRISON AND TYLER
> NO SUB-TREASURY AND BETTER TIMES.

Then followed about one hundred and twenty men on horseback, footmen, etc., etc. The moving procession presented an imposing sight. Old men and women were seen along the wayside — in their doors and some times on high hills along the road waving their hats and caps, and handkerchiefs for HARRISON AND TYLER — FREIHEIT UND VATERLAND.[13]

On September 16 New Berlin had its great celebration. The festivities really began on the previous afternoon when a committee was appointed to meet John W. Baer, "the Buckeye Blacksmith," at Hartleton and escort him to town. Baer was a homespun minstrel and orator who had exchanged Jackson for Harrison as his hero and was now touring the country in the latter's behalf. Upon his arrival, the "mechanics and farmers" repaired to his lodgings and urged him to deliver an address in the evening, "they being so anxious to hear him, that they could not wait till the day after." He consented; and, at the ringing of the courthouse bell, the people flocked, and the house was soon filled with "mechanics and laborers" anxious to hear the famed blacksmith. The meeting was organized by appointing J.A. VanValzah as President; David Schwenk, Jacob Sypher, Solomon Engle, and Archibald Thomas as Vice-Presidents; with J.J. Maclay and Samuel H. Laird as Secretaries. "The meeting was then addressed by Mr. Baer, the Buckeye Blacksmith, making some statements how some of the Van Buren party were determined to mob and kill him, because he was advocating the rights of American Industry and Economy. Mr. Baer was greatly cheered by the 'bone and sinew'."

The affair, however, was only a prelude to the main event, and the local Whig newspaper picked up the story at this point.

TREMENDOUS
HARRISON AND TYLER
COUNTY MEETING
BETWEEN 4 and 5000 FREEMEN

The most enthusiastic assemblage of the PEOPLE that has ever been seen or heard of in this section of the country, took place in New Berlin, Union County, on Wednesday the 16th inst.

The sun rose on beauty. Nature was beneficent in her smiles and her advantages. Long before the appointed hour, the people came in crowds from all portions and sections of the country. They came from the mountains, from the hills, from the vallies [sic], and last but not least from the LOG CABINS. It was the spontaneous TURN OUT of a people who knew their rights and dare maintain them. It was a guaranty of the perpetuity of our free institutions. That congregated multitude with long, loud and enthusiastic bursts of gratitude, that poured

upon the car, at times, its deafening influence — those banners that floated in the breeze and waived in proud triumph in token of respect, for a man of their choice — was a portent of his certain success at the coming contest, and struck terror and dismay to the ranks of the Van Buren spoilers and their horde of ghostly looking destructives.

The farmers, mechanics and working men themselves came, some in 'Log Cabins' with 'Hard Cider' barrels and flags floating in the air, whereon were inscribed "NO REDUCING OF WAGES FOR LABOR," on one side, and on the other, "A PROTECTIVE TARIFF." They came with six horse teams, four horse and two horse farm wagons, carriages, on horseback, on foot and with wagons drawn by oxen, so that the streets were crowded to overflow, with flags and banners too numerous to be described. . .

At 11 o'clock the multitude repaired to the place that was prepared by the committees in the following manner. A cord was stretched across the street from the Court House steeple to the Hotel of Mr. Kleckner (a distance of 120 feet) from which was suspended thirteen streamers at equal distances and joined by the same number of laurel wreaths. The officers' stand was erected across the pavement in front of the Register's office. There was a beautiful triumphal arch made of laurel and cedar erected over the stand; the back ground was releaved [sic.] by an excellent likeness of General Harrison in the centre; the battle of the Thames on the right and the battle of Tippecanoe on the left. The whole presented a most brilliant and liefly appearance, and indeed it may be said, that never did New Berlin see such a day before. . . Mr. Baer, the Buckeye Blacksmith, addressed the meeting, convincing every man under the sound of his voice, that we must have a speedy reform in the affairs of the General Government.

About 1 o'clock, the scene was enlivened by the arrival of the splendid Milton band, drawn in an Omnibus by six grey horses; next in order came a canoe drawn by four horses; then the Lewisburg band in a wagon drawn by four horses, followed by stage coaches, farm wagons, carriages, horsemen and footmen. This procession arrived with numerous splendid flags and banners.

The meeting then recessed until two o'clock to provide time for refreshments. It was then parade time.

The procession marched through the principal streets with the bands in front, presenting a sight to every beholder at once grand and imposing. The procession having arrived at the stand, the bands played a few airs, when Mr. Baer continued his splendid, powerful and convincing remarks of the corruption and misgovernment of Martin Van Buren's Administration . . . Mr. Baer concluded by singing a Log Cabin song.

Mr. Hugh Bellas being called on addressed the meeting in a very able and eloquent manner. He having concluded, the meeting adjourned.[14]

At candlelight they assembled again at the Court House. In a short time it was crowded, and loud calls from every corner were heard for Mr. Baer, the Buckeye Blacksmith. He rose and sang an appropriate log cabin song depicting the meeting held that day. He said that he was very fatigued, but when calls continued from "the mechanics and laboring men," he agreed to address them. He was followed by James Merrill. Everyone seemed satisfied now, and the celebration was finished.

The Democrats could find nothing to match log cabins, hard cider, and the indefatigable Buckeye Blacksmith and consequently went down to defeat on election day. Lewisburg Whigs held a mammoth victory celebration at a grove adjacent to town, where oratory was followed by an ox roast served by tavern keeper John Haus. In the evening a procession moved from street to street, and at Market Street marched under an arch where 300 glowing candles created a magnificent spectacle: "Language fails us to describe the beauty and gorgeousness of the scene which the [illuminated] windows presented, with the exception of here and there a dark spot, where the genius of loco-focism [radical Democrats] sat brooding with closed doors over its irretrievable overthrow. The streets presented . . . the blaze of noonday upon the dark hours of a moonless night."[15]

The Whigs of Union County won more often than they lost in the 1840s despite Harrison's death in office and Tyler's running quarrel with the party's leaders in Congress. The Democrats inadvertently contributed to the Whig successes by expending their energies on internecine quarrels. The upstate Democrats were pro-tariff, pro-internal improvements, and pro-banks, all of which set them apart from the party leadership in Washington. They chanted "fifty-four, forty or fight" in 1844; but when southern leaders pushed through the Tariff of 1846, cutting duties on European goods competing with Pennsylvania's "infant" industries, they could not be held in line. A decade later the "free soil" issue drew not only Whigs but many Democrats as well into the ranks of the newborn Republican Party, and by the Civil War Republicans had gained the ascendancy, leaving Mifflinburg the last Democratic stronghold in the county.

Meanwhile, the usual party cleavages were virtually eliminated by a local issue for a time. Union County as laid out in 1813 was a compact county with New Berlin the county seat at its center. This, however, proved to be no guarantee against a change. During the years which followed, New Berlin remained a small town which came to life only during court sessions and elections, whereas Lewisburg and Selinsgrove became thriving canal towns. Mifflinburg, Swineford / Middleburg, and Freeburg, all with rich agricultural hinterlands, also grew but at a slower pace. Residents of the communities needed no reminders that if the county were divided, two county seats would be in the works.

These political breezes were fanned into a storm by a railroad bond issue in 1852 which was advocated by "Improvement Men" in the towns but bitterly opposed by the residents of the interior, who assumed that the costs would ultimately fall upon the taxpayers. A year earlier the Susquehanna Railroad Company had obtained a charter to build along the east bank of the Susquehanna River from Harrisburg to Sunbury, with the privilege of extending northward. Lewisburg "Improvement Men," headed by William Cameron, immediately went into action to bring the railroad into Union County from Sunbury or Northumberland and extend it through Lewisburg to Williamsport. Also catching the railroad fever, residents of Selinsgrove projected a connection with the line and ultimately a branch to Lewistown. In New Berlin, too, hopes were raised for a Lewistown / Winfield connection which would run through the village. In a matter of months Lewisburg contracted to bond itself for $75,000 to purchase Susquehanna Railroad stock, and somewhat surprisingly, the County Commissioners voted to bond the county for $200,000 for the same purpose without the formality of a referendum.

Every country store at once became a forum as proponents and critics went after each other with hammer and tongs. A mass meeting at New Berlin on August 31, 1852, became one of the best-remembered political incidents of the century. The crowd — said to have been the largest public meeting ever held there — could not be accommodated in the courthouse, and the meeting was moved to the street outside. Finding it impossible to organize, the two factions separated into two camps. Ner Middleswarth mounted a wagon to address the pro-bond assemblage, but the anti-bond men seized the shafts and dashed for Penns Creek, two blocks away. The 69-year-old veteran soon reappeared, "puffing and blowing, having jumped from the wagon and escaped from his captors."[16] He then stepped into a second wagon and conducted the meeting without further interruptions. Six months later, with the furor over the bonds unresolved, citizens of New Berlin petitioned the grand jury for a report favorable to the erection of a new courthouse at the taxpayers' expense. The storm became a gale.

Ordinarily, when counties divided, the impetus came from the region being severed to form a new county, but Union County's division came about through a more subtle and unusual combination of forces. The separatist movement centered in Lewisburg, which it was assumed would remain in Union, and received strong support from Selinsgrove and environs, which would fall into the new county. Both entered into the plan with the expectation of becoming county seats; the first succeeded, but the second failed. Curiously, the majority of voters in the new county (Snyder) rejected the division, while a majority in the part remaining in Union — which would thus be reduced to half its size — sanctioned it.

Had New Berlin not sought a new courthouse or at least offered to pay the costs for one, Union County likely would not have been divided, and New Berlin would have remained the county seat indefinitely. As C. Warren Gutelius pointed out, the division of counties in Pennsylvania had almost ceased by 1855, and after Snyder County only Cameron and Lackawanna were subsequently created.[17] Today, Union and Snyder combined would be smaller than 36 of the state's counties while Lycoming would be twice as large. Only Philadelphia, Delaware, and Montour are smaller than either Union or Snyder Counties.

With modern communications there is more emphasis upon combining county services than decentralizing them, but in 1853 through 1855 the time was right, and the opportunity was not lost. The *Der Democrat* of New Berlin (its editor, Israel Gutelius, appears to have been one of two New Berliners to support county division) condemned those who had petitioned for a new courthouse and commended the grand jury for its 13-6 vote against it. New Berlin could have a new courthouse, he argued, but they should pay for a substantial portion of it by subscription as other county seats had commonly done. Echoes of the newspaper's stand reverberated around the county, where meet-

ings and petitions were the order of the day. New Berlin's bid for a new courthouse was excoriated, and, worse for its future, demands were voiced for a division of the county. Attempting to strike back, New Berliners published handbills warning the people in the southern townships that if division were consummated, the new county would be held accountable for its share of the railroad bonds even though the railroad would not cross its soil.

Lewisburg's response was an immediate denial, and its business and political leaders, meeting with representatives of adjacent townships, insisted that the bonds would not be dropped upon the tax payers. In addition to $75,000 of stock, they had made individual subscriptions for sums ranging from $30,000 to $40,000. "So far as wishing to rid ourselves of these engagements, we are able and would be willing, if necessary, in case the county is divided as proposed, to guarantee the exemption of the south side from their share of the county's liability on account of said subscription."[18] They denied that Lewisburg had concocted division or that it sought to remove the county seat from New Berlin. Resolutions adopted by a Selinsgrove "division meeting" also reassured residents of the "southern county" that the "northern county" would assume the whole responsibility for the bonds, "where it properly belongs in as much as the said railroad will pass through the entire length of the eastern line of that county."[19]

The *Lewisburg Democrat* argued that the county was large enough for division, that both counties would be larger than Montour, and that the growth of each would offset the cost of maintaining two governments. It considered time and convenience as factors also, but it placed greatest emphasis upon New Berlin's attempt to build a courthouse at public expense: "Let them stop talking of repudiation, and let them raise money [for the courthouse] by subscription, and the tax payers may listen to them."[20] Meanwhile, Eli Slifer of Lewisburg had introduced a division bill in the State Senate along with a second measure to eliminate the southern county from any responsibility for the bonds. With petitions from both sides pouring in, Slifer professed neutrality and recommended a referendum on the issue at the October election.

Election results only served to confirm the previously held views of the partisans. Ballots with a separate box with the label "DIVISION" and one marked "AGAINST DIVISION" on the inside were avoided by opponents of division, and the *Democrat* reported 1,564 votes were cast — all of them for division. A second type of ballot printed by the New Berlin faction was marked "Bonds and Division," and it asked two questions: "Against the Railroad Bonds — Yes or No" and "Against Division — Yes or No." The *Democrat* insisted that these ballots should not be accepted in that they violated the spirit of the referendum. Unable to agree on the legality of the ballots, the judges of election refused to sign the returns. The *New Berlin Star* offered its own count with a majority of 181 against division, while the *Democrat* claimed a majority of 1,564 for division!

Thus the controversy went into the state legislative session of 1854, where the local Assemblyman was Major John W. Simonton, a Whig from Buffalo Township. He had promised to accept the dictate of his constituents and after some hesitation decided that the mandate was against division. He reached this decision despite the blandishments and pressures by the leaders of his party in the Lewisburg area, and his position led to the defeat of division in the Assembly by a vote of 38 to 36. The question was thus postponed until the fall when state-wide prohibition (formulated like a Maine law), Know Nothingism (nativism), and the Kansas-Nebraska Bill (free-soil) added three divisive national issues to the perplexing bonds and division imbroglio.

Lewisburg's leaders now laid down the gauntlet. In a full-page advertisement embellished by a spreading eagle, 28 of them, including William Cameron, Eli Slifer, William Frick, Thomas Hayes, Philip Billmeyer, John Walls, James F. Linn, Peter Beaver, John Chamberlain, Jonathan Wolfe, and George F. Miller, affirmed that new public buildings in New Berlin would cost the county from $80,000 to $100,000. If, instead, the county were divided, the Lewisburg citizens would bear the cost of a courthouse in Lewisburg; and to prove that there was no trick involved, they offered a bond for the sum of $50,000.[21] Lewisburg's *Democrat*, which carried the advertisement, added that division would result in the cancellation of the county's $200,000 obligation to the Susquehanna Railroad. Failure to divide, on the other hand, would add the cost of the new buildings to the $200,000, a debt which would "mortgage the farms of their children and their children's children."[22] It further observed that the county buildings in New Berlin were in a "filthy condition" and

a fire hazard, thereby endangering the records. New Berlin could not find 28 affluent citizens to make a counteroffer.

By fall one issue was losing its impact. The Susquehanna Railroad was being consolidated, and it had dropped its claim upon the county. The election also changed the county's representation in Harrisburg; Simonton, "candidate of the New Berlin wire pullers," was defeated by Dr. James W. Crawford, a Democrat from Juniata County, who had endorsed the division — this, despite a majority of 185 for Simonton in Union County. The intensity of the division issue is suggested by the votes for Simonton and Crawford in New Berlin and Lewisburg, with the former receiving 145 votes and the latter only two in New Berlin, whereas in Lewisburg — ordinarily a Whig stronghold — Crawford was given 435 and Simonton, from neighboring Buffalo Township, just six. In the Senate, James M. Sellers, a Whig of Juniata County and an advocate of division, had replaced Eli Slifer, who did not accept a renomination.

The division bill now moved forward and was accepted by both houses but did require the Speaker's vote in the Senate to break a tie. Governor Pollock approved it on March 2, 1855. The proponents had wisely refrained from designating the county seats, and their choice of Snyder as the name of the new county was also an asset, but New Berlin's defenders had received one concession in the act — the law would go into effect only if accepted by a referendum on March 16. This allowed but two weeks to wage a campaign and in this short time both sides resorted to hand bills and posters, documents which occasionally turn up among old county papers. The New Berlin faction raised a hue and cry over the costs involved in division: in addition to building costs there would be a county enrollment fee of $500 and an expenditure of $2,000 to $3,000 to transcribe records for the new county. "Are you willing to do all this — to incur the moral certainty of greatly increased taxation and an immense county debt in order to accommodate Israel Gutelius, who has been the source of all the trouble and contention amongst the people for years?"[23]

The Lewisburg Committee hastily volunteered to pay for both the enrollment and the transcription of records; and, not to be outdone, Selinsgrove advocates, including George Schnure, Henry C. Eyer, William Colsher, John App, Charles A. Moyer, and Leonard App, distributed a poster with a similar proposal. New Berlin leaders such as Charles Merrill, Isaac Slenker, and Samuel Weirick meanwhile charged Lewisburg with an attempt to buy the votes of the people in the lower part of the county, and warned the public that the offer to pay division costs was absolutely worthless. A New Berlin committee of nine offered a reward of $50,000 to anyone who would produce the original paper purportedly signed by the Lewisburg leaders, but again New Berlin did not have the last word. John Shrack of East Buffalo distributed a poster in which he offered to copy all of the records required for $125.

On election day there were 2,553 votes for division and 2,508 against it. By such a small vote was Snyder County born. Ironically, however, a breakdown of the vote indicates that it was the eastern townships of present day Union County which foisted a new county upon reluctant Snyder County; voters in present-day Snyder County rejected division 1,767-964. Looking closer at the election results, the ambitions of Lewisburg and Selinsgrove to be county seats are obvious: Lewisburg approved division by 485-1, its neighbor East Buffalo Township agreed with it 175 -4, and Selinsgrove backed division 258-5.

New Berlin gave its expected disapproval by a 143-2 vote and unanimous disapproval came from Beaver and Centre Townships with almost unanimous disapproval also by Jackson and Franklin Townships. It is plain that most of New Berlin's friends lived south of Penns Creek.

With the division consummated, the scramble for the two county seats followed. To be eligible, the towns competing for them were required to post a subscription of $10,000. Lewisburg and Mifflinburg qualified in Union County with the former raising its guarantee to $50,000; Selinsgrove, Middleburg, and Freeburg became official contestants in Snyder County. Between March and October each community put its best foot forward. Anticipating a glowing future for Selinsgrove and finding the atmosphere frigid in New Berlin, Gutelius moved his *Der Union Demokrat* there; and while he professed no preference among the three Snyder rivals, it requires little reading between the lines of his paper to detect his choice. He found the Middleburg subscription and bond defective, alleging that it had not been given to the court on time. New Berlin, meanwhile, refusing to accept total defeat, interceded to support Middleburg, using the argument that Middleburg's choice

Portrait of Ner Middlesworth. From the collection of the Snyder County Historical Society. Photo by Jim Walter.

might require no buildings in that a slight change in the boundary of the two counties could catapult New Berlin into Snyder County with buildings ready to conduct its business and house its papers. It is doubtful that the New Berlin strategy was decisive, but with the central townships voting heavily for it Middleburg won over Selinsgrove 1,357-922; Freeburg ran a poor third.

Selinsgrove's unanimous support of its own candidacy 261-0 had not been enough. Reflecting upon its defeat, Gutelius ruefully noted in his paper that Selinsgrove's enemies had circulated rumors that the town was extremely unhealthy and that visitors might get sick by spending a single day there. He doubted that such a high-handed untruth had originated in that "civilized and Christian neighborhood," and he reassured his readers that it was as healthy as any part of the country.[24]

In Union County, Lewisburg defeated Mifflinburg by a margin of 1,436 to 1,226. In the voting districts outside of Mifflinburg and Lewisburg, however, the voters preferred Mifflinburg by more than 100 ballots, thus making Lewisburg's 519 votes cast unanimously for the home town decisive. The first court convened in Lewisburg the week before Christmas in 1855.

The rancor stirred up by the division controversy would outlive its generation, but realistic politicians accepted the new state of affairs, and, with the bond and division questions behind them, they faced up to the swirling political currents unloosed by the Kansas-Nebraska free-soil controversy. Within the span of several years, the Whig Party disintegrated, and the Democratic Party, rent by free-soilism, sectionalized. Meanwhile, the new Republican Party absorbed the Whigs and a sizable proportion of the Democrats. In the Republican Party's first presidential campaign in 1856, Union County cast 1,429 votes for Fremont and 1,092 for Buchanan, the Democratic victor. The local Democrats salvaged Mifflinburg and West Buffalo, White Deer, and Union Townships. Two years later in local contests, Mifflinburg edged into the Republican column. The *Lewisburg Chronicle* hailed its metamorphosis, gloating, "Mifflinburg, the old stronghold of 'unterrified' Democracy is for once emancipated . . . A political revolution has taken place in Pennsylvania."[25] Only Union Township went Democratic. A year later when Mifflinburg chose its first Republican burgess, the *Chronicle* returned to the subject: "The charm of their name 'Democracy' and the old motto 'stick to the ticket though the Devil is on it' is broken. The political aspect of Mifflinburg will no longer be an eyesore to the freedom-loving citizens of Union County."

The *Chronicle's* burial of the Democratic Party in Mifflinburg was somewhat premature, for it would revert to its old habits again. By 1860 hundreds of local farmers were abandoning the Democratic Party of Jackson, now identified with Southern leadership, and were joining the ranks of the Republicans. The trend helped to swell the majorities for Lincoln and Andrew Curtin, the first Republican Governor of the state. Lincoln carried Lewisburg by a margin of 3-1 and Kelly Township by 9-1, while his majority in Mifflinburg was a slender 104-91. The election of Curtin proved to be of particular interest in Union County when he chose Eli Slifer as his Secretary of the Commonwealth. Slifer's appointment resulted from his enviable record in both branches of the legislature and as State Treasurer. As Secretary of the Commonwealth, Slifer had the complete confidence of Curtin and assumed many duties ordinarily handled by the governor during Curtin's protracted illness and convalescence. Colonel Alexander K. McClure in his memoirs noted that "In all the vexatious complications which arose by the countless new problems presented by the Civil War, the one man whose judgment was always deferred to was Slifer . . . He was just the man to temper the impulsive qualities of Curtin . . . and to no man was Curtin so much indebted for the eminent success of his two administrations, as to Eli Slifer . . . He was always calm and unruffled, even in the most perilous extremities."[26]

The Civil War, of course, superseded all other issues. At the outset, Republicans invited Democrats to disregard labels and join them in a Union Party to crush the rebellion. Some tentatively accepted, and Democratic exhorters such as Major Charles H. Shriner joined erstwhile political enemies on the same platforms; but when the campaign to take Richmond faltered and the "ninety-day war" went into its second year, Democrats found much to disapprove, including the stretching of executive war powers, the arrest and imprisonment of civilians without jury trials, the suspension of newspapers, and conscription. Meanwhile, Republicans labeled their opponents "Copperheads," "Cops," or "Secesh," and organized the Union League to strengthen the war effort. By 1863 it was politics as usual, and both parties carried on vigorous campaigns during the gubernatorial election.

A Republican rally at Laurelton was one of the most colorful gatherings in the history of the West End. Carriages starting from the eastern extremities of the county were joined by others along the way, and hundreds of them, decorated with colorful banners heralding the reelections of Lincoln and Curtin, streamed into Laurelton. Reports, possibly exaggerated, estimated the crowd at 1,500; but whatever the number, it exceeded by severalfold a competing rally in a nearby field for Judge George W. Woodward, the Democratic candidate for governor. It was said that liquor was not sold that day in Laurelton and all moved peaceably and pleasantly despite the impassioned oratory from the two platforms.[27] In October the Republicans carried the county in the state elections with only West Buffalo Township and Mifflinburg dissenting.

The victory was celebrated in Lewisburg at a giant ox roast, which was said to have been the largest gathering in its history — the oxen sharing the pits

with turkeys, chickens, and a bear. A giant parade followed the oratory, and the evening glowed with torches as well as illuminated dwellings and business houses. More than 50 mottoes spelled out the sentiments of the hour: "Jeff Davis, You Shan't Come Here" and "Copperheads Beg for Peace — We Fight for It" to quote but two of them.[28]

General Grant's failure to take Richmond in the fall of 1864 despite soaring Southern casualties and the seemingly unproductive siege of Petersburg and Richmond were setbacks to Republican hopes of reelecting President Lincoln. Several plans were underway to bypass him, but they did not materialize. Republican prospects, however, revived upon the news of General Sherman's spectacular capture of Atlanta as well as his aggressive envelopment of Georgia and his march toward the sea — all crippling blows to Confederate arms and morale. In November Union County voters, with additional absentee ballots of the soldiers, polled decisive majorities for Lincoln and Johnson.

At the close of the war President Johnson's handling of Reconstruction gave the Democrats new issues. They supported his plans for an early withdrawal of troops from the South and the return of the Confederate states to a normal relationship, whereas the Republicans were dismayed at the thought of turning over these states to unrepentant "rebels." Thus the fat was in the fire. Viewing Johnson as an obstruction to "Radical Reconstruction," Republicans supported his impeachment and removal from office. George F. Miller, the local Member of Congress, voted for impeachment and justified his action in a lengthy article in the press.

The Republicans, flocking behind the standard of General Grant, the "Savior of the Nation," and strengthened by the votes of the war veterans, continued to dominate local politics. The candidacy of General John F. Hartranft for Governor in 1872 illustrates the Republican strategy in this era. Hartranft had commanded the 51st Regiment of Pennsylvania Volunteers, which included three Union County companies. One of Hartranft's press releases called on the veterans of his regiment to support their old leader: "You, who in former days took pleasure in praising the courageous conduct of your old commander — stand up. Keep position in a well-chosen line of defense, attack and rout the crew of vilifiers, and share in the well-deserved victory."[29] The scandals of the Grant administration scarcely affected his local popularity, and voters virtually ignored the Liberal Republican movement of 1872.

As indicated, Democrats seldom provided majorities for their candidates in the county; but joined with neighboring counties in assembly, senatorial, and congressional districts, they could profit from Democratic majorities in Lycoming, Northumberland, and Mifflin Counties. For example, Andrew H. Dill of Lewisburg served for one term in the Assembly and three terms in the State Senate between 1869 and 1879. In 1871 Joseph C. Bucher, also a Lewisburg Democrat, though rejected for President Judge in Union, his home county, by 278 votes, offset this deficit in Mifflin and Snyder Counties and was elected by nine votes; he was reelected for another ten-year term in 1881. These Democratic successes, however, were exceptional.

During the 1870s the county's outstanding legislator was Charles Spyker Wolfe. Born in Lewisburg in 1845, he showed intellectual promise from childhood. During his undergraduate days at Bucknell during the Civil War, Wolfe left his classes long enough to join the cavalry and was dispatched to Columbia County to quell the "Fishing Creek Confederacy."

Charles S. Wolfe

After graduation he matriculated at the Harvard Law School. By his mid-twenties he was recognized as a legal authority and a shrewd trial lawyer, and in 1872 at age 27 he was elected to the legislature. Even before Charles Spyker Wolfe had taken his seat, it was clear that he was not the usual inconspicuous freshman legislator when, in answer to the question whether he would support the reelection of Senator Simon Cameron, Wolfe declared he was pledged to no one.

In the legislature Wolfe introduced few bills, but he worked tirelessly to protect the public from venal political deals. A reporter once labeled him a "born legislator" and a "watch-dog of legislation."[30] During his first term Wolfe labored to defeat a pay increase for legislators, identified as the "big steal," and called for a vote on it at every opportunity. He failed to get a senate vote, and the increase was passed by sandwiching it into the general appropriation bill; but he had made his mark upon the lawmakers and public alike. Evidence of the latter is suggested by a short letter from a Gregg correspondent to the editor of a local newspaper: "What they said, and what they are saying about Mr. Wolfe: In 1872: Mr. Wolfe can not be elected, *as he is too youthful*. In 1873: Mr. Wolfe can not be reelected *as he is too good a man*. In 1874: There is no use of any candidate to come out on the *Assembly ticket against Charley Wolfe*."[31]

During Wolfe's third term a "Boom Bill," designed to limit the charges imposed by monopolists who controlled the logging on the West Branch of the Susquehanna, was adopted despite the opposition of a powerful lobby. Charges that the lobby had used bribery reverberated around the capitol, and a committee was appointed to investigate. As a member of the committee, Wolfe refused to let sleeping dogs lie, and he pushed the investigation with such vigor that it was observed that "he was the committee." The committee's report implicated two members of the Assembly, and they were expelled from their seats.

In Wolfe's fourth term another lobby sought legislation to commit the state to assume an obligation of $4,000,000 to pay damages in Allegheny County resulting from riots there in 1877. Wolfe fought the bill, and it was eventually defeated; and again he served upon an investigatory committee which implicated legislators — four of them this time. The House, however, rejected the committee's recommendation for expulsion. Refusing to accept the rebuff, Wolfe joined seven others to initiate a suit against the alleged bribers in the Dauphin County Court. Obtaining no funds from the legislature, the eight raised the money by subscription and, after a widely publicized trial, obtained five convictions. Wolfe's triumph was short-lived, however; within hours of the decision the State Board of Pardons freed them.

During the heat of the inquiry into the "Boom Bill," Wolfe brushed aside requests that he yield the floor, and the Democratic-controlled House reproved him with a vote of censure; but fearing that their summary treatment of him might backfire, the Democratic leadership rescinded the resolution on the last day of the session. In Wolfe's fifth and final term, a senatorial election propelled him into the spotlight. With 46 other "Independents," he refused to go into the Republican caucus, which was prepared to designate a "boss"-dictated candidate as the party's choice. Faced with the possibility of an Independent-Democratic coalition, the party machine agreed to a compromise nominee acceptable to the Independents. Wolfe was not entirely reconciled, and several months later — presumably without consulting his closest friends — he announced his candidacy for State Treasurer as an independent against the Republican and Democratic nominees. In the four weeks before election he dashed about the state upon a whirlwind campaign, scarcely pausing to rest. He ran a poor third, but polled 50,000 votes, a remarkable showing for a "lost cause" and a source of inspiration for reform groups across the state.

At age 37 Charles Spyker Wolfe retired from politics, but his restless spirit would not permit him to remain on the sidelines. In 1886 he accepted the Prohibition Party's nomination for Governor — another "lost cause" which entailed another strenuous jaunt around the state. Seven years later, a few hours after he had accepted an appointment to head the Pennsylvania Commission for the Columbian Exposition, he collapsed and died a few feet from the capitol steps in Harrisburg. Wolfe's daughter, Dr. Mary Wolfe, would carry on the family tradition for aggressive and independent leadership as Director of Laurelton State Village; and his grandson, Charles Kalp, would serve a generation later as President Judge of Union County.

While Wolfe was fighting bossism in Harrisburg, a younger contemporary in Lewisburg, the precocious and irrepressible Benjamin Kurtz Focht, was carving a niche for himself in local politics. Focht was born at New Bloomfield in 1863, the son of the Reverend David and Susan Brown Focht. His father was a Lutheran minister, author, and chaplain in the Civil War. Nicknamed the "Fighting Parson," David Focht participated in long marches and exhausting campaigns, but these strenuous activities contributed to his death in 1864, when Benjamin was just one year old. Following David Focht's death, the family moved to Lewisburg, where Benjamin attended the local schools including the Academy at Bucknell University. At fifteen he served an apprenticeship with J.R. Cornelius, publisher of the *Lewisburg Chronicle*; and in a recommendation for him two years later Cornelius noted, "He has been a most faithful, obliging, active and intelligent employee, and the best compositor, taking into consideration the short time he served at the business, that I ever knew."[32]

At eighteen, Benjamin K. Focht borrowed $500 from his mother to found the *Lewisburg Saturday News*, a newspaper which would reflect his orthodox Republican philosophy for the next 56 years. After holding several minor posts, Focht was defeated in a three-cornered contest for a seat in the state House of Representatives in 1890; but two years later, at age 29, Focht won, having qualified for preferment by his able management of the campaign of Harold M. McClure for Judge.

McClure, who had been a professional baseball star before turning to a legal career, was a young Sunbury attorney and brother-in-law of Focht. He was given little chance to upset Judge Bucher at the outset. The latter was running for a third ten-year term and, though a Democrat, had the backing of almost the entire bar and five Republican newspapers in the district.

The Democratic *Mifflinburg Times* charged that Focht had set aside a 22-9 vote by the Union County Republican Committee to take no part in the district nominating convention. The newspaper called upon the representatives from Snyder County to reject Focht's "self-constituted delegation." When McClure obtained the district nomination, the *Times* charged that it constituted "bossism and family dictation of the worst type" and asked whether voters would accept a Sunbury lawyer with little courtroom experience "simply because his brother-in-law has forced his nomination upon the district."[33] On election day McClure carried not only Union but Snyder and Mifflin Counties as well. Democrats noted that McClure ran 500 votes behind the Republican ticket in Union County, but it was no solace for their despair.

Focht's satisfaction with the results requires no comment. The 28-year-old "boss" had won his spurs.

He was reelected to the legislature in 1894 as well as in 1896 when his majority reached an unprecedented 1,265 votes. As a legislator Focht did not rock the political boat. He was a loyal party man and developed a smooth-working machine in the county. Alert to local interests and attentive to details, he spearheaded a drive for a free river bridge at Lewisburg, and, despite delays and vetoes, he eventually delivered it. Focht also endorsed better rural roads, a department of agriculture, the establishment of the Laurelton State Village, veterans' benefits, and free textbooks in the public schools; but he refused to support a minimum wage of $35 per month for teachers. Acknowledging that higher pay was desirable, he rejected the bill as a threat to home rule.

On the street Focht was a model of sartorial splendor. Closeted with friends, he was vivacious and high spirited; and on the platform he was polished and almost regal. At Memorial Day exercises he was a focus of attention — first along the line of the parade in his chauffeured Paige limousine and later on the platform where he delivered well-phrased platitudes with power and conviction. Old citizens have not forgotten the color and glamour of a Focht performance or the shake of his hand along the campaign trail; some can recall his electioneering tours via horse and buggy and the gallon jug which he passed around.

Benjamin K. Focht was defeated for reelection in 1898 when anti-machine Republicans, in a statewide movement headed by John Wanamaker, bolted the party's ticket and supported Democratic nominee, Francis Brown, a Brook Park farmer and livestock dealer. The *Mifflinburg Telegraph*, which had been less than lukewarm toward Focht in his earlier campaigns, castigated Wanamaker for interfering in Union County and attributed Focht's defeat to "boodle, rum, fraud and false pretense" — qualities which editor George W. Schoch attributed to the Democrats and the influence of the disgruntled and disappointed Wanamaker.

In the ensuing session of the legislature, Brown was the center of attention for one brief moment when he accused ex-Congressman Monroe H. Kulp of Shamokin of offering him a bribe to go to Philadelphia so he would be absent from the capitol during the voting upon Matthew Quay's reelection to the United States Senate. In his testimony before a grand jury, Kulp responded that he had simply advised Brown to take his horses to Philadelphia if he wished to obtain a higher price for them. He was not indicted, and Brown's moment had expired.

In 1900 Brown and Focht faced each other again as candidates for the State Senate, and in a closely contested race Focht won by a bare 21 votes. The same election marked the entrance of another colorful figure into the county's political arena when Albert W. Johnson, a young attorney who had moved from the West End to Lewisburg to practice law, became a candidate for the State House of Representatives in the Republican primary. He opposed another West End favorite in "Handsome" Doctor George C. Mohn, who was also in his first political trial.

As the campaign warmed up, Mohn's backers charged Johnson with defeating Focht in 1898 by secretly encouraging Independent Republicans to support Brown. An affidavit war followed, and on primary day Mohn was victorious by a 71-vote majority. Johnson, however, refused to accept defeat and, claiming irregularities, announced his candidacy as an independent. Pleased with the Republican schism, Democrats backed Johnson, and the Mohn-Johnson contest was resumed in the general election. Johnson insisted that he was running as a Republican, but he attracted independent as well as Democratic support by stating that he would oppose Senator Quay's reelection. In another stirring contest Johnson beat Mohn by a handful of votes; but Johnson's political straddling had compromised his opportunity for reelection and he was replaced by Dr. Mohn in 1902.

By 1911 Johnson decided to seek a bigger prize — the seat of President Judge Harold McClure, who had held the office for twenty years. By this time Johnson was highly regarded as trial lawyer, and enjoyed the prestige of having won a damage settlement of $200,000 for the Lewisburg Bridge Company in a suit against Union and Northumberland Counties — a trial touted as the most celebrated case ever instituted in Union County, but involving a decision which was later reversed in the appellate court. In a three-cornered primary involving Frank Wagenseller of Selinsgrove as well as the two Union County contestants, the Republican organization in Union backed McClure. In the columns of the *Saturday News*, Focht stressed the point that McClure was "very much a Union and Snyder Countian," and displayed a picture of the McClure homestead on Buffalo Creek where the ancestors of the Judge had resided. Denied was the allegation that a disproportionate share of his decisions had been reversed by appeals to the higher courts. The *Telegraph*, meanwhile, pointed to Johnson's desire to vindicate himself for betraying the party earlier when he had "hugged to his bosom a Democratic endorsement" for the House of Representatives.

Benjamin Focht posed with his son, Brown, at the Victory Club on Market Street, Lewisburg, in 1918. From the collection of the Union County Historical Society, #89.5.1.12C.

On primary day Johnson swept Union County and cut into Wagenseller's majority in Snyder County sufficiently to gain a plurality in the district. Running against William R. Follmer in the general election, Albert Johnson won Union County by merely 60 votes, but a majority of 500 in Snyder made his victory decisive. Judge McClure's experience thus paralleled that of Judge Bucher, whom he had beaten in 1891.

Johnson was regarded as a capable and hardworking judge; his unpretentious and disarming manner added to his popularity. His crackdown on liquor licenses and saloons was approved by the "drys," and his interest in the out-of-doors appealed to the sportsmen. In fact, as the close of his term approached, his reelection seemed assured. However, Snyder County had never had a President Judge, and its voters felt slighted by Union County's 60-year monopoly of the office. A pension act of 1919 also served to place Johnson on the defensive since a second term would qualify him for a pension at half-pay, when he would be 59. Noting a groundswell of oppo-

sition, Johnson let it be known that he would decline the pension and resume the practice of law at the close of his second term. Even with two Snyder County candidates in the field, Johnson went into the primary as the favorite. Then the unexpected happened — Snyder County voters unified in favor of Miles I. Potter and gave him the victory. Though Johnson had amassed a 3-1 majority in Union, Potter had carried his own county by more than 4-1, leaving Harry Coryell of Selinsgrove a distant third in the district.

Johnson thus returned to his law practice, but four years later he received the support of the Focht organization, the county bar, and the local Republican press for an appointment as Judge of the United States District Court, Middle District of Pennsylvania, a vacancy created by the death of Judge Charles B. Witmer. With the added endorsement of the state's United States Senators Pepper and Reed, the appointment was made by President Coolidge on May 25, 1925. Hailed as "alert, aggressive and successful . . . virile, progressive, of spotless integrity, and an all-around American" by

Focht's *Saturday News*, Johnson typified the American success story.[34] Twenty years later, however, Albert Johnson would resign under pressure for several alleged incidents of bribery, one of the few to face impeachment in the United States Senate.

Meanwhile, local Democrats were also beset with problems. They were unimpressed by the magic of William Jennings Bryan and "Free Silver" at the turn of the century. They did so poorly in the general elections that the excitement was confined to the Republican primaries. The emergence of Lee Francis Lybarger, however, provided them with a colorful standard bearer during the first quarter of the twentieth century. A graduate of Neff's School of Oratory in Philadelphia, Lybarger had a gift which would take him from politics to the lecture platform. Tall and handsome, with a touch of gray in his blond hair, he made a striking appearance, and his repertoire ranged from money and banking to Henry George and "The Single Tax," and from Anti-imperialism to "How to be Happy." Lybarger had remained at Neff as an instructor, where he married Lydia Kessinger, a student from Mifflinburg. When they settled in Mifflinburg in 1896, he stumped for "Free Silver," a position anathema to the more conservative of both major parties. George Schoch, staunch Republican editor of the *Telegraph*, praised his eloquence but disagreed with almost everything Lybarger said. When Lybarger declared that laborers produced the wealth of the nation but remained slaves and also called upon the Civil War veterans to vote for Bryan because they had fought to free black slaves, Schoch reminded him that veterans, Republicans and Democrats alike, had shouldered arms to save the nation. When Lybarger alleged that the Republican Party favored a large and costly naval program, Schoch answered, "not too large, Professor, just large enough for our needs."

When Lybarger berated Senator Quay as a thief, Schoch responded that thief was "a nasty word . . . You never saw a man who said he stole from him . . . He is a patriot, true and tried, who fought on the gory field at Fredericksburg." When Lybarger pointed to the hard times, his self-appointed instructor, editor Schoch, insisted that "times are good," and to document his point listed 26 businesses in Mifflinburg which were prospering. Lybarger was a fine orator, Schoch conceded, "and his arguments might be acceptable in some sections, but not in Mifflinburg." By the time Lybarger referred to Aguinaldo, the controversial Filipino leader, as a "hero and a patriot," Schoch's patience had been worn threadbare. He could find no pleasantries to mix with his condemnation.[35]

Lybarger was admitted to the Union County bar and opened a law office, but he was willing to leave it for politics and oratory. In 1902 he obtained the Democratic nomination for the state House of Representatives but lost to Dr. Mohn in the general election. Two years later Lybarger closed his practice to deliver lectures on the Lyceum and Chautauqua platforms for more than a decade.

After serving a four-year term in the Pennsylvania Senate, Focht resigned to seek election to Congress. The retirement of incumbent Thaddeus Mahon of Franklin County gave him the opportunity, and Focht seized it, gaining the endorsement of the district convention after 30 highly contested ballots. It was a notable achievement and attested to Focht's strong organization in Union and Snyder Counties since Union was one of the smallest counties in the eight-county "Shoe String" district, which extended from Union southwestward to the Maryland border. He won handily in the general election.

In Congress Benjamin K. Focht is best remembered for his introduction of the first old-age pension bill, designed to benefit men and women 65 and over who lacked sufficient income to meet their needs. It received little support at the time but was finally incorporated into the Social Security legislation of 1935. It was no longer his bill, but his vote helped to make it law. He is also remembered as the Chairman of the Committee on the District of Columbia and was frequently referred to as the "Mayor of Washington."

Beaten for reelection in 1912 by Frank L. Dershem, a Lewisburg Democrat, when the Bull Moose movement split the Republicans into two warring factions, Focht returned in 1914 to serve through World War I. He supported the war but opposed American participation in the League of Nations. In 1922 he was defeated in the Republican primary by Edward M. Beers of Huntingdon County. Possibly no one ever "retired" with more reluctance, and Focht, considering it a temporary misfortune, contested the nomination every election year, becoming a consistent loser. Beers died in office in the spring of 1932, and the way was opened for Focht's dramatic return to his old post. He won in 1932 and again in 1934 and 1936 despite Democratic landslides elsewhere. In the early morning of March 27, 1937, after a day with Union County friends at his favorite Washington haunts, Congressman Focht suffered a heart attack and succumbed a few hours later. He died as he would have wished — in political harness. Union County has had no Congressman since that time, nor has it had a public figure with his presence and stature.

ENDNOTES:

[1] John Blair Linn, *Annals of Buffalo Valley, Pennsylvania, 1755-1855*, Harrisburg, 1877, 295.

[2] Linn, 327.

[3] Linn, 342.

[4] Charles A. Beard's introduction to the *Journal of William Maclay*, Edgar S. Maclay,(ed.), New York, 1927, v.

[5] Eleanor Young, *Forgotten Patriot Robert Morris*, New York, 1950, 181.

[6] Beard, v.

[7] A claims case in which the Federal and State courts disagreed upon the application of Federal and State laws.

[8] Charles F. Snyder, "Formation and Changes in Northumberland County Prior to 1813," *Proceedings of the Northumberland County Historical Society XIX* (1952), 71-100.

[9] Linn, 392-393.

[10] Linn, 405.

[11] Linn, 471-474.

[12] *Lewisburg Chronicle*, February 28, 1873, quoting J.F. Wolfinger.

[13] *New Berlin Union Star*, April 25, 1840.

[14] *New Berlin Union Star*, September 19, 1840.

[15] *New Berlin Union Star*, November 20 and 27, 1840.

[16] Charles H. Shriner, "Reminiscences," *Mifflinburg Telegraph*, November 10, 1886; R.V.B. Lincoln's memoir in *Mifflinburg Telegraph*, November 17, 1886.

[17] C. Warren Gutelius, "The Contest for the Division of Union County," *Proceedings of the Northumberland County Historical Society XIII* (1943), 126-156.

[18] *Lewisburg Democrat*, September 13 and 27, 1854.

[19] Gutelius, 150.

[20] *Lewisburg Democrat*, March 16, 1853.

[21] *Lewisburg Democrat*, Sept. 13, 1854.

[22] *Lewisburg Democrat*, Sept. 13, 1854.

[23] Gutelius, 151.

[24] Gutelius, 152.

[25] *Lewisburg Chronicle*, October 22, 1858 and March 25, 1859.

[26] Alexander K. McClure, quoted in the *Lewisburg Saturday News*, October 1, 1904.

[27] *Lewisburg Chronicle*, October 13, 1863.

[28] *Lewisburg Chronicle*, October 23, 1863.

[29] *Lewisburg Chronicle*, September 27, 1872.

[30] *Lewisburg Saturday News*, February 4, 1902.

[31] *Lewisburg Chronicle*, October 2, 1874.

[32] May 15, 1880, Archives of the Union County Historical Society.

[33] September 26, 1891; and October 10 and 17, 1891, Archives of the Union County Historical Society.

[34] May 16, 1925, Archives of the Union County Historical Society.

[35] *Mifflinburg Telegraph*, October 12, 1900.

The Governor Snyder mansion at 121 North Market Street, Selinsgrove. Photo by Jim Walter.

Portrait of Governor Simon Snyder. Snyder was the first "common man" governor and the first of German origin. From the State Museum of Pennsylvania, Pennsylvania Historical and Museum Commission.

CHAPTER 6

NEW BERLIN AND LIMESTONE TOWNSHIP

When one reflects upon the forbidding mountains and ridges overhanging the banks of the Susquehanna River north of Harrisburg, it is scarcely surprising that the pioneers would have ventured into valleys as inviting as Penns Creek and Dry Valley at an early date. The more impetuous ones ignored Indian claims to the region; and by 1754, the year a part of it was opened to settlement by the Albany Conference with the Six Nations, they were already on the ground.

The Penns Creek Massacre in October of 1755 emptied the settlements, but a second migration began a decade later and continued until the outbreak of the American Revolution. By 1775 the family of George Overmeier lived a mile west of present-day New Berlin. Overmeier was a member of the first grand jury of Northumberland County and a captain in the war. John Rearick lived south of Penns Creek while Daniel Lewis, Samuel Mathers, and Adam Smith had settled east of White Springs. David Smith, John Scott, and Patrick Watson were tenants of Robert Barber at White Springs. Andrew Pontius had purchased the LeRoy place, and his neighbors were Philip Hoy and John Baltzer Klinesmith. Christian Shively II settled on land inherited from his father near the mouth of Cedar Run, south of White Springs; and nearby John Nees had built a small mill which stood for more than a century until it was swept away at the time of the Johnstown Flood of 1889.

Then, as the frontier became a battleground, the migration halted; and the "Great Runaway," along with its aftermath, swept most of these pioneers from the valley. During one of the raids, the Shively family found refuge in the woods on the south side of Penns Creek; but Patrick Watson was mortally wounded by a war party of Indians even as his mother was shot and scalped. The Indians also struck at Klinesmiths, ambushing Baltzer and his two teen-aged daughters, Catherine and Elizabeth, who were on their way to the harvest field. They killed Baltzer and made the girls prisoners, forcing them to cross New Berlin Mountain. An old warrior assigned to guard the girls fell asleep, enabling Elizabeth to seize his tomahawk and dash it against his skull. The girls ran into the woods, but the injured Indian's cry was heard by the other Indians, who gave chase. Catherine was shot through the shoulder and fell behind a log, where she remained undetected, while Elizabeth reached the Beatty place and sounded the alarm. Reapers

organized a search and soon found Catherine. She recovered from her ordeal and survived two husbands, Daniel Campbell, a Revolutionary War soldier, and Robert Chambers; she eventually died at her home at the Big Spring farm at White Springs.

The close of the war was the signal for a third occupation of the land; and among the newcomers in the White Springs area, no family was more notable than the Barbers. Robert and Thomas Barber's grandfather had been the first sheriff of Lancaster County, and their father had purchased a large tract of land at White Springs, which he was clearing when the war intervened. The Barber brothers were married to sisters: Robert to Sarah Boude and Thomas to Mary Boude, while their neighbor Paschall Lewis was the husband of a third sister, Elizabeth Boude.

In the 1790s Robert successively built a sawmill, a distillery, and a gristmill on White Springs Run, the latter remaining operative as the Dreibelbis Mill until the 1940s. Robert died in 1841 at age 91; and when his estate was finally settled 50 years later, it was shared by 68 descendants. Most of them lived in the Midwest, but those remaining in this area continued to live on the broad Barber lands until they retired to Mifflinburg. The stately stone mansion of Samuel Barber, the son of Robert, standing on the hill just west of White Springs Run, remains as a testimonial to this industrious and virile family.

The Chambers, early neighbors of the Barbers, were also a prominent family. Like the Barbers they did not take possession of their land until the close of the Revolution; and James Chambers was killed in an Indian attack on French Jacob's Mill at the foot of the Brush Valley Narrows. When peace returned, the widow of William Chambers and her three sons, Robert, Benjamin, and Joseph, cleared farms between Mifflinburg and White Springs. Their descendants were civic leaders in Limestone Township and Mifflinburg as well as pioneers in the Middle and Far West.

A third family to sink roots in the White Springs area was the Shivelys. They moved here from York County in 1775 and for four generations were farmers, sawyers, millers, and broom manufacturers on the ancestral land north of Penns Creek. Joining with the Bakers, Beavers, Royers, and a few other families, the Shivelys were also active in the Church of the Brethren (also called German Baptist Brethren or Dunkards) in this area. The house the Shivelys built in

LIMESTONE

Scale 1½ Inches to the Mile

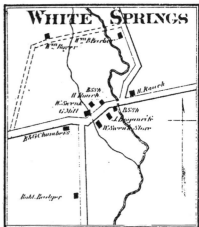

Limestone Township and White Springs. From *Pomeroy's Atlas of Union and Snyder Counties 1868.*

The Barber home in White Springs was photographed in 1968. Mary Snyder is in the foreground. Courtesy of the Mifflinburg Buggy Museum.

1796, after the barn, was constructed with folding doors which allowed for group worship — a feature found in a number of the houses built by members of the Church of the Brethren.

Under the supervision of Elder David Shellenberger and David Smith of the Lost Creek Congregation, a love feast was celebrated and baptisms were administered in the brook in front of the Baker house in 1816. John Baker had come from Lancaster County and settled at the corner of Furnace and New Berlin Mountain Roads in Buffalo Township. His parents, the Wendell Bakers, were the first Church of the Brethren members in Union County having settled in Buffalo Township in 1772.

The Church of the Brethren appears to have been formally organized in Union County in 1826 under the supervision of David Shellenberger and Elder Christian Long of Huntingdon. Shellenberger and John Royer were elected Deacons at that time. At a love feast in 1828 David Shellenberger was elected the first minister of the Buffalo Congregation. West of Mifflinburg the sons of John and Joel Royer were meeting with their neighbors in homes, schools or barns and later Royer organized a congregation near Kelly Point in Kelly Township. There was the Royer Cemetery in 1850, followed by the erection of a wooden meetinghouse in 1861. Meanwhile, two miles west of Laurelton, on land given by John Showalter, another flock erected a modest edifice in 1861.

The pacifism of the Brethren during the Civil War led to the closing of the churches in Kelly and Hartley Townships. In 1864 leaders chose a more central location on the Turnpike west of Mifflinburg, where they erected the Buffalo Church on a lot provided by Samuel B. Barber sometimes called the "Pike Meeting House." In 1904 Jacob Shively moved the Kelly meetinghouse to White Springs to accommodate the Brethren in his neighborhood. The White Springs Brethren later merged with the Buffalo congregation, and Green Shively, son of Jacob, was the pastor there for many years. The Hartley congregation joined that of the Pike Meeting House and closed its building; it sold in 1926.

In the early years of the nineteenth century, the lower valley of Switzer Run became Seebold country. Christopher Seebold, who emigrated from Wurtemberg with his parents, grew up in Berks County. In 1790 he removed to Switzer Run, midway between Youngmanstown and Penns Creek, where he farmed and operated a gristmill, which he had purchased from James Watson. His son John built and operated a sawmill at their power site on Switzer Run; he also

constructed and navigated arks on Penns Creek. Christopher Seebold II provided the lot for the courthouse in New Berlin and may have designed and erected the building. He was a tavern keeper, a justice of the peace, and treasurer of Union County. Christopher III had a carding and fulling mill near the mouth of Switzer Run, but this was destroyed by fire in 1865. John Henry Seebold was a druggist in New Berlin, and William F. Seebold was a physician in Hartleton for 50 years. Few families have been identified as long and as actively with the life of the county.

Near the head of Switzer Run a hamlet arose where two roads branched westward and one eastward from the New Berlin highway. The origin of the name Battletown is lost in folklore. The more romantic tale relates it to a continuing war between two tribes of Indians with each claiming the title of princess for one of its daughters; a second story attributes it to the repeated quarreling and feuding in the neighborhood. The name was later changed to Dice, presumably to honor a local gospel minister.

Between the forks of the plateau which rises sharply from the west bank of Switzer Run lies Miegtig's or *Mechdich Loch*, a hollow whose name has been preserved in Pennsylvania German folklore. One version, narrated by the Spangler family, who lived in the neighborhood many years ago, is that a hermit, Johann Miegtig, squatted here shortly after the American Revolution. His cabin marked the site for some years after his death, but it eventually disappeared. A row of apple trees remained longer, but it too is gone. *Mechdich Loch*, according to the Sauers tradition, in the Pennsylvania German dialect means "an extraordinarily steep short hollow (ravine), a big kettle-like hole or abrupt dip in the land." A glance across Switzer Run, a half-mile south of Dice, reveals the three steep sides and the bowl-like hollow, and it is possible that both folktales speak truthfully.[1]

A visitor who might have taken the rural road west of Dice 90 years ago would have crossed Seebold's millrace just before reaching the Switzer Run bridge and would have seen the millpond on the right and the millrace on the left, the latter extending through the fields to the gristmill along the run where the shortcut to Centreville (Penns Creek) leaves the New Berlin road. A part of the foundation, the millstones, and the tailrace remain while the old mill, moved to a Seebold farm nearby, has been used as an implement shed for many years.

In time Dice had a store, a post office, and a small cluster of houses; and on his contiguous farm John Rinkard had a cobbler's shop. In the 1870s a union

The Dunkard complex in White Springs includes the original log barn and house from the 1770s. Jacob Shively's broom-making shop, which had served as the United Church of the Bretheran's meeting house, was moved to this site when it was no longer used as a church. Photos by Jim Walter.

church was organized, and in 1886 the Evangelical Church erected a small sanctuary on the west side of the road on land given by the Sauers family. The store and the post office are gone; but the church remains, used by Limestone Township for meetings and as the polling place.

West of Dice on the old Youngmanstown/*Werick Stettle* (Penns Creek) road, Simon Wehr opened the Black Horse Inn on his farm in 1812. It was later taken over by his son Peter and became one of the best-known public houses in the area. Peter provided fencing to hold the livestock of drovers, and operated a cider press. He donated land for the first school in the neighborhood; and when the original log structure was replaced, he moved it to his farm where it was used as a butcher shop, summerhouse, and polling place. In 1930 the woodland on the higher elevations adjacent to the old Wehr School building was acquired by the Pennsylvania Game Commission for public hunting, hiking, and horseback riding.

On April 3, 1769, George Albright (Albrecht) of Lancaster County applied for a warrant for 300 acres of land on Penns Creek; and on July 8, 1774, a grant of 226 acres was confirmed by the land office in Philadelphia. Albright held title to the tract until 1787 when he sold it to George Long, also of Lancaster County, for 250 pounds lawful Pennsylvania money (estimated at $1,200). With the founding of a town in mind, Long purchased an additional 65 acres west of the original plot where he and his wife Catherine resided while he supervised the birth of Longstown (*Longa Stettle*), later called New Berlin. In 1792 George Long employed Frederick Evans to lay out the town; and on January 18, 1793, the first sales were made to Adam Sneider of Berks County, who presumably purchased a lot as a speculation, and to John Mitchel of Buffalo Township. The latter was lot 53 on the southeast corner of Front and Hazel Streets.

Obviously, Long was hopeful that the village would grow and prosper. He had several things in his favor. Penns Creek had potential as a waterway and mill site; the Haines Road crossed his plot; a bridge across Penns Creek would tie into the road from the south; and a mile west of his settlement Lick or Switzer Run cut through the high ridge extending westward from New Berlin Mountain, offering a roadway northward into the heart of Buffalo Valley.

Situated on a high bank, the site was well above the high-water mark of the spring freshets, and the sparkling springs on the lower slope of the mountain seemed to guarantee an adequate supply of water.

Also, the valley of Penns Creek to the east and west and the slopes on the south side of the creek would soon be under the plow, and the town would be a market place for the products of the field and forest.

In 1793 there were four families in residence in Longstown: Christopher Miller, a shop keeper; George Moyer, a weaver; the Beattys;[2] and the Longs. The assessment records of 1800 list William and Hugh Beatty (farmers), Philip Berger, John Clark, James Cook, Isaac Gill, George Grove, Philip Herman (carpenter), Philip Overmeier, James Parks (store-keeper), William Rerick (blacksmith), Jacob Rothrow, Christopher Seebold (tavern keeper), Peter Smith (tailor), Adam Specht (shoemaker), Martin Treaster, Andrew Wagoner (inn keeper), and George Moyer.

In 1814, when New Berlin became the county seat, there were 45 householders — all but one of them living in log houses. Seven were listed as joiners, two as carpenters, and one as a turner, suggesting the relative importance of the building trades. There were three blacksmiths, three innkeepers and two coopers (indicative of the ark trade), two gunsmiths, two merchants, two weavers, and two potters; also living there were a shoemaker, a millwright, a school-teacher, a tanner, a saddler, a tailor, a justice of the peace, a peddler, a tinker, and a physician. There were as yet no lawyers, but James Merrill would soon arrive from New England.

The bill creating Union County placed the responsibility for a courthouse upon the county seat, and the citizenry turned over the lot and unfinished courthouse to the county commissioners on March 31, 1815. The brick structure at Market and Vine Streets was embellished with an apse at the rear, which added three-directional lighting to the judge's desk. In the following November, the commissioners purchased materials to finish the upper floor and engaged unknown mechanics to do the work. Presumably, they also added a graceful Georgian cupola, which would eventually be replaced by a taller, square, Italianate one, a style popular in the 1850s.

The commissioners agreed to "sell" the erection of a stone jail and jail yard wall to Frederick Hipple of Centre Township (later Snyder County) for $4,000. He completed its stone walls in October of 1817. The venerable structure, since converted into a dwelling, still adorns the northwest corner of Market and Plum Streets. The "State House," adjacent to the courthouse, housing offices and jury rooms, seems to have been constructed at this time. In 1821 Christopher Seebold II erected the Emanuel Reformed Church, another brick edifice, across the street from the courthouse.

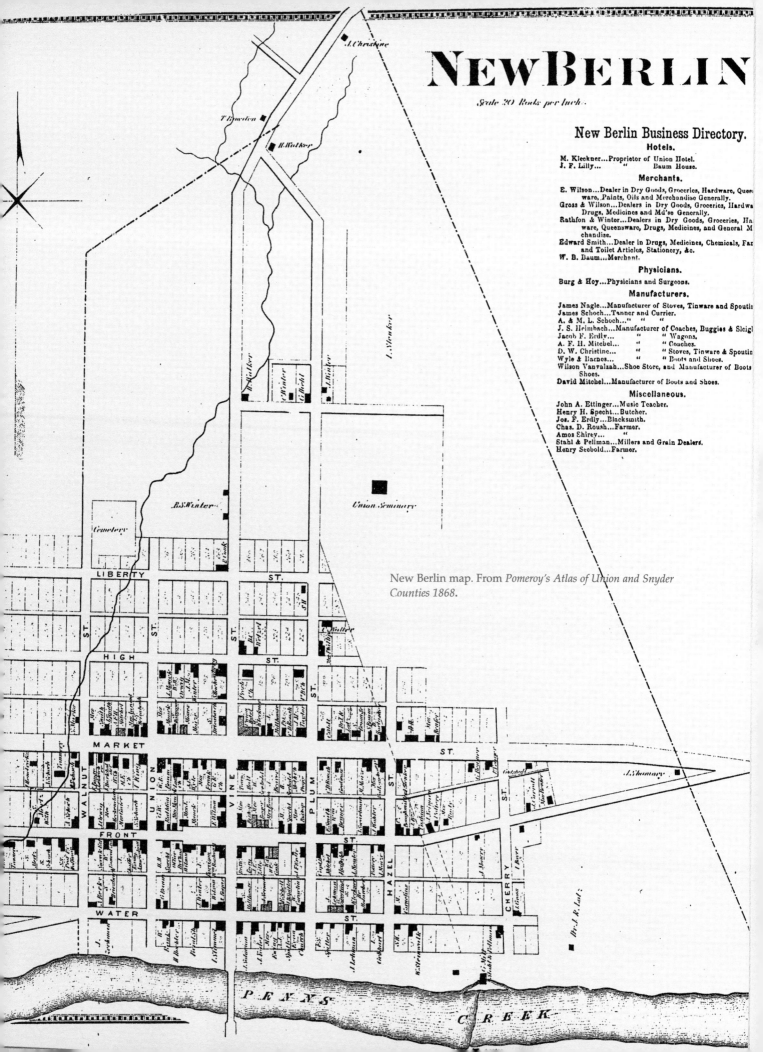

NewBerlin

Scale 20 Rods per Inch.

New Berlin map. From *Pomeroy's Atlas of Union and Snyder Counties 1868.*

TOP: County courthouse in New Berlin (1814-1855) appears in 1999 views of the north side as well as the south side with the reconstructed apse. BOTTOM: The first county jail was built of stone in 1816 at 427-429 Market Street, New Berlin. The jail was converted to a private dwelling in 1857, shortly after the county seat was relocated in Lewisburg. Photos by Jim Walter.

New Berlin expanded northward into the Springfield addition in 1816 when George Spring disposed of a number of lots through a lottery, and in 1837 the court approved a New Berlin request that it be incorporated as a borough. Meanwhile, the village was stretching eastward and westward, and vacant lots were filling with houses and shops.

The village was also taking on a more sophisticated appearance as home owners replaced older log houses with brick or frame structures. Trees were beginning to spread shade along the streets, and by 1850 there was an aura of dignity and gentility which would last for a century. Noting these changes, New Berlin's *Union Times* on January 29, 1846, commented enthusiastically about the attractive town; its industrious, intelligent, and moral townspeople; and the handsome new buildings in the most-approved styles. Samuel Wilson, it noted, had recently finished a splendid brick residence (300 Market Street), Bogar and Winter were completing a fine brick dwelling, Mr. Millhouse had a large frame house started, and Mr. Baum had refitted and greatly improved his large hotel. The town blended with nature's handiwork and the neat farms lying beyond its borders.

Remote from canals and railroads on the upper Susquehanna, New Berlin did not have any large industries, but its shops and stores were a mecca for the adjacent countryside, and the skills of its craftsmen became proverbial. New Berlin clocks, pottery, guns, books, and chairs have become highly-prized collectors' items. A Phillip Frank clock is a masterpiece of craftsmanship.

An 1840 advertisement contains descriptions of several chair makers. Daniel Lemon and Son were specializing in "fancy and Windsor chairs, Boston rocking chairs, common and children's chairs"; Leonard Stine had "settees, Boston Rocking chairs, common and children's, and black walnut, fancy and Windsor chairs"; and Jacob L. Metzgar offered settees, Boston Rockers, common and children's chairs. The latter had recently moved his shop to Old Market Street (Front Street) next door to Baum's Hotel and directly opposite Mr. Aurand's hostelry.[3] Elsewhere, Oberlin and Harmony were doing "fashionable tailoring," and Jacob Haus had opened a marble manufactory opposite the Slenker residence and a few doors from Mr. Merrill's office. Haus was prepared to supply not only Italian and Egyptian marble monuments but also mantles, window and door sills, hearths, mullers (pestles), and paint. As early as 1847,

Mr. Carscaddon was executing daguerreotype likenesses in a room in Kleckner's Hotel.

On the run at the edge of town, three generations of Schochs were tanners; on the creek Solomon Kleckner and his son Joseph were operating the large brick gristmill; and by mid-century Kleckner and Roush were general merchandisers while J.D. Spitler sold cigars shaped by John Rishel, his "master-workman."

New Berlin's principal businesses in the early years were its taverns and its print shops. As noted elsewhere, roads and thus stage routes intersected here, and court week brought an influx of lawyers, litigants, jurors, witnesses, and curiosity seekers. Christopher Seebold II opened a tavern shortly after New Berlin became the county seat, and there were others in short order. In 1839 Adam Weidensaul's Washington Hotel was available to travelers at Market and Plum while Jacob Bishop's Bull's Head Tavern gave him competition on the opposite corner. A year later, the latter had relinquished his business to Benjamin Burroughs. Samuel Aurand's hostelry burned during the night of February 19, 1839, during court week, while it was filled with guests. Some of them had narrow escapes, salvaging only their nightclothes, but there were no fatalities. Aurand rebuilt but died a short time later, and his widow Maria took over its management. Samuel Baum, Jr., and Adam Shower also ran hotels.

The best-remembered hotelier was Michael Kleckner. He purchased the Seebold hotel in 1838 and doubled its frontage on Market Street. Known thereafter as Kleckner's, the three-story brick building became a landmark. Crossing the street from the courthouse, the visitor faced five arched doorways. The one on the left opened into the parlor, the second into the hallway, the third into the bar, the fourth into the general store, and the fifth into the residence. The ell-shaped extension on Vine Street provided access to the dining room and kitchen. Kleckner and his son operated the hotel for 66 years — the latter finally disposing of it in 1904. Eight years later it burned to the ground in a spectacular blaze, and two guests escaped without injury.

Many stories have survived about the old hostelry. One told by Professor D. Paul Souders relates to Michael Kleckner's daughter, Elizabeth, a powerfully built woman with muscles to match her frame. When bartender John Maize refused to serve a customer who seemed to have already imbibed too much alcohol, the guest became obstreperous. Maize rang a bell, and

TOP: The former home of George P. Long, New Berlin's last gunsmith, is located at 327 High Street. His shop was behind the house. MIDDLE: The first frame house in New Berlin was built at 134 Front Street by John Stout, a joiner, in 1814. The 1868 local atlas shows it being owned by Francis Hoffman. BOTTOM: The building at 501 Market street was constructed as a residence in 1825; from 1836 through 1854 it served as a printing house for the Evangelical Church Association; and after 1854 different parts of the large building served as a tavern, a girl's dormitory, a law office, and a library. Photos by Jim Walter.

Both a "beginning book" and a baptismal certificate (*taufschein*) were printed by George Miller, New Berlin, in the 1840s. The *taufschein* measures 15 inches x 12 1/4 inches and is hand-colored with red and green watercolors. This certificate's recipient was Jonathan Maize, born on February 25, 1828 at 2 A.M. in Union Township, Union County, to Johannes and Barbara (Maurer) Maize. Also recorded on the *taufschein* were other significant dates, including his baptism on April 24, 1828, with his grandmother, Eva Maurer, designated as godmother, and his death on June 26, 1831. From the collection of the Union County Historical Society. Photo by the Terry Wild Studio.

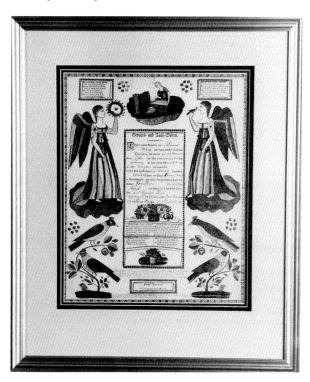

Elizabeth appeared. When she threatened to throw the guest out unless his deportment improved, he replied scornfully that he would like to see any woman try it. He was quickly gratified. Seizing him by "the scruff of the neck and the seat of his pants, out the man went and landed on the sidewalk!"[4]

As county seat of an area encompassing present-day Snyder and Union Counties, with a population speaking two languages, and as the publishing center for the Evangelical Association, New Berlin had a printing and publishing business which may have exceeded any village of its size in the state. Through most years from the 1820s to 1855, there were two weekly English newspapers as well as one, and sometimes two, German papers. Newspapers were apt to be short-lived. Oriented to a political party or an issue — Democratic Republican, Jacksonian, Antimasonic, Whig, Temperance, Know Nothing or Free Soil — they flourished and died with startling rapidity; and a list of the titles and publishers becomes encyclopedic. Antimasonry spawned *The Antimasonic Star* edited by Charles Seebold, and *Der AntiFreymaurer Advocat and Freund des Freyen Volks* (The Anti-Freemason Advocate and Friend of Free People) published by Joseph Miller. The former had at least eleven changes of management in its 27-year history and frequent modifications in its title prior to its transfer to Mifflinburg when the county seat moved to Lewisburg. In addition to newspapers, the printers turned out a variety of political tracts, miscellaneous pamphlets and handbills, birth certificates and house blessings, and books on a variety of subjects.

Between 1816 and 1854 New Berlin was also the printing house for the Evangelical Association in America. In the beginning, the outreach was limited to Pennsylvania, but it gradually expanded into the South and Midwest. In fact, its growth ultimately led to its removal to Cleveland, Ohio, nearer the center of the Association's activities. The printing house was set up next door to the church, and its first publication may have been *Das Geistliche Saitenspiel* (The Spiritual Lyre), the association's first authorized hymnal, in 1817. The first magazine of the Society, *Der Christliche Botschafter* (The Christian Ambassador), was published here in 1837 by the Reverend W.W. Orwig; a semi-monthly publication, it was printed in German until 1946. It was the oldest magazine of its kind in the United States.

Another of Orwig's works was the association's *Catechism*, the first edition of which was published in

Redware pottery pieces were made in New Berlin by potters James Neiman c. 1855-1887 and Adam, Emanuel, or Jacob Maize c. 1855-1870. From the collection of the New Berlin Heritage Association, the Union County Historical Society, Packwood House Museum, and Jim and Carol Bohn. Photo by the Terry Wild Studio, courtesy of the Oral Traditions Project.

1847. He was also the first historian of the church. In 1847 he withdrew from some of his duties to write the story of the church from its origins to 1845. It was published in Cleveland in 1857. The history was written in German but later translated into English, and a twentieth-century historian of the church has described it as "the truest portrayal of the origin of the church. It is at once the most authoritative work of the period It covers, and the finest piece of original research."[5]

Like its clocks, chairs, and pottery, New Berlin's publications are now prized by collectors. Some of the imprints can be seen in the collections of the New Berlin Heritage Association and the Union County Historical Society.

The two earliest religions in New Berlin were the Lutheran and German Reformed (German Calvinist), and both were served by traveling ministers on their rounds through Buffalo and Middle Creek Valleys — the Reverend George Geistweit, a Reformed missionary in the Shamokin area, and the Reverend Ludwig Albert William Ilgen, a Lutheran clergyman from Penns Valley. The two flocks joined to build the Emanuel Church in 1822, a building considered to be a handsome one: "Christopher Seebold, the contractor, deserves much credit for the superb manner in which the building is finished, particularly the pulpit, which is said to be a correct model of the one in the German Reformed church at Harrisburg, and which has been pronounced to be inferior to none in the state."[6] The steeple of the two-story brick edifice was surmounted by a brass winged angel with a trumpet in its hand.

In 1867 the Lutherans withdrew to build a sanctuary a few doors west of old Emanuel, and the Reformed congregation remodeled the original building, removing the second floor and steeple. However, the angel with trumpet survived and remains a highly prized keepsake. The angel, thought to be Gabriel, has in recent years become the symbol of a revived New Berlin.

The Presbyterians organized in 1841 with James Merrill, John Lashells, and Joseph Stillwell as elders and the Reverend G.W. Thompson as the regularly settled pastor. Though the congregation was small, it built an attractive Greek Revival meeting house on North Vine Street in 1844. Services ceased there after a century, but the building remained, used as a community center through 1999. The Methodists also erected a church in 1841, followed by the United

Philip Frank clock. Frank was active in New Berlin from 1817 to 1843. From the collection of the New Berlin Heritage Association. Photo by Jim Walter.

PAGE 104 TOP: The exterior of the blacksmith shop of Jessie Cornelius. From the collection of the Union County Historical Society, #89.5.1.63.; BOTTOM: Forged ironware made by Jessie Cornelius (b. 1855, d. 1943) in New Berlin includes the basic household set of skimmer, ladle, flesh fork, spatula, and taster as well as other pieces. From the collection of the Union County Historical Society. Photo by the Terry Wild Studio, courtesy of the Oral Traditions Project.

BAROUCH, BUGGY & SULKEY

MANUFACTORY.

THE subscriber respectfully informs his friends and the public generally, that he has opened shop one door east of Baum's hotel, (having erected a large and convenient brick shop for the purpose) in the borough of New Berlin, Union county, where he hopes to be able to accommodate all who may desire any article of his manufacture, and on the most reasonable terms. He is now prepared to manufacture, of the most substantial material,

BAROUCHES, BUGGIES

AND

SULKEYS.

All articles of his manufacture are warranted to be substantially put together. There is a

BLACKSMITH SHOP

attached, at which all iron works appertaining to vehicles will be manufactured. Also,

REPAIRING

done in the neatest and most durable manner.

A NEW INVENTION

The subscriber has purchased the patten right for Union County of Little's Iron Patent.

SINGLE-TREE

AND

LOCKING APPARATUS,

For Carriages and other Vehicles.

This is a discovery which is allowed to be one of the most important that has ever yet been brought before the public. It is one which may be the means of saving many valuable lives by the most simple process that could possibly be devised. It consists of a Single-Tree, which by means of springs connecting with the tips or ends of the Tree, and those springs connected with a strap leading to the hand of the driver can be in a moment disengaged from the horse, and thus freeing him from the carriage, and leaving the inmates in perfect safety—along with this is the LOCKING APPARATUS, which is a new invention, that must recommend itself to all persons who are much engaged in travelling in Carriages, &c. This machine can be operated on by the simple pressure of the foot of the person who is in the Carriage, and can in an instant stop the Vehicle, although on the steepest declivity.

These two Great Inventions deserve the serious consideration of the whole community.

The above Patent can be attached to any old Carriage or Buggy.

J. SCHWINEHART
New Berlin, June 10, 1843.

The New Berlin Union Times,
November 3, 1843.

Brethren in Christ in 1857; the former remained active for about 35 years, the latter for about 80 years.

The history of the Evangelical Church in New Berlin is indelibly linked with the story of the Evangelical movement in America. The German element of the Union County area and especially those of Dry Valley seem to have been awaiting Jacob Albrecht's (Albright) call for a new birth through conversion, and their response was both immediate and enduring. Albright never lived in Buffalo Valley, and during his short ministry of twelve years, his presence here was limited to a few evangelistic journeys. There is a tradition that he preached in the Elias Church in Mifflinburg in 1805; but this building was not erected until 1806 and he seldom preached in churches. He did deliver a sermon at the home of Martin Dreisbach near the present-day boundary of Buffalo and Limestone Townships in 1806. Albright's death occurred in 1808, yet his message had already enrolled a band of converts which included Dreisbach and his son John, John Aurand, Abraham Eyer, Michael Maize, and John Ranck of White Deer. It was in large part this little band of zealots who opened their homes to Albright and his followers and spread the message across the countryside.

Following his conversion, John Dreisbach joined Albright in 1807 and was licensed to preach at the age of eighteen. A fluent speaker in both German and English, Dreisbach was hailed as "a genius in administration."[7] At the association's second conference in 1809, he was appointed one of the four regular ministers, and he was later named a deacon and finally a bishop. It is not surprising, therefore, that the Dry Valley/New Berlin area should have become the seedbed of the Evangelical movement; and as the historian of the church notes, "Its history is New Berlin written large." The first publishing house was located in New Berlin; likewise, the first Evangelical church edifice; the first Evangelical graveyard; the second Sunday school; Union Seminary, the church's first institution of higher learning; as well as many annual and general conferences. It was near New Berlin that the first Evangelical camp meeting in America was held in 1810; the first General Conference met in the farmhouse of Martin Dreisbach in 1816; and the parent missionary society was formed in the brick house of John S. Dunkel near New Berlin in 1839.

It is not known when the first itinerant Evangelical minister preached in New Berlin, but there is a tradition that some time in 1805 John Walter, Albright's first assistant, arrived in town only to find that the schoolhouse at the corner of Old Market and Cherry Streets, where he had expected to preach, was locked to prevent his service. So he preached from its step — his voice rising until it was heard all over the village. Suddenly, the door burst open, and Walter decided to move to the inside. "God has opened us a door in New Berlin," he prophesied, "and he will establish his work here in spite of the opposition of hell and that of wicked men." The story was recorded by the Reverend Dr. Ammon Stapleton, noted Evangelical minister, author, and native of East Buffalo Township.

At the third conference of the followers of Albright in 1810, it was agreed to hold the first camp meeting at the farm of Michael Maize, two miles east of New Berlin. Since it was a novelty, crowds gathered to see what might happen, and it was said that some came to scoff but remained to become seekers and members. It is known that some of the Albright people traveled long distances and tented in the grove. On the last night of the encampment, the clergy and laity formed a large circle, joined hands, and sang hymns. Hymn singing would remain a feature of the Evangelical services for many years as would the camp meetings. It would be at a camp meeting near Middleburg in 1826 where W.W. Orwig would be converted after a ten-mile hike from Hartley Township.

The Evangelical Society in New Berlin erected the Albright Church in 1816 and dedicated it on February 13, 1817. A large concourse of people gathered to witness the ceremony, arriving in more than 200 sleds. The church was a modestly sized rectangular log structure, 34 x 38 feet, and its four windows and two doors set it apart from the other log houses on Water Street. Inside, there was the luxury of a ten-plate stove (possibly a later accession). The pulpit, set high along the wall, had the appearance of a swallow's nest and was reached by a narrow stairway. Later, a small steeple was added, a decoration which would have been unacceptable to the first generation

The Evangelical and Lutheran churches in New Berlin as they appeared in 1915. From the collection of the Union County Historical Society, #89.5.2.4-5.

of worshippers. The building was taken down in 1873 when a brick edifice was erected at the corner of Market and Plum Streets.

While the original church was under construction, the annual conference of the Association was held in the spacious stone barn of Abraham Eyer at Winfield. At this conference, the publishing arm of the church was founded, and the first missionaries were sent forth to seek converts in the Midwest. Unfortunately, the barn, which is still remembered by many residents of Winfield, was considered expendable by the highway department when Route 15 was widened.

New Berlin's first one-room subscription school was erected on land belonging to the Beatty family about 1800 and, in the words of R.V.B. Lincoln, was built of logs and architecturally "neither Tuscan, Doric, Ionic, Corinthian, Composite or Gothic, but entirely backwoods American." George Malick is said to have been the first teacher; and Mr. McCord, John Beckman, Dr. Charlton, Mr. Eppler, Joseph Stillwell, and John Mauch taught in that order — all before 1820. When the village became the county seat, its growth led to the building of two additional elementary schools: one on Water Street and the second on the Methodist lot. The latter had the first recorded blackboard in the county, with the records indicating that "Daniel Horlacker was paid $2.25 for installing a wooden blackboard 4 by 8 feet."[8]

The growth in New Berlin's population also facilitated the founding of secondary schools; a stock company provided a frame building to house the first academy at the rear of the courthouse lot in 1820. The classics were taught for the first time by J.H. Hickock, a Connecticut schoolmaster. George A. Snyder, scholarly son of Governor Simon Snyder, also taught there. An octagonal brick school house (the only one of its kind in the county) was erected at the back of the Emanual Church lot, c. 1824. (It would have been similar in shape to the octagonal stone Sodom School east of Montandon in Northumberland County.) From time to time, private schools also offered their services; at least one such school was housed on the second floor of the courthouse.

Unlike the rest of Union Township, of which it was a part in 1834, New Berlin favored the acceptance of the Public School Law. The failure of the township to adopt the measure was given as the principal reason for New Berlin seeking incorporation as a borough. In 1837, within a year after becoming a bor-

ough, New Berlin adopted the school law and elected a school board which opened public schools in three existing buildings. However, two years later, the costs of public education created an unfavorable reaction, and the borough voted to discontinue the system. A year later, though, proponents of public education reversed the reversal.

While New Berlin's nondescript one-room schools may have been as adequate as others of that period, they did not meet with the approval of John M. Baum, the crusading publisher of the *Union Times*, who admonished his fellow townspeople:

Without good, convenient and airy school houses, properly modeled within and without, it is a folly to expect good schools, even after competent teachers have been procured. In former days a school house was regarded as a kind of filthy pig sty where disorder and whispering, and kicking and fighting on the part of the scholars, and moroseness and scolding, and whipping and occasional drinking and swearing on the part of the master were the order of the day. . . . It was small, smoking and ill-ventilated, the desks or tables were awkward, clumsy and inconvenient, and were whittled and carved in a most shocking and indecent manner. Hence, children never once dreamed that a school might be a place where pleasure enters, where modesty and good breeding are cultivated, and a kind, benevolent and polite teacher might preside . . . Let us remedy these defects in our common schools by taking out the desks that are not properly constructed, that are cut and carved with lewd figures and diagrams, and replace them with new and suitable ones . . . Let us introduce a system of ventilation that will provide invigorating and pure air.[9]

Baum may not have received the response he was looking for at that time; but after the removal of the county seat, the school directors purchased the courthouse for $1,000 and remodeled the second floor to accommodate the elementary school children, thereby closing the one-room structures. School was still held there 90 years later, with the primary grades in the south room, the intermediate grades in the northeast room, and the grammar grades in the northwest room.

Meanwhile, the life expectancy of the private schools remained poor. The New Berlin Female Seminary was opened in 1840 with attorney Isaac Slenker serving as the Board's President and Samuel Weirick as its Secretary. In July of that year, the school listed as its assets the services of the Reverend B.B. Newton and a location remarkable for the general health of its inhabitants: "Their manners are plain, such as indicate the strictest frugality and economy in their expenditures." Boarding (and lodging) were available with good families on moderate terms. Offerings included Latin, French, Greek, and higher branches of

TOP: The covered bridge over Penns Creek looking south. It was built with a Burr arch-truss. This type of truss system, which eased problems with bridging wider streams and rivers, was particularly popular in the Susquehanna River watershed. The designer, Theodore Burr of Torrington, Connecticut, built some of his earliest and largest bridges in this area of Pennsylvania. From the collection of the Union County Historical Society, #89.5.8.7 and #89.5.8.10.

BOTTOM: The Commons was given to the borough of Longstown (New Berlin) in 1795 by town founder George Long and his wife, for use as a common cow pasture. In 2000 it serves as an "open space" and site for numerous recreational activities. Photo by Jim Walter.

an English education, as well as natural and moral philosophy, chemistry, geology, and botany — a formidable curriculum for a single instructor and possibly one assistant — at five dollars per twelve-week quarter. Piano lessons were offered at an additional cost.[10] One quarter later, the management was advertising still another attraction — a chemical and philosophical apparatus which would provide demonstrations in the presence of the entire school. Seven years later, the school was no longer advertising, but Mr. and Mrs. Flinn of New York were preparing to open the Mount Annata Seminary on a farm on the edge of town. They planned to offer all branches suited to the education of young ladies including history, chemistry, natural philosophy, astronomy, and natural history. The notice added that Mr. Flinn had traveled widely to attend institutions of learning in Europe.[11] If the schools lived up to their advertising, they had a curriculum considerably broader than the typical female seminaries of that time, but they seem to have been too ephemeral to have educated many of the town's young ladies. Better times were coming from an unexpected source.

In the early years the Evangelical Association did not require its clergy to have a formal education. Beyond the ability to read the Scriptures, it asked only for dedication, earnestness, morality, a love of God and their fellow-beings, and an adherence to the Catechism. A generation later the need for a better-educated leadership was becoming apparent. Sensing the changing times, John Dreisbach wrote an article, "Teachers and Preachers Should Not Be Ignorant," in 1845, in which he urged a school for "useful knowledge." Two years later, he offered a motion at the General Conference at New Berlin for the establishment of a seminary for instruction in the general sciences. Nothing came of his proposal at the time, but W.W. Orwig and others kept up the pressure and in 1854 obtained a resolution at the Western Pennsylvania Conference at York for the creation of an institution of learning.

Having won a commitment to higher education, Orwig left no stone unturned to bring the school to New Berlin. Facing the likelihood of losing the county seat to Lewisburg and the Evangelical printing office to Cleveland, Orwig's fellow townspeople rallied behind the proposal and at a town meeting on January 9, 1854, chaired by Colonel John Swineford, drafted their claims for the school. New Berlin, they insisted, was the acknowledged center of the

Evangelical Association: "There is probably no town in either the Western or Eastern Conference better located for this purpose than New Berlin. The Tempter has but few emissaries here, and as for health, good morals, and order, it is perhaps not surpassed by any other in either conference." Just eight miles from the river, the boundary separating the conferences, New Berlin was readily accessible by railroad to Sunbury and then by stage. In addition to these advantages, the community could furnish from 30 to 50 scholars and Union County from 75 to 100.[12]

Orwig's enthusiasm and perseverance gained the victory before the adjournment of the Conference at York, and he returned home with the promise that the school would indeed open in New Berlin. Three of the original seven trustees were residents of Union County: Orwig, Martin Dreisbach, and H.D. Maize. Orwig and Simon Wolf were named as solicitors to raise the sum of $15,000 to construct and equip the school. Wolf, in particular, proved his competence as a fundraiser, obtaining almost $10,000 locally. Thus Union Seminary was born.

In recognition of his leadership, Orwig was named as its principal and professor of moral science and German language. Although reluctant to accept the post due to his trusteeship and his limited formal education, W.W. Orwig was persuaded by his associates to undertake the venture. The trustees erected a three-story brick structure 78 x 45 feet, trimmed with stone and adorned with a steeple and bell, on a six-acre campus just north of town. The first two floors contained a chapel, two large study rooms, and a number of classrooms; the third floor served as a dormitory. The chapel seated 350 and was lighted by oil lamps and a central chandelier; the rooms were heated with wood stoves. Lamps and stoves were obviously fire hazards, but there was no serious fire during the life of the institution.

The trustees adopted a three-year course of study, hired a faculty of seven, and on January 3, 1856, opened the doors to approximately 60 students amidst a bustle and excitement shared by almost every citizen. Bursting with pride, Orwig declared that New Berlin had become a "little Athens." The school grew rapidly at the outset, and by the 1858-1859 school year, the enrollment reached 264 — the highest in its history — and in that spring the first class of five young women was graduated. In 1859 Orwig resigned when he was elected a bishop of the

church. He was replaced by the Reverend Francis A. Hendricks, the school's first professor of mathematics.

The Civil War, however, drained the school of its young men, so instruction was suspended from 1863 until 1865. Faced with deficits, at the end of the war the trustees issued stock certificates and sold a sufficient number of them to reopen, but enrollment did not bounce back sufficiently to prevent recurring financial strains. Only the dedication and self-sacrifice of its leaders kept the now-much-smaller school alive through the hard times of the 1870s. Faculty salaries remained in arrears from year to year, and the sheriff seized the property during one of the crises but released it when the faculty and friends reached into their savings to redeem it. Attendance varied through these years from 18 to 120. In 1883 a proposal to convert the seminary into a collegiate institution closed the school, and the trustees transferred the title to the Conference.

All was not lost, however. The trustees of the Evangelical Association incorporated the Central Pennsylvania College with scientific and classical curricula leading to the degrees of bachelor of science and bachelor of arts; remodeled and enlarged the seminary building; and made the addition of a mansard-roofed fourth floor. In turn, the newly created college trustees named the Reverend Aaron E. Gobble, who was a teacher of mathematics at the seminary, as principal, and the college opened early in 1887. Several of its upper division students were graduated the same spring.

Despite a factional struggle within the Evangelical Church which resulted in its division into two warring organizations, the college achieved an enviable reputation under Gobble's leadership. During the ensuing litigation, the trustees lost title to the property but Gobble and a supporting committee purchased it and obtained the charter rights. Gobble and his group turned the charter over to the newly organized United Evangelical Church, and a successful drive for endowments at the turn of the century, headed by the Reverend W.E. Detwiler, was hailed by Gobble as "the greatest forward movement the institution had ever made."[13]

At this time the college offered four courses of study: the classical, which led to the bachelor of arts degree; the scientific, which led to the bachelor of science degree; the academic, which provided the bachelor of education degree; and the theological, which encompassed Biblical and ecclesiastical literature. There were two literary societies, the Excelsior and the Neocosmian (New World); a library of 5,000 volumes; a museum and scientific laboratory; a faculty of nine; and 113 students, with a ratio of one young woman for every three young men.

In 1902 time ran out on New Berlin's claim to the institution. Central Pennsylvania College was consolidated with Albright College and removed to the latter's campus at Myerstown, Pennsylvania. During its brief life in New Berlin, it had graduated 180 students. The building had scarcely been emptied when a citizens' group combined with alumni to purchase the building and reopen it as an academy, using the original name, Union Seminary. With a railroad on the drawing board that would link New Berlin with the Main railroad at Winfield, it was anticipated that non-residents would supplement local young people desiring a secondary education. The school was now non-denominational, and its curriculum was comparable to the high schools in the area but with enrichment in such subjects as music and elocution.

By 1911, though, it too succumbed to change; like the many other academies, it was unable to compete with tuition-free high schools. The building was used as a silk mill for a few years, and after standing empty for a time was taken down to make room for a playground. The closing of the seminary was particularly unfortunate for New Berlin's teenagers, who, in many cases, were now deprived of a secondary education. The coming of the automobile eased the problem, permitting some of them to enroll in towns nearby; and the school consolidation solved it as students became part of the Mifflinburg District.

Because New Berlin was the political hub of the county, it was also the scene of a variety of activities which otherwise might have passed it by. It certainly had more than its share of circuses, menageries, acrobats, rope dancers and peddlers. Militia day and political rallies, parades and demonstrations added to its calendar of events. In the decade of the 1840s, there was the Washington Band, and the New Berlin Singing Association offered a program of sacred music to help liquidate the indebtedness of the local Presbyterian Society.

The town also had its home-owned circus for a few years. Returning from the Civil War, Colonel Charles Kleckner felt the lure of the sawdust and assembled a collection of wild animals, a lion trainer, a bareback rider and other performers, and a tent — the whole transported on wagons. "Billie" (W.L.) Showers recalled a performance in Mifflinburg and noted that the usual collection of goldbrickers, pickpockets, and confidence men mingled with the

Bands such as the New Berlin Band were featured at area fairs, festivals, cake walks, Sunday school picnics, and, of course, parades. From the collection of Gary W. and Donna M. Slear.

PAGE 110 TOP: Jay Napp and a friend were photographed c. 1908-1909 in a dormitory room of the Union Seminary in New Berlin. MIDDLE: The three-story seminary building was located on the north side of New Berlin. The third floor was the dormitory; while classrooms, a study, and the chapel were on the other floors. BOTTOM: Cloyd Napp (on left) and a teammate left practice to have their picture taken in New Berlin c. 1907. The Union Seminary team often played Mifflinburg High School as noted when "Mifflinburg crossed bats with Union Seminary at New Berlin last Saturday and were defeated by a score of 8-5, " *Mifflinburg Telegraph*, May 18, 1906. From the collections of Billy and Lindy Mattern, and Gary W. and Donna M. Slear.

crowd. An unscheduled event occurred when the bareback rider was beaten by her husband in Young's Hotel, where the stars were housed. The next morning the bruised bareback rider was observed seated with the lion tamer when the circus pulled out of town.[14]

In the 1870s the New Berlin Silver Cornet Band was giving concerts, alternating selections with tableaux and minstrel performances. In the 1890s there was C.D. Bogar's Brass Band; and many New Berliners can still recall the 1910 Cornet Band, with its white Palm Beach uniforms and bandwagon as it performed at Sunday school picnics, cakewalks, festivals, and holiday parades. Literature buffs formed the Excelsior Literary Society in the 1870s, and the Red Clover Dramatic Club was regaling audiences at the turn of the century.

New Berliners, like most of their neighbors in the county, paid little attention to the antislavery movement, regarding abolitionists as trouble makers and the behavior of their leaders as shocking. When C.C. Burleigh was jailed for selling abolitionist tracts on the Sabbath, the *Union Times* commented that it "served him right. His brother, C.M. Burleigh, who lectured in this place a short time ago appears to entertain the same views — violating the laws of God by preaching political sermons in one of our churches and disavowing any allegiance to the law of our country . . . Cannot his 'right hand man,' Friday Templeton, below town, have him released!"[15]

On the other hand, New Berlin people were apt to be supporters of temperance as the movement spread across the nation. In 1827 a local paper reported that Dr. E. Appleton of New Berlin created a sensation over a recipe he had concocted for drunkenness. It was in great demand for a short time but in the end proved to be of no account.[16] Samuel Barber, one of the first recruits for temperance, headed the New Berlin Temperance Society. Israel Gutelius was also a leader and advocated temperance in the columns of his *Union Times*. Little headway seems to have been made, however, while New Berlin was the county seat.

In 1857 a state-wide referendum upon a prohibitory liquor law (the Maine Law) was endorsed strongly by Lewisburg and Mifflinburg, but New Berlin and Limestone Township rejected it by a wide margin. The county (present Union and Snyder combined) turned it down by a whopping 1,171 votes. In a local option referendum in 1873, the county gave its approval by 238 votes. New Berlin went with the majority by a vote of 72 to 44 whereas Limestone Township rejected it. The law went into effect in the county, and Judge Bucher ordered the constables to

enforce it. Failing to note any action on the constables' part, temperance leaders organized a county prosecuting committee with a member in each district. Before much could be accomplished, though, the legislature repealed the law, returning the state to a licensing system, "virtually opening the flood of intemperance."[17] The action was a setback to temperance, but the momentum was restored with the advent of the Women's Christian Temperance Union.

New Berlin has had many outstanding personalities. While it remained the county seat, the legal profession was in the forefront. In 1816 James Merrill arrived from Vermont by way of Dartmouth College and York, Pennsylvania. A college friend of Thaddeus Stevens, Merrill's life in some respects paralleled that of the enigmatic Stevens. Both offered allegiance to the Antimasonic and Whig Parties; both fought for Negro suffrage in Pennsylvania; both, as delegates to the Pennsylvania Constitutional Convention of 1837, resisted innovations, preferring the conservative tradition of the founding fathers; and both, after active participation in the debates of the Convention, rejected the ratification of the amendments though Merrill signed it while Stevens refused. Merrill held a number of political offices but is remembered particularly as a legal counselor and public servant. He was instrumental in founding a library and organizing a Presbyterian Society in New Berlin, obtaining the latter during the last month of his life when he was stricken with cancer.

Isaac Slenker, a younger contemporary of Merrill, was born on a farm in Gregg Township and educated in the country schools there. He taught school for a few years and then read law with Attorney James F. Linn in Lewisburg. After admission to the bar in 1828, Slenker settled in New Berlin and remained until his death in 1873. A Jacksonian Democrat, he was elected to the state senate but failed as a candidate for president judge. During the resurgence of the Democratic Party during the Civil War, Isaac Slenker was nominated and elected as auditor-general of Pennsylvania and handled his duties competently through this difficult period. Like Merrill, Slenker was an ardent Presbyterian and a founder of the church in New Berlin. During his Harrisburg years or possibly earlier, Slenker became consumptive; the disease also took the lives of his children, leaving only his wife and granddaughter at his death.

With the loss of the county seat, some of the lawyers drifted away; Merrill's son, Charles, went to Middleburg, and the highly talented Joseph C. Casey removed to Harrisburg, where he edited the twelve volumes of *Casey's Reports of the Decisions of the Supreme Court of Pennsylvania*. Charles Merrill later moved to Washington where he served as First Chief Justice of the Court of Claims. William Van Gezer, a renowned trial lawyer, resettled in Lewisburg.

Dr. Joseph R. Lotz deserves mention as one of the leading citizens during the middle period of the nineteenth century. The son of a miller, he came to New Berlin to work in Kleckner's gristmill. However, anxious to study medicine, he walked to Selinsgrove weekly to report to a preceptor. He later matriculated at the University of Pennsylvania and returned to New Berlin in 1827 to practice medicine. In addition to handling a large country practice, Lotz became a skilled surgeon and was called upon by other surgeons in the area to operate and to consult. He also invented several surgical instruments. Students flocked to him, and twenty graduated under his tutelage. Dr. Lotz was generous to the poor and responded to requests for his services wherever they took him with a buoyancy of temperament which never seemed to flag. He died at 75 after a half century of dedicated service.

Shortly after Lotz's death, Dr. Harry M. Wilson opened his medical practice on Front Street near Vine where his quaint office building remains today. His grandfather had been an early storekeeper in New Berlin, and his father had succeeded him in the business. The Wilsons were Democrats, Presbyterians, and civic leaders. Harry Wilson attended Jefferson Medical College and upon his graduation in 1877 returned to his old home. In many respects he was the stereotype of the old-fashioned doctor — ready to relieve suffering whenever called as well as counselor and confidant to hundreds of people. A former resident of New Berlin recalled an incident illustrative of his human touch. As a boy of five, he longed for a baby sister, not knowing that his mother was pregnant. After several requests, his parents sent him to Dr. Wilson to tell the doctor about his wish. The doctor greeted him and led him into his office, where he listened to his plea. After some discussion, the doctor promised to see whether he could do something about it, and sure enough, the much-desired sister arrived a short time later.

However, Dr. Wilson did not have a monopoly as indicated by a second reminiscence of the above-mentioned individual. During his childhood, the boy contracted typhoid fever, and his nose began to bleed; the physician advised that if it did not stop, his nose would have to be plugged. Seeking to avoid such therapy, his father went to see a nearby pow-wow specialist. The latter invoked the hidden magic; and when the father returned to his home, he found that the bleeding had stopped. On another occasion, the boy had a wart on his face, and his barber volunteered to cut it out. Again the family preferred pow-wowing. The practitioner uttered a few sounds, unintelligible to the boy, and the wart soon disappeared.

At 400 Front Street, New Berlin, stands the former office of Dr. Simon Burg (active 1863-1877), which later became the office and home of Dr. Harry Wilson. Photo by Jim Walter.

Among the town's most enduring memories are those relating to Dr. Wesley Vallerchamp, doctor of dentistry. His family was of French and Welsh descent, and his father was said to have been both a physician and a dentist although he seems to have practiced neither. Instead, the elder Vallerchamp and his wife became itinerant preachers and settled in New Berlin in 1852 to educate their children. Mr. Vallerchamp died several years later, leaving his widow and three children. Wesley's older brother attended the Baltimore Dental College, and Wesley, in turn, learned dentistry from him. Dr. Vallerchamp practiced his profession for many years in the front room of his home, but he also reserved a good share of his time to take dentistry to the homes of his patients. After loading his valise with the tools of his practice: a small hand drill, a turnkey, a small hammer (tampon), a knife, and a few small paper-thin squares of gold, he would hitch his pony to a high-topped buggy and ride across the countryside, making his headquarters with a particular family while word spread about the neighborhood.

In the performance of his craft, Dr. Vallerchamp held the drill in the palm of his left hand and turned it with his right, requiring strong hands and patience from both the giver and receiver. Once the tooth had been drilled, he rolled the gold into a pellet and beat it into the cavity with his hammer. If an extraction were required, he separated the gum from the tooth with his knife, and moved the turnkey back and forth until it loosened. Some years later he installed a drill which he operated with a foot-treadle, but he never discarded the old rocking chair which he used as his dental chair. One patient recalled that she had insisted that the doctor cover his beard with a towel because she could not endure being tickled by it.

A photograph of Dr. Vallerchamp in his thirties reveals a handsome man with dark hair and a pointed beard, neatly groomed, wearing broadcloth and a brocade vest with embroidered white figures. In later years he was less attentive to his dress, and he permitted his house to deteriorate until a wag reported that he took his umbrella with him as a shelter from the water dripping from the ceiling. Other eccentricities were evident in his organic gardening and his unweeded potatoes became a yearly joke. His peculiarities did not deprive him of community interests, however, and for a time he headed the seminary's alumni organization. The demand for his services tapered off as he grew older, but Vallerchamp was still practicing at age 85. In 1928 his life ended tragically when he was struck down and killed by an automobile while crossing the street near his home. Even today, "a few New Berlin people may yet admit to having Vallerchamp's gold in their teeth."[18]

New Berlin obtained its long-awaited railroad in 1905, and electricity was initially generated by the Kleckner Mill. Still, large-scale industry continued to pass New Berlin by, and its population remained stationary for a century. The Frank Maurer Creamery assembled milk for delivery to Shamokin, and the Rosedale Dairy enlarged the business and made its products a widely-known name brand in the 1920s; but like glove making, tanning, and silk spinning, the creamery endured only for a generation and then succumbed to consolidations elsewhere. By the 1950s, however, the Q-E Machine Shop was fabricating metal products through subcontracts with national manufacturers, Marlin Industries was making furniture, and the Middleburg Sportswear Company was fashioning garments. The First National Bank of New Berlin, established in 1905, fell victim to the Great Depression, but a branch of the Snyder County Trust Company replaced it in 1974. Meanwhile, a sizable number of the town's labor force found employment in Mifflinburg, Lewisburg, Selinsgrove, and Kreamer.

Generations have come and gone in New Berlin, but the stability which has marked its history remains. No urban renewal has severed its historic ties, nor has it suffered the decay which has befallen some of the railroad and coal mining communities. Its fine early nineteenth-century structures are prized by its residents, and its Heritage Association has made the region aware of its historical significance and its unique charm.

From the collection of Mary Sassaman.

ENDNOTES

1 Reminiscences of Roy and Ray Sauers.

2 The Beatty family is well written about by William Dorwart whose ancestor Hugh Beatty served at least two tours in the Revolutionary War and spent the rest of his life in New Berlin where he is buried. He had at least seven children who reached maturity. The Beattys were known for helping others and when Dr. VanValzah came to Buffalo Valley in 1786 he had not a shilling to pay for the ferry to cross the Susquehanna at Sunbury. Hugh Beatty paid his fee. Dr., VanValzah later took in Margaret Beatty and gave her a home until she died in 1875. Alexander Beatty Jr. and James Beatty protested the building of a dam across Penns Creek in 1792 for a gristmill. They lost. It is quite likely that the dam adversely affected their tannery and after James died in 1795, Alexander moved to Ontario, Canada.

3 Union Star, March 14, 1840.

4 Second Annual Heritage Day, I, 13 (August 26, 1972).

5 Raymond W. Albright, A History of the Evangelical Church, Harrisburg, 1942, 320.

6 New Berlin Times. Quoted in John Blair Linn, Annals of Buffalo Valley, Pennsylvania, 1755-1855, Harrisburg, 1877, 481.

7 Albright, 99.

8 School Board Minutes, April 29, 1847, Frank P. Boyer Papers, Union County Historical Society.

9 Union Times, March 20, 1851.

10 July 17, 1840.

11 New Berlin Times, July 27, 1847.

12 The Evangelical Messenger, January 18, 1854, quoted by F. Wilbur Gingrich and Eugene H. Barth in A History of Albright College, Reading, PA., 43. Additional details relating to Union Seminary and Central Pennsylvania College may be found in this history. Many of them are taken from documents in the archives of the Albright College Library.

13 Reminiscence of A.E. Gobble, Lewisburg Saturday News, September 30, 1905.

14 Lewisburg Saturday News, January 31, 1914.

15 Lewisburg Saturday News, April 20, 1847.

16 Linn, 493.

17 Lewisburg Chronicle, March 19, 1875.

18 Agnes Selin Schoch, "Yester Years," Selinsgrove Times Tribune, February 3 and 10, 1949.

Rosedale Dairy items. Counterclockwise are: crate, milk can, Paramount can, and three boxes for different cream cheeses. From the collections of the Union County Historical Society #99.20.1, Peter Gardner, and the New Berlin Heritage Association. Photo by the Terry Wild Studio.

CHAPTER 7

LEWISBURG: PEOPLE AND EVENTS THAT SHAPED ITS HISTORY

by Lois M. Kalp

In 1769 when John and Thomas Penn, the Proprietors of the colony of Pennsylvania, announced that land lotteries would be held in the region of the West Branch of the Susquehanna River, a Palatinate German, Ludwig Derr, left his home in Heidelberg Township, Berks County, to take part. Although Derr encamped on a pleasant site near the mouth of Limestone Run (now called Bull Run) on the Susquehanna, he preferred a location at present-day New Columbia for his home and mill. At the lottery, someone else drew that plot, and Derr (which he spelled Dorr and pronounced Tarr) had to be satisfied with the site of his encampment. In 1770, with the help of his wife, Catherine, and his son, George, Ludwig Derr built his log house and his mill there. The house still stands today, incorporated into a larger building at 34 Brown Street. His mill was located nearby at a site presently known as 40 Brown Street. It is currently occupied by "The Brady Apartments," named for the man who operated the mill after Derr. The convergence of the land lottery and the personage of the genial, adventuresome Ludwig Derr started the town of Lewisburg.

Before Derr laid out the town in 1785, he was involved in numerous activities which were significant in developing his own business and that of this town. At his tavern he played host to both Indian and Revolutionary War councils, in addition, he served as a constable. In order to supply water for his mill, Derr almost single-handedly scooped out a wide trench from a point on Limestone Run (near where the municipal swimming pool is today) to his mill near the mouth of the run. Derr's mill race is shown in *Pomeroy's 1868 Atlas* and was extant until 1883, when the borough filled it in.

Derr's mill and mill race attested to his formidable strength of both body and character. His business acumen revealed itself in his design for the town, which provided lots for three church faiths: Lutheran, Presbyterian, and Roman Catholic. The inclusion of Catholics possibly denotes Derr's faith, for Scots Irish (Presbyterians) and Germans (Lutherans) were the more prevalent settlers in this area by far. Derr died in 1785 and his wife Catherine a year later, leaving their son George and his wife, Fanny Yentzer, to carry on German tradition, including raising a large family.

With the death of Ludwig Derr, the development of Derrstown faltered. George, his son, was not as interested in the real estate business as Ludwig had been. In 1789 George sold all but seventeen lots of land in Lewisburg to Peter Borger, a land agent, who in turn sold them to Carl Ellenkhuysen of Amsterdam, Holland. Ellenkhuysen's purpose in buying land so remote from Amsterdam was to occupy the time and energies of his son, Mathias, to whom historians give little respect. Ellenkhuysen gave Mathias the land in Lewisburg with the hope that he would develop it. It was a vain hope, for Mathias was carefree and bibulous with a lighthearted wife, Clara, whose deepest interest was ice skating.

Mathias and Clara Ellenkhuysen moved to Lewisburg (called Tarrstown at the time), accompanied by a Catholic priest, John Baptist Charles Helbron, whose task was to be a spiritual advisor as well as a land agent. Father Helbron was a missionary priest from Holy Trinity in Philadelphia. He served Milton, Selinsgrove, and Chillisquaque as well as Lewisburg. The Ellenkhuysens lived in a log house on the high west bank of South Water Street, overlooking the river and the dock for Mathias' ferry boat, which he rowed when he was not patronizing one of the region's many taverns.

The sojourn of the Ellenkhuysens in Lewisburg was brief, terminated by Mathias' early death in 1792 and the departure of Clara to Erie, Pennsylvania. Their chief contribution to the town's development was the construction of a Catholic chapel on North Second Street near the St. Mary Street intersection. The chapel, the first church building in town, was demolished when the only Catholics in town departed. Without a congregation, Helbron had no reason for staying in Lewisburg since he had not been a permanent resident, but had traveled between his frontier congregations and Holy Trinity. He returned to his duties in Philadelphia.

The legend that the Ellenkhuysens were responsible for the Saint added to the streets named for Derr's family is easily discounted by the fact that Saint appears on the 1785 map drawn by Samuel Weiser and on deeds signed by Catherine and George Derr several years before the Ellenkhuysens arrived. The other widely circulated story concerning the use of Saint, attributing it to an accident by an itinerant sign

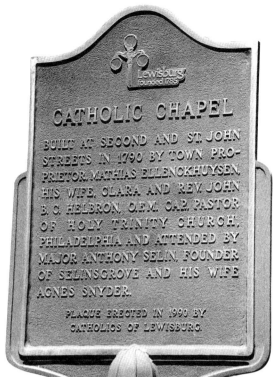

Photo by Jim Walter.

painter who ran out of room and placed "St," denoting street, at the beginning in the European tradition, is a story without basis.

An early settler who cannot be overlooked in a treatment of Lewisburg's history was Flavel Roan, the region's first "Renaissance man." He built neither mills nor churches, nor even his own house, for he lived at the mouth of Buffalo Creek in a house owned by Ludwig Derr, from which point he conducted a ferry boat business. Roan was a notary, a scrivener for persons who could not write, and a schoolteacher. He served as county commissioner, as member of the General Assembly, and as sheriff. His great contribution was his journal, which he wrote in 1803 and from 1807 through 1813 in an inimitable style filled with detailed entries of meetings, parties, balls, hops, and drinking bouts. Northumberland County was his milieu, and he knew and liked everyone. He was strong proof that lack of mechanical transportation need not be a deterrent to travel and social communication.

Upon his death in 1817, Roan was buried in the English or Presbyterian Cemetery next to Shearer's Tavern on Market Street near the Susquehanna. As a member of the Buffalo Presbyterian Church and an habitué of the tavern, he would have appreciated the proximity. Thanks to the historian, John Blair Linn, Roan's journal is preserved in the *Annals of Buffalo Valley.*

Before the construction of the Eastern Division of the Pennsylvania Canal in 1830 and the crosscut canal in 1833, works that revolutionized life in early Lewisburg, a number of events took place that influenced the region's history in a quieter way. Two schools were established: a German school in 1802 and an English one in 1805; the first was located on the site of the present Lutheran Church and the second on the site of the present Presbyterian manse. Three church groups formed, albeit without buildings: the Christian in 1801, the Lutheran in 1802, and the Methodist in 1812.

On March 31, 1812, the incorporation of "the directors of streets, lanes, and alleys" took place, followed by an election of directors the following October, and thus the town of Lewisburg began. Derr's Town became a memory. The division of Union County from Northumberland County in 1813 was an act that would have a profound effect on Lewisburg in the future. The committee appointed by the state legislature to select a site for the new county seat bypassed Lewisburg and Mifflinburg for a more central location at New Berlin. Any possible disappointment in Lewisburg's not being named the county seat did not prevent the townspeople from applying their energies to improving their village, which was showing signs of emerging from a raw, pioneer condition. By 1818 Lewisburg could boast of having two church buildings: the Methodist on the southeast corner of South Front and St. Louis Streets, and the Christian Church on North Fifth Street. For the greater convenience of the inhabitants, a toll bridge opened on February 9, 1818, relegating ferry boats to their docks forever.

The incorporation of Lewisburg as a borough occurred on March 21, 1822, and was followed several years later by one of the most significant events in the early development of the town — the construction of the Eastern Division of the Pennsylvania Canal. This was a project that not only changed the quality of life in Lewisburg but also brought to the attention of the townspeople three personalities who were themselves makers of history: General Abbott Green, William Cameron, and James Moore II.

In early nineteenth-century Lewisburg there were no more influential or capable men than Green, Cameron, and Moore, all sons of eighteenth-century pioneers. Both Green and Moore were civil engineers of considerable talent. General Green, a six-footer of immense vitality, was a pillar of the Presbyterian Church, which he attended at Buffalo Crossroads until a church was built in Lewisburg in 1833. James Moore II, a weather-beaten bridge builder and

Phillip Billmeyer & Co. boatyards on North Water Street, Lewisburg, c. 1865. The *Allentown* and *Mauch Chunk* canal boats shown were larger than those used in the West Branch of the Pennsylvania Canal, which were about 85 feet long and thirteen to fourteen feet wide. These larger boats were built for service on the larger Lehigh and Delaware Canals, and would be transported downstream when the spring flood deepened the river. From the collection of the Union County Historical Society, #89.5.21.3.

carpenter, was an ardent Baptist and a member of the Milton Baptist Church, which he had helped to found. Green and Moore were to become active in the development of the University at Lewisburg (est. 1846) — Moore as one of its founders and Green as one of its most prominent curators. William Cameron, known for his Scottish temper and intemperance, applied his attention to more mundane affairs, eventually founding the Lewisburg Dimes Savings Institution in 1853 (later the Lewisburg National Bank) and by involving himself in politics.

In 1827 Green and Cameron joined in a complicated contract to construct the Eastern Division of the Pennsylvania Canal, a contract that Cameron soon broke for reasons known only to himself; whereupon Moore assumed Cameron's obligations and with Green completed the canal on December 1, 1830. Although of great importance to those communities along the Susquehanna's east bank which it touched, the canal had to be augmented by a crosscut from the east bank to the west side of the river at Lewisburg in order to benefit the town. This section was completed in the fall of 1833 when the first cargo crossed to Lewisburg, initiating a new era in the town's social and industrial

life. At the same time, the Mifflinburg/Lewisburg Turnpike was completed. As if in immediate response to new demands, an iron foundry was opened by Nathan Mitchell and Peter Nevius (later the Marsh Foundry), and the Lutheran and Reformed Churches dedicated the cornerstone of their "gallery" church on the southeast corner of South Third and St. Louis Streets. Lewisburg was at the beginning of its growing period.

The canal's influence on Lewisburg's social, educational, and economic life during the years of its usefulness (1834-1869) was monumental, bringing, as it did, new people into the town with new businesses and new ideas. The great impact on the townspeople of the Common School Law (1834), the abolition movement (1837), the Mexican War (1846), and the Civil War (1861-1865) was mitigated by the extraordinary surge of creative and commercial endeavor within the borough, made possible by the canal. Even in the most difficult hours of national crisis, the tempo of life in Lewisburg maintained an evenness that typified the local character, and the period of 1818 to 1869 stands as the first pronounced growing period in Lewisburg's history.

During this period there was frenetic building activity: the Lewisburg Academy in 1839, the Academy of the University at Lewisburg in 1847 to 1848, the Main Administration Building of the university from 1849 through 1857, the North Ward School in 1855, the South Ward School in 1861, and the West Ward School in 1869. The first church of the Presbyterians was erected in 1833 and their second church in 1857; the Baptists built their first structure in 1845 and their second in 1869 to 1870; and the second church of the Methodists was raised in 1832 on South Third Street and their third structure on the same site in 1853. The brick gallery church of the Lutheran and Reformed Churches was built in 1834, and the Reformed Church (separated by then from the Lutheran group) in 1848, as well as St. Paul's Evangelical United Brethren in 1861 to 1862, and the Congregational Christian Church in 1854. The Union County Courthouse was constructed in 1855, the Kline Hotel in 1834, the Mt. Vernon Hotel in 1850, and the Buffalo House in 1856.

As a result of the crosscut canal's existence, Samuel Wolfe settled on South Water Street in 1841 near his grain-shipping wharf, and in 1850 William Frick and Eli Slifer moved their boatyard from the east side of the river to the river bank on North Water Street, Lewisburg. The telegraph arrived in 1851. Thriving industries established were the James Marsh Foundry in 1840; the Gas Works, built between 1859 and 1860; the Slifer, Walls, Shriner and Company, which made Buckeye Reapers and Mowers, in 1860; and Mark Halfpenny's Woolen Mills in 1866. The Palmer, Ross and Company Planing Mill was run by Lewis Palmer and J.B. Ross in 1859; the Lewisburg Water Mills, constructed by George Derr in 1813, was run by Joseph Shriner in 1867; and the Lewisburg Star Mills, started in 1874, was run by J.A. Fry and G.W. Walls. There were banks: the Lewisburg Dimes Savings Institution started in 1853, and the Union National Bank started in 1860. A music hall was built on the former site of the Baptist Church at 27 South Third Street in 1845; constructed by H.G. Swartz, its elegance represented the changing times in Lewisburg.

The growing period, spawning as it did immense business activity, was a factor in the division of the county in 1855 into Snyder and Union Counties. Likewise, the favorable result of the election naming Lewisburg as the county seat encouraged the trends of prosperity. Both events were momentous occasions in the life of the town. A third factor in the growth and prosperity was the founding of the First Baptist Church in 1845, an act that resulted in the founding in 1846 of the University at Lewisburg, later called Bucknell, one of the town's major assets. Prominent in this achievement were James Moore II, bridge builder; Dr. William Ludwig, physician; Samuel Wolfe, grain merchant; James Moore III, construction engineer and farmer; Joseph Meixell, merchant and farmer; and Eugenio Kincaid, Baptist Minister.

Of other significant events, one was of natural origin and the other of human invention. On March 17, 1865, the Susquehanna went on a rampage, surpassing all previous floods. All but one span of the bridge was destroyed, and the destruction wrought by the muddy waters in the town was significant. Following that disaster was the dreadful news of Abraham Lincoln's assassination on April 14, 1865; the impact on the town was solemn and sobering.

In 1869 an event occurred that shook the town — a train of the Lewisburg, Centre and Spruce Creek Railroad chugged across the new St. John's Street bridge into Lewisburg, its long piercing whistle sounding the end of the canal era and the beginning of a more sophisticated era on wheels. Lewisburg celebrated not only the railroad's coming but also many festive events. Two hundred people attended the elegant evening anniversary party for Eli Slifer, local businessman and politician. Townspeople turned out by the hundreds for parades commemorating the country's centennial, the meeting of the International Order of Odd Fellows, Memorial Day, or the fanfare of a circus's arrival in town.

Thousands came by foot, wagon, and rail to see the unveiling of the Civil War monument on July 4, 1901, at the juncture of University, Third, and Brown Streets. Like other Fourth of July celebrations as reported by local newspapers or recorded in private diaries like Sally Meixell's, buildings were decorated, flags waved, bands marched, liquor flowed, cannons fired, and speeches continued for hours. Churches served dinners as well as lemonade at two glasses for five cents; the fire company entertained the ladies and turned out more than twenty companies to swell the parade. It was reported that in spite of the refreshments taken, there were no "real desperate cases of drunk," and only one accident, when little Augustus Houghton came too close into contact with a revolver that was being fired. (This was an improvement over prior years, when fingers and even arms were lost when the cannon misfired.) Editors of local newspapers mentioned church suppers, visiting lecturers,

One-half of the stereo view card of Lewisburg's 1885
Centennial, taken at Market and South Third Streets. From
the collection of the Union County Historical Society,
#89.5.14.14A.

phrenologists, band concerts, and horse racing at the
fair grounds as well as fakirs or magic shows.
Lewisburg was indeed a lively place.

Many people believe that the romantic period of
the prosperous railroad era, which lasted roughly
from 1870 to 1920, saw a greater growth of industry,
business, and commerce than at any preceding time
in the town's history. Considering the extraordinary
activity of the first growing period from 1833 through
1869, the belief bears some analysis and re-evaluation.

There is no denying that there was a marked
increase in business in the railroad era, as was
evidenced in Lewisburg by the completion of the
Shamokin, Sunbury and Lewisburg Railroad (later a
branch of the Reading Railroad) in 1883, with an
architecturally impressive passenger depot; by the
opening of Joseph Musser's knitting mill located on
the west side of North Fifth Street between Cherry
Alley and St. John Street in 1880 (later used as a warehouse for C. Dreisbach Sons Wholesale Hardware
and more recently for Busser Supply Company); and
by Cyrus Hoffa's opening of the Buffalo Mills in 1833
at the juncture of the Reading and Pennsylvania
Railroads. Likewise, the Water Works started in 1883

with construction of a standpipe with the capacity of
110,000 gallons; a nail works opened in 1884 but was
short-lived; and the opening of the Lewisburg Furniture and Planing Company in 1885 was followed by a
re-opening of the old Lewisburg Planing Mill in 1886.
The Quaker Manufacturing Company was located on
the south side of St. Louis between Water and Front
Streets in 1902; the Lewisburg Trust and Safe Deposit
Company was established in 1915; the Lewisburg
Brick Yard was located west of St. Anthony Street
between present Route 15 and the former Reading
Railroad; and Benson McDowell acquired the old
Woolen Mill at the northeast corner of North Water
and St. John Streets in 1916 (now the Roller Mills
antique center). At this time, part of the width of present St. John Street was actually the rail bed of a
branch of the Pennsylvania Railroad.

The chief characteristic of the railroad era was not
Lewisburg's extraordinary growth but its appetite for
worldly things: the good things of life, culture, fine
homes, and elegant clothing, along with the concomitant of these things — good manners. This was a normal
reaction of people to a long period of pioneer living.
The trains whistling noisily in and out of town were
symbols of life projecting itself beyond provincial borders. This trend was everywhere, not just in Lewisburg.

This appetite or attitude found expression in the
buildings and houses that were designed and constructed. In Lewisburg the Baptists dedicated their
handsome new Gothic stone church in 1870 on the
northwest corner of St. Louis and South Third Streets.
It exemplified one of the most popular styles of the
time, and its minister was one of the most popular
hymn writers in America, Professor Robert Lowry
(author of "Shall We Gather at the River"), also
associated with the University at Lewisburg. That the
church was the expression of a real need for a larger
church can be discounted — it was evidence of the
hunger for beauty in an age of elegance. In 1890 the
Methodists, having demolished their church building, dedicated their magnificent Victorian structure
with understandable pride. In 1902 the members of
Christ's Evangelical Lutheran Church dedicated their
imposing church; and the Reformed Church (later
known as the United Church of Christ) laid the
cornerstone for its church on the southwest corner of
North Third and St. John Streets, a substantial edifice
with real Tiffany windows. When the congregation
constructed a new building on the north side of Route
192 near Reitz Boulevard just west of Lewisburg in
1990, the Tiffany windows were moved to the new

site, and the former church became a private home. The Evangelical church on the east side of South Fourth Street became a Methodist church when the denominations merged; at the same time the Evangelical Home and Orphanage became the United Methodist Home (now RiverWoods). Visitors to Lewisburg never failed to mention its impressively beautiful churches, typically concluding, "There must be money in this town."

The appetite for elegance indulged itself in the design and construction of beautiful homes, some in the mansion category, defined in the nineteenth century as a "great home with four chimneys"; and those that were not built in this period were renovated to be in style. All were elegantly decorated with flare and good taste, staffed with servants, and equipped with stables, fine horses, and carriage houses. The handsomest of these mansions were those that belonged to James Marsh and George F. Miller at 60 and 43/45 South Second Street; William Cameron at 201 Market Street; Dr. Samuel Beck and Charles S. Wolfe at 41 and 18 South Third Street; Daniel Bright Miller and Peter Beaver on 82 and 63 University Avenue; William Frick on 98 North Front Street; and Philip Billmeyer on 101 North Fourth Street. Of all of these homes, only Philip Billmeyer's residence has been removed.

The style of living in the great houses was pleasurably recalled by one of the members of the elegant nineteenth-century social set in Lewisburg, William Cameron Walls, president of the Lewisburg National Bank from 1927 to 1941. With a life span that included the last half of the nineteenth century and almost all of the first half of the twentieth century, Walls possessed a wealth of memories, which he shared generously with the author. He liked to recall his own father and step-mother, John and Sarah Wilson Walls, whose home at 331 Market Street was always open to friends and neighbors. (This was the Lewisburg Municipal Building from 1968 through the 1990s. It barely resembles the Victorian brick building with white trim and a white picket fence of the nineteenth century.)

Also prominent was Johnson Walls, first president of the Union National Bank, who built the Victorian house on the south side of Pine Alley at 26 South Third Street, occupied later by the family of William Cameron Walls, then by the latter's daughter, Dorothy Walls McCormick and her husband, Harry "Moose" McCormick, an early twentieth-century star, a pinch-hitter for the New York Giants' baseball team. The family was highly social, and their home was filled with beautiful objects and family heir-

Stamped tin hand and calling cards from the 1880s. From the collections of Diana M. Lasansky, and Qualitiques/Carol A. Berrigan. Photo by the Terry Wild Studio.

looms. Mrs. William Cameron Walls expressed the philosophy of the age of elegance when she advised her children "to demand the best always, in dresses, houses and friends."

W.C. Walls' admiration extended to his in-laws, Colonel and Mrs. Eli Slifer, who maintained an impressive country home, Delta Place (now the Slifer House Museum), overlooking the river. Slifer was head of the boatyard with William Frick, president of the Lewisburg-Tyrone Railroad, and president of the Company to Manufacture Buckeye Reapers and Mowers. Walls recalled the comfort of Delta Place with its richly laden dining table, its preening peacocks on the lawn, the flocks of guinea hens in the fields, and the stable of fine Kentucky thoroughbred horses.

The Buchers lived in the old General Abbott Green house at 43 Market Street. Elected in 1871 as president judge of the 20th Judicial District (now the 17th), Joseph Casper Bucher was a much-admired jurist who in private circles was known for his immense wit and good humor. His wife, Mary Ellen Walls, was the daughter of John Walls and the granddaughter of Green. Her brother, William Cameron Walls, described her in his memoirs as one of the most cultivated, intellectual, and gracious women in his life. She was, in Walls' memory, a noble woman and mother, ideals in the nineteenth century of every woman.

Across the street from the Buchers lived James Merrill Linn and his wife, Mary Ellen Billmeyer Linn, at 101 Market Street. An attorney and historian, the author of chapters on Union County in *The History of the Susquehanna and Juniata Valley*, James Merrill Linn was noted for his lively humor and mischievous proclivities. His wife was Mary Ellen, the daughter of Philip Billmeyer, official in the Boatyard Company, and she was credited with making the Linn household a combination of charm and liveliness. Walls' warmest memories were of James Merrill Linn's brother, John Blair Linn, author of *The Annals of Buffalo Valley*, who, according to Walls, was one of the funniest men alive. The latter, however, was only a visitor in Lewisburg, having made Bellefonte his home.

In the elegant tradition, also, were the Andrew Dills, who lived in the Victorian mansion at 129 Market Street (in the 1890s this house was the home of Frank Stoughton, whose daughter Jane married New York Giants' pitcher Christy Mathewson in 1903; he was among the first inductees into baseball's Hall of Fame and a member of baseball's "All-Century Team"). An attorney, Dill was a Southerner with the well-known charm of people of that region. Married to Catherine Slifer, daughter of Colonel and Mrs. Eli Slifer, Andrew Dill entered Lewisburg life with many advantages, but not enough to win him the governorship of Pennsylvania, which he sought in 1878. The Dills maintained a friendly, hospitable household.

In recalling Dill, Walls was reminded of Charles S. Wolfe, an attorney, who made an unsuccessful run for that office in 1886. As residents of the mansion that Wolfe had built in 1881, now an adjunct at the rear of Sovereign Bank (formerly Lewisburg Bank and Trust Company) on Market and South Third streets, Charles S. Wolfe and his wife, Martha Meixell Wolfe, led socially restrained lives, colored by the intensity of their political and moral principles. Both were ardent prohibitionists, the platform on which Wolfe ran for governor. Their household, like many others in Lewisburg, consisted of many servants and a governess for their children.

Across from the Wolfes and Johnson Walls at 29 South Third Street were the Elisha Shorkleys. Elisha was an official in the Marsh Foundry, and his wife, Sarah, was a daughter of Joseph and Mary Ann Moore Meixell and a sister of Mrs. Charles S. Wolfe. One feature of this comfortable, unostentatious home was the presence of a devoted servant, Eliza Cuthbert, an ex-slave, who had entered Lewisburg via the Underground Railroad.

The roster of distinguished families in Walls' memories was long. Philip Billmeyer, an official of the Boatyard Company, had a substantial mansion at 101 North Fourth Street, which was later owned and occupied by his daughter, Alice, and her husband, Henry Wolfe, also an official in the Boatyard Company. The family of William Duncan, an attorney, lived in Slifer's old house at 32 South Second Street, which was later occupied by Duncan's son, John, also an attorney, and his wife, Clara, and children, Stephen and Marguerite. William Cameron, who with his wife, Eleanor, and children, Elizabeth, Mary, Jane, and William, Jr., lived in the imposing mansion on the southwest corner of Market and South Second Streets. The family of George F. Miller, a member of the United States Congress during the Civil War, lived in the three-storied mansion at 43/45 South Second Street until he was inspired to build a "smaller" house across the street at 40. The sons of George F. Miller, both attorneys, lived in massive brick dwellings as well: George Barron Miller at 54 South Second Street and Daniel Bright Miller in the

One of the sons of Congressman George F. Miller, Daniel Bright Miller, was painted in 1848 when eight years old by itinerant portrait painter John Francis (American, b. 1808, d. 1886). Daniel Bright Miller later built his home at 82 University Avenue, which in the mid-twentieth century was converted by Bucknell University from a private home to the university's dining hall. Currently, it houses the university's development area and is called Cooley Hall. The oil on canvas painting of the young Miller boy, 36 inches x 29 inches, was purchased at Lois Kalp's sale by Bucknell University for its collection, #1981.6. Photo by Frank Hagenbuch, courtesy of the Bucknell Art Gallery.

Italianate villa at 82 University Avenue (Bucknell's Cooley Hall). The family of the Honorable Samuel D. Bates, a former state senator as well as a director and owner of numerous businesses including the Water Company and a plumbing company, lived in an austere brick house on North Fourth Street; one of his daughters, Bessie Bates Hoffman, lived in another house at the northwest corner of Second and Market until she died at age 105. George Matlack, an official of the Boatyard Company, lived with his wife, Emma Billmeyer Matlack, in the Victorian mansion opposite the Union County Courthouse at 106 South Second Street. The family of J. Thompson Baker, attorney and founder of Wildwood, New Jersey, lived in the sump-

tuously renovated Mt. Vernon Hotel at 44 Market Street; the family of Henry Eyer Spyker, owner of the Opera House, succeeded the Baker family in the Mt. Vernon house, adding a ballroom to the third floor. The family of the Honorable Harold McClure, elected president judge of the 20th Judicial District in 1891 and again in 1901, lived in the Beaver mansion (originally built by Professor George Bliss) at 63 University Avenue. James Marsh, owner of the foundry, built the ornate Italian villa at 60 South Second Street at the height of Victorian taste in the nineteenth century; the Marshes were succeeded there by the family of Benjamin K. Focht, editor of the *Lewisburg Saturday News* and a member of the United States Congress for ten terms. William Nogel, an official of the Boatyard Company, lived in a stone house along Buffalo Creek, while the family of Robert Lawshe, a merchant, resided in the Victorian frame house at 60 South Third Street. Other distinguished families including the Cyrus Hoffas and Joseph Shriners had handsome dwellings near their mills along Buffalo Creek in the country outside the borough.

Walls recalled with special pleasure the residents of the Presbyterian manse in 1901, Reverend and Mrs. Wellington Thomas; their son, Norman, later the candidate of the Socialist Party for President of the United States, loved to sit in the northwest window seat of the Himmelreich Library, reading by the hour. Both the Presbyterian manse at 14 Market Street and the William D. Himmelreich Library were good examples of an age of elegance and prosperity.

These families were certainly the most-discussed families in town, and their lifestyle was sometimes supported by the help of former slaves, some of whom had come north on the Underground Railroad. There were few parties, balls, teas, or receptions given in Lewisburg without the assistance of Henry and Mitchell Carter, the Reelers, Mrs. Taylor, and the Bells. In a picture of this period, a party at the Duncan home on South Third Street shows Mr. and Mrs. Reeler in the group of stylishly-dressed Lewisburg citizens.

The townspeople's interest in a better and more interesting way of life extended to their eager support of schools and educational matters. The University at Lewisburg (after 1886 called Bucknell University) was closely connected with all town activities; and the William D. Himmelreich Library was built and formally opened in 1902; at first it was just for the people of the Presbyterian Church, but it was opened to the townspeople in 1910. Citizens were also more devoted than they had been in the past to their news-

Lewisburg's streets. From *Pomeroy's Atlas of Union and Snyder Counties 1868*.

LEWISBURG

Scale 300 Feet to an Inch.

NORTH WARD

CREEK

BUFFALO

RIVER

The Armory of Company A, 12th Regiment, located at 221-237 South Third Street, Lewisburg, was the site for dancing classes, dinners, and balls. It is seen here c. 1905 as the subject of a real photo postcard. From the collection of the Union County Historical Society, #87.7.10.

BELOW: The imposing Lewisburg Opera House was often photographed both before and after a devastating fire razed it on December 27, 1908. From the collection of the Union County Historical Society, #87.7.1. *Peck's Bad Boy,* which appeared at the Opera House in 1900, was advertised by mailed cards such as this. From the collection of Gary W. and Donna M. Slear.

papers, which earlier in the nineteenth century had led a precarious existence. After numerous newspapers had come and gone, the *Lewisburg Chronicle,* started in 1843 and continuing until 1912, enjoyed a period of long popularity, equaled only by that of the *Lewisburg Saturday News* (briefly called the *Lewisburg Local News*), started in 1882 by Benjamin K. Focht. The newsreading public seemed to be divided in loyalty between the more restrained editor of the *Chronicle,* John Cornelius (later Lewis K. Derr), and the *Saturday News'* daring editor, Benjamin K. Focht, who was destined to have a long successful career in politics.

The people's interest in changing the tone of their lives was expressed in their enthusiasm for the Music Hall, built by H.G. Swartz in 1869, and for its rejuvenated life as the Opera House, renovated in 1900 by Henry Eyer Spyker. The center of the town's social, cultural, and entertainment life, the Opera House saw hundreds of talented actors, singers, and opera companies tread its commodious stage, including the famous Joseph Jefferson, noted for his portrayal of Bob Acres in "The Rivals," which he played in Lewisburg. The gutting of the Opera House by fire on December 27, 1908, was a tragedy for the entire community as well as for Mr. Spyker, whose financial loss was considerable.

Also popular with the socially-minded public was the Armory, located on what is now the lawn of the Zeller residence at 227 South Third Street, where the town's Assembly Balls were held with formally gowned and dressed couples dancing under Japanese lanterns. The tone of this polite form of entertainment was discreetly underplayed and very proper, for it took place in the day of quiet elegance, formal calls, calling cards, dance programs, and social protocol — a day doomed to banishment after World War I.

This glance back at the elegant railroad era in Lewisburg reveals the trend and spirit of the times. However, it does not include significant events like the 1878 burning of the Woolen Mills (later restored) and the Marsh Foundry (not replaced); the centennial celebration of Lewisburg's founding in 1885; or the horrendous floods of 1865 and 1889, the latter serving for years as the flood by which all floods were measured until the floods of 1936 and 1972 destroyed that record. It should include, however, a summation of events that changed and affected life in Lewisburg in a less dramatic way: the starting of the Buffalo Valley Telephone Company, with John P. Ruhl as Manager, in 1904; the building of the Free Bridge between 1906 and 1907; and sale of Eli Slifer's "Delta Place" by

TOP: The Pennsylvania Railroad station in Lewisburg as it appeared in 1905. The station was built on St. John Street between North Second and Third Streets in 1869 for what was then called the Lewisburg, Centre and Spruce Creek Railroad (later called the Lewisburg and Tyrone Railroad). A Pennsy Class H3 is facing east. From the collection of the Union County Historical Society, #92.9.90.25.

The post office staff and Lewisburg mail carriers posed in 1913 alongside their cars. From left to right are: Merrill Royer, rural carrier; Gregg Johnson, George Housel, Charlie Walters, and Gene Kerstetter, carriers; Mitchell Carter, janitor; Samuel Dunkle, Charlie Dunkle, Fred Slack, and Bess Brown, clerks; Fred Kuntz, postmaster; Jesse Higgins, clerk; Harry St_____, assistant postmaster; and Elmer Gramley, Clyde Gundy and _____Bastian, rural carriers. From the collection of the Union County Historical Society, #89.5.21.3.

Dr. Lamont Ross in 1915 to the Home Society of the Evangelical Church for use as an old folks home (leading to the eventual creation of the Lewisburg Evangelical Hospital in 1953). These events were important to the town's well-being.

The end of the railroad era in Lewisburg was heralded by the toot of the first "flivver" to rattle down Market Street, a toot that occurred in the early 1900s but which did not impact the life or the economy of the town until the 1920s. Although the railroads, like the great houses and families of the town, continued to serve actively up to 1950, they were beginning to show signs of decline, especially after World War II. The great houses like the George F. Miller home at 43 South Second Street were proving to be too big and expensive to maintain and were gradually being converted into apartment houses. The West Ward School on North Eighth Street was

converted from its former educational use into the Colonial Apartments by Clarence Auten and Charles Dunkle. The families who had dominated the romantic railroad period were fading into history, their ranks either depleted or their descendants attracted to other parts of the country or the world. New community leaders would come to the fore, many not born in the area but attracted by Bucknell University and new or growing businesses such as the Federal Penitentiary, General Interiors, International Paper Company, or Playworld.

To give a name to the period from 1920-1950 is difficult, including as it did the post-World War I recovery period, the Great Depression, and World War II. The period was characterized by a subservience of people to the automobile more than to any other technological invention. Suddenly, perhaps as the result of World War I, society became geared to it. This was as true in Lewisburg as elsewhere. In the

1920s the Watsontown-Lewisburg Trolley was, for example, one of the first casualties of the new age, and the little bus system that replaced it in the 1930s suffered the same fate.

The period of the 1920s was not as frenzied as it was in other sections of the country. The town was struggling to catch up to modern times, and there was much progress. The streets were paved; three-globe street lights were installed in 1916; the Lewisburg High School was built between 1927 and 1929; and the federal judge of the district, Albert W. Johnson, who was vitally interested in the town's growth, developed the Johnson Addition on the south side of West Market Street in Linntown. The Evangelical Home and Hospital added a new unit to its facilities; and to keep up with the relatively new Lewisburg Trust and Safe Deposit Company and its building constructed in 1915, the Union National Bank underwent renovation, and the Lewisburg National Bank built a handsome new building in 1927, moving from its old offices opposite the Cameron House. Dietrich and Gambrill bought Hoffa's Buffalo Mills in 1928; but even as life seemed brighter and progress seemed real, the New York Stock Market crashed in October 1929.

The dull period of the 1930s proved to be a challenge for Lewisburgers, who were trying to keep their sights high and their chins up. However, there were events that mitigated the pain of the Great Depression: the building of the Northeastern Federal Penitentiary near Lewisburg in 1932; and the construction of the Federal Courthouse and Post Office in 1934, when Albert W. Johnson, formerly judge of Snyder and Union Counties (1911-1921), ascended the bench. Likewise important for the economy were the re-opening of the Lewisburg Chair Company with Robert N. Parker as president in 1933; and the building of the Church of the Nazarene and the Roman Catholic Sacred Heart Chapel in 1934 and 1935. All of these events brought new people into town with new ideas — newcomers who were entranced by the peace and quiet of a rural community that seemed to have few law enforcement problems, a fact appreciated by the sitting judge of Snyder and Union Counties, the Honorable Curtis Lesher. It was so peaceful and so quiet that the newcomers began to make demands for more outlets for their energies, more ways to entertain themselves.

Without theatrical activity since the destruction of the Opera House in 1908, young people in the town had for some time tried to fill in the gap created by that disaster. In the 1920s Abbott Bucher, Katherine Wainwright, and Ruth Gundy successfully produced musicals in the Orpheum Motion Picture Theater (on the east side of North Third Street at Cherry Alley) and in the new high school. In the 1930s the Civic Club tried to bring entertainment to the town with the introduction of its "Flower Marts" with parades, booths of novelties, luncheons, and bridge parties; and in 1937 Reverend Edward L. Junkin, Mrs. Miller Johnson, and Mrs. Charles W. Kalp organized the Community Theater Guild with the help of the Junior Civic Club. In 1939 Edith Kelly Fetherston, Robert Pawling, and Professor Warren Garman conceived and organized the Central Pennsylvania Artists' Association.

Altogether, Lewisburg in the 1930s was not as dismal as other towns. Its shops, all on Market Street, were memorable. Manned by friendly merchants who would take time to talk to people, the shops were popular meeting places: Smith's Drug Store; Birchard's Candy Store; Bechtel's Ice Cream and Dairy Store; and Schlow's Quality Shop, where one could buy an evening dress for ten dollars. In both Herman and Leiser's Drygoods Store and Groover's Drygoods Store, the shelves were filled with bolts of cloth and spools and spools of thread. Popular spots were Ed Noll's Feed Store; Wainwright's Pool Hall, where there was always an assemblage of loafers on the front steps; Elmer Wagner's Grocery Store; Flavio's Fruit Store; and the dime-store where items were really a dime. There was Clint Aurand's and Mr. Ward's Barber Shop with Mr. Aurand expressing his dry humor, and Donehower's Sporting Goods Store with Mr. William Donehower expounding politics. Other Market Street businesses were C. Dreisbach's Sons Wholesale and Retail Hardware, Max Harris Clothing, and Joseph Wolfe's University Book Store. Providing more amenities were the Grenoble, Nogle, and Zeller jewelry stores; Martin's Flower Shop, where George Bender dispensed information about flowers and New York shows; and Margaret Gundy's Hat Shop, where the age of elegance still prevailed. Less genteel was the old Orpheum Theater, where it was hazardous to sit directly under the balcony; even so, the townspeople went there to watch the favorites of the day, stars such as Tom Mix, Greta Garbo, Norma Shearer, and Mary Pickford.

There was an air of peace and contentment in the air of Lewisburg during this very depressed and disturbed time, thanks largely to the durable character of the natives. The clergy, the bar association, and the schools were working overtime; and Congressman Benjamin K. Focht, "the father of old age pensions," working diligently in Washington, D. C., exceeded his own strength, and he died on March 27, 1937.

Ruth Gundy Watson ran an elegant millinery shop at 412 Market Street, Lewisburg; some of her hats are owned by the Union County Historical Society. From the collection of the Union County Historical Society, #89.5.1.39.

BELOW: Lewisburg photographer Donald Ross photographed the W.W. Watkins Building at the northwest corner of Third and Market Streets in 1942. It once housed the J.J. Newberry Company; presently Rea and Derick Drugs occupies it. From the collection of the Union County Historical Society, #89.5.15.34.

The most disastrous event of the 1930s was the flood in March of 1936, which washed into town with greater force than had been known in any previous flood. For days Lewisburgers wandered around the town, staring in disbelief at the debris and destruction. The flood gave a warning not heeded, for 1972 would have an even greater flood, followed by a good-sized one three years later, in 1975. Other disasters of the 1930s were the fires that destroyed Old Main on the Bucknell campus, the Sunday school rooms of the Baptist Church, the Dreisbach Hardware Building at the northeast corner of Fourth and Market streets, and the J.J. Newberry Building on the northwest corner of Third and Market streets.

During the Great Depression a greater public consciousness developed of the social needs of people, especially of young people. An increase in juvenile delinquency prompted civic-minded people to take action, as did the courts, suddenly bereft of the services of the Honorable Curtis Lesher who died in 1941. Briefly under the judicial offices of the Honorable Cloyd Steininger, who had been appointed to take Judge Lesher's place, the court had as its permanent judge during the 1940s the Honorable Francis Gilbert of Middleburg, Snyder County. He dispensed justice fairly but firmly.

In 1941, as the result of public pressure, the borough council appointed a community projects director, Oscar Smeal; it also established the Lewisburg Activities Council with Reverend Perry L. Smith as chairman, a council that with the help and sponsorship of the Civic Club made possible the opening of a community house in 1944. Even the smashing attack of the Japanese on Pearl Harbor, December 7, 1941, did not deter the people of Lewisburg from continuing their civic projects and responsibilities. With their customary self-control, they assumed war duties with civic duties, "carrying on" in the spirit of the favorite slogan of the day. In 1944 the American Association of University Women campaigned for the employment by the county of a child welfare worker and for the improvement of the schools.

Newcomers to the community were unhappy with the mid-nineteenth-century buildings that housed the schools and particularly with the one-room schools in the rural districts which were rapidly becoming suburbs. It was not surprising that the leaders of the effort to build a new school in Linntown were the first persons to build a house in College Park, Professor and Mrs. Philip Harriman. In 1946 the East Buffalo School in Linntown became the first consolidated school in the Lewisburg district with Professor Harry

Bourne as principal. Following this move, Lewisburg began to make plans for the replacement of its old 1861 South Ward School with a modern structure. The movement to improve and merge schools had begun.

In keeping with the upsurge of interest in progress, Jay P. Mathias with his brothers, Earl and Roy, and mother, Margaret, started the JPM Company in 1949, an industry geared to serving the television business. Activity, whether educational or industrial, stemmed from the technological age, and all depended upon the automobile as the mode of transportation.

If it is difficult to give a title to the period of 1920 to 1950, the labeling of the period of 1950 to 1975 is even more so, for it included the Korean and Vietnam Wars; some of the most intricate national and international political maneuvers in the nation's history; the assassination of one President of the United States and the unseating of another; and the civil rights movement, which resulted in more equal treatment of all citizens. There are inherent in the age, which for practical reasons shall be called "the nuclear-space age," elements that destined it to be frenetic, spasmodic, and nerve-racking, propelling people into the feverish action of building more roads, more bridges, more schools, more buildings, and more factories. This period saw the displacement of elegance, manners, morals, and discipline with informality and lack of discipline, made acceptable by the anonymity which the automobile and airplane afforded people. With swiftly moving people, there were rapidly moving events that catapulted individuals into notoriety or fame, for a week or a month, then tossed them back into limbo. The emergence of a permanent hero was becoming an impossibility. The homogenizing of the elements of society, caused by the tempo of the nuclear-space age, made more difficult the existence of strong, individualistic characters. The mad tempo and the feverish activity of this time produced a restlessness among both old and young that was reflected in the increased caseloads of the courts and concern among the presiding judges of the period: the Honorable William L. Showers (1951-1961), the Honorable Paul Showalter (1961-1962), and the Honorable Charles W. Kalp (1962-1973), both of the latter two judges dying while in office.

Beginning with the list of the town's achievements in 1950, one must take a deep breath in order to read to the end without gasping. In 1950 the school jointures, which required massive projects of school construction, started their long journeys to completion; and the Friends of the Himmelreich Library began a campaign for funds to build a children's room in the library. In 1951 the East Buffalo Consolidated School prepared for a building expansion with Professor Harry U. Heckart as principal. In 1952 JPM opened a new building between Sixth and Seventh Streets on St. Mary's, and Charles R. Smith sold the *Lewisburg News Journal* to Ivan Boxell of Danville.

The new Lewisburg Evangelical Community Hospital neared completion and opened in 1953. Also in that year, William Hastings of Milton purchased the *Lewisburg News Journal*, merging it with the *Union County Standard* to become the *Union County Journal*, which continued for nearly 40 years; the Lewisburg High School planned an expansion of its buildings; the Buffalo Valley Telephone Company adopted the seven-digit dial system to accommodate the great increase of subscribers; while a bequest from Daniel Green, late president of the Lewisburg Trust and Safe Deposit Company, provided funds for the construction of a recreation field, as well as improvements to the Lewisburg Club and the Lewisburg Evangelical Community Hospital. In 1955 the Beaver Memorial Church renovated and modernized its Victorian sanctuary, once so admired in 1890; and in 1956 Richard DuWors and Wendell Smith of Bucknell University started the Susquehanna Economic Development Association for the encouragement of new industries in the area. Christ Lutheran Church opened its education building in 1958 and the Beaver Memorial Church planned for a new education building made possible by a generous bequest from the estate of Robert N. Parker, late president of the Lewisburg Chair and Furniture Company. In 1959 the Wolfe Athletic Field was opened, the gift of General Samuel Wolfe; Newberry's Store was gutted by fire, necessitating the construction of a new building; and the Chair Company expanded by acquiring the Woolen Mills from Benson McDowell.

In 1960 JPM built a large new factory on Route 15 (in 1996 the company would go public on the New York Stock Exchange, and by 1999 it would have operations in six foreign countries). St. John's United Church of Christ (formerly the Reformed Church) dedicated its renovated church in 1961 and a new Quaker Manufacturing Plant was planned for construction in the Mary Brown Industrial Park. In 1962 the Keystone Shortway (later named Interstate 80) was under construction, and the First Baptist Church thoroughly renovated its sanctuary. In 1964 the Colonial Printing Company bought the Royal Imprint Company at the northwest corner of North Third and St. John Streets; in 1965 the new junior high

ABOVE AND BOTTOM OF PAGE 132: Pennsylvania House catalog and photo of chair production from the 1950s. From the collection of Pennsylvania House.

The furnituremaking tradition in Lewisburg includes an advertising photograph and ruler for W.B. Bartholomew, furniture dealer and undertaker at 206 Market Street, Lewisburg. Bartholomew was selling the oak bedroom suite pictured here for $19.50. From the collection of the Union County Historical Society, #97.4.3, and Gary M. and Donna W. Slear. Photo by the Terry Wild Studio.

PENNSYLVANIA HOUSE

An early traditional furnituremaker was David Ginter.
A matching set of six chairs and rocker were stamped
GINTER/LEWISBURG for this chairmaker, who was active
in Lewisburg c. 1831-1873. From the collection of Roger
and Arletta Zimmerman. Photo by the Terry Wild Studio,
courtesy of the Oral Traditions Project.

school was dedicated; and the new William Cameron Engine Company, designed by architect Malcolm Clinger, was built in 1966. In 1968, the borough, having recently acquired the old John Walls house for a borough building, began to plan for a parking lot at its rear; in the name of progress, the Weidensaul buildings (the site of the First Baptist Church and Opera House) on the southwest corner of Pine Alley and South Third Street as well as the 1877 William Cameron Fire Engine House on the southeast corner of Pine Alley and South Fourth Street were razed. This municipal parking lot was completed in 1969.

In the 1960s a group of Quakers began to meet at Bucknell, and a Unitarian Fellowship was formed by three families from Union and Snyder Counties. After two years of meeting together as a growing group, the Joseph Priestly Unitarian Universalist Fellowship was officially accepted by the Unitarian Universalist Association. It has varied in size as its members have come and gone, serving between 25 and 35 members over four decades, meeting regularly on Sundays, mostly in members' homes. Another recent religious body to organize formally was St. Andrews Episcopalian Church, and the members situated their building at Route 15 and Curtin Avenue, south of Route 45. In 1969 the United Methodist Church's Riverview Manor received its first occupants in assisted living, and ground was broken for a nursing home — the beginning of an ambitious expansion of these facilities (now called RiverWoods) under the direction of David Reed. Reed became the first layman of his church to serve as administrator.

In 1972 this commendable flow of activity was interrupted abruptly by the worst flood in the town's history. Following Hurricane Agnes in June 1972, the flood caused massive damage and the deaths of three persons: Police Chief Gordon Hufnagle, Mrs. Joseph Murphy, and Mrs. William Minium. Stricken, the members of the Lewisburg Borough Council decided, since the town had suffered from a century and a half of floods, to apply themselves immediately to the problem of how to prevent a recurrence of the 1972 disaster. Uppermost in their minds was the necessity of passing a Flood Plain Ordinance to control building in low-lying areas and to redevelop the sections of the town that had experienced the worst damage.

The Union County Courthouse Authority had been established in 1970, with Professor Earl Thomas of Mifflinburg as chairman, with the express purpose of adding a section to the old courthouse and renovating the latter. In May 1973, with the town still recovering from the flood, the renovated Union County Court-

house was dedicated with impressive ceremony, including introductory remarks by John F. Zeller III and addresses by the Honorable Benjamin R. Jones, Chief Justice of the Supreme Court; Lewis Van Dusen, president-elect of the Pennsylvania Bar Association; and Raymond Lobos, president of the Union County Bar Association. Tribute was paid to the court's stricken judge, the Honorable Charles W. Kalp, whose death followed thereafter on August 4, 1973.

By 1974 the Flood Plain Ordinance and the redevelopment of the town were receiving the full attention of the town's mayor, John Baker, and the borough Council with Lewis Hendricks, Jr., as president; Mrs. Jennie S. Erdley, vice-president; and members Raymond Minium, Sr., John M. Book, Thomas Groninger, Walter J. Bechtel, Russell E. Richard, Jr., and Harold E. Sones. Also active was the Lewisburg Planning Commission, a member of which, Evelyn Kim, became an authority on this issue. Problems were being compounded by the decline of the town's business section as the result of the growth of large shopping plazas being built on Route 15. All suggestions on how to restore the business section were considered, such as be creation of a shopping mall on Market Street and the construction of an apartment house for senior citizens, but the problem's solution was elusive.

The sudden interest in the welfare of the elderly, encouraged by both state and federal governments, was showing results in Lewisburg with lunches being served at the Union County Courthouse for senior citizens and Meals on Wheels being delivered to those persons who were unable to leave their homes. The purchase of the Buffalo Valley Lutheran Village by the Tressler-Lutheran Service Association in 1975 not only maintained an already excellent nursing home service but also established another church-oriented institution in the area with plans to build an apartment compound similar to that being constructed by the United Methodist services. When the Bicentennial Commission for the celebration of the United States' 200th birthday was appointed, its local members found themselves overwhelmed by the quantity of material on the town's achievements. There was every reason to be proud of Lewisburg.

In summarizing the significant events of Lewisburg in this fast-moving "nuclear-space age" (1950-1975), one must look at some of the less spectacular events of the time to sense that in the hearts of many people was growing the feeling that there was a need to slow down. Although building and economic growth was admirable, its rate was recognizably something that could go out of control. As a result, movements were

started everywhere to encourage control of technology; conservation of land, air, and water; and preservation of the nation's landmarks and heritage.

In Lewisburg, for example, the destruction of historic landmarks like the Reading Railroad's Passenger Depot, the Congregational Christian Church, the old fire engine house, and numerous structures along Route 15 for the widening of that thoroughfare, reminded people that in the haste of modern development, something precious was being sacrificed. As the result of this feeling there came into being the movement for historic preservation, initiated in the 1960s by John B. Deans. When in 1963 Deans and his son, Thomas, organized and produced an entertaining and educational Sesquicentennial Celebration of the founding in 1813 of Union County, public enthusiasm was great. Under John Dean's direction, a group of citizens organized the Union County Historical Society (its third organization), and proceeded to save from destruction both the Ray's Church near Hartleton and the first Union County Courthouse in New Berlin. Some of the society's founding members like Jeanne Sampsell and George A. Ruhl continued their work for three decades.

Also saved was Delta Place, the home of Eli Slifer. It had been purchased in 1916 by the Evangelical Church to establish a home for old people. By the 1970s it had outlived its usefulness and was scheduled for demolition. Through the efforts of the home's administrator, David Reed; his wife, Doris; and a group of Lewisburg citizens named "The History Committee," the house was placed on the National Register of Historic Places and thus saved from the wrecking ball. It now stands proudly as the Slifer House Museum, with its mission to interpret Victorian life. In the rush of modern times, the less hurried past seemed more attractive. When Edith Kelly Fetherston died in 1972, leaving her home, Packwood House, as a privately endowed museum, Lewisburg was afforded another important opportunity to preserve its heritage and contemplate its values.

ABOVE: Real photo postcard of the William Cameron Engine Company's Stanley Steamer. The steamer was last used in fighting the fire at Bucknell's Old Main on August 27, 1932. Regularly shown in Lewisburg parades, it is now on display in a building renovated by the fire company in 1999 on the occasion of its 150th anniversary. The original firehall in the background was razed in the late 1960s, as seen at left. The South Fourth Street site became part of the first municipal parking lot. From the collection of the Union County Historical Society, #92.9.91.136 and #89.5.16.4.

THE UNIVERSITY OF LEWISBURGH.

CHAPTER 8

BUCKNELL UNIVERSITY

Like the history of Lewisburg, the history of Bucknell University consists of the people and events that shaped it. The people who founded Bucknell were especially inspired individuals, and the course of Bucknell's existence has always reflected their hopes and ideals. Its career started on a cold night in December 1843, when a small group of people assembled in the abandoned Presbyterian log schoolhouse on Market Street, Lewisburg, to listen to evangelist Reverend William Grant, a Baptist minister from New York. They had two purposes in mind: organizing a Baptist church and establishing a Baptist university, an incredibly ambitious project even then. Neither the Northumberland Baptist Association nor the Philadelphia Baptist Association considered the plan feasible, practical, or desirable in view of the rural area in which the proposed institution would be located.

The small number of Baptists in the community were of another opinion. In Lewisburg itself there were not many of that faith: Catherine Lawshe Wolfe, whose husband, Samuel, was a successful grain shipper with a wharf on South Water Street; and Rebecca VanDyke Moore Ludwig, whose father, James Moore II, was a prominent bridge-builder, and whose husband, Dr. William Ludwig, was a physician in Lewisburg. Near Lewisburg there were James Moore II and his wife, Mary Ott Clark Moore, as well as their son, James Moore III, who, with his wife, Mary Ann Ludwig Moore, lived at Brook Park; Joseph Meixell, a farmer, and his wife, Mary Ann Moore Meixell, lived near Lewisburg at Housel's Run on the Northumberland side of the Susquehanna; and Reverend Anson Hewitt, pastor of the Milton Baptist Church, and his wife, Martha Wilkinson Moore Hewitt, lived in the area also. Since James Moore II and his son and son-in-law were the originators of the idea to found both a church and university, the entire project was distinctly a family affair.

What was especially interesting about the founders, aside from their family relationships, was their apparent lack of credentials for undertaking such an enterprise. Wolfe, drawn into the activity by his wife, who was the descendent of Palatinate Germans who had entered the country in 1720, was a Lutheran by persuasion. Catherine Lawshe Wolfe was the granddaughter of Colonel William Chamberlin, the first Baptist to enter Buffalo Valley in 1794, a soldier by profession and a miller by trade. Although

of English origin, James Moore II, because of unusual circumstances that separated his parents during the American Revolution, had received his upbringing from the German carpenter to whom he had been apprenticed, an influence that was reflected in Moore's manner of speech and writing to the end of his life. Of the group, only Dr. Ludwig had received the kind of training that would inspire dreams of higher education. So improbable as founders of a church and university did the group seem that for years they were referred to by town and university historians as "a little band of poor Baptists." They deserved better treatment, for it was their effort and money that produced both the Baptist Church and Bucknell University.

In January 1844 the Northumberland Baptist Association formally recognized the First Baptist Church of Lewisburg; and by September of 1845 a church building was being erected on the site of what is now the Lewisburg municipal parking lot on South Third Street, its basement ready for Sunday school and church services. Impatient, however, to complete their objectives with the establishment of a university, Wolfe, both Moores, Ludwig, and Meixell conferred at length with a member of the Northumberland Baptist Association, Reverend Eugenio Kincaid, one of America's first missionaries to Burma. The doctor, merchants, and construction engineers were intelligent enough to realize that they would need professional guidance to undertake an educational project with the great scope that they had envisioned.

A graduate of the Hamilton Literary and Theological Institute of Hamilton, New York, Kincaid remembered a college classmate and friend, Professor Stephen Taylor, who had recently resigned from the faculty of Madison University (now Colgate University) in Hamilton and was without a position. Describing Professor Taylor to the others, Kincaid was glowing in his recommendation of Taylor, urging that he be invited to visit Lewisburg with the idea of acquiring his services to organize the new university. Impressed by Kincaid's enthusiasm, the five men agreed to finance Kincaid's trip to New York and his return with Taylor — a journey that was accomplished by stagecoach and canal boat. The wait in Lewisburg must have been tense, prolonged as it was by a lack of any easy means of communication. The arrival of Taylor and Kincaid in Lewisburg was greeted with relief by the founders, who established their lone professor in modest quarters in the Kline Hotel (now the Lewisburg Hotel) on Market Street.

Professor Taylor lost no time in starting his work, beginning at once to write a charter for the new university, which was accepted by the state legislature and signed by Governor Francis Shunk on February 5, 1846. Providing for the establishment of a board of curators and a board of trustees — the former to consist of members other than Baptists and the latter to consist only of Baptists — the charter also stipulated that the university could not be started until $100,000 had been subscribed to the venture. With a generous sprinkling of Philadelphians and Chester Countians in their ranks, both curators and trustees began their heavy duties with zeal. In order of their appearance in the charter, the trustees were: James Moore II, James Moore III, Joseph Meixell, Dr. William Ludwig (the first chairman of the board), Samuel Wolfe, Henry Funk, Benjamin Bear, William Kean, William Bucknell, Thomas Wattson, James McMullin Linnard, Lewis Vastine, Oliver Blackburn, Caleb Lee, and Daniel Moore.

Among the curators were some very prominent figures: General Abbott Green, one of the builders of the Eastern Division of the Pennsylvania Canal; the Honorable Simon Cameron, brother of Lewisburg banker William Cameron and a future secretary of war in President Abraham Lincoln's first cabinet; George F. Miller, a Lewisburg attorney and later a congressman during the Civil War; and James Buchanan, eventually president of the United States. William Bucknell, for whom the university was to be named in 1886, was not prominent in its early history when it was known as the University at Lewisburg; for as a Philadelphia Baptist, he was convinced that distant Lewisburg was not a good location for a university, and his best efforts were spent in trying to move the institution to Philadelphia.

The selection of a site for the university fell to the younger Moore, Ludwig, and Wolfe, who chose a section of the John Brown farm, including a hill overlooking the Susquehanna, for the school's location. In the meantime, the Academy (high school) of the University at Lewisburg opened in the basement of the First Baptist Church on October 6, 1846, while the church was still under construction, with workmen busily placing the wooden belfry on the roof. By 1848 the students of the academy were able to move their school equipment from the Baptist Church to the new Academy Building on the hill.

By 1849 Professor Taylor could report that the University at Lewisburg had its charter, a farm of 70 acres in the borough of Lewisburg, and the Academy Building, the Primary Department, and the English Department. The Classical Department and a library had been started, and the foundation of the west wing of the main administration building had been laid out by architect Thomas U. Walter (who was to help design the dome of the United States Capitol and its wings), employed to complete the work. Two financial agents had been secured to raise money for the university: Reverend William Shadrach and Reverend J.V. Allison. By 1850 the teaching staff numbered five members. The university was in the promising early stages of its career even though time was taking a toll of its loyal founders and supporters: Ludwig died in 1848, Wolfe in 1850, and Green in 1851, the year in which the University at Lewisburg held its first commencement.

Moving slowly from the Academy Building (later Taylor Hall) to the First Baptist Church on South Third Street, the procession of academic persons, friends, relatives, and graduates entered the little church for the baccalaureate service; they returned again to the Academy Building for the August 1851 commencement program, which honored not only the graduates but the retiring Professor Taylor and a new president, Dr. Howard Malcom. The main address of the occasion was delivered by James Buchanan, future president of the United States. The University at Lewisburg was preparing to start a new phase of its career.

The first president of the University at Lewisburg (Professor Taylor never received the title), Dr. Malcom was a man of extensive intellectual gifts and talents. A Welsh Quaker and a graduate of Dickinson College at Carlisle, Pennsylvania, Dr. Malcom enjoyed many interests. Trained in medicine and widely traveled, he was musical and held a firm belief in the abolition of slavery. He brought a new dimension of learning to the University at Lewisburg, a humanitarianism that evidenced itself in his interest in people and their needs. He was responsible for the development of the University Extension of Lewisburg, consisting of the construction of faculty homes on University Avenue; he also oversaw the establishment of the Female Institute (1852), the Department of Theology (1854-1855), as well as the Collegiate, Academic, and

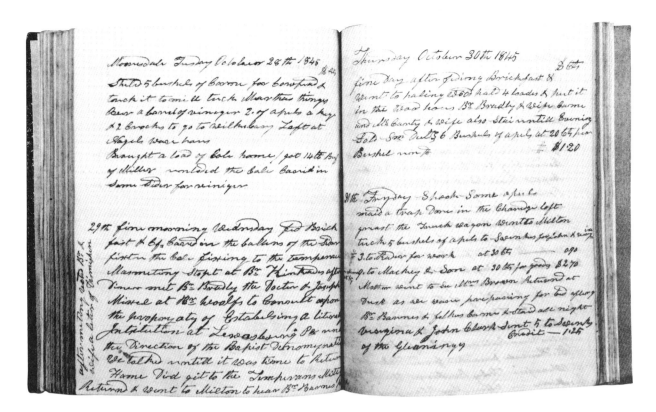

Seminarial Departments. During Malcolm's administration, the Female Institute moved from South Second Street to the lower campus in 1856. At the same time there was contention among the trustees over the attempt in July 1856 by John Price Crozer, abetted by William Bucknell, to move the university to Chester, Pennsylvania, a move that was thwarted by the combined efforts of the Lewisburg members of the board of trustees led by James Moore III.

In 1857, with Union County in the throes of an economic crisis and the university floundering in debt and dissension, Dr. Malcom tendered his resignation and was succeeded in 1858 by Professor Justin Loomis, a giant of a man and character, who was to guide the university through days of financial crisis and the Civil War. A graduate of Brown University (1835), Dr. Loomis was a dedicated Baptist and a scholar of distinction. He was a man with no-nonsense ideas (he disliked fraternities and sports, both of which he banned) about the quality of education that he wanted to encourage in all departments of the University at Lewisburg — ideas which seemed to conflict with those of two of the most influential and wealthy trustees: Crozer of Chester, Pennsylvania and Bucknell of Philadelphia, who resigned from the board of trustees in 1863. In the midst of the Civil War, the university could ill afford a break in its

TOP: James Moore III, who first proposed founding a Baptist college in Lewisburg, wrote a manuscript account of the founding of the school which became Bucknell University. Courtesy of Bucknell University Archives.

BOTTOM: Bucknell faculty members were photographed by William M. Ginter of Lewisburg in 1874. Seated are: Professor G.R. Bliss and President Justin R. Loomis; standing left to right are: Professors F.W. Tustin, Robert Lowry, and C.S. James. Courtesy of Bucknell University Archives.

Old Main as it appeared on President Malcolm's letterhead c.1851-1858. Courtesy of Bucknell University Archives.

Katherine Larison, first dean of women students and former principal of the Female Institute, c. 1872. Courtesy of Bucknell University Archives.

PAGE 141: William Bucknell, cast bronze sculpture, 16-1/4 inches high and 10-1/4 inches wide, by artist and Bucknell professor William Lasansky (1938-) is located in Bucknell Hall. Commissioned by Bucknell University and part of the permanent collection, #1988.9. Photo by Frank Hagenbuch, courtesy of the Bucknell Art Gallery.

administrative or official ranks, and its survival can be attributed to Dr. Loomis' indomitable courage and faith. With resignation the university accepted the removal in 1868 of the Department of Theology to Upland, Pennsylvania, where it became a part of Crozer Theological Seminary. Only Dr. Loomis' refusal to admit failure kept the university going during the difficult Civil War and post-war years. His great strength of character and heart, however, could not save him in 1878 when, beset by financial reverses and an academic scandal involving his dismissal of a popular professor, Charles Sexton James, he left the presidency in defeat and retired to his Victorian gothic house on South Third Street.

Dr. Loomis' successor in 1879 was David Jayne Hill, a graduate of the University at Lewisburg, Class of 1874, and a man of great personal charm and intellectual ability. He was also a diplomat, a talent that he was to use later in life as minister to the Netherlands and as ambassador to Germany. His first task as president of the University at Lewisburg was to woo back the offended trustees, Bucknell and Crozer, to the university's family. Crozer had shown signs of relenting in 1866 with his endowment of a Chair of Belles Lettres, but Bucknell was still intransigent. That Hill succeeded in winning over the irascible Bucknell was a tribute to Hill's charm and his appreciation of the financier's sensitivities. This effort was rewarded in 1881 by Bucknell's offer to give the university $50,000 if the trustees would raise the same amount and if the university would revise its charter and re-organize its

administration to abolish the board of curators and to permit the board of trustees to consist of four-fifths Baptists and one-fifth other denominations. When the latter was accomplished in 1882, Bucknell was in full control of the board of trustees and the University at Lewisburg was on its way to being non-denominational. This was also the year that James Moore III, returning to Lewisburg after a long sojourn in Missouri, died.

During this period of rejuvenation and reorganization, President Hill strengthened the Female Institute which was prospering under Katherine Larison's direction. He hired the first woman instructor at the University in 1885, Edith Hedges, who proved to be an inspiration to her students; that same year the first woman, Chella Scott, graduated from the university. With women now enrolled in and graduating from the university, the days of the Female Institute were numbered. Pursuing his liberal course of action, Dr. Hill restored fraternities and sports to the campus, encouraging both football and baseball; and he aided the development of drama courses and a dramatic society under the directorship of Edith Hedges. As a rhetorician, he emphasized "belles lettres"; and, with the financial help of William Bucknell, he oversaw the construction of

Bucknell Hall (a chapel), the annex to Taylor Hall, Bucknell Cottage, the astronomical observatory, and the chemistry laboratory. His resignation in 1888 was a blow to the university, now formally called Bucknell University — so named in 1886 in honor of the university's chief benefactor, William Bucknell.

President Hill's successor was also a graduate of the University at Lewisburg, Class of 1869, Dr. John Howard Harris of the Keystone Academy (which he had founded) in Factoryville, Pennsylvania. His character combined the qualities of his predecessors, Loomis and Hill. Like Loomis he was an autocrat and a man of great determination, even stubbornness of character; and like Hill he could be a man of charm and persuasiveness. On the subjects of strict moral standards and religion, Dr. Harris was unshakable in his belief that both were fundamental to education. His whole administration was permeated with this spirit, and every change in the educational program and curricula reflected Dr. Harris' principles.

During his administration (1889-1919), Dr. Harris encouraged the development of the university to the exclusion of the Female Institute and the academy, which were discontinued in 1916 and 1917, respectively; and with great care he guided the university

through the trying years of World War I, 1914-1918. Two new dormitories for men (now Kress Hall and Trax Hall), the Carnegie Library, a physical laboratory, a heating and lighting plant, and a foundry were constructed. After a long and fruitful service, Dr. Harris retired in 1919; and long after his departure from Lewisburg for Scranton, Pennsylvania, where he died in 1925, his words and deeds were remembered.

The man who in 1919 succeeded Dr. Harris in the increasingly burdensome position of president of Bucknell University was Dr. Emory Hunt, former president of Denison University in Ohio. Able, gentlemanly, learned, and religious without being pious, Dr. Hunt began his administration in a period almost as revolutionary as the 1960s — both eras of social change and unrest. Public pressures to modernize the college curricula, combined with a change in moral attitudes and behavior of the students, created real problems for Dr. Hunt and his faculty. A new day in education and social theory had dawned. The emphasis began to be placed on teaching subjects that were in demand rather than on the traditional classical courses which were not considered to be relevant to modern life. Even the earlier-held ideals of a classical education would eventually be abandoned.

It was during Dr. Hunt's administration that athletics — notably football — were emphasized, resulting in the construction of the Memorial Stadium; and it was during his administration, with the modernizing of the curriculum, that the engineering building (one wing) and the botany building were constructed. The Charles J. Wolfe property was acquired as a music school, and Hunt Hall was built to meet the needs of a growing student population in addition to the Ziegler Infirmary. Dr. Hunt's resignation in 1931 at the beginning of the Great Depression did not stop the university from taking firm action to complete the modernizing of university politics and curriculum.

The students and faculty, however, were unprepared for the radical changes that occurred during the administration of Dr. Homer P. Rainey (1931-1935). This was apparent in their reaction to the new "survey courses" and an educational program that stressed a broad, cultural preparation of at least two years before specialization in studies began. The program was Dr. Rainey's way of combining the old classical ideal of a general education with the modern idea of specialization, but its success was impaired by the effects of the Depression and by the costs engendered by the partial destruction by fire of Old Main in the summer of 1932. Even so, modernization continued.

Football is played and watched c. 1900 on Loomis Field, Bucknell's first athletic field. Loomis Field was later replaced by the stadium at the other end of campus. From the collection of the Union County Historical Society, #89.5.3.27.

Christy Mathewson is seen on the extreme left in the second row, along with other members of Bucknell's football team, in this c. 1898-1900 photograph. He was a legendary sportsman in football, basketball, and baseball as well as a scholar during the two and one-half years he attended Bucknell. Mathewson excelled as a pitcher for the New York Giants Courtesy of Bucknell University Archives.

In line with Dr. Rainey's ideas of broadening education was the university's founding in 1933 of Bucknell Junior College in Wilkes-Barre (now Wilkes College), the construction of Vaughn Literature Building in 1933 to 1934, and the completion of a comprehensive building plan for the university. All these were signficant accomplishments, but the strain of financial problems exacerbated by the unpopularity of his educational programs brought about Dr. Rainey's resignation in 1935.

Dr. Rainey's successor was a member of the university's board of trustees, Arnaud C. Marts, a partner and owner of the fund-raising firm of Marts and Lundy of New York City. Attuned more to the world of business and finance then that of education, Dr. Marts was the answer in this period to the financial problems that were plaguing the university and to the critical ones facing its survival during World War II. Dr. Marts undertook the restoration of Old Main, the

completion of the engineering building, and the beginning of the construction of Davis Gymnasium for the men, with the women relegated to the old Tustin Gymnasium.

With the double burdens of his business in New York and his services as a captain in the United States Coast Guard, Dr. Marts resigned his presidency in 1945 to Dr. Herbert L. Spencer, former president of the Pennsylvania College for Women, now Chatham College, in Pittsburgh, Pennsylvania. A graduate of Carnegie Institute of Technology with a Ph.D. degree from the University of Pittsburgh, Dr. Spencer was an educator of long experience and a humanitarian with an impressive record of helping people. His dean of the university, was Dr. William H. Coleman, formerly of the university's Department of English, whose name would be given to Coleman Hall. Although Dr. Spencer's administration was successful from every

Bucknell students pose for a studio shot along with their scientific equipment. Courtesy of Bucknell University Achives.

PAGE 144: Blanchard Gummo, professor of art and a graduate of Yale University, taught at Bucknell as early as 1931 and then from 1946 to 1974. Courtesy of Bucknell University Archives.

PAGE 144: The exterior and interior of Bucknell's Carnegie Library is the subject of two real photo postcards c. 1905. The university's first observatory is seen in the background. From the collection of the Union County Historical Society, #92.9.90.38-39.

point of view, it was brief, ending in 1949 with his becoming director of the Kress Foundation, a position in keeping with his philanthropic interests.

With the appointment in 1949 of the Honorable Horace Hildreth, former governor of Maine, to the presidency of Bucknell University, a new era began for the institution. Beset by the problems posed by the post-World War II period, the administration proceeded with dispatch to cope with housing an increased student population by building Bucknell Village and Faculty Court. In addition, the educational program was upgraded, and less emphasis was put on sports. The establishment of an ROTC in 1950 and the completion of the Ellen Clarke Bertrand Library in 1951 were significant accomplishments of the Hildreth administration. Most important, however, was the amendment of the university's charter to change the Baptist membership of the board of trustees from a majority to a minority. Occurring in 1953, this action changed the course of the university's history. For all practical purposes, the University was no longer a Baptist institution. Dr. Hildreth's resignation as president in 1953 to become the United States' ambassador to Pakistan was accepted regretfully.

Hildreth's successor in 1954 was Dr. Merle Odgers, former president of Girard College in Philadelphia, Pennsylvania. A scholarly, reserved man, Dr. Odgers led the university through very prosperous years, which allowed an ambitious building program and the reorganization of the curriculum. During his administration the institution increased its income and endowment, built the Olin Science Building, Coleman Hall, the James Swartz Residence Hall, the Freas-Rooke Swimming Pool, the Recreation Center at Cowan (later named for Forrest Brown, longtime head of the Christian Association), the Marts Hall, and a new observatory. In addition to these accomplishments, there were extensive renovations of Tustin Gymnasium, the Carnegie Building, the women's dormitories, and Kress and Trax Halls. The retirement of Dr. Odgers in 1964 concluded a most fruitful career as an educator and a developer of Bucknell University.

Charles H. Watts, at age 37, began his duties on August 1, 1964, as the eleventh president of Bucknell. The recipient of a B.A. and Ph.D. from Brown University and a specialist in American literature, he had joined the Brown staff as a faculty member and dean. Dr. Watts came to Bucknell after serving two years as the executive director of the

American Council on Education. His tasks at Bucknell were formidable.

The rush of World War II veterans into higher education had almost overwhelmed institutions in the late 1940s and early 1950s, but ended after over $19 billion were spent on educational benefits. Now there were new problems to solve on campuses across the nation. In response to the Russian space launches of Sputnik I and II in 1957, NASA was established to administer the scientific exploration of space; and in 1958 the National Defense Education Act was passed, which supported a change in education to emphasize science and mathematics as being in the national interest. The NDEA was reinforced in the Kennedy/ Johnson era amidst the struggles for civil rights and the desegregation of public schools. President Kennedy pledged "to seek a system of higher education where every young American can be educated, not according to his race or means, but according to his capacity." Legislation was enacted which made available construction funds and the first large-scale federal scholarship/ loan/job programs to assist individual students as well as provide the first significant support for humanities and academic libraries. One problem for private institutions like Bucknell was the impact of these financial relationships with Washington. About 80 percent of the 2,200 institutions of higher education participated in one or more of the federally-supported programs, but even those which did not participate directly were affected since they had to compete for faculty, students, and private funding with those institutions that did receive federal funds.

New fields of study were rapidly added to the older professions in an age of science and high technology. It was the duty of Bucknell's president and faculty to develop ways to prepare students for an emerging global economy and for the intellectual and ethical challenges in their future roles in modern society. One of the central problems was to create courses, curricula, and programs that would include novel ways to address the traditional tension between the need to provide a broad liberal arts education and the needs of the professions for highly trained men and women. While the University Center, completed in 1971, was a major achievement during the tenure of Watts, there was interest but not the funds for a life sciences building as well as facilities for music and art — projects that would be deferred to future administrations.

President Watts won especially high praise for his able handling of a series of protests and demonstra-

The fire at Old Main, Bucknell, was captured by several photographers at approximately 5 A.M. on August 27, 1932. Firefighters from Watsontown, Milton, Northumberland, Sunbury, and Mifflinburg helped Lewisburg's fire department fight the blaze. From the collection of Gary W. and Donna M. Slear.

The College Park Motel's card reads: "Located in Historic Buffalo Valley, and along the Susquehanna River, near Bucknell University, the home of the Bison. We are surrounded by Mountains which have many parks and historic spots. We are located on top of a plateau, overlooking many valleys, and are seldom without a breeze. Our Dutch generosity and atmosphere will add to your pleasant stay with us." From the collection of the Union County Historical Society, #92.9.92.67.

COLLEGE PARK MOTEL
SOUTH OF LEWISBURG, PENNA.
ON U. S. ROUTE 15

tions against the Vietnam War as well as against some of the regulations governing student life. With grace, wit, and a willingness to listen and communicate, he recognized early on the high degree of intellectual and emotional stress that all parties were under during those years. Civility prevailed. Each issue was examined and a dialogue sustained over an extended period. In the end, curfew regulations for women were abolished; dining and residence facilities were no longer segregated by gender; and students won a new role in university governance with the creation of a University Senate. In like manner, communal efforts addressed the damages sustained on the lower campus and in the adjacent community during severe floods triggered by Hurricane Agnes in 1972.

President Watts resigned on July 1, 1976 after twelve years of leadership. Despite the fact that the economy was sagging, with a national unemployment rate at 8.2 percent in late 1975, Bucknell continued to prosper as its growing number of graduates added to an established reputation for sound scholarship and teaching excellence. Amidst continued inflation and economic recession, Americans were busy marking their nation's birth when Bucknell's trustees elected Dennis O'Brien as the university's new president on May 17, 1976. A graduate of Yale University and the recipient of a Ph.D. from the University of Chicago, Dr. O'Brien came from Middlebury College, where he taught philosophy and was dean of the college; previously he had spent three years as assistant dean of the faculty at Princeton University. The new president made clear from the start his intention to teach philosophy as well as to fulfill the administrative duties at Bucknell. He also addressed the issue of heavily tenured departments — an issue on the minds of other college administrators at the time.

President O'Brien had inherited a $4 million fund drive for a field house amid some warning signs of pressure on the university budget caused in part by a recent 9.5 percent inflation rate. The campaign was a success, however, and the new Recreation Sports Center was completed in early 1978. The Terrace Room and the Center Gallery became important parts of the University Center while a building for the Freas-Rooke Computer Center was added on to Dana Engineering, and the groundwork was laid for a performing arts center made possible by a major bequest from the estate of Mrs. Claire G. Weis.

At the completion of his first five years in office, O'Brien insisted that he and all segments of the university undergo a critical performance evaluation,

and he received high praise for his leadership abilities and his many accomplishments. Bucknell's physical growth and comprehensive development had been shaped by the campus design created by Jens Larsen under the direction of President Rainey in the 1930s. That plan, with some modifications, remains in use as the model for the locations of buildings, but there were emerging disciplines and new needs. President O'Brien observed in May 1979, upon the receipt of a $1 million gift from the Sherman Fairchild Foundation for the design, construction, and equipping of a new computer center, "There have been previous moments in our history when a crucial gift at a crucial time proved all-important. This gift may be one of those turning points." Indeed the university was well beyond the resources of its first generation Burroughs E103 computer, the second generation IBM 1620, or the third generation Sigma 7. In 1981, with the Fairchild gift, the university acquired the fourth generation Honeywell CP-6.

In October 1982 the trustees petitioned the court for a change in the university's charter that prohibited indebtedness, thus allowing Bucknell to borrow $30 million through a bond issue for the construction of much-needed residence halls (completed in 1986) and to accelerate plans for renovation and expansion. By May 1983 , when the capital campaign was formally opened, approximately $28.5 million had already been donated or pledged, including $13 million by members of the university's board of trustees.

By the time that Dennis O'Brien announced that he would be assuming the presidency of the University of Rochester in 1984, Bucknell's growing stature was confirmed by admission statistics, gifts, and endowment figures, all of which were record-breaking. The school repeatedly received recognition of its position relative to that of other schools in *Newsweek Magazine*'s annual college report. In addition, an idea that O'Brien helped to foster was the formation of the Colonial League (later called the Patriot League), which included some traditional rivals like Lafayette, Colgate, and Lehigh, as well as members of the Ivy League.

Renovations on the president's house were only partially completed when Dr. Gary Sojka, the former dean of the College of Arts and Sciences at Indiana University, Bloomington, Indiana, arrived in August 1984 to become the new President of Bucknell. A graduate of Coe College, Sojka had a Ph.D. in microbiology from Purdue University and was the recipient of several awards for excellence in teaching. Like his predecessor, President Sojka indicated his intention to

Bucknell's quadrangle ("The Quad") was photographed by Donald Ross of Lewisburg in the mid-1940s. The engineering building and Vaughn Literature Building are seen behind the Navy V-12 unit being reviewed. Courtesy of Bucknell University Archives.

continue his research and teaching, and to return to them more earnestly when he would retire.

President Sojka's first priority was to conduct and complete the $58.5 million capital campaign begun two years earlier; the plan earmarked $2 million for renovations and additions to Dana Engineering, $10 million for greatly expanded science facilities, $9.5 million for the Bertrand Library additions and major renovations, and $9 million for the construction of a new performing arts center. There also were also additional goals of $20 million for the university's endowment fund and $8 million for the annual giving fund. When the 100th Anniversary of the institution's designation as Bucknell University was marked in the 1986-1987 academic year, it began on a triumphant note. The $58.5 million goal of the capital campaign — unprecedented in its aims and ambitions — was exceeded in 1986. The campaign was extended from 1987 through 1990 and a new $86.5 million goal was established. Again passing the goal, the campaign ultimately raised $91 million.

For his leadership of the university and many accomplishments, President Sojka received a unanimous vote of confidence from the trustees after his first five years in office. In 1995 President Sojka stepped down to become professor of biology at Bucknell. In his new role he remains proud of the generosity of graduates, parents, friends, and members of the campus community who made possible a wide range of achievements during his tenure as president, a part of which is embodied in new and renovated structures.

President Sojka had overseen renovations to the first floor of the Elaine Langone Center (previously called the University Center); as well as restoration of Cooley Hall, the president's house, Bucknell Hall, and Taylor Hall, with all of the latter preserving a sense of the past. Construction of the Sigmund and Clare Weis Center for the Performing Arts, the renovation of Stadler Center for Poetry and the Tustin Studio Theater, and expansion of the Center Gallery' provided new strengths for teaching as well as regional resources in the fine and performing arts. Additional instructional resources for the sciences, mathematics, management, art, and engineering were completed.

The fourteenth president of Bucknell, William D. Adams, assumed his duties in March 1995. President Adams was a magna cum laude graduate of Colorado College in 1972, a Fulbright Scholar in France in 1977, and earned his Ph.D. from the University of California at Santa Cruz in 1982. He began his academic career as an assistant professor of political science at the University of North Carolina at Chapel Hill. Adams has produced scholarly work in social and political philosophy which has been widely published.

Since 1986, Adams was in university administration at Stanford and then at Wesleyan University in Connecticut before assuming the presidency at Bucknell. He led Bucknell into the next century during a period of continued physical growth and social challenges. Bucknell University, like many other academic institutions, faced a myriad of social challenges—in particular gender and diversity issues; social drinking — with concomitant responsibility and liability implications. These were issues which cropped up repeatedly beginning in the early 1970s. Adams also stressed the university's need for continuous planning and assessment; after his second year at Bucknell, he completed a strategic financial plan which has led to a continuous planning and assessment process for the university.

During Adam's tenure the Bucknell faculty was increased by 12 percent as part of a concerted effort to reduce the student-faculty ratio to less than 12 to 1. Even as unprecedented numbers of students from a more diverse applicant pool were applying, more needed financial aid. New teaching facilities were planned for the Sigfried Weis Music Building and the O'Leary Center for Psychology and Geology, as well as a new athletic center and a large residential complex. These buildings as well as an increased endowment and financial aid program were goals set in "The Bucknell Campaign" launched a little more than a year after Adams arrived. The campaign had secured $143 million of its $150 million goal as the new century dawned. As in recent capital campaigns, this one was adjusted to meet additional goals which included a new art building. The success of the campaign, along with sound investment strategies, which were among the best in the nation for academic institutions, had resulted in an endowment that had nearly doubled during Adam's tenure. Bucknell's endowment was valued at $392 million by the end of June 1999.

Less visible, however, was the steady growth in Bucknell's academic stature. Regarded for many years as a premiere "regional" undergraduate institution, the university won ever-increasing recognition from educators for the quality and strength of its faculty, the breadth of its academic programs, and the distinction of its graduates. Its current status as a respected "national" institution has been confirmed in its ability to recruit outstanding faculty and students from coast to coast in America and around the world. The founders of the University at Lewisburg, meeting together in the old log school on Market Street on that cold night in December of 1843, would have been gratified had they known how the fruits of their labors, their hopes, and their dreams would turn out.

The Maypole Dance, an annual ritual at Bucknell's Spring Festival, is being practiced near Loomis Field in 1935. Courtesy of Bucknell University Archives.

A detail of a silk fundraising quilt made by Bucknell University students from the classes of 1896 and 1898 in support of the Vincent Chapel in West Chillisquaque Township, Northumberland County. Bucknell students , in charge of the non-denominational services held at the chapel, were paid two dollars and an evening meal for conducting services there, which they did until the 1920s. From the collection of Catherine K. Stahl. Photo by the Terry Wild Studio, courtesy of the Oral Traditions Project.

CHAPTER 9

MIFFLINBURG, THE BUGGY TOWN

Mifflinburg's origins go back to an inspiration of Elias Youngman just before 1792. Eleven years earlier he had acquired a part of a military lot assigned to Ensign McMeen. While there was little evidence that the uncultivated land might blossom into a town, Youngman was aware that it lay at the center of Buffalo Valley and in a direct line between the Susquehanna River and Penns Valley (Centre County). He took the plunge and in 1792 laid out a town extending from present-day Third Street westward; not surprisingly, he called it Youngmanstown, or as the early German residents preferred, *Younkman's Stettle.* The former appears to have been Elias Youngman's choice as he often used it in deeds beginning as early as 1806.

His timing was right, for within the span of a year Elias Youngman sold 32 lots in town each 60 x 120 feet; and 56 outlots, each consisting of a one-acre plot at the southern edge of the plat. More significant than the number of immediate purchases, which were sometimes taken by absentee owners and simply held for speculation, was the arrival of actual settlers, who filled the air with the music of the ax and hammer. Youngman was not averse to combining philanthropy with land development, offering a lot at a token price to the Lutheran and German Presbyterian (German Reformed) congregations and another to a bi-denominational committee for a school. He also provided a cemetery lot. By the end of the first year the residents were:

Dreisbach, John, gunsmith. (In 1796, he had a hewed log house, brick kitchen, frame shop and stable.)
Earnhart, John, blacksmith, hewed log house and smith shop.
Gettig, Ludwig [Getgen], mason, log house.
Holmes, Robert, storekeeper, hewed log house and chipped stable.
Holmes, Jonathan, small hewed log house.
Irvine, John, storekeeper, hewed log house and round log stable.
Longabauth, Henry, weaver, hewed log house.
Neal, Henry, tailor, hewed log house.
Ritter, Israel.
Reedy, Nicholas, jobber.
Sampsel, Nicholas, carpenter, hewed log house.
Wagner, Christopher, carpenter, hewed log house.
Welker, Jacob, tailor, hewed log house.
Welker, William, jobber, hewed log house.
Withington, Martin, tavern keeper.
Youngman, Elias.
Youngman, Thomas.
Youngman, George, storekeeper.[1]

A glance at the list suggests the village's Germanic flavor with a variety of occupations. (George and Thomas Youngman were sons of Elias.)

Youngman's success invited competition, and in 1797 George Rote laid out a village just east of Youngmanstown, which was identified locally as Rotestown or Rhodestown. By contrast, however, Rote's plot remained almost undeveloped through several generations. Motorists might wish that Rote could have met with Youngman at Withington's tavern and shared plans. Streets and lots might have been joined more harmoniously and a central avenue agreed upon.

By 1799 Youngmanstown had 53 taxables, a gain of threefold in six years, and momentarily seems to have been larger than Derr's Town. It now contained a broader spectrum of occupations, including three tavern keepers, a school teacher, and a brewer, though there was no minister of the gospel in residence.[2]

Perhaps the most notable arrival at this time was the Gutelius family, (Adam) Frederick Gutelius (b. 1766, d. 1839) and his wife, Anna Catherine Bistel (b. 1773, d. 1828), from Lancaster County. The Guteliuses settled at the northeastern corner of Thomas and High Streets (present-day Green and Fifth) in one of several enclaves within the village. Frederick was a surveyor, a justice of the peace, and a county commissioner in the newly created Union County. He and his wife were founders and pillars of the Reformed Church. Most of their twelve children lived and died in the vicinity, and in 1900 there were more persons bearing the name Gutelius in Mifflinburg than any other. Older residents still recall the identification of three branches of the family within the buggy industry.

When Union County was created on March 22, 1813, Mifflinburg had 107 taxables and it became the county seat until the first county buildings were constructed in New Berlin.[3] The commissioners chose a log house at 406 Green Street, Mifflinburg, to serve as the temporary courthouse which it did until March 28, 1815. The building was owned by George Lehman, a schoolteacher. On February 14, 1814, the first court session of Union County was convened there. For reasons of space, court sessions were later moved down the street to the old German School. The grand jurors of the first court were John Boal, Adam Regar, Arthur Thomas, Jacob Musser, John Fisher, James Madden, Robert Chambers, Valentine Haas, Jacob Houseworth,

John Nogel, James McClure, John Williams, Aaron Chamberlin, Levi Zimmerman, Philip Gemberling, Frederick Wertz, James Caldwell, Andrew Grove, David Simmons, John Aurand, Abraham TenBrooke, John Seidel, and John German. Attorneys sworn in at this time were Enoch Smith, E.G. Bradford, Samuel Hepburn, Ebenezer Greenough, Charles Maus, William Erwin, John Lashells, John Johnston, Ethan Baldwin, Charles Hall, George Frick, Alem Marr, and Hugh Bellas, with William Irwin as deputy district attorney.

In 1827 Youngmanstown and Rotestown were combined and incorporated as one borough with a new name. Obviously, Thomas Mifflin, the state's first governor, had not been forgotten in Central Pennsylvania; many towns, like Mifflin, Mifflinville, and Mifflintown, and now Mifflinburg, were renamed in his honor. More significant for the town's growth than its incorporation or name was the construction of the Lewisburg-Youngmanstown Turnpike, as well as the Bellefonte-Aaronsburg-Youngmanstown Turnpike at this time. The turnpikes placed Mifflinburg on a main artery of transportation eastward and westward, and the wagons heavy with Centre County grain were soon passing down its main thoroughfare while stage and mail coaches were offering their services to Easton, Pittsburgh, and Philadelphia.

In the 1830s and 1840s, Mifflinburg's principal business district on George (later Chestnut) Street between Third and Fifth was becoming a cluster of small shops and stores. Businesses' life cycles were surprisingly short in this restless age, but the rare old newspapers suggest their transitory nature, though some allowance must be made for exaggeration, a situation not unknown to consumers more than a century later. In 1840 Roush and Shaffer listed "dry goods, silks, bonnets, teas, hollow ware, hardware and steel and iron products."[4] In 1846 Dr. W.A. Piper and Henry offered "fresh drugs and medicines, paints and dye stuffs, confectioneries, fine chemicals, tobacco and cigars, oil, fruits, patent medicine, perfumery and soaps," in what would appear to have been a forerunner of a late-twentieth-century drug store.[5] A year later D. Carskaddon, a Mifflinburg daguerreotypist, was heralded in the *New Berlin Union Times* as an artist whose work "far surpasses any others that we have ever seen in point of neatness of style, finish, and life-like appearance. Mr. Carskaddon is perfect in his profession. We hope citizens of Mifflinburg will patronize him liberally."[6] The same editor, after a visit to Mifflinburg, noted William Young's "most beautiful

The Youngmans' graves are located in the Mifflinburg Cemetery. Photo by Jim Walter.

and richest assortment of new goods displayed with great taste. His new style of bustles should please the ladies."[7] He also had praise for the fine quality, elegance, and beauty of Hassenplug's boots and shoes. In 1861 the Drug and Chemical Emporium advertised "Confectioneries, toys and Yankee notions, pocket knives and umbrellas; lamps and coal oil (kerosene) which for brilliance of light surpasses any oil in use."[8] This claim was just two years after Colonel Drake's first gusher near Oil City, Pennsylvania.

Though the names of business owners came and went with confusing rapidity, a few bucked the trend to remain business leaders for many years, notably Henry Gast, Henry Wolf, William Young, and Henry Strunk. Johann Christian Gast, founder of the family in America, earned his passage from Germany to Philadelphia by working as an indentured servant. After serving his time he settled on the Susquehanna River below Sunbury. His son, John Nicholas, was a pioneer in Centre County and died there when his son Henry was five. Henry Gast first drove a peddler's cart in Aaronsburg; but in 1830, when 28 years old, he moved to Mifflinburg, where he opened a general store on Chestnut Street in partnership with George Wolf. The latter withdrew in a few years, and Gast invited his nephew, Henry Gast Wolf, to work for him. Six years later Wolf opened a store of his own a block west of his uncle's store on Chestnut, and there proved to be enough trade for both of them to prosper. In 1883 Gast and his son, J.D.S. (Spyker), moved the business to the north side of the street, where they erected a massive brick storeroom. J.D.S. and his son Harry continued the business there until 1934.

Henry Gast built one of the village's mansions in the 1840s at the southwest corner of Market and Fourth Streets, adorning the front facade with hard pink brick from Philadelphia and marble on the foundation and sills. Gast built wooden conduits to pipe in water from a spring that was on the border of the cemetery and his house, providing the adjacent spring house with running water. In later years Gast became a gentleman farmer in West Buffalo Township and purchased timberland along the mountains beyond, accumulating thousands of acres, which he later sold to Ryan, Thompson and Company of Williamsport and the Laurelton Lumber Company for a handsome profit. Gast enjoyed his wealth and liked to do things on a large scale. On a family anniversary he once presented each of his three surviving children, Spyker, Dr. J.R. Gast, and Kate (Mrs. J.A. Montelius), with costly grand pianos. Gast lived to be 91 years old and at his death on November 6, 1897, was the town's oldest resident.

Henry Wolf, meanwhile, constructed a substantial home and business in 1867; he also broadened his investments to include milling and banking. For many years he was an office holder in the Lutheran Church and Sunday school, and he also headed the Centennial Anniversary of the town in 1892. He married Ellen Moss of Mifflinburg, and their daughters, in turn, married into prominent familes — Emma Jane becoming the wife of Professor Paul M. Bikle of Pennsylvania College at Gettysburg and Edith, the wife of Congressman Benjamin K. Focht. A son, Harry, preferred banking to merchandising. Tiring of store keeping, Wolf closed his store in 1897. Years later, his grandson, Dr. Paul Bikle, resided in the Wolf mansion and practiced medicine there, but the old storehouse thereafter produced limited profits for its users and stood empty for many years.

A third successful general merchandiser was Henry Strunk. Beginning as a tailor in 1862, he expanded his shop to include general merchandise in 1873 and housed his wares in a frame building on the north side of Chestnut Street. His business grew steadily. When Gast moved from the south side to the north side of the street in 1883 to occupy new quarters and Augustus Heiter erected his tonsorial parlor next door, Strunk found himself next to the most elegant business section in town. Not wishing to suffer from comparisons, he improved his own store and home.

The *Mifflinburg Telegraph,* noting that he would now look out from a brick edifice that would compete with his neighbors, Heiter and Gast, commented, "Good! Competition is what builds up a town, and may their enterprise meet with success."[9] Not to be outdone, each of the three merchants extended substantial frame awnings in front of their establishments. Strunk added a final touch five years later when he laid a sidewalk of Cleveland sandstone, starting a fad in town as the more affluent property holders followed suit. The days of brick and board walks were numbered. A pedestrian may still find sections of the "flagstone," and older devotees of roller skating may recall the smooth glide over their surfaces. Gast, Heiter, and Strunk remained the heart of the town's shopping center for many years, even well into the twentieth century.

During the 1880s it might be noted much of the business block between Third and Fourth Streets was substantially rebuilt to give it the appearance which would last through much of the twentieth century. While Gast, Heiter, and Strunk were building their impressive row, the Snodgrass family, Samuel W. and his sons, Robert E., and James H., were building a costly brick structure on the south side of the street near the eastern end of the block to house their hardware business. Samuel had come to Mifflinburg in

Henry Gast

Albert Snyder of Mifflinburg poses in his dairy wagon in front of James Beaver's fruit store on the west side of Fourth Street, Mifflinburg. From the collection of the Union County Historical Society, #89.5.11.58.

1855 from Dauphin County and had engaged in milling with his brother-in-law, William Young. They also had a produce and grocery business and, for a time, operated a tannery.

In 1869 Samuel Snodgrass opened a hardware store, the only establishment dealing exclusively in that line. He was successful from the start. The new building extended from the street to the alley and had show windows of French plate glass, which the *Telegraph* described as "Mammoth in size, where Jim, the proprietor's son, will evince his good taste in displaying fancy hardware." There were wide counters of walnut and maple, beautifully finished, and a handsome stairway at the rear led to a spacious showroom on the second floor. At the press of a button a counter "flopped out of sight, a door opened, and we could pop down a stairway to a ware-room for bar iron." The newspaper also had compliments for the builder, Enoch Miller, Mifflinburg's noted architect, who had supervised the work, and for Bowes and Swineford, who had painted the interior.[10]

Earlier in the decade, the Mifflinburg Bank had erected a fine brick building two doors west of the Snodgrass establishment, the second floor of which housed the Masonic Lodge. Across the street Minadore Schwartz built an attractive commercial building used for many purposes through the years, including a half-century as a restaurant and lodge hall. Finally, in 1884, on the site of the old Gast store,

clothier J. Wilson Barber erected a brick storeroom and house; and Strunk's would later have their mortuary establishment at that location. Were Gast and his contemporaries able to return after over one hundred years, they would have no difficulty recognizing and finding their way around their elegant block.

Mifflinburg's most exciting business tycoon during the second half of the nineteenth century was William Young. Born on a farm in Kelly Township in 1816, he clerked in stores at Northumberland and Danville during his teens; at age 21 he came to Mifflinburg to work for his uncle, Berryhill Bell, a general merchandiser. A few years later he bought the store and opened another in Hartleton; later, broadening his investments, he also dealt in coal and grain. In 1857 he erected the town's most elegant residence on the south side of Chestnut Street midway between Third and Fourth Streets. Designed by Lewis Palmer, the noted Lewisburg architect, and superintended by Thomas T. Baker, a Lewisburg builder, the three-story Italianate brick structure with twin Victorian porches and square tower was the "last word" in contemporary architecture. A local newspaper spoke only modestly when referring to it as "a little superior in style and conveniences to any building in town."[11] Members of the family lived there for two generations before it was acquired by the town for the borough hall.

William Young married Eleanor Snodgrass, and they were blessed with seven daughters and six sons. Mifflinburg residents still recall Hadwin, one of the younger sons, the tallest man in town — jovial, yet dignified, sitting with friends on the porch or playing chess with one of his brothers. During the Civil War William organized and became the first president of the First National Bank of Mifflinburg, the earliest banking institution. With a nod toward tourism, he also built Young's Hotel at Fifth and Chestnut Streets in the early 1860s, a hostelry remembered as the Buffalo Valley Inn. There is a story, probably apocryphal, that Young and Harry Robbins of Mt. Carmel purchased valuable properties in Philadelphia at panic prices just after General Lee invaded Pennsylvania and was expected momentarily to march on that city. After the battle at Gettysburg, they sold them at inflated prices. Even if this tradition is without foundation, the fact remains that Young was an astute businessman. An old Mifflinburg maxim,

not far from the mark, alleged that Young made more money at his grain mill at Fourth and Railroad Streets before breakfast than any other businessman earned all day.[12]

Young organized and was president of a bank in Reading as well as a director of banks in Williamsport, Scranton, Pittston, Chester, and Philadelphia. In addition to his business dealings, William Young also served for a term in the state House of Representatives in 1871, elected on the Democratic ticket in the Union, Snyder and Lycoming district. After 38 years in Mifflinburg, Young moved to Germantown, where he built another fine home, helped to found the Northern Bank of Philadelphia, and joined Robert F. Whitmer in a lumber and planing mill business on

A detail of the Mifflinburg street layout. From Pomeroy's Atlas for Union and Snyder Counties 1868.

Broad Street. He left his sons in charge of his banking and mercantile interests in Mifflinburg.

Two of Young's ventures ran upon shoals, but he salvaged his investments. The National Bank of Mifflinburg prospered for a time, returning dividends in excess of the original cost of the stock within twelve years. However, it fell victim to the panic of 1873 and was liquidated in 1880. A second ill-fated venture involved the purchase of a graphite mine near Phoenixville. Veins of ore which the sellers had represented proved non-existent so Young went to court, where he was eventually awarded damages. "Winning that big suit," the *Telegraph* exulted, "makes him look at least ten years younger."[13] The erstwhile merchant, miller, and banker died at age 88 in 1904 while visiting his sons in Mifflinburg.

The termination of the First National Bank did not leave the town without the services of a banking institution. The Mifflinburg Bank was organized in 1872 and incorporated a year later. Its growth was less impressive than that of the First National, but it weathered the panic and in 1880 purchased the building, vault, and furnishings of its former competitor. The Mifflinburg Bank continued to prosper, and the organization celebrated its centennial in 1972.

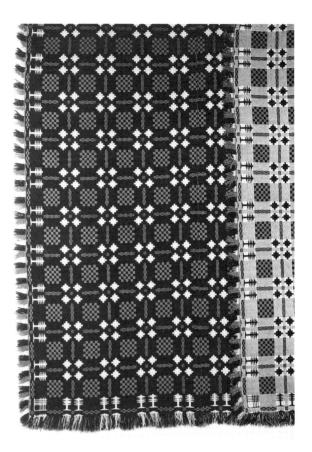

Through the first half of the nineteenth century, Mifflinburg's economy centered upon its stores, shops and hostelries. A visitor at mid-century would have had few clues to anticipate its future specialization. There were several small foundries, a tannery, a brewery, the Dreisbach gun shop, several hatters and tailors, a nailer, and two buggy shops. One of the latter was opened by John S. Stitzer in 1841 but discontinued a few years later; the second belonged to Thomas Gutelius. It would be Gutelius and his brothers and sons who would demonstrate the economical potential of buggymaking.

Thomas was the oldest son of Frederick and Anna Gutelius and perhaps acquired the skills of the trade from Stitzer. Gutelius opened his shop in 1846, employing his brother, Jacob. In time Jacob went into business for himself, employing another brother, John, as millwright. John, in turn, opened a shop in 1875. Meanwhile, the sons of the Gutelius brothers worked with their fathers. Thomas' shop was on Walnut Street near Fourth, Jacob's at the corner of Market and Third, and John's on the south side of Market midway between Fifth and Sixth Streets. The Gutelius family moved into the buggy business at an opportune time. During the half-century following the

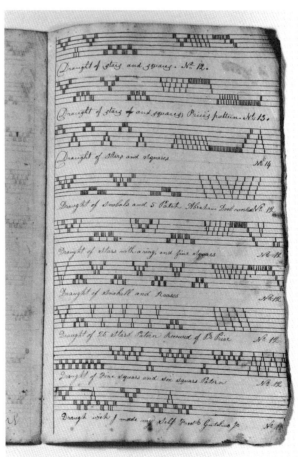

Civil War, the public demand for small, light, and relatively inexpensive family vehicles mounted steadily; and producers were soon turning out a broad variety of four-wheeled, one-seated vehicles for as little as $50 and, for the winter season, produced sleighs for as small a sum as $28.

J.H. Condon opened a buggy shop about 1870 and found markets as distant as Kansas. He specialized in more costly models at his Keystone Coach Works on Market Street; his prize-winning Phaeton at the Bloomsburg Fair was described as dazzling, pleasing to the eyes, and a tribute to his eleven "stalwart sons of toil."[14] Unfortunately, Condon's vehicles were too costly during the panic of 1873 and the sheriff sold his shop and house in 1880. Condon subsequently moved to Altoona, where he again became a successful buggy manufacturer.

George Moss began to turn out buggies on West Chestnut Street in 1862; T.B. Taylor, on Market Street in 1869; William H. Hursh, at Third and Walnut in 1870; John G. Miller, on Green Street in 1877; and H.A. Taylor near the depot in 1878. By 1886 they had been joined by James Moss, Solomon Miller, John Kreisher, William Heiss, Daniel B. Miller, G.F. Shell, William Brown, Oliver P. Mensch, Robert A. Wendell, Samuel Wilson, the Berry Brothers, Wilbur Blair, George W. Rissel, George Hummel, and James Hoover. The list is by no means definitive since smaller builders worked part-time, particularly during the winter months, in shops which accommodated a single buggy. Others, like the Frederick brothers, specialized in painting or building the bodies and forging the metal axles and gears.

In later years a sizable number of women were employed as upholsterers (trimmers), and boys frequently obtained their first employment as helpers. At the turn of the century, a twelve-year-old assisted a painter in William Brown's shop on Market Street near Sixth for 25¢ a week. When he was told to beat carpets, he asked for an additional 15¢, explaining that he was hired to learn the trade. He was denied and found employment at Hopp's shop for 50¢ a week. A sixteen-year-old in 1910 found employment at Brown's (now at Fifth and Railroad Streets) at $9 for a 60-hour week. By cutting his noon hour to 50 minutes each day, the young worker completed the work on Saturday at five, enabling him to go "up town" an hour earlier for his weekend celebration.[15]

At the outset the components of the buggies, sleighs, and wagons were fashioned by the builders in their shops or by local blacksmiths and foundrymen. Elm was cut into short pieces and stored in oats through the winter. In the spring, when "just right," they were worked into hubs and mortised to hold the spokes. Hickory, meanwhile, was shaped into spokes and felloes; hickory and oak were boiled in linseed oil in lieu of painting. Elsewhere, Stayman's foundry was casting axles from Union and Centre County iron. Later, with higher quality iron ore coming from Minnesota's Mesabi Range and from Sweden, the buggy makers purchased axles from large manufacturers such as the Sheldon Iron Works in Scranton, and the Snodgrass and Young Hardware Stores were stocked with parts for the smaller builders, including everything from the wheels to the whip. The magnitude of the latter's stock for the buggy-building trade is suggested by the variety of its purchases. From 1895 through 1896, its orders embraced 327 different supply houses and manufacturers. Some buggy builders also supplied other shops with parts. John Gutelius was an expert wheelwright; and years after he had turned over his buggy-making business to his sons, he continued to work at this earlier trade. Robert Wendell turned out shafts, wheels, and other millwork for his customers.

Marketing soon became a major consideration as the buggy supply out-stripped local markets. The best advertising was the product itself. The managers or their agents drove them to the agricultural fairs, exhibits, political rallies, reunions, and parks — wherever crowds were expected — to demonstrate their beauty and utility. Mifflinburg became identified as the buggy capital of Pennsylvania, and was known far and wide as the "buggy town." A Mifflinburg buggy became an object of pride and satisfaction. The Berry Brothers focused upon Centre County and for a time drove two buggies up the Fourteen Mile Narrows weekly, hitching them in tandem. Jacob Gutelius, a large producer, found markets in western Pennsylvania and displayed his vehicles annually at the Armstrong and Jefferson County fairs. In November of 1884 he dispatched two railroad carloads of sleighs to Indiana County in a single week. A few days later he shipped a carload of buggies and an elegant bus-sleigh with a capacity of fourteen persons to Brookville in the same neighborhood. John Gutelius shipped "many carloads to the extreme South and West."

The town's premier salesman was James R. Ritter, who seemed to find profits wherever he turned his hand. He was a dealer in agricultural products and a keen judge of real estate, his dealings in the latter filling page after page of the county records. Vivacious and a lover of fine foods and beverages, his receptions were a "must" among the community's "elite" and consistently newsworthy. Though he personally built no buggies, he purchased them wholesale and organized his own sales campaigns. In July of 1886 the *Telegraph* noted that he had sold 80 buggies that season — evidence that it would be a good year. On another occasion he was seen moving toward the coal region with a string of twenty buggies. Ritter served a term in the state House of Representatives, defeating young Benjamin K. Focht in the Republican primary — only 23 Mifflinburg voters failing to support him; but business, not politics, was his forte.

Statistics are elusive, but as early as 1881 the production of sleighs was reported to be 597. Thomas Gutelius headed the list with 138 and was followed by brother Jacob with 90 and brother John with 71. A.A. Hopp made 45 and D.B. Miller, 32. Of the 38 producers named, 24 turned out fewer than ten. Additional shops did the woodwork only. Robert Wendell, for example, built 21 for other manufacturers.[16] Production continued to grow through the next 30 years even though the number of producers declined. Thomas Gutelius' failure in 1888 was attributed by his descendants to his endorsing the notes of friends rather than paying attention to the business itself, while H.A. Taylor was foreclosed in 1895.

A significant shift in the manufacturing process occurred in 1897 when the Mifflinburg Buggy Company was founded on the site of the Thomas Gutelius plant on Walnut Street near Fourth. It was organized as a partnership by Robert S. Gutelius (a son of Jacob), A.A. Hopp, and Harry F. Blair, "all practical mechanics and first-class business men." They substantially enlarged the Gutelius works and soon outdistanced their competitors. A front-page advertisement claimed that they were the largest producer in Central Pennsylvania and that their size and efficiency permitted them to sell at ten to twenty percent below the prices

TOP: An advertisement for the newly opened Mifflinburg Body and Gear Company appeared in *The Spokesman* in 1912. Courtesy of the Mifflinburg Buggy Museum.

BOTTOM: A William A. Heiss advertisement offers stoves to supplement buggy sales, which were slowing by 1909. Courtesy of the Heiss family.

PAGE 157: A ledger page from the account book of C.W. Haslet Men's Clothing Store, Mifflinburg, covering transactions from 1887 through 1896. From the collection of the Union County Historical Society, #83.3.2.

1887		Thomas O. Gutelius					
June	11	Pants					1 25
Aug	20	By cash			1 00		
"	20	Pants					4 00
"	20	Knee Pants					90
Sep	17	Credited by cash			1 00		
Oct	8	" " "			2 00		
Oct	4	Boys Suit	v. a. r				4 25
"	4	Shirts	a. k. k				2 50
"	22	Shirts	a. t. r				3 25
"	22	Boys Rubbers					60
Nov	19	By cash			1 00		
"	26	By cash			1 00		
		See page 24			#6 00	#16	65
1887		George Schoch					
June	11	Hose					25
"	11	Scarf					40
"	11	Collar Buttons					05
"	11	Linen Collars					30
July	5	Hat By Haley					50
Aug	6	Shoes	Milt			2	50
"	6	Gauze Shirt	"				25
Sep	10	Cuffs	l. s. 3				25
"	10	Scarf	v. t. k				60
"	10	Collar	o ½				15
Dec	28	Shirt	l. k. k. Elmer			1	25
1888 April	4	Shoes	R. K. K. Indian			3	75
"	4	Scarf	v. K. "				75
Dec	8	Drawers & Shirt Elmer t o				1	00
"	24	Rubbers	v. K. Sutton				65
1889 June	24	Shoes Elmer	find our			3	75
July	20	" "				1	25

of their competitors. They employed only experienced mechanics, offered new styles, and guaranteed that their axles would run for 1000 miles without oiling. "Compressed Band Wood hubs and Sarvan and Warner Patent wheels" were provided without additional cost.[17] A bit later, they offered the "Stanhope," a "noiseless and pretty" buggy with rubber tires and springs in the upholstery.

On a tour of the spacious three-story factory, *Telegraph* editor George W. Schoch found its magnitude "astonishing." He also noted the efficiency of its 30 mechanics, including the several ladies in the trimming department. He reported the capacity to be twelve vehicles per day. In 1900 he estimated the production to be 700 annually and still growing.[18] The company was reorganized in 1903, after A.A. Hopp sold out to his associates following an unexplained disagreement. Blair and Gutelius, joined by Hadwin B. Young, Horace P. Glover, and David L. Glover, incorporated The Mifflinburg Buggy Company at $20,000.

Hopp was reported to be "looking around," and within a few months, with financial backing from James R. Ritter, he purchased two lots just west of his recent partners, where the old town hall and the Kurtz tannery stood. (Samuel G. Grove hastily dismantled the latter and wheeled it to his farm on North Eighth Street, where it continues to serve as a barn.) At this location, Hopp erected a three-story brick building extending along Fourth Street to the alley. There were now two "giants" competing for the buggy trade, and competition was keen. Both companies subsequently built additions to their plants and fought in the courts for a disputed fifteen inches of land along their common boundary. Meanwhile, officials of the Buggy Company went to Cleveland, Ohio, to induce William F. Sterling, Manager of the Columbia Carriage Company, to direct plant operations. He came and remained the driving force of the company during its halcyon years.

Productivity in buggy manufacture had tailed off during the hard times of the 1890s, and the popularity of the recently invented bicycle doubtless contributed to the lag. Business rebounded at the turn of the century and reached its zenith in the first fifteen years of the new century. Early in this period, John Gutelius, William F. Brown, Daniel B. Miller, John G. Miller, the Berry Brothers, and Oberdorf and Son (who had replaced Solomon B. Miller) expanded their operations. In 1903 the *Telegraph* estimated the total yearly production at 6,000 vehicles, 1,500 of which were built by the Mifflinburg Buggy Company. While local pride may have exaggerated the figure, the volume

continued to climb when Hopp got into production in 1905. Presumably, the automobile did not yet pose a threat, though the smooth concrete-macadam stretch of road completed in 1907 between Lewisburg and Mifflinburg might have served as a warning. In 1909 Samuel G. Grove observed in his "Jottings" that "The farsighted buggy maker considers the sign of the times and betakes himself to auto making. Surely the horseless carriage is here to stay, and he who would profit by it must get into the procession."[19]

As late as 1911, Horace Orwig headed a syndicate which organized the Mifflinburg Body and Gear Company at Eighth and Walnut Streets, designed to turn out running gears and other parts for buggies. Five years later Gutelius and Sterling bought out the Body and Gear Company and merged it with the Mifflinburg Buggy Company to create the Mifflinburg Body Company. The company soon began to phase out buggies and to build bodies for cars and trucks. At this time auto and truck companies ordinarily manufactured the chassis only, leaving the body to be added by the purchaser. The body company thus filled a vacuum and survived, even as other buggy builders folded. Hastily converting to the wood bodies, the business was profitable in its second year and at Christmas in 1917 a bonus of $1,000 was divided with its workers. In 1920 the older frame building was destroyed by fire, but most of the production had already been transferred to the newer plant at Eighth and Walnut.

During the 1920s the company manufactured a varied line including bodies for open stake and panel trucks and estate (station) wagons. Sales were made to distributors in the major cities, and hundreds were mounted upon trucks driven to the plant. Exporters often made large purchases, dismantling them for shipment to the place where trucks were to be sold. By 1928 production reached twenty bodies a day, employment approached 300, annual sales equaled $1 million, and its payroll represented about one-half of the town's total income. Meanwhile, it erected a second three-story brick building in 1922.

The Great Depression was the Mifflinburg Body Company's undoing. The death of William Sterling, its dynamic president, accelerated the crisis. The business was faced with declining sales as the Ford Motor Company and, soon thereafter, other auto makers began to build their own bodies. The body company built its last station wagon body in 1932. A United States government contract for post office trucks and orders for custom bodies — ambulance bodies for

A view of the Mifflinburg Body and Gear Company on North Eighth Street and the area south and west, as it appeared in an aerial photo shot in the 1940s. Courtesy of Mary Koons.

Hawaii, for example — gave the plant sporadic work in the Depression years, but by 1941 the company was bankrupt. Meanwhile, all of the smaller buggy makers had ceased operations, and Mifflinburg's buggy-body days were only an absorbing memory.

During the horse and buggy days, farm implement manufacture also contributed to the town's prosperity. James H. Albright had opened a foundry near Laurelton (Laurel Park) shortly after the Civil War, where he experimented with castings for the farm. Albright perfected a self-dumping hay rake, and he and his three sons manufactured and marketed it in the area. In 1891 they bought out the inactive Stayman foundry in Mifflinburg and enlarged it. Over the next 30 years they manufactured cultivators, harrows, corn planters, and hay rakes, distributing them across Central Pennsylvania. Like the buggy builders, the Albrights displayed their wares at the fairs and demonstrated

them wherever farmers gathered. Their business was steady and offered employment to about fifteen operatives in the molding, wood, and paint departments, and most of the workers lived in or near the Thompson Street addition. Again, like the buggy makers, the Albrights closed their plant in 1920 because the gas engine, in the guise of the tractor, virtually terminated the market for horse-drawn equipment.

As might be expected, Mifflinburg's growth until 1940 was tied closely to the buggy and truck body industry. Prior to that its population grew slowly from decade to decade. In the 30 years between 1840 and 1870, the village added 248 residents, whereas during the next twenty years — paralleling the rise of the buggy industry and the building of the railroad — the population increased by more than 600 to reach 1,417 in 1890. Maps published in 1868 and 1884 show the manner in which this population burst was shaping the community. From the former it is evident that Rotestown on the east had scarcely developed except along Chestnut Street where there were scattered houses, "nearly all logged up, and all on the turn-pike."[20] Otherwise, Chestnut Street was occupied to Eighth Street. Market Street was filled in between Third and Fifth, with a few additional buildings west of Sixth. Green Street was developed from Third Street to Fifth, but beyond the latter there was only the academy. Walnut had several houses adjacent to Berry's Shop at Third; Thomas Gutelius' buggy plant near Fourth; and Andrew J. Katherman's cabinet and coffin shop near Fifth; otherwise, the street remained unopened. Thompson and Green Streets east of Third were also undeveloped.

By 1884 Chestnut Street was pushing west from Eighth; Market had reached Seventh on the west and was moving eastward between Third and Second. Green had edged westward to Sixth; and Walnut was filling in between Third and Fourth as was Thompson between Fourth and Fifth. There was a lull in the 1890s during the panic of 1893; but by the turn of the century Green and Walnut Streets were expanding from Third to Second, and Thompson from Fourth to Third — an auction of 40 lots in 1907 stimulating the latter. Between 1905 and 1910 Mrs. Kitty Romig and her husband, William, built much of the block on Walnut between Sixth and Seventh, and in the 1920s Samuel Strickler added a row of double dwellings on the south side of Walnut between Fifth and Sixth. The town's growth virtually ceased amidst the Great Depression and the closure of the Body Company. After World War II developments were built in eastward expansion and covered the hills to the north and south.

The population changes can be seen in the structures fashioned by the town's master builders through more than a century. The slow growth of the village during the 1840s and 1850s and the high cost of Greek Revival architecture in this period leaves the community almost devoid of the columns, pilasters, and elliptical arches of this era; and the same might be said of the Italianate style of the 1850s and 1860s, represented only by the Young home (present Mifflinburg Borough Building). Instead of innovative architecture, Mifflinburg's builders preferred the older modes of southeastern Pennsylvania — comparatively plain, rectangular, frame or brick structures set almost flush with the street. Henry Gast's house was one of the finer of these: with narrow rectangular windows below the cornice suggesting ornamentation. Smaller brick structures of this style occupied the four corners of Chestnut and Fourth Streets and the northwest corner of Chestnut and Third. If these buildings were similar to their counterparts in other parts of the county, they originally had double chimneys at the two sides and central hallways.

The builders of these early structures were seldom recorded; but by the 1850s the outstanding architect and builder was Joseph Boob, son of George Boob, who had helped to build the First Presbyterian Church in 1844. At the time of Joseph's death in 1878, the *Telegraph* noted that he had built more houses in the town than any other carpenter, "and good buildings, too." Three of his buildings, undoubtedly among his most ambitious, survive: the Samuel H. Orwig house at the southwest corner of Chestnut and Fifth; the James R. Ritter home at the southeastern corner of Chestnut and Third; and the J. Philip Cronmiller homestead on Chestnut Street near Ninth. The Orwig house is one of the few "Victorian cottages" in the town, and is the oldest of the three; its appearance was altered by the addition of a concrete-block porch about 1920. The Ritter and Cronmiller houses made their appearances during the 1870s, and the latter remained unfinished at the time of Boob's death. It was completed by his son Charles. They remain splendid Victorian structures with nicely turned brackets and distinctive quoins. Charles Boob moved to Kansas, where he became a well-known architect, leaving the field to Enoch Miller, a former apprentice of Boob, who remained the area's out-standing builder for more than 40 years.

Enoch Miller was born in West Buffalo Township in 1835, his parents having migrated from Berks County a few months earlier. He was apprenticed to Boob at fifteen to learn the carpenter's trade, and at twenty he went into business for himself, erecting a shop at Market and Sixth Streets. Miller soon made his mark as a painstaking yet imaginative builder, and he and Boob shared most of the local construction. In 1878 Miller built a handsome brick residence for Dr. J.R. Gast at 422 Market Street, several doors west of the Lutheran Church. In the words of the *Telegraph*, it was "an ornament . . . a beauty, and most convenient, which speaks well for the architect and builder." It did speak well for Miller, who went on to build the present Presbyterian (1881), the Wesley Methodist (1894), the United Methodist (1881; earlier Presbyterian and Evangelical), and Lutheran (1901)

Enoch Miller's planing mill was located on North Eighth Street beside the railroad track. Appearing in the 1900 photograph from left to right are: Harry Shirey, unknown, Benjamin Little, Harry Smith, Eli Groover, Harry Wilkinson, and George Solomon. From the collection of the Mifflinburg Buggy Museum.

Enoch Miller

churches. He also built the United Church of Christ (Reformed) in Lewisburg in 1903, the Lincoln Chapel (Methodist) near Laurelton in 1891, and the Ray's Church (Lutheran and Reformed) in 1883. He expanded afield and was responsible for the Lutheran Church in Lewistown (1900) and the Mifflin County Courthouse in Lewistown (1904). Miller also

built the Gast and Strunk stores, the Snodgrass Hardware Store, the Mifflinburg Bank (1880; later the fire house, now gone), and the Farmers' Bank on Chestnut Street (1889). In addition, he constructed many private homes: the Kurtz house at the corner of Walnut and Fourth Streets in 1888, the residence of Dr. Dimm across Third from the Ritter house in 1906, and his own home on Market Street at the corner of Sixth in 1875. (The wide porch as well as other similar porches in the neighborhood were later additions also fashioned by Miller.)

Most of Miller's buildings, of course, were more modest than the structures mentioned above. One-room school houses such as the Green Grove (1888) and the White Springs (1909), barns, and renovations required a good deal of his time. When a challenge was presented — church interiors, the delicate wood carvings in a mansion such as storekeeper Raudenbush's in Vicksburg (1887), or the blending of fine hardwoods in the Reformed Parsonage of Mifflinburg (1895) — architect Enoch Miller had perfectionists such as Mike Noll and Eli Groover to execute them.

In 1883 Miller opened a planing mill in North Eighth Street just south of the railroad. He advertised custom work and "plans, designs and estimates on short notice and on reasonable terms," and "flooring, siding, doors, sash, blinds, shutters, moulding, brackets and everything that pertains to the trade."[21] When Miller was not at the mill or at the construction site, he was in his garden or at the Reformed Church, where he directed the choir. Old age slowed him down, but he stayed on the job — a Mifflinburg resident

Enoch Miller's buildings. From top to bottom, left column: 307, 329, and 330 Market Street; top to bottom, right column: 411, 422 Market Street and 411 Walnut Street.

PAGE 163: commercial buildings at 315 and 407 Chestnut Street, all in Mifflinburg; and the Ray's Church west of Mifflinburg. Enoch Miller's personal residence before 1870 was at 601 Market Street and after that at 537 Market Street. Photos by Jim Walter.

Bird's-eye view of Mifflinburg looking north and west from the cemetery. From the collection of the Union County Historical Society, #85.7.6.

recalls that he saw him go up the ramp to the second floor of his mill on his hands and knees. When Miller died at age 88 in 1923, he left a legacy on almost every block of Mifflinburg. Notwithstanding all his successes, Miller's life was marred by tragedies that were not untypical of his time. Both of his sons and a daughter died in childhood, a son-in-law committed suicide, and two married daughters who had moved to Alabama died within a few months of each other in 1901.

During the Enoch Miller era there were limited opportunities for other builders. The Rudy family, consisting of Jacob and his sons, Elmer and Charles, were also highly regarded carpenters. Jacob, a West Buffalo Township pump maker and carpenter, moved to town and built a frame house with Victorian trim for his residence at the southwest corner of Walnut and First Streets, and a few years later he erected another next door for Charlie. Elmer is identified with the houses at 83 and 85 Chestnut Street and 225 Walnut. He built a residence for his family at 200 Market Street in the Queen Anne style and trimmed its interior with handsome oak woodwork including the door knobs. He added handmade tables and mirror framing. When work was slack in the winters, Rudy laid hardwood floors in Philadelphia and, for a time, operated a shirt factory in his barn.

Charles Rudy built a fine residence at 201 Chestnut Street with cast iron gables and broad porches, replacing the dilapidated Mader foundry which had stood there. During the prosperous 1920s he constructed a number of houses upon the vacant lots on Walnut Street between Second and Third as well as several of the bungalows scattered through the town. During the difficult 1930s Rudy sometimes built houses to sell, thereby giving employment to himself and his workmen. Accustomed to the older ways, he was reluctant to substitute synthetic sheathing for diagonal pine or narrow baseboards for broader traditional widths. On one occasion he refused to wall-in a bathroom which was devoid of a window. He also liked to see a pitch on a house roof and had no taste for the newfangled "ranch" house.

When "Charlie" put away his tools, only Hoyt Zimmerman, who had been an apprentice to Enoch Miller, along with his brothers, John and Ralph, remained the principal builders. Their bungalows and rectangular frame structures may be seen on Maple and Green Streets east of Third. Eventually, the Shipton family came to town from the Swengel area in time to handle much of the post-World War II housing expansion.

ENDNOTES:

1 R.V.B. Lincoln, *Mifflinburg Telegraph*, July 13, 1900.

2 John Blair Linn, *Annals of Buffalo Valley, Pennsylvania, 1755-1855*, Harrisburg, 1877, 279.

3 Archives, Union County Courthouse.

4 *New Berlin Union Star*, May 22, 1840.

5 *New Berlin Union Star*, June 3, 1846.

6 *New Berlin Union Times*, January 12, 1847.

7 *New Berlin Union Times*, January 12, 1847.

8 *Mifflinburg Union County Press*, August 7, 1861.

9 *Mifflinburg Telegraph*, April 9, 1884.

10 *Mifflinburg Telegraph*, April 30, 1884.

11 *Lewisburg Chronicle*, June 19, 1857.

12 Reminiscence of Cloyd A. Frederick.

13 *Mifflinburg Telegraph*, April 18, 1888.

14 *Mifflinburg Telegraph*, October 2, 1873.

15 Reminiscence of Harry C. Stuck.

16 *Mifflinburg Telegraph*, February 9, 1881.

17 *Mifflinburg Telegraph*, March 25, 1898.

18 *Mifflinburg Telegraph*, February 24, 1899.

19 *Mifflinburg Telegraph*, November 19, 1909.

20 *Mifflinburg Telegraph*, December 17, 1884.

21 *Mifflinburg Telegraph*, January 17, 1883.

CHAPTER 10

MIFFLINBURG AND THE LIFESTYLES OF SEVEN GENERATIONS

To write about the olden times is to be confronted with a multitude of problems, not the least of which is the fact that while change did not occur as rapidly as it has in more modern times, it occurred nevertheless, generation after generation. The times of Elias Youngman were different from those of Henry Gast, and from the latter to those of his son Spyker and his grandson Harry. Hence generalizations are apt to be misleading. Some indication of the changes wrought by inventions in transportation, on the farm, in industry, and in home building, have been noted; but there were also transformations in community life and lifestyles, and the town of Mifflinburg was no exception.

When the town fathers took over the management of the new borough in 1827, there were relatively few items of business to transact. Necessary roads and alleys had been opened and a constable chosen to enforce the laws. There were no water or sewer systems to regulate, no street lights to fill or trim, no street signs to keep up-to-date, and no fire apparatus to house or service. Livestock grazing in the streets, overindulgence at the local taverns, thieving, and gullies in the sloping roadways provided the town council with its business agenda. Unfortunately, the early minutes of the council are missing, and newspapers were sporadic until 1863. However, incidents were sometimes reported in the Lewisburg and New Berlin newspapers, and reminiscences occasionally appeared in the papers of a later date.

Undoubtedly reflecting a need, town leaders organized an extra legal agency just three years after incorporation, which they termed "The Society for the Prevention of Vice and Immorality." A secretarial report indicates that the principal focus was upon horse racing — presumably on the streets of the town — which it regarded as a serious offense. The society agreed to enforce local and state laws and to pay informers a share of the fines. They also resolved to prevent intoxication, card playing, and all other unlawful games and misbehavior. Henry Yearick was its president and Elias Youngman, its treasurer; and among its 100 members were four Dreisbachs, four Guteliuses, and three Monteliuses.[1] The effectiveness of the Society cannot be appraised, but its life appears to have been brief. It might be noted that the objection to horse racing was not so much endangerment as it was the side effects — the gambling, heavy drinking, and the roistering which it seemed to invite. Prevention and the avoidance of crises seem to have been the goals of the society. With only a sheriff in New Berlin and a local constable normally responsible for law enforcement, the assistance of the citizenry in emergencies was salutary. In time, the horse racing menace seems to have abated or been transferred to the local fairs, and card playing became less objectionable despite strenuous opposition from Methodists and kindred sects, but intoxication remained endemic.

A small corps of workers, receiving inspiration from national agitation for temperance in the second quarter of the nineteenth century, attempted to educate the public upon the evils of alcohol and to promote temperance through a state-wide Maine Law (prohibition) or local option legislation designed to stop the sale of alcoholic beverages in districts where the voters approved. Temperance reformers were more durable than successful through the nineteenth century, but, without planning it, the agitators opened the way for women to get involved in a social issue and eventually take a leadership in it.

Not being the county seat, Mifflinburg did not always share in the special events which came to its neighbors, New Berlin and Lewisburg. Circuses and menageries as well as more modest shows were apt to coincide with court week at the county seat. Even so, Mifflinburg did not seem to lack an active social life for those who sought it. A reminiscence relating to John Dreisbach, one of the village's most colorful personalities in the second quarter of the nineteenth century, mentions that he was a gun maker, a bachelor, a veteran of the War of 1812, a Jacksonian Democrat and Whig hater, and a ladies' man, who "loved his bitters but did not use to excess, as he did snuff. His blue coat with brass buttons, and foppish manner, his wiry form, swinging cane and hurried step, quickened into a run, hop-step and jump before ladies, occasioned laughter and provoked remark whenever he promenaded the streets of old Mifflinburg." It was also recalled that he had a meadow where the railroad depot stood later and that year after year it always rained when he mowed the grass. When he was told that it was due to his wickedness, he swore that he would thereafter mow only when the Reverend Anspach cut his grass.[2]

Dennison's patriotic honeycomb garland from 1898. Photo by the Terry Wild Studio.

If Mifflinburg were not a mecca for traveling shows, it had its Fourth of July. At the outset the Revolutionary War veterans mingled with the crowd and received the adulation of the orator — a local clergyman or possibly a lawyer from Sunbury or New Berlin. The celebration of 1854, surely one of the better-remembered commemorations, included a parade featuring the veterans of the War of 1812. Having passed through the principal streets, it moved eastward to a grove east of town, where J. Philip Cronmiller, a young teacher and law student, read the Declaration of Independence, and the Honorable Joseph Casey, a New Berlin lawyer and former member of Congress, delivered the principal oration. While Casey was exhorting, Thomas Crotzer, manager of the Columbia House, was cooking dinner. After a sumptuous repast the crowd gathered at the platform for a second address, this one by the Reverend Ephriam Kieffer, pastor of the Reformed Church. At its conclusion Captain Yearick's Brass Band offered martial music, and a male quartet rendered "exquisite singing." The celebration as a whole was "an honor to Mifflinburg."[3]

After the Civil War, the Fourth of July yielded to Memorial Day as the town's foremost holiday. At the initial celebration on May 30, 1873, in the absence of a local post of the Grand Army of the Republic, the state department of the Grand Army of the Republic decorated the graves of the Civil War dead with the assistance of the Spyker Graham Post no. 52 of Lewisburg. Delegations from both organizations reached town on the newly constructed railroad. Lewisburg, with Post no. 52 to spark it, had commemorated Decoration Day as early as 1869. The parade moved at 1:00 P.M. with Captain J.R. Orwig, one of the town's war heroes, serving as Marshal. He was followed by the Lewisburg Silver Cornet Band, Post no. 52 "clad in black with white gloves, badges of mourning, and regulation belts and caps," the Mifflinburg Cornet Band of fourteen, the survivors of the War of 1812, and the veterans of the Civil War. After the decoration of graves, Major Charles H. Shriner, the town's most eloquent orator, delivered the address. At its conclusion the Lewisburgers hastened to the depot to catch a train for home, where they repeated the ceremony a few hours later.[4]

In 1884 Mifflinburg's war veterans organized the William B. Foster Post no. 247, and from that year to World War I they headed the Memorial Day observances in town and assisted in the services at the rural cemeteries in the vicinity. The participation of children carrying bouquets of flowers — mostly wild varieties — became a fixture as early as 1874, and the ritual varied little through the next century.

Summer, of course, was picnicking and camping season. Four miles to the south, Penns Creek's wooded banks awaited the pleasure seeker, and five miles northward sparkling brooks gushed from the hemlock-covered ravines along Jones Mountain. The first outing to the latter reported in the local press occurred in late July of 1846; it appears also to be the first use of the word "picnic." Thirty couples seated in wagons left town at seven in the morning, bound for Buffalo Mountain and enjoying a "feast of nature's green garb" enroute. At the foot of the mountain they separated to engage in angling for the "speckled fin tribe." After several hours they returned to the grove for a sumptuous dinner and appropriate remarks by Dr. John Rothrock. As they returned, "evening shades, clouds of purple and most delicate crimson tints" hovered over the western horizon.[5]

A quite different variation of a picnic took place in 1855 at Sampsell's Dam on the south side of Buffalo

Valley when "twenty couples of young men and maidens" set out in a farm wagon for Penns Creek. Arriving at noon, they set up tents and enjoyed a big picnic dinner. In the afternoon they divided into couples, rods in hand for fishing, and the afternoon passed quickly. Some went horseback riding; some clowned as cavaliers; others toured the countryside, returning at sunset when a camp fire awaited them. In the evening there was play-acting, with Indian scenes, and green corn and rattlesnake dances predominating. At midnight lights were extinguished, but there was little sleep. Some joined the guard at the camp fire. Later, the stillness was broken by the driver, who rushed from his bed in the wagon shouting "robbers." None could be found, but the horses had vanished and had to be pursued in the darkness. By this time "the spirit of mischief was rife." It was an "eventful" night, but dawn was a "welcome sight." In the morning there was hunting for small game, and at noon a grand dinner. The rumbling of thunder and threat of a storm "hastened the adieus."[6] The picnic's activities would scarcely conform with the twentieth century's notion of Victorian deportment.

One of the favorite gathering places in late summer for at least half a century was the Sugar Camp, a grove of sugar maples on the south side of Penns Creek. Referred to also as Smith's and Shively's Camp, it had a dancing platform in the 1870s and 1880s. There young people gathered on Saturday evenings to dance to the music of fiddler Charles Hummel of White Springs. Later, it was used as a camping ground by several generations of White Springs/Mifflinburg families. Another variety of the picnic was the huckleberry party — a trip to the mountains by a group of friends to find recreation in berry-picking. Similar arrangements took people to the fields for wild strawberries and to the woodlots for raspberries and blackberries. In the fall tiresome and blister-prone corn husking was sometimes lightened with parties, and gathering chestnuts was a pleasantly rewarding way to wind up a hike.

The coming of the railroad opened the West End to outings. In fact, the laying of the last rail to Laurel Park initiated a veritable round of festivities at Weidensaul's (later Albright's) Grove on the bank of Penns Creek. Other favorite picnic and camping spots — all near whistle stops on Penns Creek — were Cherry Run, Lindale, and, at the turn of the century, Thomas' Dam or Trail's End between Glen Iron and Weikert.

Changing times in the "horse and buggy" era may be seen in the kaleidoscope of recreations. As early as 1820 debating was a favorite. A contest between Mifflinburg and Lewisburg, staged at Taggert's Tavern at Buffalo Cross Roads, which the chairman awarded to the former, so incensed the Lewisburg team that they took their case to the press, "cudgeling the Mifflinburg Society in a pretty lively

Laurelton Lumber Company outing on May 31, 1902. Some of the participants were: Charles Mohn and wife (with parasol), Samuel Rutherford, Dr. Glover, Florence Rutherford, Clara Pursley, and Pete Pursley (with bow tie). From the collection of the Union County Historical Society, #89.5.14.16.

BOTTOM: Excursions on the narrow-gauge White Deer/Loganton Railroad, taken to Tea Springs, were extremely popular from 1906 to 1916. The line, which connected Buffalo Valley to Sugar Valley, was never profitable. This real photo postcard was sent in 1909 to Helen Kennedy of New Columbia. From the collection of Gary W. and Donna M. Slear.

way."[7] In the 1840s and again in the 1870s, spelling bees were the rage in both towns and in the country schools. Shooting matches were a favorite for several generations but seem to have enjoyed their greatest popularity in the 1840s.

Baseball was introduced in Lewisburg by Clifford and Charlie Hade in 1858 and popularized during the Civil War. Teams were organized in Lewisburg by 1866 and in the smaller towns shortly thereafter. A Lewisburg town team, the McLaughlins, defeated a college group, the Star Club, by a prodigious 85-35, obviously a triumph of batters over pitchers and fielders.[8] In a few years the sport attracted so much interest that a skeptic noted, "Too much play, a bad business." He conceded that amusement was desirable, "But hilarity should not over-leap the limits of prudence, morality, temperance, or any other kindred virtue . . . . Baseball gives health to the system and elasticity to the muscles, but there is a limit to the time expended . . . and it may be a nuisance and an absolute evil." He deplored the betting, which reduced the sport to "common gambling." "Young men neglect their shops, books and families to indulge in it . . . . They have baseball in their conversation, and baseball on the brain." He hoped that the participants would not permit its fascination to "unseat their better judgment."[9] Despite such misgivings of some, baseball was here to stay.

Mifflinburg's teams played in various fields on the margin of town and after the erection of the new school in 1876 on the slope east of it. The right fielder looked down from an elevation which gave him a breathtaking view of Buffalo Valley, but one which undoubtedly impeded his efficiency. In 1905 a public subscription permitted the fields relocation to Fifth and Railroad Streets, where twenty years later "Irish" Tom Murphy of Northumberland would leave Mifflinburg fans speechless when he smote three tape-measure home runs across the ditch in left field against the town's hapless pitching.

In 1867 French croquet was introduced in Union County, and it immediately caught on. Men and women competed in pairs. It became a popular family game as it could be played on a small lawn and the mallets, balls, and wickets could be easily transported to picnics and camping sites. In the 1870s quoits had its finest hour. Almost overnight clay boxes, iron hubs, and the doughnut-like discs appeared near barber shops and other loafing places. It was a game for both young and old, and participants were soon rated according to their expertise. Like croquet, quoits went along to the picnic groves. In the 1880s checkers

caught the public's fancy, and again a pecking order evolved. A.A. Hopp and Dr. James Kleckner were rated highly, but the champion was acknowledged to be the Reverend W.K. Forster, pastor of the Presbyterian Church.[10]

By the 1880s football arrived in Buffalo Valley, first at Bucknell and twenty years later as a town sport. The game was accepted at Bucknell by the students despite, or possibly because of, its ferocity. Townspeople were more skeptical of its contributions to education. Editor Schoch observed in the fall of 1893 that "Football is all the rage now, and about as much danger in it as a slugging match . . . . State College and Bucknell will play on Saturday in Lewisburg. Go down and see them trying to break each other's ribs." The following week he returned to the subject. "Score: 36 to 18, State College winning. The game was characterized by brutal and uncalled-for slugging on the part of State College. It became so serious at one time that the spectators stopped the game and demanded

Croquet set. Courtesy of Bernie & Peg's Antiques. Photo by the Terry Wild Studio.

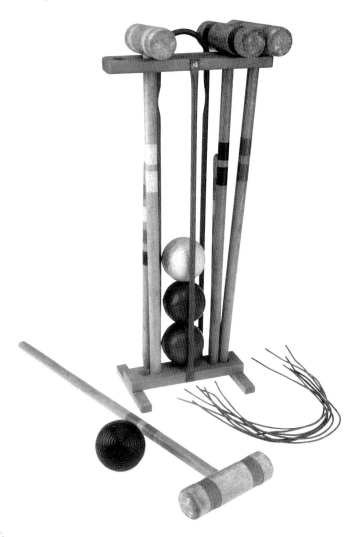

that it cease."[11] Football found a defender in editor George W. Foote of the *Mifflinburg Times*, who noted, "An occasional consequence of a football game is a deplorable accident. A frequent consequence of a pleasure trip by rail, an excursion on a yacht, or a bath in the lake or ocean is an accident equally deplorable. Just why these persons who condemn the game of football because of one accident do not condemn pleasure travel, yachting and bathing for the same reason probably will never be known."[12] Despite disagreements regarding its merits, by the turn of the century Mifflinburg, Laurelton, and Lewisburg each had town teams, the latter sponsored by the Furniture Factory. Harry "Pat" Gilbert, a massive butcher, was Mifflinburg's star. After a victory over Milton, Gilbert's picture appeared in the *Philadelphia Inquirer*, but he was mistakenly identified as a member of the Bucknell team. The *Telegraph* called upon the university to correct the error or risk the wrath of a P.O.T.F.C. (pugilist of the first class).[13]

Costs seem to have been the factor that turned the game back to the collegians if Lewisburg's game at Laurelton in November of 1900 was typical. The Laurelton team won by a decisive 40-0, with Harry Pursley and Captain Hoover in starring roles, but gate receipts were less than ten dollars. Some spectators contributed a second time to meet expenses, but others had climbed the back fence and would pay nothing. "It takes a mean man to steal his way into a game," a spectator moralized. The team, he insisted, did not wish to take money and would admit anyone too poor to pay.[14] No more box scores were recorded in the local press. A quarter century later, football was given a new lease on life when the high schools in the area introduced it into their athletic programs. In time, football became the most popular spectator sport in the region, although wrestling would have its fair share of devotees, particularly in Mifflinburg.

The decade of the 1890s was the golden age of the bicycle. The "wheel," of course, was invented earlier, but its popularity awaited rubber tires, ball bearings, free wheels, and coaster hubs — all of which appealed to people of all ages. One of the first bicycle rides featured in the newspapers occurred in 1884 when the "Buffalo Bits" correspondent noted that Charles Seeman, a bookkeeper at the Central Foundry in Lewisburg, paid his friends at Boyertown (Mazeppa) a visit when "He came on a bicycle and made the time from Lewisburg up the pike through Lochiel and then via Buffalo Cross Roads to Boyertown in fifty minutes."[15] It will never be known how many heads turned at the sight of this bicycle, or velocipede as it was called in the early days, but by the 1890s it was becoming available at shops and hardware stores.

The enthusiasm may be seen in the number of purchasers. In 1899 more than 800 were reported, and the number of unregistered wheels was anyone's guess. Its popularity may also be seen in a borough ordinance prohibiting bicycles on the sidewalks, and in the number of bicycle clubs. The Mifflinburg Club cycled to Penns Cave in August of 1896, wheeling out of town at 4:30 A.M. They breakfasted at Millheim 23 miles away and arrived at their destination at 9:30 A.M. After an hour's rowboat tour of the cavern, they were winging their way to Millheim, where they lunched at two. Still unexhausted, they separated — some heading for Milesburg, others for Rebersburg, and the less adventurous for home — the latter arriving before dark after logging 71 miles.[16]

A year later the club made an even more ambitious round-trip to the Gettysburg Battlefield. For the less athletic, the club sponsored a bicycle parade with both the wheels and riders decorated in colorful regalia; there were 59 in line, ladies in front, with the gentlemen and young boys following. To be sure, the unusual rather than the commonplace was ordinarily reported by the press, but small items occasionally noted information such as Harry Wilkinson's quick trip to Milton and Benneville Mensch's occasional business trips to Lewisburg from his farm west of town.

With many inexperienced riders and the temptation to move at high speeds, accidents were inevitable. A young cyclist "chock full of fire water, who scorched up town on last Saturday evening, caused no little excitement," the *Telegraph* noted, "especially when he took a ten or fifteen foot plunge from his wheel. Doubtless his well-earned header had a sobering effect."[17] Ladies as well as men were sometimes involved. "Miss 'Bess' Brubaker and Dr. Gast, whilst on their bicycles and going it a mile a minute, collided at Chestnut and Fifth streets on Monday last, when something dropped — yes, both dropped like a flash. Apologies were exchanged, showing a reciprocity of feeling, which was most commendable."[18] As it was with buggies and would be with automobiles later, the slope of the Cemetery Hill was a test of bicycles. The leader of a group of young ladies enroute from New Berlin was unable to retard her vehicle and was thrown upon the gravel roadbed, but women were also complimented for their skill using the wheel. "Wheelmen should profit by the example of the wheelwomen. They scorch not, neither do they hump themselves, nor run blindly into obstructions; but sit erect and beautiful sail gracefully along and get there on time."[19]

Bicycles created a demand for sales and services. Shops were soon meeting the cyclists' needs; Frank H. Forster's on South Fifth Street seems to have been the first of its kind in town, and Charles F. Lontz was its genial salesman and mechanic. When editor Schoch gave it an inspection, he found 30 new bicycles ranging in price from $20 for the Cadorus to $75 for the magnificent Columbia. "This industry has come to stay without a fraction of a doubt," he prophesied. "There was a time when wheels were indulged in just for the fun of it, but now it's business with the great majority."[20]

Just a year after his forecast an automobile was driven into town. "Monday afternoon, July 29 [1901] a very neat and pretty automobile, having three occupants glided into this office," Schoch reported, "exciting the curiosity and admiration of all witnesses of the sight." The chassis was manufactured by W.E. Ritter of Milton and the body by Charles Harter, a buggy mechanic of Mifflinburg. A year later adventuresome Dr. O.K. Pellman purchased a one-cylinder Cadillac. After only a short time, he and his mother had an accident at the Barber farm two miles west of town. The steering lever had dropped out, and the unguided car had hit a post, throwing Mrs. Pellman out of the car and breaking her left arm. The age of the automobile had arrived, and with it the romantic era of the bicycle departed.

Mifflinburg had no opera house to be compared with Lewisburg's impressive Schwartz Hall; and if they wished to hear people such as Frances Willard, Frederick Douglass, "Petroleum" Nasby or Henry Ward Beecher, they had to go to Lewisburg or Milton. Sankey Hall, a ramshackle structure on Walnut Street near Fourth, was available to touring shows and local talent. There was no regular schedule of events; but if one were patient, something possibly exciting would come along. It might be J.W. Donavin's Original Tennesseeans; The Original Slave Cabin Singers; Uncle Tom's Cabin; an address on liberty or taxes by Lee Francis Lybarger; a concert by Mifflinburg's own string band; or the community's first exposure to a "Talking Machine" (Graphophone), with cornet and banjo solos, a rendition of the Twenty Third Psalm and the Lord's Prayer.

By the 1890s women were participating actively in musicals, drama, and declamations. Bessie Brubaker was a standout as a dramatist, and her role as the Irish maid in "Chaperone" was the hit of 1898;

Virginia Anspach and Carrie Mensch were fine pianists in the first quarter of the new century; and a string quartet composed of Anspach, Virginia Miller, Minnie Kurtz, and Edith Bogenrief performed for audiences in the churches of the area. Sue Stapleton Brubaker was renowned as elocutionist, poet, and teacher.

Women were also participating more actively in intellectual and civic activities. The Shakespeare Society as well as the Twentieth Century and the Athenaeum clubs date from the turn of the century, and the Order of Eastern Star and the Scarlet Rebecca Lodge both began in 1913. During its early years the benches in the Lyric Theatre could be removed and the auditorium transformed into a ballroom, and it was the scene of the annual assembly. The Assembly of 1909 was heralded as "the most brilliant social event of the season for Mifflinburg's society and friends."[21] The Imperial Orchestra of Lewisburg offered a dance program of 24 numbers.

Visits and parties might occur any time of the year, but they were concentrated in the sleighing season, which usually extended from December through February. Work was not apt to be as pressing in mid-winter, and the advantages of travel in a light sleigh on hard-packed snow needs no elaboration. An evening in Milton was not unusual; and trips to Lewisburg, New Berlin, and the West End were commonplace. As indicated elsewhere, a winter's evening might be disastrous if interrupted by heavy snow and wind, but the uncertainty of the weather was seldom a deterrent. The quest might be a jolly party with friends; it might be a bob-sled ride into the country in Strawser's or Bender's sled; it might be simply a "family call" with apples and paring knives before the kitchen stove; or it could be sledding on Cemetery Hill. Until the coming of the automobile, Third and Fourth Streets were frequently toboggan-like raceways carrying the riders as far as the cindered railroad crossings.

Children looked forward to Christmas when there was gift exchanging, albeit quite modest when compared with twentieth-century practices. The week following Christmas was even more enticing. On these evenings they dressed in bizarre costumes and went "belsnikelling" — moving from door to door in their neighborhoods, "begging for goodies." On New Year's Eve they might wait for the stroke of twelve to hear the bells and gun blasts which greeted the new year. Hallowe'en was a night of petty mischief, carried on without masks or costumes.

Though there are real photo postcards of many of the county's town bands, including Mifflinburg's string band, Glen Iron's is the only orchestra so photographed. From the collection of Gary W. and Donna M. Slear.

An invitation to a Grand March on New Year's Eve. From the collection of Glenn and Ruth Wehr Zimmerman.

Kreider Kurtz, Guy Roush, David VanDueson, Newton Kurtz, and David L. Glover (left to right) being playful at Camp Westfall, Hartley Township, in the 1920s. From the collection of David Goehring.

Bellings (charivari) were opportunities to harass newly wedded couples with bells and other noise-making devices, ending in the couple's capitulation, symbolized by their offer of sweetmeats to the merrymakers.

Of course, there was also Sunday school, a weekly fellowship with one's friends. The Sunday school movement reached Mifflinburg in 1820 when the Society of the Mifflinburg Sunday and Adult School was founded. Though non-denominational, its membership was made up largely of members of the Lutheran and German Reformed congregations. After an organizational meeting at the Franklin School, twelve managers were elected and proceeded to adopt a set of bylaws and appoint superintendents for the two schools, the German and English. Frederick Gutelius headed the former and Joseph Musser, the latter. The schools were divided into male and female sections, presumably without reference to age. Class meetings were held each Sunday, with one in the morning and the other in the afternoon.

Class I was designed for scholars able to read the Bible; Class II, for those capable of reading the New Testament; Class III, for students who could read "indifferently"; Class IV, for pupils unable to read but who could spell in one or more syllables; and Class V, for those who could read the alphabet and spell in one syllable. For textual materials Class I read from the Bible and catechisms; Class II from the New Testament; Classes III and IV from spelling books and hymnals; and Class V from the alphabet. Rewards in the form of blue and red cards were provided for all classes. A Class I student, for example, qualified for a blue card by reciting six verses of scripture or one page of catechism, while a Class II or IV pupil received a blue card for punctual attendance and good behavior. Six blue cards were exchangeable for a red one, and a red one was valued at a half cent — redeemable in religious tracts suitable to the reading capacity of the recipient. If a student could not read the tract, it was assumed that it would be of value to the parents. It was not entirely a one-way street, however, in that a penalty for misbehavior was the forfeiture of a prescribed number of cards. The managers too were subject to disciplinary action in this highly structured system. To miss a meeting without an acceptable excuse incurred a fine of six cents.

The schools operated upon a quarterly basis; and at the conclusion of each term, two clergymen were invited to deliver appropriate sermons to the students, parents, teachers, and administrators, with one sermon in English, and the second in German. Ministers conversant in German were close at hand, and the Reverend J.H. Fries, pastor of the German Reformed Church in Mifflinburg, was a frequent invitee. The managers went as far as the Milton Presbyterian Church to obtain the Reverend George Junkin and the Reverend David Kirkpatrick, and to the Buffalo Presbyterian Church for the Reverend Thomas Hood. An authorization for the purchase of books in 1826 indicates that the English-reading students outnumbered the German readers by a ratio of more than three to one. In 1839, 104 females and 78 males were enrolled, with the girls excelling the boys in earning blue tickets by a ratio of four to one.

At the outset the instructors appear to have been men; but in 1829 Margaret Geddis was appointed school librarian, and six women were named to the

and several generations of Cowan children attended Sunday school at the Red Bank School. The churches eventually provided religious instruction for their own membership, and the doors of the one-room schoolhouses once again remained closed on Sundays. The Union County Sabbath School Association celebrated its centennial in 1973.

For young and old there were the medicine shows and the more controversial gypsies. People were intrigued by their fortunetelling but frequently critical of their behavior. In 1908 the gypsies camped for several weeks in a shed at the cemetery while they solicited scrap iron, paper, and rags. Several years later the gypsies were ordered to leave town after being charged with "lifting goods" in the local stores. After spending a few more days in the Laurel Park area, they drifted on to Centre County. There were also Italian organ grinders and musicians. Two of the latter equipped with a harp and violin, "made choice

The Mifflinburg Telegraph.

VOL. 60 NO.12.   MIFFLINBURG, PA., THURSDAY, OCTOBER 27, 1921.   WHOLE NO. 4071

OCTOBER'S EVER CHANGING SCENE, SHOWS LAST OF ALL, OUR HALLOWE'EN

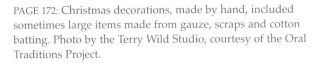

PAGE 172: Christmas decorations, made by hand, included sometimes large items made from gauze, scraps and cotton batting. Photo by the Terry Wild Studio, courtesy of the Oral Traditions Project.

Hallowe'en tricksters in White Deer c. 1910 as photographed by Mary E. Hagey. From the collection of Betty Herald.

teaching staff.[22] The ecumenical approach to a Sunday school began to erode after a few years when the Methodists withdrew. In 1855 the First Presbyterians separated also, and in 1858 the Lutherans left the Elias Church to move into their new edifice. Finally, the Reformed and Lutheran congregations formally dissolved the association. After the acceptance of the Public School Law, the Sunday school movement spread to the one-room schoolhouses in the country. An active program was conducted in the Green Grove School in Limestone Township for many years,

music on our streets the other day to the delight of every listener, who voiced their appreciation in dropping many nickels in the collector's hat."23 There were itinerant gymnasts who performed at the street corners, scissors sharpeners, umbrella menders, and a variety of other vendors.

Movies became popular almost instantly. The first were presented by itinerants at the high school or Sankey Hall. One resident recalls the "Black Diamond Express" at the latter and the anguished cries of the audience as the train appeared to rush toward them. The nickelodeon offered pictures for several years. In 1908 Kathryn (Kitty) and William Romig built the Lyric Theatre next door to their home on Chestnut Street, and it soon became a Mifflinburg institution. Fortified with bags of roasted peanuts to occupy the intermissions between each reel of the show, the children crowded into the front rows, leaving their parents seated farther back with larger bags of peanuts. Saturday night featured a western, hopefully with Tom Mix, the local champion. Thursday was reserved for more serious drama, with fewer children and peanuts.

Mifflinburg men found much of their relaxation at their favorite congregating places. At the turn of the century, John Klingler's (later Jacob Boop's) tobacco shop was a popular spot; but the favorite appears to have been Lincoln (Link) Hoffman's tinning and plumbing shop or "entertainment room," where the "boys" grouped to discuss "politics, religion, progress of the village, history — both ancient and up-to-date — deaths and 'what did he leave,' law, marriage and divorce, etc., etc." Perhaps the best-remembered evening occurred in March of 1901:

Just two-thirds of the Mifflinburg Buggy Company, Al [Hopp] and Bob [Gutelius] had located itself on a beautiful porcelain ivory-like tub (all the chairs and lounges, upholstered and otherwise, being occupied by the early callers) and just as the gentlemen named were warming up to the discussion before the house there was a crash beneath them — the tub and the two-thirds going to earth with a thud that shook the building, threatened to extinguish the acetylene lights and jar the store teeth from the jaws of those who were dropping in to pay their water bills. . . . When the shock was fairly over and reason once more ruled, an inspection [revealed] that its feet had only slipped out of place and no damage sustained. The business of the house then proceeded in its usual decorous manner, and on adjournment all voted that Hoffman's bath fixtures will safely withstand all the customary tests and a few unusual ones to boot.24

More formal gathering places for the males were provided by the Odd Fellows (est. 1846), the Masons (1866),

the Knights of the Golden Eagle (1888), the Modern Woodmen (1901), the Patriotic Order Sons of America (1907), and the Loyal Order of the Moose (1923).

The best-remembered event of the late nineteenth century was the town's centennial celebration on Tuesday, October 4, 1892. The streets were thronged from the first gray lines of approaching dawn until late at night, and special trains helped to swell the crowd, estimated at 10,000. Arches and banners spanned the streets, and almost every home was decorated. A grand military, civic, and industrial parade was highlighted by the inspiring presence of old Mexican War fifers and drummers from Centreville (Penns Creek) — most of them past 70. John B. Linn, distinguished author and state historian, delivered the principal address from a platform in front of the Reformed church. For the young there were bicycle races, a balloon which failed to ascend due to high winds, and a great display of fireworks from the top of Cemetery Hill.

Not as spectacular as Mifflinburg's Centennial but of incalculable influence upon the thinking of a generation of Mifflinburgers was the Chautauqua. Beginning in 1912 the great tent served as a town meeting place, where hundreds gathered for lectures, drama, and music. Each afternoon and evening for five days they saw a series of programs prepared by the Swarthmore Division of Chautauqua from its nationwide outreach. The children, too, participated, meeting in the mornings with college students majoring in dramatics, who shaped the talents of their pupils into a Saturday afternoon program for their parents and friends. Public-spirited citizens sponsored the Chautauqua and paid the deficits when they occurred. After a sizable loss in 1925, it was decided to enlarge the tent and cut the price to one dollar — less than one-half the usual cost for the five days. The stratagem worked; the tickets were sold, and Mifflinburg had a "first" in Chautauqua history. The district superintendent made a special trip to see the 1,500 spectators under the mammoth canvas. The experiment was successful a second year. In 1928, however, time ran out for the Chautauqua as the radio and the automobile decimated its popular support. Many local participants, however, mourned its loss.

PAGE 175: Chautauquas came to both Mifflinburg and Lewisburg from 1912 through 1931. The Chautauquas — a cultural, religious, and recreational movement that presented daytime educational seminars and evening performances — were held under tents in the summertime in the two communities. From the collection of Katherine Roush.

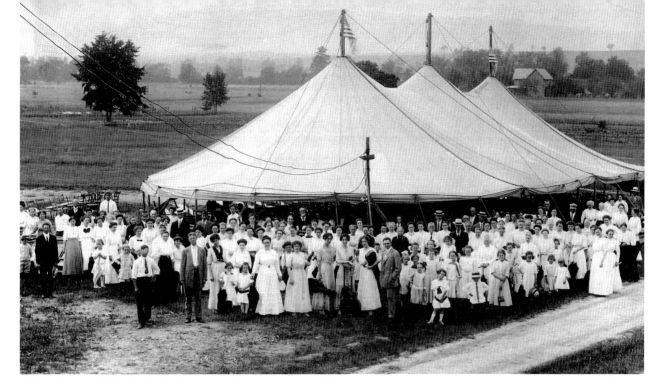

In the civic life of Mifflinburg between the Civil War and World War I, no one exerted a greater influence than George Washington Schoch. Born there in 1842, he learned the printer's trade in Lewisburg; and after an enlistment in the Civil War, he purchased the *Mifflinburg Telegraph* from Reuben G. and Thomas G. Orwig. He distributed his first issue of the paper on January 1, 1873. With a keen eye for news, he filled two or three columns weekly with personal items and one or two with civic and business developments. An ardent Republican, he hewed to the party line at home as well as in Harrisburg and Washington. He advocated veterans' benefits and reported individual pensions as they were legislated, and he apparently never found any not deserving.

George Shoch had an unflagging enthusiasm for Mifflinburg and repeatedly advocated changes which he believed would improve it. Almost with the first issue of the paper, he pointed out the need for fire protection. When Lewisburg, through William Cameron's generosity, purchased a Silsby Steamer in 1874, Schoch pressed for action in Mifflinburg; and he assisted in bringing the Lewisburg fire company to town for a demonstration. The results were impressive as the engine and personnel met every test before a large audience. "The day of the leather bucket is gone," he insisted. "We hope the demonstration today will open the eyes of some of our people that this is the year 1875, a better way to put out a fire than was known when Adam smoked his cigar in the shade of the apple tree, and Eve washed her clothes in the creek." However, the cost seemed prohibitive to most townspeople, and the leather bucket remained.[25]

Ten years later Schoch again tried to provide the community with fire protection, advocating the purchase of two J.M. Connelly chemical extinguishers. "Do the people of Mifflinburg want protection against fire?" he asked. Answering his own question in the affirmative, he urged the citizens to sign petitions for the purchase of the machines, and a few weeks later he estimated that three-fifths of the voters had signed. The town council agreed to a referendum, but the taxpayers objected to the cost, and the proposal went down to defeat by a 173-86 vote. Schoch accepted the action as a delay, not a defeat, and decided to await another opportunity.

As with fire protection, Lewisburg's organization of a water works in 1883 caught the attention of Mifflinburg's citizenry — and particularly that of George Schoch. It might be noted that at this time the borough provided two hand pumps, one on Chestnut between Third and Fourth, and another on Market between Fourth and Fifth; and some of the property holders dug wells on their lots. There was also an ice pond on East Walnut Street fed by springs a few blocks away, and some householders obtained ice by cutting it on Buffalo Creek. Despite the apparent inadequacy of water, there appear to have been few complaints.

Samuel Gutelius Grove, in one of his hundreds of columns in the *Telegraph*, offered an explanation for the tendency of householders to use a neighbor's pump rather than dig wells of their own. In 1887 he had a well drilled on his farm just north of town — a technique which was replacing the older dug wells. The new well cost just over $100 and provided him with plenty of water. Earlier, he noted, there were few dug wells. Buildings were erected, when possible, at springs or streams, some convenient and others inconvenient. For himself, Grove added, he would rather have a good well to honor his memory than a monument. The old well, which he was abandoning, was 48 feet deep. It had cost 48 full days' work as well as $50 for the digging and $30 for the pump. It had required five years to complete since it could only be deepened a few feet at a time during dry weather. By contrast, a drilled well could be completed in several days and be superior to a dug one.

Now that Lewisburg was lifting its water from the Susquehanna, Schoch urged support for the Spring Water Company of Mifflinburg, organized for the purpose of tapping springs along "Yonder Towering Hills." Nothing materialized. A year later, following his comments upon Al Stuck's sprinkling service on the streets in front of subscribers, he opined, "Oh that we had a reservoir on the big hill sufficient to supply the entire burg with the same sort of water. How handy it would be in case of fire, and from $8,000-$10,000 ought to secure Mifflinburg with a blessing of this kind. Why not raise a stock company for this purpose? It would pay." Again, his advice went unheeded.[26]

The town's centennial celebration in 1892 and the Columbian Exposition at Chicago the following year with its use of water and fountains to beautify the grounds seem to have stimulated local interest in a water works. At a public meeting, leaders decided to seek a municipal system and a bond issue of $35,000 to meet the costs. Organizing as a "Peoples' Ticket," they called for the property holders to support them in a referendum. The balloting revealed a sentiment in favor of public ownership by a vote of 185 to 109, but it turned out to be only the first of a series of developments over the next five years. With the borough council divided, opponents refused to accept the word of engineers that a source of water at the foot of Buffalo Mountain eight miles northwest of town would flow by gravity to the proposed reservoir atop Cemetery Hill despite reassurances that the intake at the mountain was 200 feet higher. The doubters also questioned whether the water would have sufficient pressure to reach the upper streets.

Editor Schoch agreed that there was a need for caution and that there were honest differences of opinion; but he solicited letters from former residents, in whom the citizenry would have confidence and who lived in places where there were water works. They responded with letters of praise for running water and pointed to the industrial advantages which

would accrue. He next presented a petition for water to the council with the signatures of 284 male and female taxables, but the council postponed action from month to month. In February of 1895 the Mifflinburg Borough Council finally approved another referendum, and again water was approved by a 193-76 vote. However, the council failed to apply to the state for permission to bond. A public meeting called for action upon water and for a sewage system as well, but the latter was at once divisive. One optimist observed that sewers were not required and that the water system would help to flush the wastes which accumulated in the gutters during dry weather. The more water used, he explained, the more runoff. The high cost of the right of way was also voiced, and proponents, in turn, charged that obstructionists sought to increase this cost and labeled their behavior as malicious.

The contest dragged on through 1896 and 1897 with Schoch grinding out editorial after editorial. In July of 1897 the council agreed unanimously to yet another referendum, and the opponents of water girded themselves for a last stand, making the proposed bonding their principal target. They were now joined by the *Mifflinburg Times*, which had been ambivalent heretofore. In one of Shoch's rare criticisms of its editor, he wrote that Foote had been so long in opposition to everything going on that it might make him seem queer to be in any other position. Schoch noted that the churches and the school had bonded, "without hurting anybody." He also found space to report a disastrous fire at Hawley, which had failed to provide local firefighting equipment.

The weather was fine on referendum day, but there were noisy arguments along the streets leading to the polling places. The result was a victory for bonding by 194 to 123. By the spring of 1898, contracts had been let for the construction of the water works; the dirt was flying from 80 hand-propelled shovels; and Hoffman's advertisements for sanitary plumbing, steam and hot water fittings, galvanized, enameled, copper, and cast iron tubs, were appearing in the local papers. Achievement was in the air as proposals for a trolley, electric plant, sewage system, town hall, fire department, cannery, knitting and shirt factories, athletic park, and a town clock were rolling from the tongues of the townspeople. The borough council made a start in the direction of fire protection by purchasing hose and hose wagons.

On June 3 the water was turned on to test the hydrants and flush out the pipes. In Schoch's words, "As it gushed forth we felt like appropriating some of the hurrahs for Schley [Spanish-American War hero at Santiago de Cuba] for the Mifflinburg water system. Now the young men in town should be up and doing in the way of organizing a fire department."[27] "Solomon B. Miller wanted the honor and credit of being the first citizen to 'take the water,' and we mean the pure water right from the mountain.... Last Monday [June 26] Mr. Hoffman's plumber did the necessary work in the Miller mansion [southwest corner of Green and Fourth Streets] and now 'Sollie' can turn it on."[28] That evening the town council formally accepted the work, and "Sollie" had his wish. Of course, few homes were as yet connected, but the curious gathered at Miller's and at the hydrants to see the "miracle." The demonstrations were not disappointing.

The running water served to relieve most of the tension which had accumulated. Before that, however, several proponents of the water system took their revenge upon John Sortman, who had insisted that the water would never reach the second floor of his house at the northwest corner of Thompson and Fourth Streets. Connecting a section of the new fire hose to a nearby hydrant, they unleashed a stream of water against his chimney top and scattered the bricks across the roof. Sortman moved to Lewis Township a short time later. Thus Mifflinburg had its water system at a cost of $30,000, $5,000 less than the estimate.

The jubilation had scarcely subsided when typhoid fever broke out. Some of the opponents of the system at once attributed it to the water, but it was more widely believed that the pipe laying had opened a seepage between the outhouses and the wells which were still in use. In a few days the cases increased to five or six, and unconfirmed reports placed the number at 20 or 30 with eight resulting deaths. Advocates of a sewerage system at once launched a campaign to draw off the effluvia into Buffalo Creek, and within several months two companies were organized to install the sewers: one system for the east side of town, and one for the west. Again the dirt was flying.

Schoch, of course, advocated its consummation, and he reached back to the Civil War to find a metaphor to justify it. "As to sewerage," he wrote, "Mifflinburg now has a fine water plant, and patrons of the same will want a sewer .... A good substantial tent has been erected, and now like wise occupants of it, we want a drain around it." He maintained that a sewer would increase the number of water subscribers, expand the revenues, and cut the cost to the user; and insisted that the expense of $8-10,000 was

"not a mountain that cannot be crossed easily."[29] During the construction of the sewers (which were later taken over by the borough), Schoch continued to promote the mountain water to those who remained undecided, but his tone was now relaxed and jovial. "You long and snoring sleepers miss a grand sight every morning of your life, depend upon it. Get up, grasp the nozzle from fair maiden hands and see how the spray will cheer you all the day through." He lauded the Woman's Christian Temperance Union for a public water trough they had installed at Chestnut and Fourth Streets, writing, "It is a God-inspiring gift . . . a great blessing, liberally used and very greatly appreciated."[30] Henry Strunk, he added, had introduced water motors in his store to grind coffee, run sewing machines, and operate fans; and he had installed toilet rooms for his customers as well. Only the street water sprinkler had been affected adversely, but instead of the rambling sprinkler there was now the efficient pavement street wash. The mountain spring water source continues to be used even now.

With running water assured, Schoch returned to the long-delayed question of a fire department. In March of 1898 he observed in the *Mifflinburg Telegraph* that a bucket brigade did not work automatically. Three months later an organizational meeting was held; and David L. Glover, a young attorney, was chosen as president, and H.O. Bower, a local butcher, was named chief. Drills followed, and the following January the fire company met its first test successfully. The old barn of the Thompson marble works, now filled with hay and straw, was discovered to be on fire, with the blaze bursting through the roof. The fire company responded promptly and soon had two hoses on the barn and the buildings adjacent to it. In Schoch's words: "The reliability of the waterworks and the promptness of the firemen saved the village a very disastrous conflagration; the water plant paid for itself at its first test."[31]

At the same time Mifflinburg people had their first demonstration of acetylene gas lighting at Link Hoffman's plumbing establishment. The light was described as brilliant, and Hoffman soon installed a generator and fixtures. In larger towns, electricity was already replacing kerosene for lighting, but at the moment it seemed years away for Mifflinburg. Gast's store was next in line, and, after correcting some defects, it too glowed with an astonishing brilliance. Other local businesses followed suit, but its growth was cut short by the inevitable arrival of electricity.

Schoch, as might have been expected, was in the forefront of the movement for electricity also; but he shared the leadership with Thomas O. Gutelius, president of the borough council, who championed municipal ownership and led the drive to a successful conclusion. Under Gutelius' guidance in the fall of 1902, the Mifflinburg Borough Council authorized a debt of $6,000 to provide a power plant, and the voters gave it their approval. Negotiations began for the water power site at Halfpenny and Grove's Mill on Penns Creek, for a dynamo and generator, and for a substation. Poles and wire followed, and by the following fall contracts were signed. The *Telegraph* could exult, "All hail to the Council and the good people back of them."[32] Meanwhile, the citizens were waiting impatiently for its consummation. Finally on June 13, 1904, the "beautiful electric light" came unexpectedly like "a flash from a clear sky, in broad daylight, when no one seemed to be on the 'skirmish line.' It thrilled the hearts of all our people with joy supreme in that now they have a modern electric plant all their own."[33] The power was turned on first along the north side of Chestnut; and that night crowds gathered to look into Heiter's Barber Shop, Strunk's Department Store, and Feese's Shoe Bazaar, feasting their eyes upon the glittering display. The arc lights at the street corners malfunctioned, and James R. Ritter's bulbs popped, but these few untoward incidents did not dampen the general enthusiasm.

Penns Creek, however, proved capricious. In December low water dimmed the lights, and during the winter ice shut off the flow of water altogether. The current continued to be unreliable during the decade which followed. Samuel G. Grove's advice was scarcely reassuring: "Close your eyes and think of our great grandfathers — without matches, with no lamp, no stove, perhaps a few tallow dips for company occasions, but a big chimney for light and heat. The flap jacks baked in a pan on the fire, and tasted sweeter than your white bread of luxury does to you. Oh, do learn to reflect to appreciate, and be grateful."[34] Mifflinburg learned to live with such uncertainties but eventually added an oil-powered generator for supplementary power. Its voters twice refused to sell out to utility companies. Finally, in 1931 a contract was signed with the Pennsylvania Power and Light Company to supply electricity to the borough's transformer. In the otherwise dark financial period of the 1930s, Mifflinburg's distribution of its water and electricity paid dividends. Though rates for both were moderate, the profits enabled the borough to extinguish its bonded indebtedness. In 1938 the tax rate was reduced to five mills, and the following year the town took an action almost unique in municipal history when it eliminated its tax entirely.

While establishment of the water and sewer systems created public controversies, the telephone came to town more quietly. The local driving force for this revolutionary invention in communications was generated in Lewisburg, where in 1895 a group of civic leaders headed by J. Thompson Baker organized the Home Telephone Company. Starting at Lewisburg, the company erected poles and strung wire along Buffalo Road (Route 192) to Forest Hill with branches reaching to Vicksburg and Mifflinburg as well as along the river road to Milton. Four years later they had acquired 89 subscribers in Lewisburg; 22 in Mifflinburg; nine in New Berlin; six in Millmont; four in Laurelton and Vicksburg; three in Glen Iron and West Milton; two in Winfield, New Columbia, Cowan, and Forest Hill; and one each in Hartleton, Swengel, Dry Valley, Buffalo Cross Roads, and Blue Hill; as well as nine in the Montandon/Pottsgrove section — all reached through the Lewisburg exchange. The company also served three customers in West Milton and two each in Kelly and White Deer Townships from its Milton office. Most of the subscribers were businesses; few householders were as yet in the network.[35]

Expansion ceased about 1900 when United Telephone bought out the local company and proceeded to increase rates and restrict free calls. As a result of the growing dissatisfaction, a second locally-sponsored organization entered the field in 1904 in the guise of the Buffalo Valley Telephone Company, incorporated with a capital stock of $10,000. The new company was in large part the handiwork of John P. Ruhl, the largest investor and its first manager — a position which would stretch through 39 years. Ruhl had served briefly as manager of the Home Telephone and was described as a young man with progressive ideas and with the business and technical qualifications fitting him admirably for telephone management. He was also the first secretary and later the treasurer of the company. President Judge Harold M. McClure was the company's initial president, William M. Dreisbach its vice president, and A.W. Brown its treasurer. In addition to the officers, the principal investors included Dr. G.C. Mohn, Dr. O.W.H. Glover, Samuel W. Rutherford, and Charles M. Cook, all of the West End, as well as T.C. Thornton of Lewisburg.[36]

During the first year the company acquired 56 users in Lewisburg and 22 in Mifflinburg, constructed a toll trunk line to Sunbury, and extended poles and wires to the Laurelton and Glen Iron areas. By 1907 it had more subscribers than United Telephone, and the latter's users were now transferring to the new organization. The Buffalo Valley Telephone Company operated switchboards leased from the Bell System in the W.C. Walls Building on Market Street in Lewisburg and in a loft at the corner of Fourth Street and Cherry Alley in Mifflinburg. Service was provided from 7:00 A.M. to 10:00 P.M. daily, Monday through Saturday, and more sparingly on Sundays. Night service was added by employing "night boys," who slept on cots near the switchboards. By 1913 the company employed Benjamin Eberhart as construction foreman, David Ream and G. Ralph Klingman as "trouble shooters," and eleven young women as switchboard operators with seven in the Lewisburg office and four in Mifflinburg.[37]

Once the public had overcome the initial embarrassment of talking into the "wire," the "magneto," or the "organ grinder," and there were enough users to facilitate personal calls between friends and neighbors, installations increased dramatically; and by 1920 the original 81 telephones had multiplied to 1,800. On April 27, 1928, an unseasonable snowstorm felled most of the poles between Lewisburg and Mifflinburg — a scene yet remembered by many county residents. To restore travel, the poles had to be cut in half and dragged from the roadway, and months were required to completely restore the service. Four years later another gale created a similar carnage, but the company survived, and by 1930 there were more than 2,000 subscribers.

In 1935 the dial system was installed in the Buffalo Valley Telephone Company's new headquarters on South Second Street in Lewisburg; and as a part of the inaugural ceremony John P. Ruhl called Charles R. Ruhl, a director of the company, at his home near Millmont. The call went through without a hitch, a bit reminiscent of Alexander Graham Bell's famous call to his assistant, Mr. Watson. Upon John P. Ruhl's death in 1943, he was succeeded by his great-nephew, George A. Ruhl, who served as manager for 41 years. James Davis followed him as manager until his retirement. In 1996 the company became part of a larger diverse communications system, Conestoga Enterprises, of Birdsboro, Pennsylvania. Buffalo Valley Telephone remains a separate subsidiary, serving the county under the management of Kenneth A. Benner.

While Schoch was sparking community development, one of his contemporaries, Samuel Gutelius Grove, was also exerting a pervasive influence upon the community and the adjacent countryside. Born in Mifflinburg in 1845, he grew up on a farm in West Buffalo Township. His formal schooling was rather limited, but he acquired a thirst for learning which was never satiated. He worked at farming, masonry, and lumbering during his early teens and enlisted in the 131st Regiment of the Pennsylvania Volunteers in August of 1862 when not yet seventeen. Like so many others of his generation, he looked back to the war for inspiration, but it did not divert his attention from the present. He was deeply concerned with the general welfare of mankind and was a good neighbor as well as a public-spirited citizen. Unpretentious and almost humble in demeanor, his "folksy" ways and ready wit made him a center of conversation at any gathering. When an issue arose, "What does Sammy say about it?" was asked repeatedly. For almost 40 years, Samuel Grove's news and views found a weekly outlet in the *Telegraph* under the by-line "Jottings"; and when he needed more space, he resorted to a letter to the editor with the signature "G" or "S.G.G." The "Jottings" consisted of current events largely relating to West Buffalo Township and Mifflinburg; these were often mixed with short items global in scope which caught his fancy, bits of advice, and reflections upon the passing scene. A complete collection of Grove's "Jottings" fills two stout volumes.

One of Samuel Grove's repeated themes was the need for better roads, in which he dealt in both generalities and specifics, frequently listing problem streets and blocks, and even the pothole involved. In one such complaint in 1901, he noted that there was not a single street marker in town and the resulting havoc for the stranger, writing, "Then we wonder why our most progressive young people go away. . . . The stranger takes no stock in such a community. . . . It is only a small matter, yet time, money, comfort and lives are involved."[38] Street signs soon appeared.

After residing for a number of years on a farm on North Eighth Street, Grove purchased a lot at the west end of Thompson Street and built on it a house which he considered ample for the needs of his wife and himself. With dimensions 20 x 30 feet and 10-1/2 feet high, he admitted that its appearance was somewhat novel — "good and solid but unplanned outside." Noting comments emanating from observers and catching the words, "Sammy has made a mistake, [it is] a shed," he offered a bit of his philosophy to his readers. He acknowledged that it had been a mistake to be born poor and to have no pension; but if he had $50,000, he would not change a board but instead build 50 houses for 50 poor families.[39]

When the Reformed Church in Mifflinburg sold its parsonage on Green Street and built a more costly one east of the church property in 1895, Grove deplored the decision. In a rambling article in which he recalled his childhood in the old Elias Church, he sighed over the abandonment of the hallowed structure while admiring its handsome replacement. Turning to the present, he saw a greater need for sheds for horses than for a new parsonage. Country people, he scolded, had to tie their horses in a small space and "run the gauntlet of a snow slide from the church roof and a scorching summer sun. [One] can scarcely worship God inside, when worrying about the animals outside!" Having expressed his opinion, he reassured his readers that he was censuring none. The past could not be undone; there was work for all, and the only direction was forward.[40]

Grove's interest in agriculture and possibly his columns in the paper recommended him to the United States Department of Agriculture, and in 1893 he was appointed statistical reporter for the county. It was a two way-street — he plied Washington with Union County's news and in turn received the federal department's handouts crammed with material for his "Jottings."

In 1906 Samuel Grove served as health officer of Mifflinburg. As might be expected, he made himself into a task force of one to guard the health of his clients. Clad in a long white smock with headgear to match and armed with bottles of chemicals, galvanized containers, and quarantine cards, Grove made his rounds. He looked over back fences, inspected food handling, and fumigated to eradicate diseases considered to be communicable, including scarlet fever, diphtheria, chicken pox, measles, and pink eye. He gave Roush's Excelsior Bakery a qualified bill of health, terming the materials pure and the locality not filthy, "although some places needed improvement."[41] His efficiency was labeled snooping and spying by his critics, and the borough was soon receiving complaints. It might be added that he held the same position in West Buffalo and Limestone Townships for several years and received similar reactions. Grove had defenders too; a correspondent observed that "he trod on our corns a trifle, but we have removed them and now feel better."[42] When asked why he did it for a pittance, Grove replied that his ancestors had lived and died here and that he expected to live out his time here also and be buried plainly. "That is why the health officer walks the streets, ferrets out the alleys . . . . It is not the dirt we are after, but lives, health, comfort, pride and souls."[43]

After a survey in the spring of 1908, Samuel Grove reported that in 400 homes there was not a sick

card and wrote, "May it ever be thus, is our desire"[44]; but the borough's new garbage and trash dump in North Eighth Street drew his wrath. He complained that it was a harbor for rats and was becoming increasingly unsightly, and he recommended that the borough dig trenches and bury the garbage. The cost, he argued, would be moderate, and it would put idle men to work; but his plea was ignored by the town council. In 1910 Grove recommended a public hospital for Mifflinburg. Pointing out the difficulties of isolating the sick in private homes, he noted that cities were building such institutions and that the armies had hospitals and nurses and wondered, "Why not do as well for our home people?" His challenge was answered, not by Mifflinburg, but by Lewisburg and the Evangelical Church some years later. After concluding his role as health officer, Grove continued to inform, amuse, and edify the community in his "Jottings" until a few weeks before his death in 1919 at age 74.

Elias Youngman and his wife, Catharina, considered the importance of meeting the educational as well as the religious needs of their embryonic community. On September 29, 1799, they deeded a lot at the southwest corner of Fifth and Green Streets to the trustees of the German Presbyterian (Reformed) and the German Lutheran congregations for the "absolute use of a German School." The gesture was not entirely philanthropic since the two boards paid the Youngmans eight pounds for it. The trustees erected a two-room log cabin on the site, one for the pupils and the second as a residence for the schoolmaster, some time before 1813. The date is uncertain, and the question of whether the children of the village were first offered their ABCs in German or English cannot be answered. There were both "Yankee" and German teachers in the early days, and the Franklin School on the north side of Market Street between Third and Fourth Streets was opened as early as the German school.

In 1827, the same year the village was incorporated, the state chartered the Mifflinburg Academy and turned it over to a local board of trustees along with an appropriation of $2,000. It opened in 1829 in rented quarters, but in 1839 the trustees erected a building at the northeast corner of Green and Sixth Streets. The Mifflinburg Academy became renowned for the quality of its instruction and drew a sizable proportion of its 50-75 students from adjacent counties. The Reverend Nathaniel Todd was the first principal; James McClure (1839-1844), Henry G. McGuire

German School, Mifflinburg. Photo by Jim Walter.

(1844-1851), and Aaron Crosby Fisher (1851-1854) were outstanding teachers; and to have been one of "Bossy" McGuire's "boys" or "girls" was a lifelong source of pride.

In an age when discipline and formalism were considered cardinal principles of teaching, it is refreshing to observe both the philosophy and the innate modesty of McGuire. In a letter recalling his experience at the academy after an interval of more than 30 years, McGuire refused to take credit for the school's fine reputation, explaining that he was a young instructor and lacked the skills which come with experience but "I know that I dearly loved to teach, and I loved my scholars too." He had not governed them, he said; "No, they governed themselves. . . . We were a family; I was in no sense a master. I was an instructor only, an 'elder brother' to whom they all came in perfect confidence and trust."[45]

The coming of Aaron Fisher, a young graduate of Amherst College, was termed by one of his students "an educational epoch"; "He filled the academy with new life and made it an intellectual center, not only for the town and its neighborhood, but also for the surrounding counties." He added that Fisher had "a mind-kindling mind" and had awakened his youthful intellect. Strict and exacting, Fisher had "opened the gate into a new world, extensive, opulent, ever beautiful and fair. In his classroom 'dead languages' [Greek and Latin] came alive."[46] Frail of body, Fisher went home at noon one day and failed to return. He died a few days later of consumption at age 34.

Competition from the many other academies across the state and the new public high schools led to the decline of the academy, and by 1860 classes were suspended. In 1864 a public subscription made possible its rebuilding; but it failed to attract a sufficient enrollment to be sustainable, and in 1870 it closed its doors for the last time. This building has since been razed; and a modern home was built on the site in the early 1980s, and it, in turn, is to be converted into an educational interpretive center for the Mifflinburg Buggy Museum in 2000.

Meanwhile, Mifflinburg accepted the Public School Law in 1838 after a five-year delay. Overcrowding in the Franklin and German Schools prompted the school board to purchase the empty Elias Church property in 1857 and convert it into an elementary school. In the early 1870s, a movement evolved to erect a building adequate for the entire system. The cost was high; but the Elias School was considered to be a firetrap, and adolescents were deprived of an education unless they could afford to go to the private academies.

The school board answered the challenge by purchasing three acres of land at the foot of Cemetery Hill, but a dogged battle was required to overcome the objections of a dissident group which carried its case to court, only to obtain the dissatisfaction of having to pay the court costs as well as losing their case. Contracts were let in the spring of 1876, and on February 22, 1877, the children took their seats. The cost was high — $12,237, which included $8,900 to the builders, Keeley and Wagner of Selinsgrove; $1,500 for the grounds; and $962 for furniture — especially during a depression period. Even so, they built well, almost elegantly, and even the halls were heated. The high Victorian structure with a massive Italianate cupola was justifiably the pride of the community — or at least most of its residents — and elicited the praise of visitors. One such observer praised it as magnificent, the equal of many college structures. Editor Schoch noted that taxes would be higher, "but we will now receive ample return for the money invested."[47]

The new school was graded so as to provide a first primary (grades one and two), a second primary (grades three and four), a first intermediate (grades five and six), a second intermediate (grades seven and eight), a preparatory (grades nine and ten), and a grammar (grades eleven and twelve). Ten years later, the preparatory and grammar grades were formally organized to create a high school, and graduation diplomas were awarded in 1889.

The Elias School stood empty for a time, but it was eventually sold and used for storing hay and straw as well as for buggymaking by John Gutelius. In 1927 it was stripped of its belfry and converted into apartments, leaving nothing to suggest its earlier elegance.

As Mifflinburg continued to grow, some of the elementary classes were transferred to the old academy building, which had been used for some years as a meeting place for the Grand Army of the Republic. In 1924 the children were moved to a substantial addition onto the central building, which also housed a new auditorium and the town's first gymnasium. Great changes occurred again in 1953 when the consolidation of the county's schools resulted in the erection of a new junior-senior high school on a 28-acre plot at the east end of town; a middle school was added in 1974 and a modern elementary school in 1980.

With their German heritage, most of Mifflinburg's early families had ties linking them to the Lutheran and German Reformed denominations. At the outset, some of them affiliated with their respective congregations at the Dreisbach Church in Buffalo Township; but in 1798 the Lutherans organized formally and in 1806 joined with the Reformed congregation to build the Elias Church, which they would share for half a century. The Youngmans were among the principal donors; others included the Kleckner, Pontius, Dreisbach, Schoch, and Hoy families. The masonry of the rectangular plank structure was laid by Ludwig Getchen, and Michael Schoch was the chief carpenter. Reminiscences of "Old Elias" indicate that an elevated wineglass-shaped pulpit on the south wall gave the minister a sweeping view of the sanctuary, including the gallery extending from three sides. Everyone seems to have had a designated seating place: elderly women at the southeast; elderly men at the southwest; and the young unmarried women at the northeast corner. In the gallery on the minister's left were the boys, and on his right the choir and organ. The married men were seated directly in front of him. Below, and in front of the older men's corner, was the bench for the elders and deacons.

The exterior of the building was modified in 1820 when an oversized belfry enclosing a bell was added. The latter sounded the call to services and served as the harbinger of special events through the years which followed. The first Lutheran services were conducted by the Reverend Ludwig Albrecht Wilhelm Ilgen, a son and grandson of Lutheran clergymen in Germany, who came to America at age seventeen as an "Ansbach Jaeger" in the British Army during the American Revolution. Afterward he took the oath of allegiance to the Commonwealth of Pennsylvania, studied theology, and was ordained in the Evangelical Lutheran Church. Ministering to a host of frontier congregations in Centre, Union, and Northumberland Counties, Reverend Ilgen was the pastor in Mifflinburg from 1806 to 1809. He also wrote a hymnal.

Early Presbyterians also had a church to serve them at Buffalo Cross Roads; but distance posed problems, and beginning in 1808 the Reverend Thomas Hood of the Buffalo Church held services in Mifflinburg. In 1818 doctrinal disagreements led to the formation of a second congregation, the First Presbyterian Society, which met in homes and in other churches until 1846, when it erected a brick structure on the site of the present church on Green Street. Meanwhile, the Buffalo church group in Mifflinburg remained alive though lacking a meeting house and, at times, a minister as well.

Possibly the earliest church structure in Mifflinburg used exclusively for religious purposes was a small log cabin on the site of the present Wesleyan United Methodist Church at Third and Market Streets. Methodist circuit riders preached in Mifflinburg as early as the 1790s, and in 1803 they organized the Communion Christian Church. At that time or shortly thereafter, the group built the log sanctuary on land donated by John Aurand and his wife. It served its purpose until 1856, when, following the collapse of the ceiling during a revival service, it was replaced by a brick building.

By the 1850s the Lutherans and German Reformed congregations had outgrown the Elias Church, and each erected its own building on Market Street between Fourth and Fifth streets — the Reformed on the south side of the street and the Lutherans on the north. In the 1890s the Evangelicals organized in Mifflinburg; and thus as the nineteenth century closed, five congregations shared the town's churchgoers.

The Mifflinburg clergy were the most highly educated residents of the community, and some of them exerted an influence far beyond the membership of their respective congregations. Such was surely the case of Jost Henry Fries, pastor of the Reformed church, who arrived in town in time to exhort the militia departing for the War of 1812 and remained until his death in 1839. Born in the Duchy of Westphalia, Germany, and ambitious to seek a future in America, he obtained passage as a "redemptioner," like so many of his countrymen. The purchaser of his labor encouraged him to study for the ministry, and he was licensed as a Reformed preacher at age 33.

Watercolor portrait of Reverend Ludwig Albrecht Wilhelm Ilgen painted by schoolmaster and fraktur artist Henry Young in 1823. From the Abby Aldrich Rockefeller Folk Art Museum, Williamsburg, Virginia. Photo courtesy of Harvey W. Ilgen.

Two years later he accepted a charge which extended from Lower Penns Valley to Bloomsburg and from Muncy to Selinsgrove, with a residence in Mifflinburg. Short, stout, nearsighted, powerful of voice, and distinct in enunciation, his sermons were never dull or equivocal. Hating sham and hypocrisy, he was "constantly in danger of falling into blunt frankness, without giving due attention to that suavity of manner, which is to an open heart what the fragrance is to an open flower."[48] Once, when he debated on the negative side of the proposition, "Is there such a thing as witchcraft?" and the verdict went to the affirmative, he presented an indignant protest, accusing the judge of deciding it through ignorance. During the Antimasonic controversy, he remained a staunch advocate of President Jackson, and apparently he never hesitated to mix politics with religion despite the popularity of Antimasonry with his Germanic parishioners. For a number of years, he drove regularly to attend a flock in Rebersburg. Disapproving of their behavior, he is said

to have quit in disgust with the following peroration, "Geld regiert der weld, aber dumheit Brush Valley" (Money rules the world, but ignorance Brush Valley.)[49]

Like many others of his generation, Fries buoyed his spirits with alcohol. The matter eventually came before the synod, which advised him to withdraw from Mifflinburg. Returning to his home, he obtained a hearing with the elders of his churches; but none rose to charge him, and the officers voted him innocent. Several years before his death, he lost his sight, but his amazing memory permitted him to handle the service and to preach with his usual eloquence.

As Fries' career drew to a close, those of Isaac Grier and John George Anspach were getting underway. Anspach, born of German parentage in Centre County in 1801, was licensed to preach by the Lutheran Synod of Western Pennsylvania in 1830. He came to Mifflinburg two years later and spent his entire professional life preaching in the churches of the region. Indefatigable, his ministrations seem almost unbelievable: 7,397 sermons, 1,613 funerals, 3,407 baptisms of infants and children, 548 adult baptisms, and 2,861 confirmations; most of these were delivered in the German tongue, of which he was a master. Anspach is remembered particularly for his record as a builder of churches. He preached at the Ray's Church for 53 years and was partially responsible for two buildings at that site; at Mifflinburg, 30 years and one building; at Lewisburg, fourteen years and one building; at White Deer, 50 years and one building; at New Berlin, nineteen years and one building; and Mazeppa, 40 years and one building. Father Anspach, as he was affectionately called, was revered by all who knew him. Retiring at 84, he died three years later.

One son, Luther Anspach, was an outstanding scholar, principal of the Mifflinburg Academy, and a talented musician. Luther Anspach's children, in turn, were gifted musicians, and townspeople still remember the talent and enthusiasm of Miss Virginia, who gave instruction on the piano in her old home on South Fifth Street. A second son, John Malancton, was also a prominent Lutheran clergyman, serving for a few years in Mifflinburg and for many years in Easton and Williamsport.

Isaac Grier was born at Jersey Shore in 1806, one of the twelve children of Dr. Isaac Grier, Senior, a Presbyterian minister and teacher, and Elizabeth Cooper Grier. His father died when he was just eight; but by alternating teaching with study, Isaac attended Dickinson College and the Princeton Theological Seminary. One of his brothers was a general in the

United States Army, and another, Robert C., became an associate justice of the Supreme Court of the United States. Isaac Grier was licensed by the Presbytery of Northumberland at the age of 26 and became a supply to the congregations of Shamokin and Washington in White Deer Valley. He went to the Buffalo Church at Buffalo Cross Roads in 1835 and was the pastor there when the Greek Revival brick meetinghouse was built in 1846. In 1853 he moved to Mifflinburg, adding the Buffalo congregation there to his duties. His leadership of the Buffalo Presbyterian Church in Mifflinburg was marked by controversy with the First Presbyterians. In 1868 the synod resolved that Grier "be enjoined to cease preaching and administering the Lord's Supper in the town of Mifflinburg unless it be done with the consent of the Mifflinburg Church, and that said church be requested to grant Dr. Grier the privilege of occupying their house of worship at the convenience of the congregation."[50] Neither Presbyterian congregation seemed willing to compromise, and Grier's flock continued to meet in other sanctuaries.

Under Grier's leadership, the Buffalo Presbyterians erected a meeting house in 1881 on the south side of Market Street between Third and Fourth Streets. Coincidentally, an unusually heavy snow crushed the roof and flattened the walls of the First Presbyterian edifice, requiring its reconstruction from the foundation. Thus the two small congregations were struggling simultaneously for building funds. Both succeeded, and both structures were tributes to the skill of architect Enoch Miller and his craftsmen.

As a preacher, Grier gave emphasis to the great themes of the gospel. He was clear, forceful, and direct; and he held attention by the quality of his intellect rather than the flourish of oratory. An avid reader of literature and history, he kept abreast of the times, and his mental vigor remained unimpaired when "full of years." A boy who went into the ministry under Grier's guidance recalled many years later that the day Grier called at his home to hear his recitation of the catechism savored of the final Day of Judgment. He also recalled that this visitation implanted the significance of religion and truth upon his tractable mind.[51] Upon the fiftieth anniversary of Grier's ordination, the clergy of the town conducted a testimonial service and unveiled a portrait of the venerable churchman painted by the Reverend A.M. Barnitz of the Methodist Church. On the Sunday preceding his death, Isaac Grier preached at Buffalo Cross Roads in the morning and in Mifflinburg in the afternoon, but on account of weakness he kept his seat during the delivery of the second sermon.

Under the leadership of Dr. M.L. Ross, minister of the First Presbyterian Church, the two Presbyterian denominations finally merged in 1899 in what was described as a "joyous God-blessed scene, never to be forgotten."[52] The empty building on Market Street was then taken over by the Evangelical Church, which had organized about twenty years earlier.

ENDNOTES:

[1] *Lewisburg Journal*, May 1, 1830.

[2] *Mifflinburg Telegraph*, July 20, 1876.

[3] *Lewisburg Democrat,* July 5, 1854.

[4] *Mifflinburg Telegraph*, May 29 and June 5, 1873.

[5] *New Berlin Union Times*, August 1, 1846.

[6] *Lewisburg Chronicle*, July 6, 1855.

[7] John Blair Linn, *Annals of Buffalo Valley, Pennsylvania, 1755-1855*, Harrisburg, 1877, 91. The event was held on February 16, 1827.

[8] *Lewisburg Chronicle*, June 22, 1866.

[9] *Lewisburg Chronicle*, November 10, 1866.

[10] *Mifflinburg Telegraph*, January 6, 1886.

[11] *Mifflinburg Telegraph*, November 10, 1893.

[12] *Mifflinburg Times*, November 24, 1900.

[13] *Mifflinburg Telegraph*, January 10, 1902.

[14] *Mifflinburg Times*, November 24, 1900.

[15] *Mifflinburg Telegraph*, November 5, 1884.

[16] *Mifflinburg Telegraph*, August 21, 1896.

[17] *Mifflinburg Telegraph*, August 13, 1897.

[18] *Mifflinburg Telegraph*, August 17, 1894.

[19] *Mifflinburg Telegraph*, June 8, 1900.

[20] *Mifflinburg Telegraph*, April 13, 1900.

[21] *Mifflinburg Telegraph*, March 26, 1909.

[22] Archives, First Lutheran Church, Mifflinburg.

[23] *Mifflinburg Telegraph*, August 11, 1886.

[24] *Mifflinburg Telegraph*, April 12, 1901.

[25] *Mifflinburg Telegraph*, August 12, 1875.

[26] *Mifflinburg Telegraph*, May 21, 1884.

[27] *Mifflinburg Telegraph*, June 3, 1898.

[28] *Mifflinburg Telegraph*, July 1, 1898.

[29] *Mifflinburg Telegraph*, September 9, 1898.

[30] *Mifflinburg Telegraph*, July 7, 1899.

[31] *Mifflinburg Telegraph*, February 3, 1899.

[32] *Mifflinburg Telegraph*, July 17, 1903.

[33] *Mifflinburg Telegraph*, June 17, 1904.

[34] *Mifflinburg Telegraph*, July 10, 1908.

[35] Subscription list, Home Telephone Company, 1899.

[36] *Mifflinburg Telegraph*, September 16, 1904.

[37] G. Howard Klingman, *Buffalo Valley Telephone Company 1904-1974*, Lewisburg, 1975.

[38] *Mifflinburg Telegraph*, January 18, 1901.

[39] *Mifflinburg Telegraph*, November 2, 1887.

[40] *Mifflinburg Telegraph*, March 4, 1904.

[41] *Mifflinburg Telegraph*, September 7, 1906.

42 *Mifflinburg Telegraph,* September 21, 1906.

43 *Mifflinburg Telegraph,* September 21, 1906.

44 *Mifflinburg Telegraph,* May 8, 1908.

45 *Mifflinburg Telegraph,* March 24, 1886.

46 Reminiscence of the Rev. Dr. J.S. Kieffer; *Mifflinburg Telegraph,* February 19, 1904.

47 *Mifflinburg Telegraph,* March 15, 1877.

48 Henry Harbaugh, *The Fathers of the German Reformed Church III,* Lancaster, 1872, 245.

49 Linn, 535.

50 *Lewisburg Chronicle,* May 1, 1868.

51 Rev. W.T.L. Kieffer, delivered at the third annual pilgrimage to the Buffalo Church on Sept. 5, 1920.

52 *Mifflinburg Telegraph,* May 11, 1900.

Badges from the Patriotic Order of the Sons of America and the Independent Order of Odd Fellows. From the collection of the Union County Historical Society, #92.9.32a, 92.9.41-2 and .44 , and #97.17.2. Photo by the Terry Wild Studio.

Circuses provided entertainment in Union County. This rare shot was taken as circus elephants were heading north on South Sixth Street, Lewisburg. From the collection of the Union County Historical Society, #89.5.14.23.

CHAPTER 11

UNION, EAST BUFFALO, BUFFALO, AND WEST BUFFALO TOWNSHIPS

With its fertile acres accessible from the Susquehanna River and Penns Creek as well as its proximity to the Tulpehocken Road and Fort Hunter, the region between Penns Creek and Lewisburg attracted more than its share of land seekers. The absence of bridges to link it with Sunbury and Northumberland in the early days, and the forbidding slopes of Shamokin and Chestnut Ridges limiting outlets to the south, on the other hand, tended to discourage commercial activity. Thus the population of what would later be Union and East Buffalo Townships grew rapidly at the outset but growth leveled off by the mid-nineteenth century.

This area was a part of Buffalo Township when Northumberland County was divided into townships in 1772. In 1792 it became East Buffalo Township; in 1815 another subdivision split it further, with Union Township established on the south side of Shamokin and New Berlin Ridges, and East Buffalo Township on the north. The division of the county in 1855 cut off the southern portion of Buffalo Township while the creation of Limestone Township removed a section on the west.

The first settler in the Dry Valley area, west of Winfield, may have been Jacob Brylinger. He was living on land long known as Maize's in 1755 when he was killed by the same marauding Indians who committed the LeRoy massacre on the other side of New Berlin Ridge on October 16 of that year. Other settlers moved into the area after the French and Indian War, some of them becoming victims of Indian depredations during the Revolutionary War. David Emerick, who settled near the future site of Winfield in 1772, was soon joined by Thomas Sutherland, James Hunter, George Olds, Henry Bickel, and John Lee. Abraham Eyer of Lancaster County cleared a farm near Dry Valley Cross Roads (what is now called Dry Valley), but later moved to his river farm at Winfield, where he built a large stone barn. The barn is remembered as one of the landmarks of the early Evangelical Church. Folklore also made it a refuge from Indians, but their incursions were only memories when Eyer erected it in 1805.

For Dry Valley farmers the nearest mills were on Penns Creek. Jacob Maurer, who came from the Goschenhoppen region of Montgomery County with his brothers, Frederick and Andrew, purchased the mill

property about two miles east of New Berlin from Henry Drinker in 1796. He dismantled the old mill and rebuilt it in 1805. Grist and sawmills were dangerous places to work, and Jacob's son, Frederick, was killed in a mill accident c. 1827. Undaunted, the Maurer family continued in the milling business for many decades. Competition came from an even older mill about a half a mile upstream, known later as Arbogast's.

John MacPherson, who occupied the river bank south of Winfield in 1778, served in the American Navy during the Revolutionary War and was an associate judge of Northumberland County for many years. Some of his descendants lived in Dry Valley and in Hartley Township, while others found homes in the West. James Cawley operated a ferry to Northumberland, and R.V.B. Lincoln remembered that his sons were remarkable for their stature, towering above their fellow men "like the Israelites' King Saul."[1] The Cawleys also conducted a grain and coal business, poling the latter from Sunbury on the river in flatboats. Robert King, another early resident of Dry Valley, was the first constable in Buffalo Township and an officer in the American Revolution.

In 1772 John Aurand settled at the mouth of Turtle Creek, the only stream in the area with a power seat. He built a grist and sawmill, and became the founder of what would later be the thriving village of Turtleville. His son, John Dietrich, was a soldier in the Revolution and a preacher in the German Reformed Church, serving at the Dreisbach and New Berlin churches. In 1778 James Jenkins purchased the Aurand property and built a stone millhouse, where his neighbors took refuge when exposed to Indian attacks during the Revolution. During the flood of 1846, the mill dam gave way, washing Thomas Follmer, a local storekeeper, his son, and William Gundy to their deaths. The mill was rebuilt in 1853 by Alfred Kneass, who was married to a great-granddaughter of James Jenkins; it was modernized in 1884 by A.O. Van Alen, a son-in-law of Kneass. Descendants of Jenkins continued to operate the mill for more than a century. By the 1860s, in addition to the grist mill, Turtleville had a sawmill, a blacksmith shop, a carpenter's shop, a school, and a cluster of possibly ten houses. Today, the mills and dam are gone, and only a small bridge and several weather-worn buildings just off the highway remain to mark the site.

UNION

Scale 1¼ inches to the mile

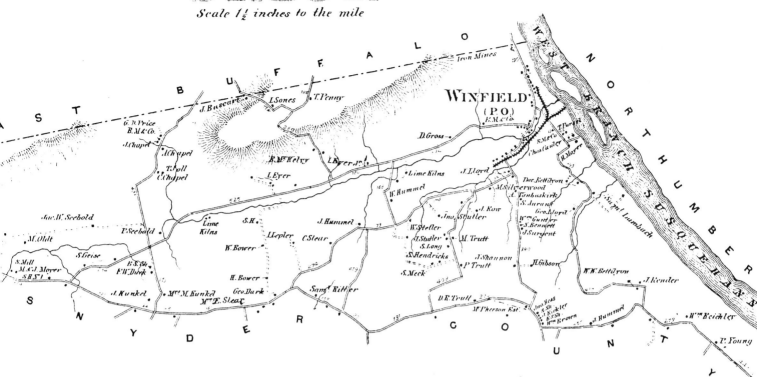

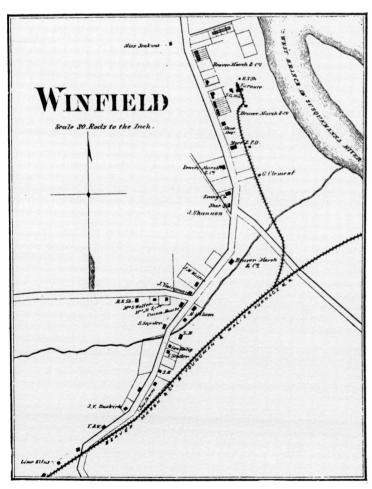

Union Township and the town of Winfield. From *Pomeroy's Atlas of Union and Snyder Counties 1868.*

Two miles farther north on the Susquehanna and just below the future site of Lewisburg, Christian Van Gundy established a tavern and ferry in 1773. The title to the site was also claimed by Ludwig Derr, and a long court fight ended in Van Gundy's ejection and removal to Ohio. The loss, however, did not prevent VanGundy's son, Christian, Jr., from acquiring another homestead in the neighborhood; and his sons in turn, John, Adam, and Jacob, were among the most successful farmers in the region. Though Jacob VanGundy's formal education was quite limited, he became an advocate of scientific farming and wrote extensively upon the subject. He was instrumental in founding the Union County Agricultural Society and was an officer in the Pennsylvania Agricultural Society. He was an advocate of temperance also, and it was said that he erected the first barn in the county without the use of liquor. The Van Gundy farm was later purchased by the Strohecker family, who have occupied it through four generations. The farm is located on River Road just south of the easterly Seventh Street entrance to Bucknell.

In 1770 William Speddy, a Connecticut "Yankee," settled on Turtle Creek about a mile from its mouth at a place long known as Brown's or Supplee's Mill, claiming the title to the land upon a deed granted by the Susquehanna Land Company of Connecticut. Actually, the location was several miles below the 41st degree of latitude and beyond the Connecticut claim, but surveys were incomplete, and he was not disturbed for a time. Later he joined his old associates in the Wyoming Valley, where he was arrested by Pennsylvania officials and lodged in the Philadelphia jail. After his release, Speddy returned to Buffalo Valley, content to benefit from a hands-off policy on the territorial dispute; in the meantime, his active service in the Northumberland County Committee of Public Safety and the local militia during the war won the friendship of his neighbors. His deed, however, remained defective, and he lost his land to a Pennsylvania claimant. He died at Speddy's Gap in Lost Creek Valley, Juniata County.

Captain John Brady, head of a family renowned in the Susquehanna Valley for its Indian fighters, owned a farm at the top of Smoketown hill, but he made his home on the east side of the river at Muncy. Following his death in battle in 1779, his widow and sons made their residence at the Smoketown farm; but with the return of the Indians, the widow moved to Jenkins "fort," where she remained until the close of the war. Due to a defective title, the Bradys eventually lost the Smoketown farm, and it was taken over by Japhet Morton, who laid out the village of Mortonsville; that settlement later became identified as Smoketown (for the smoke from a pitch-fired brick kiln).[2] Smoketown was located on the early road from Lewisburg to Penns Valley, just a few hundred yards south of the turnpike. In 1868 Smoketown (called Fairville by others) had ten houses, a store, a blacksmith, and a carpenter's shop.

The most common family name in the neighborhood was Brown after descendants of John Brown purchased land near Smoketown in 1804. Five of his sons and a daughter resided here as well as many of their children. The cabin of Adam Grove stood between Smoketown and the turnpike in the early days. He and his three brothers, Wendell, Michael, and Peter, were among the region's foremost Indian fighters. Over the hill south of Smoketown, on Turtle Creek, lived the descendants of George Wendell Wolfe, who migrated from Berks County in 1796. Three of George's sons settled on land adjacent to the homestead, and a grandson, Samuel, engaged in the grain and mercantile business in Lewisburg. Samuel and his wife, Catherine Lawshe, were the parents of Senator Charles S. Wolfe.

Samuel Reber opened a tavern on the turnpike at Lochiel in 1830. For many years it was the only public house between Lewisburg and Mifflinburg; it served as a rendezvous for drovers moving their herds from Ohio and western Pennsylvania to eastern markets, as well as for Penns Valley farmers delivering grain to the canal at Lewisburg. Reber later sold out to Gideon Riehl, one of the area's early Amish settlers, and the latter, in turn, to David Royer. With the coming of the railroad, the hamlet, originally known as Reber's or Riehl's received a post office, where Noah Slear served as postmaster. It was renamed Lochiel — presumably in remembrance of the headquarters of the Cameron clan in Scotland.

In the second half of the nineteenth century, Lewisburg's growth westward created the village of Linnville or Linntown, which took its name from the Linn family, who owned several farms on the south side of the turnpike there. For a time the village consisted of only of a few houses strung along the north side of the turnpike, but the railroad stimulated commercial activity. At the turn of the century, the Kulp Lumber Mill and railroad junction at this location handled millions of board feet of timber drawn from the Spruce Run and White Deer Creek watersheds on a narrow gauge railroad network. Later, the Lewisburg Chair Factory, the forerunner of Pennsylvania House, located on the railroad. In the 1920s the Linn farms were carved into building lots by a syndicate headed by Judge Albert Johnson, and Linntown's population exploded. Older residents can still recall when only three houses stood on the south side of the turnpike between Lewisburg and the Fairgrounds at Brook Park.

Meanwhile, Winfield in 1840 was little more than the junction of the Dry Valley and River Roads, with three or four houses, a store, a tavern, and a blacksmith shop. It had neither a railroad nor a turnpike and was simply called Dry Valley until 1851, when a post office was opened bearing the name Winfield. In 1841 Napoleon Hughes, a prospector from Franklin County, opened a drift of iron ore at Yankee Spring near Winfield and another a short time later at Miner's Hollow. The bright-hued ore was loaded into wagons and hauled to the Susquehanna, where it was taken by water to the iron furnaces at Danville. Reasoning that ore good enough for the Danville iron mongers was worth smelting at its source, Samuel Geddes, James S. Marsh, Elisha C. Marsh, and Joseph Shriner of Lewisburg operated a foundry there under the firm name of Geddes, Marsh, and Company. In 1853 they purchased twenty acres of land south of the mouth of Turtle Creek, took leases on various ore properties, and commenced the construction of the Union Furnace. Finding a need for more capital, the firm first admitted Thomas Beaver of Danville, his brother, Peter, of Lewisburg, and Charles E. Morris of Chester County; and in 1856 Dr. Levi Rooke joined them as a partner.

John F. Hackenberg stands in front of his blacksmith shop near the stone quarry in Winfield in October 1897. He later worked at shops in Hartleton (1920s) and Vicksburg (1925). Known for being able to "shoe the tough ones," he shod horses at the Lewisburg Fair for years. Courtesy of Mrs. Horace V. Stimel.

Rooke was a native of Chester County and a graduate of Jefferson Medical College. He practiced medicine for a time but abandoned it to pursue iron manufacture. After a few years at the Berlin Iron Works at Glen Iron, Rooke came to the Union Furnace to direct the ore mining; a few years later he became the superintendent of the entire operation, continuing in this capacity until the plant was closed. Through the years he established the Dry Valley Lime Manufacturing Company, invested in lumbering, and served as president of the Union National Bank in Lewisburg. A civic leader as well, he was elected as a member of the Pennsylvania Constitutional Convention of 1873. The Rooke family went on to develop an important and long-lasting relationship with Bucknell University in the twentieth century.

When the Union Furnace opened in 1854, the plant comprised a large furnace stack, stock house, casting room, engine and blowing tub room, four large boilers, a hot blast, and a flue stack nearly 100 feet tall. For its workmen, the firm erected five blocks of houses and a store. The company added a brick grist mill, from which it obtained its power, close to the furnace and built a large double brick house for Morris and Rooke. The first tap of iron on October 30, 1854, was a joyous moment, but the owners found little

to cheer about during the years immediately following. Breakdowns required drilling and blasting to remove huge blocks of metal from the furnace while the panic of 1857 flattened sales. Only heavy contributions from Thomas Beaver kept the business out of bankruptcy; in 1864 the ownership was taken over by Peter Beaver, James S. Marsh, and Levi Rooke, and the business name changed to Beaver, Marsh and Company.

The Civil War was the company's salvation as iron skyrocketed to $90 a ton. It was commonly said in Lewisburg that each exhaust of the furnace (which could clearly be heard there) meant a dollar in the pockets of the company. In 1866 the income taxes of the owners were the highest in the county. Returns were lean during the panic years from 1873 through 1879, but better times returned during the next decade. By the 1890s, however, mass production and richer Michigan ores had cut prices below local production costs, and in 1891 the last casting was made.

Years later, Charles Reagan, who represented the county in the state House of Representatives, in recalling his boyhood in Winfield spoke of the four-mile-long caravan of brick-colored wagons creaking under loads of five tons as they moved from the mines along Shamokin (New Berlin) Ridge to the furnace. He also noted that in the early days, the iron was hauled to Northumberland or ferried across the Susquehanna to Kapp's Siding. During mid-winter a mule, hitched with a long lead to a small bobsled bearing a half-ton of iron, was driven across the ice on the river — a procedure that came to grief many times when either the mule or the sled broke through the ice. Anthracite coal, used to fuel the furnace, was shoveled from canal barges at the Northumberland bridge and towed up the river by horses, with the projecting rocks along Blue Hill at one point forcing the horses to enter the water.[3]

The limestone used in fluxing was quarried just west of the village and transported to the furnace upon a horse-drawn narrow-gauge railway. After construction of the Shamokin Branch of the Reading Railroad in 1882, the coal and iron were moved by rail. After the closing of the Union Furnace, the quarries were worked by the Rooke family and as many as eighteen lime kilns were kept in blast. The area continues to be quarried at present by Eastern Industries, which is also excavating at the Dale Ridge in Buffalo Township.

Winfield, for a short period in the 1870s and 1880s, was also a logging center. A log boom extending into the Susquehanna reportedly held several million feet of logs in 1873. However, it could not withstand the pressure of high water in the Great Flood of 1889 and

Union Furnace January 30th 1869

Furnace	Dr To Sundries			
Lary Tierney	For 32 days work			68 57
John Quigley	" 32 " "			50 28
William Drum	" 33¾ " "			65 96
John Connery	" 32 " "			50 28
Charles Williams	" 32 " "			50 28
John R. Trull	" 32 " "			50 28
Francis Stanford	" 33 " "			51 85
George Campbell	" 32 " "			50 28
Edward Brinan	" 32 " "			50 28
Patrick Power	" 31½ " "			65 14
P. S. Myer				48 71
William McC				55 44
Patrick Ca				
"				93 4
John Care				42 46
Jos. H. Figr				46 35
Jacob Cam				52 04
Crist. Mill				47 14
Asbury Gill				
" "				81 64
William D				47 14
John Parker	" 27½ " "	⌐25⌐		43 46
John Drum	" 22¾ " "			51 18
John Moser	" 25¼ " "			63 12
Uriah McCollum	" 22¼ " "			33 38
Peter Sero	" 27 " "	⌐96⌐		45 9
Peter Clements	" 27 " "	⌐96⌐		45 9
Philip Fetter	" 24½ " "			36 75

was swept away, leaving a mass of logs on both sides of the river and the dockets of the courts crowded with cases relating to their ownership.[4]

During the winter of 1853-54, the Susquehanna Railroad, a short-lived company which projected — but failed to build — a railroad along the west bank of the river between Harrisburg and Williamsport, dispatched a gang of Irish laborers to Gundy's Lane near Winfield to do some grading. It appears to have been one of the first encounters between the predominantly teutonic Protestant populace of the region and the Gaelic Catholic immigrants. The incident serves to document the preconceptions and misgivings felt by the former as they adjusted to the presence of the latter, who were streaming to America in the wake of disaster on their native isle.

The death of one of the laborers precipitated a quarrel with the township officials regarding a proper burial place. When the overseers proposed the "potter's field" in the Lewisburg cemetery, the Irish called it "unhallowed ground" and, in the words of the local press, told them to "pit wan ov their own min into it." The Irish found their own solution to the problem by carrying the body to Milton and burying it in the Catholic cemetery there. Returning to their camp, they celebrated, "with copious spiritous libations, a wake which awoke all their long-slumbering belligerent passions." An ensuing brawl continued from Saturday night into Sunday with "spades and pickaxes, blood flowing as freely as whiskey and even women with fiery tongues and scalding water mingling freely in the fray." The constable invoked the "Sunday Law"; but when his admonitions proved futile, he sent an express to Lewisburg requesting an armed *posse comitatus*. The sheriff interrupted religious services to round up volunteers and proceeded to Gundy's Lane with 80 men armed with muskets and 150 camp followers.

Arriving at its destination, the posse neither saw nor heard any sign of human habitation. Concluding that the Irish were feigning sleep, the Lewisburg men formed on three sides of the citadel (the river being the fourth) and advanced. A shutter opened and a voice called from within, "What is wanted?" "Prisoners," was the sheriff's reply. "The fight is all over, and all of the men have gone to bed, ready to work tomorrow." "Must execute my commission and capture the outlaws." "Go to the arch-enemy of man." The advance was resumed, guns in hand; and so complete was the investiture that there was no resistance. Some of the Irish ran but soon came back; and the

ABOVE: Scene near the old Gundy Farm on River Road south of Lewisburg (near the present-day Glen Pool). From the collection of the Union County Historical Society, #89.5.19.8.

PAGE 190: A ledger page of the Union Furnace, Winfield, which shows the pay of those working there in January 1869. Those who lived in company housing were paying $2.50 of their wages for a month's housing. From the collection of the Union County Historical Society, #89.5.15.27 and #91.34.1. INSET: Ruins of the Union Ironworks in Winfield c. 1912.

moment they surrendered, all was peaceful. The posse returned to Lewisburg with the ringleaders, and a head count revealed: "Killed, none; wounded, none; heads, etc. broken, thirty-two; frightened, forty; missing, four; total - eighty [?]." The editor rejoiced that the riot had been nipped in the bud, and he assumed that the action would deter potential revellers from any "further bacchanalian and Sabbath polluting orgies."[5]

The work gang was soon disbanded, and most county residents continued to form their impressions of the Irish from the biased and often lurid tales in the press. Few were to be seen in the flesh since the tidal wave of Irish as well as German migration bypassed Buffalo Valley. In 1860, for example, of the 14,145 residents of Union County, only 319 were foreign-born, and the number dropped each census year thereafter. The 319 were divided almost evenly between those of German, Irish, and English extraction; and, as might be expected, males outnumbered females by a substantial margin. The Roman Catholic element remained small

The barn of Abraham Eyer in Winfield, built in 1805, was the site of an important Evangelical Church conference in 1816. The barn was demolished when Route 15 (the former Lewisburg/Winfield Road) was widened in the early 1960s. From the collection of Gary W. and Donna M. Slear.

Charles R. Reagan in front of Dyer's Store in Winfield at the time of the 1936 flood. From the collection of the Union County Historical Society, #2000.2.3.

John A. Van Buskirk, a rural mail carrier for 52 years, worked out of the Winfield post office. From the collection of the Union County Historical Society, #2000.2.2.

through the decades which followed, and there was no Catholic church in Union County until 1935 when the Chapel of the Sacred Heart was erected in Lewisburg.

The census of 1860 also indicated the presence of 55 blacks, almost evenly divided between male and female, about half of whom were under 21 years old. Twenty-eight of them resided in Lewisburg and eleven each in Hartley and East Buffalo Townships. Most of the other villages and townships had none.

The proximity of Lewisburg and New Berlin undoubtedly retarded the organization of churches in East Buffalo and Union Townships. The Evangelicals in Winfield, however, built a brick edifice in 1856. In 1868 a handful of Winfield Baptists who had heretofore affiliated with the congregation in Lewisburg began to hold services in the Evangelical church. The following winter they conducted a month-long revival, which must have been one of the most inspirational among the many held in the late nineteenth century in the county. It was reported that between 60 and 70 "returned to their Heavenly Father's House and eighty-nine professed hope in Jesus for the first time, and several wanderers returned home." Twenty-three were baptized in the river on January 17 and thirteen more a week later.[6] Dr. Rooke, who does not appear to have been a member of the Baptist congregation, arose from his seat during a service, proposed that "the laborer is worthy of his hire," and asked the audience for $200 for the converts, leading off himself with a "liberal" contribution. The service was halted, and in less than one-half hour the $200 was on the plate.[7] The organization of the congregation was formalized the following March, and in 1874 they erected a brick church. Both Winfield churches were constructed on lots donated by the Union Furnace Company.

At Dry Valley Cross Roads, several miles to the west, the Lutheran and Reformed residents of the area united in 1909 to build the St. John's Union Church. In 1849, the Evangelical Association erected the Salem Church, a classical brick structure with stout columns, in a small grove of oaks on the hill southwest of Smoketown. The Amish organized a district among the families along the Furnace Road under the guidance of Elias Riehl. A self-educated farmer, Riehl had been called by lot to preach the gospel in 1847 and served for thirteen years.

There have been four different periods in which members of the plain sects, Amish, Dunkards, and Mennonites, immigrated into Union County. The first was in 1755 when a Swiss, John Jacob King, came to Buffalo Valley, Northumberland County (now

Union), from Berks County, Pennsylvania, in order to escape conscription. Though he averted conscription, both he and his family were victims of an Indian rampage in Buffalo Valley, which resulted in the death and capture of several, and retreat to Berks County for the survivors. King had changed his name to the French "LeRoy" in order to protect himself and his family on the French-controlled frontier during the French and Indian War, and hence historians have always described the events as the LeRoy Massacre.[8]

In the 1770s the Dunkards, another plain sect, settled near White Springs. Some stayed close to Penns Creek, which they used for baptisms involving total submersion. Like the Amish, the Dunkards worshipped in their homes. Employing very wide interior doorways and sliding panels, the homes were designed to accommodate 20-30 families in worship. Nearly a century later the group built their first churches: one at the juncture of Brethren Church Road with the Old Turnpike in Limestone Township (used 1864 to the present); a second in Hartley Township two miles west of Laurelton on the Showalter farm built in 1861; and the third at Kelly Point, Kelly Township, at the Royer farm, also constructed in 1861. The group is now known as the Church of the Brethren.

In 1836 the third wave of plain sect settlement began, prompted in part because the canal system had opened up central Pennsylvania for commerce and easy transportation. This wave was comprised primarily of Amish coming from Berks, Chester, Lancaster, and Mifflin Counties. It has been said that "an Amish man can smell limestone 100 miles away," and that is just about how far they traveled in order to establish the second and more successful Amish settlement in Union County. This second group of Amish included the Lantz, Esh, Riehl, Beiler, Yoder, Glick, and Stoltzfus families.[9]

Many settled on farms along Furnace Road and the Old Turnpike as well as the farmland in between, in East and West Buffalo Townships. One can see evidence of this nineteenth-century settlement in their cemeteries, which were cared for by the Amish, even in the period of 1924 to 1949, when no Amish lived in Buffalo Valley. The easiest to see is the Lantz Cemetery on the south side of Route 45 midway between Lewisburg and Mifflinburg. Samuel Lantz was the founder of the Buffalo Valley Amish community, and the cemetery was established on the 113-acre farm he purchased in 1837. The last burial there took place in 1862. Lantz had one son and six daughters. He and his wife returned to Lancaster as she was homesick. Near the Samuel Lantz farm was the 158-acre farm his son, Christian Lantz, bought in 1838 (sold in 1859

The presence of the plain sects, both now and in the past, is very evident in Union County today. From top to bottom: are: the land formation they and others refer to as "the bowl" is near the juncture of Furnace and Dreisbach Church Roads. Nearby, the meetinghouse and horse stalls located near Vicksburg are on the eastern side of their settlement area.

Evidence of much earlier settlements are the walled Lantz Cemetery on Salem Church Road south of Route 45 and, nearby, the former farm of Amishmen, Christian and Fisher Lantz. Photos by Jim Walter.

to Fisher Lantz); today, it remains distinctive with its white and green checkerboard silo.

Between the Old Turnpike and Furnace Road, on the Old Salem Church Road, were two farms owned by another Amishman, Joel Riehl. He was the brother of Elias Riehl, the group's second bishop. Elias Riehl's two maiden sisters lived on Iron Cave Road. One of them, Sarah, was a quilt maker and weaver, and she is said to have made a "Buffalo Valley" quilt which had the names of all her community's members sewn into it.

Many of the farms along Furnace Road, starting at its junction with Old Salem Church Road, that are home today for several of the present plain-sect Mennonite families, had previously been Amish in the 1830s-1860s with one or two "English" families in between. The farms of John and Samuel Kennel, Joseph and Joel Zook, John Beiler, Elias Riehl, Samuel Kauffman, Josiah Beiler, and John Stoltzfus (the first farm in Union County to have a windmill) lined Furnace Road on both the north and south sides as far as "Glick's Corner" (the juncture of New Berlin Mountain Road and Furnace Road).

At this crossroads was the farm of Samuel Glick, who had married Barbara Lantz, one of the daughters of Samuel Lantz. Nearby were the farms of Michael Beiler, Jonathan Glick, and Michael Jacob Swartz on Pheasant Ridge Road just before its juncture with Dreisbach Church Road. There, two who were closer than second cousins were married — one of several

incidents in the late 1860s that caused the Lancaster County Amish to deny requests from their Union County brethren and created dissension within the Union County group. At this time many of the more conservative Amish, not pleased by Bishop Riehl's handling of matters and by internal strife, moved back to Lancaster County.

Closer to Mifflinburg on Furnace Road, near Stitzler Road, lived David and Magdelena Lantz Glick. He was a prosperous farmer and coppersmith, who also owned woodland on New Berlin Mountain and sold tree bark to tanners. In 1877 David Glick rented three train cars for those who wanted to leave and go to Lancaster County. Many did, and from 1873 to 1880 the Amish held only one semi-annual communion in Union County.

During this period of controversy, the Amish community was led by Bishop Elias Riehl. A powerful preacher, community leader, and Union County resident for 63 years, Bishop Riehl, who succeeded the area's first bishop, Solomon Yoder, made several controversial rulings on the application of doctrine. The group's differences caused a split in the Union County Amish community and eventually its demise by the turn of the century. Among Riehl's controversial decisions were permitting the marriage of first cousins, allowing winemaking by Simeon Stoltzfus, and promoting Sunday school. Riehl also stood by his sons, who were troublemakers, and further split his community in so doing. Eventually he was silenced, but he continued to preach in Juniata County for the Evangelicals. Creating further contention, Riehl also preached at a funeral at the Salem Church after he was silenced. Other sources of dissension were his position as a school director and, although a pacifist, a supporter of "the Boys in Blue" during the Civil War. Also, Riehl felt it was one's duty to vote for the presidency, and he convinced members of his sect to speak English as well as Pennsylvania Dutch so that they could use the public school system. Riehl's retirement home was on the Old Turnpike just west of Lewisburg (beside the present Smeltz garage). Elias Riehl died on March 9, 1901.

The fourth period of immigration of plain sects began in 1949 when some Lancaster Conference Mennonites moved into Union County; they were followed by the Beachy Amish under Noah Yoder, who in 1955 settled in the Kelly Point area. In 1961 team Mennonites occupied western Union County; among them was Daniel Zimmerman, harness maker and barn raiser. Eleven Groffdale Conference Old Order Mennonite families, led by Amos B. Hoover of Denver, Lancaster County, arrived in 1968. Currently among Union County's plain sects there are nine distinct Mennonite groups, three Beachy Amish groups, the Church of the Brethren (formerly Dunkard), the Old Order Amish, and the Nebraska Amish or "white toppers," the latter of which have settled in the Dry Valley area of Union County.

Union Township refused to accept the public school law by a unanimous vote while East Buffalo rejected it almost as decisively by an 87-3 margin. In fact, support of the system was so exceptional that Captain John Gundy, Benjamin Winegardner, and Major John Gundy were remembered for their "yes" votes, though once the sentiment had been reversed, there were other claimants for the honor. Both districts eventually had second thoughts, and Union built a school at Winfield and a second midway between Winfield and New Berlin. When Snyder County was separated, residents at the western end of Union Township and the northeastern corner of Jackson Township felt that their interests were ignored and petitioned for an independent school district. Obtaining one in 1861, the petitioners erected the Union Independent School on a lot taken from the Miller and Moyer farms close to the county line. The Independent District endured for a century until consolidation merged the Union County portion with the Mifflinburg Area School District. In 1838 East Buffalo approved the school law, and the directors acquired

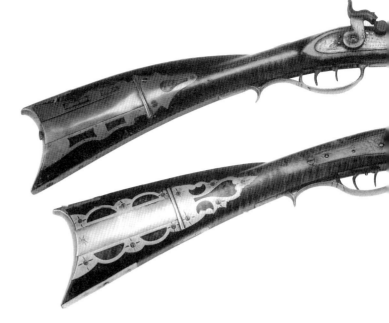

Details of Pennsylvania long rifles made by Union County gunsmiths. TOP: A 54 inch-long rifle made by Levi Kaup, West Buffalo Township; and BOTTOM: a 50 1/2 inch rifle made by Isaac L. Beck, Mifflinburg (active c. 1835-1850). Both stocks are of curly maple and have similar patch boxes; Kaup's has brass decoration; and Beck's silver-decorated rifle is a swivel breach model. Beck was the son-in-law of gunsmith John Dreisbach. From a private collection. Photo by the Terry Wild Studio.

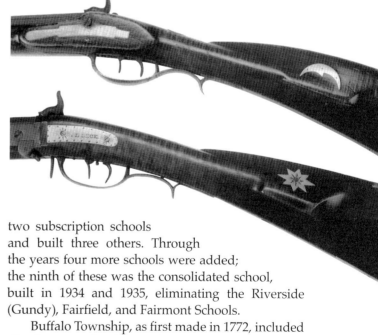

two subscription schools and built three others. Through the years four more schools were added; the ninth of these was the consolidated school, built in 1934 and 1935, eliminating the Riverside (Gundy), Fairfield, and Fairmont Schools.

Buffalo Township, as first made in 1772, included all of present-day Union County as well as a large part of Snyder, Centre, Clinton, and Lycoming Counties. It was quickly subdivided as the area became populated. The bottomland and rolling hills along the banks of Buffalo Creek were too rich to remain unnoticed; and when the land office was

Hand-painted baptismal certificate (*taufschein*) by the Flat Tulip Artist for Magdelena Getz, who was born in West Buffalo Township, Union County, on June 16, 1817, at 4 A.M. in the sign of the crab. Magdelena Getz was baptized in October 1817. Her parents were Henry and Barbara (Noll) Getz, and her godparents were Henry and Esther Billman. From the collection of the Union County Historical Society, #99.13.1. Photo by the Terry Wild Studio.

Only one coverlet woven by J. Clapham of West Buffalo Township, Union County, has been found. Photo by the Terry Wild Studio, courtesy of the Oral Traditions Project.

opened, there was a flood of applications for it. Surveys were made the same year, and the sound of the ax was soon commonplace. In July 1775 when the Reverend Philip Fithian came north on the West Branch of the Susquehanna on a missionary tour and held services near Buffalo Cross Roads, he was pleasantly surprised by both the number and quality of his audience:

> The people are building a log meeting house up the valley about four miles from the river. There is a numerous society here, and it is a growing, promising place. We had a good number today. But I was put to my trumps; there is no house; I must preach from among the trees. I mounted, therefore, upon a little bench before the people; but O it is hard to preach in the air, entirely "sub Jove."

> The assembly was very attentive; I could not avoid smiling at the new appearance, to see them peeping at me through the bushes. I saw here the greatest number and the greatest variety of silk gowns among the ladies that I have yet seen on my course. It, is and shall be therefore, the "silk gowned congregation."[10]

Unfortunately, the young Princeton College graduate did not record the names of his listeners, but William McCandlish was probably in the audience. He had settled on the site of the future Billmyer tavern just east of Dale's Ridge on the Lewisburg/Buffalo Cross Roads road a year earlier; here he built an enormous log structure, which became a gathering place for the Committee of Public Safety and a refuge during the Revolutionary War. Wendell Baker, William Irvine, and their families, who lived several miles west of Buffalo Cross Roads, may have also attended the service; and surely James McLenahan and Samuel Allen, the first ruling elders of the congregation, were on hand. Fithian's hosts during his short stop in Buffalo Valley, William Gray and family, lived near the Susquehanna just north of Buffalo Creek and were in all likelihood among the group; their neighbors, the Fruits and Clarks, were also likely present. Walter Clark contributed twenty shillings toward Fithian's mission on behalf of the congregation. The Kellys and Linns, who lived across the creek from the meeting place, were also probably among the group.

Since an ordained minister was a rarity at this early date, it can be assumed that the Maclays from the Dreisbach Church area, the Barbers of White Springs, the Fosters of West Buffalo, and the Glovers of Hartley may have made the arduous trip to the meeting place. The German element, including the Dreisbachs, Wolfes, and Sierers, were more doubtful attendants but may have been present on this special occasion. It is known that Dr. William Plunket, who held an officer's grant on Chillisquaque Creek, was at the service, since he invited Fithian to accept his

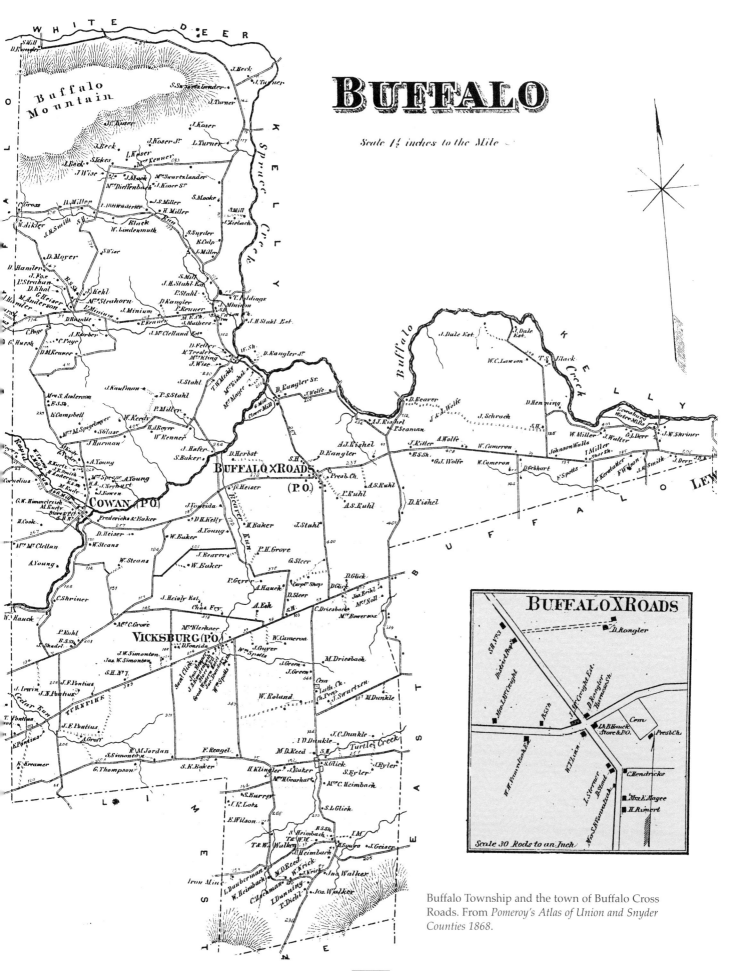

Buffalo Township and the town of Buffalo Cross Roads. From *Pomeroy's Atlas of Union and Snyder Counties 1868.*

hospitality. Fithian declined Plunket's offer, deciding to remain with the Grays for a day of fasting called by the Continental Congress to unify public support against British aggression.

The Revolutionary War precipitated withdrawals from the region, and some did not return, but peace let loose another avalanche of home seekers. Even before the war's close, Christian Van Gundy built a mill near the mouth of Buffalo Creek. He lost it after a drawn-out law suit with the heirs of Ludwig Derr, but it was operated by many owners through the next century, including Joseph Shriner, the foremost miller in Buffalo Valley. Long identified as the Campbell Mill, it was still using water power in the 1950s. The old mill race remains visible from the road adjacent to it.

In 1783 Philip Billmyer purchased the McCandlish property and opened a tavern there; and in 1800 William Clingan and his wife, Jane Roan, of Lancaster County settled near the mouth of Little Buffalo Creek; there they were joined by Jane's brother, Flavel, a teacher and diarist. West of the Clingans, John Baer of Lancaster built a mill in the 1780s; known to future generations as the Chamberlain, then Hoffa, then Grove Mill, it is still geared for water power. William Linn of Franklin County purchased land just beyond the mill and became the founder of that family in Buffalo Valley. At a mill seat another mile upstream near the mouth of Spruce Run, Michael Rentschler, his wife, and son, John, erected grist and sawmills. The former remained a family enterprise for several generations and continued to grind until 1981, when that mill was closed by owner F. Eugene Johnson.

Meanwhile, possibly in 1784, the Buffalo Presbyterians erected a log meeting house at the intersection soon to be identified as Buffalo Roads or Buffalo Cross Roads. It appears to have been the first church edifice in Union County. It is known that the Buffalo Church, formally organized in 1773, was the first church established west of the West Branch of the Susquehanna River, a mere five years after the territory was opened to settlement as a result of the Albany Purchase. Thus, Reverend Fithian, in his 1775 visit, was preaching to a formally constituted congregation, albeit one without a building. During the ministry of the Reverend Hugh Morrison, the first pastor, the congregation was divided by a controversy between Morrison, a Federalist partisan, and some of his Republican-minded parishioners, and several members ceased attending. During the tenure of his successor, the Reverend Thomas Hood, an even greater controversy over the psalmody question emerged, and several members left, forming their own congregation in Mifflinburg.

Even so, the congregation grew again from 60 after the 1818 split to 273 in 1828. During this period, a larger stone structure was built in 1816 on land given by Edward and Joseph Shippen of Philadelphia. However, its foundation mortar was faulty, and the stone church was replaced in 1846 by the brick Greek Revival structure which occupies the site today.

At the same time, however, three more churches were formed from congregants who wanted to worship closer to home. Therefore, by the time the Reverend Isaac Grier assumed the pastorate in 1835, there were only 58 members. His ministry, which continued until his death in 1874, saw an increase in communicants despite formation of yet a fifth church from its membership. However, at the turn of the century, 91 members petitioned to join other congregations, and only 19 members remained. After considerable thought and discussion, most of those transferred their membership to the Lewisburg church in 1918. On January 27, 1919, the last six members dissolved Buffalo Church and transferred their membership. Annual historical pilgrimages during the years which followed revealed a continuing interest in its heritage.

In the years that followed, two Mennonite congregations leased the building. In 1975 the church and the surrounding grove of trees were purchased by the 1773 Buffalo Church Association, composed of Mary Ruhl Maher, Ethel D. Ruhl, and George A. Ruhl, for the

Old Buffalo (Presbyterian) Church at Buffalo Cross Roads. Photo by Jim Walter.

purpose of preserving the historic religious structure. The restored building, now used only for religious and historical purposes, honors the "Mother of Churches," as Old Buffalo is called, in recognition of the five congregations formed from it: Mifflinburg (1818), Bethel in White Deer (1831), Laurel Run in Hartley (1832), Lewisburg (1833), and New Berlin (1841).

Title for the cemetery was given to another group, the Old Buffalo Presbyterian Church Cemetery Association, Inc.; its first president was Robert L. Donehower, followed by the present officeholder, Linn M. Kieffer. Revolutionary War veterans who attended Buffalo Church included John Campbell, Colonel William Chamberlin, Captain Samuel Dale, William Irwin, Colonel John Kelly, George Lashells, Senator Samuel Maclay, James Magee, Captain Alexander McEwen, Jacob V. Ross (brother-in-law of Betsy Ross), Captain James Thompson, and Hugh Wilson. Many of these were interred in the cemetery, but the remains were removed from several of the graves to active cemeteries after the dissolution of the church.

About 1793 Christopher Baldy built a tannery at Buffalo Cross Roads. At the same time George Frederick opened a hotel on the northwest corner, which Baldy took over a few years later. Glimpses of the varied civic and social activities under its roof have been preserved in the diary of Flavel Roan. James McCreight bought the hotel property in 1831 and kept a store there until 1862; J.O. Glover, scion of Robert Glover, pioneer of Hartleton, was the next storekeeper. In 1863 William T. Linn built a brick house and storeroom on the southeastern corner of Buffalo Crossroads; this remained in continuous use as a general store until 1974, when it was converted into apartments. Clustered nearby in the mid-nineteenth century were harness, wagon, and blacksmith shops. In the 1870s the Buffalo Grange erected a hall, and the chapter remains active after more than 120 years.

Dr. Robert Van Valzah was an outstanding citizen from the time of his arrival at Buffalo Cross Roads in 1796 until his death in 1850. Of Dutch ancestry, he reached Sunbury with all of his earthly possessions, a horse and saddle. According to an oft-told story, he had to borrow a shilling from a stranger to cross the river, an act of kindness which he never forgot — providing in his will for an indigent member of this family as long as she lived. Dedicated to his profession, his practice extended over the countryside and occasionally into Northumberland and Centre Counties as well. Of his seven sons, five became physicians, several of whom practiced in Union and Centre Counties, while others moved West. A third

generation of Van Valzahs — the whole adding up to eighteen — were practicing medicine as the nineteenth century closed, a record possibly unequaled in the nation. The family homestead, a spacious brick structure, stands several doors west of the intersection.

Children at Buffalo Cross Roads sometimes attended the classical school of the Reverend Thomas Hood, but in 1807 John Sierer and Christopher Baldy donated two acres of land for a German school just a few yards north of the crossroad. Adjacent to Buffalo Cross Roads was the farm of James Dale Chamberlin, who, by experimentation, found that vegetables could be preserved by hermetically sealing them in cans. His products were exhibited at Philadelphia in addition to regional fairs, and within a few decades his invention was revolutionizing food preservation in the home and factory.

John Sierer also lived nearby on Buffalo Creek (formerly the Henry Sies tract), arriving there from Berks County around 1769. In 1795 he erected a stone house, which retains an unusual interest to this day because of the markings he placed high on the eastern gable. A piece of marble depicting the dial of a clock has hands positioned at 11:45, and below it cut into the stone appear "I.H.S/1.7.9.5/S.N.S," the initials in German (with J appearing as I, and the S carved backward) of Sierer and his wife, Susanna. The clock, according to a tradition recorded more than a century ago, indicates the hour and minute when the family escaped being massacred by hiding in a rye field — even the dog did not bark — while hostile Indians combed their cabin and outbuildings. Just west of the Sierer home, Wendell Baker diverted water from Buffalo Creek to operate a sawmill, and his son Jacob added fulling and carding mills. The remains of the Baker and Kelly families are interred in a small walled burial plot there.

Colonel John Kelly, one of the region's heroes in the Revolutionary War and a legend in his own time, lived on his estate on the north side of Buffalo Creek and east of Spruce Run. It was said that "he exhibited the same anxiety to do right and disregard himself" which had marked his military service.[11] As a justice of the peace, he often overlooked his own fees and sometimes paid the constable from his own pocket to facilitate an amicable settlement. Well over six feet tall and muscular, he lost little of his vigor until the closing years of his long life. His wife, Sarah Poak, died in 1831, and he died a year later at 88. On April 8, 1835, a monument was erected in his memory in the English (Presbyterian) Cemetery on Market Street in Lewisburg with appropriate pomp and an imposing military and civic parade. His remains and marker were moved to the Lewisburg Cemetery when the Presbyterian church was built on the site of the early cemetery.

Through the years, Colonel Kelly's image became larger than life, and his deeds became proverbial, with truth and myth blending to become almost inseparable. It was related that he was a great hunter and that he shot the last buffalo in Buffalo Valley. Riding on his trusted horse, Brandywine, which had carried him through the arduous campaigns of the war, on a misty morning near Buffalo Cross Roads in 1801, the steed snorted and swerved, dodging the attacking beast which Kelly had not observed. Dismounting, Kelly, "taking leisurely aim, shot the bison through the heart." Supposedly, the buffalo's head was nailed to a tree, and there it hung until 1820, when the tree was blown down. It was then taken to

the Kleckner home (relatives of the Kellys), where it was thoughtlessly destroyed some years later.[12]

An anecdote recorded by Linn relates that Kelly's dog awoke him one night during the Revolutionary War, when he was at home in his cabin. Sensing that an Indian was prowling outside, he watched through a hole he had cut in his door for such emergencies and at daylight spotted an Indian who was partially concealed behind a log. When the Indian raised his head, Kelly fired and killed him. Kelly buried the body in a lot by the spring under a heavy stone but said nothing, not even telling his nearest neighbor, in order to protect himself from the vengeance of the Indian's next of kin. Shortly before his death, Kelly employed a neighbor's boy to clean up the lot but warned him not to disturb the stone. The boy became curious and at the first opportunity grubbed out the stone and discovered the skeleton under it. He took out the skull — an exceptionally large one — with a hole through the center of the forehead. He pushed back the stone and hid the skull under the porch of the house. Some time later, Dr. Van Valzah stopped to talk with the Colonel, and the subject of large heads came up in the conversation. The boy, who happened to be listening, brought out the skull from its hiding place. When he told where he had found it, Kelly's anger was almost uncontrollable, and he would have whaled the lad if Dr. Van Valzah had not intervened.[13]

Jacob Stahl, a wagon maker, lived with his sons and daughters near Spruce Run. Here a hamlet emerged, stretching irregularly toward Rentschler's Mill near the confluence of Spruce Run with Buffalo Creek. It was called Union in the early days, and later Boyertown after the Boyers in the vicinity; it is now known as Mazeppa. In 1841 the German Reformed and Lutheran flocks joined to organize a union church there. They purchased a lot from Peter Stahl, transferring the title to trustees Jacob Kauffman, George Miller, Abraham Brower, Daniel Giddings, and John Minium. The congregations bound themselves, "the one to the other, that we will [act], appertaining to these matters, in common together as long as the sun and moon shall shine, or

The Emery Store in Mazeppa c. 1908. In the buggy are Clark Miller and Miriam Emery Feaster, while Irvin and Maggie Emery stand on the porch. From the collection of the Union County Historical Society, courtesy of Dorothy Johnson.

Portrait of Cyrus Hoffa, miller, as a young boy. From the collection of the Union County Historical Society, #89.5.1.45.

until we ourselves shall dissolve the unity between us." The agreement continues after 159 years.

During 1841 the trustees erected a one-story brick building, measuring 45 x 60 feet, under the direction of Samuel Noll. John Long of Smoketown did the masonry with bricks from the kiln there. It was completed in the fall and dedicated on Christmas Day. It is recalled that John Minium, who served as sexton without pay, trimmed the lamps, cut the wood, and took care of the pastor's horse. In 1885 a small belfry was added; in 1891 a union Sunday school was officially organized, followed in two years by a union choir. In 1915 an ell was added to the building, the belfry was replaced by a larger steeple, and stained glass windows were installed. A union communion service was initiated in 1938, continuing the long, harmonious relationship of the two sects. The Mazeppa Union Church is apparently the oldest in Union County holding continuous services in the same building.

In 1859 the Union Immanuel Evangelical Church was organized, and construction begun upon a house of worship on the west side of Mazeppa's main street. Its original trustees were John Hartman, David Herbst, Jacob Zeiback, Peter S. Stahl, and E.M. Kling. The frame structure was remodeled and enlarged in 1875 and 1897, but it had to be substantially rebuilt after the destructive tornado of July 22, 1926, hurled the steeple and bell to the street and ripped away much of the roof. The Evangelical Church also conducted a camp meeting in the 1890s in a grove a mile north of the village; extending through eight days of August, it attracted hundreds of campers and visitors.

The village's growth accelerated in the closing years of the nineteenth century. At the turn of the century Mazeppa contained a wagon shop, a slaughterhouse, a shoemaker, a gunsmith, a sawmill and sorghum mill, a maple bush, and a boarding house, which overflowed during camp meetings. A number of farm families retired to the village, occupying newly built homes which today retain architectural details of this period. John L. Bitting was named postmaster in 1886 and handled the mail in his general store. In 1916 Mazeppa was struck by a devastating fire, which started in the stable behind Shuck's store. A high wind spread it down the street. Before the Lewisburg fire department could halt the fire, it had consumed seven houses, four barns, a blacksmith shop, and a meat market in addition to Shuck's store.

Meanwhile, the old Rentschler (anglicized to Rengler) Mill continued to operate. It remained in the family until 1874, when it was purchased by William Cameron of Lewisburg. Upon his death it became the property of the Packer family of Sunbury, who leased it to millers. It was purchased by Clarence Auten in 1922 and Fred I. Johnson in 1930. The latter's son, Eugene, took over operation of the mill in 1946, a year after its conversion from water to diesel power, which was used until it closed in 1981.

Prior to the adoption of the public school law by Buffalo Township, a crude log cabin served as a school for the scattered families of the Boyertown area. Shortly after 1838 the school directors erected a brick structure just north of the present Mazeppa Union Church. In 1895 it was replaced by a larger frame building, which housed the elementary children in the south room and the grammar school in the north. Under the able direction of Professor Clement E. Edmunds, the latter offered the equivalent of the first two years of high school.

It was Edmunds who is credited with renaming Boyertown in 1886, when the post office required a change (as Pennsylvania had another Boyertown in Berks County). Noting the many turnings in the road between Rengler's Mill and the far end of the village, he proposed the name Mazeppa in honor of a figure in Ukrainian folklore, known to Edmunds through the poetry of Byron. The hapless Ivan Stepanovitch Mazeppa, a page in the Polish court, was tied naked to a wild horse and set loose as a punishment for intrigue. The horse fell dead in the Ukraine, but Mazeppa was rescued by the Cossacks and eventually to Sweden and in remorse committed suicide.

South of the turnpike (Route 45) was the home of Martin Dreisbach, a native of Germany, who was living there as early as 1773. A deeply religious man, he opened his door to the itinerant clergy of the Evangelical and United Brethren churches and donated seven acres of land near his farm to the Lutheran and German Reformed congregations for a church, as well as several additional acres for a school. His descendants owned farms there for four generations, and several of them also became prominent merchants and tradesmen in Lewisburg and Mifflinburg.

The Lutheran and Reformed (or German Presbyterian) adherents jointly erected a log church in 1788, and rebuilt it of brick in 1839 and 1860. The latter was later embellished with a massive tower and a squared steeple — a landmark for a full century — but its foundation was accidentally undermined while undergoing renovations in 1963 and the building had to be razed. The Dreisbach United Church of Christ

Great Western Hotel and the Roudenbush home appeared as printed postcards. From the collection of the Union County Historical Society, #92.9.89.36 and #82.2.5.0.

PAGE 203: Rockey's Mill in Buffalo Township with Charles Meese, unknown, Isaac Moyer (owner), and D.P. Stapleton on a real photo postcard sent in 1910. From the collection of Gary W. and Donna M. Slear.

(formerly the Reformed) now occupies the site by itself, since the Lutherans in the meantime built Faith Church just west of Lewisburg.

Charles Dreisbach, a son of Martin Dreisbach II, built the Great Western Hotel on the south side of the Lewisburg/Youngmanstown Turnpike a short distance west of the ancestral farm. The large, rectangular, three-storied structure with long porches on the southern and eastern exposures became a favorite stopping place for hungry and thirsty riders. Beginning in the 1880s, during the tenure of Daniel F. Bingaman, it drew farmers from near and far to the western horse auctions held at its stables. Dealers sometimes hand-picked the horses in Illinois and Indiana; and in later years in locations as distant as South Dakota. During summers at the turn of the century, the hostelry became a resort patronized by visitors from as far away as Shamokin and even Philadelphia. A tennis court and croquet green offered entertainment, and the fine food served by the Everett family was always an attraction.

The commercial activity at the hotel drew the discerning eye of Joseph S. Raudenbush of White Springs, and in 1865 he opened a general store on the lot west of it. He was also named postmaster and is credited with the recommendation that the nascent village be named Vicksburg, in honor of General Grant's siege and capture of Vicksburg, Mississippi, during the Civil War. Raudenbush appears to have prospered from the start, and the arrival of the railroad added another dimension to his business — a weekly boxcar filled with grain and other produce that was then shipped from his elevator on the siding to Hazleton. In 1883 he employed Enoch Miller to build an Eastlake Victorian mansion. With its five tall chimneys, "gingerbread" porches and balconies, stained glass windows, and steam-heated interior, the home is as elegant as any residence in Buffalo Valley and currently functions as a bed and breakfast.

Raudenbush's success inevitably attracted competition. H.A. Cook and Jerry Burrey opened general stores, also shipping produce to the coal regions. Descendants of Cook and Burrey continued the businesses until the 1950s. Meanwhile, Addison Baker laid out lots on the north side of the highway in 1885, and a village evolved. More than a century later its architecture conforms to its Victorian origins.

At the turn of the century, in addition to the three general stores and hotel, there were an agricultural implement sales and repair shop, blacksmith, barber, coal yard, and creamery; a new ballroom in the Great Western Hotel was installed by Robert Hopkins, its congenial owner. In 1900 a nucleus from congregations at Dreisbach and Mifflinburg erected the St. Paul's Reformed Church, an attractive Gothic structure on the north side of the street. It was originally attached to the White Deer charge, and later to the Lewisburg Reformed Church.

Once the automobile opened markets in Lewisburg and Sunbury, even the four daily passenger trains, trolley, and freight services could not maintain Vicksburg's economy. Stores closed, one by one, and by 1985 none remained. In 1913 the Great Western lost its liquor license, and its clientele departed. The Everetts continued to live in the building, from which they operated an extensive antiques business for many years. The Great Western Hotel was razed in 1971, revealing its mammoth wooden beams. A sprawling mobile home sales area now occupies its site. Declining support led to the closure of the church in the 1940s, but a citizens' group converted the building into a community center and library.

At the eastern edge of Vicksburg are businesses and other buildings associated with the "team Mennonites," who came to Union County from Lancaster County in significant numbers, starting in the late 1960s. Isaac Reiff operates a buggy shop for his plain sect community just north of Route 45 on Beaver Run Road, and James Yoder operates an oak furniture shop nearby, while on the south side, about a half mile farther south is one of two Groffdale meetinghouses in Buffalo Valley (the westernmost one being behind Ray's Church near Hartleton). This meetinghouse and carriage sheds were constructed in 1979.

Cowan's origins centered around a gristmill, the shell of which still stands on Rapid Run about 100 yards from its confluence with Buffalo Creek. The first mill was built by Adam Wagoner and "found its patronage for many miles around by people coming on horseback through the trackless wilderness and along the rude bridle paths."[14] It burned about 1812 and was rebuilt by Jacob Baker, but it was again destroyed by fire. Jacob Rengler, Baker's son-in-law, constructed the third mill on the site and after a few years sold it to Daniel D. Guldin of Berks County. It remained in "Guldy's" hands until mid-century, though only the timely intervention of a plucky bucket brigade saved it from a threatened conflagration in 1844. In time a hamlet grew up adjacent to the intersection. S.L. Shoemaker opened a general store in 1848, but he sold it to Martin Rudy, who also operated

Guldy's Mill. John Hildebrand had a chair shop on another corner; cooper and carpenter shops stood nearby. First known as Guldy's Mill, Farmersville later caught on as the village's name; but with the coming of the post office in 1886, the name was changed to Cowan in honor of United States Senator Edgar Cowan of Westmoreland County.

The career of George W. Himmelreich exemplifies the opportunities afforded to a village businessman in the nineteenth century. At age 22, with but several hundred dollars to invest, Himmelreich became a junior partner to Martin Rudy in Cowan's general store. Ten years later, in 1866, he bought out Rudy, and subsequently opened stores in Forest Hill and Mazeppa. Himmelreich was also a founder and director of the Mifflinburg Bank. Much the same might be said of the Mussina brothers, William and Henry, who came to Cowan from Aaronsburg by way of Mt. Carmel in 1873. They purchased the gristmill, opened a general store, and became successful managers of both. They rebuilt the store property in 1882 and were reported by the local press to be "as happy as birds taken out of an old cage and put in a nice new one."[15] The store burned in 1902, but the brothers promptly rebuilt it and added a lumber and shingle business to their enterprises. The mill changed hands several times in the twentieth century, but the milling business ended when it was gutted by fire on February 12, 1942. It is presently the site of a pottery business.

The Lutherans erected a church at the northern margin of Cowan in 1872 and enlarged it twenty years later. The Evangelicals also built a sanctuary north of the center of the village in 1882; it was later consolidated with the Forest Hill congregation, and its timbers were used to provide an addition to the latter. In the 1830s a log school stood near the Buffalo Creek bridge, and in 1870 a more adequate brick structure was erected on a plot just north of the Lutheran Church. By 1884 it overflowed with more than 80 pupils, and its enlargement necessitated the employment of an assistant teacher. Three years later a grammar school was built in front of the elementary school, and the schools were graded. By 1918, with the school population decreasing, the grammar school was closed, and in 1956 the Cowan children were bused to Mifflinburg.

Farther upstream on Rapid Run, near Forest Hill, the Reish family operated distilleries for many years. Daniel Reish, a native of Berks County, settled here in 1820 and built a sawmill, gristmill, and distillery. His son, Benivel, also a distiller, was proprietor of the Forest House, a hostelry at the entrance to the Fourteen Mile Narrows. By the 1890s Benivel's sons, James K. and Joel, were running the businesses. For a time Joel also retailed his whiskey, but this was terminated by action of the court in 1913 under the local option law. The plant burned in 1897 — a fate common to many of the small distilleries — with the loss of 400 barrels in bond. The Reishes rebuilt and continued the business until the Volstead Act rang its death knell in 1920. In 1899 the distillery was described as "the most complete and best kept in the district. All of the latest improvements are in use, and everything is kept clean and neat."[16] Many of its account books survive to give a more detailed picture and are in the Union County Historical Society's collection.

In 1847 Ammon Lutz, a young Mifflinburg merchant, opened a store near the beginning of the Fourteen Mile Narrows, where the Mifflinburg road intersected the Brush Valley highway. In addition to merchandise found in a typical country store, he added a saddlery and tailor shop. Several years later he was named postmaster of the hamlet, which was designated Forest Hill. Lutz moved away, but the store remained. A subscription school was erected near the store, and after the school law was accepted by West Buffalo Township, a new building was constructed on the site. About 1857 the Reverend Samuel

Creighton, the Methodist minister in charge of the Mifflinburg circuit, began preaching in the schoolhouse. He received a warm response, and a union church was soon rising on a lot near the store. The Methodists shared the sanctuary with the Evangelicals and Lutherans for a number of years, but in 1916 it was acquired by the Evangelical Association and enlarged. Today, the hamlet's activities ebb and flow each year with the seasons, as devotees of winter sports, fishing, camping, and hunting find their way into the adjoining mountains.

West of Rapid Run, the north branch of Buffalo Creek, cascading from Jones and Buffalo Mountains, once provided power for a number of small mills used to produce grist, cider, lumber, and woolens; and in the late nineteenth century the country road paralleling the stream was dotted with cottages and identified locally as Johnstown. The homes remain, but the mills are now gone, and the utilization of the stream is recreational rather than industrial.

At the confluence of the north branch of Buffalo Creek with the main stream east of Mifflinburg, Jacob Fought purchased 216 acres of Captain Joseph Green's military tract and built the first gristmill on the site in 1771. For a time it was the polling place for the third election district of Northumberland County, encompassing White Deer, Buffalo, and Potter Townships. The first election under the Pennsylvania Constitution of 1776 was held here. William Rockey acquired the mill in 1789, and it remained in the Rockey family for two generations; the name Rockey's Mills lingered there for many more years, even during its occupancy by Charles H. Shriner and C.W. Thomas. In the twentieth century, the Voneida and Moyer families operated the mill during the first quarter; they were followed by the Taylor, Oberlin, and Fisher families. Its wheel stopped running in September of 1971, when it was consumed by fire, leaving only the foundation and the mill race as visible evidence of its two centuries of service.

Along Cedar Run, just east of Mifflinburg, were the extensive farms of John Frederick Pontius and his sons. Pontius and his wife, natives of Switzerland, had come to Buffalo Valley by way of Berks County. He purchased the Captain Bucher military tract, 600 acres of prime land, and his seven sons carved out farms for themselves, which remained in the family through four generations. In 1775 John Frederick Pontius was one of the viewers who laid out the first public road through the heart of Buffalo Valley,

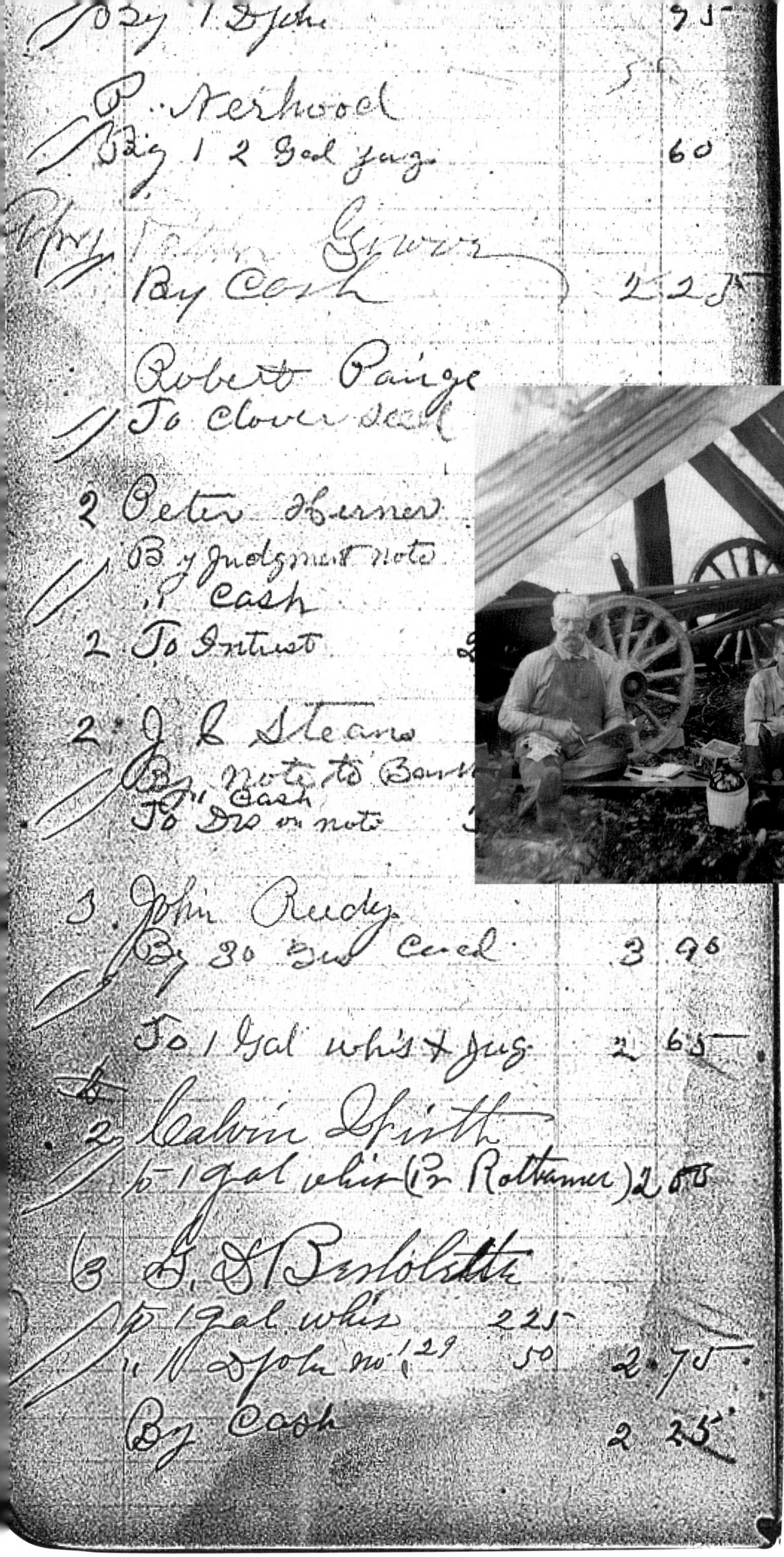

By 1 Djue ... 95

P. Nerhood ... 5
By 1 2 Gad jug ... 60

John Grove
By Cash ... 2 20

Robert Painge
1 To Clover seed

2 Peter Harner
By Judgment note
" Cash
2 To Intrust ... 9

2 J R Steans
By Note to Bonn
" Cash
To Dis on note ... 5

3 John Rudy
By 30 Bus Cord ... 3 96

To 1 Gal whis & Jug ... 2 65

2 Calvin Smith
To 1 gal whis (Pr Rothamer) 2 00

6 G. D. Berloletti
To 1 gal whis ... 225
" Djue no 129 50 ... 2 75
By Cash ... 2 25

Joel Reish, who is posed with an account book and pencil, and Cling Reish (second from right) are seated with others at the Reish Distillery on Rapid Run near Forest Hill. Joel was the grandson of the distillery's founder, Daniel Reish, who had come to Buffalo Valley from Berks County. Joel's father, Benivel, also operated the Forest House at the foot of the Fourteen Mile Narrows. Joel and his brother, James, ran the distillery until 1920. From the collection of Billy and Lindy Mattern.

Page from the Reish Distillery account book covering transactions from 1896 to 1902. From the collection of the Union County Historical Society, #92.2.3, a gift of Ethel D. Ruhl.

connecting it to the Reuben Haines Road near Hartleton; and in 1792 he was a viewer to divide Buffalo Township. The Pontius burial lot on the Furnace Road marks the site of their Big Spring Farm, a nineteenth-century garden spot.

Norman Saunders made baskets of ash and maple near Forest Hill. From the collections of the Union County Historical Society, and Jeannette Lasansky. Photo by William Irwin, courtesy of the Oral Traditions Project.

The Forest Hill Store was photographed by Stephen Horton sometime between 1907 and 1911, and then issued as a real photo postcard. Ammon Lutz started the store in 1847, and L. H. Miller was operating it about 60 years later. From the collection of the Union County Historical Society, #89.5.15.5.

ENDNOTES:

1 *Mifflinburg Telegraph*, July 18, 1902.

2 Smoketown folklore attributes the name of the hamlet to smoke rising from the cabins, where the women were puffing on their pipes.

3 Charles Reagan, "Early Iron Industry at Winfield," *Union County Heritage I* (1968), 15.

4 *Lewisburg Saturday News*, August 30, 1930.

5 *Lewisburg Chronicle*, January 20, 1854.

6 *Lewisburg Chronicle*, January 29, 1869.

7 *Lewisburg Chronicle*, January 29, 1869.

8 Donald Carpenter in his presentation at the John B. Deans Annual Dinner, November 9, 1995, discussed this matter as well as much of the information that follows on the early Amish settlements in Union County.

9 David Luthy, *The Amish in America: Settlements that Failed, 1840-1960*, Aylmer, Ontario, 421-429.

10 Robert G. Albion and Leonidas Dodson, eds., *Philip Vickers Fithian: Journal, 1775-1776*, Princeton, NJ., 1934, 52.

11 R.V.B. Lincoln, *Mifflinburg Telegraph*, October 10, 1901.

12 This particular version of the tale was related by Colonel Henry W. Shoemaker in *A Pennsylvania Bison Hunt*, Middleburg Post Press, 1915, 40, written 83 years after Kelly's death and more than a century after the alleged incident. Linn did not mention it. I.H. Mauser may have first recorded it in his *History of Lewisburg*, published in 1886. His account of the "last" Buffalo is less dramatic than Shoemaker's. According to Mauser, Kelly was hunting on a neighbor's land some time between 1790 and 1800, and coming upon a buffalo he shot it. It ran, however, and as it was late in the evening he did not pursue it. Several days later he learned that a buffalo had been found several miles away. He went to get it, but found that a great part of it had been devoured by wolves. In documenting the account Mauser observed that Colonel Kelly had related the incident to Dr. S.L. Beck, who told it some years later to the Rev. Justin R. Loomis, who in turn, published it in Haydin's *Geological Reports* for 1875. Dr. Beck, a Lewisburg physician, had opened a medical practice several years prior to Kelly's death.

13 John Blair Linn, *Annals of Buffalo Valley, Pennsylvania, 1755-1855*, Harrisburg, 1877, 172.

14 Reminiscences of Samuel G. Frey (1897), published in the Lewisburg *Saturday News*, August 14, 1907.

15 *Mifflinburg Telegraph*, Aug. 22, 1882.

16 *Mifflinburg Telegraph*, May 26, 1899.

CHAPTER 12

WHITE DEER, KELLY AND GREGG TOWNSHIPS

A veritable paradise for the land-hungry lay athwart the West Branch of the Susquehanna River north of Winfield, where the river sliced between the Montour and Shamokin ridges. Reports of its fertility induced a rush to the land office when it opened in 1769. The officers' warrants exempted much of Buffalo Valley between Lewisburg and Mifflinburg, but there were many acres available within the present-day boundaries of Kelly, White Deer, and Gregg Townships.

A tract on the river just north of Buffalo Creek containing 675 acres was surveyed on a special warrant for the Reverend John Ewing, who divided it into six plots, five of which were almost immediately taken up by settlers from Paxton, near Harrisburg. Walter Clark had the first farm (later Eli Slifer's homestead, and more recently the United Methodist Home, and now RiverWoods); Robert Fruit, the second; William Gray, the third; Robert Clark, the fourth; and William Clark, the fifth. To the north of those, Michael Weyland obtained a patent for the land where historians have sometimes located Shikellamy's initial settlement on a limestone ridge overlooking the river. John Fisher occupied the site of West Milton in 1769, and some of his descendants still reside in the neighborhood. John Hoffman located and surveyed 300 acres on the Susquehanna north of Fisher's land while Dietrich Rees' later survey became the site of New Columbia. Nearby, Hawkins Boone, a cousin and former neighbor of Daniel Boone in Berks County, built a cabin in 1771. North of his tract the John Zimmerman survey was occupied by Robert McCurley in 1784; he and his son would later be active in White Deer's politics. James Potter resided north of the Zimmerman survey for a few years prior to 1774 and again after the Revolutionary War, but he subsequently removed to Penns Valley where he founded a settlement at Old Fort, adjacent to Centre Hall. North of the Potter survey William Blythe received a grant of land from Governor Penn for his assistance in apprehending Frederick Stump and John Eisenhauer, who had jeopardized the peace with their mass killings of Indians on Middle Creek in present-day Snyder County. Beyond Blythe's grant, at the mouth of White Deer Creek, Jessie Lukens purchased the Charles Iredell survey in 1772. Finding that a Peter Smith had settled there, he brought suit for ejectment; but when Smith died, the

suit abated, and his widow Catherine and her sons remained undisturbed for a time.

In February of 1776 the occupation of the west side of the river led to the creation of White Deer Township, which was set off from Buffalo. It extended from Buffalo Creek and Spruce Run on the south, to Potter Township (later Centre County) on the west, and northeast to the West Branch of the Susquehanna River. Its birth thus preceded that of the nation by five months. Like Buffalo Township, most of White Deer Township's expansive mountains and valleys would later be divided to form other municipalities.

The American Revolution exposed the region to marauding bands of Indians, culminating in the Great Runaway. Few of the inhabitants moved to safety at the outset, preferring to risk their lives rather than lose their hard-won possessions. The example of widow Catherine Smith and her sons is a record of courage and sacrifice, and helps to explain the ultimate triumph of the cause of independence. With only a squatter's rights to the land and in the face of litigation to eject her, Catherine Smith erected a gristmill and a sawmill, both propelled by the water of White Deer Creek. When resistance to British rule turned into armed conflict, she added a hemp mill and a gun-boring shop. Confirmation is lacking, but tradition holds that she supplied the local militia with arms and that her settlement became a place of refuge in times of danger. At the time of the Great Runaway, however, Indians burned her buildings and forced Widow Smith to flee to Fort Augusta. She returned after the war but was compelled to expend her time and energy in fighting eviction. While the case dragged on in court, she petitioned the legislature in Philadelphia for relief; but it did not respond, and Widow Smith finally lost her property in 1801.

During the lengthy controversy, Catherine Smith did not lose hope; instead, tradition relates that she walked to Philadelphia and back thirteen times — 160 miles each way — in repeated attempts to legalize her claim. One account, written many years later, indicates that she walked barefooted, reserving shoes for her passage through the villages and towns enroute. Worn out by her labors, she died shortly after her eviction and was buried in a plot in the Old Settlers' Grave Yard, located on the old mill property.

The Iredells again took possession of the mill site and erected a three-storied gristmill with two pairs of overshot wheels, a sawmill, and a stone house. About 1810 Daniel Caldwell purchased the property and operated the mills for 25 years. Caldwell was a civic leader and served on Union County's first Board of Commissioners in 1813. He was elected to the legislature in 1820, and he was to serve as a member of the Constitutional Convention of 1837 but died before taking his seat. Caldwell was also a champion of public education and led the battle for White Deer's acceptance of the law. He was a member of the first school board and was serving a second term at the time of his death. The tribute of his colleagues on the board of directors has been preserved and reads in part: "His high sense of public and private duty in matters pertaining to the welfare of our community, will linger as a standard for each generation. . . . He knew that virtue and intelligence are the pillars of republican government .... Consequently he was the sturdiest active friend of the Free Public School Law. . . . May the school children of White Deer revere his memory and emulate his devotion to the cause of public instruction."[1]

During the early years, a hamlet, at first called White Deer Mills, grew up around the mills on the two sides of the creek, and the village became a stopping place along the river road connecting Northumberland with Bald Eagle. The assessment records of 1814, taken just after White Deer Township had been reduced to what are now White Deer and Kelly Townships, provides a glimpse of its development at that time. There were 160 houses, 110 of which were of logs; 37 were termed "small"; eight were built of stone; and four were identified as "good." Of the 235 adult males, there were 91 laborers; 80 farmers; seventeen weavers; ten carpenters; seven blacksmiths; six distillers; five shoemakers; four millers; three masons and three tailors; two coopers, wheelwrights, and ferrymen; and one tanner, comb maker, and schoolmaster. The absence of storekeepers suggests that residents did their trading in the villages adjacent to White Deer Township and with peddlers, who traveled the roads at that time.

The people of White Deer Township were largely of Scots-Irish and English ancestry, with the German element smaller than in other parts of the county. Ethnic diversity came later as a byproduct of economic forces which successively planted and uprooted industries in the area. At White Deer, Henry High purchased the mills from the Caldwell estate; and he soon added a stone hotel, a row of substantial brick dwellings, and a post office. In fact, the village was

called Hightown for some years even though the post office was designated White Deer.

In 1824 a state road was laid out from Bellefonte to White Deer by way of Sugar Valley. The Union County portion of the road passed through the mountains of Lewis, West Buffalo, and White Deer Townships and was frequently in poor repair. Though it was later taken over by the White Deer and Sugar Valley Turnpike Company, it was not greatly improved. Nevertheless, it enabled Sugar Valley farmers to market their grain at White Deer and purchase their supplies at its store. A ferry there also gave them access to the canal at Watsontown.

The flouring mill was destroyed by fire in 1850, but Henry High rebuilt it, engaging the services of Benjamin Griffoy, a local millwright, mason, bridge builder, and architect. The panic of 1857 wiped him out, but Dr. W.F. Danowsky and his son, Augustus, took it over. Danowsky was born in Poland, the son of a cavalry officer. He practiced medicine in Hanover, Germany, and on ocean liners plying the seas between Hanover and ports in the New World. Danowsky emigrated to Allentown, Pennsylvania, in 1846 and built a drugstore there. He experimented with coal gas for lighting in his store and was so successful that he was soon installing municipal systems, first in Bethlehem and later in Tamaqua, Danville, and Williamsport. Deciding to remove to the country, he purchased the flouring mill in White Deer and subsequently added a pottery. He also acquired the Caldwell farm and enlarged the imposing brick homestead. Folklore associates a small stone structure behind the house with Widow Smith, though her mill would have been on the bank of the creek. Danowsky later disposed of the mill to Thompson Bower and J.N. Messinger, who expanded its capacity by installing two Reliance Turbines. The massive, five-story stone structure remained the heart of White Deer's commercial life until 1928, when it was again consumed by fire.

In 1845 a mile to the west in the valley, on the site of an early gristmill, Dr. G.W. Green and Joseph Green of Lewisburg and David Howard of Kelly Township erected a furnace for the production of pig iron. Ore was found in many places in the vicinity as was limestone, and an almost unlimited supply of charcoal was near at hand. A race leading from White Deer Creek powered the blast. The Forest Iron Works opened with high hopes. The Whig tariff of 1842 offered protection for domestic iron, and a small community of workers moved to the site; but a year

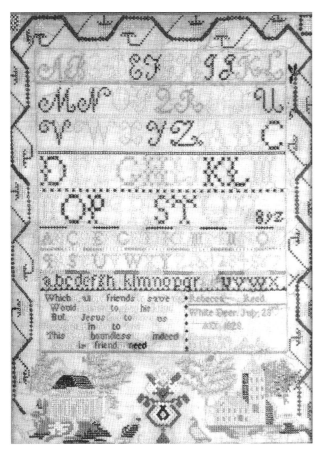

after the furnace was lighted, the Walker tariff of 1846 reduced the duty on iron, and production halted. The Forest Iron Works was purchased by Berks County ironmasters at sheriff's sale, but they too failed. Ario Pardee, the coal and lumber magnate, resumed operations for several years, but the business was still not profitable, and the furnace ceased operations for the third and last time. Many of its ledgers are in the collection of the Union County Historical Society.

The impact of these failures, though serious, was mitigated by a large enterprise midway between the furnace and White Deer village. Here, at a third power site on White Deer Creek, Statten, Marr, and Company, composed of Isaac Statten, David Marr, John Finner, and David Steininger, erected the White Deer Woolen Mills between 1848 and 1850, and began operations in 1851. The factory was housed in a six-story wooden structure built by Benjamin Griffey, and driven by a powerful 85-horsepower overshot waterwheel. The enterprise was highly successful for a time, turning out a variety of woolen goods: cassimeres, trieste, diagonal, tweed, flannels, worsteds, and yarns. During the Civil War it manufactured thousands of blankets for the Union Army.

Sampler of Rebecca Reed of White Deer, Union County, dated July 28, 1828. Silks and linens on linen, 14 1/2 inches x 19 3/4 inches. Photo by the Terry Wild Studio, from the collection of the Union County Historical Society, #87.21.1.

The White Deer Flour Mill was photographed c. 1906, well before the mill's final devastating fire in 1928. From the collection of Gary W. and Donna M. Slear.

The company provided cottages or shanties for some of its more than 100 operatives recruited from beyond Buffalo Valley, and a village grew up adjacent to the mill. *Pomeroy's Atlas of 1868* shows eight private and ten company houses, and some of the former have survived to this time.

In 1867 a sudden freshet tore out the dam and damaged the factory. All work ceased, and the operatives gradually drifted away; some of them eventually found work in the Halfpenny Woolen Plant in Lewisburg. In 1873 Ario Pardee formed a partnership with Benjamin Griffey under the firm name of B. Griffey and Company; they restored the property and added a hat manufactory. Griffey and Pardee constructed additional housing to accommodate the enlarged work force, but in 1879 a second tragedy struck the community when the mill caught fire and burned to the ground. It was partially insured; but times were hard during the lingering panic of 1873, and it was not rebuilt. The closing was a shock to the region. Some of the workers found jobs with Pardee at his lumbering, milling, and mining operations in Hartley Township, Watsontown, and the coal regions while others moved away. The giant waterwheel and the furnace stack a little farther upstream remained for many years to remind the onlooker of the palmy days gone by.

Lumbering contributed substantially to White Deer Valley's economy from the early years onward. Large stands of virgin forest remained virtually untouched until late in the nineteenth century. Dr. Samuel L. Beck of White Deer and Lewisburg acquired thousands of acres of timberland but marketed little lumber, preferring to hold the land for speculation. John McCall, a native of Scotland, on the other hand, built a camp on the upper watershed of White Deer Creek in the 1860s and used splash dams to float the logs to his mill. Later, Ario Pardee enlarged upon the technique to bring logs to the mouth of the creek, where he ferried them to Watsontown for milling. His success attracted other "lumber barons" to the area, including John F. Duncan of Lewisburg, who gained access to the distant White Deer watershed by building a tram line westward from White Deer to Loganton. His extensive timberlands and railroad were subsequently acquired by Whitmer, Steel and Company in 1903; and they, in turn, erected a large mill at White Deer with sidings on the Reading Railroad. They continued to operate there until 1916.

The largest operation along the borders of Union, Lycoming, and Clinton Counties was headed by Monroe H. Kulp, one of the biggest "prop merchants" in the state. A member of Congress, real estate magnate, and developer of Shamokin's municipal transportation and parks, Kulp had lumbering enterprises which extended into three states as well as nine counties of Pennsylvania, and encompassed more than 100,000 acres. In 1897 Kulp constructed a sawmill at West Lewisburg with rail connections to the Lewisburg and Tyrone Railroad as well as the Reading Railroad. He ran a thirty-six-inch-gauge tram line northwestward from the mill into the Spruce Run watershed with spurs extending into Sugar Valley and the upper forks of White Deer Creek. The line, chartered as the Lewisburg and Buffalo Valley Railroad Company, proceeded through Kelly Point to Kulp's Station or Woolheater's Camp near the present-day Spruce Creek Reservoir. For a short time trains along this section provided transport for passengers and freight, but the service proved to be unprofitable. Beyond Kulp's Station, spurs extended between and across the mountains to such colorfully designated campsites as Crabapple, McCall Fields, Tunis Road, Dog Town, Black Gap, Kettle Hole, and Pine Swamp; the spurs finally reached Eastville and Livonia as well as Lost Corner and Zimmerman Run on the border of Lycoming County.

While Kulp's tram roads were better-engineered than most, sharp curves and steep grades inevitably produced accidents. One crash at an ice-weakened trestle across Buffalo Creek hurled the locomotive into the stream, but the engineer waded out only slightly injured. On another occasion a "flat wheel" toppled a barrel of crackers into a run on the north slope of Naked Mountain, and the spot was identified by lumbermen from that day on as "Cracker Bridge."

During the years which followed, Kulp acquired new timberland as the older tracts were stripped, so the tracks and camps were relocated time after time. Ten different lumber camps and stables accommodated as many as 150 horses and mules each. At its peak the company marketed as many as 500 carloads of prop timber per month to the anthracite mines. Kulp paid the sawyers monthly in silver — often in person — from a special pay train. For him, recruiting a work gang was seldom a problem.

Tama Thompson of Loganton moved from one camp to another with her grandparents, Mr. and Mrs. Daniel Mark, who ran a boarding house and did the cooking. She recalled the arrival of foodstuffs, the flatcars piled high with boxes and barrels, and a harrowing experience which remained as vivid "as though it happened yesterday." During a weekend in the spring of 1901, the camp was deserted; only she, her grandmother, and two stablemen remained on duty. Some time on Saturday the men slipped away, presumably to a tavern some miles distant, and they did not return that night. The following day the crazed horses were pounding their hooves and tearing at their straps. Ignoring the order of her grandmother to remain away from the stable, Tama inched into the stalls, unsnapped the halters one by one, and finally emerged unscathed. When the camp superintendent learned of the incident, he warned the stablemen not to set foot on the camp again, and on his next trip to town he returned with a fine piece of blue silk for a dress for Tama.

Kulp's sawmill at Lewisburg burned in 1905, and it was promptly rebuilt. A year later, however, the last timber was cut on Sand Mountain; and the track, rolling stock, and a sizable number of the workmen were transferred to another Kulp sawmill in western Maryland. What appears to have been the last stand of virgin forest in White Deer Township was removed by the Watsontown Door and Sash Company in 1917. It was a 200-acre tract on the "furnace farm," which the Pardee Estate had kept intact and protected from encroachment by other lumbermen. It contained an estimated two million board feet, readily accessible on a gentle slope, and thus a veritable lumberer's paradise. Cutting this tract marked the end of an era.

In the decades which followed, the automobile enabled White Deer Township workers to reach job opportunities in Watsontown and Milton. More recently, however, industry has been moving into its river plain to take advantage of markets served by the interstate highways, and White Deer stands at another economic threshold.

White Deer's immediate acceptance of the Public School Law of 1834 was no accident. Assessment records indicate that several teachers were living there before 1800, though no schools can be dated that early. There were at least three subscription schools, however, within the present boundaries of the township before 1834: two in the rural areas and one in New Columbia.

The first school directors, elected in accordance with the school law, were Jacob McCurley, Daniel Caldwell, John Ranck, Joseph Moore, and James Miller. They agreed to build five schools of brick construction on good stone foundations, and they contracted with John Fisher to erect them for $1,450.

The high cost precipitated a mass meeting, chaired by Samuel Engleman, where it was charged that the law benefited only the few, and enabled the rich and poor to appropriate the hard-won earnings of the farmers and mechanics. The opponents claimed it added a burdensome levy to be added to the county, the roads, the poor, personal property, and state taxes, ". . . a load so unjust and beyond endurance, that they will be compelled to leave the homes of their children and the graves of their fathers and emigrate to the 'far west'."[2] When allegations were made that the state would never pay its share of the costs, Ranck hurried to Harrisburg with the power of attorney from the county treasurer and returned with the money.

With the new schools a reality, a referendum was demanded by opponents of the system seeking to close their doors, but the directors led the campaign to keep them open and had the satisfaction of winning by 60 votes. The continuing zeal of the directors was evidenced in a decision to add a two-month summer session in 1836, and in its emphatic rejection of a petition signed by a number of property holders asking that they be exonerated from the school tax because they were sending their children to a private school. Thus the cause of public education was off to an exceptional start in rural White Deer.

The response of the residents is evident in the growth of the system. By 1854 there were seven schools and 560 scholars, an average of 80 per school. One hundred and two pupils were enrolled at New Columbia by 1858, and the board agreed to employ an assistant teacher for the winter term. Four years later they built a two-room school to handle the overflow. The quaint structure still stands amidst the playground and maple trees near the center of the village and serves the area as a community center. Also, in 1862, the board decided that the schools were not to be used for certain types of traveling shows: namely, performances by Indians, Negroes, and fortunetellers.

Two township schools added in 1868 were Furnace and Leiser's #2. The board erected the Applegate Mills and Sunrise or "Swamp Poodle" Schools in 1870, and the Ramsey School was rebuilt in 1872. The Robin's School was built in 1876, High or Central School in 1885, and Yocum's in 1892; also in 1892 the Sunrise School was rebuilt on the ridge farther east than the original site. In 1902 the Washington School in West Milton reflected the growing population there. The peak attendance in White Deer Township was reached in 1870 when the school population stood at 680 — the largest district enrollment in Union County.

With the closing of the mills in White Deer Valley, the school population gradually fell off. By 1940 there were 356 pupils in eleven elementary schools, and 103 in high schools: 68 in Milton, 26 in Watsontown, and nine in Lewisburg. In the consolidations of the 1950s, the first four grades of the surviving schools, New Columbia, Washington, Leiser's, Central, Ramsey's, Yocum, Sunrise, and Factory, were combined to create the White Deer Elementary School near New Columbia. Middle school and high school students were bused to the Milton District School.

The earliest religious activity in White Deer is identified with the Presbyterians, who affiliated for a time with the Buffalo Cross Roads congregation. In 1831 Andrew McLenahan and his neighbor, Matthew Laird, were instrumental in founding the Bethel Church as an offshoot of the Buffalo Church, with McLenahan and Laird becoming its first elders. The church, a small brick edifice, was served for a number of years by the pastor of the Buffalo Church, but removals from the area led to its closure.

In 1843 members of the Evangelical faith built a brick house of worship in New Columbia, which they shared with the Lutherans. A second Evangelical church was constructed near the woolen factory in 1874; a third was built at White Deer Mills; and a

fourth was erected by the Esherite branch of the church in New Columbia in 1896. The two New Columbia congregations united about 1906 and sold the older structure to the Lutherans, who made a substantial addition to it in 1974. Meanwhile, the Dill Chapel of the Methodist church in New Columbia, which had been erected in 1881, was disbanded. The Evangelicals built a church at Sunrise in the western part of the township, adjacent to the school, in 1908; and in 1966 the Evangelical United Brethren constructed Faith Chapel on the old turnpike a short distance west of White Deer.

While the White Deer Valley's fortunes were fluctuating, New Columbia found a place on the map in 1818 when David Yoder, with the help of Henry Hertz, a surveyor, laid out a plan for a town on Dog Run. The 132 lots on the original plat were on the south side of Main Street; those on the north side were a later addition taken from the farm of John Fisher. Yoder and his son Moses were obviously hopeful that a town on this site would prosper, but there was no river bridge there, nor was there a power seat on the river or run. There was rafting on the river and clay for brickmaking on its bank, but its greatest potential was the fine farm land on the river plain and the hills to the west.

There was no rush for lots, but New Columbia gradually evolved into a compact village with several general stores, a hardware shop, two blacksmiths, a

Gregg Township's Washington Presbyterian Church was photographed in 1908; built in 1830, it has since been razed. From the collection of Gary W. and Donna M. Slear.

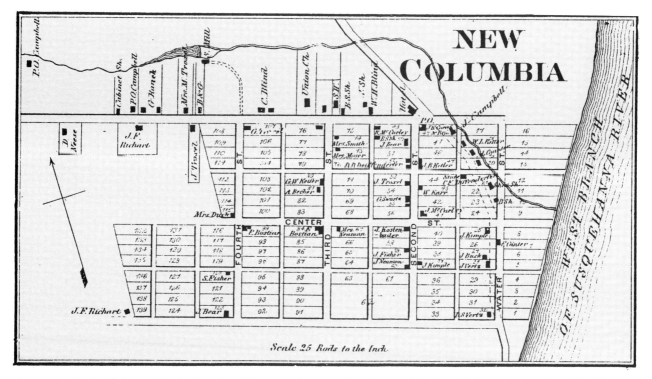

Pomeroy's Atlas for Union and Snyder Counties 1868 shows the sawmill, cabinet and blacksmith shops, the hotel, and the Union Church, all in New Columbia.

shoemaker who also doubled as a constable, a coach-maker, and a boat shop. The arrival of the Reading Railroad in 1871 furthered its growth. Two coal and lumber yards in addition to a chop mill soon faced the tracks; and by the 1890s business establishments included a baker, a confectioner, an ice cream parlor, and a bicycle shop. At the turn of the century New Columbia's population was about 350.

Notable among the business community were the Fisher and Ranck families. William Fisher learned the hardware trade as a clerk for William H. Dennis and eventually purchased the business. He carried a full line of shelf goods and heavy hardware: stoves, heaters, and ranges; the store also featured cutlery, paints and oils, flour, and feed, as well as a variety of farm machinery. Fisher huckstered stoves and hardware in his earlier years. He was also postmaster, and it was from his store that rural mail was first delivered in 1917. In 1900 William Fisher added Atlantic Gasoline to his stock, and 70 years later his son and daughter were the second-oldest dealers of Atlantic-Arco products in the company's distribution system.

John and Barbara Martin Ranck, the founders of the family in the area, came to the future site of New Columbia in 1797; part of their homestead remained in the family for four generations. Their son,

Jonathan, and his wife, Mary Dieffenderfer, were parents of ten children, most of whom found homes nearby. One of these children, Edward, who married Sara Goodlander of White Deer, had eleven children. Two of the latter, John Jefferson Ranck and Samuel C. Ranck, were longtime New Columbia businessmen. The former learned the coach trade from William H. Blind; and after working as a journeyman at various places, he returned home and built a shop and residence. He prospered and subsequently added an undertaking business. Samuel clerked in the general store of his brother-in-law, H.H. Trumfeller, and later bought the business. His daughter, Martha Ranck Farley, recalled that a Williamsport druggist spent several weeks with him to qualify him to handle drugs. She also remembered the demand for laudanum and patented remedies as well as the need for restraint in dispensing them. Other specialties of the store were furniture and wallpaper. Samuel added a small overall factory to his businesses, employing several women. The two brothers, laid out the New Columbia Cemetery, which was later moved to make room for highway construction. Martha Ranck Farley also remembered that her grandfather, Edward, had led a movement to grade the New Columbia school. When she and three schoolmates entered Milton High School with the assistance of her Ranck kinsmen,

This "bird's-eye view" is of West Milton, also called Datesman's Station. The photograph was taken from the hill north of town, looking south towards the Susquehanna River and the road to Lewisburg. From the collection of Gary W. and Donna M. Slear.

they had broken down the resistance of the school directors to the payment of tuition there. Other members of the Ranck family were teachers, physicians, and farmers while Dayton Ranck was treasurer of Bucknell University for many years.

In the twentieth century New Columbia shared West Milton's boom times. In the war years many of its wage earners found employment in Milton and Watsontown; and after World War II, they worked in the new industries which lined the river bank north of the village.

The rise of West Milton is associated with the growth of Milton across the Susquehanna; but this was not evident at the outset, when the only commercial crossings were made by ferries. The building of the Milton/West Milton bridge in 1823, however, put the ferries out of business and placed West Milton upon a main highway. Even this, however, was not a sufficient incentive to spawn a settlement, and for a time only the Hoffman and Bennage farms lay athwart the road. Jost Hoffman, of Lebanon County, had settled there in 1793, and the old Hoffman homestead built in 1844 by his grandson, George, still stands on High Street just east of the railroad.

About 1834 the John Datesman and Jacob Keiser families removed here from Northampton County. Datesman built a store at the entrance to the bridge, and Keiser bought the George Bennage farm and erected a fine brick house on it. Like the Hoffman residence it has survived the vicissitudes of West Milton's history. For a number of years thereafter, the two farmhouses and Datesman's storehouse remained the only buildings on the site.

Datesman's arrival was timely — the West Branch Canal had just opened, facilitating trade with Baltimore and Philadelphia. He was soon exchanging the wares of his well-stocked store for grain since his reputation for fair dealing attracted the grain and lumber of Penns and Brush Valleys in Centre County to his door, much of it carried on sleds during the winter months. His son, Ephraim, later recalled that as many as 50 teams would be tied to the hitching posts in a single day. From the morning through the afternoon and evening, the conversation was a mixture of business and pleasure, with the conviviality enhanced by the warmth of the store and the whiskey, cheese, and crackers on the counter. The following morning the drivers would start back with dry goods and metal wares — and possibly a few gallons of whiskey. Ephraim also remembered that he paid as much as $3.15 per bushel of wheat at the close of the Civil War, but as little as 50¢ for wheat, 20¢ for corn, and 14¢ for oats during the panic of 1893.

Through the 73 years that Datesman and his son operated the store, they were exposed many times to high water. The flood of 1865 swept away the bridge and reached a depth of eighteen inches in the storeroom. When neighbors offered to clean up the cellar, where the whiskey was stored, he accepted the offer and handed each volunteer a tin cup. Their initial determination did not sustain them long enough to complete the job; instead, they came out staggering. The Johnstown flood of 1889 swept six-and-one-half feet of water through the store, but a work gang had moved most of the goods to the second floor before the onslaught. Three hundred loads of ground were required to fill the crater in front of the store. Five years later another disastrous wall of water engulfed the store. Ephraim sold the store in 1906, but he continued to operate a grain exchange in Milton, where he died in 1934, two years before the then-record-breaking flood of 1936. The old Datesman property was at last razed in 1972 after a final battering from Hurricane Agnes, which precipitated the greatest flood of all.

In 1871 the Catawissa branch of the Reading Railroad came to West Milton. The track crossed the Susquehanna a few hundred yards south of the highway bridge and then continued northward to Williamsport. Change was now in the air. Ephraim Datesman became the passenger agent, selling the tickets across the counter of his store, and the whistle stop was called Datesman's Station for a time. However, when the Shamokin branch of the railroad made a juncture with the Catawissa line in the village in 1882, the name was changed to West Milton.

Meanwhile, in 1872 the Keisers began to parcel their farm into lots, and in 1883 they laid out a more extensive area. Sales apparently were not active at the beginning; but in 1901 the railroad built shops and yards to service the northern section of the two divisions, so West Milton at last blossomed. A survey of its architecture bears testimony to its rapid growth since most of the buildings suggest the popular styles of the first quarter of the twentieth century.

In a few years the village had a population of 750 as well as a hotel, stores, shops, schools, and churches. John Datesman had been named its first postmaster in 1862, and together he and Ephraim held the post for 40 years. The heart of the village was the railroad. About 75 of its residents were employed in the roundhouse and shops. There were section and work train gangs, yard men, ash and coal dock men, air men, oilers, train men, and telegraphers. Four of the latter were employed at the West Milton tower; others included one each at New Columbia and White Deer, three at Allenwood, and 40 between West Milton and Newberry. In the course of a day as many as seventeen to nineteen passenger trains required servicing in addition to the freight trains. There was also an annex — a short line connecting the station with the Pennsylvania Railroad terminal in Milton, from which the last of four daily runs returned at midnight; some West Miltonians still remember the scramble to catch it after spending an evening in Milton — and the long hike when they missed it.

A sizable number of workmen moved to West Milton from Catawissa, where the Reading had closed a substation; others came from Shamokin. Among these railroad families were the Krells, Highs, and Kochs. Another new resident was Ed Begley, who worked on the track gang and married Amanda Huff. Ed was regarded as good company and was often referred to

Byrly's Store in West Milton. From the collection of the Union County Historical Society, #94.9.1.

as "happy-go-lucky," and a bit "off-beat." He drifted away after a few years to get into radio, eventually starring on the stage and screen. His portrayal of William Jennings Bryan in the movie version of the Scopes trial remains an American classic.

The railroad helped to make West Milton a well-traveled community, for railroad passes permitted employee trips to Philadelphia and New York or locally to Shamokin and Williamsport, and, of course, to Milton on the annex. With its converging lines and the many trains stopping at the station or yards, West Milton was a logical stopping place for "tramps" who were "riding the rails." Residents could almost forecast the state of the economy by the number of hoboes gathered at their camp fires by the water tank, where the lines joined. Ordinarily, they did not disrupt the even tenor of the village, but some of the exceptions are still remembered. In 1914, when several tramps were "whiskied up with 50-cent booze," a fracas resulted in the shooting of one participant as well as the holding of two for assault and six others as witnesses. The wounded man was taken to the Williamsport Hospital and the others to the county jail in Lewisburg. The incident was back in the news a few weeks later when the sheriff's five-year-old son foiled an attempted jail break. Eventually, the victim recovered, and the men were given a safe passage out of the county.

In perspective, West Milton's railroad era lasted little longer than a generation. Its rail traffic slowed during the Great Depression. The diesel engines, introduced in the 1940s, did not require the laborious servicing which had been lavished upon the steam locomotives. Interstate trucking also took its toll in the post-World War II years. By the 1970s massive tractor-trailers were roaring across the center of the village on an elevated expressway, and the Susquehanna Trucking Company's terminal looked down upon the ruins of the old railroad shops and yards.

By happenstance, West Milton spread out into two townships, with High Street the dividing line between Kelly and White Deer; two-thirds of the residents lived in the former and the remainder in the latter. It did not seem to matter in the beginning, but problems occasionally arose. Children on the south side of Broad Street, for example, attended a school on Third Street in Kelly Township while the children on the north side went to Washington School on the hill in White Deer Township.

The Reformed congregation built a sanctuary in 1902 and made a substantial addition to the church in 1963. In 1909 J.C. Winter founded Central Oak Heights, a church camp affiliated with the Evangelical Church, on an oak-covered ridge just south of the village. Starting with a tabernacle, the camp was expanded to encompass a dining hall and a community of summer homes and tents; more recently, a swimming pool was added. Throughout the years it has attracted thousands of summer residents and visitors and conducted countless church-oriented activities. Several years ago the church conference sold the facility to a group which formed a non-profit organization called Central Oak Heights Association. Sixty-two of the cabins (which long ago replaced the tents) are now privately owned. Facilities that can be rented include four cabins, five clusters of log cabins, the dining hall, two pavilions, and a swimming pool. Services are held in the tabernacle every Sunday from Memorial Day to Labor Day and many Saturday evening concerts are also performed. Currently, some of the facilities are being used by the Bethesda Day Treatment Center.

Three miles west of West Milton, where the road crosses Little Buffalo Creek, is the hamlet of Kelly Cross Roads. Joseph Spotts settled there about 1800, and the Spotts family has been identified with the neighborhood ever since. Joseph Spotts, Jr., built the first brick house in 1821, and William H. Spotts was a justice of the peace during the last quarter of the nineteenth century. A country store was opened in 1847 and a post office established in 1864. A short distance upstream on Little Buffalo Creek, Henry Titzell built a gristmill and a sawmill in 1775. He abandoned it during the Great Runaway and never returned, but his mill was a patriot rendezvous

during the war. The mill was purchased by Nagel Gray after the war and changed hands frequently during the nineteenth century. Some buildings were removed many years ago but the fort itself (a small but sturdy building that could shelter settlers during Indian attacks) and the old mill race remain visible on the east side of the road.

The nearby Kelly Point area in the latter half of the nineteenth century had a concentration of Amish familes, again revealed by one of their cemeteries with low white walls, the Stoltzfus cemetery. An Amish woman, Betsy Beiler, held Sunday school at the nearby Red Hill School and at the Fairmont School on alternate Sundays in 1860s. From the Red Hill School's vantage point, one can view many of the Kelly Point area's formerly Amish farms, including those of Isaac, Christian, and Simeon Stoltzfus. During the Civil War, the Amish in Union County supported the Union army by giving their crops, after having them ground at the nearby Hoffa (now Grove) Mill. A short distance to the west was John Lapp's house (former Sierer house), on the grounds of which is the burial site for Shem Esh, as well as Sarah and Elizabeth Lapp, the wife and daughter of John Lapp. To the east of Kelly Point on the grounds of the federal penitentiary on the north side of

Buffalo Creek, still stands the house of Christian King, where the last Amish church meeting was held in 1883 before most of the remaining Kelly Point area Amish left for Lyon County, Kansas. Nearby is the former Jacob Stoltzfus farm, which still has its Amish interiors.

There had been no communion in the Buffalo Valley for seven and one-half years because of the split within the Amish community. Deacon Christian

Stoltzfus, very old and desiring communion, illustrated how bad the situation had become when he observed that love had grown cold in Union County. His wish was fulfilled, and the last Amish communion was held c. 1880, probably in the Buffalo Church. After Stoltzfus's death's, his widow and sons were among others from the Old Order Amish community who left for Kansas.

Vicksburg, further toward the center of the county, was the center of the Amish community, not unlike the role it plays today for the team (Groffdale) Mennonites. An Amish couple, David and Barbara Beiler Smucker, had a store and home there. They were among the last to leave Buffalo Valley, going first to Troxelville, Snyder County, then Big Valley, Mifflin County, in the 1890s. Also near Vicksburg were the Samuel F. Glick (later, Michael Beiler) farm and his eventual retirement house. On January 20, 1883, the *Lewisburg Chronicle* noted that area Amish had chartered a train and left from the Vicksburg train station for Lyon County, Kansas, hoping to be as successful in farming there as they had been in Union County. Six years later the Union Countians were destitute as the land they bought there proved worthless for raising crops. In fact, when the families returned eastward to an Amish community in Ohio, they could find no buyers.

A mile east of Kelly Cross Roads, a short distance south of the road from West Milton, stand two country churches on opposite sides of a rural road. Their histories have been intertwined for more than 150 years. Known as the White Deer churches — though they are in Kelly Township — they are more properly identified as St. Peter's United Church of Christ (Reformed) and the St. John's United Lutheran Church. The churches grew out of a wish of Philip Stahl, a wagonmaker and farmer, who migrated from Bucks County to the mouth of Black Run, just north of Mazeppa, in 1793. In his will Stahl provided for either an endowment or land, to pay for preachers in the region — a wish which eventually produced seven acres and 91 perches in trust for the use of a school house, a German Lutheran church, and a burying ground. A congregation of Lutherans accepted the challenge and erected a log building in 1802. They shared the pulpit with ministers of the German Reformed church, and in 1819 the two congregations agreed to erect a house of worship and share its use and costs. The new building was another log structure, which was enlarged and weather-boarded in 1848.

The Vicksburg train station saw a major contingent of Amish residents leave Buffalo Valley for Kansas in 1883. The station still stands on the west side of the road. From the collection of Gary W. and Donna M. Slear.

PAGE 216: Tents and family members at Central Oak Heights photographed by John D. Swanger of Milton. He photographed the activities, buildings, and visitors until 1923, although the site remained active until 1944. Many of Swanger's photographs were released as postcards. From the collection of Gary W. and Donna M. Slear.

The twin churches in Kelly Township photographed from the cemetery of St. John's Lutheran Church in 1909 by amateur photographer Urs H. Eisenhauer of Millmont. From the collection of Gary W. and Donna M. Slear.

In 1877 the Lutherans decided to sever their connection with the Reformed congregation and erected a rectangular two-story brick edifice surmounted by a bell platform and a six-columned cupola. Like other churches of its time, the sanctuary was located on the second floor, leaving the ground floor to the church school. Stained glass windows and many other changes were made through the next century, and in 1969 a new wing substantially enlarged its

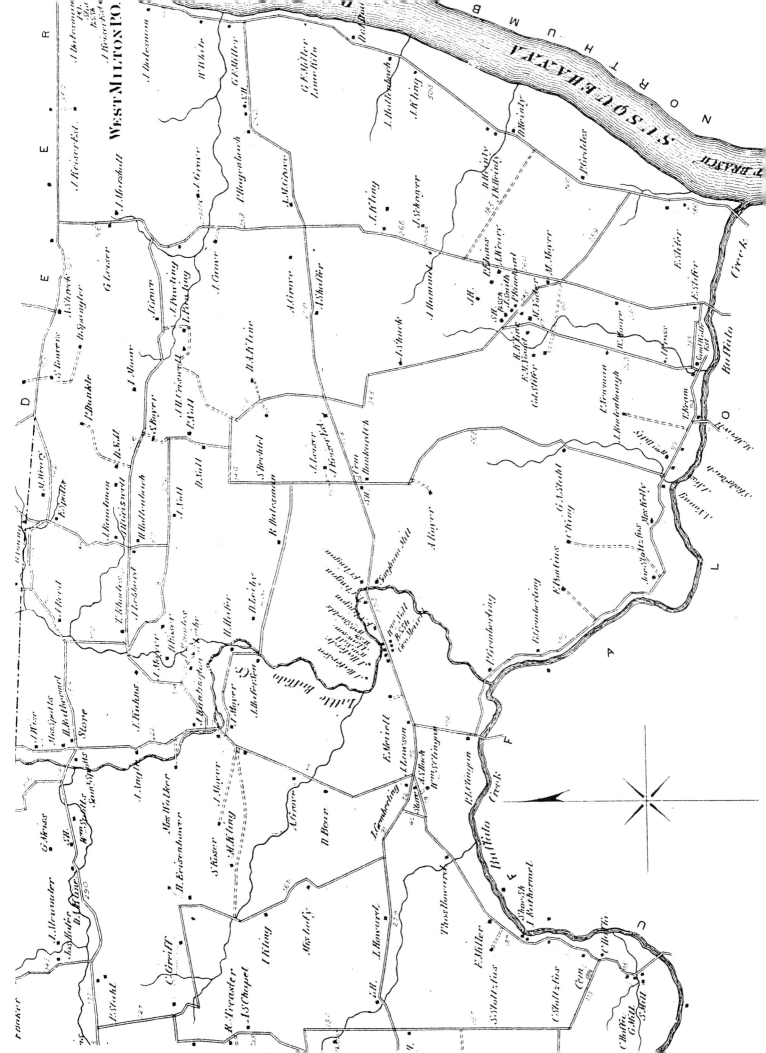

TOP: A printed post card from c. 1940 featured Betty's Coffee Pot at Sunset Village. It was located just south of the present Country Cupboard/Great Western complex on Route 15 (then Route 404). From the collection of Joseph W. Epler.

ABOVE: Starting in 1917 produce was sold and displayed at each summer's Anniversary Day on the grounds of the Evangelical Home (later called the United Methodist Home, now RiverWoods). This was one of many real photo postcards by the Swanger Studios of Milton c. 1917-1923. From the collection of Gary W. and Donna M. Slear.

PAGE 218: Detail of Kelly Township. From *Pomeroy's Atlas for Union and Snyder Counties 1868.*

physical capacity, and a spire of more modern design replaced the original cupola. The Reformed congregation remained in the older log structure three years and then raised a new building on the same ground. The exterior of the new building was strikingly similar to the Lutheran edifice — so similar, in fact, that the expression "Twin Churches" soon caught on. The main differences in appearance are its belfry and stately Gothic spire. The two handsome buildings in their rural setting offer a nostalgic glimpse of old America seldom encountered in the beginning of the twenty-first century.

When Matthew Brown, from Lancaster County, rounded the spur of White Deer Mountain to settle upon an 800-acre tract in White Deer Hole Valley, he was founding yet another township which would successively bear the name Buffalo, White Deer, Washington, Brady, and Gregg; this would also, by turns, be a part of Northumberland, Lycoming, and Union Counties. In the few years remaining to him, Brown would be a member of the Pennsylvania Constitutional Convention of 1776, a member of the Committee of Public Safety of Northumberland County, an overseer of the poor, and a soldier in the Continental Army. While serving in the latter, he contracted camp fever and died in 1777. His family remained in Buffalo Valley, and his great-grandson, Robert, served two terms as county commissioner just over 100 years later. The township which the Browns founded lay in the White Deer Hole Valley, a beautiful and fertile region bordered with mountains on the south and west and the West Branch of the Susquehanna River on the east. The land was appropriated and surveyed shortly after the opening of the land office in 1769, and by 1787 there were fourteen families on the banks of the creek and its tributaries, Spring and South Creeks.

When New Berlin became the county seat of Union County, the residents of White Deer Hole Valley found that they were twenty miles and two mountains distant from it. Displeased with their lot, they petitioned for annexation to Lycoming County. Their wish was granted, and the valley was attached to Washington Township. A few years later Washington Township was divided, and the area became Brady Township. When the county seat of Union County was shifted to Lewisburg in 1855, public opinion did an about-face, and petitions were soon reaching Harrisburg in support of reannexation. The Legislature acceded to a referendum, and

the transfer was approved in 1861 by a small majority but not without arousing bitter passions. One observer noted that Williamsport men were spending hundreds of dollars to keep it in Lycoming County. "You never saw as mad a set of men as the beat party was. And they had to move quietly or they would have been handsomely licked, for the men was on the ground to do it."[3] In 1865 the name of the township was changed from Brady to Gregg to honor State Senator Andrew Gregg of Bellefonte, who had guided the reannexation bill through the legislature.

Among the families which migrated to the White Deer Hole Creek were the Farleys of New Jersey. They cleared the land at the mouth of the creek and built a small gristmill there, the first in the valley. John Farley returned to New Jersey, but his sons remained. Through the years which followed, the Farleys were farmers, civic leaders, and teachers. Their reunions at an ancestral log cabin along White Deer Mountain continued as long as the White Deer/Loganton Railroad offered transportation. The Vollmers (anglicized to Follmer) were also early arrivals, and Frederick Follmer built the first mill on the site of Spring Garden. After his death the mill passed to David Hunter, a native of North Ireland, and at his death to his son James P. Hunter, who also acquired extensive farm land and operated a pottery on the road leading south from Spring Garden.

About 1814, Ludwig Stitzel, who had emigrated from Germany, bought the Farley mill and added an oil mill and forge. He also erected a stone residence. After his death the property was managed by his son-in-law, Charles Gudykunst, formerly of Lehigh County, who in time became the leading businessman in the area and owner of several of the valley's finest farms. Gudykunst was a prime mover in the return of Brady Township to Union County. The mill property was subsequently modernized by John H. Follmer in 1883.

In 1815 John McCurdy laid out a village on the public road leading upriver, a short distance north of White Deer Hole Creek. McCurdy had a tavern here and obviously had an optimistic frame of mind. He called it Uniontown, but its name was changed so often thereafter that in identifying it a journalist jokingly referred to it with all four of its titles: Uniontown (its traditional name), Slifer (its post office named in honor of Eli Slifer), Cairo (the railroad depot), and Allenwood (a name which was catching on). The slow growth of the hamlet must

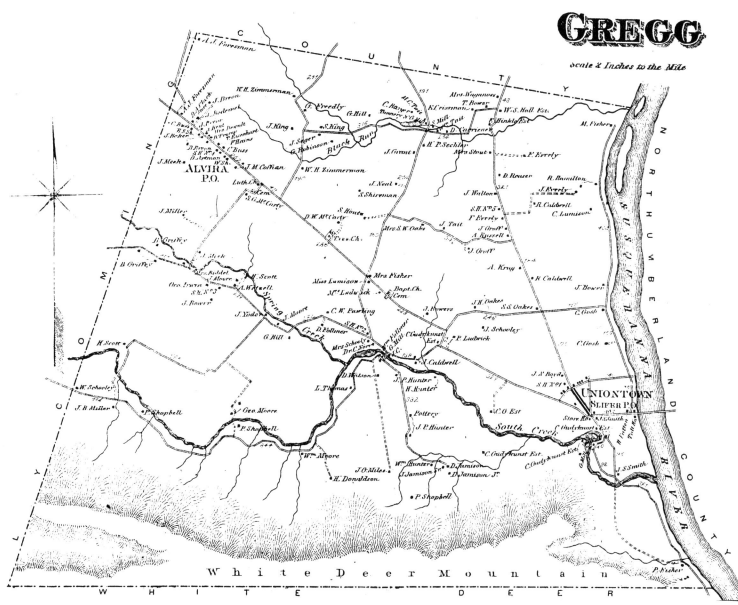

GREGG

Scale 2 Inches to the Mile

Gregg Township and the town of Uniontown (Allenwood).
From *Pomeroy's Atlas for Union and Snyder Counties 1868.*

have disappointed McCurdy, but a river bridge, constructed in 1852, connected Allenwood with Dewart on the Pennsylvania and Erie Railroad. The extension of the Reading Railroad into the area was a good omen for further growth. H.P. Allen, who owned the land between McCurdy's and the Susquehanna, had opened a general store in 1861; he laid out 80 additional lots in 1872 and donated land for the railroad depot. He also built a handsome storeroom in 1880, which he labeled the "Universal Provider." Under Allen's son, Frank, the store was expanded to handle farm machinery and automobiles. The hustle of the Allens earned the name Allenwood for the entire settlement.

At the turn of the century Allenwood was also the outlet for a logging operation along the north slopes of White Deer Mountain conducted by the Vincent Lumber Company of Danville. At the outset the

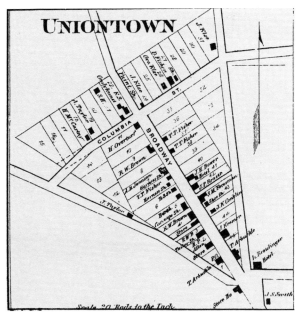

TOP: "Compliments of the Allenwood Hotel," a real photo postcard from c. 1907-1911. From the collection of the Union County Historical Society, #95.2.1.

MIDDLE: George A. Sypher's Store in Spring Garden photographed by Stephen Horton c. 1907-1911. Spring Gardens and Alvira, two towns in Gregg Township, disappeared when the Federal government appropriated 9,000 acres for the Letterkenny Ordnance (now the Allenwood Federal Prison) during World War II. From the collection of Gary W. and Donna M. Slear.

BOTTOM: Baptismal mill pond at Spring Garden, Gregg Township c. 1905. From the collection of the Union County Historical Society, #89.5.2.20.

Vincents drew their logs by sled or wagon, but in 1901, using Italian labor, they laid a forty-two-inch-gauge tramroad across the valley with a terminal at the Reading Railroad. An unusually heavy blast of black powder, inserted to remove the last rock obstruction at Allenwood, scattered boulders across the Reading tracks and hurled smaller stones across the river. Fortunately, there were no serious casualties. By 1904 the timber was gone, and the company removed the track and Gray geared locomotive to other cuttings.

At the turn of the century, Allenwood had two hotels, two stores, a gristmill, a lumber yard, a planing mill, a school, a Presbyterian chapel, and a population of about 300. The automotive age opened the stores of Watsontown, Milton, and Montgomery to local shoppers, and businesses in the village declined; the gristmill closed, and the planing mill burned to the ground. World War II momentarily stimulated a wartime euphoria since a railroad depot handled the traffic of the giant Allenwood subdepot of the Letterkenny Ordnance Plant near the village. Jobs were plentiful then, but the ordnance plant closed at the war's end, leaving only a federal prison camp, an adjunct of the Northeastern Federal Penitentiary at Lewisburg, on the 9,000-acre site. In the 1990s that prison site was greatly expanded with the addition of separate maximum, medium and minimum security prison units making it the largest federal prison complex in the United States.

As in White Deer, a sizable number of Gregg's pioneers were Scots-Irish, and as early as 1790 the Reverend Hugh Morrison of the Buffalo Presbyterian Church helped to found the Washington congregation. The Presbyterians built a log church with a gallery and high-backed pews near the center of Gregg Township, replacing it in 1830 with a white frame structure with Greek Revival detail. In 1808 Elder Thomas Smiley assembled a few Baptists at Spring Garden and organized the White Deer Baptist Society. They built a small log house at the edge of the hamlet and in 1837 erected a neat frame edifice, which continues to serve the community to this day. About 1850 the German Reformed congregation constructed a small frame sanctuary a half-mile west of the Washington Church; this was identified for many years as the "Pine Knot Church." In 1889 the Washington Church added a chapel in Allenwood, and in 1885 the Evangelical Association built a small church in Alvira. Thus the four churches in Gregg Township at one time stood on the same highway

between Spring Garden and Alvira. In 1942, however, a dramatic turn of events befell three of these religious bodies when the federal government appropriated their properties for its ordnance plant. The historic Washington meeting house was razed, and its congregation merged with the branch at Allenwood. Today a magnificent grove of oaks towers over the rubble of the old sanctuary and the walled cemetery at its side. The Reformed and Evangelical churches also lie in ruins near the cellar holes of Alvira — a village which fell victim to the exigencies of war. The ordnance ruins add to the scene of desolation.

Gregg Township accepted the Public School Law in 1837, when it was a part of Lycoming County. The directors first selected Uniontown (#1) and Spring Garden (#2) as school sites; they subsequently added Wetzell on Spring Creek, Alvira at the northwest corner of the township, and Russell (Fair View) on the Uniontown-Williamsport road. In 1865, after the township had become a part of Union County, the County Superintendent reported that its five schools were "of brick, and of ample dimensions, and with sufficient playgrounds — a set of houses of which the district may well be proud." The Allenwood school was later graded to include a grammar department, which had a "good library" by 1898. In 1909 graduation exercises were held, and a year later a township high school was opened; but the latter remained too small to withstand pressure for consolidation, and the secondary pupils matriculated at the Watsontown and Montgomery high schools.

The continuing decline in rural population led to the closure of the Fair View School in 1921. In 1942, just prior to the dislocations resulting from the ordnance plant, the school population was 135, more than half of whom attended the Allenwood primary and grammar school. Alvira had 25 students; Spring Garden had twenty, and Wetzell had only seventeen. In the 1950s the Gregg district joined the Warrior Run consolidation despite a preference for Montgomery among the families in the northern part of the township.

In 1912 Dr. William Devitt of Philadelphia opened a treatment center for his patients suffering from tuberculosis on the slope of White Deer Mountain a short distance southwest of Allenwood. He began in a small way; his facility was located in a barn, with a manager and a local physician to administer it. Other physicians were soon recommending it, and Devitt's Camp expanded cottage by cottage so that by 1918 it housed 30 patients. At the close of World War I, the United States Public Health Service and the Veterans'

TOP: Aerial view of Devitt Camp . From the collection of the Union County Historical Society, #97.1.23.

BOTTOM: The federal penitentiary opened in Lewisburg on November 14, 1932. This real photo postcard illustrated its construction Fom the collection of the Union County Historical Society, #92.9.92.65.

Bureau sent veterans who had been gassed for rehabilitation there, and they soon constituted more than one-half of its 70 patients. Private and corporate contributions added to the physical facilities; while school, civic, and church groups, such as the "Workers for Devitt" of the St. Peter's United Church of Christ in Kelly Township, contributed many hours of labor and helped to provide social programs.

In 1923 Dr. Devitt moved with his family to the sanitarium to head the medical staff. By 1927 it housed 128 patients and was still growing, subsequently adding a dairy farm and a two-story dormitory for 48 women. However, new and more effective therapy sharply reduced the incidence of tuberculosis during the years which followed, and in 1956 Devitt sold the establishment to the United Church of Christ for the sum of one dollar for use as a home for the aged. The administration of this newly acquired facility was managed by the church's Phoebe Home of Allentown with a local pastor, the Reverend Thomas B. Musser, serving as acting superintendent, assisted by Thomas Walter Wilson of Milton. The Reverend Herman Snyder was named superintendent in 1956, and during the 1960s the home accommodated about 100 residents. By 1968, with the group facing budget problems and the wooden cottages no longer meeting state standards, the church closed the institution and moved the residents to the Phoebe Home. The site is now used by White Deer Run, a drug and alcohol rehabilitation center. Since 1970 White Deer Run has treated more than 30,000 patients in its 180-bed facility and is the center of a nine-site treatment system.

At the approach of the fourth quarter of the twentieth century, Gregg Township, having lost a sizable portion of its taxable land to the federal government during WW II, found itself once again the target of government. Lands taken during the war for a munitions plant were never offered back to area residents at the end of the war as local citizens insisted they had been promised. To add insult to injury, Lycoming County, immediately north of Union County, needed a new municipal landfill; and in the 1970s Lycoming County officials worked quietly with the federal government to secure a lease on some of the land that had been taken during the war. The landfill was to be placed at the southern border of Lycoming County where it abutted Union County — where any escaped leachate would drain. Sitting on land honeycombed by underground limestone caverns, an area described by one hydrogeologist as the worst possible site for a landfill, the location was politically popular with

Lycoming residents. Plans for the project proceeded; but strong and prolonged opposition by residents in Gregg Township held off the proposal for a number of years, as a grassroots movement called Organizations United for Ecology (OUE) was formed. Despite tenacious opposition to the project, Lycoming County prevailed, and the landfill became a reality. Within a year, convincing evidence showed that the landfill's impervious liner had failed and toxic leachate was finding its way into the underground, but neither Lycoming County nor Department of Environmental Protection (DEP) officials have ever openly acknowledged these problems.

By 1990 OUE had dwindled to a small group of diehards who monitored the landfill operation and continued to push for more safeguards. Meanwhile, on several hundred acres of land south of the landfill, a federal three-prison complex was under construction, soon to house more than 3,000 prisoners. On the east side of Route 15, meanwhile, 700 acres of farm and woodland adjoining the village of Allenwood became the subject of rumors. The acreage had remained agricultural despite having been zoned industrial by the Gregg Township Supervisors years earlier. In 1990 a company called Pennswood Development began buying options on individual parcels. Company officials claimed the land would be used to build a light industrial park with a campus-like environment, but a few OUE members quickly discovered that the land was, in fact, being purchased for a giant waste company called United States Pollution Control, Inc. (USPCI), a subsidiary of Union Pacific Corporation. By September 1990, USPCI acknowledged its plan to build a hazardous industrial waste incinerator on the property. By then OUE — renamed Organizations United for the Environment — having reorganized and rebuilt its membership, was determined to derail the project. Having learned from past mistakes, the organization immediately went on the offensive. Within ten months membership soared to 17,000 area residents and businesses. Members of the group began giving speeches, writing newsletters, organizing meetings, and motivating citizens to make telephone calls and write letters of protest. OUE opened an office, hired a paid coordinator, and encouraged elected officials to jump into the fight on the side of citizens. It quickly became a power that stunned USPCI.

For four years a coalition of organizations joined OUE in fighting the intrusion of outside interests in Gregg Township; most prominent among these were the Union County commissioners, the Union County Planning Commission, Gregg Township supervisors, the Susquehanna Economic Development Agency-Council of Governments (SEDA-COG), and State Representative Russell Fairchild, as well as a host of other politicians and organizations. In 1994 USPCI admitted defeat and announced its intent to pull out of Gregg Township. The giant corporation quickly sold the 700 acres to Laidlaw, another waste industry company. Embattled OUE members worried about yet another attempt at waste disposal, but Laidlaw decided it wanted no part of Gregg Township nor a repeat what USPCI had been through with local citizens. Instead, Laidlaw put the land on the open market. Fortunately Laidlaw offered Union County a first right of refusal. Seeing a rare opportunity to end the controversial development, the Union County commissioners agreed to back the Union County Industrial Development Corporation (UCIDC), which purchased the land. The land was back in local hands, but by that time, the agricultural lands had become too expensive to continue farming there. The UCIDC board of directors set out to make the best of the situation: if the land could no longer remain as farmland, it could become an environmentally friendly corporate park with adjoining housing that preserved as much open space as possible. The idea for "Great Stream Commons" was born. With local citizen input, UCIDC's vision was to retain the land's original topography and existing tree lines, and tightly control the types of industries that moved into the park. Implementing that vision is the challenge for Gregg Township and its residents as it enters the twenty-first century.

ENDNOTES:

1 White Deer Township School Records, Dr. Frank P. Boyer Papers, Union County Historical Society.

2 *New Berlin Anti-Masonic Star,* August 7, 1835; from a copy in the Boyer Papers, Union County Historical Society.

3 Charles Gudy Kunst to Eli Slifer, February 25 and July 11, 1861, Eli Slifer-Dill Papers, Archives of Dickinson College.

CHAPTER 13

HARTLEY AND LEWIS TOWNSHIPS AND HARTLETON

Though situated geographically along the western and eastern extremities of Union County respectively, the histories of Hartley and White Deer Townships suggest a number of parallels. Both encompass sizable mountainous areas interspersed with narrow valleys, leaving a limited acreage suited to agriculture. Both have had large-scale lumbering and railroading operations, which multiplied employment opportunities in one decade and eliminated them in another. Hence, there has been a greater mobility of population and a greater instability in the economies of these regions.

The eastern part of Hartley (later Lewis) Township was opened to a handful of intrepid frontiersmen and absentee landholders in 1769. At least four families, the Coles, Glovers, Shivelys and Weirbachs, were settled in the clearings which they had shaped with their axes, when the resurgence of the Indians in the course of the Revolutionary War forced their withdrawal to Fort Augusta and points south. Of the four, only the Glovers and Shivelys came back after the war. These families were soon joined by others from the area encompassing Berks, Schuylkill, Northumberland, Snyder, and Mifflin Counties. Reaching Hartley by way of New Berlin or Mifflinburg, settlers scattered westward; and within the span of two generations they were opening the last frontier in the county on the upper reaches of Penns Creek, where Buffalo Valley narrows to the "Tight End" and is finally pinched off by the convergence of Paddy and White Mountains.

The pioneers who arrived prior to 1792 were settling in what was then called Buffalo Township; those coming between 1792 and 1811 in West Buffalo; and in Hartley after 1811, when the latter was separated from West Buffalo. The township was named for Thomas Hartley, an absentee landholder who had commanded a militia regiment recruited in Buffalo Valley in 1776. Hartley purchased Philip Cole's land in 1784 and laid out Hartleton. In 1857 Hartley Township lost a broad strip of its most fertile land when Lewis Township was cut away from its eastern section.

According to Union County's first assessment in 1814, there were 97 householders in the township, of whom seventeen were tenants. Despite the sizable number of removals through the years which followed, it is obvious that some had come to sink their roots — a fact which can be verified by a glance at the names in a current telephone directory. Among the early householders were: Boop (Boob), Braucher (Browther), Catherman (Coderman), Cook, Corl, Dorman, Frederick, Glover, Hoffman, Galer (Kaler), Heise, Hendricks, Keister (Kester), Kleckner, Klingman, Lincoln, Miller, Reed, Rote, Roush, Royer, Ruhl, Schnure (Snure), Shively, Showalter, Smith, Spigelmyer, Stitzer, Voneida, Wise, Weiker (Wiker), and Zimmerman — many of whose descendants continue to dwell near the firesides of their forefathers.

As might be expected, a large majority of the residents were farmers, but there were also ten men employed in sawmills and three in gristmills; six were weavers, four each were distillers, leather workers, and shoemakers. There were also several carpenters, blacksmiths, and coopers.

It is difficult to select families for special mention, but the Glovers could scarcely be overlooked. John Glover and his wife, Sophia Duncan, founders of the family in Hartley Township, migrated from the Shenandoah Valley in Virginia in 1772 and settled approximately a mile west of Hartleton. In 1775 John Glover was assessed for five acres of cultivable land, two horses, and two cows. The nearest and only neighbor was John Cole at Hartleton. During the Great Runaway, the Glovers went back to Virginia but returned in 1789. In 1804 Glover was taxed for one slave; and in 1814 his occupation was listed as "gentleman," and, with his son, John Jr., he was assessed for 480 acres of land (most of it uncleared), a house, and a barn.

A grandson of John Sr., Robert V. Glover, moved to Hartleton, where he was a storekeeper for 45 years. He was also the first cashier of the Mifflinburg Bank and later its president. His sons, Horace P. and David L., in turn, were lawyers in Mifflinburg; both served in the state legislature and were outstanding civic leaders. Another descendant of John and Sophia, Dr. Oliver Wendell Holmes Glover, was Laurelton's beloved "country doctor" at the turn of the twentieth century, presiding at the birth of many of Hartley's elder citizens. The old homestead was divided to provide farms for the children and grandchildren of the founders, with several of them remaining in the Glover family until the 1930s.

A second "landed family" identified with leadership through several generations was founded by John and Hannah Lincoln. John's father, Michael, of Berks County, had fought in the West Branch Valley during the Revolution and settled on a farm near Mifflinburg at its close. John grew up there and married Hannah, the daughter of Richard Van Buskirk, a Mifflinburg tavernkeeper. John and Hannah subsequently moved to a farm just south of the future site of the Lincoln Chapel and later donated the land for this Methodist Church. Their son, Richard Van Buskirk Lincoln, attended the Mifflinburg Academy and graduated from Dickinson College in 1841 — one of the few college men of his generation. He was one of the first teachers in Hartley's schools following the township's acceptance of the Public School Law in 1841 and served on the school board for more than twenty years. He later turned to farming, and his farm on the north side of Penns Creek downstream from Laurel Park was a veritable garden spot as he applied the latest developments in scientific agriculture. He was a founder and officer of the county agricultural society. Also active in politics, he served as a county commissioner and was a Republican nominee for Congress.

A student of literature and a local historian, Lincoln's essays on Union County remain the most comprehensive and scholarly studies of the nineteenth century. He traced his ancestry to the lineage of Abraham Lincoln and exemplified the manners associated with a landlord of the old English countryside. An octogenarian recalls the aging "R.V.B.," as he was called, directing farm operations from the back of a magnificent sorrel gelding. The informant also remembers that he and his friends, when enroute to the country school adjacent to the Lincoln farm, avoided shortcuts across Lincoln's fields rather than risk a scolding from the "grouchy" landlord.[1]

Families identified for more than a century with the rich farm lands in the eastern portion of the township (later Lewis Township) included the Ruhls, Menschs, and Orwigs. Like most of their neighbors, these families were of German stock and came to Hartley by way of Berks and Lancaster Counties. George Orwig, a veteran of the Revolutionary War, was a founder of Orwigsburg. In a quest for better land, he settled on a farm in West Buffalo Township with his wife, Magdalina, and their eight sons and four daughters. Some of the children later removed to Ohio and Iowa, but Abraham bought a farm at Pleasant Grove, where he and his son Henry operated a distillery and gristmill. A second son, Samuel, fathered three sons, all of whom were officers in the Civil War, with one of them later becoming assistant state librarian. A fourth son, Samuel H., an outstand-

ing lawyer and orator in Mifflinburg as well as Lewisburg, erected a fine Victorian cottage at the corner of Fifth and Chestnut Streets in Mifflinburg.

Abraham Mensch grew up in Berks County and arrived in Hartley (Lewis) about 1825, occupying a farm near Swengel. Abraham Jr. later took over the homestead, and three grandsons lived on adjacent farms north of the Ray's Church. Another son, John, settled in Limestone Township, and three of his sons, in turn, purchased farms there. Descendants included ministers, teachers, and merchants; but most of them remained on the land, and it is likely that no other family except possibly the Gundys of East Buffalo Township cultivated more of Buffalo Valley's fine farms.

The Ruhls were also keen judges of prime farmland. Philip Sr. migrated from Lancaster County in 1806 and took up land south of the Ray's Church. Four of his sons subsequently farmed in the neighborhood. Five generations of Ruhls lived on the original homestead, and Philip Sr.'s son, John, erected the splendid brick residence which graces it. Other of Philip Sr.'s descendants lived on the Mifflinburg-Swengel Road, and one of them owned the mill property on Penns Creek nearby. Philip Jr. moved to Buffalo Township, where he represented the county for three terms in the legislature. Few of the first-generation families would appear to have as many descendants still living in the Buffalo Valley as the Ruhls.

While the above-mentioned families tended their crops, the Roush family, Henry and his sons, managed a more complex business on the Reuben Haines Road (later the turnpike) where it entered the Penns Valley Narrows. Michael Shirtz had built saw and gristmills there, using water power from Laurel Run. In 1800 Adam Wilt, a surveyor from Cumberland County, took over the business and added a hotel; these he sold to Roush, who enlarged the operations to include a store and distillery. It was soon the principal business in the western part of the county. With no hotel or store west of Hartleton and no mill west of Laurel Park, farmers took their wheat, corn, and rye to Roush, who milled the wheat and converted the corn and rye into whiskey. When he did not have a market for them locally, he hauled them to Penns Creek, for storage in his warehouse until they could be taken by arks to Chesapeake Bay and Baltimore.

Since navigating arks from Centre County was extremely hazardous, farmers in Penns Valley also delivered their grain to Roush rather than risk a year's profits on Butter Rock or other unnamed obstacles.

Interior of the Halfpenny Mill near Swengel. From the collection of the Union County Historical Society, #89.5.6.4.

According to tradition, a cargo of Penns Valley butter had once crashed on this rock, giving it an immortality. With the opening of the turnpike, Roush's Hotel became a stopping place for stagecoaches and teamsters on the long haul from Pittsburgh to Northumberland and Philadelphia. Until 1840 Roush's place was the hub for much of the commercial activity in Hartley Township. Henry's prestige grew with his business, and in 1837 he was elected to the legislature.

Then, almost overnight, Roush's operation became obsolete. In 1839 George Braucher built a gristmill farther downstream on Laurel Run on the site of Slabtown (Laurelton) in the heart of Buffalo Valley, more accessible to the farm trade. During this decade as well, the canals took the commerce away from the streams. As a result, the Roush family was forced to liquidate their properties, which included 311 acres of land; a large merchant gristmill with three runs of stones; a pair of shellers; a sawmill; a distillery; and a commodious dwelling house used as a tavern and a storehouse as well as the miller's house; in addition to all the necessary barns and stabling. The Roushes subsequently moved west.

David Stitzer attempted to run the business, but a fire destroyed the gristmill and distillery; and although he rebuilt them, they were never profitable. He sold off the buildings, several of which were moved to Laurelton, but continued to operate the tavern. After his death, however, it was acquired by the township and used as a poorhouse. All traces of the establishment have now disappeared.

By the 1840s pressure for agricultural land had propelled land seekers into the narrow flats between Penns Creek and Jacks Mountain. The Keisters were joined by the Cathermans, Dormans, and Boops. It was on the north slope of the mountain, tradition records, that Lewis Dorman shot the last panthers. "A great man," his 90-year-old grandson called him. At "Tight End" the Weiker brothers, George and Jacob, early occupants of this remote area who gave their name to Weikert Run, were selling out and going west. Benjamin Goodlander bought George's land across Penns Creek from Weikert Run and divided it among his sons. About this time, also, the Johnsons and Pursleys entered the region coming by way of Milroy in Mifflin County, Musser Valley, and the Glen Iron Gap.

William Johnson was born in Staten Island, New York in 1800 and while yet a boy traveled widely in the United States and Canada. It was said that at thirteen he witnessed Perry's victory on Lake Erie, that he fought in the Mexican War, and that he served briefly in the Civil War with his sons, William Jr. and Alanson. It was also said that he was a personal friend of Generals Scott and Grant. A jeweler by trade, William Johnson seems to have preferred farming and lumbering once he had married and settled down with his wife, Catherine Switzer, in the vicinity of Weikert. In 1846 his real estate, which included 300 acres (30 of which were cleared), two log houses, a printer's ink factory, a stable, and a grain house, was foreclosed and sold at sheriff's sale. Later, Johnson amassed 18,000 acres of woodland, but financial reverses again forced him to dispose of it at a disadvantage.

The vicissitudes of Johnson's business life, however, failed to dampen his enthusiasm for literature and science; and when he was 90, his grandson, Albert, valedictorian of his college class, a practicing attorney, and professor of law, found him a formidable adversary when they locked horns on an intellectual issue. William Johnson could outwalk many younger men, and he found it no task to hike through mountain trails to Centre County. He died at 98 — his life almost spanning the century. His brother, David, had a similar longevity and much the same wanderlust.

William P. Pursley appears to have moved to Weikert about the same time as William Johnson, and his wife, Eliza Switzer, may have been a sister of Catherine Switzer Johnson. A farmer by occupation, he was also a woodsman, hunter, trapper, and fisherman; but his foremost talent was story-telling — "tall tales," for the most part, relating to his adventures in the woods. His repertoire was seemingly inexhaustible. Pursley's fame spread through the region, even as far as Sunbury and Shamokin once the railroad made the Tight End accessible to campers. Sportsmen such as Judge Charles B. Witmer and Attorney James Merrill Linn sought him out as a guide, and he regaled them with his stories around the campfire. A tale of his falling 300 feet from the top of a pine tree that stood on a high bank of Penns Creek without receiving a scratch — he had climbed there to shake down a raccoon — was reproduced in three Union and Snyder papers with the *Middleburg Post* asking, "How high is that for high?" When William Pursley turned up in Mifflinburg or Lewisburg, the word soon spread and he was invited to converse with the press and escorted about the town to see the sights.

In later years the Pursleys moved into Weikert, where Eliza was often engaged as a midwife. Following William's death at 98, the *Telegraph* noted, "Mr. Pursley was of a jolly disposition, of sunny temperament, and could tell a story equal to the best entertainer in that line. Because of this fact, he was known all over the county, many seeking his company to hear him relate his experiences in hunting and fishing. His adventures thus freely given would fill a volume and prove very interesting fireside reading."[2] The Pursleys' son, James, went to fight in the Civil War at eighteen, returned to marry Sarah Swank, who was just fifteen, and settled upon a farm near his parents. James speculated in lumber tracts, and in 1891 moved to Laurelton, where he was a farmer and tavernkeeper as well as a horse and cattle dealer. A Democrat in politics, he was elected as a Union County commissioner in 1896. His son, David R., generally known as "Pete," helped manage the tavern and in 1911 purchased the Raudenbush block and general store from the Laurelton Lumber Company, which he operated for many years. Also a Democratic politician, he served the county as a commissioner (1911-1915) and associate judge (1922-1928).

Like his father and grandfather, Pete Pursley was an ardent sportsman, as were many of his West End neighbors. Hartley Township is home to excellent trout streams, and the existing native brook trout population was enhanced with juvenile fish provided by the Pennsylvania Fish Commission. Unlike the modern practice of stocking streams with mature fish, mostly brown and rainbow trout which are not native to the region, the Fish Commission in early years distributed native brook trout fry to individual sportsmen, who placed them in the streams. In one year alone, Pursley and 49 other Union Countians received a total of 75,000 fry for stocking.[3]

Despite the misfortunes of Roush and Stitzer, the milling trade remained basic to the economy of Hartley. A gristmill on Penns Creek was built near the mouth of Laurel Run in 1797 by Peter Fisher, who tapped Laurel Run with two immense overshot wheels. A second owner added a distillery but appears to have neglected the mill, while a third user enlarged the distillery to house machinery for the manufacture of woolen goods. However, in the 1860s Samuel Weidensaul was milling grain in a second mill on the same site. He sold the property to the Albright brothers in 1895, and they built an implement factory adjacent to it. When they, in turn, moved their implement business to Mifflinburg, the mill came into the possession of C.C. Yagel, who continued milling into the 1920s.

The third mill — and the first to tap Penns Creek — was constructed south of Swengel on the site of the mill which later furnished Mifflinburg with its electric power during the first quarter of the twentieth century. It was built by Adam Smith and owned later by members of the Barber, Ruhl, Knauer, Grove, and Halfpenny families. Like the Yagel Mill, it was eventually abandoned as a power site, and it was finally converted into a chicken pen. Perhaps the most productive of the gristmills was the Braucher mill at Laurelton — a large brick structure which passed through many hands: Charles H. Shriner of Buffalo Township (who at one time owned at least four mills in Buffalo Valley), R.V.B. Lincoln, O.K. Pellman, and Andrew Herbster. It ceased to grind on December 23, 1961, and has been converted into a home.

Hartley's most ambitious manufacturing enterprises in the nineteenth century were the iron works at Glen Iron and the Halfpenny Woolens Mill just north of Laurelton. The former dates back to the 1820s, when David Beaver, who operated a sawmill on the south side of Penns Creek at the Glen Iron bridge, added an iron forge to his operations. It appears to have been a small forge, yet it proved large enough to attract Charles and Clement Brooks, prominent iron manufacturers of Chester County, who bought it and erected a furnace which they styled the Berlin Iron Works. Their furnace was situated against the rising hill on the south side of the creek and connected to the hill by a ramp, permitting workmen to carry baskets of charcoal, limestone, and iron ore to the rim of the stone stack. At the outset a waterwheel, fed by the race of the saw mill, appears

TOP: Charcoal pit crew at Camp Laurelton near Glen Iron. From the collection of the Union County Historical Society, #89.5.15.6.

Glen Iron Furnace as it looked on July 4, 1909. The iron furnace, operational in 1820s, was known then as the Berlin Ironworks. The enterprise suffered a series of setbacks with major fires in 1887, 1892, 1903, and 1905. The last owner, John T. Church, after attempting several comebacks, finally closed the ironworks in the 1920s. From the collection of Gary W. and Donna M. Slear.

to have moved the bellows to provide the blast, but later a steam engine was used for this purpose. In the beginning Jacks Mountain provided wood for the charcoal, which was charred in pits there. The iron ore was dug out of the mountain and, as richer veins were discovered, from small mines along Penns Creek. At times of peak production, the search for ore became feverish, and dozens of farmers dug into their hillsides in search of the elusive hematite. For a time these now-forgotten sites were familiar place names: the William Pursley Perforated Hill Mine, the Libby and Sholter, the Lincoln, the Galer and Aumiller, the Johnson #1 and #2 mines, and the Walls and Linn diggings. Despite these many enterprises, a newspaper reported truthfully that no "Emma" had been discovered — a reference to the spectacular but short-lasting silver mine in Utah.

The Brooks brothers operated the furnace for several years but then closed it. They leased the forge to John C. Wilson, another Chester County ironmaster, who operated it successfully for a time. In 1842 Wilson joined with Robert B. Green and Nathan Mitchell of Lewisburg to restore the furnace and improve it with a hot blast, but profits were not forthcoming; and when a fire destroyed the store house, the blast was blown out. Again, Chester County investors came to the rescue in the form of Dr. Levi Rooke and his brother, Jonathan, and John H. Church. The latter was a nephew of Clement Brooks and learned ironmaking at the Hopewell Furnace and Forge in Berks County, famous for its fine six-plate stoves. The checkered career of the Berlin Works was linked to Church and his son for the next half-century.

Dr. Rooke and his brother remained for only a few years before removing to Winfield, where they helped to manage the Union Iron Furnace. Meanwhile, Church and his father-in-law, Samuel Knauer, persevered for a few years with little success. It was becoming obvious by this time that the Berlin Works was not competitive. Its ore was not of a high quality, and the forge had to add pig iron from Centre County to the mix to produce a tough metal. Lacking rail transportation, its pig and forged iron had to be hauled to Lewisburg for distribution on the canal. By this time also, coal and coke were replacing charcoal, and mass production was lowering prices.

The coming of the railroad to Glen Iron encouraged investors to try again, and in 1880 Church leased the plant to a Berwick group composed of the Jackson brothers and B.F. Crispin. They rejuvenated the works — erecting new buildings, restoring the stack, and adding a steam engine. The charcoal burners, wagoners, miners, and laborers at the furnace were soon on the job; and during the euphoria the railroad depot for Laurelton was moved from Laurel Park to the iron works and named Glen Iron. Within a few years mounting deficits closed the business, and laborers were casting about for employment. There was another reorganization and another revival in 1890. It was reported that 150 men were in the woods cutting charcoal wood; but, as before, the activity was not sustained, and in 1892 it was noted that the "golden sun has gone down gently on the Berlin Iron Works and the furnace has produced its last iron."[4] "Quite a number" were said to be out of employment.

The Church family were not quitters. With Philadelphia capital, John T. Church resumed operations again in 1901 as the Glen Iron Furnace Company. Older residents in the mid-twentieth century recalled this boon to the village — the smoking charcoal wagons enroute to the furnace, the molten iron running into the molds, and the cluster of shanties adjacent to the plant. One elderly citizen had vivid memories of going to housekeeping there, his "miserable" wages, and the "White House" where the bosses lived.[5] However, the activity did not last long. In 1903 a fire consumed the buildings, leaving only the casting house, and there was no insurance.

Church remained undaunted and made at least two further attempts to revive the business during the next few years. "John is a hustler, and the West End people will soon see the smoke fly along the mountain," the *Saturday News* predicted in 1918. In 1923, twenty years after the disastrous fire, John Church made what would really be his final bid to revive the defunct iron works. His grandiose plan envisioned an integrated iron manufactory powered by electricity furnished by a hydroelectric plant; and the company would specialize in the production of two patented wrenches; the first, "The New Perfection Wrench," invented by R.F. Boop, a neighbor, was said to be the only pipe wrench which would turn a four-inch pipe without the use of a chain and without crimping the pipe; the second, designed by J.W. Shook of the Titan Metal Company of Bellefonte, was described as an improved nut wrench. It was said that electric power in excess of the company's needs would light the homes of Glen Iron and Laurelton.

The enterprise was formalized as the Glen Iron Power and Tool Company, with Church as President, Shook as Vice President, Marlin W.L. Boop as Secretary, and R.F. Boop as Treasurer. The public was invited to purchase stock at $10 per share. The *Saturday News* anticipated that Glen Iron would be ". . . put on the boom. The old John Church furnace is to be blown in, water power developed, and a steel casting factory installed; a patent wrench will be manufactured, and a half- million dollars invested. Many men will be employed, and a real industrial awakening in the West End is assured."[6] It reported that

Church had advised that more ore remained in the ground than had ever been taken out.

In a news release a few months later, Church indicated that there had been delays due to the state's new "Blue Sky Law," but that the firm had now received a clean bill of health. Calling upon the public to purchase the stock and give the West End the great enterprise, he declared that the benefits would be a boon to the entire county. The value of the stock, Church predicted, would double by the time the building program was completed. Perhaps the collapse of the Dollings Company at this time — an investment trust in which hundreds of the county's residents had invested — made the public cautious. Perhaps the furnace had opened and closed too many times to radiate confidence. In any event, much of the stock remained unsold. Two years later, the newspapers reported that construction was to begin the following week. The power site was said to be excellent, and the demand for the Boop wrench was declared to be unlimited; but construction was postponed yet again, and the press did not find the "great enterprise" again newsworthy. Today only the old stack, with trees growing up around it, remains to recall the Berlin Iron Works and John T. Church.

During the "good years" of the furnace, Glen Iron came alive. Its railroad depot hummed with activity, and Frank Church's three-storied hotel as well as the Fessenden store flourished. The former catered to the Philadelphia summer vacation trade. Following Church's death, his widow employed Sam Dunlap, a retired iron worker, to manage the resort house. One of Dunlap's daughters married a Mr. Mills and moved to Harrisburg. Their sons later won nationwide acclaim as the Mills Brothers Quartet.

With the population at an all-time high in the 1890s, Glen Iron's residents sought a school, feeling that their growth warranted it and that it was an inconvenience for their children to walk to the Feese (or Creek) School, one and one-half miles west of the village. They petitioned the Hartley Township School Board, made up of R.V.B. Lincoln, Daniel M. Showalter, David M. McCool, Alanson Johnson, and Lemuel Fessenden, but were rejected with only Fessenden dissenting. Feeling that he had a mandate from the residents, Fessenden circulated petitions and presented them to the court, alleging that four members of the board were delinquent in the performance of their duties and should be dismissed. His action touched off a row unprecedented in the school history of the West End. The court complied, leaving Fessenden the only survivor, and he promptly named Howard H.

Yarger, William H. Showalter, David Eley, Thomas Libby, and Robert J. Bingaman as replacements. All were friends of the Glen Iron project. As expected, they lost no time in voting to build the school, and then entering into a contract for its construction.

R.V.B. Lincoln, president of the original board, denounced the action as " 'Punica Fides,' or in plain English — Treachery," and predicted that it would needlessly multiply the school taxes. He also claimed that the board would have granted a school to Glen Iron once the district was out of debt but that Fessenden would not agree, "and backed by a couple of individuals with spirits as imperious and impetuous as his own, he would brook no delay."[7] The original board appealed the court's decision and obtained a reversal, with the supreme court declaring that Fessenden's appointment of the "rump" was irregular. The same court then proceeded to name the "rump" as the official board. The official termination of the controversy followed quickly. The reconstituted board accepted the previous contract, and Glen Iron got its one-room school.[8] Unofficially, however, it took several years to cool the passions which had been aroused. Statistics tended to bear out Glen Iron's bid for a school. In January of 1897 its teacher, W.E. Yarger, reported sixteen males and 30 females attending.[9]

The Halfpenny Woolens, while it lasted, was one of the most successful business enterprises in the West End, but like the iron works it too had an untimely demise. Mark Halfpenny came to Northumberland County about 1806 and lived at Washingtonville and Muncy. In Muncy he and his sons learned the woolens trade. They later opened a mill of their own at Millheim and in 1841 removed to Laurel Park, where they operated a woolens factory until 1851, when Mark II purchased the sawmill property of Leonard Smith on Laurel Run just north of Laurelton and built the Winfield Woolen Factory there. He also continued to operate a sumac mill on the property and opened a store as an outlet for his products. Meanwhile, Halfpenny obtained an appointment as postmaster of Laurelton, paying the costs of delivery from Hartleton out of his own pockets until the office was placed on the regular mail route from Lewisburg to Centre County.

In time some of his workers constructed homes near the factory, and a prospective village was forming. However, shortly after the plant was enlarged in 1866, a fire destroyed the factory as well as the saw and sumac mills. Halfpenny considered rebuilding and restocked his store with merchandise from a Larry's Creek mill in which he had an interest.

Rich⁰. V.B. Lincoln

Halfpenny's stock included cassimeres, satinettes, jeans, flannels, blankets, and yarn. He at last concluded, however, to rebuild in Lewisburg, with the expectation that the canal and railroad connections there offered better prospects for the future. Halfpenny's decision was obviously a blow to Laurelton, and only a part of the old mill race remains today.

For more than a century lumbering was second only to agriculture in sustaining the economy of Hartley Township. At the outset, the mills served the local market, though surpluses were sometimes rafted to the lower Susquehanna Valley. The first large-scale operation was initiated in 1852 by absentee Maine entrepreneurs at a time when other Maine men were making Williamsport the lumber capital of the world. David Scribner and Nathan Perkins of Topsham, Maine, purchased 14,000 acres of mountain land on the two sides of Penns Creek along Paddy and White Mountains and erected the Maine Saw Mill just north of Selinsgrove where Penns Creek and the canal ran side by side.

The time was well chosen. Before the mill had sawed its first board, an order was received for the lumber to build a Susquehanna River bridge at Port Trevorton, and the business was off to a flying start. The partners engaged Alvah Marston, Scribner's son-in-law and an experienced lumberman, to direct the lumbering, and Daniel Carey, also a Maine "Yankee," to run the mill. Additional lumbermen, including William Brawn, Thomas Libby, and Philip Fessenden, joined the exodus from Maine to become residents of Weikert and marry local young women. Their descendants, in R.V.B. Lincoln's words, became some of the "most respectable, thrifty and law-abiding citizens of the township."[10]

After the timber was cut, it was hauled by oxen to the creek and floated to Selinsgrove during high water, where it was caught by a boom. Where feasible they built slides — trough-like inclined planes — on which one or two horses could draw a dozen or more logs. On the larger streams such as Weikert Run, they also built splash dams, which they filled with logs. When the water rose, they opened the dam and floated the logs to the next splash dam. By repeating the process one or more times, the logs reached Penns Creek, where they continued their journey to Selinsgrove. A gang of men followed the logs to guide them as needed. If all went well, the logs reached their destination on the third or fourth day. After Perkins' death in 1868, the land and mill were sold to Daniel Carey and George Schnure of Selinsgrove, who continued the business for a number of years. By the late 1870s, however, the good timber had been removed and the log drive was abandoned.

Logging activity gave rise to the hamlet of Weikert. It might have succumbed once the lumbering stopped, but the railroad revived it a few years later, and the flag stop, post office, and country store helped to stabilize it. In 1880 a union church was founded, its small frame edifice erected by contributions of time and materials. The Articles of Agreement were signed by Charles H. Marston, Perry Grubb, F.B. McCurdy, and Lewis Shaffer, who deeded it to trustees representing five sects: Lutheran, United Evangelical, Methodist, German Baptist (Church of the Brethren), and Reformed. It was named the Hironimus Church in recognition of Andrew Hironimus, who had donated a part of the land for the church and churchyard. In practice, however, the Evangelical Church was the only one to conduct services in the quaint structure, a practice which they continued for the next 83 years.[11] A few yards from the churchyard, a country school was erected in 1898.

Meanwhile, in York Valley, at the northern tip of Hartley Township where it borders Clinton and Centre Counties, John McCall was using splash dams to propel logs down the south branch of White Deer Creek for delivery to the village of White Deer. The ruins of several of these dams and a road to them from the Fourteen Mile Narrows road still bear his name. While splash dams were useful, large stands of timber were beyond their reach, and it was the rail-

Sholter's General Store at Weikert was the place where many shopped when staying in the Tight End. Courtesy of the Mifflinburg Buggy Museum.

road which probed the depths of this magnificent virgin forest and wrote the last chapter of large-scale lumbering.

One such enterprise in the western part of the county was centered at Buffalo Mills at the foot of Jones Mountain in Lewis Township, in close proximity to Mifflinburg's water intake. The railroad at Mifflinburg had brought the timberland close enough to markets to attract a large operator, Ryan, Thompson, and Company, headed by John R. Ryan and James M. Thompson of Williamsport. As mentioned elsewhere, Henry Gast had purchased an extensive tract of timberland on the south slopes of Jones and Little Buffalo Mountains, and in the summer of 1882 he agreed to sell about half of his holdings — some 3,400 acres — for a reported $37,000 to Ryan, Thompson, and Company. Concurrently, the latter announced its intention to build a five-mile railroad from Mifflinburg to Buffalo Mills through West Buffalo and Lewis Townships.

The local response was mixed. Some farmers offered a passage free of charge; others waited to hear the company's offer. Editor George Schoch of the *Mifflinburg Telegraph* urged landholders to be liberal, arguing that while railroads were at some times injurious to property, they were blessings in the long run, stating "Had it not been for the Lewisburg and Tyrone Railroad Mr. Gast would not have realized $37,000."[12] Reluctant owners were eventually won over with sums ranging from $15 to $475; and by the following spring the mill was completed, the road was graded and the railhead had crossed Buffalo Creek. Meanwhile, the company built a "shanty," which one mill hand termed "a boss one, you can bet." It was described as a two-story, frame structure with a lobby, dining room, and kitchen/storehouse, in nearly equal proportions. There were also a large stable, granary, and loft. Three miles west of the mill, an upper camp was also constructed for the sawyers.

By October, they were "slashing" the hemlock which lined the creek; in this process, the workmen removed the bark, discarding the wood or using it to fire the boiler, and prepared to assault the pine. The latter was truly one of the finest stands of timber in the state. Horace Orwig, a young axman, who later lumbered tracts in Central Pennsylvania and West Virginia, when revisiting Buffalo Mills fifteen years later, pointed to a gigantic white pine stump about the size of "an overstuffed living room chair." Here, he said, was the largest pine tree he had ever seen — 70 feet to the first limbs and containing 6,500 board feet of timber.[13] It would not appear that he exaggerated its enormity. Some years later, when old lumbermen were shown the magnificent virgin hemlocks in Snyder/Middleswarth Park, they insisted that they had sawed larger ones in the old days.

A reminiscence appearing in a Lewisburg paper testified, also, to the massive oaks on the Buffalo Mills tract. "The biggest stick ever seen in Lewisburg, a white oak forty-five feet long, and weighing eight tons," came down the pike in mid-winter on a sled driven by Ollie Wagner and drawn by four horses. "Ollie kept the big, broad kind of horses, that could get home with a load that was worth going after." On this trip, though, he hitched four additional horses to reach the summit of the Vicksburg hill. He brought the "stick" safely to Billmeyer's boat yard, where the big boilers under maximum pressure sliced it into timber for canal boats.[14]

The mill closed down during the winter, and the dinkeys stopped running; but the lumberjacks remained in the woods cutting and skidding the logs in preparation for spring, and they stopped only when "a mountain of logs were in the dam." By early March the saw was again turning, and "thirty big-hoofed hemlock fiends" were in the woods; but logging was slowed by the mud, and it required "four horses instead of two to drag a log to the skidway."[15] By June, however, the place was buzzing with activity.

In July, with the woods unseasonably dry, a fire destroyed the woods, timber, and bark at the upper camp, and the wind swept the flames toward the main mill. The superintendent dispatched a dinkey locomotive and gondola to Mifflinburg for help, where more than 100 men and buckets were hastily assembled and rushed to the mill. They extinguished the flames before they reached the compound. Meanwhile, the telegraph operator at Mifflinburg had also alerted Lewisburg, and the Cameron Fire Company — 60 men strong — with its steamer and hose carriage was soon enroute on a flatcar of the Lewisburg and Tyrone Railroad. At Mifflinburg they transferred the apparatus to the narrow-gauge and made a record run to the mill, but, on arrival, found they were no longer needed.

Over the next several years the work went on apace, and it required the unusual to break into print. Occasionally on Saturday night the lumbermen strained their welcome in Mifflinburg. The *Telegraph* once likened them to Comanche Indians after several had annoyed the citizenry by shrieking and staggering in the streets. "A lock up and an hour's shower bath would be a proper medicine for bummers of this

TOP: The Laurelton Lumber Company with: Bert Lohr, Jim Olmstead, unknown, Fred Snyder, William Bogenreif, Ed Lohr, and David Kahler. BOTTOM: a company sawmill with Samuel Rutherford on the far left, both c. 1894. From the collection of the Union County Historical Society, #89.5.5.7-8.

sort," it scolded.[16] (The town had a one-man jail at this time, but shower baths were something for the future.) After five years the timber was gone, and Henry Gast would sell no more of his land. In the fall of 1888, Ryan, Thompson, and Company shipped their mill and store goods to other sites, sold their furnishings at auction, and pulled up their track. George Aumiller bought the office for use as a springhouse and hog stable, leaving only the "shanty" and dam. The former became a hunting camp, and the latter endured to remind Mifflinburg that it had a water works ready to be tapped.

Ario Pardee, a resident of Hazleton and one of the largest owners and operators of anthracite mining in Pennsylvania, did not invent "wildcatting," but he introduced it in Hartley Township shortly after the advent of the railroad there to satisfy his seemingly insatiable need for prop-timber. In 1873 he purchased 30,000 acres of forest land (subsequently enlarged to 80,000) extending from Hartley Township into Snyder, Mifflin, and Centre Counties. In the early 1880s he initiated operations at Pardee (the post office was called Cohn) on the railroad four miles west of Glen Iron. From a siding there he threw a bridge across Penns Creek and erected a sawmill on the south side of the stream, a site commonly referred to as McColmville after William McColm, who tended the furnace. From the mill tram, roads were built into Lick and Hoofnaugle gaps to the south and west respectively, using "wildcatting" and horse power to bring the logs to the mill. Wooden rails (and later iron ones) were placed upon stringers of sufficient size to hold "trucks" — four-wheeled, narrow-gauge flat cars, which might hold twelve to fifteen good-sized logs. The loaded trucks were released at loading points and taken by gravity to the mill. The emptied trucks were then drawn back to the loading platforms by mules. Gravity propelled the trucks, but hand brakes were required to control their speed. At best, the trucking was dangerous; and when drivers competed for speed records, the descent could be suicidal. In one year there were four deaths and and the number of injuries was not recorded.

Lewis Dorman, who wildcatted, blamed the accidents on "high flyers who wanted to show off." One of the most reckless, in his opinion was, "a Mr. Jordan, who at dinner one day said, 'Next meal I'll eat will be in hell.' After finishing his meal he cut the truck out sitting high on the load and went flying down. It jumped the track at Pardee gap. The truck lay there marking the spot for many years." By 1889 they had substituted a Climax steam engine for the mules and

had pushed into the mountains by a series of switchbacks and laterals until the narrow-gauge network encompassed more than 50 miles of tracks and such colorful place names as Coral Run, Gold Spring, Buckwheat Shanty Gap, Sheep Pen Springs, and Hen Step Gap.

Back at Pardee a row of hastily built houses and stores served the needs of the lumbermen. There was the superintendent's home and store, the post office (named after the first postmaster, Benjamin Cohn), and an assortment of clapboard homes and boarding houses; and in time there was a school as well. At least three stores vended merchandise in a period of ten years. There was also an engine house, a storage shed for dinkeys, and a repair shop for trucks.

In the woods were several boarding camps, which were built and maintained by the cutting contractors — three of them boarding as many as 50 men. Pay was about $1.55 per day, less 50¢ for board (and lodging). The mill, which employed 36 men in 1886, turned out vast quantities of sawed lumber and about 70 carloads of "props" a month. The labor force, drawn largely from the West End but supplemented by sawyers from Snyder, Mifflin, and Centre Counties, also had its share of drifters and characters. Tall tales were soon circulating and growing with the telling. One story, relating to Albert Lichtenwalter, the superintendent, reveals the devil-may-care attitude of the wildcatter as it contrasted with the more sober outlook of the boss. After overseeing the logging on a higher elevation, Lichtenwalter looked about for a ride to the Treaster Valley mill, and, not trusting a wildcat truck, he asked Jim Havice to take him down on a hand car. Havice agreed. "I knew the track well," he recalled, "and after passing the danger points, tapped Lichtenwalter on the shoulder and when he turned, I threw the brake handle away and seated myself. We attained a high rate of speed, but as we approached the mill, we began to slow down. I jumped off as we passed it but the hand car continued onward for close to a mile before Lichtenwalter would get off. Al never said a word that day, but took his train to Pardee. He would never again approach anything that even resembled a wildcat truck."[17]

Ario Pardee died in 1892 without ever visiting the village and mill named for him. Two years later Lichtenwalter failed financially, with liabilities estimated at $30,000. His store, eleven houses, and a blacksmith shop at Pardee, in addition to other pieces of real estate, were knocked off at a sheriff's sale at panic prices of less than $100 each. Even so, the work was continued at a diminishing pace until 1904, when the dinkeys were sold and the bridge and mill were dismantled. Prospects for the village were now gloomy. The stores were closed, some of the houses were razed, others were simply abandoned, and at least one was floated down Penns Creek to Glen Iron. Later travelers on the railroad recall the remaining row of unpainted houses along the railroad right of way. Today, several are used as cottages, and the ghost town revives each year during camping season. Only the long, cindered siding bed, stripped of its rails and ties, remains to suggest the bustle of its former days.

Pardee's extensive lumbering operation did not go unobserved at Laurelton, where two of its leading citizens decided to emulate it on the north side of the valley. Samuel W. Rutherford was a storekeeper who liked to dabble in real estate and western horses,

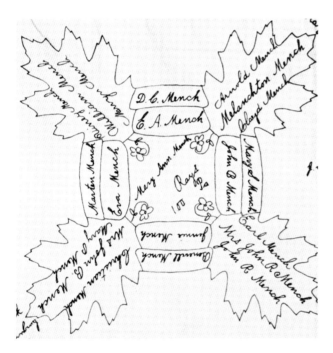

Detail of quilt top made as a fundraiser by members of St. Peter's Aid and the Missionary Society of Ray's Lutheran Church, Hartley Township, and dated "1897." White whole cloth with red embroidery, 83" square. From the collection of Helen Ruhl Kerstetter. Photo by the Terry Wild Studio, courtesy of the Oral Traditions Project.

while Dr. George Calvin Mohn was a local physician and druggist with a penchant for business and politics. In 1885 Rutherford bought a timber tract in the Sheesley Gap area north of the turnpike and several miles east of what would later be Hairy John's Park. It was one of a number of tracts in the region which had been partially worked over but discontinued

because of their isolation from markets. Rutherford installed a portable sawmill but did not appear to fare better than his predecessor. His prospects took a turn for the better, however, when he entered into partnership with Mohn as the Laurelton Lumber Company. They leased land at Laurel Park adjacent to the railroad and installed a portable mill on it. Then they ran a narrow-gauge track from the mill through Laurelton to the south slope of Paddy Mountain, where they had obtained title to several thousand acres of fine timberland. Scarcely had the operations begun when a fire destroyed the mill, but the Laurelton Lumber Company replaced it with a larger steam mill and dug a pond which was fed by Laurel Run. A letterhead of 1895 notes that they were manufacturers and dealers in white pine, hemlock, oak and all kinds of hardwoods, prop timber, bark, and stone.

To expand their operations, the Laurelton Lumber Company incorporated in 1896, thereby adding the resources of Robert F. Whitmer of Sunbury, a native of Hartleton, and Charles M. Steele of Northumberland, two of the rising young lumbermen in the state. Rutherford was the company's first president; Whitmer, the vice president; and Steele, the secretary and treasurer. With capital of $100,000 the company purchased or leased 25,000 acres north of the turnpike and moved the track toward the headwaters of Laurel Run into Sheesley Gap and across Buffalo Mountain with the help of a switchback. Later they laid another branch into the Pine Creek flats and continued it along Pine Creek to Woodward. They also extended the network to the Walker Tract east of Livonia by way of Stover's Gap, and finally, in 1905, they ran the tramway down the south side of Little Mountain into the Hayes Tract near the older Buffalo Mills operation. A letter written by William Boop, while working at the Walker site, provides a glimpse into the lumberman's life in the winter of 1904:

I am working in the woods fourteen miles from the Laurelton Lumber Company's mill, one mile from Stover's in Brush Valley. The camp is in a ravine at a spring, but our work is on a mountain a mile or so away. We go in to dinner, so we walk four to eight miles a day. It is a fresh air camp and very healthy, although we can see through the roof and the snow comes in. Here it is all beef, and I wouldn't mind having some of your sausages. On a recent day we cut a white pine tree that had 2400 feet of lumber. We were at a larger one when I left. I took particular notice of a yellow pine seventy feet to the limbs, thirty inches at the butt, and perfectly straight. We have eight inches of snow. The work goes on all winter regardless of the weather.[18]

Finding that motive power was needed to reach the recesses of the mountains, the company utilized dinkey engines while wildcatting on some of the

Hemlock or oak bark for tanning was loaded in Millmont. From the collection of the Union County Historical Society, #89.15.5.

branches. At Laurel Park the mill was run year-round, with exhaust steam keeping the mill pond from freezing in winter. Utilizing a band saw, lath mill, shingle mill, edger, trimmer, planer, three steam engines, and carbide lights, mill production reached 85,000 board feet daily, filling five boxcars. The need for growth capital seems to have exceeded the means of Dr. Mohn and Rutherford, and both eventually sold out to Whitmer and Steele. In fact the luckless Rutherford was in bankruptcy by 1902, whereas Whitmer and Steele were well on their way to becoming millionaires.

As in the case of the Pardee operation, the Laurelton Lumber Company employed many local people. An old photograph shows a truck crew of fifteen; another taken at the camp at Walker's contains just over 100 men and six women. An early picture of the mill reveals 21 employees; a later one, more than 40. The Laurel Park area became dotted with the houses of the lumbermen, and boarders were a part of most households. Laurelton, Glen Iron, and Millmont also supplied a part of the labor force, and employees from Pardee's mill found jobs with Laurelton as their old company phased out its sawing. Otto Goerdel and his family came all the way from Germany to find employment, but they were exceptions.

Since Whitmer, Steele and Company continued operations at Laurel Park until 1909, older citizens still remember the mill and the pond — the latter being a favorite skating rink after the mill was dismantled. They also recall the old station house in Laurelton, the tram roads and dinkeys, and also the huckleberry trips on the trucks. No surviving workman has forgotten the spectacular "explosion" of the main flywheel of the mill engine in May of 1904. The wheel was flawed and out of balance but had worked satisfactorily at normal speed. A breakage of the governor belt, while the engineer was momentarily absent, permitted the engine to accelerate. Several mill hands still recall that they heard the change of speed. Before the steam valve could be turned off, the flywheel flew apart. One section hurtled upward through the mill floor and roof, killing one workman and severely injuring several others. Older residents also remember the great fire on December 14, 1907, when the entire mill was leveled.

With the cutting almost finished, the company rebuilt the mill in sections to facilitate its removal, and in the summer of 1909 the last log was hoisted by the bull-chain to the cutting floor. Laurel Park was never the same again. Some families followed Whitmer, Steele to its mills at White Deer and Philipsburg, and later to Clearfield and West Virginia; Hartley's lumbering days were gone — never to return. If Chief Bald Eagle or other legendary Indians of the region had been able to return to their native forests at this time, they would have been shocked at the carnage. The virgin forests were gone, and in their place the "scars made by ruthless logging and the greater forest enemy, forest fires." During the drought of 1909 thousands of acres had been burned over; some had been set afire by the sparks from the dinkey engines; some by farmers for pasture or by pickers aware that wild berries multiplied in burned-over areas; but most by careless hunters, fishermen, and campers. In many places "nothing was left but bare rocks and mineral soil."[19]

Fortunately, some roots survived, and seeds were borne by the wind into the desolated regions. The public, at last, was becoming aware of the enormity of the loss and beginning to make amends. Pennsylvania's Governor Gifford Pinchot became one of the nation's foremost advocates of conservation and reforestation, and in 1910 a program of reforestation was initiated by the commonwealth. During that year, also, Raymond B. Winter, a recent graduate of the Mont Alto State Forest School of the Pennsylvania State College, was assigned as guardian over the White Deer State Forest of 20,000 acres, with his headquarters in the Forest House at the north edge of the Fourteen Mile or Brush Valley Narrows. He would remain the principal spokesman for the reclamation of the county's forest lands for the next half-century.

The focus at the outset was fire protection, but in 1914 tree planting was started locally — a quarter of a million trees in the Buffalo and White Deer forests and a smaller planting on the farm of Carrie Lincoln near Laurelton in 1916. Two years later, a reforestation project was begun in the Winkleblech region just across the Centre County line. In the 1930s a Civilian Conservation Corps unit in the Fourteen Mile Narrows planted thousands of seedlings. By 1957 the ruins of the old Half Way Dam, surrounded by a fine stand of second-growth pines, was restored and appropriately dedicated as the Raymond B. Winter State Forest Park. Meanwhile, the state was purchasing private forest land, tract by tract, and by 1975 the state forest acreage in the county encompassed approximately 59,000 acres, surely one of the area's greatest assets.

Laurelton profited more from the lumbering era than Pardee, Weikert, or Laurel Park. For a time it had been little more than two small clusters of dwellings: one near the Braucher mill and the other adjacent to Halfpenny's Woolens. In the 1870s the community began to stir. It discarded the name Slabtown and erected two churches, the Reformed and Lutheran, replacing an older, partially dilapidated structure which the two congregations had shared. R.V.B. Lincoln purchased the Braucher gristmill and enlarged it. The decision of the railroad to follow a route through Laurel Park and Glen Iron was, of course, a setback, but Laurelton remained the principal crossroads at the West End.

Beginning in the 1880s Laurelton's men found work at Buffalo Mills, Pardee, and Laurel Park. They throttled and fired the dinkeys, wildcatted, and handled the picks and shovels on the track gang. They walked back and forth to Glen Iron to tend the iron furnace, and climbed the slopes of Paddy Mountain to burn charcoal and haul it to the furnace. The business activity precipitated a housing boom, and J. Russell Slayman, the Hartleton carpenter, could not keep up with the increased demand.

Most conspicuous among the new structures was Joseph Raudenbush's three-storied brick "Palace Store and West End Hotel" and residence at the main intersection, a block which Laurelton residents claimed "would adorn even a county seat." Across the street a new post office, also housing the offices of Doctors Mohn and Glover and the former's drug store, replaced an older building. Raudenbush's suicide was "like a clap of thunder," but his business was continued by the Laurelton Lumber Company. A brick grammar school built in 1884 was another

TOP: Raymond B. Winter is fourth from the left in group photo probably taken at the Civilian Conservation Corps Camp near Rapid Run. Courtesy of R.B. Winter State Park.

BOTTOM: From 1933 to 1942 the Civilian Conservation Corps was involved in extensive reforestation efforts, bridge and trail building, and road maintenance, as well as the construction of a masonry dam and bath pavilion at Rapid Run (later called the Raymond B. Winter State Park). The CCC camp at Weikert (location of present Union County Sportsmen's Club) on Hassenplug Road was exclusively for older men—veterans of World War I. The 1394th Company's PX and Recreation Hall is seen here. From the collection of the Union County Historical Society, #92.9.9.6.

HARTLETON

Scale 35 Rods to the Inch

Hartleton as seen in *Pomeroy's Atlas for Union and Snyder Counties, 1868.*

some addition to the community. Twenty years later the building would house the first high school in the area.

In 1891 the Methodists rebuilt the Lincoln Chapel at the intersection just to the west of the village, an unusually attractive Gothic edifice designed by Mifflinburg's noted architect and builder, Enoch Miller. Meanwhile, one property holder after another placed a board walk in front of his residence, and it was boasted that one day Laurelton would spread out to reach Glen Iron. Then the sawmills closed, and the region stopped growing. Architecturally, Laurelton retains much of the charm of a later Victorian village.

By contrast with Laurelton, Hartleton scarcely felt the bustle of the lumber camps, although Shem Spigelmyer, Horace Orwig, and Harvey Brungard timbered sizable tracts along the rim of the valley between 1870 and 1910. The origins of Hartleton go back to the Haines Road and the Bellefonte/Aaronsburg/Youngmanstown Turnpike, which succeeded it. At that time its taverns were the focal points of activity. Hugh Wilson seems to have opened the first one in 1793 on Colonel Hartley's property. The hamlet was first called Kester's since it was the home of Peter Kester (or Keister), Hartley's tenant. Considering the site favorable for future growth, Colonel Hartley laid out the village on a gentle slope just west of an ever flowing-spring. It was the post town for the upper end of Buffalo Valley, and John Thomas had a store there as early as 1811.

When Union County was formed in 1813, there were nine taxpayers in Hartleton; two were storekeepers and two were hostelers. There were also a joiner, a shoemaker, a leather worker, a weaver, and a wheelwright. The turnpike sparked business activity, and by the 1840s there were three taverns and three stores; Wilt and Eilert, Samuel Haupt, and Robert V. Glover were merchants as was Shem Spigelmyer, who advertised liquor by the pint or barrel. Dr. William F. Seebold practiced medicine there from 1843 until the 1890s.

Stimulated by the separation of Lewis from Hartley Township, residents petitioned the court in 1858 for incorporation as a borough, and their appeal was granted. Hartleton's population of about 300 varied little through the next century; neither did its general appearance. Only New Berlin changed as little among the communities in Union County. The prosperity of Hartleton's early merchants and tavernkeepers endured in the solid, even elegant, homesteads lining its single street; its pre-Victorian architecture was interrupted only by the Victorian gables of the Wilt and Wagner residences in addition to the Presbyterian Church.

Hartleton's commercial affluence permitted a sizable number of its families to send their children to the academies for a secondary education. Daughters of the Haupt, Lodge, and Catherman families became schoolteachers, while the Glover and Hayes families provided collegiate educations for their sons. Meanwhile, the town's literary societies found public approval through many a long winter's evening.

As mentioned elsewhere, Hartleton's failure to obtain the railroad was a bitter disappointment; and as the traffic on the turnpike declined, its taverns and businesses suffered. The decline of the former is suggested by the activity of the temperance movement, which held a temperance festival in 1879 at Yarger's Grove just to the east of the borough, for the benefit of the Hartleton Sabbath School. With its music furnished by the Laurelton and Hartleton brass bands, the temperance festival was said to have attracted 1,500-2,000 spectators. Further evidence of Hartleton's decline as a stopover for travelers is reflected in its decision to refuse liquor licenses in the borough, and by the commentary in the *Mifflinburg Telegraph* in 1890 which alleged that an adjacent village (Laurelton) had become a place of wickedness equal to Sodom and Gomorrah due to the rum traffic there.[20]

TOP: The exterior of the Union Church in Hartleton c. 1907. From the collection of the Union County Historical Society, #94.6.1.

BOTTOM: Donald Hayes restored the interior and exterior of the Hartleton Church in the mid-1970s, and his personal preservation effort was recognized with a citation from the American Association of State and Local History. From the collection of the Union County Historical Society, #89.5.1.43.

In the 1920s the opening of the Laurelton State Village gave needed employment to some of Hartleton's residents, and the automobile and the paving of the highways permitted other citizens to commute to jobs in Union and Northumberland Counties. The village was in response to the urging of township leaders, headed by Dr. Glover and D.R. Pursley. Three thousand dollars was raised to purchase 230 acres of farm land to establish the Laurelton State Village for Feeble-minded Women of Child-

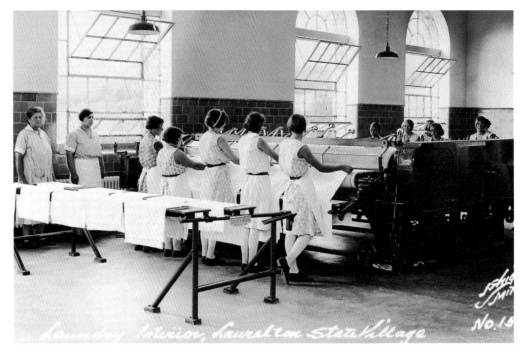

The laundry room at the Laurelton State School was photographed by Arthur R. Ishiguro, Milton photographer, c. 1924. From the collection of the Union County Historical Society, #86.3.15.

bearing Age at the foot of the Seven Mile Narrows. The first building was completed by 1917. Twenty years later it provided employment for 132 and was still growing, and it had become the township's largest employer. In the mid-1960s the facility was home to over 1,000 individuals, and in the mid-1980s its workforce reached a peak at over 540 employees.

When the village opened, laws were such that committing a woman was relatively uncomplicated and its rural setting reflected the prevailing popular belief that "feeble-minded" women should be removed from the general population. This setting was also conducive to the facility's initial concept of self-sufficiency. Women living there tended livestock and raised food crops as well as worked in the laundry, the dairy, the cannery, the rootcellar and in food service.

In its approximately 80-year history, the facility evolved to match the needs of its population and society's changing approach to dealing with people having mental retardation. The average level of need for assistance, both mentally and physically, increased over the years. The facility's name changed from the Village to Laurelton State School and Hospital to Laurelton Center. People living there were first identified as "inmates," then "students," then "residents," then "clients," and, finally, "individuals." Men were first admitted in 1968. Anti-peonage laws were passed which ended work for individuals

unless it was paid and part of a vocational training program. New laws made commitment more difficult as treatment options became available in non-institutional settings and community-based treatment came to be viewed as most acceptable; new admissions slowed and almost stopped by the early 1990s.

Laurelton Center had a history of returning individuals to the community beginning shortly after its opening. This movement expanded as community programs were able to accept more individuals and rules governing federal funding fostered it. Laurelton was one of the smaller facilities of its kind operated by Pennsylvania's Department of Public Welfare, and was special for its closeness among employes as well as between employees and individuals. The separation caused by community placement of long-time friends was difficult for some individuals and for some direct-care workers, as well, as if a family member moved away not to return.

The movement to community-based services resulted in Laurelton Center's closing in June, 1998. What re-use will be made of "the Village," as many Tight End residents still call it, remains unknown at the start of 2000.

Hartleton had no churches within its village limits until 1876. Its worshipers were affiliated with the Lutheran and Reformed congregations at Ray's Church or Laurel Run. Ray's Church, a mile east on the turnpike was erected about 1802 on land given by George Ray for a token payment. It was a hewn log structure, which was neglected after a time and virtually abandoned.

R.V.B. Lincoln recalled that the superstitious told weird tales of apparitions around the aging log church and the little cemetery adjoining it. One such report relating to a mysterious opening and closing of its doors was exposed when it was discovered that sheep were seeking shelter at night and leaving in the morning. A variation of this tale, handed down by word of mouth by members of the congregations, adds that rumors that the church was haunted traveled to Mifflinburg, and a group of young fellows decided to expose the myth. Entering the church one night, one of the more adventuresome mounted the pulpit, and pounding his fist, shouted, *"lus divil lose"* (let the devil loose). The noise startled the unseen sheep in the gallery, and they fled noisily down the stairs. It was said that the Mifflinburg boys did not stop running until they reached town.

Perhaps the most exciting issue to rock the two congregations during the earlier years was the controversy in 1834 over the second coming of Christ. This was precipitated by the Reverend William Miller of Massachusetts, who interpreted passages in the Old Testament to reveal that the world would end and the faithful would be gathered into heaven the following year. Some of his followers, going a step further, predicted the day and the hour. The excitement spread through Pennsylvania, where it became the inspiration for hundreds of protracted church meetings, dividing churchgoers into believers and doubters. It is known that groups gathered at the appointed hour at the Dreisbach Church, the Evangelical and Lutheran churches in New Berlin, the Elias Church of Mifflinburg, and the Ray's Church, where they awaited the predicted cataclysmic moment clad in white robes.

The diary of Theodore Christ, a teen-aged schoolboy from Lewisburg, portrays the emotional fervor aroused by the issue.[21] A Mr. French, an itinerant Millerite from New England preaching in the Christian church, declared that only God knew the day and hour of the coming but that it was near at hand. The services at the church almost emptied the school, but Theodore remained somewhat skeptical. The Reverend Hugh Pollock, a Presbyterian minister and principal of the Lewisburg Academy, as well as several other clergymen, disputed French's assertions, but Theodore noted that "he [French] answered every question given him." Meanwhile, the Methodists were holding nightly meetings and baptising unusually large numbers. Even after Mr. French

had gone, the Christian church continued ". . . doing a big business. Today they baptized sixteen men and women; some are our scholars." He expected that as a result of the conversions his teacher, Mr. A. Kennedy, would have fewer disciplinary problems "now that so many scholars profess to have religion. . . . There are meetings enough to have the whole town converted. The Lutherans will have protracted meetings as soon as the Methodist meeting is over." Two months later, Theo observed that 60 had joined the Presbyterian church and that the revival was continuing. Unfortunately, the Christ diary does not record Lewisburg's response on the nights (there were several) when the second coming was expected, but, obviously, many of Mr. Miller's followers were disillusioned, and religious revivals abated for a time.

In 1851 a renewal of interest at Ray's Church led to the razing of the dilapidated log building and the erection of a brick sanctuary on the same site. This building, too, seems to have been unsatisfactory as 32 years later it was rebuilt on the north side of the road on a lot donated by the Ruhl family. This last building was a credit to the parishioners and to the architect and builder, Enoch Miller; its Gothic lines and graceful spire still make it landmark along the turnpike.

Meanwhile, in 1841, a union church was erected just to the south of Hartleton. The plain brick structure, graced with a small but attractive tower, soon suggested an antiquity beyond its age. It was used at times by the Methodists, Presbyterians, Evangelicals, and Lutherans; but they eventually withdrew, one by one, leaving the quaint structure empty and forlorn until it was restored in 1976 by area resident Donald Hayes. It is currently owned and maintained by the Borough of Hartleton and used occasionally for public events.

The Lutherans subsequently erected a church of their own on the south side of the main thoroughfare. It, too, was of Gothic design and appears to have been one of Enoch Miller's earlier structures. The response to the drive for funds was substantial, and on its dedication day, June 29, 1876, the sum of $1,600 was raised, thereby canceling the debt. In 1885 the Presbyterians also decided to build and, despite a small membership, erected a meetinghouse two doors east of the Lutheran Church; much of the driving force for its construction was contributed by Robert V. Glover.

When Hartleton became a borough, it was served by two one-room schools — one just to the east and the other just to the west of the village. Shortly thereafter, a frame school building with two rooms on the

TOP: Round oak rod baskets made by members of the Boop and Shively families, along with some of their tools. Photo by Bridget Allen, courtesy of the Oral Traditions Project.

ACROSS: Ledger entries of Henry Edward Smith, tinsmith in Hartleton from 1865 to 1902. From the collection of the Union County Historical Society, #80.7.16.

ACROSS: Cake cutters, funnels, dippers, and scoops were production items made by Laurelton tinsmith Samuel H. Bingman (b. 1835, d. 1922) starting in 1854. Many are in the collection of the Union County Historical Society. Photo by William Irwin, courtesy of the Oral Traditions Project.

BOTTOM. Miller's barber shop in Laurelton was photographed by Stephen B. Horton c. 1907-1910, when it was postmarked. From the collection of the Union County Historical Society, #92.9.89.11.

first floor was erected at the west end of the community. A second floor was added by subscription as an auditorium, and the villagers found many uses for it. By 1887 a grammar school, incorporating the first two years of high school, was also accommodated here; but when high schools were organized in Hartley and Lewis Townships, its enrollment fell off, and it was discontinued in 1911.

As the industries of the West End declined, the township's economy was bolstered by the construction of summer cottages on Penns Creek. With the railroad providing daily service at numerous "whistle stops," people from other areas, and residents of Northumberland County in particular — where many of the streams were blackened by drainage from the coal mines — turned to the sparkling waters of Penns Creek and its forest-fringed banks for their outings. Beginning at Lindale, west of Weikert, the vacation belt edged downstream from one wooded area to another until it extended east of Millmont. Of course the automobile increased the momentum, and scout and church camps as well as year-round dwellings were added to the creek communities.

ENDNOTES:

[1] Interview with Robert Jones Smith.

[2] February 16, 1894.

[3] *Report of the Fish Commissioners of the State of Pennsylvania for the Year 1903*, 61-62.

[4] *Mifflinburg Telegraph*, March 4, 1892.

[5] Interview with Lewis Dorman, February 23, 1974.

[6] July 7 and 28, 1923.

[7] *Mifflinburg Telegraph*, April 19, 1895.

[8] *Mifflinburg Telegraph*, April 19, 1895.

[9] *Lewisburg Saturday News*, February 13, 1897.

[10] *Mifflinburg Telegraph*, September 1, 1899.

[11] Helen Bauer, *The Story of Hironimus Union Church*, 1970, 5-7.

[12] *Mifflinburg Telegraph*, August 9, 1882.

[13] Told to Floyd Frederick by Horace Orwig.

[14] *Lewisburg Saturday News*, December 26, 1914.

[15] *Mifflinburg Telegraph*, March 12, 1884.

[16] September 16, 1885.

[17] Benjamin F.G. Kline, Jr., *Wild Catting on the Mountain*, 1970, 221-222.

[18] *Mifflinburg Telegraph*, January 15, 1904.

[19] Raymond B. Winter, "Halfway to Winter," August, 1967, 5.

[20] March 14, 1890.

[21] Bucknell University Archives.

Isaac Rieff

1868				
Feb 10	To 10 pie dishes			1 00
" "	To 1 stue ketel			1 15
" "	To 1 wash bason			55
" "	To 1 coffe pot stand			15
" "	To 2 dipper			20
" "	To 1 oil can			15
" "	To 1 culender			50
" 17	To 5 pie plates			50
"	To 2 coffee pot stand			30
" "	by 1 plank		75	00
	by 1 string of bells		1 50	00
	by 2 qts of wine		55	00
March 22	To 8¾ lbs sheet iron at 10cts			
	To 1 treet			
	2 lbs cirld hair			
J[illegible] 24	1 coffee pot stand			
	To 1 dipper			
Dec 24	Settled the above			
	To 2 frying pan			1 [illegible]
	To [illegible] pudding pans			2 [illegible]
	To [illegible] coffee pot			[illegible]
	by 1[illegible] lbs iron		[illegible] 50	00
	To 1 egg wip			1[illegible]
	1 mach safe			2[illegible]
	To [illegible] label spoons			7[illegible]
	To [illegible] tea spoons			2
Jan 1	by [illegible] & top props		[illegible] 90	

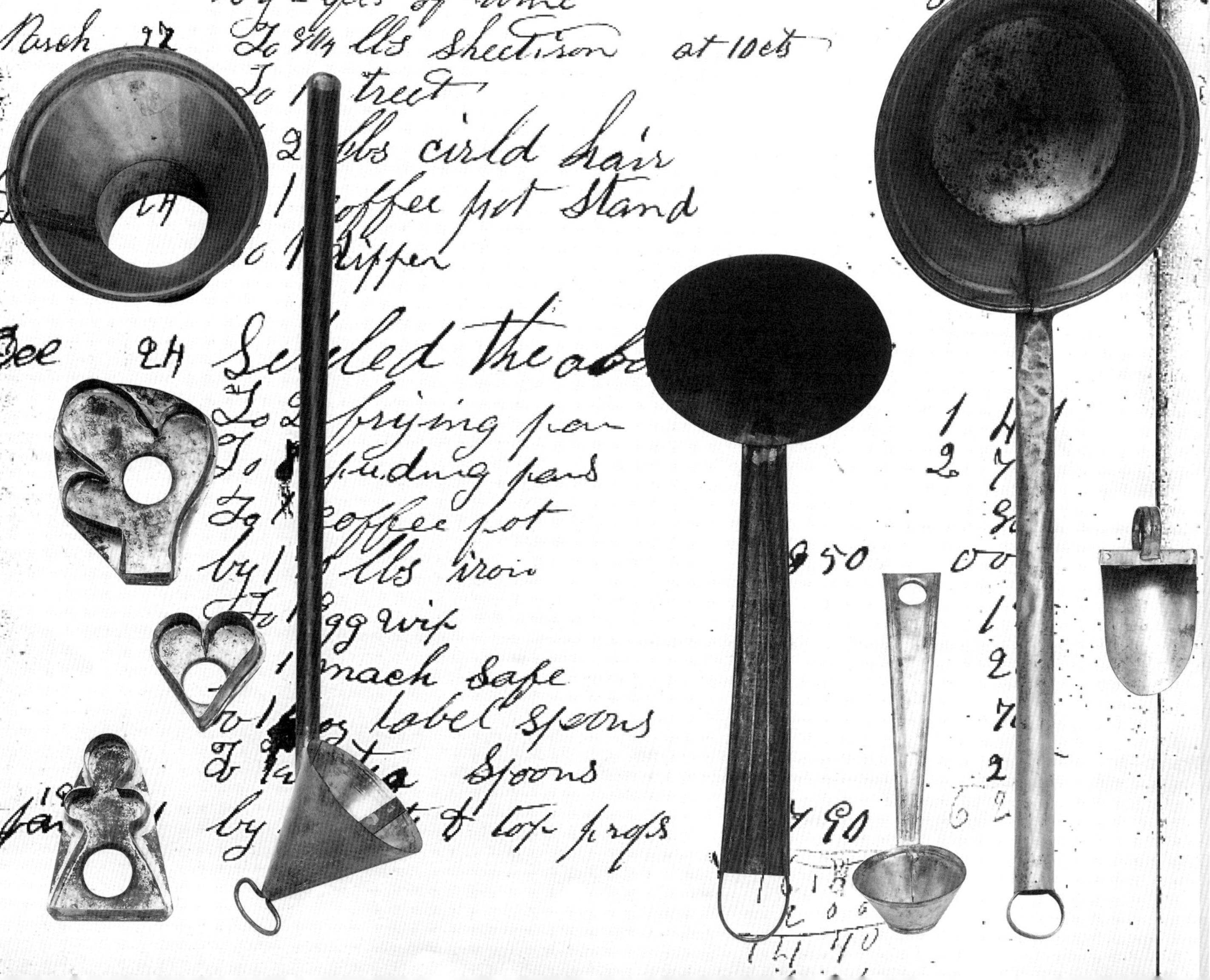

CHAPTER 14

SCHOOLS AND SCHOOL LIFE

One can only speculate upon the educational background of the pioneer generation in Union County. At the time of the colonial migration to America, the working classes, with few exceptions, were illiterate. On the other hand, the middle class — particularly the Calvinists, which included the English Puritans, the Scots-Irish Presbyterians, the French Huguenots, the German and Dutch Reformed, and the Pietists — placed a high value upon literacy as a key to the scriptures and an asset to business. The aristocracy, of course, could afford tutored instruction for their children, but few of them came to the New World.

As communities evolved in the Berks/Lancaster area, the seedbed for the settlement of Buffalo Valley, private subscription and church schools became available; but, in the absence of statutory regulations, attendance remained a personal matter. Furthermore, many Germans and Scots-Irish, in their quest for land, pushed beyond the settlements to a frontier remote from schools; and if the children were not instructed to read and write at home, they remained illiterate.

The Germans formed their own communities, with characteristics reminiscent of their former life in Europe. They spoke Pennsylvania German, popularly known as Pennsylvania Dutch, a southern German dialect most closely related to the dialects of the German Palatinate region. This Pennsylvania German, often studded with word borrowings from English, was the language of the schools in these communities until the statutes mandated that schools teach in English. Churches in these communities also maintained worship in German until the dearth of German-speaking ministers forced a switch to English. By that time, congregations could barely understand the classical European German that was the official church language, much like the Roman Catholic use of Latin; that German was quite different from their own Palatinate Pennsylvania German. The Old Order Amish and Old Order Mennonites continue to run their own parochial schools; and while Pennsylvania German is still spoken in Old Order Amish and Mennonite homes and communities, the schools teach only in English. Pennsylvania German can still be heard in the rural areas of Union County, among Amish and Mennonites and also among some of the elderly non-plain sect Pennsylvania Germans. Outsiders are often surprised to hear it at farmers markets and farm auctions throughout the county. Many older residents still recall that their parents and grandparents conversed in Pennsylvania German when they wished to keep subject matter from the prying ears of the younger generation.

When the problems involved in setting up educational institutions in a thinly populated region are considered, it is surprising to note the early appearance of several schools. It is recorded that Jane McClennan opened a school at Derr's Town (Lewisburg) in 1790, just five years after Ludwig Derr had laid out the village. Even more remarkable, the Reverend William Colbert, a Methodist circuit-rider, mentioned a school on the Barber farm at the still-remote White Springs in 1792. In 1795 Anna M. Smith of East Buffalo left 30 pounds in her will for a school for poor children; that school stood near the mouth of Turtle Creek for a number of years. In the same year, George Keister, Hartley's tenant, provided for the erection of a school on his land two miles west of Laurelton. It was known as the Keister or Kester School and later as the White School. Today the site can be identified by the small cemetery which was located adjacent to it.

By 1800 there were schools in White Deer, Buffalo and West Buffalo Townships as well as in New Berlin. Terms were short, and three months was probably typical. The income of teachers was meager — good enough to attract New England and New York teachers — but poor enough to require them to seek alternate employment during periods when the schools were not in session. With few exceptions the early teachers were males, a sizable portion of whom made teaching a steppingstone to law, medicine, theology, or political office. Their general knowledge and penmanship also fitted them to be scriveners and vendue clerks.

The best-remembered of the first generation of teachers was Flavel Roan, a native of Lancaster County of Scots-Irish descent and the son of a Presbyterian minister. Educated in the classics, he objected to his father's wishes that he study for the ministry, ran away from home when seventeen, and joined the Revolutionary Army. After serving seven years, he removed to Buffalo Valley and conducted a trading business near the mouth of Buffalo Creek. A gregarious bachelor possessing a quick mind, a ready wit, and high spirits, his social life was filled to overflowing. "He was the general scribe for the valley and clerk at the elections and public sales, wrote obituary and marriage notices for the newspapers, and attended social gatherings of the young people, where he was always a favorite."[1] Roan also engaged actively in politics. Appointed sheriff of Northumberland County in 1791 and commissioned in the same year as a notary public, he held the former position for three years and the latter until his death in 1817. Flavel Roan was twice elected to the state legislature and served as a commissioner of Northumberland County; and, after the separation of Union County from Northumberland, he became the commissioners' clerk of the former. His fine penmanship in the old records of the two counties is a model of excellence. From 1799 to 1806 Flavel Roan conducted an English and military school in Lewisburg. Rural folk found its spirited parades well worth a trip to town. Between 1807 and 1813, Roan headed an English school for boys and girls in a small building near Buffalo Creek, about two miles west of Lewisburg.

Except for the occasional appearance of his name in the old records, Roan might have been forgotten, but John Blair Linn found his journal invaluable and incorporated much material from it in his *Annals*.[2] Linn's quotations from Roan's diary provide not only many details from his busy — and at times exciting — life but unmatched vignettes of the social and political life of the times as well. Flavel Roan had much more to say about out-of-school hours than those in the classroom, and with regard to his country school experience he observed only:

March 18, 1809: Mr. [Roan] McClure's family, Richard Fruit and wife, Judge [W.M.] Wilson and wife, came to my school today to hear the boys speak.

August 23, 1809: Jamey Wilson hauled the stuff for the fence at my schoolhouse, and Cherry helped me put it up. Send Joseph Wallis for another bottle of whiskey for them.

October 8, 1810: Planted two lombardys at the schoolhouse.

But elsewhere his breadth of interests and zest rise from the pages of his diary over and over again:

Called at Giddy Smith's to get signers to the petition for a new county. . . . Ate cakes and drank cider with a number of young ladies and gentlemen at Granny Philips'. . . . Great horse race at Derrs Town. . . . A blazing star, like a comet, appeared in the north for some time. . . . Great ball at Baldy's . . . . Rode twenty-four miles, a good Sabbath-Day's journey. . . . Governor Snyder's Message of December 3rd 1811 is worthy of remark as containing an emphatic protest against slavery, and also a strong recommendation of the canal system. . . . Met Esquire Vincent, Esquire Brown, and Mr. Iredell on a road view. They are very jacose, sociable, and funny men. . . . Had psalm singing the old way [Presbyterian] at George Wood's, also prayers. He is a very religious man. . . . It commenced to rain as sermon closed, and we were kept there two hours.

In one of his gay moods Roan traced the title for a lot in Lewisburg back to the creation of the world and Adam and Eve. In another, when 34, he wrote a poem for the local newspaper asking for a bride:

I am an old man, my case is quite common,
I want me a wife, a likely young woman.
I late had an old one, but three years ago,
She sickened and died and left me in woe . . .
A girl that will warm my old bones in the winter,
Let them leave the intelligence with Mr. Printer.

When death removed the debonair bachelor from the Valley in 1817, it must have seemed that an essence of gaiety and spontaneity went with him.

The language of the early schools was usually English, but German subscription schools were founded in Mifflinburg and Lewisburg before 1810. There were also German schools by this time near the Dreisbach Church and at Buffalo Cross Roads. The one on Dreisbach Church Road seems to have been built about 1800, and John Betz may have been the first teacher. The building contained two rooms: one housing the school and the second housing the schoolmaster and his wife. At Buffalo Cross Roads, John Sierer and Christopher Baldy and their wives provided a plot just to the north of the intersection in 1807, and again Betz was the initial instructor. Some years later, after it had become a public school, the heirs of Sierer attempted to recover the money received by the directors from the sale of the property to the school district. They were not successful, and the receipts were used as an endowment adding a few weeks to the school term.

The fate of the German schools was predictable. With the passage of time, fewer students were conversant in German, and one by one they were closed or reorganized. The beginning of the end was evident in Lewisburg as early as 1809 when subscribers to the German school signed their names in English instead of German script.

A rivalry remained, however, between students who preferred Pennsylvania Dutch (German) and their counterparts who were reared in English-speaking homes, long after the last German school had closed. Samuel Ruhl of Swengel recalled in 1935 that in the White Springs area, students living on the Penns Creek side of the hamlet were of Pennsylvania German stock and attended the Cedar Run School — usually referred to as the "Dutch School" by the English-oriented families living on the north side of White Springs. Children of the latter usually attended the Barber School, identified by the "Dutch School" faction as the "British School." In the winter of 1868,

The cover and interior pages from *ABC and Reading Book* was published by Heinrich Fisher in New Berlin in 1848. From the collection of the Union County Historical Society.

young men from the two schools agreed to debate the subject, "Fire is more destructive than water," in the English language. The Cedar Run debaters adhered to the arrangement through the opening presentations, but, feeling that they were losing, switched to Pennsylvania Dutch in the rebuttals — to the obvious annoyance of their opponents. When the judges awarded the decision to Cedar Run, supporters of the Barber School could scarcely be restrained. To intensify their anger, a subsequent investigation revealed that two of the imported judges had decided German proclivities. Needless to add, plans for additional debates were dropped.

At least two secondary schools were offering English and classical studies by 1810. A tiny log cabin academy, financed by subscriptions, was opened in Lewisburg in 1805; and at Kelly Point the Reverend Thomas Hood, pastor of the Buffalo Presbyterian Church, was instructing nineteen boys in the classics. He continued the school for only a few years but during that time recruited the sons of the more prominent families in the region: Maclay, Wilson, Hayes, Graham, Potter, Clingan, Dougal, McClure, Wood, and Youngman.

Despite the proliferation of schools during the first third of the nineteenth century, many children were not enrolled, and the attendance at many others was erratic and limited to a few short terms. Aware of the inadequacies of educational endeavors, the framers of the state's Constitution of 1776 had inserted a provision for a school or schools in each county for the instruction of youths at public expense. The legislature, however, had not implemented it. The Constitution of 1790 reiterated the principle, but again the legislature failed to act. In 1809 a law, soon to be labeled the "pauper school law," was enacted. It instructed the assessors to ascertain the names of all families unable to pay for the schooling of their children. The parents could then send their children to school at public expense, provided that they would declare themselves paupers. Teachers recorded the attendance of these pupils and received two cents per student for each day of actual attendance from the county commissioners, who, in turn, added the cost to the local taxes.

A few lists of these children, with ages varying from five to twelve, appear in the assessors' reports. For example, White Deer Township had 21 poor children recorded in 1814; West Buffalo Township had 25 in 1820; Union Township, four in 1823 and Hartley Township, sixteen that same year; while in 1826 Kelly Township had seven and New Berlin twelve. The stigma of pauperism was detested, and parents frequently preferred to keep their children at home rather than publicly acknowledge their poverty. In 1834 it was estimated that in the entire state, only 17,500 of the eligible students were in school, while 250,000 were receiving no schooling.

Public dissatisfaction gave impetus to a public school movement initiated by the Pennsylvania Society for the Promotion of Public Schools and led by Philadelphia humanitarian and workingmen's societies. In 1829 Governor George Wolf placed himself squarely behind the movement in his first annual message, and he returned to the subject each year thereafter. In the 1833-1834 session, the legislature responded and fashioned a free, tax-supported, statewide system of public education with a provision that it be accepted or rejected by local option. The bill passed the legislature with little opposition, and Wolf signed it on April 1, 1834. It had not been a party issue, but it quickly took on a political significance, particularly in the German counties, where the double specter of taxation and the discarding of their mother tongue raised a storm of protest.

The reaction in Union County was typical. "The aristocratic school law" was denounced on the streets and at district and county rallies. Hundreds of signatures were appended to petitions demanding repeal. At a mass meeting in New Berlin, committees were

N.B. You are like wise to receive from the Parents the Names of all their Children between the ages of five and twelve years who resides within your township and whose Parents are unable to pay for their Schooling per act of Assembly passed the 4th of April 1809 and enter the same on a Separate Leaf in your duplicate

The local tax assessments listed the poor children in all the townships. Their education was supported by local tax money. This page from the tax assessments from 1809 included a memo on the enabling legislation. From the Union County Courthouse Archives.

organized to lead the campaign for repeal in the boroughs and townships, in addition to adopting resolutions which deplored the "unjust and unequal" taxation. For a state appropriation of $1,000, it was alleged that the county would have to raise $2,200 and each district would have to pay "at least $800" to build as many schools as six directors might think proper. Teachers' salaries would add hundreds of dollars to the total which would reach the staggering sum of $40,600 for the first year, "all to be paid by the people by various taxations."[3]

The ensuing vote — with two exceptions — was all that the proponents of repeal could have asked for. Only White Deer Township and Lewisburg endorsed the law — the former by a 52-26 vote and the latter by 71-55, with the comparatively small German vote in these districts presumably making passage possible. Mifflinburg rejected public education by a margin of 67-41; Hartley (including Lewis) Township, by 144-30; Kelly Township, by 70-7; West Buffalo (including Buffalo and Limestone) Township, by 187-7; East Buffalo Township, by 87-3; and Union Township, which straddled Penns Creek, by 205-0. If White Deer needed plaudits from a neighbor, it received them from the *Miltonian* across the river: "The little township of White Deer has contracted with a mechanic for the building of five schoolhouses — all to be built of brick and to be 25 x 30 feet. Go ye and do likewise!"[4]

The momentum of repeal in Union County swept the local incumbent members of the legislature from office and replaced them with anti-school leaders: Isaac Slenker in the Senate, and Ner Middlesworth and John Montelius in the House. At Harrisburg a bill for repeal passed the Senate and was taken up for consideration by the House. It was at this juncture that Thaddeus Stevens experienced his finest hour as a Pennsylvania legislator. After his impassioned defense of public education, the repeal was defeated, and Stevens won the sobriquet, "Savior of the Public Schools." Behind the scenes Governor Wolf and others also had a hand in saving the school law, and Stevens' role may have been exaggerated. In any event, instead of repealing the law, the House membership strengthened it, and the Senate finally reversed itself and accepted it also.

In Union County, however, Stevens' heroics did not signal a turnabout. Most districts continued to reject the option for two, three, four or more years; in several districts where it had been accepted, it was turned down in subsequent referenda. However, time was on the side of public education, and the state softened the opposition by making its subsidies cumulative, thus permitting a district to pick up the sums it had rejected in previous years. By 1840 a district could obtain $6 per taxable by levying a tax of 60¢ upon each taxpayer; but if it refused, the money would go back into the state's school fund. Most districts succumbed, a lesson not lost upon the state and federal governments in the twentieth century.

As the school law was accepted, the villages sometimes took over the older subscription schools; but in the rural areas acceptance precipitated building programs. Most of the buildings, new as well as old, however, were crude log structures, poorly lighted and poorly heated. Floors were apt to be bare earth at the outset, but plank floors were added later, and stoves replaced fireplaces. Samuel G. Frey recalled the first use of coal in a stove in the school on the turnpike just to the east of Vicksburg in 1849, an experi-

The Fairfield School picture was taken on January 24, 1895. C. Dale Wolf was the teacher, and he posed with his pupils in the well-appointed classroom/schoolhouse. From the collection of the Union County Historical Society, #89.5.3.9.A.

ment which proved to be a learning experience for students and teacher alike, since neither had seen a coal stove before. The teacher was unable to light the coal and after several attempts transferred it from the fire box to the ash pit below, with the same results. The children, meanwhile, passed an uncomfortable day. He discarded the coal for a time and returned to the wood box for his fuel; but later, almost by chance, he discovered that a roaring wood fire would ignite a few chunks of the black stuff. The laborious wood chopping ceased, and the teacher and scholars were won over to coal.

Furnishings in the early schools were almost as primitive as the exteriors. Along the unplastered walls, pins were inserted in the logs to hold planks which served as desks. Benches were split logs mounted on stout legs. Children thus faced the wall, their backs visible to the teacher despite the murky atmosphere. The schools were set on small plots of land, usually without playgrounds. Once the buildings were in use, little thought was given to repairs or improvements, with the result that the primitive structures became even less desirable with the passage of time.

The teachers were apt to be male New England itinerants, capable of instructing reading, writing,

and ciphering. If his qualifications were questionable, the teacher would be tested by a local minister. Directors could save money by having the teacher board and lodge with residents of the neighborhood, and they could offer country produce in lieu of cash; but both practices were unpopular with teachers. Whatever the arrangement, wages were low — $8-10 a month in the early years or $25 for a term of 27 days.

It was essential that the teacher maintain strict discipline — sometimes with the rod — to maintain orderly procedure, for his or her attention had to be focused upon the recitation group, seated on benches near the center, while other age groups remained at their stations. A day's routine could include as many as four reading and four spelling recitations with some ciphering in between. Some schools were identified as difficult to manage, and disciplinarians would be transferred to these to restore order. O.L.B. Thompson is recalled by older rural residents as an able teacher and lover of music, who made his school a "singing school," but he is also remembered for his ability to restore tranquillity to a "tough" school. In 55 years Thompson moved more than 30 times and taught in nineteen schools — almost always as a trouble shooter.

Perhaps the longest step forward taken during the century of one-room schools was the provision for county superintendents of schools. Until that time there had been almost no supervision except that given by the local lay boards, whose focus was frequently upon cost saving rather than standards; but, beginning in 1854, superintendents were made responsible for the general supervision of the public schools. The position required leadership, tact, patience, dogged perseverance, and unusual durability. The challenge faced by J.S. Whitman, the county's first superintendent of schools, is reflected in his first annual report:

I gave public notice when and where I would meet directors of the various districts of the county for the purpose of examining teachers and others designing to enter the profession. Some of the meetings were well attended, but I regret to say that in three districts, neither teachers, directors, nor spectators were to be found.

In these meetings I endeavored to explain the design of the new phase of the law, and to enlist the cooperation of the directors, and people in carrying out their provisions. The examinations were always made public, and conducted in such a manner as to satisfy myself of the requirements of the applicants, and also to interest and satisfy their employers. . . . I have examined 184 teachers: males 172, females 12.

Many of the schools which I have visited, I am compelled to say, are far from what the friends of education and progress could wish them to be. Among the obstacles in the way of their improvement, the most prominent are — insufficient salaries of teachers, and too short the time of their employment; the use of improper books, indifference on the part of parents, and irregular attendance.

Whitman and his successors continued to combat these roadblocks to quality education through the years which followed. Whitman's tenure was limited to a single year — he later became a distinguished professor at Farmers' High School (Pennsylvania State University) and a county superintendent of schools in Kansas — and it remained for his successor, David H. Heckendorn (1855-1863), to establish the working relationship between the superintendent and the schools. His acceptance by the latter in his almost daily visitations is suggested in his correspondence with a young niece:

January 10, 1860: Shall I tell you of the 3850 boys and girls in our visits to our public schools? How I am dreaded by some and entreated by others to revisit their schools. See me enter a school of 60 or 65 little children. Little hands go up requesting help in their lessons, to which I gladly respond. Now go with me to the next school and you find the children frightened as a flock of sheep when a stray dog comes among them. What makes the difference in feeling? That question I cannot answer at present. Perhaps you can guess. [5]

A comparison of the conditions in the schools in 1862 with previous decades, as viewed through his annual report, reveals solid progress. The buildings constructed that year were larger and higher than the early ones and built of brick rather than logs; each had three large windows on both sides and a ventilator extending into the bell tower; there was a coal stove at the center of the room, and a blackboard extended the length of the back wall. The more adequate and comfortable classrooms were attracting more parental visitation, and the children complained less frequently of headaches. With but several exceptions, the schools were now supplied with double desks, and all of them had blackboards. Globes, maps, and charts were still lacking in most of the buildings. The larger schools had been graded during the past seven years; and in New Columbia directors were erecting a double building, which would permit the graded system.

In the course of the year, Heckendorn had traveled 1,095 miles, most of them on foot, and had made 188 school visits and examined 105 teachers. In the same period district institutes had been held in Buffalo, West Buffalo, Lewis, Hartley, Kelly, and White Deer Townships. They had all been successful and were "the most efficient agents to overcome the prejudice still existing in some localities against new measures intended to improve the conditions of the schools." The superintendent noted that he had been unable to attend all of them since he reserved Saturdays for teachers and others who wished to consult with him in his office.

Heckendorn also presided over the first annual county-wide teachers' institute in 1855. At these gatherings outstanding local teachers shared the platform with visiting educators during the morning and afternoon; evening sessions were devoted to music and literature. Frances Willard was the principal attraction at the institute of 1859, and other notables appeared in the years which followed.

In evaluating teachers, Heckendorn included both oral and written examinations, varying them from year to year as he searched for better methods. He found that the female applicants had higher qualifications than males and were more zealous in their work, yet he believed that a majority of them accomplished less. Perhaps his views reflected the conservatism of the German counties in accepting female teachers. In counties with an English ethnic origin, more than one-half of the teachers were women; but in the German counties the number was much smaller. In 1862 there were 58 men and 27 women teaching in

Union County, with possibly the shortage of manpower during the Civil War making the difference. In Snyder County there were eleven males for each female. Summer schools were held in Buffalo, West Buffalo, and Kelly Townships; but there were objections to them in other districts because, it was argued, the poor needed their children at home and should not be taxed to educate children whose parents could afford to send them to school. The strength of this argument can be seen in the prevalence of subscription schools in the summer months, ranging from 33 to 40 in the county.

The "boarding 'round" of teachers had been abandoned by 1862; but when visiting schools somewhat remote from his home in New Berlin, Heckendorn frequently found hospitality among his friends, terming the practice "a social institution that merits my highest commendation." In his statistical report, Superintendent Heckendorn noted that there were 75 schools in the county; the average term was five months; the average salary per month was $24.39 for male teachers and $16.98 for females; there were 3,888 pupils, 2,151 of them boys and 1,737 girls; the average daily attendance was 2,583; the average cost per pupil per month was 51¢; and teaching in German had been discontinued.[6] After completing his report, Heckendorn resigned to become a photographer with the Army of the Potomac. He was captured by the Confederates and taken to a Richmond prison, but he was later paroled and returned to his home, where he died after a short illness. A tribute in his obituary testifies to his service for education:

All who knew him well will be witness that he was a most faithful, energetic, and efficient officer, beloved and esteemed for his many noble qualities of heart and mind, by every true teacher in the county. How eagerly we used to look for his visits to our school, and how the little eyes sparkled and the little faces brightened as he entered the schoolroom . . . Teachers, your old leader has laid down his armor! Toil on faithfully, as he did to advance the cause of Universal Education.

During the regimes of John A. Owens and C. Van Gundy, the post-Civil War boom facilitated the erection of new buildings. Owens termed Brady (Gregg) Township's brick structures a source of pride, and he also commended Lewis and Limestone Townships for their building programs. In this period, also, the towns provided facilities to grade their schools. Lewisburg, for example, had two grammar, two intermediate, two secondary, and four primary schools; Mifflinburg had a high school as well as one each grammar, intermediate, secondary, and primary schools; New Berlin had three and Hartleton two

Oaklyn School was closed in the 1930s after serving children of school age for nearly 70 years. It is located at the rear service gate to the Northeastern Federal Penitentiary on the Colonel John Kelly Road and has been converted into a private home. From the collection of Gary M. and Donna W. Slear.

A winter scene of the Mifflinburg High School taken c. 1914 and issued as a real photo postcard by Grover Bierly. From the collection of the Union County Historical Society #85.7.5.

graded schools; while Green Grove in Limestone Township and New Columbia had made a start in that direction. Elsewhere the county schools remained ungraded.

The school directors chose another outstanding educator in 1872, when they named Albin S. Burrows as county superintendent. Born in England, reared in Susquehanna County, and a graduate of Bloomsburg Normal School, Burrows taught in Illinois, New York, and Delaware before coming to Union County. Between school assignments, he had fought with the

Army of the Potomac and ridden with General Custer in the Shenandoah Valley of Virginia. Like Heckendorn he was captured and incarcerated in Libby Prison, where he remained until the war's end.

Burrows was a dynamic and articulate speaker as well as an indefatigable worker, and it was once said that no officer in the state devoted himself more scrupulously or zealously to his duties. He found the schools in Mifflinburg antiquated and overcrowded, and he was largely responsible for the movement which led to the building of the stately Victorian edifice there in 1876. He encouraged young teachers to make a career of the profession rather than a stepping-stone to another, and he induced directors to adopt a coordinated series of schoolbooks and to purchase unabridged dictionaries. Burrows' wife, Fannie, a native of Montrose, was also an outstanding teacher and administrator. She opened a select school for girls in the academy building in Mifflinburg in 1874, and this was soon accepted as a model. Both wife and husband participated actively in the county and district teachers' institutes. After serving as county superintendent for ten years, Burrows resigned to enter business in Grand Forks, North Dakota.

Between 1895 and 1908, the county's schools were guided by Daniel P. Stapleton, another gifted teacher and administrator. A native of East Buffalo Township, whose parents had come from Berks County by canal, Stapleton was a farm boy who began a teaching career while picking up an education, course by course, when school was not in session. He attended Central Pennsylvania College in New Berlin and eventually graduated from Mansfield Normal School. After teaching in several county schools, Stapleton obtained a position in the Boys' Grammar School in Lewisburg (1879-1885), where he importuned the school board to create a coeducational high school. The board acceded in 1886, despite strong objections from opponents of coeducation. Young Benjamin K. Focht characterized the result as "Mr. Stapleton's triumph over public opinion."[7] Stapleton was named as the school's first principal, and under his guidance the coeducational institution was soon accepted. He was later elected county superintendent and served for four terms.

Residents of the county can still recall Stapleton's visits to the schools, his love of history, and his popular tales of old Union County. The sound of his horse and buggy as he entered the school yard was the signal for another stirring chapter. During his tenure in 1893, free textbooks were provided for the children of the state, a policy which was particularly advantageous to rural children, many of whom had been handicapped by their inability to buy the textbooks prescribed by the directors.

In 1908 Stapleton was defeated for reelection by William W. Spigelmyer, another exceptional teacher. Spigelmyer, too, was a farm boy who taught in the country schools of the area while earning his way through college. He graduated from Susquehanna University in 1900 with honors. Accepting a position in the Lewis Grammar School, he upgraded it to a high school in his first year and remained as its principal for the next seven years. As county superintendent, Spigelmyer enriched the courses of study and broadened community services. Gregg High School was organized at this time, and the initial step toward consolidation was taken when Hartley Township transported some of its pupils to Laurelton. In his annual report in 1912, Spigelmyer hailed the organization of the county's first Parent-Teacher Association as a milestone in school-community relations. He also commended the work of the county's first women school directors in Lewisburg: "In every phase of their new duties they have performed them with ability; in fact it would be hard to find more progressive directors anywhere."

Dr. Frank P. Boyer, an inspiring teacher and progressive educator, was still another county superintendent (1930-1954) who was steeped in the lore of the county. Amidst the tedious and controversial details of the school consolidation process, Boyer made time to revive the moribund Union County Historical Society, collect hundreds of memoirs from former teachers and students, and write a comprehensive history of public education in the county.

Running through the administrations of Union County's superintendents for a full century was their continuing struggle for both quality and quantity. The two goals were interrelated; longer terms made possible a greater pupil achievement, and higher salaries encouraged teachers to remain in the profession and to use the summers for self-improvement. By 1920 the school term had been increased to eight months in the country and nine months in the towns.

The Public School Law of 1834 was a boon to elementary education, but it did little for teenage boys and girls. This need was met after a fashion by academies and select schools for girls. The former provided a classical background for the ministry or the other professions, and a broader curriculum, including mathematics, science, and bookkeeping, for careers in business. Mifflinburg had an academy in

1829; Lewisburg, the Brick or Randolph Academy in 1839 and the Academy at the college in 1849; and New Berlin, Union Seminary in 1856. Meanwhile, Maria Geddes opened a select school in Lewisburg in 1835, and the Reverend P.B. Marr headed another between 1852 and 1857. The Female Institute, associated with the University at Lewisburg, was founded in 1852 and moved to the lower campus in 1858. It admitted a few boys at the outset, but the "convulsion" overturned coeducation for nearly 30 years. New Berlin and Mifflinburg also had select female schools at mid-century.

Two developments of the public schools during the second half of the nineteenth century formalized their secondary offerings. The first was the grammar school, introduced in Lewisburg, Mifflinburg, and Hartleton in the 1860s, and in the 1890s in Cowan, Mazeppa, and Lewis Township. In Mazeppa, for example, a student could elect algebra, physical geography, American literature, advanced civics, single-entry bookkeeping, geometry, and beginning Latin — subjects ordinarily reserved for secondary schools. As mentioned above, Lewisburg's high school was founded in 1886; Mifflinburg's opened its doors two years later and the following spring had its first graduating class of three. Lewis Township saw the inception of a high school in 1902 and Hartley Township in 1904; meanwhile, students in Gregg, White Deer and Kelly Townships were crossing the river to matriculate in Watsontown and Milton high schools. It should be noted, however, that the number of high school students remained small for many years. With a general population in Lewisburg of more than 3,000 in 1916, the high school had a graduating class of but nineteen.

Pupils who did not go to high school sometimes remained in the elementary or grammar schools from year to year after completing the eighth grade, receiving additional instruction at the discretion of the teacher and occasionally assisting with the instruction of the younger pupils. After thus marking time for several years, these students sometimes enrolled in the neighboring high school at the "advanced" age of sixteen or seventeen.

The availability of auto transportation in the 1920s substantially increased the number of country boys and girls in the high schools, while the addition of domestic science (home economics or homemaking), industrial arts, and agriculture in the 1930s and 1940s helped retain many more in the schools. A great change — probably the most revolutionary in the history of the county's public schools — occurred during the 1940s and 1950s when more than 70 schools were consolidated into nine, and fifteen districts into four.

The attachment of country and village people to their local schools and their reluctance to lose them scarcely needs documentation. Many one-room schools had existed, frequently on the same sites, for a century or more, and as many as four generations of the same families had attended them. While people resisted for a time, they could not long withstand the pressure of centralization emanating from the state capital, and the promise of an enriched program partially subsidized by the commonwealth gradually wore down the opposition. Consolidation began in Hartley Township in 1917, when the directors erected an annex to the building in Laurelton and bused the pupils of the township to it; this led to the closing of the Pike, Pine Grove, White, Centre Point, Lincoln, and Feese Schools over the course of several years; the Glen Iron school was thus eliminated in 1930, and the Hironimous school, the most distant from Laurelton, in 1942. East Buffalo built a new elementary school in Linntown in 1934 and consolidated the Fairfield, Riverside (Gundy), and Fairmount Schools in the new structure, and an addition to the consolidated school in 1941 permitted the closing of the older one-room Linntown School across the road.

In 1947 the General Assembly mandated jointures to provide rural children with a high school education, leaving the details to the district school directors and the implementation to the county superintendents of schools. Dr. Frank P. Boyer had been elected county superintendent in 1930 after serving as a teacher and administrator in the county for fifteen years. An innovative and resourceful teacher and administrator, he tackled the problem with his usual vigor and enthusiasm — aware that no plan would fully satisfy the various sections of the county.

A tentative proposal to create a single administrative unit, with one senior high school, presumably between Lewisburg and Mifflinburg, two junior high schools in Lewisburg and Mifflinburg, and six elementary schools in Lewisburg, Mifflinburg, New Berlin, Laurelton, White Deer Township, and Buffalo Township, was discarded when three of the districts dissented. After a county-wide hearing early in 1950 failed to break the deadlock, nine of the twelve districts represented at the meeting, Buffalo, West Buffalo, Hartley, Lewis, and Limestone Townships, and the boroughs of Hartleton, Mifflinburg, and New Berlin, together with Union Independent District, agreed to organize the Western Area Joint School District. The plan called for a new junior-senior high school in Mifflinburg, new elementary schools at Laurelton, Buffalo Cross Roads and New Berlin, and the remodeling and

The pupils of the Sandel School, Union Township 1932-33. Front row: "Tiny" Hess, Ruth Berge, Mary Alice Roush, Martha Felmey and Wilma Reitz; 2nd row: Marguerite Bailey, Mildred Sandel, Geneva Hess, and Doris Geise; 3rd row: Martin Felmey, Ethelene Bailey, Madelene Felmey, Doris Roush, and Mark Berge; top row: Tennyson Reitz and Lester Willow. Their teacher, Carolyn Roller, is not pictured but signed the photograph. From the collection of the Union County Historical Society, gift of George F. Sandel.

The Scholars Monthly Reports of Raymond Kline for English in the Lewisburg High School. From the collection of the Union County Historical Society, gift of George F. Sandel.

enlargement of the 1876 building in Mifflinburg. Buffalo Township, stretching almost all the way from Lewisburg to Mifflinburg, was won over to the agreement by an arrangement permitting their secondary students to choose either the Lewisburg or Mifflinburg schools. The merger closed the old Hartleton and New Berlin Schools as well as the Laurelton Consolidated School; in Limestone Township, the White Springs and Green Grove Schools; in Union Township, the Union Independent School; in West Buffalo Township, the Creek, Red Bank, Forest Hill, Centennial, and Rand Schools; in Buffalo Township, the Steans, Black Run, Buffalo Cross Roads, Mazeppa, and Reed Schools; and in Lewis Township, the Salem, Spring Creek, Pike, Millmont, and Swengel Schools as well as the Lewis Township High School.

At that time, the Pike School was housed in the east side of the Lewis Township High School. The original Pike School was located on the south side of Route 45 about half a mile west of the Ray's Church. It burned in 1929, due to a chimney fire. At the time, rather than construct a new building, the decision was made to utilize the vacant side of the high school building. That room became vacant when the high school was downgraded to a two-year school. The children were bused to a new location; and the bus driver, Henry Moll, who owned the bus and a local dairy, would deliver milk to some customers along the bus route. On the same route, high school students were picked up. More high school students from Millmont and Swengel were met at the high school, and all were transported to Mifflinburg for their last two years of high school. The jointure ended that busing arrangement. It also ended an arrangement whereby rural school students could take an examination, given by the county superintendent, and go on to high school if they passed the examination. Under this system, some students had entered high school at a rather early age without completing all grades.

Professor Boyer retired in 1954 due to ill health and was succeeded by W. Earl Thomas, the supervising principal of the Mifflinburg schools. He at once found himself involved in the twisting currents of consolidation.

Meanwhile, between 1951 and 1952, East Buffalo and Union Townships agreed to a jointure, whereby the latter's elementary students would be bused to the Linntown school. The action led to the closure of the Trutt, Eyre, Sandel, and Winfield Schools. In 1956 Kelly Township formed a jointure with Lewisburg in which Kelly obtained an elementary school, and shortly thereafter the East Buffalo district fell into line.

The school bus used by Lewis Township pupils. Courtesy of Nessie Watson.

Kelly Township School's twelfth Commencement program from 1907. Admission of five and ten cents was charged. From the collection of Harold Danowsky.

KELLY TOWNSHIP SCHOOLS

—‡—

DIRECTORS

J. S. Pawling, President

E. E. Smith, Secretary

C. A. Noll, Treasurer

William Hoffman

C. A. Grove

U. C. Moore

—‡—

TEACHERS

G. O. Keiser

G. R. Cornelius

Mary Bucher

Mabel Farley

W. W. Ridge

S. R. Spotts

...PROGRAM...

March—''Nation's Honor,''...............Chas. E. Bronnell.
Invocation,...................... .....Rev. E. E. Weaver.
March—"Loop the Loop,''................ .....Jos. Thorne.
''Importance of Character and Reputation,''
Winifred Werkheiser.
''Buttoned Up People,''....................Mary Anna Lau.
"The Path to Success,''...........Effie Clara Peterson.
Serenade Waltz—"To Thee,''........... .....Otto J. Muller.
"Symbol of Americanism,''...........Dessie Mae Reedy.
''True Politeness,''....................Maud Ellen Arner.
''Benefits of Inventions and Discoveries,''
George Edwin Rhodes.
Overture—''Benefactor,''............................J. T. Heed.
''The Jamestown Exposition,''.....Miriam Ruth Hoffa.
''Pleasures of Home,''............. Lillie Augusta Lau.
Une Bagatelle Mazurka...........................P. V. Olker.
"Invasion of the Mongolians,'' Thomas Guy Hartman.
''Influence and the Power,'' ...... Carrie Jane Grugan.
March—''Diamond Flush,''............... Edmund Braham.
''The Value of Character,'' Carrie Elizabeth Fetzer.
Valedictory,......................... Miriam Ruth Hoffa.
Waltz—"Auf Weidersehn,''......................E. H. Bailey.
Presentation of Diplomas,
Prof. D. P. Stapleton, County Superintendent.
Concert—"Czardas Styuenne,''.................G. Michaels.
Benediction,..................................Rev. D. B. Lau.
Music by Progressive Orchestra, J. G. App, Mgr., Lewisburg, Pa.

Junior high school pupils were bused to a new school at Linntown and the high school students to Lewisburg Joint High School. The Kelly consolidation closed the Evangelical Orphanage, Pine Grove, Oakland, Spotts, and West Milton Elementary Schools. Kelly Township's decision to merge with Lewisburg was hard to accept by residents of the West Milton area, who had had close ties with Milton High School for many years.

Elsewhere, White Deer joined the Milton district, obtaining a new elementary school at New Columbia; Gregg Township, after wavering for a time between Montgomery and Watsontown, joined the latter; this jointure was later expanded to form the Warrior Run District. In the process White Deer closed the New Columbia, Washington, Leiser, Central, Ramsey, Yocum, and Factory Schools; and Gregg Township shut down the Allenwood, Wetzel, and Spring Garden Schools.

The solution to the enigma seemed in sight until 1963, when the legislature again threw the districts into a quandary by defining the minimum size of a district as 4,000 pupils. If enforced, the action would have eliminated both the eastern and western area districts and required the merger of the two. After a round of discussions, most of the district boards seemed prepared to accept the inevitable, but, again, the legislature changed the rules. The jointures were now slated for transformation into districts, with nine elective board members each; the Western Area Joint School District would be renamed the Mifflinburg Area School District, and the Eastern Area Joint District, the Lewisburg Area School District.

Buffalo Township, however, was again "caught in the middle." Its secondary students living in the Lewisburg "panhandle" were attending the eastern area high school (Lewisburg) and most of the others were enrolled at the western area high school (Mifflinburg). Buffalo district directors interpreted the changes as an opportunity to go back to a single district plan, but, failing to get the support of other districts and facing liquidation, the directors resolved on January 20, 1964 to become a part of the Western Area Joint School District. Their condition for acceptance was that after reorganization, the western district would "afford to all secondary school pupils in Buffalo Township the right and privilege to attend the Eastern Area Unit secondary schools on a tuition basis to be paid for by the Western Area Unit together with the costs of transportation." A few weeks later the Western Area Joint School Board found that proposal acceptable.

The May Queen at the Lewisburg High School in 1954. From the collection of the Union County Historical Society, #89.5.3.22.1-n.

In the course of the next several years, the newly-created Lewisburg and Mifflinburg Area School Districts became realities, and the old district boards were eliminated. In 1971 the directors of the Mifflinburg Area School Board sought to eliminate tuition payments for students in Buffalo Township who were attending the Lewisburg Area High School, but Buffalo residents went to court to prevent the action and won their suit, with Judge Charles W. Kalp ruling that the above-mentioned resolutions were binding upon the successor districts. Three years later, however, the Mifflinburg board appealed the decision in the Commonwealth Court and obtained a reversal. As a result, Buffalo Township students living in the periphery of Lewisburg are bused to the Mifflinburg Middle and Senior High Schools.

With consolidation reducing the districts wholly within the county from fifteen to two, each staffed with a superintendent, the office of county superintendent was phased out on July 13, 1974, and replaced by an intermediate unit, a multi-county regional organization. Union County became part of the Central Susquehanna Intermediate Unit, containing Columbia, Montour, Northumberland, Snyder, and

SUN Area Career & Technology Center , located in New Berlin, was formerly called SUN VO-TECH. Photo by Jim Walter.

Union Counties. The CSIU was headed by an executive director, Dr. Patrick Toole, an advisory council, and an elected board of directors starting in 1971. Unlike the county offices, the intermediate units were strictly service organizations charged with "developing a program of services to meet the educational needs of constituent school districts." The governing legislation for the intermediate units suggested providing services such as curriculum development, instructional improvement, research and planning, continuing professional education, as well as that the intermediate units act as a state and federal liaisons; later other tasks were added, such as aid to nonpublic schools and the collection of data, as well as being a conduit for information for and from the State's Department of Education. The administrative duties once performed by a county superintendent were now handled by the two district school superintendents.

The erection of the SUN Area Vocational Technical School in New Berlin in 1971 marked the culmination of a five-year effort to provide a more meaningful and relevant educational program for youths in an area comprising Snyder and Union Counties and the Shikellamy School District of Northumberland County (centered in Sunbury). Believing that a multi-district approach would facilitate an expanded vocational-technical offering, financially beyond the reach of a single district, the nineteen school districts of Snyder County joined with the two districts in Union County and the Shikellamy district to pool resources. During the negotiation stage, the consolidation of schools in Snyder County reduced the number of districts there to two, and by 1971 this cooperative venture — which was unique in the region — included West Snyder, Middleburg, Selinsgrove, Lewisburg, Mifflinburg, and Shikellamy High Schools.

Students who selected the SUN vocational-technical program entered it in the tenth grade and rotated (shifting every few weeks) from academic studies in their respective high schools to the course offerings of their choice at the vocational technical school. In 1974 they could choose from twenty courses, starting alphabetically with Agricultural Technology and ending with Welding. Courses were open to boys and girls alike, but the latter were concentrated in the apparel manufacturing, commercial art, cosmetology and dental assistant specializations. Just over 800 students, divided into two sections, were enrolled. In 1974 students in the various programs combined their training to construct a house on a lot in Chestnut Acres on Park Road in Monroe Township, Snyder County. The quality of the workmanship elicited a host of bids when it was subsequently offered for sale. This combination of academic and technical education helped to meet a nationwide need as the third quarter of the century closed.

ENDNOTES:

[1] R.V.B. Lincoln, *Mifflinburg Telegraph*, October 18, 1901.

[2] John Blair Linn, *Annals of Buffalo Valley, Pennsylvania, 1755-1855*, Harrisburg, 1877.

[3] Dr. G.G. Groff, "Early Schools in Union County," reporting a meeting on September 23, 1834, *Lewisburg Saturday News*, April 29, 1905.

[4] *Milton Miltonian*, May 2, 1835.

[5] Dr. Frank P. Boyer Papers, Union County Historical Society.

[6] County Superintendent David H. Heckendorn's *Annual Report of 1862*.

[7] *Lewisburg Saturday News*, May 15, 1886.

CHAPTER 15

WOMEN THROUGH THE PASSING GENERATIONS

Unlike the Gold Rush to California, in which men were predominate, the migration to Union County was by families, with wives and daughters arriving simultaneously with husbands and sons. Unfortunately, surviving records have little to say about the role of women in the process. Census reports, assessment rolls, and military and legal documents are almost entirely in the masculine gender. The early newspapers virtually ignored women as well; the few columns reserved for local news related primarily political and business matters, in which women had almost no part. Marriages and deaths among the more prominent families were apt to be newsworthy, but births were seldom mentioned.

Fortunately, descendants of the pioneer generation, impressed by the contributions of their ancestors in founding a civilization in the wilderness, acted in time to save some of the details. In this respect historians are thankful to John Blair Linn, Richard V.B. Lincoln, and the publishers of the *History of the Susquehanna and Juniata Valleys* and the *Commemorative Biographical Record of Central Pennsylvania*. While their treatment of women was typically peripheral, they did incorporate considerable genealogical detail.

The old land titles supply the given names of hundreds of the wives of sellers of property, not because they handled the sales or the money, but because the law required the signature or mark of the wife, given after she had sworn before a justice of the peace that she had not been coerced to give her consent to the transaction by her husband. The diary of Flavel Roan provides brief references to the women of his generation; and researchers for the descendants of Revolutionary War soldiers can find the names of wives in service and pension records. Speculation upon the influence of women in the founding of early churches and schools, and in the abolition and temperance movements brings more questions than answers.

There are exceptions. The most notable woman in the Revolutionary War generation was the widow Catherine Smith, who ran a gristmill and gun-boring shop at White Deer despite harassment from mortgagors and hostile Indians. Her contemporary, Mary Quigley Brady, was the wife of Captain John Brady, and mother of Samuel, James, and John — all Revolutionary War heroes and Indian fighters. Mary Brady is remembered for her stoic refusal to take refuge in her old Cumberland County home and her insistence upon remaining with her family when

Buffalo Valley became a bloody battleground. Brady survived the death of her husband on the battlefield and the scalping of James, and lived until peace was restored and the Indians were driven away. Her death occurred on October 20, 1873, a few months after the restoration of peace.

A generation later, Jane McClennan of Lewisburg was probably the first school teacher in Buffalo Valley at a time when the other teachers in the area were males. Later, women were accepted as teachers in the public schools, but they were usually paid less than men and assigned to the short terms which were shunned by their male competitors. Widows occasionally managed small businesses or did sewing, spinning, or weaving on a piece-work basis in their homes. Once the Sunday school movement spread through the county in the 1830s, women were entrusted with the training of the children. They could also qualify as organists and sing in the choirs, once these innovations became a part of the church services; but they never were allowed to serve on church boards or participate in annual meetings.

A few women joined their husbands to hear the itinerant abolitionists in Lewisburg, New Berlin, and Mifflinburg, risking the unpopularity of their neighbors, who frequently regarded abolitionists as troublemakers. Several Lewisburg women may have heard Miller McKim, a lecturer for abolition in 1837. A "small riot" occurred several days later when a second lecture was proposed.[1] The mere eight votes given to James G. Birney, the Liberty (Abolition) nominee for president in 1844, by Lewisburg voters emphasizes the weakness of the movement. Even so, at least three places in Lewisburg served as "stations" on one of the routes of the Underground Railroad, the system of paths taken by fugitive slaves during their escape from bondage in the South to freedom in Canada, in the years prior to the Civil War. Lucy Bliss recalled many years later that she had made up beds in a barn behind her home on University Avenue, where fugitive slaves were sequestered while awaiting the next segment of their northward journey. Her father, Professor George R. Bliss, along with Professor Thomas F. Curtis and President Howard Malcom of the College at Lewisburg, were credited with instituting the "railroad" in this area.[2]

The Civil War opened opportunities for women denied to them in less troublesome times. Beyond supplying the armed forces with bedding, hospital supplies, and foodstuffs, women filled vacancies in the federal departments heretofore closed to them. Margaret P. Steese succeeded her husband as postmaster in Mifflinburg in 1861 and held the office for eight years; a decade later Julia Steadman followed her husband in the same position, retaining it for ten years. Women also obtained the right to vote for the officers in some of the local churches in this period, although officeholding itself would await the coming of the twentieth century.

At least six young women left the county to serve as war nurses — another opportunity for their gender. Melinda Spigelmyer of Hartleton worked at the St. Elizabeth Hospital for Insane Soldiers in Washington. Sara Dysart, Annie Bell, and Sallie Chamberlain, students at the Female Seminary of the University at Lewisburg, departed together for duty with the 12th Army Corps and served at Harper's Ferry, Nashville, and Gettysburg; and Dysart received a corps citation for bravery. Belle Vorse and Lida Houghton, residents of Lewisburg, found employment at the military headquarters at Nashville, Tennessee.

Despite the shackling effects of the Victorian psyche, women did not lose all of the gains won during the war. The temperance movement, which they had shared as silent partners with their husbands in the 1840s and 1850s, had been a casualty of the conflict; but, by the 1870s the crusade was renewed with increased vigor. Leadership remained a male prerogative during this time, when the goal was prohibition through local option and regeneration rather than a statewide "Maine Law." In 1873 the legislature permitted each county to reach a decision through a referendum, and Union County went "dry." The boroughs, obviously more friendly toward temperance than rural areas, piled up substantial majorities for prohibition, whereas most of the townships rejected it. Finding that no provision had been made to handle offenders, a prosecuting committee was elected. However, before enforcement had progressed very far, the legislature repealed the law, and the question was turned over to the local courts, which could grant or withhold licenses for the sale of alcoholic beverages, basing their decision upon the sentiment of the local populace.

Hartleton was the first to respond. Sixteen residents signed a remonstrance against issuing liquor licenses in the borough; the pro-license faction could not match it, and the community was thus "entitled to the banner." In 1879 the anti-license party in

---

PROGRAM

of the

Forty-Ninth Annual Convention

Union County Women's Christian Temperance Union

United Evangelical Church, New Columbia, Pa.

THURSDAY, SEPTEMBER 14th, 1933

* * * * *

OFFICERS

President.....................................Mrs. Jennie M. Follmer, Lewisburg
Vice President..................... ....Mrs. Romeyn Rivenburg, Lewisburg
Corresponding and Recording Secretary, Miss Maud C. Kaup, Vicksburg
Treasurer...................................Miss Blanche Speigelmeyer, Vicksburg

PROGRAM—THURSDAY, 2 P. M.

Praise Service............................Led by Mrs. R. F. Heiser, New Columbia
Devotions...Mrs. Annie Rooke, Winfield
Roll Call by Recording Secretary:
          Officers and Directors
          Presidents and Delegates
          Reading of Minutes
Appointment of Committees:
          Courtesies
          Press
          Membership
Words of Greeting...........................Mrs. Francis Farley, New Columbia
Response.........................Mrs. Elwood Hoffman, West Milton
Report of Corresponding Secretary...........Miss Maud C. Kaup, Vicksburg
Report of Treasurer.....................Miss Blanche Speigelmeyer, Vicksburg
Report of Flower Missions................Mrs. Harry Thomas, Lewisburg
Report of Department of Temperance and Missions:
          Mrs. Wm. G. Owens, Lewisburg
Report of Scientific Temperance Instruction, Mrs. Wm. Erdley, Vicksburg

MEMORIAL SERVICE

In Charge of...Mrs. C. A. Kniss, Mifflinburg
Election of Officers:
Supper,...............................Served by Ladies of Hostess Union at 5:30 P. M.

EVENING SESSION—7:30 P. M.

Devotions..Rev. B. F. Heiser, New Columbia
Music: Girls' Saxaphone Ensemble of Evangelical Orphanage, Lewisburg
Address: Dr. A. A. Winter, Superintendent of the Evangelical Home
Music: Girls' Saxaphone Ensemble of Evangelical Orphanage, Lewisburg
Collection
Benediction.

Mifflinburg overwhelmed the "wets" in the battle for signatures, and licenses for the Deckard and Showers hotels were denied. The Hartleton and Mifflinburg contests hold particular interest because they reveal the expanding role of women in the movement. In the former, women not only joined the local temperance union but were elected to several of the offices, and in Mifflinburg they signed and circulated anti-license petitions with an unprecedented vigor. Of the 400-plus signatures submitted by the anti-license faction, more than one-half were those of women.[3]

In the late 1870s women and children joined their husbands and fathers in "Bush Meetings," which were organized by the clergy to redeem the drunkards and extract abstinence pledges from the better-disciplined

he W.C.T.U. of Lewisburgh, being the only one
the County, called a meeting of all the ladies
the County who were interested in the work of
mperance. The pastors of the various churches
e requested to appoint two ladies as delegates.

The meeting was held at Lewisburgh on
sday. Sept. 30th 1884.
Mrs. Dr. Loomis. of Lewisburgh was called to the
in. and Mrs. A. E. Waffle appointed Sec. pro. tem.
motion was made and carried that all ladies
esent be considered delegates. and entitled to
ote.

The question of organizing a County Convention
in arose. and a motion was made and unan-
mously carried that such a Convention be organ-
ed.

The Constitution of the W.C.T.U. was read
d Unanimously adopted.
The Convention then proceeded to the election
officers with the following result:—

TOP AND PAGE 260: An entry in the Woman's Christian
Temperance Union (WCTU) minute book and program.
From the collection of the Union County Historical Society,
#2000.3.1-2.

Temperance map as it appeared in the *Mifflinburg Telegraph* of
March 24, 1914.

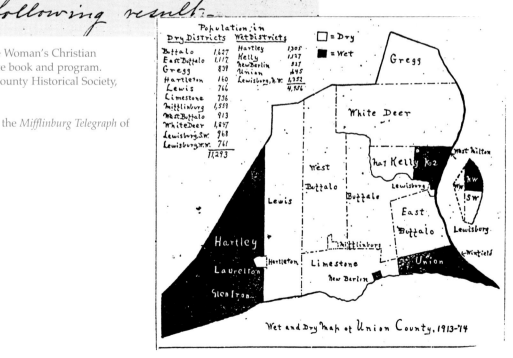

Population in

Dry Districts		Wet Districts	
Buffalo	1,627	Hartley	1,305
East Buffalo	1,117	Kelly	1,137
Gregg	839	New Berlin	927
Hartleton	160	Union	645
Lewis	766	Lewisburg, N.W.	6,252
Limestone	736		4,156
Mifflinburg	1,559		
West Buffalo	913		
White Deer	1,847		
Lewisburg S.W.	968		
Lewisburg N.W.	761		
	11,293		

☐ = Dry
■ = Wet

Wet and Dry Map of Union County, 1913-14

drinkers. The appeal was to the emotions, and the approach was not unlike that of traditional camp meetings. One of these gatherings in a grove near Cowan, directed by the Reverend William McCool of Laurelton, extended through five days and attracted more than 700 at the Saturday sessions. A smaller attendance on Monday was attributed to the absence of women, who were assumed to be too busy with their washing (laundry) at home to attend. At the meeting's close the list of abstinence pledges totaled 54 — a very satisfactory figure. The Cowan meeting had followed one near Hartleton, and another near Vicksburg succeeded it.[4]

Temperance momentum slowed thereafter, and by sheer persistence most of the taverns won renewals for their licenses. Meanwhile, the Woman's Christian Temperance Union (founded in 1874) had organized local chapters as early as 1879, and in 1884 the first county convention assembled. They continued to gather annually until nationwide prohibition became a reality. The organization provided women with their own vehicle to carry forward the drive against "demon rum" and the means to bring their quarry to bay when the time was right.

By the first quarter of the twentieth century the millennium seemed at hand. Reform was in the air. On the national scene the progressivism of Presidents Theodore Roosevelt and Woodrow Wilson was having its impact, and in the West and South prohibition was winning victories. Joining forces with the Anti-Saloon League, the WCTU directed its attention to both statewide prohibition by constitutional amendment and local prohibition by local option. A death in 1913 in Mifflinburg, attributed to a blow from a whiskey bottle in a barroom brawl, proved persuasive. Armed with long lists of petitioners, the prohibitionists found Judge Albert Johnson, and Associate Judges A.K. Dieffenderfer and Gottlieb Rowe receptive, and their refusal to renew the licenses of the two Mifflinburg hotels made the town officially dry.

When the *Lewisburg Chronicle* editor, Benjamin Focht, qualified his congratulations with an observation that "the world's consumption of rum has not been lessened by one drink," his judgment was immediately challenged. Mifflinburg grocers testified that their business had spurted upon the closure of the bars. Others noted that there were fewer drunks on the streets and that men who had been habitually intemperate had more money for their families, were paying their bills more promptly, and had opened bank accounts.[5] Their evidence was not altogether convincing, however. Reports of bootlegging from Milton on the trolley and by motor car were widely repeated. Allegations were made that drinking in homes and barns was on the rise.

The Mifflinburg victory was the signal for a county-wide drive for prohibition. Susanna Brubaker of Mifflinburg "sprang a sensation" when she reported that she found six empty beer bottles in a Snyder County schoolhouse just after a meeting of the school board there, and young Dr. Mary Wolfe lectured on alcohol as a cause of insanity. Petitions were circulated against the renewal of licenses for the remaining taverns in the county. With the court responding to their wishes, the bars were closed in Winfield, Vicksburg, New Columbia, Allenwood, Lochiel, Glen Iron, Forest Hill, White Deer, and West Milton. By the spring of 1914, only the Baker and Cameron houses in Lewisburg, Pursley's in Laurelton, and the Union Hotel in New Berlin remained open. A year later Pursley's and the Union Hotel were eliminated, and only the Lewisburg bars were open.

The battle of Lewisburg was now joined. "Wets" noted that both men and women were gathering at "gambling dens" and "speakeasies" where "booze" carted from Milton was flowing freely, but they could not stop the "dry" momentum. Petitions to close the two bars were signed by more than 1,000 Lewisburg men and women, and the court responded favorably; thus, on April 1, 1916, Union County became dry — the eleventh county in the state to take the action.

The prohibitionists celebrated their success with birch beer and sarsaparilla, but they were the first to admit that their job was not finished. At Harrisburg votes were not forthcoming to initiate statewide prohibition. Across the river in Northumberland County, no fewer than 310 bars were dispensing alcohol as usual, and a statistically-minded individual could have identified sixteen in Snyder County as well. With trolleys running regularly to Milton and Montandon, oases were near at hand.

The prohibitionists, of course, hailed the ratification of the Twentieth Amendment to the Constitution in 1920, which had been hastened by the crusading spirit generated by World War I. Again the victory was flawed by the unwillingness of the public to accept it. Nevertheless, the repeal of Prohibition by the Twenty-First Amendment in 1933 did not divert a hard core of the WCTU from the century-old struggle.

Two young women out for a summer ride pose under their runabout's fringed parasol top, in front of the Union Hotel in New Berlin. From the collection of the Union County Historical Society, courtesy of Gloria Maize.

While the once-familiar white banners are seldom seen, the old spirit lives on among its thinning ranks.

While a sizable number of women were finding an outlet in the temperance movement, others were seeking fulfillment in the professions and industry. Careers in teaching were opening to them in the elementary schools — less frequently in the secondary schools — and they could qualify inexpensively by merely graduating from the local high schools. In time female teachers outnumbered the male teachers and made elementary education almost exclusively a feminine bailiwick. Teaching might also be a passport to distant lands. Two Gutelius sisters, Margaret and Emma of Mifflinburg, entered the teaching profession at the Carlisle Indian School, and their experience led them later to reservations in Nevada, Washington, Minnesota, Michigan, and South Dakota. Katherine Johnson of Lewisburg became a teacher in a mission school at Puebla, Mexico. Mary B. Harris, daughter of the Bucknell University President and his wife, John H. and Lucy B. Harris, taught at a girls' school in Rome.

By the century's close, women were staking out new roles in local industries. In Mifflinburg they found employment in the buggy industry as stitchers and upholsterers, and they operated sewing machines at the Kurtz Overall factory. In Lewisburg women stitched shoes and spun wool; in New Berlin, Millmont, and Lewisburg, they operated sewing machines in the garment trades; and when the opportunity was presented, they took over the new telephone switchboards and edged into many of the commercial establishments as clerks and typists.

A half century-earlier, in 1853, Mary Ellen Wolfe, daughter of Samuel and Catherine Lawshe Wolfe of Lewisburg, entered the Penn Medical School at Philadelphia, just six years after Elizabeth Blackball had broken the male stranglehold on the medical profession by gaining admission to the Medical School of Geneva, New York. Wolfe found that instructors refused to admit her to their lectures and laboratories, so the dean provided her with special admission cards, which are testimony to her attendance at anatomy, obstetrics, surgical and microscopic laboratories and demonstrations. Wolfe completed the three-year course of study but was unable to initiate a medical practice, having contracted tuberculosis from which she did not recover.

Meanwhile, Sara Kleckner was also preparing for a medical career. The daughter of David and Esther Wingard Kleckner of West Buffalo Township, Sara grew up on a farm just to the west of Mifflinburg, where her grandfather, John Kleckner, a native of Wurtemburg, Germany, had settled in 1785. Despite the financial burden involved, the Kleckner's provided a secondary education for each of their nine daughters, five of whom became teachers prior to marriage. "Dr. Sallie," as Sara was called, studied with Dr. Charles Brundage at White Springs and then attended the recently opened Women's Medical College of Pennsylvania in Philadelphia. After her graduation in 1861, she returned to Mifflinburg and opened a practice.

Kleckner partially overcame the prevailing prejudice against female practitioners by accepting requests to deliver babies, heretofore the function of midwives, and one of the poorest-paying specializations in the profession. Her warm and buoyant temperament and her dedication to her work were also assets. A former neighbor recalls that she was "all doctor; strong, and good on her feet," despite her heavy frame.[6] Like many other physicians, she added a drugstore at Chestnut and Fourth Streets to her practice.

In 1885 Dr. Kleckner cast about for a more rewarding practice. Apparently accompanying the family of the Reverend Samuel Henry, the Lutheran minister of Mifflinburg, to Ottawa on the Kansas frontier, she accepted a position as a medical missionary. However, after eight months she returned to her practice in Mifflinburg. In 1891, when 58, she married George Saltzgiver, a hatter of York, Pennsylvania — the highlight of the social season that year. They lived for a time in York, where she seems to have continued her practice. When they returned to Mifflinburg several years later, she retired from an active practice but continued to minister to her family and neighbors. She also found more time to attend to her lifelong work in the Lutheran Church. Her husband's business does not appear to have been profitable, and it was said that she had been "too easy in business"; thus, during her last years they lived abstemiously upon their dwindling resources. Sara Kleckner Saltzgiver died in 1905 at age 72, and she was buried, as she had requested, with her head facing the sun.[7] She bequeathed her medical library to the York County Medical Society and the York County Hospital. Presumably included in the volumes going to the latter was a journal with the record of the babies she had delivered, with names, dates and other particulars. The journal turned up recently at a flea market in York County.

A generation after Dr. Sallie had fought to overcome the prejudice against female physicians, Mary Moore Wolfe, a daughter of Charles S. and Martha Meixell Wolfe of Lewisburg and niece of the earlier Dr. Mary Wolfe, entered the profession. An honors graduate of Bucknell University, the younger Mary Wolfe obtained a medical degree from the College of Medicine, University of Michigan, in 1900. She served on the staff of the Norristown State Hospital until 1914 and shortly after her resignation there was named as superintendent of the Laurelton State Village for Feeble-Minded Women of Childbearing Age.

Operating on the assumption that mental retardation was hereditary, the institution was conceived as a means of removing mentally defective women of childbearing age from society, where they would otherwise breed and multiply. The school was designed to care for them and to train them, when feasible, for employment in domestic service and agriculture. Once they were beyond the childbearing age, the more competent could be paroled and hopefully become self-sustaining. The emphasis at the outset, however, seems to have been upon removal and isolation rather than upon reclamation. Having authorized the institution, the legislature was reluctant to provide it with funds, and the first "cottage" was not opened until late in 1919. During these seemingly endless delays, Dr. Wolfe accepted a second challenge, that of women's suffrage.

The women's suffrage movement, founded by Lucretia Mott and Elizabeth Cady Stanton at the now-famous convention at Seneca Falls, New York, in 1848, seems to have had little impact upon Union County at that time. The same might be said for the National Woman's Suffrage Association which met annually after its initial 1869 meeting. However, news that the territories of Wyoming and Utah had given women the right to vote was heard with interest, and right-to-vote wins in the states of Washington and California in 1910 and 1911 served as calls for local action.

Evidence of a women's movement in Union County became manifest in the activities of the Lewisburg Civic Club, founded in 1907 for the purpose of making the town a better place in which to live. In 1911, dissatisfied with the management of the local schools, the club decided to back two of its members for election to the school board, even though women could not cast ballots to elect them. When the Democrats did not nominate anyone, the club was able to place Emma Thomas and Annie Van

Gundy on the ballot; and they entered vigorously into the campaign, conducting a door-to-door solicitation with the slogan, "Are you interested in the welfare of your children? If men haven't the time, let women do it." In the ensuing election both women were winners, and Thomas, wife of Presbyterian clergyman Welling E. Thomas, was chosen as president of the board. She was also the mother of 26-year-old Norman Thomas, a recent graduate of Union Theological Seminary, who would later be the Socialist Party's six-time nominee for President of the United States.

Emma Thomas' qualifications were impeccable. Born of missionary parents in India, she was a graduate of Elmira College and a mother of six. She had served on the school board in Marion, Ohio. Tall and indefatigable, like her son, Norman, and dedicated to the improvement of the quality of education, the school board could scarcely have acted otherwise. Proof that the public's willingness to share the management of its schools with women was not a mere whim is evidenced by Van Gundy's re-election in 1915 and the election of Grace Drum to replace Thomas when the latter moved from Lewisburg.

The election of these women to the school board undoubtedly encouraged young Edith Cummings Wilson to run for a county office. A native of Watsontown, she had commuted daily by train to Williamsport to attend the Williamsport Commercial College. Moving to Lewisburg upon the completion of her studies, she found that men were entrenched in the commercial positions including bookkeeping and typing. However, she found occasional employment in the register and recorder's office in the courthouse; and in 1912 she received an appointment as deputy, thus breaking the sex barrier in that male stronghold. When Francis Baker retired as register and recorder in 1915, he and other leaders of the Washington (Bull Moose) faction of the Republican Party encouraged Cummings to run for the office, and, not without misgivings, she agreed.

Learning of her candidacy, the *Philadelphia North American* featured it in a column entitled, "Woman is Candidate for a County Office," obviously furnished to the paper by the Washington faction. Noting that the Republicans in Union County were badly divided and that Baker had won his office by bucking the "Focht Gang," the paper predicted that many traditional Republicans would bolt the ticket and come over to her support.[8] Cummings had no illusions and felt certain that she "would fall on her face." Yet the element of surprise was not entirely absent on elec-

tion day, when she obtained majorities in New Berlin, Mifflinburg, and the south ward of Lewisburg. Having lost her position in the register's office, she crossed the corridor to the prothonotary's office, where she served for fourteen years as deputy to C. Dale Wolfe and awaited the coming of women's suffrage before tossing her hat into the ring again.

Moved by the feminist ferment, women in Laurelton organized the "Ladies of the Concrete Sidewalk," dedicated to lifting pedestrians above the sea of mud which frequently covered that low-lying village. Through 1912 and 1913 they held an incredible number of chicken and waffle dinners, graphaphone concerts, and festivals (guess cakes were a favorite). Their leadership paid off. "Where heretofore you waded the mud, shoe deep, or walked over loose boards at the risk of breaking your neck, you can now go to any part of town . . . with safety and comfort."[9] They built well, and many blocks of the sidewalk remain intact after more than 60 years. Stimulated by their success, the Laurelton women held a work project on Arbor Day in October of 1913 to convert a "stony batter" into a manicured lawn and playing field. Again, the women demonstrated their ability to execute civic improvements.

Meanwhile, the Lewisburg Civic Club, under its dynamic president, Emma J. Matlack, transformed the riverfront between the two bridges from the town's dump into a park. Purchasing several tracts of land and receiving another as a donation from the Norton Estate, they leveled and planted the wasteland. Its restoration was a source of pride and joy to the entire community. While the Civic Club's primary goal remained the creation of a better Lewisburg, its leaders moved into the forefront of the broader women's crusade. The new emphasis may be seen in its programs. On February 19, 1913, Emma Thomas spoke on women's suffrage; the following spring Mrs. William G. Owens' topic was "The Feminist Movement in the Modern World," and a few months later Eveline Stanton Gundy delivered an address entitled "Preparation for the Vote."

The movement entered the political arena in 1914 as the legislature came to grips with the suffrage issue, and women across the state organized to promote it. The first guns of the county campaign were fired in the late summer of 1914 in Mifflinburg, where, under the leadership of Blanche Gast, women gathered at the Lyric Theatre to organize a suffrage association and to listen to an address by Dr. Mary Wolfe.[10] The following week, leaders of the Civic Club in Lewisburg sponsored an organizing meeting in the home of Mary Linn; that evening, in a county-wide mass rally attended by about 300, Mrs. Frank M. Roessburg, president of the Pennsylvania Woman's Suffrage Association, joined Dr. Wolfe and Emma Matlack in a call for action. Growing out of these meetings was the creation of the Woman Suffrage Party of Union County, with Dr. Wolfe as its first president, Eveline Gundy as secretary, Frieda Thompson as treasurer, and Blanche Gast and Dorothy Walls as borough leaders of Mifflinburg and Lewisburg, respectively. The legislature, responding favorably to the suffrage campaign, passed the proposed amendment along to the voters in 1915 for their ratification or rejection. The suffragists now shifted their emphasis to the men, who would have the last word at the polls.

In February the Mifflinburg committee turned to music to persuade the opposite sex. Under the guidance of Blanche Gast, they held "a delightful banquet, musical, and old-time social" at the Buffalo Valley Inn. The decorations, acclaimed as spectacular, included an immense yellow banner (the suffragist color) proclaiming "VOTES FOR WOMEN" and hand-made badges bearing the same message. A great white dove held a streamer in its bill spelling "PEACE." The musical was shared by local men and women, and included an original composition by Kreider Kurtz entitled "When Jennie Come Home to Vote." Lee Francis Lybarger concluded with a testimonial to womanhood.[11]

In May the Mifflinburg Woman Suffrage Association held a rally at the Lyric Theatre. Sharing the platform were Emma McAlarney, member of a former Mifflinburg family, a Wellesley College graduate and instructor, and a touring speaker; and D. Effinger Reber, a native of the county who had drafted the Kansas suffrage bill. A witness recalls the enthusiasm generated in the packed hall.[12] In both Mifflinburg and Lewisburg during this period, the Chautauqua exerted a subtle pressure for women's rights. Women appeared frequently on its platform; and in August of 1915, directors of the childrens' activities in Lewisburg staged a parade with 100 youthful marchers, resplendent in derby hats and yellow silk sashes spelling out "Votes for Women," and carrying ribbon-bedecked umbrellas.

The climax of the 1915 drive was the tour of the "Woman's Liberty Bell" through the county. Designed to catch the spirit of the immortal Liberty Bell, which the suffragists alleged proclaimed liberty for males only, this 2,000-pound replica served as the symbol of the crusade. Mounted on a truck body with conventional hard rubber tires and driven around the state, its appearance was a call for demonstrations. Its bronze tongue, however, remained motionless and was not to be heard "until the men of Pennsylvania see fit to give the same privilege of citizenship to their women-folk that they themselves now enjoy."[13] The entourage entered Gregg Township by way of Montgomery on Saturday afternoon, September 18, and made its first

The Woman's Suffrage Movement Bell toured Pennsylvania towns including some in Union County in 1915. From the collection of the Union County Historical Society, #89.5.14.1.

The Chatauqua Parade held on August 16, 1915, had suffragettes from Union County: Rae Seaman (Reiner), Ruth Weidenhamer, Sara Bernhart (Derr), Katherine Wainwright, Anna Belle Zimmerman, Florence Perry (Kunkle), Martha Leiser, Anna Mae Spease, Emmalene Fisher (Grice), Edith Cumings Wilson. From the collection of the Union County Historical Society, #89.5.14.21.

stop at Allenwood, which was gaily decorated for the occasion. A good-sized crowd gathered to hear Mary Bakewell, a suffragist from Pittsburgh, and Professor T.F. Hamblin of the Bucknell faculty. At New Columbia, school children in yellow and white sashes turned out, and at West Milton railroad yardmen paused to view the colorful spectacle.

Arriving at Lewisburg at six o'clock, the Citizens' Band led the procession through the principal streets and thence to the town square where Bakewell, Bucknell President Rev. John H. Harris, and Adele Potter, a touring suffragist, added their voices to the suffrage drive. After resting on Sunday, the belltruck and an accompanying motorcade resumed the journey westward, seldom out of sight of yellow bunting. It paused briefly at Vicksburg, Millmont, and Hartleton before returning at 12:30 to Mifflinburg, where a motorcar parade, interspersed with Camp Fire Girls, Boy Scouts, pony carts, and children in historic costumes — including youthful Spessard Strunk, dressed as "Uncle Sam"— awaited them. "Mifflinburg did itself proud," the *Lewisburg Journal* noted, "and all must hand it to Mifflinburg for its royal entertainment, due largely to its local chairman, Blanche Gast."[14]

After a luncheon and speeches at the Buffalo Valley Inn, the caravan entrained for New Berlin, where an enthusiastic assemblage awaited it on the village green. Later in the afternoon the belltruck and its attendants moved through Dry Valley to Winfield and finally crossed Chestnut Ridge enroute to Snyder County. Speaking of the experience later, Dr. Wolfe recalled stopping the caravan to tell a farmer in a field along the highway about the bell's mission. Finding that he was deaf, she shouted (her voice was awesome), "The bell, the bell, it's the bell." Whereupon the startled agriculturist responded, "You can go to hell, too!"[15]

Editor George Schoch gave the campaign a ringing endorsement on the front page of the *Mifflinburg Telegraph*. After reviewing historical highlights of the American Revolution and the Civil War, he turned to the sacrifices of women in both wars and concluded: "God bless woman-kind. Give women the well earned right to vote — and pass a new and well earned declaration of independence — all males and females are free and equal." He asked doubters to tour the town with him, declaring that at the school they would observe that all teachers except the principal were women, and that they would find talented women employed at the buggy factories, the department stores, the overall factory, and the post office, and as seamstresses. He was confident that no one would remain unconvinced that they were competent to vote. He followed his testimonial with weekly tributes to women until election day.[16]

By contrast, Benjamin Focht, convinced that the voters would reject suffrage at the polls, avoided a commitment in the *Saturday News*. He proved to be the realist. On election day the male voters rejected the amendment by a decisive 150,000 votes in the state, and only the south ward of Lewisburg voted favorably in Union County. Focht's silence did not endear him to the suffragists, nor did his negative vote on the Nineteenth Amendment when it came before the House of Representatives in Washington in 1919. Pointing out that every one of the eight counties in his district had voted against it four years earlier, Focht insisted that "a vast majority of women do not want the vote nor do they need it for their protection."[17] Thereafter, the women's vote came back to haunt him repeatedly in his unsuccessful campaigns for Congress in the 1920s.

The defeat did not destroy the suffrage movement in Union County. In 1916 Dorothy Walls was chosen as chairwoman of the Suffrage Party, with Mrs. George Ocker and Mrs. C.L. Blind of New Columbia as vice chairwomen. Margaret Stoughton headed the Lewisburg Association, and a leader was named for each ward; but the immediacy of the cause was lost as the war and the prohibition crusade absorbed public attention during the next several years. The ratification of the Nineteenth Amendment to the Federal Constitution in 1920 was the culmination of their drive; but many women declined to use the voting privilege in the presidential election later that year, and the women's vote did not appear to affect the results.

Women who aspired to county offices were seldom viable candidates. In 1929 Emily S. Frock, after succeeding her husband as sheriff by appointment, failed to win election; and Edith Cummings Wilson, the deputy prothonotary, was defeated in a bid to become prothonotary by eighteen votes. In Lewisburg Grace Drum, after serving several terms on the school board, was rejected for reelection.

Yet time was working in favor of an acceptance of women by the voters. In 1951 Eleanor Middlesworth Bingaman broke precedent when she defeated two male rivals in the Republican primary for county treasurer, and she went on to victory in November. Four years later, Thelma J. Showalter was elected to the first of two terms to the board of county commissioners and Cora Spotts was chosen as county auditor. In 1988 Ruth Wehr Zimmerman was elected to the first of three terms as county commissioner. By this time it was more common than not for women to be main row officers for the county: Kitty Henry (1976-1979), Dorothy Dersham (1980-1995), and Lorraine Lenhart

(1996-present) as register and recorder of deeds; Miriam Oberdorf (1976-1980), Jean Derr (1981-1999) and Diana Auten Weikel (2000-present) as county treasurer; Bertha Boyer (1981-1987) and Dianne Brouse Lynch (1988-present) as prothonotary and clerk of court. One did need to be a member of the Republican party to be elected, it appeared, as all were. In 1998 Louise Knight became the first woman to serve as judge in Union County. Initially appointed by Governor Tom Ridge to fill a vacancy, Knight was subsequently elected in 1999 to a full ten-year term.

In 1922 a Union County chapter of the League of Women Voters was organized with Elizabeth Vance of Winfield as chairperson. She and Mary Linn toured the county, meeting delegations from Lewisburg, Mifflinburg, West Milton, and Allenwood. They also conducted a rally in Mifflinburg chaired by Alma Shaffer, but the interest was not sustained, and the league was not reactivated until 1954. In March of 1954, women from three neighboring counties gathered in Lewisburg at the call of the International Relations Study Group of the American Association of University Women to consider a new start. At this meeting Elizabeth Hitchcock's resolution that a League of Women Voters was necessary in the area was approved, and plans were initiated to implement it. Full recognition of the local unit was received in August of 1955.[18] Since that time, the league has remained a vital force in civic affairs.

Whatever its impact on politics, however, the broader role of women was increasingly apparent in other areas. One of the most outstanding local success stories was the career of Mary Belle Harris. After graduation from Bucknell University with summa cum laude honors in 1894, she attended the graduate school of the University of Chicago, where she earned the degree of doctor of philosophy. While in Chicago, she worked with Jane Addams at Hull House. A few years later Harris joined the drive in Maryland for a ten-hour law for working women; and in 1914 she went on to New York where she received a six months' appointment as acting superintendent in charge of the women's prison in the Blackwell Island Workhouse. Harris was named as superintendent of the New Jersey State Reform School for Women at Clinton in 1919, and subsequently headed the New Jersey Reformatory for Women at Trenton for six years. In 1925 she was appointed as director of the Federal Industrial Institution for Women at Alderson, West Virginia. An innovative experiment in the reclamation of erring women, there were no walls, no iron bars, and no armed guards — nothing but mosquito

Judge Louise Knight. Photo by Jim Walter.

Dr. Mary Wolfe. Courtesy of Bucknell University.

netting on the sleeping porches separating them from the outside world. The cottages stood in a rural setting near a dairy, poultry farm, school, and hospital. Here for the next twenty years Dr. Harris demonstrated the feasibility of reclamation. In the mid-1940s she retired to Lewisburg, where she continued to be active in literary pursuits and civic affairs.

After many delays, resulting in part from the stress of war, the Laurelton State Village finally opened in 1920 with 36 women housed in a single cottage. During the next decade, six additional buildings were constructed, and the population grew to more than 500 under Dr. Mary Wolfe's dedicated — albeit authoritarian — administration. The institution was accepted as a landmark in the care and training of the "feeble-minded." Changes of attitude relating to the causes of mental retardation and corrective therapy led to the questioning of some of the premises of its founders however; and the unvaried daily regimen, spartan-like in its execution in isolation from the world outside, did not harmonize with the newer concepts. In the 1930s, Dr. Wolfe acceded to a program of paroles or furloughs, in which selected patients were permitted to return to society; and, under the direction of Dr. Mary Vanuxem, more than 100 patients were being supervised in private homes by 1938.

Complicating the situation also was its vulnerability to the whims of politics. From the naming of its directors to the employment of a pig farmer, the overriding considerations were always political; so when Dr. Wolfe broke with the local Republican organization over the candidacies of Gifford Pinchot for Governor and Edward M. Beers for Congress, she was pilloried in the columns of the *Lewisburg Saturday News*. In 1930, at a tension-filled meeting of the directors, Wolfe submitted her resignation; but supporters rallied to her defense, and the Board asked her to reconsider. In 1934 the Democrats carried the state for the first time in many years, and dismissals from state offices became the order of the day. By changing her political registration, Dr. Wolfe survived the onslaught, but she was never forgiven by Republican stalwarts.

The return of the Republicans to power in the state in 1938 left Dr. Wolfe in an untenable position. At a meeting of the directors in June of 1940, a motion to reappoint her for another one-year term was not passed as a result of a tie vote. A proxy in her favor from an absentee was refused by the same vote. A few weeks later the veteran administrator stepped down and accepted a permissible retirement. Dr. Effie C. Ireland, a Bucknell University and University of

Pennsylvania Medical School graduate who had served with Dr. Wolfe for twelve years, was named as her successor.

Dr. Ireland served as the administrator until February of 1955, when politics again precipitated an explosion. Allegations that unwarranted restraints and locked doors were used to harass patients led Governor George Leader, a Democrat, to call upon the board of directors to conduct an investigation; and amidst charges and countercharges, the Republican-dominated board sustained the superintendent. The Department of Welfare thereupon instituted an investigation of the directors, and the latter resigned in a body; Dr. Ireland followed suit and was joined by Dr. C. DeEtte Edgett, her able associate. The legislature subsequently modified the charter of the institution to permit the appointment of a male superintendent. In 1962 the Village was renamed the Laurelton State School and Hospital in recognition of its changing role.

Four women from Union County have been honored as "Distinguished Daughters of Pennsylvania" since that organization's founding in 1948. Recognized by Pennsylvania governors have been Mary Belle Harris, the prison reformer described earlier, (1950); Ruth Sprague Downs (1952); Nancy Neuman (1987); and Martha Zeller (1994). Ruth Sprague Downs, Bucknell Class of 1898, came to live in Lewisburg with her family when her father, John Sprague, retired as a mining engineer. She distinguished herself in a career devoted to the blind, becoming chief of transcription for Volunteer Services for the Blind. She transcribed books of all categories into Braille and worked out a code for Amharic, the language of Ethiopia, at a time when blindness was widely prevalent there. She was married to Edgar Downs and lived in Ardmore, Pennsylvania.

Seldom found on the front pages of the newspapers during the past century were items illustrative of the changes taking place that affected the lives of girls and young women of school age. One such change was marked by the graduation of the first woman from Bucknell University in 1885. In 1892 there were sixteen women enrolled, and by 1915 the number had jumped to 194. Also in 1915, the Female Institute or Seminary at Bucknell was disbanded, as the growth of high schools had rendered it obsolete. Earlier, in 1892, girls were permitted to participate in

Martha Zeller.

PAGE 270: The Democratic Primary Debate was hosted by National League of Women Voters President Nancy Neuman of Lewisburg . It was held in New Hampshire in February 1988. Participants were: Neuman, Senator Paul Simon, Governor Michael Dukakis, Senator Gary Hart, Reverend Jesse Jackson, Representative Richard Gephart, Senator Bruce Babbitt, Moderator Edwin Newman, Senator Al Gore, and Brother Joachim Froehlich, OSB, president of St. Anselm College. Courtesy of Nancy Neuman.

a mixed-doubles tennis tournament at Bucknell. By 1895 girls in the seminary participated in a one-mile bicycle race, and a year later they played a game of basketball with the college girls — the uniforms of both sweeping the floor. In 1922 Bucknell University young women had their own debating society, and by 1926 they were competing with men for positions on the desegregated college debating team.

In Mifflinburg, high school girls were playing basketball between basket standards on the school ground in 1915, and a year later Lewisburg girls were playing inter-mural basketball. The Lewisburg girls team enjoyed an undefeated season in 1919 under the direction of Professor Harold W. Musser and their chaperone, Lucille Owens; Katherine Owens was the team's leading scorer. In 1926 Mifflinburg High School became the champions of the Central Pennsylvania Debating League with a team composed of five girls and three boys. By the 1930s, girls were an integral part of the high school bands and filling elective offices in school societies.

In an address given when only four or five members of the Bucknell Female Seminary's class of 1869 remained, Emma Billmeyer Matlack, recalled the

gains women had made during the intervening 50 years. Matlack rated coeducation highly, for it had opened opportunities for higher education. She also had praise for the organization of women's civic and patriotic societies and lauded the congressional passage of the Susan B. Anthony Amendment (the Nineteenth), which was still awaiting ratification by the states. As soon as 36 states had ratified it, she added, "Women of our land will be citizens of the United States, and now whatever a women proves herself able to do, society will be thankful to see her do it, just as if she were a man. If she is scientific, science will welcome her . . . if capable of political thought and action, women will obtain even that."[19]

If Emma Matlack's forecast was too simplistic, her vision was on target. By World War II, both Union County's mothers and daughters were at the threshold of new challenges; and in the post-war era, new stirrings, designated as Women's Liberation, would continue to sweep away old barriers and win new victories.

ENDNOTES:

[1] John Blair Linn, *Annals of Buffalo Valley, Pennsylvania, 1755-1855*, Harrisburg, 1877, 527.

[2] Emma Matlack, Address before Shikelimo Chapter, Daughters of the American Revolution, *Mifflinburg Telegraph*, June 6, 1924.

[3] *Mifflinburg Telegraph*, July 12, 1877, May 7 and July 16, 1879.

[4] *Mifflinburg Telegraph*, July 16, 1879.

[5] *Mifflinburg Telegraph*, April 5, 1913.

[6] Reminiscence of Miss Jessie Sankey.

[7] Dr. C. DeEtte Edgett Papers, Union County Historical Society.

[8] Letter to *Public Ledger* dated October 4, 1915; Interview with Edith Cummings Wilson.

[9] *Mifflinburg Telegraph*, July 27, August 17, October 5, and November 2, 1912.

[10] *Mifflinburg Telegraph*, September 4, 1914.

[11] *Mifflinburg Telegraph*, March 5, 1915.

[12] *Mifflinburg Telegraph*, May 7, 1915.

[13] *Mifflinburg Telegraph*, September 17, 1915.

[14] *Mifflinburg Telegraph*, September 24, 1915; *Lewisburg Journal*, September 24, 1915.

[15] Reminiscence of Lois Kalp.

[16] *Mifflinburg Telegraph*, September 24, 1915.

[17] *Congressional Record*, U.S. Government Printing Office, Washington, 1919.

[18] Secretarial Minutes, League of Women Voters.

[19] Archives of the Union County Historical Society.

CHAPTER 16

UNION COUNTY AND THE WAR
BETWEEN THE STATES

Sectionalism, threatening to dismember the Union, had cast a darkening shadow over Union County's citizenry for a full decade before 1861. Looking back into this tragic period, historians have noted the gradual takeover by extremists in the North as well as the South, a stiffening of sectional attitudes, and an almost inevitable drift toward disruption. To most Americans of that era with a shared heritage stretching back to the revered Washington and the other "giants" of the Revolutionary generation, fragmentation of the country bordered upon the unbelievable. Even "Bleeding Kansas," the election of a sectional president, committed "Free Soil" advocates, and the secession process itself did not altogether shatter their faith in a reconciliation; but, seemingly overnight, the bombardment of Fort Sumter in Charleston Harbor on April 12, 1861, and Lincoln's call for 75,000 militiamen to quell "combinations" obstructing the operation of federal laws broke the spell. The unthinkable had become a reality. "Grim-visaged" war was upon them.

The local response was almost spontaneous. In Lewisburg an eyewitness recalled that the busiest place in town was the recruiting office in Chamberlain's store at the corner of Fifth and Market, "but the fire burned everywhere":

Young men came home from work Monday evening to be told by their mothers that other young men, their comrades or neighbors, had enlisted. Before bed time these young men had themselves enrolled. Company G, Fourth Pennsylvania, Captain J. Wesley Chamberlain, seemed to spring up like the five hundred warriors of Roderick Dhu, from the earth. . . . The boys were sent away with proper patriotic demonstrations, processions, music and speeches. We all marched with them across the old Market Street bridge to Montandon, breaking step, lest under the strain of solid tramp the spans might break. Open lumber cars were the best means of transportation the Pennsylvania Railroad could then furnish in the stress of emergency. But patriotism was not crying for luxury, and the new soldiers sat down on planks stretched across the cars. With cheers and tears, as the train pulled out, we bade them adieu.[1]

Attorney James Merrill Linn was conducting a trial in the courthouse at Middleburg, when he heard the news. He hurried to Lewisburg, where by prodigious efforts he not only enrolled in the company but recruited enough others to win election as second lieutenant. The company was mustered at Harrisburg on April 20 but was barred from a direct passage to

Washington by mob violence in Baltimore. Instead, they proceeded to Philadelphia and then to Annapolis, where they occupied the grounds of the United States Naval Academy. Poorly equipped and provisioned, and thrown together upon an improvised camp site, the men were soon dispirited. In a letter to his father, Linn noted:

Everything is abused. The houses have been rendered unfit to live in. . . the waste of food — piles of beef, pork, crackers, beans and salt lying around wasted. . . . The grounds are not properly policed. A regiment comes in at noon, leaves perhaps at night, and don't clean their quarters. Then another comes in with no expectation of staying, and they clean up a place to stand in, or squat in the dirt. . . . Our company has lived cleanly, [but there are] always two or three companies lying along side, over whom we have no control, [who] fall into filthy habits from neglect of their officers.[2]

The company was transferred to Washington several weeks later, but, lacking tents, they were crowded into public buildings in the city, where a growing sick list added to their miseries. Having at last received uniforms and garrison equipage, they crossed the Potomac River, where they were assigned to the First Brigade, Third Division of the army commanded by General McDowell. Here on July 20 their three-month enlistment expired; and despite an appeal from General McDowell to remain for two more weeks, opinions were so divided that he decided to release them. Thus, they missed seeing action in the famous Battle of Bull Run by one day. In justice to most of the personnel of Company G, records show a large percentage of them later enrolled in other companies as they were formed.

Meanwhile, men who had volunteered too late to get into Company G were organized as Company D of the Fifth Pennsylvania Reserve, identified locally as the Slifer Guards. Its personnel, like its predecessor, was made up largely of Lewisburg men, and its commanding officer, Thomas Chamberlain, was a brother of J. Wesley Chamberlain of the ill-fated Company G.

Lost amidst the flags and drums as the recruits departed for the front were the heartaches among the families whose sons were so suddenly torn from their midst. The dilemma of George W. Schoch of Lewisburg would be repeated again and again. A nineteen-year-old printer, Schoch found his mother unwilling to let him go. In her judgment he was too

A group musters at Market Street near Fifth in Lewisburg. From the collection of the Union County Historical Society, #89.5.10.3.

young, and no argument could persuade her otherwise. "Full of the war spirit," he sweated over the matter for several weeks and finally "decided to run away." Swearing two of his friends to secrecy, he told them of his plan, and they agreed to help him. On the appointed evening, under cover of darkness, they escorted him along a circuitous path to the station, where he got away undetected, and arrived at Harrisburg at two o'clock the next morning. Unable to sleep, he groped for words to draft a confession:

Dearest Ones at home,

I have put this off longer than I expected, but the time has at length arrived when I can no longer inhale the same atmosphere that some people of Lewisburg do.

Dearest ones, I cannot remain behind when I think duty calls me; although I owe a duty to home.

Now judge rightly, and not harshly. I have thought over it long, and the longer I have been thinking the more has it increased my determination to go. If I have erred I pray to God for his forgiveness. I have formed the determination to refrain from all intoxicating drink and the temptations besetting the Soldier; and I hope and pray you will all intercede to Him who rules supreme to enable me to keep good my determination. This is one reason that prompts me to leave Lewisburg, and I think it is a good one. If I should fall in this cause, do not grieve over my death, for I feel (and you all know) that I am engaged in the cause of *Truth, Justice and Right* in which all lovers of *Freedom* have a deep interest. So, fare-you-well dearest ones.

I remain your affectionate and absent one engaged in the duty of preserving good Government.

Geo. W. Schoch

In a letter to a sister a short time later, Schoch added, "I know mother mourns for me. Now, do please try and comfort her, and tell her I am engaged in a good cause. . . . Dinner is now ready, and I will now pitch in for my rice, beans, fresh bread, cracker and coffee. . . . Dinner is now over, and I feel better." The silent disapproval of his family continued to bother him for several weeks, but at last a letter in his father's familiar hand brought a small measure of relief, though the disapproval continued. "You mention the word 'desert.' Why, I scorn the idea. No, never will it be said that I proved a deserter to my country. . . . Do, therefore, yield, and join me in my wish to remain."[3] He remained for a three-year enlistment; and if his ardor waned, it was never revealed in his correspondence.

While no Union County unit participated at Bull Run, the unexpected defeat and panic brought home the gravity of the conflict. The North became painfully aware that strenuous recruitment program would be required, and the nation would have to be girded to face its greatest crisis. Union County's response was an almost simultaneous enrollment of five companies: E, H, and K of the 51st Pennsylvania Volunteers; D of the 52nd; and E of the 53rd, totaling more than 500 recruits from a county with about 3,000 taxables and a population of 15,000. The nucleus of the 51st was the men from the former Company G of the Fourth Regiment, but volunteers were also drawn from the length and breadth of Buffalo Valley. The 51st was assigned to General Burnside for amphibious operations along the Carolina coast, while the 52nd and 53rd augmented the Grand Army of the Potomac, which General McClellan was preparing for the repeatedly postponed march on Richmond.

With but limited military activity during the winter of 1861-1862, there was a respite from recruitment; but the situation changed dramatically in the spring, when McClellan launched his Peninsula Campaign against the Confederate capital. Casualties by the thousands were soon thinning the ranks, and he had scarcely withdrawn to the safety of the Virginia tidewater before General Pope's army was shattered by Generals Lee and Jackson at the Second Battle of Bull Run. In the resulting emergency, Lincoln called for 300,000 more men as Congress enacted the First Conscription Act.

Each borough and township was now given a quota, based on its population, and those failing to meet it were required to invoke the draft. Conscription was so unpopular, however, that officials postponed it as long as possible, hoping to find additional volunteers. To make armed service more palatable, they also sought bounties for enlistees; and in August the Union County commissioners, yielding to public pressure, granted $25 to each nine-month and $50 dollars to each three-year enrollee.

Awaiting the results of voluntary recruitment, boards were at work examining men claiming exemption; and in September the *Mifflinburg Telegraph* noted that on examination day, "the town was full of the lame and blind and deaf and toothless and fingerless, and others crippled in various ways."[4] While the comment was obviously an exaggeration, it suggests the sagging morale. A year earlier, George Schoch had noted that a muscular member of his company had appeared for inspection at least three times in place of fellow enlistees who feared that they might be rejected for physical infirmities.

With a few exceptions, the threat of conscription sufficed to obtain the enlistments, and Company A, 131st Regiment (nine months), Company E, 142nd Regiment (three years), and Company D, 150th Regiment (three years) were soon enroute to the war zone. The three new companies involved the combined efforts of many recruiters, but most of the credit for the 131st belonged to Jacob M. Moyer of Kelly Township and Joseph R. Orwig of Mifflinburg, both of whom were veterans of the short-lived Fourth Regiment, as well as J.W. Kepler, a young Lewisburg postal worker. Orwig had become co-editor of the *Telegraph*, but "thinking that in the emergency the

sword was mightier than the pen," he left the paper to campaign for volunteers. His reminiscence provides insights into the recruitment process. He first met with Moyer and Kepler, and they divided the county and set to work. Turning to the West End, Orwig found the Laurelton Woolens Mill "a veritable recruiting station and a commissary for hapless ones left in the rear of our armies." The Halfpenny brothers, R V.B. Lincoln, John Diehl, Samuel Hartman, the Smiths and others "rendered all possible encouragement." He left Laurelton with eleven names. Judge William F. Wilson, the Whitmers, Glovers, Reeds, Mr. Geddes, and others were equally helpful at Hartleton, where four recruits were enrolled. In Mifflinburg he obtained the assistance of the irrepressible Major Charles H. Shriner, John Hayes, S.W. Snodgrass, the Gutelius family, James Chambers, and J.E. Herr, and rounded up nine — some of them from the adjacent townships. Finally at New Berlin, where the venerable Michael Kleckner, the hosteler, E. Smith, and the Schochs offered their assistance, he added five more to the roll.

With his list in hand, Orwig conferred with Moyer and Kepler, only to discover that some of the Lewisburg recruits had objected to the claims of the threesome to monopolize the commissions. After a hurried conference with the Lewisburg Recruitment Board, the original arrangement was approved, "though the outcome left a rankling which was never entirely healed."[5]

The 142nd was rightfully identified with John A. Owens. A native of Pittsburgh who came to Lewisburg to attend Bucknell Academy, he matriculated at the college but withdrew after a year to pursue a teaching career in the local schools. His roving spirit subsequently propelled him into the recently opened oil fields of eastern Kentucky, but at the outbreak of the war he returned to East Buffalo Township and organized a drill team at the Gundy School. During the recruitment of the 142nd Regiment, seventeen members of his troop offered to join, provided that he would enroll with them. He agreed; and as the word spread, his former students and acquaintances enlisted in clusters. To no one's surprise, when the regiment's Company E was mustered, Owens was elected as its captain.

Henry W. Crotzer, a former Mifflinburg teacher and later a merchant in Lewisburg, headed the recruitment of Company D of the 150th Regiment. His work appears to have been lightened by the fortuitous naming of Colonel Langhorne Wister, a captain of the colorful "Bucktails" from the northern tier of the state, as commander of the new regiment, and the equally good selection of Thomas Chamberlain of Lewisburg, former captain of Company D of the 5th Pennsylvania Reserve Regiment, as its major. The 150th was at once identified as the Bucktails, despite its tenuous tie with the original, and retained this identification as long as the Civil War generation survived. The new company drew recruits from all parts of Union County, but Dry Valley and New Berlin contributed more than their shares, and the company's popularity extended beyond Penns Creek into Snyder County as well.

The new regiments had barely departed from Camp Curtin in Harrisburg when General Lee's unexpected crossing of the Potomac into Maryland threatened to carry the war into Pennsylvania. On September 4 Governor Curtin ordered the people to arm, and a week later he called for 50,000 militia. Forty-eight hours later the Lewisburg South Ward Militia (Company B, Third Regiment), headed by Charles C. Shorkley, a Lewisburg iron founder, departed for Camp Curtin; two days later the North Lewisburg Militia, led by George W. Forrest, moved out. The former included men in their forties and fifties — Private Justin Loomis of the college was 52, and Levi Christ, a local justice of the peace, was 56. Other companies in New Berlin and Hartleton were not activated. The two companies remained in Harrisburg during the bloody Battle of Antietam on September 17 but later advanced as far as Hagerstown. Lee's withdrawal spared them from further service, and they were back in Lewisburg before the close of the month.

Lee's second crossing of the Potomac in June of 1863 precipitated another emergency in Pennsylvania. Business virtually stopped, and partisan issues were laid aside while crowds gathered at the corners. At Northumberland, residents jammed hay into the tri-county West Branch bridge, preparing to burn it rather than allow it to become a crossing for the Confederate invaders. Editorializing on one of the pressing questions, "Who Should Go?" the *Lewisburg Chronicle* advised,

> Those who could contribute and not be a burden, the best men, returned soldiers and others accustomed to arms . . . who would be useful at once to guard our mountain passes, which may become necessary to save Union County, and the Juniata and North and West Branch Valleys from the fate of Virginia and the Cumberland Valley. [6]

Three companies were hastily mustered in Lewisburg as Companies A, D, and F of the 28th Regiment, commanded by Colonel James Chamberlain. Company A was made up largely of

Eli Slifer [signature]

ELI SLIFER

Home, 1861-1888, of Civil War Secretary of the Commonwealth, who as assistant to Governor Andrew Curtin had leading role in mobilizing State's men and resources for war. Elected State Assemblyman, State Treasurer. Born 1818, died 1888. House is now office of Evangelical Home.

PENNSYLVANIA HISTORICAL AND MUSEUM COMMISSION

Photo by Jim Walter.

college students, and at its departure not more than ten males remained on campus. With pardonable exaggeration, Professor J.S. James, a lieutenant in the company, recalled years later that "cobwebs curtained the windows of the West Wing, and hinges of the Main Building grew stiff with rust." Companies D and F contained many of the personnel who had heeded the earlier call during the Antietam crisis.

As these companies marched out of Lewisburg, 40 carriages with over 100 volunteers from New Berlin, Mifflinburg, Hartleton, and the upper townships arrived under the combined commands of Captains C.D. Roush of New Berlin and Thomas Church, both of whom had seen service in local companies. After hurried formalities, they too crossed the bridge and, joining the other companies, boarded a special troop train bearing more than 1,000 volunteers.

Company A occupied a bridgehead north of Harrisburg during the Battle of Gettysburg, and the other companies took stations in the neighborhood. The Lewisburg units later marched through the Cumberland Valley, billeting in barns and schoolhouses, whereas the Roush-Church militiamen bivouacked near Reading. With the emergency behind them, they returned to their homes, with the college students arriving just in time for commencement exercises on July 30.

An additional call for militia was made in August of 1864, when General Early's cavalry swept through the Shenandoah Valley and entered Maryland just north of the outskirts of Washington. During this alarm Captain Bruce Lambert's Independent Company in Lewisburg answered the summons and served for a term of 100 days. Other companies were recruited by Captains William Harrison McCall and C.D. Roush, both of whom were momentarily between terms of enlistment. Early's hasty turnabout eased the crisis, and the companies were not called.

Meanwhile, the casualty toll at Chancellorsville and Gettysburg required new quotas and more intensive recruiting. The county's most eloquent orators spoke from platforms in every village and hamlet, and the gifted Charles H. Shriner delivered his message in English or German, depending upon the composition of his audience. Particular attention was given to the filling of depleted ranks in the old regiments. By the spring of 1863, Company D of the Fifth Reserves had just 31 men on duty from an original muster of 105. Officers of these companies proved to be effectual recruiters and, as they could be spared, were detached for this purpose. A bounty and a month-long furlough just prior to the expiration of a

term of service in return for reenlistment were also dangled before the veterans, and the terms of several companies were extended in this manner.

No measure could delay the draft indefinitely, however, and in August of 1863 the drum was again spun and the names drawn. The *Chronicle,* urging Union men not to substitute for Copperheads (Southern sympathizers), exhorted, "Let them fill their own ranks." Despite disturbances elsewhere, the drawing went off peacefully. At the next turn of the drum the following winter, the government offered what would have been considered exorbitant bounties in less critical times: $300 to a man without military experience, and $400 to a returning veteran. Obviously, the war was reaching the bottom of the manpower barrel.

The stimulation provided by high bounties permitted the postponement of the next draft through the spring of 1864, but the unprecedented losses in dead and wounded at the Wilderness, Spottsylvania, and Cold Harbor in May and June as a result of General Grant's frontal push against Richmond required new quotas. With so many paying the commutation fee of $300 in lieu of military service, more and more names had to be called. In near desperation, Lewisburg found a solution by raising $14,000 through personal subscriptions — a sum sufficient to pay 35 substitutes at the current rate of $400 each. They repeated the solicitation the following February and thereby fulfilled their last commitment. Other districts were soon resorting to the same expedient. As it turned out, only a handful of draftees ever wore a uniform in Union County, but the draft had served as a goad to the public to furnish its share of military personnel.

A comprehensive history of Union County's contributions on the battlefields has not been written, and only a bare outline can be offered here. The Fifth Reserves (34th Regiment, Pennsylvania Volunteer Infantry), nicknamed the Slifer Guards, was assigned to McDowell's Corps for the defense of Washington during McClellan's Peninsula Campaign against Richmond. The latter's appeal for more troops led to its transfer to the Peninsula, where they arrived in time to participate in the Seven Days' Battle at Mechanicsville, in which they sustained 50 casualties. Positioned at the rear of McClellan's retreat to the James River, they remained under fire as they crossed the Chickahominy River and the swamps which bordered it. Reaching Harrison's Landing on the James, they were transferred to General Pope's command, arriving there in time to participate in the disastrous Second Battle of Bull Run. They saw limited action at Antietam, Fredericksburg, and Gettysburg, and later accompanied Grant on his campaign against Richmond. They fought their last battle at Bethesda Church on May 30, 1864, leaving the field a few days later at the expiration of their three-year term.

The 51st Regiment, containing three Union County companies, was the most traveled and actively engaged of the local regiments. After a few weeks of intensive drill at Annapolis, they endured a rough passage to Cape Hatteras and joined in the amphibious assault on Roanoke Island, which guarded the channel into Pamlico Sound. Captain J. Merrill Linn's experience, though it varied in the details, was doubtless typical of that of hundreds of Union County's soldiers who faced the enemy for the first time. After shelling the island's fortifications, the 51st disembarked from the *Cosack* at dusk on February 7, 1862.

> When we reached the shore it was boggy and very uncertain footing. I sent [Lieutenant David] Brewer ahead to pilot the way. He hadn't gone ten yards when he suddenly disappeared — then saw his head coming up. "Look out Captain here's a well." Dave crawled out, and then we waded along in the dark, half the time up to your knees in mud. . . . We went about a half mile through swamp and mire, and at last got on solid ground. We stacked arms and had a most wretched night. It rained all night; we had no shelter. Wood was scarce, and we sat shivering over the scanty fires . . . my boots smoking, my feet swelling until they became painful.
>
> An alarm occurred early in the morning, and it wasn't two minutes until the whole army were in ranks. The first brigade moved off. We stood in the rain and snow for an hour or two — at half past seven we heard the scattered reports of musketry close by. . . and soon the bang of cannon. The front of our brigade commenced moving . . . when the first wounded were carried back. That was very trying — the hardest thing we had to bear. We moved on through a road all thick with trees and underbrush. The musketry became more distinct. . . . Double quick, away we went along the winding road . . . you could not see ten feet. Just imagine such a road as leads from Chappel's Hollow in the valley [a primitive road below the New Berlin Mountain]. We came past the field hospital. There they lay in all sorts of mangled shape. Skulls split, brains oozing out . . . one with his arm off at the shoulder. . . . A fellow was limping along with a hole in each leg. "Go it boys." I gave them thirty-five rounds.
>
> We waited for the Rhode Island regiment which came across at right angles to pass, then we put double quick down the road. . . . Soon saw our battery of artillery — all lying down, bullets whistling. We had to squat low. . . . We got up, waded on through the swamp up to the middle — full of thick underbrush and tangled vines and briars. Oh horrors what a place. . . .
>
> We emerged on the right and rear of the battery, but the enemy had disappeared. . . . I went into the battery. There were only six or seven dead lying inside, and it seemed queer to see

> them lie there like logs. . . . Two wounded officers were there. One struck at some of my men with his sword as they came near him. . . . He said he had heard that we gave no quarter. I went around looking at the dead; the buzzards had been at them already. . . .
>
> I met General J.G. Foster on horseback. "Well boys," he said, "We have gained a great victory; two or three thousand have just surrendered to me, and all the batteries." Better believe we yelled! I tramped on — it got nightfall, lost our way — at last I got into one of the camps. [7]

Thus the 51st had its "baptism of fire" and earned the first battle inscription on its regimental flag. During the weeks which followed, the regiment fought its second engagement in the occupation of New Bern and carried out raids against strategic points in the interior of North Carolina. In July the 51st left the occupation of the Carolina coast to others and joined Pope's army where it held a defensive position at Second Bull Run. Dispatched hastily to Maryland, the 51st fought its way through the Confederate rear guard at South Mountain; and on the afternoon of September 17, the regiment led the left flank of Burnside's Corps across the famous stone bridge at Antietam in the face of a hail of bullets from the heights on the opposite bank. In this brief action, the regiment sustained more than 100 casualties.

The following December, the 51st was in the left flank of Burnside's costly assault against the Confederates on Marye's Heights, where more than 80 were killed and wounded. In the spring of 1863, they were transported by rail to Cincinnati and thence by the Ohio and Mississippi Rivers to the siege of Vicksburg, arriving in time to help General Grant force the surrender of the city on July 4. After additional engagements in central Mississippi, the regiment was assigned to the Middle Front in Tennessee, where in January of 1864 most of the men reenlisted.

After a heartwarming homecoming during the reenlistment bonus furlough, the regiment returned to the eastern theater of war, crossing the Rapidan River with General Grant to participate in the campaign against Richmond. At the siege of Petersburg on July 30, the 51st was in the charge following the explosion of the mine. Fortunately, the men were halted just short of the crater and thereby saved from the withering counterattack which followed. In the weeks just prior to the fall of Richmond and Lee's surrender, the 51st was engaged in severing Confederate supply lines south and west of the city.

In the course of its three and one-half year service, the 51st Regiment fought in twenty battles, and traveled by rail 3,311 miles, by water 5,390 miles, and on foot 1,738 miles — certainly a remarkable record.

Two of Dr. Theo Christ's diaries from the 1860s and a small notebook taken by him when he was a delegate to the National GAR Encampment in California in 1886. In it Christ copied from his diary some of his entries from 1862 such as, "Left Washington today Sunday — General McClellan Commander." From the Christ Collection, Union County Historical Society.

Company D of the 52nd Volunteer Infantry, the Cameron Guards, was the recruiting project of James Chamberlain of Lewisburg. Mustered at Camp Curtin in November of 1861, it wintered on Meridian Hill on the outskirts of Washington. In the spring the 52nd Regiment joined McClellan's Army of the Potomac on the Peninsula as it edged north toward Richmond, stopping only when it was barely five miles away. There, on May 31 and June 1, the 52nd engaged in the Battle of Fair Oaks. Fighting desperately at close range, the regiment, numbering 249, sustained 125 casualties, with Captain Chamberlain and two lieutenants in Company D among the wounded.

In December the 52nd Regiment was transferred to South Carolina and stationed on the sand spits outside the port of Charleston. Through the next twenty months, it participated in abortive actions against the fortifications of the city without obtaining a breakthrough. In an assault on Fort Johnson (the Confederate name for Sumter) in July of 1864, the entire attacking party was isolated and captured; more than 50 of them later perished in the prison pens of Columbia, Florence, and Andersonville, six of those members of Company D. At last, on February 18, 1865, the regiment entered the abandoned seaport

and ran up the stars and stripes over battered Fort Sumter. They joined Sherman's concluding march northward into North Carolina and there heard the glorious news of Lee's surrender.

Company E of the 53rd Regiment, the Rooke Guards, mustered at Camp Curtin and spent the winter at Alexandria, Virginia. Like the 52nd, it was dispatched to the Peninsula, and similarly faced the Confederate counteroffensive at Fair Oaks, where it suffered grievous losses, including the death of Major Thomas Yeager of Allentown. The 53rd was rushed to the Washington front in July to stem Lee's threat in that sector; but arriving too late to see action in the Second Battle of Bull Run, it joined the march into Maryland, and at Antietam fought its way through the "Corn Field," a name which symbolized blood and carnage as long as the Civil War generation lived. At Fredericksburg, on December 13, 1862, the 53rd was in one of the assault columns hurled against the heavily guarded Marye's Heights, and in minutes 158 of its 283 men were killed or wounded.

The remnant of the company wintered at Falmouth. In the spring, strengthened by fresh recruits, it engaged in the Battle of Chancellorsville and shortly thereafter crossed the Potomac River to block Lee's invasion of Pennsylvania. Arriving at Gettysburg on the second day of the battle, the 53rd was ordered to the left flank of the Union position on Cemetery Ridge, reaching the exposed area adjacent to Little Round Top in time to help hold it and prevent the Confederates from flanking the Union line. The regiment witnessed the unprecedented cannonading and Pickett's Charge on the third day, but it was not actively involved. After a veterans' furlough in December, the 53rd Regiment returned to Virginia, where it joined the campaign against Richmond in May. At Spottsylvania and again at Cold Harbor, it was exposed to the relentless fire of the enemy; and on June 16 it joined in the costly and unproductive assault on Petersburg. On the day of Lee's surrender, the regiment was sealing off potential Confederate escape routes in the vicinity of Appomattox.

Company A of the 131st Pennsylvania Reserves was the only nine-month military organization from the county. Mention has been made of its recruitment in the summer of 1862. It was on the field at the Second Battle of Bull Run and at Antietam, but did not see action. Its luck ran out at Marye's Heights in the Battle of Fredericksburg, where it received 153 casualties as five of the commissioned officers fell wounded. It supported batteries at Chancellorsville just a few days before the expiration of its term of enlistment. Many of its veterans later reenlisted in other organizations.

Company E of the 142nd Regiment had a grim awakening to the horrors of war below Marye's Heights at Fredericksburg. In the words of Samuel P. Bates, author of the state-authorized history of Pennsylvania's armed forces in the Civil War:

Exposed to a destructive fire, from which the rest of the brigade was shielded, [the 142nd Regiment] could only await destruction, without the privilege of returning it, and with no prospect of gaining an advantage, but with a nerve which veterans might envy, it heroically maintained its position till ordered to retire. Out of 550 men who stood in well-ordered ranks in the morning, 250 in one brief hour were stricken down.

The regiment spent the winter at Belle Plain Landing and in the spring marched to Chancellorsville. They saw no action there; but two months later they were one of the first units to reach Gettysburg, where they were deployed just west of the town to intercept the Confederate advance along the Cashtown Road. Though outnumbered and outgunned, they slowed the enemy's penetration through the afternoon, enabling the Union army to occupy Cemetery Ridge, the key to the ultimate victory. Compelled at last to retreat, the regiment left more than 100 killed

and wounded, with another 84 missing, most of them prisoners. Colonel Robert P. Cummins of Somerset was killed; and Captain Charles R. Evans and Lieutenant Andrew G. Tucker of Company E, and Major Thomas Chamberlain of the 150th Regiment were among the wounded in Confederate hands. They were taken to the seminary, which was converted into a field hospital, where they were given medical attention:

The three young men were together in the Seminary hospital, and for the next four days in the hands of the enemy. The major was able, during the progress of the battle to climb the steep, narrow, winding stairs leading to the seminary cupola, and after taking observations, bring down reports to his comrades on the ground floor. The result seemed uncertain until the rebels finally retreated on the morning of Sunday [July 5]. It was yet dim daylight when the major came down with the report. Young Tucker's face was even then pale and his eye glazed in death. Mid all his agony he had manifested keen interest and bright hope for victory. Chamberlain kneeled on the floor beside the dying boy and shouted in his ear the glad news; but it came too late to the nineteen year old officer, whose life had been given to help in bringing it about.[8]

On May 4, 1864, the 142nd Regiment joined in the campaign against Richmond and the next day was heavily engaged in the holocaust remembered as the Battle of the Wilderness. After seeing additional action at Cold Harbor, it took a position on the Petersburg siege line and at war's end was still in combat a short distance from Appomattox.

The youngest member of Company D, 150th Regiment, Pennsylvania Volunteers (the second Bucktails), sixteen-year-old Henry Kieffer, a drummer boy from Mifflinburg, recalled the drama incidental to the birth of a military organization. At the Mifflinburg Academy he and his classmates were smitten with the "war fever" and could not keep their minds on their lessons. They thrilled to the martial atmosphere of the war meetings: the fiery speeches by Henry W. Crotzer, who was soon to be their captain; the stirring tempo of "Hail Columbia" and "Away down South in Dixie"; and the wild excitement when Joe Gutelius, at the heels of his brothers, Sam and Charlie, stepped up and declared that he was going too. Joe's decision set off a chain reaction among the others, who went home to importune their parents.

Before dawn on departure day, households were astir. The local band joined relatives and friends to give them a sendoff; and as the carriages bearing the enlistees moved east on Chestnut Street, they were followed by a line of well-wishers. At almost every crossroads along the turnpike, additional convey-

Joseph S. Gutelius sent his photograph to his sister Kate on October 22, 1862. His picture was taken at the R.W. Addis Studio at 308 Pennsylvania Avenue, Washington, D.C. Courtesy of Ethel D. Ruhl.

ances moved into line. Reaching Lewisburg at 9 A.M., they found the main streets in a holiday atmosphere, and the crowds and bunting indicated that most work had ceased. Joining contingents already waiting for them, they marched to Montandon amidst huzzas from the mass of spectators — boys with red, white, and blue neckties and fatigue caps; girls carrying flags and flowers; women waving handkerchiefs; and old men waving their walking sticks. At the depot:

there was scarcely a man, woman or child in that great crowd around us but had to press up for a last shake of the hand, a last goodby, and a last "God bless you boys!" And so amid cheering and hand-shaking, and flag-waving and band-play, the train at last come thundering in, and we were off, with the "Star Spangled Banner" sounding fainter and farther away, until it was drowned and lost to the ear in the noise of the swiftly rushing train.[9]

The 150th Regiment went into training on Meridian Hill in Washington, and for a time Companies D and K were assigned to guard detail at the Soldiers' Home to protect President Lincoln and his family, who were using a cottage there as a summer home. During the years which followed, local audiences never seemed to tire of William Hursh's oft-repeated story of his meeting the President and Mrs. Lincoln.

After pitching their tents in a nearby field, Hursh and a comrade, being short of rations, had walked to the cottage, where they found the Lincolns seated on the porch. After Lincoln had returned their salute, they told him that they were from the company sent to guard him, and he replied that since General Pope's defeat many dangerous characters had been seen around the house. After a time the conversation drifted to the main purpose of their visit — their hunger.

Mrs. Lincoln went to the kitchen and ordered a meal for us. When it was ready a little bell rang, and she escorted us to the table. We then enjoyed a fine meal composed chiefly of corn cakes and bacon floating in fat. I can tell you we kept the cook busy baking!

When they had finished and were about to leave, the President surprised them by asking them to remain and sit down with him for awhile. When they told him they were in the detail for guard duty, he replied, "Never mind, I am the Commander-in-Chief of the army! You sit still." He asked them what sort of men were in their company; and when they told him they were largely students, farmers and mechanics, he replied that he had once been a soldier in the Black Hawk War. His remarks turned to the demoralized condition of the army, and he appeared to be downcast. He also spoke of his grandparents, who, he said, had been Pennsylvania Mennonites, and he expressed a desire to visit relatives there once his term had expired.

Hursh also recalled that Mrs. Lincoln had brought sandwiches and cakes to the men on guard — as late at night as 12 midnight; that Lincoln's face had been jolly after McClellan had stopped Lee at Antietam; and that as he drove out of the gate, he had raised his hat and said, "It is all right boys." One night an over-cautious guard had bayoneted an opossum, confusing it with a spy. Mrs. Lincoln had inquired about the noise and later repeated the story to Lincoln. She told the guardsmen that the president had never laughed more heartily. "He taunted us about it," Hursh added, "and he said he could depend on us to protect them in time of danger — even from opossums!"[10]

In May of 1863, the 150th Regiment, known as "The Bucktail Brigade," which included many of Union County's young men, moved with the army of General Hooker to Chancellorsville. Six weeks later the 150th made a forced march into Pennsylvania in the wake of Lee's invasion, and, arriving at Gettysburg about noon on July 1, was almost at once rushed into the battle at McPherson's Ridge. Fighting near the seminary, the Bucktails faced the same withering fire loosed upon the 142nd Regiment. As the Bucktails fell back into the town of Gettysburg, the color sergeant, who carried the brigade flag, around which all the men of the 150th would rally, was killed, and the rest of the color guard badly injured. Corporal Joseph Gutelius of Mifflinburg, possibly the only color guardsman able to bear the flag despite his wounds, carried the flag into Gettysburg. As he paused to rest on a doorstep, a pursuing Confederate squad spotted him and demanded that he surrender the flag. Rather than comply, Gutelius wrapped the flag around himself before the Confederates killed him and seized the flag as a trophy. The flag was eventually given to the Confederate president, Jefferson Davis, who kept it with his personal possessions until the war's end. After the war the flag was returned to Pennsylvania and displayed in the capitol at Harrisburg.

The heroic death of Joseph Gutelius was witnessed by two citizens of Gettysburg, who, under the cover of darkness, retrieved his body and buried it. He was reinterred with honors in grave #11, Pennsylvania section, of the Soldiers' National Cemetery in Gettysburg. The body of Joseph Ruhl, another youthful Union County casualty, was buried on the battlefield. When Ruhl's family learned of his death, his sister, Sara, hurried to Gettysburg. She found his burial place, had the body disinterred, and returned home with it. After a service in the front yard of their home, Joseph Ruhl was reburied in the Ray's Church cemetery.

After wintering at Culpepper, Virginia, the 150th advanced upon Richmond with the other Union County regiments. It was engaged in the Wilderness, where Captain Roland Stoughton of Company D was mortally wounded, and the regiment fought in the sector remembered as the "Bloody Angle" at Spottsylvania. In August it took its place at the siege of Petersburg. In the spring of 1865, the 150th was

dispatched to Elmira, New York, to guard the prisoner of war camp, remaining on duty there until the termination of the war.

Following the recruitment of the 150th Regiment, most Union County enlistees went into the older regiments as replacements. Two exceptions were made, however, when Company I of the 192nd and Company I of the 202nd Regiments were drawn from the county. The former was recruited for a term of one year only a few weeks before the end of the war and was commanded by Captain J. Wilson Hess of Lewisburg. The 192nd set up headquarters at Harper's Ferry and moved north through the Shenandoah Valley; but the fighting had virtually stopped, and it saw limited action. The 202nd rendezvoused at Camp Curtin in August of 1864 and went into training at Chambersburg under Captain Jacob Neyhart, a veteran of the 51st Regiment. For a short while, Colonel Charles Albright was called to Columbia County to handle the so-called Orange Creek Conspiracy, and his place was filled by Lieutenant Colonel John A. Maus of Union County. The regiment was dispatched to Thoroughfare Gap, Virginia, where it guarded the Manassas Gap Railroad, which provisioned General Sheridan during his brilliant campaign against General Early in the Shenandoah Valley. It saw no action but suffered some harassment from Southern guerrillas, who wrecked a locomotive and ambushed the survivors. Colonel Albright retaliated by burning every building in the vicinity and holding alleged guerrillas as hostages. With Early's forces scattered, the 202nd shifted to the line of the Orange and Alexandria Railroad and ended its service here a few weeks after the South's surrender at Appomattox.

The tradition of the Civil War was one of heroism, self-sacrifice, and service beyond the call of duty. Lewisburg could boast of the Chamberlain family — one brother following another as leaders of local companies. Mifflinburg had George H. Hassenplug, captain of Company E of the 51st Regiment, whose bravery, verve, and bearing seemed to epitomize the model officer. West Buffalo Township would brag about the Kline family, which had six sons in Captain Hassenplug's company and a seventh serving elsewhere; and the father, Jacob, had remained behind only because he was denied enlistment because of his age.

There was also the amazing career of William Harrison McCall, son of John McCall, a Scottish immigrant who had extensive lumber operations on the upper White Deer Creek watershed. He enlisted

The regimental flag of the 150th PennsylvaniaVolunteers.
Courtesy of the Capitol Preservation Committee, #1985.273.

PAGE 283: Joseph R. Ruhl was photographed in uniform
by Bell & Brother Studio at 480 Pennsylvania Avenue,
Washington D.C., c. 1862. Note the buck tail on his hat.
Courtesy of Ethel D. Ruhl.

take charge of the alleged assassins; and following their convictions, he oversaw their hangings at the Washington arsenal. He remained in the army after the war and died in Arizona in 1888.

While the focus of the Civil War must remain on the battlefields, the homefront also girded for the crisis; and the conflict has been appropriately described as an entire nation under arms as few families escaped its impact. Farmers planted more seeds and tended them more assiduously. The factories and shops turned out more goods, and mechanics worked longer hours. In Lewisburg more reapers and more canal boats were sent to market, and a newly founded shoe factory produced 1,500 pairs of "stout, serviceable" army shoes during the spring of 1862. At the west end of the county the "Penns Creek Oil Fever" set a number of "wild catters to boring for the hidden treasure." News dispatches appeared regularly, and predictions of "fifty-barrel wells" were rife; but no significant strikes were made, and the derricks were soon dismantled. The Berlin Iron Works at Glen Iron, the Union Furnace at Winfield, and the White Deer Furnace enjoyed their most productive years; and some of the county's industrialists shared in the unprecedented wartime profit making. Though the hastily improvised income tax returns are not infallible indices of earnings, they do provide bases for comparison. During the last year of the war Peter Beaver (iron industry) paid the largest income tax in the county — $14,715, reflecting an income of more than $80,000. He was followed by Levi Rooke (iron) paying $13,845; James Marsh (reapers), $13,314; and William Cameron (contracts for public and private construction), $12,768. No other resident paid more than $4,000.[11]

The initial war work of Union County women took place in their homes, producing shirts, socks, handkerchiefs, haversacks, and other necessities for the servicemen as they left for the war. Once the men were settled in training camps, they were soon packing foodstuffs by the boxful: dried fruits, butter, jellies, breads, cakes, and meats including chickens and turkeys in cold weather. The soldiers conveyed their thanks through the columns of the press, but they were soon discouraging the sending of bread and cakes as well as meats due to spoilage. Visitors leaving for the camps were apt to be loaded with home cooking, and they returned with their pockets filled with letters and money for the relatives back home.

"Woman's work" took on a greater urgency in the summer of 1862 as the massive armies went into

at age nineteen in the Fifth Pennsylvania Reserve Corps, and was mustered out three years later as a captain. Reenlisting in 1864, McCall was named as lieutenant colonel of the 200th Regiment and subsequently promoted to colonel. A few weeks before the fall of Richmond, he was again promoted to the rank of brigadier general for gallant service at the head of a brigade which captured Forts Sedgwick and Steadman at the Petersburg siege. He was then 23, possibly the youngest man of his rank in the service. After the assassination of President Lincoln, he was chosen by President Johnson and General Hancock to action on the James Peninsula. The Lewisburg's Soldiers' Aid Society was organized on July 17 and branches were soon operating in the other towns and villages. The immediate need was bandages, clothing, and other hospital supplies, and workshops were opened for this service. In Lewisburg a workshop was set up in a room at the home of William Frick at Third and Market; in Mifflinburg, at Wolf's Hall; and in Buffalo Township, at the Great Western Hotel. Girls, returning from school, stopped at these centers to pick or scrape lint. The work was coordinated by the United States Christian Commission at the outset and later by the United States Sanitary Commission. Dr. Lemuel Moss, a professor at the college in Lewisburg, served as home secretary of the former and edited its annals.

The debacle at the Second Battle of Manassas brought another call for lint, bandages, and physicians. Doctors David H. Miller, Charles Brundage, Samuel B. Van Valzah, Benjamin Thompson, and Sallie Kleckner responded. At Washington, however, they discovered that their services would not be needed. Bloody Antietam elicited another call; then came Gettysburg. The impact of the latter in Lewisburg is suggested by entries in Sallie Meixell's diary:

She had been busier than a bee in the morning. There were lots of folks at the work shop, preparing and collecting provisions. At eleven she paused to see the militia off, and joined the pilgrimage to the depot at Montandon. Word of the victory was received, but the joy was tempered by unofficial reports of local casualties. In the afternoon the women mobilized to produce bandages, cotton and flannel shirts and socks, and assemble arrow root, farina, and corn starch, jellies, dried and canned fruits, pickles, onions and beans; also syrup and butters of all kinds, "and articles too numerous to mention."[12]

Much of the work during the last two years of the war was done in behalf of the United States Sanitary Commission, a forerunner of the Red Cross. Local sanitary fairs were popular and yielded sizable sums for the cause. The Juvenile Female Aid Society of Mifflinburg raised $80 at a two-night Christmas fair. Perhaps the most strenuous drive was made in June of 1864 in conjunction with the great Philadelphia Fair, where President Lincoln was the honored guest. East Buffalo Township women contributed $142 in goods and money; and in Lewisburg both James S. Marsh and Company, and Slifer, Walls and Shriner presented their latest models of horse-drawn reapers. In the absence of a governmental agency to provide necessities for families which lost their breadwinners through enlistment or death on the battlefields, local committees solicited contributions for them, and occasionally soldiers passed the hat in their camps to help dependents of fallen comrades.

Union County people also responded individually to needs which pricked their consciences. In January of 1864, a Reverend Waters, a Unionist refugee from Tennessee, opened a school for blacks — some of them former slaves — in Lewisburg, where he assembled more than 30 pupils; the school continued for several years after the war. B.C. Youngman and W.P. Montelius of Mifflinburg, learning of the influx of freedmen into Nashville in 1864, volunteered to go there to teach in the schools which the Christian Commission was opening for them.

No fewer than eleven of Union County's physicians were commissioned as surgeons and served with the armed forces. Dr. J. Reynolds Gast of Mifflinburg interrupted his practice to serve in the military hospital at Camp Chase near Chicago. Serving as surgeons in regimental hospitals were Drs. George S. Kemble, John Noteling, Harris C. Steadman, and J.H. Hassenplug, all of Mifflinburg; George Lotz of New Berlin; and Theodore S. Christ, William Hayes, Thomas C. Thornton, Samuel Blair and P.F. Hyatt from Lewisburg. [Theodore Christ's diary includes his period of service and is in the collection of the Union County Historical Society.]

At the outset of the war, the dissidence typical in a democratic society was quieted by the general agreement that a Southern conspiracy had created the rebellion, and that it had to be suppressed whatever the cost. However, when the "90-day campaign" to quell the uprising and occupy the Confederate capital dragged into a second year, at the cost of thousands of lives, opposition to the handling of the war became commonplace. Some expressed doubts that General McClellan had sought a decisive victory, whereas his defenders alleged that the fault lay among the politicians in Washington. Lincoln was accused of wielding dictatorial power by some of his critics and moving too slowly by others. Costly defeats at Second Manassas and Fredericksburg added to the depression. Writing from General Burnside's Headquarters near the Antietam battlefield a few weeks after the battle, a young Union County officer gave vent to his feelings:

There is a devil of a row brewing somewhere. Burnside denounces McClellan openly, and you know he is not the man to do so without sufficient cause. . . . Two hundred levies have been lost, and we are worse off today than we were a year ago. I am willing to fight and die in the sacred cause of maintaining the government, but I am not willing to die for the purpose of promoting the ambition of a man, be he general or politician. . . .

I am afraid I have been talking treason. If telling what you hear and think in this matter be treason, then I am a traitor. You do not know what condition our army is in. I am sick and tired of this carnage, apparently for no purpose. . . . My comrades in arms know that I would risk and dare as much as any of them, but how can we stand idly by and see such men as [General Jesse L.] Reno, our dear friend [Jacob B.] Beaver and many others sacrificed, and nothing done. But when Beaver was slain . . . and when I heard the result of the battle . . . I felt as if they were leading our men to the grave for nothing. . . . Evidence, overwhelming evidence, force us unwillingly to believe in the imbecility of our leaders.[13]

Several months later, writing from the battlefield of Fredericksburg, where several days earlier Burnside's poorly conceived battle plan had cost so many lives, a second county officer poured out his despair:

I have just returned from the hospital — awful scenes, legs and arms by the cords; I intend to resign. . . . I don't mean to have my life at the disposal of a set of miserable military gamblers. Joe. Hooker wants to succeed General Burnside, and refused to obey orders on the field. . . . I thank God I am safe, and out of the massacre of the innocents. I am too weary and heart sick to write any more. Our army is too badly used up. It can do no more fighting this winter.[14]

As the crisis worsened, local supporters of the administration were apt to overlook the difference between methods and goals and to regard any criticism as harmful and as evidence of Southern sympathies. The label "Copperhead" was thrown about almost indiscriminately so as to encompass not only a military cell organized to assist the Southern cause (none of which existed in the county), but also a candidate for a local office on the Democratic ticket. When a young New Berlin man objected to Bible reading in the schools, the *Telegraph* warned that it proved him to be "a Copperhead of the highest magnitude."

Without question the most unpopular voice of dissent in the valley was the Lewisburg *Argus*, published by J. Gundy Winegartner. Unfortunately, few issues of the paper have survived, and quotations from the other papers are limited to its most abrasive outbursts. During the war-weary spring of 1863, the *Argus* advocated a negotiated peace, arguing that a peace platform was not unlike the Federalist opposition to the War of 1812. It was taken to task by the Republican papers, and the *Chronicle* predicted that the peace faction would go to oblivion in the manner of the Federalists in 1812. A more devastating response came from the soldiers in the field. Resolutions adopted by Company D of the 150th Regiment

noted "the artful manner" in which articles in the *Argus* had been designed "to mislead the masses. The whole tone of the sheet is of a nature to depress the cause of liberty, to dishearten those in the field and to discourage those at home." Castigating it as injurious to the cause, the resolutions asked loyal friends "to return to the grand jury at its next session, a paper so much at variance with true loyalty."[15]

When the *Argus* alleged that pressure in the army denied the expression of a minority opinion, it was rebuffed by a resolution adopted in Company E of the 142nd Regiment and signed by a sizable number of its personnel; the resolution declared it a "sacred duty" to give the administration undivided support and to refrain from expressions of doubt. Deploring the formation of a party hostile to the administration, which was a "corrupting influence over our friends and neighbors," the resolution declared that those who lead and those who follow it "are traitors at heart." By contrast, it lauded the Union League as a means of combating such "base designs."[16] The pervasive influence of the soldiers' viewpoint was observed by the *Chronicle* upon the return of the 131st Regiment from its nine-month tour of duty. Loyalty to the Union was having a decided effect upon the Copperhead newspapers, it declared, "making them discharge less venom than heretofore." The veterans left no doubt about their views when, at a dinner tendered by a grateful public in Lewisburg, they adopted resolutions calling for the support of the war and denouncing Southern sympathies.

The *Argus* continued to draw the wrath of the armed forces in the months which followed. Fisher Gutelius of Company D of the 150th Regiment advised the *Telegraph* that the men had received a copy of the *Argus* and found it full of censure against the president and the army but with no criticism of Jefferson Davis. Gutelius complained, "Such a filthy abusive and slanderous sheet, we never chanced to see before, and we hope and pray that another may never be found in our camp."[17] Whether the *Argus* again circulated in the camp remains unanswered, but the election of 1864 intensified the verbal warfare between the newspapers. In October the *Argus* represented the Republican Party as a collection of "howling, blood-thirsty fanatics" and its clergy as "bloody, infidel monsters who have literally turned the churches into dens of thieves." The *Argus* also labeled President Lincoln a "tyrant whose name blisters our tongue."[18]

Despite the apparent unpopularity of anti-Union sentiments, freedom of speech was not eliminated in

Union County in the stress of the Civil War. It might be noted, also, that despite the many imprecations hurled at the *Argus,* it was not taken to court nor was its publication interrupted by violence, as was a "Copperhead" paper in Sunbury. Members of a New York regiment during a train stop in Sunbury rushed from the cars and broke into the office of the *Northumberland Democrat,* where they scattered the type and damaged the press.

Aside from the *Argus,* members of the clergy were the principal targets of the critics of nonconformity. Had the Reverend John W. Hedges, pastor of the Methodist church in Lewisburg, been in a different occupation, his dislike for the war and the policies of the Lincoln administration might never have found their way into print. Even so, his "dismissal" might have remained an "open secret" in the community if political partisanship had not become involved, and if a political issue had not fanned the smoldering embers of disharmony. Hedges had advocated a reconciliation between the North and South; and after the war erupted, he continued to urge a negotiated peace. His unpopular position led to the withdrawal of a sizable number of parishioners; and the council insisted that he and the Reverend Thomas M. Reese, who alternated in the pulpit, "pledge themselves to the thirty-four stars and thirteen stripes." Hedges noted that he had voted but once in a dozen years but that he had always been loyal to the Methodist Episcopal Church of the United States and the government at Washington. However, in March of 1862, at a meeting of the East Baltimore Methodist Episcopal Conference, Hedges voted against a resolution calling for approval of the "wise and patriotic" policies of the administration. Aware that a majority of the congregation disapproved of his position, Hedges agreed to resign; but prior to his departure, a minority element in the church, headed by Henry W. Crotzer, arranged a reception for him at the parsonage, where he was presented with a gift of money.

The matter might have ended there quietly had not Crotzer declared that the behavior of the congregation exhibited a spirit of persecution. Assuming that they had been duped and made to appear that they endorsed Hedges' views by their participation in the reception, the majority thereupon went on record to observe that patriotism was a Christian duty, that the action of the Baltimore Conference met with their approval, and that Crotzer's charge of a spirit of persecution was unjustified. In explaining the action of the congregation, the *Chronicle* added:

Had his friends made their ostentatious gift of gold and silver privately, it might have passed as a personal matter only, but since he has permitted himself to be used by a little "knot of politicians" for a party and disloyal end, and has joined in giving credence to charges of "persecution" and "slander," he cannot complain if those most concerned repel the charge.

Hedges, it added, had been considered "a weak brother," and his explanation for his vote at Baltimore was unsatisfactory.[19] I.H. Mauser in his *History of Lewisburg* noted only that the membership of the church had dropped from 327 to 236, "owing no doubt to the outspoken manner in which the ministers discoursed on political subjects." Crotzer, it might be noted, was the Lewisburg postmaster during Buchanan's presidency, and he eventually led Company D of the 150th Regiment.

A year later, the *Chronicle* reported a union service where a "Democratic preacher" called for an armistice of three months and, declaring slavery scripturally defensible, traced the practice back to Ham, the second son of Noah. It did not otherwise identify the speaker, but noted that "patriotic" ministers such as Hugh S. Dickson of the Lewisburg Presbyterian church and Thomas M. Reese of the Lewisburg Methodist church were victims of "vile and libelous epithets."

Several Mifflinburg clergy likewise came under fire. At a Methodist service when the Reverend Shannon "unfortunately" called upon the Reverend William Hesser to deliver the closing prayer, "a large number of respectable citizens and members of the church rose and left the house . . . unmistakably a manifestation of supreme disgust toward a notorious Copperhead, who we trust will take the lesson of his stinging rebuke to heart and profit by it."[20] Hesser, a young Methodist minister supplying rural churches in the area, had been a teacher in the Mifflinburg schools before attending the Allegheny Theological School. He later served successfully in the Lycoming Circuit of the Methodist church and returned to Mifflinburg to retire in 1901.

Again, in a Thanksgiving sermon in November of 1863, a minister was charged with preaching a sermon "which we can say with truth would have been as appropriate in Richmond as in Mifflinburg," and with castigating "political preachers" as "ragamuffins and liars." The writer resumed the attack several weeks later; and while he did not name the minister, he identified him with the German Reformed church; with the title of his sermon, "The Position which a Christian Minister Should Occupy in these Troublous Times" and with the gist of his argument, that the war was a political issue and that sermonizing upon it would only give offense and create dissensions. He reminded the minister that the venerated Just Fries had sent the militia to war in 1812 from the pulpit of the same church with the promise that their patriotism had the blessing of God; but instead of such a forthright position, "this man has pretended to be a Republican with Republicans and a Democrat with Democrats, refusing to vote because he could not fix his tickets [there was no secret ballot, and they could be identified by their color], so no one could tell how he voted."[21] It would appear unlikely that readers of the article could have remained unaware of the identity of the clergyman; but if there were, the pseudonym used by the writer, "Pataskala," would have dispelled all doubts as "Cook's Pataskala Syrup" was the name of a medicine advertised weekly in the paper and "sold exclusively" in the region by the Reverend I. (Israel) S. Weisz. The death of Weisz's son on the battlefield a few months later may have silenced his critic, as Weisz remained in his position until the war closed.

The Reverend J.M. Anspach, son of the venerable J.G. Anspach, came as pastor to the Lutheran church in Mifflinburg in 1863 shortly after his graduation from theological school. He seems to have barely begun his ministry when it was alleged that he was a Copperhead and that he "affected to believe" that slavery was a divine institution. It was also reported that Anspach had made the statement that he would be willing to ask "Mr. B." (identified only as a Presbyterian minister who had been an army chaplain) to substitute for him in the pulpit if he were not such a Black Abolitionist. In a column in the local paper, a certain "Wesley" editorialized, "It ill becomes a mere BABE in knowledge and religion to blabber forth his feeble opposition. J.M.A. might just as well attempt to turn back the current of the Mississippi with his foot as to stem the advancing tide of liberty." In the manner of the *Argus*, he concluded his umbrage with an imaginative conversation between J.M.A. and the Devil. The former explained that he claimed to be loyal so that he might thrust a dagger into the country's heart, "as a friend." "I was a traitor at heart but lacked the courage to be a Rebel." His confession apparently greatly pleased Satan, for he seated him at his side.[22]

Pointing to a general conference of the Methodist Episcopal church, which excluded slaveholders from membership and endorsed abolition, and to a conference of the Lutheran church, which acknowledged that the war was righteous, the *Telegraph* soliloquized:

if only all of our ministers had the courage and the will to instill such doctrine into the hearts and minds of their members. If only some whom we could name would quit prating about this "unjust, ungodly, wicked" war and teach their people that it is a "righteous" war — a war for freedom — a war for humanity — a war for our very Nationality.

The Copperhead issue spilled over into the election of the county superintendent of schools in May of 1863. Luther Anspach, son of J.G. Anspach and brother of J.M. Anspach, was, like his father and brother, a prominent Democrat. He and Captain John A. Owens, a Republican who had recently retired from the army, were the rivals. Before proceeding to a vote, the directors asked the candidates to respond to a resolution in support of the Constitutions of the United States and Pennsylvania and in support of the constituted authorities in suppressing rebellion, punishing treason, and maintaining the government without compromise with traitors. In response Anspach explained that he thought he could accept it while Owens' reply was a cryptic, "Now and forever." Owens was elected by a vote of 36-23.[23]

Charges that John Randolph was a Copperhead also closed the Lewisburg Academy. Randolph, a Southerner by birth, had operated the school for eighteen years; but his criticisms of the administration's war policy did not please the parents of his pupils, and they withdrew their children in such numbers that he was unable to reopen the school in the fall of 1863. "Professor Randolph's school did not start Monday," a Lewisburg resident informed Eli Slifer. "He has printed a card asking the good people not to allow party feelings to enter into educational affairs;"[24] but they did, and the small Greek temple became a private home.

Particularly satisfying to administration Republicans in the presidential election of 1864 were the votes of the soldiers, which were cast overwhelmingly for Lincoln as well as for local Republican candidates. Almost equally gratifying was the demise of the *Argus*, which ceased publication shortly after Lincoln's triumph. Victory now seemed increasingly a matter of time.

The fall of Richmond on April 3, 1865, symbolizing the close of the war, was the first of a fortnight of glorious and tragic occurrences. News of the surrender came to Buffalo Valley in a proclamation by Eli Slifer, Pennsylvania's secretary of the commonwealth:

The last center of treason has fallen . . . Richmond is ours . . . . Let us give glory to the Lord, who hath given us the victory. The Republic is saved . . . I call on the people of the

Commonwealth to assemble to their places of worship on Sunday and give thanks to almighty God for all his mercies, and especially that he has made us the instruments to establish Right, to vindicate the principles of Free Government, and to prove the certainty of Divine Justice.[25]

That night throughout Union County bonfires were kindled, salutes were fired from the anvils, flags were displayed, "and the greatest joy was manifested."

The surrender of General Lee six days later set off another spontaneous round of celebrations. "This morning the news came that the Rebel General Lee had surrendered his army, and such a time of rejoicing I am sure this town has never seen," Sally Meixell noted in her diary. "Flags of all sizes and descriptions were displayed everywhere this afternoon. At four-thirty o'clock all bells were rung for almost an hour, and the firing of anvils has not ceased, nor bonfires, burning balls, martial music, and noise and racket of every description."[26]

Elisha Shorkley, Lewisburg foundryman, was enroute to his home from a business trip to Lewistown on the following Friday; and as the stage jolted along, his mind strayed to the great celebration planned for the morrow. After spending the night in New Berlin, he started for home. When he arrived at ten, he found all the banners draped in mourning and many of his friends in tears. President Lincoln had been shot the evening before, and the word of his death had just come over the telegraph wire. A little while later, a special single column edition of the *Chronicle* added a few of the shocking details:

Lewisburg Chronicle
— **EXTRA** —

Saturday Morning, April 15, 1865

Awful Assassination!
The Nation in Mourning!
OUR NOBLE PRESIDENT
IS DEAD!!
Seward Mortally Wounded
Frederick Seward also Assassinated!

The nation has been overwhelmed with grief by the tidings of assassination of President Lincoln, Sec. Seward and Frederick Seward, and the death of the former, contained in the following despatches. Truly, "our joy is turned to mourning."
WASHINGTON, April 15 — midnight.
GEN. DIX, N.Y.: About 9:30 P.M., at Ford's Theatre, the President, while sitting in his private box with Mrs. Lincoln, Miss Harris and Mayor Rathburn, was shot by an Assassin who suddenly entered the box and approached behind the President. The assassin then leaped upon the stage, brandishing a large dagger or knife, and made his escape through the rear of the theatre. The pistol ball entered the back of the President's head, and penetrated nearly through it. The wound was mortal. The President has been insensible ever since it was inflicted, and is now dying.

About the same time, an assassin, whether the same or another is not known, entered Mr. Seward's house, and under pretense of having a prescription, was shown the bed the Secretary was in, and rushing to the bed inflicted one or two stabs in the throat and two in the face. It is hoped the wounds may not be mortal. My apprehension is that they will prove fatal.
The noise alarmed Frederick Seward, who slept in an adjoining room, when he met the assassin who inflicted upon him one or more dangerous wounds. The recovery of Frederick Seward is doubtful.
It is not probable that the President will live through the night.
E.M. STANTON.

HARRISBURG, APRIL 15 — 8 A.M.
J.R. CORNELIUS, Lewisburg: The President died at 2:15 this morning.
J. BRADY LYNDALL, Opr.[27]

Sallie Meixell recorded her impressions of that terrible day also:

It has crushed us; saddened every heart; even strong men shed tears and muttered vows to vengeance. We could talk [and] think today of but one thing. . . . Never in any nation's history have so many tears, and so much true mourning been given to any man.[28]

That remorse could be transformed into vengeance was brought home to the Reverend W. Lee Spottswood, the newly appointed minister of the Methodist church in Lewisburg. According to his reminiscence, a workman at a local shop several days later declared that the man who shot Lincoln "did right"; and that if he could find him, he would give him a quarter of a dollar. He soon discovered he had stirred a hornet's nest, and, fearing bodily harm, he attempted to get out of town. He got into a boat and tried to cross the river (the bridge had been washed away in the St. Patrick's Day flood) but was apprehended. A maddened crowd surrounded him in front of the Revere House, and shouts of "hang him" drowned out his protests that he was a good citizen. Standing at the outskirts of the "raging" crowd, Spottswood feared for the life of the "wretch," but he could think of nothing which might save him. At the critical moment Sheriff Church arrived and escorted the man to the county jail. The war had ended, but reconciliation had only begun.

It is difficult to evaluate the impact of the war upon the generation which lived through it; but until 1917, any mention made of "the war" clearly referred to the war between the states. No war has ever been "fought over" as many times; none has elicited as many publications. Veterans were still writing their memoirs 50 years after the last shot was fired. Certainly Supreme Court Justice Oliver Wendell Holmes, who was gravely wounded at Antietam, sensed the war's impact when he wrote, "Through

TOP: A collection of Civil War souvenirs owned by Lewisburg native and surgeon Dr. Theo Christ include a ceremonial sword and participant medals from the 1886, 1889, 1891, and 1894 GAR annual encampments. The tin cup is embossed on its reverse and commemorates the 20th National GAR Encampment in California. From the Christ Collection, Union County Historical Society.

Entries from the pension record ledger kept by Lewisburg attorney D.H. Getz show the Civil War and Spanish American applicants— both soldiers and widows of soldiers — for pensions, their disabilities, and the rulings. From the collection of the Union County Historical Society, #2000.1.1, gift of Alfred Hause.

Cynthia Cornelius –

Widow of Jesse M. Corneli..
Co. I. 202 Pa. Vols.
Enrolled Aug. 23 – 1864.
Discharged Aug. 3 – 1865.
Married under name of Cynthe..
Houghton, to said Jesse M. Corne..
December 28 – 1865. by Rev. Gre..
at Mifflinburgh, Pa.
Died April 18 – 1897.
Children under 16 years of a..
Donald, born Jany 2 – 1882
Florence, " March 2 – 1885.
neither of them had been previ..
married!
Soldier was pensioned by Certf. 614, 7..
Declaration mailed April 26 – 189..
Address – Lewisburgh, Pa.
Claim No. 653,239 –

Dec. 28 – 1898 allowed o..
granted at "8. – and "2. –
add. for each of i..

our great, good fortune in our youth our hearts were touched with fire. It was given to us to learn at the outset that life is a profound and passionate thing."[29]

Veterans returned to occupy prominent positions in the business, professional, and political life of their communities. Even before the advent of peace, Captain Thomas Church was elected sheriff of Union County and Captain John Owens, county superintendent of schools. Veterans dominated the councils of the Republican Party in the post-war years and revered it with a loyalty akin to patriotism. They expressed their comradeship at countless reunions, and their reverence for those who had fallen made Memorial Day a national requiem. In time, scarcely a town and few villages were without a commemorative monument, and Union County was no exception. On July 4, 1901, the public assembled at South Third Street and University Avenue in Lewisburg to share in the dedication of the Union County Soldiers and Sailors Memorial monument. It still stands; and after being refurbished, the monument was rededicated in a ceremony July 4, 1995.

ENDNOTES:

[1] *Roderick Dhu, Scottish Chieftain in Walter Scott's Lady of the Lake*, reminiscence of Professor J.S. James, then a student at the University at Lewisburg, Bucknell University Archives.

[2] Linn Papers, May 6, 1861, Bucknell University Archives.

[3] Mrs. Franklin Earnest Papers.

[4] *Mifflinburg Telegraph*, September 16, 1862.

[5] *Mifflinburg Telegraph*, March 1 and 8, 1895.

[6] *Lewisburg Chronicle*, June 30, 1863.

[7] Linn Papers, Bucknell University Archives.

[8] Reminiscence of Professor J.S. James, Bucknell University Archives.

[9] Harry M. Kieffer, *Recollections of a Drummer Boy*, Boston, 1883, 25-27.

[10] *Mifflinburg Telegraph*, March 27, 1924.

[11] *Lewisburg Chronicle*, August 9, 1867.

[12] Meixell Papers, Bucknell University Archives.

[13] Lt. John A. Morris, Linn Papers, Bucknell University Archives.

[14] Lt. John B. Linn, December 16, 1862, Linn papers, Bucknell University Archives.

[15] *Lewisburg Chronicle*, April 7, 1863.

[16] *Lewisburg Chronicle*, May 22, 1863.

[17] *Lewisburg Chronicle*, February 18, 1864.

[18] Reprinted in the *Lewisburg Chronicle*, October 6, 1865.

[19] *Lewisburg Chronicle*, April 4 and 8, 1862.

[20] *Mifflinburg Telegraph*, August 27, 1863.

[21] *Mifflinburg Telegraph*, November 26 and December 24, 1863.

[22] *Mifflinburg Telegraph*, July 14, 1864.

[23] *Lewisburg Chronicle*, May 8 and 15, 1863.

[24] Oliver N. Worden, September 29, 1863, Dickinson College Archives.

[25] *Mifflinburg Telegraph*, April 6, 1865.

[26] Meixell Papers, April 10, 1865, Bucknell University Archives.

[27] *Lewisburg Chronicle*, April 15, 1865.

[28] Meixell Papers, Bucknell University Archives.

[29] *Lewisburg Saturday News*, May 7, 1921.

Many took the train to Lewisburg on July 4, 1901, for the dedication of the Soldiers' Monument at South Third and Market Streets. From the collection of the Union County Historical Society, #82.4.3.26.Ba

CHAPTER 17

UNION COUNTY'S ROLE IN WORLD WAR I

It was not easy for Americans to decide to become involved in World War I. Recurring crises arising from competition for empires, disagreements over boundaries, expanding militarism, and the growth of nationalism among minorities were considered to be European, not American problems, since we were shielded by the Atlantic and Pacific Oceans. Thus we were neutrals, at least officially. Yet we were not neutral in thought and action.

The British Navy, still "ruling the seas," blocked the ports of the Central Powers: Germany, Austria-Hungary, and Turkey, while the delivery of manufactures and raw materials from the United States to Great Britain and France was increased dramatically. After the war, some historians charged that the American involvement in the success of the Allied Powers tipped the balance, and that we went to war to save our economy, including the munitions makers.

An accounting of the causes for our eventual participation remains more complicated. A more substantive reason for going to war was the German submarine warfare upon neutral shipping, including the taking of American lives. There were also factors which might be termed psychological; as communications were severed with the Central Powers, the war was interpreted for us by the British, who stressed German militarism — reaching back to Frederick the Great and Chancellor Bismarck.

In Central Pennsylvania, many German descendants were reluctant to go to war against their mother country (though most Pennsylvania Dutch had come from southern Germany and Switzerland rather than Prussia, which was identified with militarism). Congressman Benjamin K. Focht of Lewisburg had testified many times to the high quality of the German population, and he distributed a last-minute questionnaire among the voters asking for their opinion upon a declaration of war. German submarines, however, intervened; and he voted with the majority for war on April 2, 1917, without waiting for a response.

Except for the Spanish-American War of 1898, the nation had not been at war since 1865, and was poorly prepared to immediately enter the conflict. Once undertaken, no war in which the nation had been involved was less controversial.

With a standing army of just over 200,000 and an expected need for more than a million more, the focus in Union County was immediately upon Troop

M, a company of cavalry in Lewisburg, which was one of four — including troops I of Sunbury, L of Bellefonte, K of Lock Haven — collectively identified as the MILK Squadron. It was commanded by Major Wallace W. Fetzer of Milton, while Major General Charles Clement of Sunbury commanded the regiment. Captain Samuel B. Wolfe of Lewisburg had recently been promoted to head Troop M.[1]

The troop had been mobilized on July 6, 1916, and dispatched to the Mexican border in Texas a year earlier following Pancho Villa's raid into New Mexico; but it had returned in January of 1917 and was mustered out of service. Awaiting formal reactivation, married men were permitted to withdraw, and an active drive was undertaken for recruits. On April 20 Troop M led a preparedness parade along with the Lewisburg Band, Civil War veterans in automobiles, schoolchildren by grades carrying flags, a "platoon" of Bucknell faculty, and "two companies" of Bucknell students. Troop M was mounted on its "thirty-two chargers," supplemented with additional mounts borrowed from Troop I of Sunbury. Their troop gun was pulled by four mules. Following the parade, the troop drilled near the fountain; but it became a problem, even though they moved at a walk. The horses were not shod to handle the smooth brick road surface, and several of the riders were thrown.

A second preparedness feature was a program at the Orpheum Theatre consisting of 50 still photographs of the troop while at Camp Stewart on the Mexican border. Benefits were used to purchase auto accessories and other supplies. Troop M's reactivation was held on August 5. Forming in line then dismounting at the town square as the names were called, they moved forward two steps to enter the federal service.

On September 11 the troop departed for the war. An estimated 3,000-4,000 citizens were on the streets at 11:30 A.M. when the Lewisburg Band led the procession to the Pennsylvania Railroad Station. Above the music and cheers, the whistles at the Chair Factory and Buffalo Mills could occasionally be heard. At the depot Colonel William R. Follmer and Captain Cloyd Steininger delivered farewell messages; Follmer had headed the troop for many years, and Steininger had been its captain, but both had been retired due to their ages.[2] The train was late and didn't pull out until two o'clock, but fortunately the troop was well supplied with box lunches prepared by "the young ladies." There was now the realization of war as spectators waved their farewells.

The personnel of Troop M leaving for boot-camp were: Captain Samuel B. Wolfe, First Lieutenant Grover C. Yost, 2nd Lieutenant Paul Kline, and:

Sergeants:
Robert Donaldson	Joseph W. Snyder
Albert A. Everett	Hiram M. Wolfe, Jr.
Oliver Heiter	Donald J. Zimmerman
Herbert B. Marsh	

Corporals:
Derben W. Bartholomew	Baker Kohler
Abram W. Farley	Ralph Kohler
Robert C. Gregg	Edward L. Shannon
Joseph C. Johnson,	Baker F. Spyker

Privates:
Harry M. Albright	Stoughton Meyers
William E. Allen	William H. Middlesworth
William Aurand	Corbett G. Miller
Newton E. Baker	Thomas G. Miller
William F. Bender	Albert E. North
Harry M. Bennett	Budd Owen
William E. Bickel	William G. Painter
Harry L. Byers	Elmer D. Pierce
Harry L. Cahn	Leon C. Pierce
William A. Cawley	Harry H. Pursell
Thomas C. Cockrill, Jr.	Benjamin R. Rearick
Joseph H. Cornelius	Lester R. Ruhl
Leo J. Cromley	John F. Schneider
Ralph J. Dull	Thornton M. Sechler
Benjamin Elliot	David C. Shilling
John M. Fisher	Charles E. Siglin
D. Andrew Gearhart	Alvin L. Simons
Henry W. Graden	Bromley R. Smith, Jr.
Reber L. Groover	Daniel G. Snyder
William G.D.D. Guyer	Roy L. Stahl
Arthur J. Hafer,	Archie J. Steese
Melvin M. Harshbarger	Ralph O. Strasner
Bynum T. Hartley	Roy N. Straub
Harvey A. Hemrer	Lester C. Swanger
John C. Hendren	Harry J. Swinehart
Fred L. Hoffa	Burton H. Switzer
Harry E. Katherman	Walter S. White
Walter G. Kniss	Joshua S. Whitmoyer
Emery R. Koch	Fred B. Wolfe
Bright L. Kratzer	Joseph P. Wolfe
William L. Kratzer	John F. Yeisley
Charles T. Kreisher	James F. Young
Joseph A. Logan	John B. Youngman
William B. Lower	George R. Zeiber

Cooks:
John Aurand	Lloyd Zellner

Stable Sergeant:
Jacob E. Winkelblech

Saddler:
Charles W. Swinehart

Buglers:
Don Harpham	Watson Wagner[3]

They were joined enroute by Cavalry Troops I, L, and K, the machine gun troop from Boalsburg and the Governor's Troop. Boarding a train at Harrisburg, the contingent required 25 cars, with nine Pullman, six horse, seven box and three flat cars. After a stop at Rocky Mount in North Carolina to exercise and water the horses, they continued to what would be their training center, Fort Hancock, several miles from Augusta in northern Georgia. In a report from Camp Hancock a few weeks later, Captain Wolfe observed that the shoe polish provided by Charlie Bell, the Lewisburg "shoe-shine artist," furnished "everbright" polish for their shoes; and that he had used the $10 given by the Rev. John Judd from the Red Cross to buy bread, since none had been issued. The troop, a unit of the First Cavalry, 28th Division, was housed in seventeen tents, fourteen of which were pyramidal and held eight men each.

The Company had scarcely settled into a routine, however, when the army decided that the cavalry was expendable. The startling news reached Lewisburg on November 3 and was headlined in the *Saturday News*:

Sad fate of Troop M boys; Wiped out by war order; in small groups they are scattered elsewhere; much regret that Lewisburg and Union County will cease to be represented by an organization. A more solemn body of men never occupied a tented city than the First Cavalry. On the Border it ranked with the best in the United States.

Two weeks later the decision was countermanded, and there was "great joy" in camp. It was only a brief reprieve, however since on December 1, the troop was again "shattered" when the cavalry was "scrapped," with its personnel separated into several different services. The largest group was transferred to the 103d Trench Mortar Battery, and some others were sent to Company B, 103rd Engineers and the Military Police of the 103rd. Several of the men, including Captain Wolfe, were reassigned to the 106th U.S. Cavalry at Fort Clark, Eagle Pass, Texas, for border patrol. Pausing long enough for a wedding, Wolfe and his wife proceeded to this remote outpost.[4]

In retrospect, it might be noted that the United States mobilized for war in 1917 at a pace and to a degree never experienced earlier. During the Civil War, conscription was improvised to keep armies in the field; special taxes were levied, with one following another; and paper money, which soon depreciated in value (greenbacks), was issued. Military courts sometimes curbed traditional freedoms. In World War I, by contrast, in a matter of weeks President Wilson used emergency wartime powers to mobilize men, arms, money, energy, and food; the government sought to influence public opinion, as well.

A drive for enlistments in the armed forces was initiated immediately, and in the House of Representatives Benjamin K. Focht urged that volunteers be used to fill the ranks. In the Civil War, with a population less than one-third of that in 1917, enlistments had gathered several millions for the services; and Focht argued that Americans would once again rally just as they had done a half-century before.

Six weeks after the declaration of war, Wilson signed the Selective Service Bill, and on June 5 registration for the first draft was held. One thousand fifty names of men between the ages of 21 and 31 were recorded in Union County. On July 20 the first names were drawn in Washington, including 55 from Union County to fill sixteen slots. When the first drawing did not provide the sixteen, 45 additional names were drawn. No married men were included in this draft. A second registration, embracing males between 19 and 35 not included in the first draft, followed. The initial sixteen departed for Camp Meade at Annapolis, Maryland, on September 19, an occasion described graphically by the *Saturday News* as "a sad scene at the Pennsylvania Station" in Lewisburg."[5]

Another quota of 32 was selected and dispatched to Camp Lee in Virginia in June of 1918. Those taken from Mifflinburg and the western townships gathered first in town and were then conveyed to the courthouse in Lewisburg in autos for a second farewell; attended by "a large concourse," they received words of advice from Colonel Follmer. Following the ceremony, they were accompanied to the Pennsylvania Railroad Station for transportation to camp. Mifflinburg's draft board at this time consisted of Kreider Kurtz, Thomas M. Getgen, Dr. Charles H. Dimm, and David L. Glover (who would later receive a commendation from President Wilson for his chairmanship of this board.)

While former members of Troop M and draftees were training at various camps in the United States, volunteers in ambulance companies were enroute to Europe. Two of them were recruited at Bucknell University in the spring of 1917 from younger faculty members, graduates, and students from Bucknell and other colleges. The first unit departed for training at Allentown during the first week of June. News came back from their headquarters that they were displaying the orange and blue of Bucknell, and were participating in camp entertainment and the kitchen detail. Arriving in France in December, they were among the first to witness Europe at war, and their letters to

The recruitment office in the 200 block of Market Street, Lewisburg. From the collection of the Union County Historical Society, #92.9.92.18.

waiting families and friends apprised those at home of what they were finding there. Fortunately, the letters were sometimes released to the local newspapers and can still be shared again over 80 years later.

One of the first correspondents was Wade Earle, a young instructor at Bucknell, and son of Mr. and Mrs. I.N. Earle of Lewisburg. He revealed that he was attached to the French Army and was driving "a big Fiat ambulance with a capacity of four lying and eight sitting wounded." With the French artillery behind him and the German in front, shells were flying overhead, and it was "an awesome thing, especially when driving at night without lights hoping to avoid shell holes and mud. There were brilliant star shellings and sporadic whistles and whining shells as they passed over." Near the front at night, when shelling was renewed, he would hurry into an *abri* (dug-out) cut into a hillside and covered with a heavy roof; he noted, "Some were built by the Germans when they occupied this position." A village he passed through was "shell-riddled, deserted and ghastly"; and as he picked his way through the devastation his *blesses* (wounded) kept calling *allez vite* (go quickly) or *doucement* (gently) at every jolt. On another day, when driving through "death valley" during a gas attack, he noted, "It is a nightmare. . . the shriek and pop of a gas attack shell are the worst sounds I ever want to hear. But I am getting hardened." After several weeks near the front, he was *en repos* behind the lines while billeted in a stable. Lying in bed, Earle could see holes in the tile roof, but he was keeping warm with straw mattresses on top of and under him. In a lighter mood, in a reference to French food, he told how he had cut off the mold from cheese, only to discover he was "wasting the best part of it." He accepted other French delicacies until offered toasted snails at a hotel, served "with small spoons to dig them out."[6]

The second of the Bucknell ambulance units, Company 525, arrived in France in January of 1918. In addition to the students, Harry Mathers of Lewisburg, T. Burns Rearick of Mifflinburg, Cyrus Follmer (later in the U.S. Diplomatic service for many years), and Philip Shay of Milton, were members of this company. Burns Rearick, son of Rev. William M. and Ida M. Rearick, supplied his parents with his impressions of France and ambulance duty. He had traveled 40 hours by rail to reach his headquarters and described the train as "junk." The steam power was so weak it had to stop to blow its whistle, but he was pleased with the "dandy" YMCA facility where he was living. It had movies, a basketball court, and plenty of candy, chocolate, and tobacco. Later, at his base, Burns reported taking a wrong road; and before he was aware of it, he was halted by barbed wire and trenches. "It was a desolate place." Soldiers on duty there helped him to find the way to the rear.

In the spring Rearick found dandelion near his quarters, and searched eggs to prepare with it. He was unsuccessful, but a friend walked two miles and found two; "It sure was good." "A nice day brings out Boche planes. Allied planes are flying over today. Just now Germans are shelling an observation balloon. You can see shells burst. Boches shell railroads here most every night."

On another occasion, when he was near the front line, Rearick hurried to a dugout 40 feet under ground. Months later he was on duty for a 49-hour stretch getting ambulances out of shell holes and repairing collisions:

Had to wear gas masks; you can imagine what it is like to repair a battered automobile in the dark without a light, and wearing a gas mask. We generally get into towns [during the offensive] about the second day after the Germans left them. In some towns there wasn't a house standing. It is common to see shell craters with five dead horses thrown in; and Germans they didn't have time to bury. The Boche surely are on the run, and we expect to run them into the North Sea. About the fiercest looking thing I ever saw are the French tanks just coming out of an attack, hanging full of barbed wire, and full of dents where the shells struck them. Our section was cited for bravery, and we received a *Croix de Guerre*.[7]

Months earlier William J. McWilliams, a member of the same ambulance company, who had moved from Mifflinburg to Easton just prior to the war, described his impressions of France and his opinion of French bread:

Had a huge lunch of apple butter. Oh that French bread. It is baked in loaves as big as dish pans, or as long as a yard stick. By the time you get through the crust you begin to dig into the bottom crust. The regular war bread in content is brown in color and tough. I like it as well as any American bread. . . We are quartered in the top of a barn, and high and dry; mud everywhere. The French can farm and economize. Empty tobacco cans of Americans are carefully stored away, and there is scarcely a scrap of paper to be found. Their fruit trees are wonderfully trimmed. There are apparently no rocks in the soil for several feet down. The trains are toys, but cars ride wonderfully easy. It is like riding in a big farm spring wagon. . . We are detached for service with the French Army.[8]

Later, like Burns Rearick, McWilliams saw the war nearer the front during the final German advance; "Two days of retreat, slow, orderly, overpowered by masses of Germans. Last cars in convoy peppered with machine bullets, but no men lost. Loss of (our) baggage voluntary. Had to throw it off to carry final *blesses*, as it was the only way they could be saved." He termed the cheerfulness of the French, even in retreat, as "simply amazing. . . I have seen American troops in battle (also) doing more than first class fighting."

Eager to show their response to the Declaration of War in the weeks following April 2, 1917, Union County communities engaged in flag raisings or "floating Old Glory." They were apt to be arranged on short notice and had a similar format. One in West Lewisburg at the Chair Factory, for example, was held on a Thursday at 5 o'clock. The Lewisburg Town Band led the way to the site, and the invocation was followed by patriotic songs and music by a male quartet. After speeches by Colonel William R. Follmer and Captain Cloyd Steininger, Ruth Cromley raised the Stars and Stripes. The following Saturday, May 19, the Junior Order of the United American Mechanics of Williamsport arrived in Mifflinburg on an excursion train to assist the community in testifying to its support of the war. A "gala parade" was followed by speeches and awards for the best-decorated houses and places of business.

County chapters of the Young Men's Christian Association and the Red Cross were organized hastily to supply non-military services. The Rev. John J. Judd, pastor of the Baptist church in Lewisburg, was instrumental in founding the Red Cross, and Emma Billmeyer was the vice president. Anne Dreisbach

Troop K 1st Cavalry PNG practice on April 17, 1921. From the collection of the Union County Historical Society, #89.5.14.2.

was the Lewisburg chairman; Professor Frank Simpson, the treasurer; and Mrs. C. A. Gundy, the secretary; and Dr. Mary Wolfe, Harry Stahl, and Dr. L. H. Ross served on the board. In Mifflinburg the chairman was Annie Wolf; Laura Gutelius headed the campaign for contributions in the East Ward and Georgia Glover, in the West Ward. In a few weeks a sum of $13,000 was raised, well above the quota.

Faced with pressing demands for contributions for war-related services, Mifflinburg considered the advice of Robert S. Gutelius, president of the Mifflinburg Body Company. He had just returned from a sales trip to the Middle West, where he had found that communities were creating war chests, "thereby placing charity upon a business basis." When he presented the plan at a town meeting, it was enthusiastically accepted. Thirty solicitors were soon working in teams to canvass every householder in the town. They flooded the community with "dodgers," and posters were displayed in the stores. A "thermometer" with a goal of $12,000 was hung from a storefront at Fourth and Chestnut Streets; the sum, which represented $8 from each man, woman and child, was met![9]

Urgent requests from Washington were also soon heard for investments in "War Bonds," since taxes would not meet the costs of war; and, again,

states, counties, and municipalities were expected to contribute more. Within the span of 18 months, four drives were held, and a "Victory Loan" campaign followed the close of the war. For those unable to buy bonds, war-savings stamps, as modest in price as 25¢, were issued; and children in the schools were urged to participate. Older residents may recall the brightly colored posters and banners displayed in the post offices, banks, and places of business, especially those of artist James Montgomery Flagg. Communities competed for "Honor Flags," which were given to those which excelled in fundraising.

Mifflinburg's response to the third of the drives might serve as an illustration of the activity which they generated. A parade, led by its widely known string band, played numbers with "spirit and pep," followed by Civil War veterans riding in cars, women and children with flags, and floats fashioned for the occasion. After touring the principal streets, the parade stopped at the front of the school (then at Maple and South Third Streets), where a platform had been erected. Patriotic addresses were delivered by Anne Dreisbach of Lewisburg and Dr. Charles H. Dimm (Professor Lee Francis Lybarger was ill that day), while attorney David L. Glover read President Wilson's proclamation. On the platform also was "the Goddess of Liberty" in the form of "Miss Olive," (Olive Thompson Hoover), in a graceful white costume modeled from the Liberty Loan Poster, "Columbia Calls." She was "supporting in the left hand a large American flag, while in the right hand was a beautiful sword." She arose and sang "in her usual attractive manner one stanza of the National Hymn of France."

After three war bond drives in little more than a year, it can be assumed that a fourth drive would require some additional "priming of the pump" in Washington; and it did.

Few Americans at that time had ever seen an airplane in the sky, and fewer yet had actually viewed one on the ground. Knowing the possible excitement of the public that planes might arouse, the Government decided to use them to invigorate the war bond drive. Thirty of them were released to Pennsylvania for flights in small squadrons during the final days of the promotion. Evidence of their rarity is found in a column of the *Mifflinburg Telegraph*, which mentioned that "a single plane several weeks ago stirred up great excitement in this section." It added that while few acknowledged seeing it, others insisted that they had heard it. The paper speculated that it might have been assigned to a mail service which the Post Office

Department had in mind. Obviously, many Pennsylvanians may have seen their first plane in flight on the days they were designated to appear, weather permitting.

A second incentive to purchase bonds was the "War Exhibit Train," which zigzagged across Pennsylvania from one railroad system to another. It consisted of a string of cars filled with German war trophies, including guns, shells, uniforms, insignia, etc., which had been picked up from the battlefields after the Germans had retreated. Parked on the railroad sidings, the train drew thousands of people. Still another practice during the fourth war bond drive was the publishing of the names of purchasers in the press. In Mifflinburg the first name listed was Ruth Leopold, daughter of Mr. and Mrs. Max Leopold, who operated a men's clothing store. The names of each of the ten employees in the J.D.S. Gast Department Store were printed, representing 100 percent. The E.J. Gutelius Grocery Store was ranked at 87-1/2 percent, but no names were listed. The following week, all the names of its six employees were listed as 100 percent participation.

Beyond contributions to the YMCA, the Red Cross, the Salvation Army, and subscriptions for war bonds, many of Union County's citizens found additional ways to contribute to the war effort. There were hundreds of "victory gardens" planted on waste lots. Others without sons in the service made a practice of corresponding with sons of their friends who were wearing khaki. Buffalo Township women gathered in Vicksburg to organize the Buffalo Emergency and Improvement Association, designed to "bring women together to do helpful work," and they met regularly to sew and knit for the needs of the soldiers. A single contribution to the Red Cross included "233 triangular slings, 290 gauze compressors, 180 rest pillows, 131 handkerchiefs, 93 pieces of wearing apparel, and lesser numbers of bedside bags, eye bandages and crocheted wipes."[10]

Freewill contributions undoubtedly shortened the war, but there were shortages which required strict controls. The Allies needed food as well as munitions and manpower, and transporting them 3,000 miles by sea required ships and almost incalculable tons of coal. To meet food shortages, both production and conservation were needed; the Food Administration was created, and president Wilson named Herbert Hoover its director. Its administrator in Union County was Guy F. Roush of Mifflinburg, who was soon enforcing a strict code of regulation upon the use of flour. The flour was severely rationed; to stretch out white flour, a buyer was required to purchase a substitute, whole wheat flour, in the proportion of 20 percent white and 80 percent whole wheat. Hoarding was prohibited, and wheatless days were enforced. Eggs became a scarce item, and at one point the selling of live chickens was prohibited. Sugar was also rationed. When a rumor was spread that Union County was being discriminated against in its use of sugar, Roush denied the charge and noted that two pounds per week was in effect across the nation. He added that people speaking such falsehoods were either "German or very good friends of the Kaiser." For purposes of canning, a housewife could buy as much as five pounds per purchase, but any of the sugar not used for canning had to be returned.[11]

Some Mifflinburg citizens gave food conservation their commendation by mounting a giant sign in an empty lot on Chestnut Street just to the west of the Farmers' Bank. The Body Company supplied the lumber; Musser's Hardware Store, the hardware; electrician Paul Halfpenny, the wiring; and the borough, the power. Draymen Gilbert Lenhart and Clarence Valentine hauled the materials; while William F. Romig, a talented painter as well as proprietor of the Lyric Theatre, with assistance from Kreider Kurtz, painted the sign, which was said to have been "beautiful and attractive." In giant letters it read:

FOOD WILL WIN THE WAR. DON'T WASTE IT. AMERICA'S PROBLEM: SHIPS AND FOOD! TO SEND THE MOST FOOD POSSIBLE IN LEAST SHIPPING SPACE. EAT LESS WHEAT, BEEF AND PORK, FATS AND SUGAR. GET BEHIND OUR SAILORS, SOLDIERS AND ALLIES.[12]

During World War I, coal was in short supply. The reason for it was obvious; heating, shipping, and steam and electric power were almost wholly dependent upon it. J. Rudolph Garfield served as national administrator of coal rationing, and his representative in Union County was William L. Donehower of Lewisburg. Heatless Mondays were required through the winter of 1917-1918, and this order applied to both home heating and industry. War industries were excepted; but in Mifflinburg, Hopp's Carriage Works had to close despite the fact that it was working on war contracts. The Albright Foundry was also shut down. In Lewisburg the Chair Factory, the town's largest employer, suffered the same fate. An interesting sidelight to coal conservation was the role of school children. Tags with reminders to save coal were printed and distributed by the children from door to door, and attached to the coal shovels.[13]

Gasoline was conserved by "gasless Sundays," and the writer recalls that his father walked along the railroad track from Mifflinburg to the family farm west of Glen Iron to see his sick mother; it was more than ten miles one way. On another Sunday, he rented a carriage at the Beaver livery stable to make the trip, which was probably the author's longest ride behind a team of horses. "Gasless Sundays must be observed by all," was Donehower's order published in local newspapers:

The keen sense of patriotism and duty is such that all that should be required is to point to the necessity for self-denial, so that gasoline can be saved to enable our ambulances, and motor trucks on the field to move forward freely all the time to meet military necessities.

A week later this order was followed by another, "Burn no coal until November 1 is the Fuel Administration's request — or even longer if weather is pleasant."[14] To conserve electricity and kerosene for lighting, an experimental "daylight saving" was adopted by moving clocks one hour ahead on the last day of March in 1918, but "God's time" returned on October 27, when the "stolen" hour was given back to the public.

There was some grumbling over the maze of regulations and the temporary factory and business closings. Meanwhile, Milton's metal industries were expanded, including a shell plant and an electrical power plant. Dozens of local workmen found work there and received as much as $8 per day, a sum three times as high as labor ordinarily received. One young Union County employee remembered that he bought his first (and only) silk shirt, and that a pair of shoes cost him $10, a 300 percent hike during the war.

In New Berlin a movement was afoot to discard its name, since it was identified with Hohenzollern rule, and substitute Verdun (one of the heroic defenses by Allied troops) or St. Mihiel (a spectacular counterattack by American forces). The matter was scheduled for a town meeting; but no name could be agreed upon, and the town remained New Berlin.[15] Organizations, including the Patriotic Sons of America, exerted pressure upon high schools and colleges to discontinue the teaching of the German language. Both Bucknell and Susquehanna Universities complied. German family names were sometimes modified; in Milton, Kaiser, in some cases, became Keiser. German operas and symphonies were no longer heard. A widely-used cartoon depicted the German soldier as a barbaric Hun tramping on children with his hobnailed boots, and blood dripping from his hands. But once the war ended, American generosity in the form of food and other essentials enabled people in Western Europe, former allies and foes alike, to survive.

Meanwhile, local women were making their mark in World War I. A month after the American entry into the conflict in 1917, Georgia Glover of Mifflinburg addressed the Shikelimo Chapter of the Daughters of the American Revolution on the effects of the war upon the women of England. The "nerve" of women there, she declared, had enabled them to prove their worth, and they had taken their places in the factories and transportation. They had also cared for the wounded in France and had shown their mettle "even in politics."

Women remaining at home found employment in industry in unprecedented numbers and assisted in many war-related activities. They raised money for the Red Cross; directed Liberty Bond sales campaigns; increased the supply of food by gardening and canning; conserved food, fuel, gasoline, and other war essentials; and accepted the challenge, "Don't be a slacker, ladies."

While women were not conscripted during World War I, several Union County nurses, who volunteered to serve in the Medical Corps, accompanied the armed forces to France. One of these was Helen Fairchild (b. Turbut Township, Northumberland County) of Gregg Township. Helen grew up on the Griffey-Fairchild (later the Reaser) farm between Allenwood and Elimsport along Route 44. She studied nursing at the Philadelphia General Hospital, an institution founded by Benjamin Franklin, the first of its kind in the American Colonies. On May 7, 1917, Fairchild went overseas as an Army Reserve nurse.

Fairchild was among the 64 nurses and a number of doctors who were assigned to British hospital 16 located at LeTreport on the French coast (later called Base Hospital 10). When Americans were sent to support the British Expeditionary Forces, Fairchild volunteered to become the surgical nurse in a team consisting of two doctors, an anesthetist, and herself. Her team was sent to Casualty Clearing Station 4 on July 31, 1917, the start of the Third Battle of Ypres-Passchendaele. Long hours were spent in the operating tents, located in the mud of Flanders, under the bombardment of shellfire, as well as mustard and chlorine gases.

In late December, nurse Fairchild became ill, and surgery revealed not ulcers, but a thickening at the pylorus. Her condition worsened and she died on January 18, 1918, at age 33. Army medical records

Nurse Helen Fairchild volunteered for service in World War I. She died in Europe while in service on January 18, 1918.

Mifflinburg High School and the School of Nursing of the University of Pennsylvania, Philadelphia, Class of 1912, where she remained upon graduation as a member of the nursing staff, she subsequently served as supervisor of the operating room. Upon the outbreak of the war, she helped to organize Unit Base Hospital 20; and after special training at the Walter Reed Hospital in Washington and at Ellis Island, Irwin went to France with the unit and spent eleven months at Chatel-Guion.

In one of her letters home, Irwin described her arrival at a French port, the rail trip to camp, the French compartment cars, and the lack of dining cars or sleepers. She and four other nurses ate canned foods, using a towel over a suitcase for a table. She "couldn't have believed" she would enjoy cold sweet potatoes, tomatoes, baked beans, corned beef, and salmon; but there was sweet chocolate for dessert. The train stopped several times for water on the two-day trip. One time there was simply a water barrel permitting them to wash their faces. Irwin was favorably impressed by the countryside. The small fields resembled colored patches; but with the lack of fences, she wondered how the farmers kept them separate, "and know which is which." The French men lived in stone houses in villages and walked to their fields.

In March 1918 the nurses arrived at Base Hospital 20, a former summer resort with hotels spaced amidst the wooded hills. Their first trainload of French patients arrived in June. Irwin admired their morale: "They are wonderfully brave, and they thought the place looked like heaven." The staff had now performed their first operation, "and it seemed like old times, since I like operating better than anything else." She noted that the hospital's capacity was larger than the student body of the University of Pennsylvania. Operating teams of physicians and nurses were being sent to field hospitals at the front, but as chief nurse she would not have this opportunity to get away.

Irwin had met some very nice French people, and had tea for two groups:

Nearly all of the women here smoke and drink wine. The men could not be more polite. Each time we passed anything to them they would rise. On the other hand it almost breaks your heart to see how hard women work, and especially the old women (who) make hay and do all sorts of work. They drive oxen and cows, in fact you see few horses.

In a sudden change of thought she added,

The other day I went into the kitchen, and made fifteen lemon meringue pies, enough for my whole 'family' of seventy. . . Mother, even you would have been proud of the crust. It was a complete surprise, and they almost went wild over it.[16]

show she died of "acute yellow atrophy of the liver." Her death resulted from a reaction the chloroform anesthesia and the effects of exposure to wartime poison gases. Reports were that she had given her gas mask to a soldier. Letters tell of her being buried in the uniform of a U.S. Army nurse with full military honors, attended by an entire garrison of officers, nurses, and troops. She was buried in Somme American Military Cemetery, Bony (Aisne), France, where some 1,800 other military personnel rest under simple stone crosses.

In 1920 women veterans organized the Helen Fairchild American Legion Post 412 in Philadelphia. In 1977, on the 60th anniversary of her departure for France, a memorial marker was dedicated to her in the Watsontown Cemetery. Her war correspondence and other mementos are in the Women In Military Service Memorial, Arlington, VA, and excerpts are on the Internet at www.lib.byu.edu/~rdh~wwi under Commentary articles-medical front-nursing. Her story is also taught to British schoolchildren, as emblematic of American nurses' sacrifices for the British in World War I, at another Internet site.

A second nurse to volunteer during World War I was Edith Irwin of Mifflinburg, a daughter of J. Clayton and Annie Jodon Irwin. A graduate of

Following the war, Edith Irwin moved to Greensburg, Pennsylvania, where she became administrator of Westmoreland Hospital.

Katherine Baker of Lewisburg was a third Union County woman to serve as a nurse in France. A talented daughter of J. Thompson Baker of Lewisburg, founder of Wildwood-on-the-Sea in New Jersey and a member of Congress, Katherine was a graduate of Goucher College and practiced law with her father in Lewisburg — the first female to be admitted to practice in Union County. She was also successful as a writer of short stories, which were published in the *Atlantic Monthly*, the *Forum*, *Scribner's*, and *Collier's*, among the foremost literary journals of the era.

Katherine Baker volunteered as a war nurse in 1917, when Germany unleashed unrestricted submarine warfare prior to the American declaration of war. After handling supplies in Paris for several months after arriving from the United States, she entered Dr. Alexis Carrel's hospital at Compiégne, where she learned the Carrel technique of suturing blood vessels and the Carrel-Dakin treatment of wounds (sterilizing infected areas), which saved lives and reduced the need for amputations. Baker was made a corporal in the 17th Regiment of the Third French Army, and was subsequently decorated with a *Fourragère* and the *Croix de Guerre*. She was nursing in Dr. Cuneo's hospital at Cannes during the advance at Château-Thierry with its thousands of casualties. Seeking to serve closer to the war front, she moved to Bruyeres in the Vosges Mountains. Ignoring her health, she suffered a physical collapse from which she failed to recover. Returning to the United States at the close of the war she was admitted to the sanitorium at Saranac Lake, New York, where she died in September of 1919. She was the second female casualty from Union County.[17]

Elsie Owens was the fourth from Union County to become a nurse in France during World War I. A daughter of Professor William G. Owens, chairman of the Chemistry Department at Bucknell, and Jeannette Owens, Elsie attended the Lewisburg schools and, like her brothers and sisters, matriculated at Bucknell, where she graduated in the Class of 1908. She was a public health nurse with the school system of Kansas City, Missouri, for some years prior to enlisting as a Red Cross nurse when thirty-one. After further training at Roosevelt Hospital in New York, she first served at Base Hospital 116, a tent hospital just beyond the walls of Paris. When not on duty, she found opportunities to tour the historic sites in the region including a visit to Versailles.

Owens was assigned to Mobile Hospital 5, located on the northern flank of the Allied line on the Belgian frontier, an area which had been occupied by Germany for four years. Operating there took place in a sea of mud; furnishings had to be placed on blocks of wood or stone, while clothes were strung on poles. She hated to see "our big strapping boys arrive in such a pitiful condition," and to find "the dead buried here where their people will never get over it; that is why I am tired of war — not the work." But she regarded their "little hospital" as a "big success." Belgian refugees were returning and their plight appeared to her to be be desperate. "[I] haven't seen a chicken, and only one or two cows," she advised her family. "Poor things they huddle into corners, and build a little fire; then try to make a little shelter to sleep under."

When the war ended, Owens visited the Riviera, taking side trips to view the hill towns and to visit Monte Carlo, where she was admitted to the game room prior to opening hours, as uniforms were not allowed there while the games were in progress.[18] Returning to Lewisburg, she married Dr. William W. Long.

By the spring of 1918, Union County's soldiers were among the hundreds of thousands crossing the Atlantic Ocean. Curious and intrigued by their strange surroundings, they responded with letters to their families and friends. Most of them commented upon the beauty of the countryside, the fine crops, and the high quality of the livestock; but they found the French methods of farming antiquated and the home life behind the times. Lt. Raymond Young of Lewisburg, while moving from one village to another, advised his mother (Mrs. George W. Young) that farmers lived in villages instead of on the farms: "The cows are taken through the streets daily to pasture, so you know what streets are like. The word sanitation is surely 'Dutch' with them." But when he was quartered temporarily in a French home he had only praise for his hosts:

The first evening they gave me a supper of fine eggs, butter, cheese and bread, mighty good after living on canned junk (on the transport) for several weeks. Now I am off to bed. The Madam leads the way with a candle, opens up the skyscraper which I am to sleep in, steps outside the room until I undress, just as you used to, Mother, when I was smaller. She then wishes me good night, and departs. Such a wonderful bed. If I ever remember anything about France it will be their wonderful sleeping quarters. No wonder the people are sort of slow and lazy. Next morning the lady of the house brings me a bowl of water. This all seems so strange after having running water all my life. Nothing but candles are used here for light. They think it strange we wash so often; a bath is unheard of, but I managed to get a bath in a tub used for making wine. I forgot to tell you about roads. They are simply wonderful. I think it would be a good idea for some of the grafters in Pennsylvania to come over here and get an idea of French road making.[19]

Arriving at Liverpool, Derben W. Bartholomew, also of Lewisburg, crossed England by train, which he termed a joke:

We had lots of fun in them. We have logging trains back in the states much better. Crossing France there are castles, chateaus, high walls, moats and dungeons, and all of them many hundred years old. But closer to the war front in a town about the size of Sunbury scarcely a house hasn't been hit by the artillery. By the looks of things Germans hurriedly left it. Every house has been looted, also they left much behind — helmets, letters, clothing, rifles, machine guns. We are continually moving like gypsies.[20]

This war saw the use of many new weapons as well as tactics. The submarine was a focus of attention during World War I, and the torpedoing of neutral shipping was one of the principal reasons for the entry of the United States into the war in April 1917. The rapid-firing machine gun was more deadly than gunnery of previous wars, and tank warfare was also introduced in this war. Poisonous gas, released first by the Germans, was still another horrible and destructive addition to combat. But no innovation in tactics excited as much attention from the public as the airplane. It was an American invention; but it was developed as a weapon of war by the Germans, while England and France hurried to do the same. Meanwhile, the airplane remained undeveloped in the United States. American flyers got into combat by joining the English and French air forces, and first saw action in the latter's Lafayette Escadrille.

Upon the declaration of war, President Wilson initiated a crash program to provide an air force, but production did not become sizable until February 1918. Standardization of tools and designs enabled mass production during the next eight months, and 15,000 Liberty Engines were delivered by factories from California to Connecticut. Meanwhile, potential aviators were dispatched to England and France, where they were given final training and sent into combat in French Nieuports and Spads. Unassembled plane parts were ferried to France and put together there at eight improvised sites.

Lester R. Ruhl of Mifflinburg was on duty at one of these bases. A graduate of Mifflinburg High School in 1912, he had obtained work at a buggy shop. During the late-summer lull in production he found a similar job at York. Returning later to Mifflinburg, he spent a winter shifting freight cars at the Northumberland yards. When war was declared, Ruhl went to Harrisburg seeking to volunteer in the army, but he was refused due to his light weight and advised that he would qualify for the cavalry. Upon his return he enlisted in Troop M, and thus he was at Camp Hancock in Georgia when the cavalry was disbanded. Ruhl and some other men were transferred to the 108th Field Artillery.

Arriving at Brest, Ruhl was separated from others in his company due to his knowledge of woodwork, and was assigned to help enlarge the docks there. Finishing this work, he was dispatched to Romorantin, in the Loire Valley about 60 miles southwest of Paris, to an airfield camouflaged to prevent its identification by German planes. The French had imported Chinese laborers to convert 600 acres of swamp into an airport by bundling brush and burying it, grading the surface, and planting grass. The unassembled planes were brought from the ports by rail, and Ruhl assisted with the unpacking and assemblage. Otherwise, he was engaged in constructing storage sheds from the packing. After the planes were assembled, they were flown to landing fields closer to the front. Once the field was in use, the areas adjacent to the landing strips were converted into gardens. During Ruhl's duty there, the airfield was never subjected to a German bombing.

In a letter to his mother just after the German surrender, Ruhl noted that "every day since the armistice battered planes come limping home to the flying field." The first plane to use the 600-acre facility had arrived there on May 11, 1918, and during the following six months 1,213 planes were assembled there — as many as 60 in a single day.

I remember one morning the night crew worked overtime in order to get out a certain order as there was a big drive on, and many planes were needed. The aviators were on the field at 3 A.M. and there was a continuous line of planes from the field. This continued until dark. [They were] salvaging the used planes for parts and everything an airplane needs from an engine to a copper key, from a pair of goggles to a seat strap. . . 2706 Liberty Motors passed through this department. . . . This camp was the cradle of the American airplane in France.

At least three men from Union County served in the air corps. Marion Marmaduke Earle of Lewisburg, brother of Wade Earle (mentioned previously), enlisted in the air force and trained at Ellington Field, Texas. He was killed there when his plane failed to come out of a loop on March 14, 1918. He was one of the first casualties of the war.

Ernest W. Hewitt of Mifflinburg was another county aviator in the war. Born in 1895, Hewitt grew up in Mifflinburg and enjoyed athletics, bicycling and horseback riding. After graduating from high school, he entered Bucknell, but he left college to join the air corps. He trained first in Texas and later at the Issondun air base south of Romorantin. He spent a furlough in Paris admiring its beauty, attending operas, including *Rigoletto, Aida,* and *Faust,* and visiting the square at night to witness air raids.[21] Hewitt was assigned to the First American Pursuit Group with such distinguished flyers as Eddie Rickenbacker and Quentin Roosevelt, son of President Theodore Roosevelt. Hewitt flew with Rickenbacker's squadron during the counterattack over Château-Thierry in July and August 1918, the Argonne Forest, and Verdun in October; he was piloting a French Nieuport, a monoplane fighter, "one of the fastest." He destroyed three planes, was shot down twice, and shared a commendation presented by General Pershing to the Chief of the Air Service for its "praiseworthy record."

Elmer R. Vanatta, like Hewitt, was thrilled with the challenge of flying. Born in 1893 near Hartleton, he attended Spruce Run School and the Hartley Township High School in Laurelton. Following graduation, he enlisted in the United States Army and served a three-year term. Upon the outbreak of the war, he enlisted in the 141st Air Squadron at San Diego and qualified as a pilot. In France he participated in action over the Meuse-Argonne Sector.

Following the war, both Vanatta and Hewitt engaged in commercial aviation. After surviving a number of accidents, Vanatta lost his life in another at the edge of Mitchell Field, Long Island, in 1921, while Hewitt was killed in a crash near Altoona in 1937.

During the spring of 1918, thousands of American troops were reaching France weekly, and General Pershing was preparing to take over a sector of the Allied front. On March 21 Germany launched an offensive with five massive assaults. The British line on the north was severed, and Pershing accepted General Foch's plea to divert the American troops to stem the Allied retreat, including the crossing of the Marne River and the possible loss of Paris just 40 miles beyond. Heavy losses of American troops occurred, but their support stabilized the line.

On July 18, the Allied counteroffensive was launched, with American divisions participating in each of the six advances. Two of these at the southern end of the line were strictly American operations, directed by American commanders. At St. Mihiel a wedge held by the Germans reaching fourteen miles into the French front was assaulted by a half-million

Elmer R. Vanatta of Millmont was an aviator of World War I, after which he flew for the government's mail service. He died in a plane accident at Mitchell Air Field on Long Island, New York in April 1921 when he was 28 years old. Elmer Vanatta is shown here with one of his planes. Courtesy of Russell Vanatta.

troops, and on the Meuse-Argonne front Pershing sent the First Army into battle in rough terrain. With French air support, the Americans inched forward through the following 47 days, taking tremendous casualties, but stopping only with the German surrender. During this advance Union County was not spared.

The *Saturday News* heralded the participation of local troops. On July 7 it observed, "the brilliant achievement of our Boys; the first time a German offensive stopped on the first day since 1914." On August 3, it added that former "Troop M Boys are at the Front. Pennsylvania soldiers compose the entire 28th Division of the Second Army Corps." Later, on September 14, it acknowledged the tragedy of war: the death of Colonel Wallace Fetzer of Milton, former commander of Troop M, who was struck by a shell burst. Several days later, on September 26, the *Saturday News* announced the deaths of five local soldiers, all of which had occurred at the Argonne

Sector, each killed by a single explosion: Bright Kratzer, Ralph J. Dull, and Robert Rimert, all of Lewisburg; Leon Pierce of Milton; and Sergeant Edward Shannon of Mazeppa.

Few of the soldiers found time to correspond during these difficult weeks, but Tennyson Steininger of Vicksburg dashed off a few words, "A soldier must bring himself to a state of mind to see suffering, bleeding and dying — a brutal harness, but very necessary. Will I ever get back to normal?"

During the last weeks of the war, Steininger's division was shifted to the Belgian front, where the "horror of France was no comparison with the awful destruction, distress and terror of Belgium." For a distance of 30 miles, he added, there was not as much as a live tree or any other living thing:

with trees shot off from two to ten feet from the ground, and where fighting was thickest ground was as (though) churned. . . . Towns and villages of good size are entirely wiped off the earth . . . the city of Ypres is so totally destroyed that rebuilding is out of the question. . . . The sight of it in so many of the Belgian towns got my nerve (and) when I saw groups of women and children in Ypres huddled together hunting around for some belongings my heart melted.[22]

Lieutenant Miller Johnson, son of Judge Albert Johnson of Lewisburg, described the beginning of the last assault:

Artillery at 2:30 A.M., over the top at 5:30, smoke screen, wire not well cut. Fired into brush, moved into woods at 500 yards. German trenches deserted. Difficulty of keeping lines in woods. Crawled along 150 yards in 15 minutes. Not a German. Looked up and into a German machine gun, but two Germans with sickly grins said 'Un-Kommen.' Killed one, injured the other. Went forward, checked 10 men out of 50. Others lost contact. At other edge of woods about 10 A.M.; crossed field and into woods again. Wiped out machine-gun nests; readied for night. Had gone about a mile, and had 400 prisoners. Next morning move gun nests. First objective on September 27, a town on a high hill, where the Crown Prince of Germany had witnessed Verdun. Through town; barrage from Germans from woods. Stopped 1000 yards from town. A yell, (French) tanks were coming behind us in single file; passed us, and every one on feet following them. Germans stopped tanks, and some Frenchmen left them, running to rear. Lay there for hours. Night; three days no sleep, few hard tacks to eat. Order to attack and did in open field; advanced one mile into woods. Stopped, dug in rain. Relieved, and Monday evening marched back in dark; bivouacked about five miles in rear; men almost too weak to walk. Remained three days; food. . . . Now on another front. Officers carried guns and weren't picked off. Is said we encountered more resistance than at Château-Thierry. Have been on front a month. No signs of a rest.[23]

Several days before the cessation of hostilities, Miller was wounded, but he recovered.

In Mifflinburg news of the Armistice arrived by telegraph on November 11, and a parade was improvised in a matter of a few hours. The parade, which assembled in the street in front of the Lutheran church, included marching groups, a few floats, and automobiles decked with bunting. The focus was concentrated upon the Kaiser, who was invited to be hanged. One of the floats had a replica (unflattering, to be sure) of him with a placard urging watchers to "Swat Him." Five days later, the *Saturday News* announced that "pure wheat bread may now be eaten"; and three weeks later it advised, "Buy all the sugar you want."

Suggesting that the termination of the war was unexpected might be illustrated by the Student Army Training Corps. Hundreds of units were instituted scarcely six weeks before the German surrender. At Bucknell 360 high school graduates were admitted to the program, housed in West College (now Kress Hall), and fed in an improvised dining room in the Academy building (Taylor Hall). The government provided uniforms and paid them $30 per month. The corpsmen registered for the usual academic program with especial emphasis upon technical subjects. For military drills they were divided into three companies and fourteen squads. To clarify for the public the role of the student corps, Marlyn Steese, a member from Mifflinburg, wrote an article for the *Telegraph*, in which he reminded the public that "its men belong to the United States Army just as much as those who are serving in foreign fields." Three weeks after the German capitulation, the Student Army Training Corps was liquidated.

During the twenty months of the war, the spirit of the public did not waver. Both sacrifices and inconveniences were as well accepted on the last day as on the first. However, once the war was won, the public pressure for "normalcy," a word accidentally coined by Warren G. Harding while campaigning for the presidency in 1920, was overpowering. The dream of President Wilson for a League of Nations, designed to maintain world peace, was rejected by the United States Senate, even though Wilson was its architect and spokesman. A part of the drive for normalcy was to "get the boys back home." Public opinion insisted upon it, leaving the former Allies to muddle through post-war readjustments. An exception, however, should be noted. Food relief for devastated Europe was provided by the United States through the American Relief Administration, organized in February 1919. As its director, Herbert Hoover was tireless in his desire to save lives, and it is estimated that as many as two hundred million people, largely in central and eastern Europe, received its benefits.

Possibly the outstanding single action was the feeding of Russian people in the famine of 1921. The relief was continued into 1923 until the need had eased.

With the war won, public opinion exerted pressure upon the government to return the war veterans from Europe; but with more than a million of them to transport, more than six months were required. The first sizable contingent from Union County to make the return crossing consisted of members of the 103rd Trench Mortar Battalion, a segment of the original Troop M; and its arrival in New York City on the Battleship New Jersey was announced in the *Lewisburg Saturday News* on March 29, 1919. They were then dispatched to Camp Merritt in New Jersey. A few days later, word was received that they would be mustered out there and were expected to arrive in Lewisburg on Saturday, April 12.

During the morning of April 12, buildings were decorated along the line of march, and by afternoon throngs were gathering on the streets. About 7:00 P.M. word was passed along that they would arrive at Montandon at midnight on the "Buffalo Flyer," and

during the evening the Calhoun Military Band of Northumberland furnished music at various street corners. At 10 o'clock William L. Kratzer and Roy Straub arrived unexpectedly at the Lewisburg station, and they were escorted to Market Street. At midnight autos were at Montandon to carry the troops across the river bridge; and when they entered Market Street, "pandemonium reigned." Plans for the parade at this late hour had been dropped; but the three bands on hand wedged their way to the town square, where the "heroes of Argonne" received a "royal welcome amidst cheers and tears." Among the 25 arrivals from the 103rd were seventeen from Lewisburg, three from Milton, two from Watsontown, two from Mifflinburg and one from Vicksburg. As the testimonial to the 103rd Trench Mortar closed, a flag with golden stars was displayed at the platform, "symbolizing the dead, now lying in France. The

The Homecoming Parade for World War I soldiers and nurses was photographed by Nelson A. Caulkins (two of over a dozen different views he took) and others on July 17, 1919. From the collection of Gary W. and Donna M. Slear.

The Lewisburg Chair Company welcomed home the World War I soldiers. From the collection of the Union County Historical Society, #89.5.14.20.

multitude gazed on it with solemn hearts." At 6:30 the following morning two additional veterans arrived, and at 10:15 four more made an appearance. The Lewisburg Band reassembled and drew a sizable crowd to an informal welcoming ceremony.

The Bucknell Ambulance Unit 525 came home on May 1 to find the town decorated and a reception awaiting them. The college and most of the businesses closed for the day. Already decorated with the French *Croix de Guerre*, the 22 ambulance drivers, led by Lieutenant H.L. Parsons, proceeded to the college, where they were welcomed by Weber Gerhart, president of the Senior Class, and Judge Albert Johnson. Sergeant G.S. Meredith, Class of 1915, read the engraved citation signed by General Petain, Chief-in-Command of the French Armies. It included ribbons for service at Les Eparges, Verdun-at-Hill 304, Aisne-Marne, Meuse-Argonne, and Alsace.[24]

Several weeks later, on Thursday, July 17, 1919, the homecoming for all of the veterans of Union County, numbering 399, was held in Lewisburg. It was estimated that 8,000-10,000 area people lined the streets to see, if not hear, the ceremony conducted by Rev. William M. Rearick and Professor E.O. Bickel of Mifflinburg, and the speech of welcome by General Charles Clement of Sunbury, head of the 28th Division and former commander of the cavalry regiment in the region. The parade was organized into six divisions, each with a band: the Calhoun Military Band, the West Milton Band, the City Band of Sunbury, the Middleburg Band, the Independent Order of Odd Fellows Band of Sunbury, and the Montgomery Band. At the fountain at Third and Market Streets, a bell was tolled 31 times to commemorate those who had given their lives; and as each name was called, a young local girl stepped forward to present a wreath in memory.[25]

The July homecoming would not be the last of the commemorative ceremonies. During the months which followed, bodies of the dead were returned from France. Among them were Irvin Brown of Lewisburg, June 19, 1921, 103rd Trench Mortar; Walter H. Knauss of Swengel and Milton, September 4, 1921, 6th Machine Gun Battery, 23rd Company; George W. Zimmerman of Millmont, September 18, 1921, 314th Infantry, Co. F. (buried in Ray's Church Cemetery); Bromley Smith, Jr., September 18, 1921, 107th Machine Gun Battalion, Co. A. (buried in Factoryville); James A. Yost of White Deer, September 28, 1921, 109th Infantry; Leon C. Pierce of Milton, October 16, 1921, 103rd Trench Mortar, (buried in the Harmony Cemetery); Ralph Dull, Robert D. Rimert, Bright L. Kratzer and Edward Shannon, October 16, 1921, 103rd Trench Mortar.

A different sort of homecoming awaited Glenn W. Leitzel, a 31-year-old sergeant from Mifflinburg, who was among those on the American expeditionary force on the Archangel front in Russia. He left home in July 1918, and after a stop in England was transported to Archangel, where the American weapons were exchanged for Russian ones so that the men could use the ammunition available there. The battalion in which Leitzel served was fighting a new enemy, the Russian revolutionary Bolsheviks. Leitzel's group held its position against Bolshevik advances through the winter despite their heavy artillery (recently captured from the Germans) and more adaptive machine guns, designed for sub-freezing temperatures. Occupying a position but two degrees below the Arctic Circle, in heavy snow with temperatures as low as 50 degrees below zero, the troops were "housed" in tents, and were saved from frostbite only by the use of sheepskin sleeping bags, piles of blankets, and fur-lined clothing, including their shoes. Peasants living in the region occupied log houses "with dove-tailed corners, and nails were unfamiliar to them." These people grew tiny potatoes and onions, but subsisted largely upon buckwheat flour, baked into cakes, and dried fish. To communicate they used Eskimos with reindeer.

In March, while he was walking near the camp, a band of Bolsheviks with grenades and pistols darted out from the woods and made Leitzel a captive. With several other prisoners, he was marched into Bolshevik territory. Guards on snowshoes moved with them on four sides. Passing through villages, the prisoners were "spat at," and forced to dodge whips and clubs, but their captors protected them from further injuries. During the first night, Leitzel was lodged with about twenty other prisoners and received a share of a single loaf of bread, but it was frozen so hard that a knife wouldn't cut it and an axe was applied. To his share was added a dried herring and a cup of hot water to soften the bread. By morning his blouse and his money and trinkets were missing, but he found a Russian shirt in its place as "The Bolsheviks had a particularly keen eye for American O.D. (olive drab)."

After a week the prisoners reached a railroad, and received quarters permitting a bath, the first in "a long while." It was Russian style: a heated stone, splashed with water, throwing out a cloud of steam to lie in. Their supper was served in a large bucket, "and thirty-five or forty of us ate out of it; the soup consisting of sour cabbage, and once in a while there was a small piece of horse meat." The following day they were placed in a boxcar and taken to Moscow. Arriving as a prisoner in Moscow, Leitzel with four others was lodged in "fairly clean and decent quarters." They were issued very little food but were permitted to roam about the city during daylight. The Red Cross and YMCA were still operating there, and they supplied the prisoners with essentials. Leitzel and his companions also did some marketing and cooking. It

was their good fortune to meet Frank Taylor, a United Press correspondent, who managed to cut red tape for their removal to Finland. Meanwhile, they had seen Moscow in the throes of one of the most controversial revolutions in modern times. When Taylor interviewed them in Finland and recorded their comments for the press, he made their impressions available to the nation. By way of introduction, Taylor observed:

This is what they had to say, when in the spring sun on the grass outside the quarantine hospital, after they were in Finland and in friends' hands. They had been given an unwelcome course of lectures on Bolshevism in Moscow designed to convert them and send them home primed for agitation in America. The speakers were Russian Bolsheviks who had escaped from Czars and police earlier but had now returned as Lenin and Trotsky had done. But the Yanks didn't bother themselves with theories. What impressed them was Bolshevism in practice.

Turning then to Leitzel, to whom he referred as a fine "young American red head," the reporter asked for his views. The Union Countian asserted:

They're not making any Bolsheviks of American prisoners. They'd take (Russian) men with brains, who have accomplished something with ability and work, and reduce them to the lowest level. . . . The leaders are preaching that everyone should have the same amount of money, but every leader has a pile of rubles stuck away that would knock your eyes out. They all believe in the principle the "Bolos" (Bolsheviks in the army) believe, that "what's yours is mine."

Glenn Leitzel was astonished by the role of Russian women during the war. "Women," he said, "do nearly all of the work. They dug a lot of the trenches and a lot of the hauling of supplies, and in our section of the front would cut logs and fell trees as well as a man." Others among the released captives also mentioned the enormity of the work forced upon Russian women, one of them declaring that "If it weren't for the women, they'd never get anything done. You see them carrying enormous loads, while some big bum of a Bolshevik walks along carrying nothing."

Upon Leitzel's arrival back home in Mifflinburg on July 12, 1919, a sizable crowd came to the depot to meet him, and the Rev. William H. Clipman, pastor of the Presbyterian church, lauded him for his service to his country. Glenn followed with a short resume of his impressions of Russia and his return from Finland:

We were sent next to Sweden and put up in a fine hotel, and told to order anything we wanted, and we sure took advantage of it. Two of the boys gained 40 pounds in the 10 days we were there. We stopped in a Holland port next, and from there we went to Paris, then to Brest, and finally came back to God's Country on the U.S. Troy which was carrying 6,500 troops.

Glenn was the oldest of the three sons of Harry and Lillian (Ayres) Leitzel. The emotions of Glenn's parents, when they met him at the station, can not adequately be described. After his disappearance in Russia, their son had been reported as missing and presumed dead.

Another local soldier deserves special recognition: General Tasker Howard Bliss. One of the thirteen children of Professor George R. and Mary Ann Raymond Bliss, he was born in the family home at 115 South Front Street in Lewisburg on December 31, 1853. (The house is appropriately marked, and its exterior has scarcely changed.) The family subsequently moved to a residence built for them at 63 University Avenue. Young Bliss attended the local public schools, the Academy and the University at Lewisburg (later Bucknell) before entering the United States Military Academy at West Point. One of his favorite anecdotes, as printed in the *New York Times* at the time of his death, reads:

General Tasker H. Bliss, who died today after a distinguished career in the Army, walked 10 miles in his bare feet to obtain an appointment in the U.S. Military Academy at West Point. And it was not necessary, for he had a new pair of shoes slung over his shoulder as he trudged through the dust to see his Representative in Congress about going to West Point. "I didn't wear the shoes," the General explained later "because I knew they would be dusty. I wanted to save them until time for the conference so I would look nice."

The youth, then about seventeen, got the appointment. (The ten miles he walked were likely between Lewisburg and Sunbury, where Member of Congress John B. Packer lived.)

Following graduation with honors in the West Point Class of 1875, Bliss acted upon projects requiring technical matters beyond routine strategy and tactics, and in 1884 he was the recorder on a board investigating the military value of the interior waterways in the United States. During this decade also, he was a professor of military science at the United States Naval War College. In the 1890s he was Military Attache at the American legation in Madrid, Spain. During the brief Spanish-American War, he served in Puerto Rico and Cuba. Following the war, he was in the Philippines assisting in the restoration of civil and military law as commander of the Department of Insurrection there; and with peace restored, he was named Assistant Chief of Staff in 1909. With revolution creating problems in Mexico in 1911, Bliss was stationed on the California border, and in 1915 he was promoted to Major General.

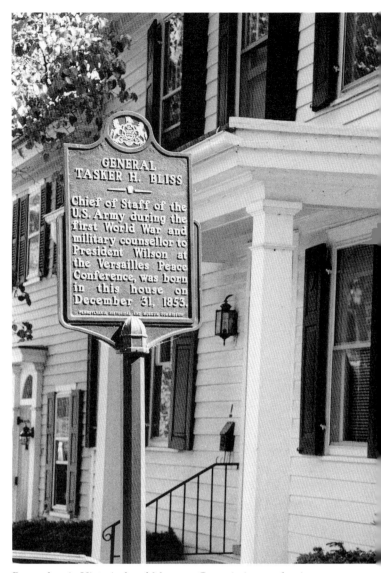

Pennsylvania Historical and Museum Commission marker in front of the home of Tasker Bliss. Photo by Jim Walter.

Following the Declaration of War in 1917, Tasker Bliss was named Chief of Staff of the Army and a member of the Supreme War Council in France. Following the war, President Wilson chose him as a member of the American Commission to Negotiate Peace as his military advisor. He accompanied Wilson to Paris in January 1919 to negotiate the Treaty of Versailles, and he was one of its signers the following June. Shortly thereafter he retired from the Army and made his home in Washington. He died there on November 9, 1930, and was buried in Arlington Cemetery. Army personnel who had attended him at Walter Reed Hospital bore his body to the grave, and honorary pallbearers included E.M. House, diplomat and confidant of President Wilson; former Secretary of War Newton D. Baker; Generals Pershing and Summerall; Admirals Benson and Rodman, and Colonel U.S. Grant, III. General of the Armies Pershing, with whom Bliss had served many years, declared, "The Army loses a great soldier, and the country, one of its distinguished citizens. He lived his life in fulfillment of his alma mater, 'Duty-Honor-Country'." Patrick J. Hurley, secretary of war, observed that America had lost "one of her most loyal and able public servants. In his long military career he won by sheer ability the highest positions open to a professional soldier."[26]

Thus the "war to end all wars" brought to a close the second decade of the twentieth century; but before the century was finished, there would be other conflicts which would involve many Union Countians on the battlefield and at home: World War II in the 1940s, the Korean conflict in the 1950s, and the Vietnam War straddling the 1960s.

ENDNOTES:

[1] Lester R. Ruhl, "A History of Troop M, First Pennsylvania Cavalry," manuscript, Union County Historical Society.

[2] *Lewisburg Saturday News*, September 15, 1917.

[3] Lester R. Ruhl.

[4] *Lewisburg Saturday News*, November 3, 1917.

[5] *Lewisburg Saturday News*, May 25, 1918.

[6] *Lewisburg Saturday News*, January 5, 1918; February 9, 1918; and March 2, 1918.

[7] *Mifflinburg Telegraph*, March 15, 1918.

[8] *Lewisburg Saturday News*, March 22, 1918; and June 10, 1918.

[9] *Lewisburg Saturday News*, June 1, 1918.

[10] *Lewisburg Saturday News*, January 12, 1918.

[11] *Lewisburg Saturday News*, March 23, 1918.

[12] *Mifflinburg Telegraph*, August 16, 1918.

[13] *Mifflinburg Telegraph*, January 26, 1918.

[14] *Lewisburg Saturday News*, September 14, 1918.

[15] *Lewisburg Saturday News*, October 19, 1918.

[16] *Mifflinburg Telegraph*. June 14, 1918; July 12, 1918 and August 16, 1918.

[17] *Lewisburg Saturday News*, October 27, 1923.

[18] *Lewisburg Saturday News*, October 7 and 13, 1918; November 9, 1918; December 7, 1918; February 8 and 15, 1919; and March 8, 1919.

[19] *Lewisburg Saturday News*, September 14, 1918.

[20] *Lewisburg Saturday News*, September 21, 1918.

[21] *Mifflinburg Telegraph*, May 17, 1918.

[22] *Lewisburg Saturday News*, November 30, 1918.

[23] *Lewisburg Saturday News*, November 19, 1918.

[24] *Lewisburg Saturday News*, May 3, 1919.

[25] *Lewisburg Saturday News*, July 19, 1919.

[26] *Lewisburg Saturday News*, November 15, 1930.

Service was held at the Methodist church in Lewisburg on October 16, 1921, for Robert D. Rimert, Edward L. Shannon, Ralph J. Dull, and Bright Kratzer of the 3rd Battery, 103rd Trench Mortar, all killed in Argonne on September 26, 1918. From the collection of the Union County Historical Society, #89.5.10.4.

CHAPTER 18

1970-2000: TOWARD A NEW MILLENNIUM

by Jeannette Lasansky

Progress in Union County was measured in its earliest days by the establishment of tanneries, gristmills and sawmills. Later, in the nineteenth century, progress was measured by the number of country stores, railroad stations, and town bands. Now success is measured by cutting-edge school buildings and medical facilities, the use of new technologies in communications and service support, as well as by state and national recognition for excellence in local endeavors.[1]

Population growth, the local economy, transportation issues, health care and social support systems, cultural institutions and education, environmental concerns — even the weather — are in flux. As the earlier modes of transportation and communication affected the area — the canal, train, automobile, phone or rural electrification — so too are local institutions and decisions greatly impacted by external forces now. With the exception of local politics where patterns have remained constant and Republicans have dominated for decades,[2] changes are happening quickly and are very interrelated.

Some recent changes challenge Union County residents by presenting conflicting values. There is the struggle between state/regional planning and the desire to preserve small-town individualism. There is a tension between traditional farming, with open space sensibilities, and development, with its need to widen highways and add bypasses and connectors. Institutions both old and new have become involved in this struggle. Coordinated police forces, library support, tourist promotion, and controlled growth become hot-button issues. The trend toward regionalism has been mirrored in the evolution from the 1970s Lewisburg Chamber of Commerce, to the Union County Chamber of Commerce headed by Herbert Bendt, to the two-county Susquehanna Valley Visitors' Bureau directed by Mark Hoy; a variety of institutional spin offs — the Union County Economic Development Committee, the Union County Industrial Development Corporation, and Leadership Susquehanna — also operate based on the concept of coordination of efforts.

Many local institutions experienced basic changes in the last quarter of the twentieth century. Bucknell, making the transition in this period from a strong regional university to one of national stature, was

recognized in 1999 as the 31st most prestigious university in the United States by *US News and World Report*. Some of the institutional changes were driven by state or federal mandates or economic opportunities. The federal prison system grew exponentially;[3] and a countywide library system was created; while the Laurelton State School closed, leaving its buildings to be occupied and used by an institution which has yet to be definitely designated.

A large conglomerate, the Union Pacific Railroad, sought to utilize Union County's central location in the state to build a major waste incinerator in Gregg Township. The resolve of local government, citizens' groups, area legislators, and a lot of ordinary individual citizens showed that change, when decided by the majority to be negative, could be stopped. How the county-sponsored alternative use of that land, the Great Stream Commons Industrial Park, develops on that very site will be testimony to harnessing change to local, not external, initiatives.

Second- or third-generation bridges in the county, at West Milton, Millmont, and Lewisburg, were paid for by PennDOT. Trains, once so vital to the expansion of the local economy by opening up markets for local goods, were largely replaced by highway trucks. The West Shore Rail Excursions, the dream of the late Richard Sanders, was enjoyed as a tourist attraction starting in 1984 but is no longer operating. While rail lines were removed west of Mifflinburg and north of White Deer, other local lines were left in place and are used occasionally by the West Shore Rail Corporation.[4] In a reversal of the trend toward less rail traffic, money is being appropriated to restore rail service to the Great Stream Commons Industrial Park. Looming ahead in the arena of transportation is the Route 15/Shamokin Dam bypass, as well as the completion of Route 147, which will require infrastructure changes to Route 45.

The abandonment and eventual dismantling of the railroad tracks west of Mifflinburg in the late 1960s and early 1970s was a symbolic loss, particularly for towns like Swengel and Millmont. Millmont had developed around the five-acre tract donated to the railroad nearly 100 years ago by Jacob E. and Elizabeth Royer for the establishment of the rail line and freight station. That rail line had been a particularly important part of the landscape and local economy. Today this parcel of land, located in the center of town and known locally as the village green, is owned by Lewis Township. In June 1989 a picnic pavilion was constructed near where the former freight/passenger station stood; later a memorial and flag pole were erected; and in 1997 a newly constructed municipal building was dedicated.

Attempts at public transportation have proved successful only in the Union/Snyder Transportation Alliance (USTA) shared ride services, which began in 1979. While anyone can arrange for USTA transportation, the primary service group is the elderly, who ride at reduced rates — ten to fifteen percent of full-fare charges within the 63-mile radius. The service operates from 6:30 A.M. to 4:30 P.M. In 1999 sixty percent of USTA's ridership consisted of the elderly, while nearly 40 percent were handicapped and low-income residents. An average of 430 trips per day are requested, resulting in 630,000 miles per year from a fleet of 26 vehicles. On the whole, however, area residents have resisted public transportation, and local taxi service is currently available but supplied from neighboring communities.

In the last three decades of the twentieth century, women took leadership roles in increasing numbers, originally by learning and working in groups like the League of Women Voters or local service organizations such as the Sunrise Rotary,[5] and later by assuming leadership roles in municipal organizations and businesses. Nada Gray, Lewisburg borough manager (1990-present); Stacy Hinck, borough council president (1996-1999), succeeded by Yvonne Morgan; and Helen Strunk, president of the Mifflinburg Bank and Trust Company (1980-1990),[6] are examples of this trend. On the county level, Ruth Wehr Zimmerman became the second female county commissioner as well as the top vote-getter in 1988; she became the chief commissioner from 1992 until she retired at the end of 1999. Martha Zeller[7] and Nancy Neuman,[8] who had headed local nonprofit organizations, the American Association of University Women and the League of Women Voters respectively, advanced to head their organizations' state offices; and Neuman eventually led the national League. Farida Zaid[9] and others in the public service sector provided insightful and imaginative leadership to groups such as the Area Agency for the Aging (1974-present). Other females have integrated formerly all-male bastions like the local Little League.

Although local corporate boards during this time were still dominated by white males, nonprofit boards were more reflective of the interests and strengths of a diverse population, and women in particular. Martha Barrick, for example, has headed a successful business as well as a public service organization. She still chairs the Union County Planning Commission, which in 1999 received statewide recognition for the most outstanding county comprehensive plan.[10]

In 1976, in order to provide support for divorced women, Susquehanna Valley Women in Transition (SVWIT) was formed in Sunbury, Pennsylvania. SVWIT evolved quickly and provided a hot line, manned 24 hours a day by trained volunteers, to take calls from women about abusive situations. In 1981 the group relocated to Lewisburg and four years later opened its first shelter, which was augmented in 1999 with a second shelter in Coal Township, Northumberland County. In 1981 SVWIT's funding came from the Pennsylvania Coalition Against Domestic Violence, later from the Pennsylvania Coalition Against Rape. Its director, Marty Gates, currently heads a professional staff of 19 along with 40 volunteers who service the hotline. In 1999 direct services were provided to approximately 2,500 area women and children residing in Snyder/Union/ Northumberland (SUN) Counties.

In spite of opportunities becoming more diverse, many women and educated young people in general have had to leave the area to pursue careers.[11] As a state, Pennsylvania suffers from the loss of highly educated and skilled occupational workers, particularly those in the 20-29 age bracket. Although this trend is less than in 1975 (10,000 moved away between 1995 and 1997, as compared to 18,000 in the 1975-1980 period), the loss of such residents since World War II has been staggering. There is also a higher net migration loss of women than men.[12] Locally, although there has been discussion of this issue from time to time by Penn State, Bucknell, SEDA-COG, and the CSIU, there is no public policy nor action plan to stop the drain.

Since 1970 the population of Union County has increased from 28,608 to 40,897 (this includes federal prison inmates: c. 1,500 in 1970 and c. 4,000 in 1998).[13] Today's median age in Union County is about 31, in contrast to a median age of 26 just 30 years ago. Most people moving here did not come as a result of broad population movements west, as in the days when they walked or rode on the Tulpehocken Road from southeastern Pennsylvania. Part of Union County's growth is driven by retirees. Some are former Bucknellians who return to Union County to live in a bucolic setting with strong academic/cultural/health facilities, where a good standard of living can be

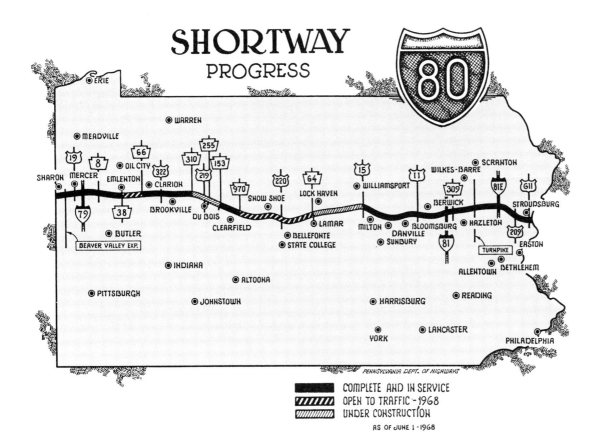

TOP: Map from "More State-wide Shortway News Releases —Pro & Con," June/July 1968. Courtesy of Paul R. Ernst.

ABOVE: Dedication and opening of the bridge on Route 80 (Keystone Shortway) which spanned the Susquehanna north of Milton and Lewisburg, c. 1966. Pictured are: Herbert Bendt, secretary of the Lewisburg Area Chamber of Commerce; Governor William Scranton; Merrill Derr, president of the Lewisburg Area Chamber of Commerce; Paul R. Ernst, Union County representative to Shortway Committee; and the Reverend George K. Bowers of the Christ Evangelical Lutheran Church in Lewisburg. Courtesy of Paul R. Ernst.

PAGE 311: Interchange of Route 15 and Route 80. Photo by Jim Walter.

attained with reasonable home prices and local land taxes. Others seeking that mix put their queries out on the Internet and find that Union County has an attractive quality of life and is only 3-4 hours away from three major metropolitan areas: New York City, Philadelphia, and Washington, D.C. Traveling to these cities was made easier in the last three decades by the completion of an interstate highway system.

In particular, Lewisburg was destined to attract new residents when it was described in volume one of Norman Cranston's *100 Best Small Towns in America* as one of the top ten rural towns (defined as 5,000 or under) in the nation in 1993.[14] Ironically, the borough itself, because of boundary limits, was not able to grow, while contiguous areas were able to do so.[15] Older people in the county do not have a tradition of moving to the Sun Belt, but rather of staying in their homes or sometimes moving into the towns from their farms, or into places which offer both independent living units and tiered care. Some of the traditional nursing home facilities like United Methodist Homes (now RiverWoods) and Buffalo Valley Lutheran Village (including Rhodesmere) became complexes with a variety of living accommodations, while an assisted living unit like Outlook Pointe Commons is entirely new to the area (est. 1998).

Part of the population growth has been a direct result of enlargement of institutions and major employers in the county. Bucknell has experienced a gradual increase from approximately 2,500 to 3,550 students over a 30-year period. The prison expansion was more sudden. A small minimum-security correctional facility

or "camp" near Allenwood housed Vietnam War conscientious objectors in the 1960s and 1970s — many of them members of the plain sects and Jehovah's Witnesses — and Watergate notables like G. Gordon Liddy and Charles Colson as well as white-collar criminals. In the early 1990s, however, the Allenwood site changed drastically, becoming a modern stand-alone prison complex renamed the Allenwood Correctional Complex; situated on 4,245 acres in northeast Union County with low-, medium-, and high-security areas, the prison population presently numbers about 3,500 inmates, with 930 employees.

Population growth has been accompanied by diversity. Though still mainly a white Anglo-Saxon/Germanic-based population,[16] the county now has some Asian, African-American, and Hispanic residents. The 1990 census figures for Union County show a population about 96.2 percent white, 2.7 percent black, 1.8 percent Hispanic, and 1.2 percent other. Some of the minorities are scattered through Kelly and Gregg Townships, where the federal penitentiary and the Allenwood complex are located. Only Lewisburg has significant minorities: 1.8 percent black, 1.8 percent Hispanic, and 2.2 percent other (including Asian). Some of the Lewisburg minority residents are students at Bucknell University which seeks diversity in its staff and student body.[17]

Though Union County does not yet have a synagogue or mosque, there are today 72 churches consisting of most Christian denominations except Orthodox. Lutherans are the most numerous of the mainstream churches,[18] and there are at least five or six Protestant

congregations which date back to the early nineteenth century. A Christian radio station and a religious book store are located in Lewisburg, and an increasing number of families do home schooling or send their children to small private schools for religious reasons.[19] Some of those coming into the area say they feel especially comfortable with what is advertised by word-of-mouth as a " Bible belt."

The major segment of the local economy in early 2000 continues to be agriculture, but this segment has been changing rapidly. The number of farms in the county decreased in the period between 1970 and 2000 from 513 to 451, while the acreage per farm stayed fairly constant.[20] Until 1960, farming had remained steady at 90,000 acres or 44 percent of the county's land mass. There was a precipitous drop in the early 1970s to about 75,000 acres. Since then there has been a loss of 10,000-15,000 acres over a 25-year period. This loss is directly attributable to development. At the same time, there has been a move toward the consolidation of farms. Cash receipts remained steady (allowing for inflation), increasing from $13.7 million in 1975 to $45.5 million in 1995. However, the costs of farming outpace the prices received for farm commodities, whether dairy, grains, livestock, or produce. In some instances, such as with dairy, farm families get the same or a lower price today than in 1975.

In order to keep farming viable, area farmers have begun a more concentrated effort to sell directly to consumers. The produce stands that now dot the landscape as well as the larger markets like Ard's and Dorman's, both on Route 45, are evidence of this trend. They complement Wednesday's Farmers' Market in Lewisburg, which attracts record crowds from within and without the county, and even tour buses. A Satur-

day farmers' market was initiated in spring 2000 in Mifflinburg where local items were sold exclusively.

Vertical integration in agriculture has also become evident. Farmers enter into contracts with large conglomerates in the poultry and hog industry. In these arrangements, the farmer tends the wholesaler's animals with the wholesaler's feed, but the farmer assumes the risk of renovating or erecting buildings for this purpose.

Farms in Union County have continued to mechanize. This has been accelerated by consolidation. Another result of consolidation, the gathering and storage of grain has been transformed. The visual landscape — the tower silos and the Swiss-style bank barns — that so many take for granted is threatened. The commodious bank barn epitomized the diversity of past farming practices with its grain storage, threshing floor, and stalls for horses and cows. The bank barn's usefulness has diminished as farming becomes more monoculture. While many farmers continue to innovate within the existing structures, often converting horse stalls to open animal housing, it is the upper two-thirds of the space that is underutilized. Bank barns were able to accommodate the transition from loose hay and straw storage to square bales, but they are not efficient with the current predominance of large bales. Not as useful either are the tower silos, which functioned well with hand labor but not with today's large-capacity storage needs. Trench silos or the caterpillar-like plastic-wrapped bales on the ground are the trend, and the demise of many tower silos can be expected.

Starting in the 1970s, reduction in traditional tillage became pronounced here. Residue or minimum tillage and more direct planting, with its reliance on chemicals, is practiced even by the plain sect farmers, who generally hew to more traditional methods. The Mennonite farming practices in Union County have been felt since their arrival here in the late 1960s — both in the retention of open space and their direct marketing approaches such as the Buffalo Valley Produce Auction located on Ridge Road. Today, Mennonites own 70 percent of the dairy and 63 percent of the poultry operations,[21] as well as about half of those farms concentrating on produce such as strawberries, cantaloupes, watermelons, and tomatoes.

The area's new architecture as well as the reuse of older buildings provide clues to other transitions. A casual glance at the east side of Mifflinburg reveals major changes. Though a few of the buildings such as the Carriage Corner (formerly Mifflinburg Farm

PAGE 312: Nebraska or "White Top" Amish women at Pennsylvania House flood sale. From the collection of the Union County Historical Society, #89.5.1.9.8.

BELOW: The Sierer farm house and barn are nearly dwarfed by the newer farm buildings. Photo by Jim Walter.

BOTTOM: Silage being wrapped for outside storage. Photos by Jim Walter.

Three-car garages are not unusual on some of the newer homes. Photo by Jim Walter.

Sheetz Gas pumps, canopy, and sign as they appeared on the east side of Mifflinburg when new in 1999. Photo by Jim Walter.

Supply) reflect adaptive use of old structures, most are new structures. While John Wilcox's Mifflinburg Lanes, built in 1961, has achieved a certain architectural cachet and status as a Maya-influenced cement block structure complete with its original signs, it is now dwarfed by its adjacent neighbor, the Sheetz gasoline emporium built in 1999. The Sheetz building, sign, and gas pump area convey a strong architectural statement in their large scale, bright colors, and height, as well as the size of the technologically innovative stretched-canopy cover. Does this site foretell the arrival of Brobdingnags?[22]

The arrival of regional and national store chains makes the survival of small, family-run businesses dependent on the support of local people. Country stores were becoming a rarity in the late 1960s and are now even more so. For example, Millmont had four country stores operating simultaneously in 1889. Today, at the beginning of the twenty-first century, only one survives: Shirks General Store. First opened for business in 1885, it was operated by brothers Philip S. and Charles H. Orwig. The next owner, Harry Mitchell, sold the business to Newton Shirk in 1912, and "Newt's" son, Donald, took over in 1960. Donald's wife, Delphia, and her daughter, Brenda Rowe, now operate the store which represents a symbolic stand against the trend to large, owned-outside-the-area establishments. Another interesting country store is Johnny Dyer's in Winfield.

Local manufacturers like Pennsylvania House, Ritz-Craft, and Playworld have worked to retain their competitive edge. Some like JPM and Playworld are now global and have experienced strong growth in the decade just preceding the twenty-first century; meanwhile, others like Pennsylvania House, having gone through cyclical ups and downs, are no longer locally owned but are part of large conglomerates based outside the area. In addition, there are many farm- and construction-related businesses.

Banking institutions, as in other parts of the United States, have merged and made name changes with dizzying frequency. As banking became more competitive, local banks were sold or merged into regional banks (by the banks' boards of directors and stockholders), beginning in the 1970s. What had been the Lewisburg Trust and Safe Deposit Company (established in 1907), was renamed Lewisburg Trust in the late 1970s; it became Commonwealth Bank (based in Williamsport) in 1984; and within a 14-year time span, the bank became Meridian (1994), Core States (1996), and Sovereign Bank (1998). The Union National Bank became part of Mellon Bank through a

two-step merger; and the Lewisburg National Bank was absorbed by Northern Central, which in turn became Keystone Financial. This trend has left the West Milton State Bank and the Mifflinburg Bank and Trust Company as the only locally-owned community banks operating at the close of the century.

Banks that were located in the heart of the old business districts are either establishing branches or moving to newer, edge-of-town locations, leaving inner business districts like Mifflinburg without banking. Late-Friday-night banking hours, that once complemented store hours, have shrunk and are destined to be a thing of the past. The continued, not-so-subtle necessity to get in a vehicle to bank or shop continues in the face of traffic congestion and land consumption.

Although local utilities like Citizens Electric and Buffalo Valley Telephone Company retain their decades-old names, these are no longer owned and controlled by local boards. The electric company was purchased in 1999 by C&T Enterprises, Inc., formerly of Wysox but now located in Lewisburg; and the telephone company was acquired by Conestoga Enterprises, Inc., of Birdsboro, Pennsylvania, in 1996.

Growing sectors of the local economy are the flea markets and antique malls. These did not exist in this area before the mid-1970s. Dealers began coming every Sunday morning to the parking area and covered walkway at the Ames/McDonald's mall on Route 15 outside Lewisburg. Vendors included regulars as well as occasional and one-time sellers. From a few dozen, the number of tables grew until there were several hundred tables both outside and in the walkway. In 1989 the management of the mall stopped this Sunday flea market activity, and many of the vendors relocated to the Interstate Flea Market near Watsontown and to the former Silver Moon Drive-in Theater a mile north of Lewisburg on Route 15. The 32-acre Silver Moon site has grown from 10 vendors to about 600 on Sundays. The site also has an antique mall with 250 dealers, a restaurant, and a facility for auctions, banquets, and weddings. The Sunday flea market is both under roof and outside in the warmer months. Another antique market opened at the former Roller Mills in 1990. Organized by local entrepreneur Craig Bennett, the mill has dealers in traditional booth settings and exhibits of smaller items in glass case displays, as well as a restaurant. In 1997 Bennett opened a second facility for larger furniture and collectibles at the former Lewisburg Woolen Mills (later Pennsylvania House) building on North Water Street.

Yard sales became an important part of social life as well as the economy, starting in the 1970s. Some communities or local neighborhoods have annual yard sale dates. For example, in the spring of each year, Swengel and Millmont hold their annual flea market and yard sales; and since 1974 Millmont's proceeds have benefited the Frank Long Community Ball Field, which was built in 1979. The Linntown and Ikeler Park areas of Lewisburg also hold annual yard sale events.

The completion of what was locally called the "Shortway," later Interstate 80, in 1970, and its intersection with U.S. Route 15 in the northern part of Union County interestingly has not radically changed the adjacent towns of Allenwood, White Deer, and New Columbia as much as other parts of the county. In fact, except for the erection of a Comfort Inn and more recently a Holiday Inn Express at the 80/15 Commerce Park nearby, these three towns are remarkably unchanged from decades before — with small post offices, community centers, and the physical presence — though not the use — of former rail stations.

The impact of these major transportation networks (going east/west and north/south) evidences itself most in the amount of traffic going to and through the eastern edge of Union County (also, increasingly so between Lewisburg and Mifflinburg). When coupled with population growth and the number of families with multiple vehicles, the lack of public transportation translates into congestion, additional traffic lights, and widened roads — with the pressure to do more of the same. Union County has not bucked the statewide trend toward rapid land consumption; the total number of land parcels has increased by 25 percent from 1980 through 1995, and 41 percent of houses in the county have been built since 1970.[23] Land consumption has usually been at the expense of particularly rich farm land.

This land-consumptive pattern has prompted the formation of several groups devoted in large part to open space and special land preservation efforts. In conjunction with other planning tools such as Agriculture Security Areas, the Agriculture Preservation Program was designed to help stem the voracious devouring of prime farm land. With state and county support, the Union County Agricultural Land Preservation Board was formed in 1989 to make use of a statewide $100 million bond issue dedicated to the purchase of development rights from eligible farmers. The Union County Commissioners quickly responded

to what was felt to be a very worthwhile program. Since 1989, twenty-two farms (a total of 2,865 acres) have had their development rights purchased in perpetuity by the match of county and state funds. This program, which started off slowly, has built up sustained interest among area farmers. Annually there are more than twenty farmers interested in having a conservation easement placed on their acreage, but funds have generally been available only for three or four each year. The selection process is based on strict criteria focusing on soil type and productivity as well as the potential for creating larger zones of protected agricultural land. As the next century approached, the Ag/Land Preservation Board, under the direction of Bill Deitrick, administrator, and Ted Retallack, secretary, set higher goals of preservation of 40,000 total acres by 2020.

Complementing such public preservation efforts is the work of the Merrill W. Linn Land & Waterways Conservancy, formed by private citizens in 1988 as a nonprofit organization devoted to the protection of open space, preservation of special plant and animal habitats, and public education on environmental issues and land protection techniques. Bucknell ecologists, local public school science teachers, and business and community leaders formed the group, which now numbers over 300 area families and businesses willing to support and work on local environmental issues. The Linn Conservancy works with older environmentally oriented groups like the local chapters of the Seven Mountains Chapter of the Audubon Society and the Otzinachson Chapter of the Sierra Club;[24] also active are local garden clubs as well as state and government agencies like the Bureau of Forestry, the Fish and Game Commission, and the Department of Conservation and Natural Resources. Like other land trusts and conservancies in Pennsylvania, this locally oriented group looks to accomplish more and diverse projects in the twenty-first century.

Recycling became the clarion call of the 1980s and 1990s, in part driven by statewide mandates as well as by individual and collective consciousness-raising. Bucknell students and employees led the way on the university's campus; courthouse employees became careful about sorting their recyclable paper products, sending only non-reusable glued and labeled goods to the landfill. In the meantime, the towns of Mifflinburg and Lewisburg began recycling slowly, often at the insistence of local citizens. Private concerns, such as the recycling station in Montandon, accepted a greater range of items and at more convenient hours than the recycling stations operated by local municipalities.

While other areas in the state have once-a-week recycling, Union County has lagged behind, with only monthly pickups of restricted items. In 1998 the county was recycling 11 percent of its waste as compared to an average of 32.6 percent statewide.[25] Area farmers have helped with their own recycling initiatives by placing containers for newspapers where their farm lanes join local roads; the newspapers are shredded by the farmers and used as animal bedding. This has proved a direct, innovative, and individualistic approach to a mounting problem.

Recyling Center at Bucknell University's barn c. 1979-80. Courtesy of Mike Molesevich.

While the area has become increasing affluent during the 1970s through the 1990s it has not happened without diligence on the part of community leaders.[26] Towns sought to continue to be viable economic entities. With increased traffic on Route 15, businesses gravitated to the business "strip" that grew up along the highway. Fast food was no longer just the locally owned sub shop or pizza parlor, but regional and national franchises like Subway. The first national fast food restaurant in Union County was a Kentucky Fried Chicken on Route 15 in 1969, followed by McDonald's in 1976, then Pizza Hut, Wendy's, Hardee's, and Burger King. In the 1970s the strip development trend was accelerated with the move of Weis Markets from downtown Lewisburg to Route 15. A petition with nearly a thousand signatures opposed to the relocation was presented to the locally owned supermarket firm, but to no avail; and in 1974 Weis Markets left its downtown location. In 1995 the Route 15 store became even larger than its

strip predecessor. Joining Weis on or near Route 15 were national chain stores like Wal-Mart in 1991 and Staples in 1996. Motorists on Route 15 were often unaware of the attractive small-town shopping and living environment just a few blocks east of the four-lane federal highway. This trend was not limited to Lewisburg; national fast-food stops arrived in Mifflinburg when Hardee's came in 1990, followed by McDonald's in 1995. Traffic lights kept popping up as well, on both Routes 15 and 45. Mifflinburg went from two to four lights in four years, all on the rapidly developing eastern half of town.

Affluence was also mirrored in this period by larger homes, not occupied by growing farm families who could work on the family enterprise, but by empty-nesters building dream homes of 2,400-3,000 square feet.[27] Three-car garages began to appear with frequency. Most often the new housing was built in land-consumptive patterns, and was centered on a lifestyle associated with these developments. Such developments entailed driving everywhere in one of several family vehicles. Young families often had two wage earners to support this lifestyle.

Subsidized housing began to develop in this era — first in Mifflinburg (1975) and Kelly Township (1981); later housing projects included the White Deer Commons of New Columbia, and the Rosedale Apartments in New Berlin among others. Some of these were private endeavors, while others were projects of the Housing Authority of Union County, which was established in August 1972.[28] The housing authority provides a comprehensive program of housing services, including rental assistance, elderly housing, family housing, housing education, residential rehabilitation, and building and sewage code enforcement. The scope of the housing authority's work has been incremental; it has included the Inter-Municipal Code Enforcement Program, which started with Lewisburg Borough and East Buffalo Township in 1987 and embraces nine of the fourteen county governing bodies by 2000, as well as the sewage code enforcement program for eleven of the fourteen. The authority was the driving force behind the establishment in 1993 of the Union County Community Service Complex, a newly renovated building which had under one roof many related county services.

One HUD-subsidized senior citizen housing project slated for Lewisburg in 1978 epitomized some of the conflicting values emerging in this era; a large six-story generic housing project was proposed for the flood plain on the south side of Market Street between Fifth and Sixth Streets. A coalition of community leaders

White Deer Commons outside of New Columbia and near the interchange of Routes 15 and 80. Photo by Jim Walter.

fought the location, design, and construction of the building, and it was rejected by the Lewisburg Planning Commission. Totally redesigned, it was built instead on North Third Street on the former Weis parking lot in 1980. Called "Heritage House," the finished building's architectural elements reflect modern adaptation of neighboring buildings' mass, proportions, and details. In 1985, the original site became the public park named for Gordon Hufnagle, Lewisburg Safety Officer who drowned in the 1972 flood.

Groups concentrating on local history were established in the mid-1970s and have flourished. The New Berlin Heritage Association, the Slifer House Museum, the Mifflinburg Buggy Museum, the Packwood House Museum, and the White Deer & Reading Station and Museum (owned and operated by the Central Pennsylvania Chapter of the National Railway Historical Society) were started, while the previously established Union County Historical Society continued to strengthen its efforts as an advocate for countywide and regional preservation efforts and educational programming. The Union County Historical Society has informally lent support and knowledge to some of the newer groups, including

the Consortium of Union County Historical Groups. More recent historic preservation efforts are those of the Mifflinburg Historical Society and Preservation Mifflinburg, both formed in the late 1990s.

In the last three decades of the twentieth century, numerous community centers were started in New Berlin, New Columbia, Vicksburg, and Laurelton, among other area towns. The largest of these was in the county seat. After repeated grassroots attempts at organizing and maintaining a community center, Lewisburg coalesced its efforts with the availability of the former Minium storage building on North Fifth Street. Now called the Donald L. Heiter Community Center, in honor of the late police "Chief Heiter," the center was started by local citizens, with support from the Area Agency on Aging, in 1993; the group incorporated in 1994 and, after a successful capital campaign of $218,000, purchased the building in 1997. Today it is a locally owned and operated multipurpose facility, with diverse youth and adult programming, as well as both a paid and a volunteer staff to provide the programs and maintain the center.

A similar daunting task, the building of the Public Library for Union County, was delayed several times. The most difficult decision for the library was to move from the former Himmelreich Library on Market

Street in Lewisburg. Once Martha Root and the board of directors made that decision, land on the former Reitz Farm (now Brook Park) on the western edge of Lewisburg (East Buffalo Township) was donated by Dan and Audrey Baylor. The effort to raise a million dollars for the construction and endowment of the 11,200-square-foot modern facility was nearly completed within a year of the capital campaign's inauguration in June 1988 as $825,000 had been raised or pledged within that time. Ground was broken on September 6, 1988, and the library was open for readers on April 24, 1989. Growth of book borrowers climbed from 4,860 card holders to over 12,000 in 1999; and the circulation of 90,600 items in 1988 grew to nearly 220,000 items in 1999 — fulfillment of a prediction that only a few had dared to make in the beginning of the project. In 1996 a children's wing of 3,000 square feet was added with the support of the Edna Sheary Trust. In 1998 the county commissioners were persuaded, after a decade of petitioning, to support, through tax millage, the concept of a countywide library system. As a result, the Herr Library in Mifflinburg built a major addition, paid for in part by

a bequest from Joseph Gutelius Foster in addition to county funds, and the library in Laurelton was also established and prospered at the Hartley Township Community Center.

The Edna M. Sheary Charitable Trust, started in 1991, provided a tremendous support to many local nonprofit organizations. After teaching at East Lewisburg and the Sand Hill School in West Chillisquaque Township, Edna Moyer Sheary began her banking career in 1926 as a clerk at the Union National Bank of Lewisburg (later Mellon Bank, N.A.). She later served as cashier, and eventually became first vice president and trust officer before retiring in 1972. Sheary was the first woman in Lewisburg bank history to serve in the latter three capacities. After her death at age 88, a charitable trust was established for "religious, charitable, scientific, literary, or educational purposes." The trust provided opportunities for often hard-pressed but increasingly professional and ambitious groups and their constituencies. Nonprofit organizations have benefited greatly; the Mifflinburg Buggy Museum is building an educational/interpretive center; the Union County

The Public Library for Union County in Brook Park Farm. Photo by Jim Walter.

Historical Society started new educational programming and the restoration of the Red Bank one-room school in West Buffalo Township; the Linn Conservancy has been able to support construction of an educational amphitheater and environmental center at R.B. Winter State Park; and the Union County Chapter of the Red Cross has built a new facility in Brook Park, which has eight times the square footage of its former space.

While the 1970-2000 period saw new sports activities, such as the midget football and American Youth Soccer Organization's (AYSO) programs for youth, start and flourish, an even larger change was the growth of "lifetime" sport and exercise regimes. This broad cultural change was reflected in walking/running and general exercise tracks built both by Bucknell and the Evangelical Community Hospital. Many area residents now jog or walk at these outdoor facilities, in Bucknell's Field House, or on roads throughout the county (sidewalks and designated paths are not yet available).

Union County did not have a large hall for presenting musical and theatrical events for 70 years after the Opera House in Lewisburg burned to the ground in 1908. The local high school auditoriums and churches, as well as Bucknell's Coleman Hall and Rooke Chapel were the sites of concerts and plays, but musical events of any size were forced into gymnasiums. In 1987 that changed with the completion of the Sigmund and Claire Weis Center for the Performing Arts, which was largely supported by a lead trust gift to Bucknell from the estate of Claire Weis, the mother of Sigfried Weis, then-president of Weis Markets and of the Bucknell Board of Trustees. The Weis Center inaugurated its opening season with performances by violinist Itzhak Perlman, the Philadelphia Orchestra, Mark Russell, Philip Glass, the Alvin Ailey Dance Theatre, and the Pittsburgh Symphony Orchestra, among other attractions. Local musical groups such as the West Branch Chorus and the Susquehanna Valley Chorale have since rented the facility for concerts on occasion.

Art — sculpture, painting, printmaking, and photography — was not as fortunate. In 1983 part of the Bucknell student center's third floor was finished as an art exhibition and storage care facility. Its inaugural show was "Faces Since the '50s," curated by director Joseph Jacobs. To run the Center Gallery, (renamed the Bucknell Art Gallery in the late 1990s), the university hired a director and assistant. Although several of the exhibitions over the next seventeen years focused on area material culture[29] as well as the work of artists teaching at Bucknell who had made Union County their home, the exhibition space was not accessible for showcasing local work.

Health care and social services availability and delivery have changed dramatically between 1970 and 2000. As 1999 closed, the Evangelical Community Hospital (the county's third largest employer) was in an enviable position as a well-managed institution. The hospital, which dates back to 1926 when a community infirmary opened at the Evangelical Home, saw tremendous growth in the second half of the twentieth century. Under the continuing administration of Lystra Rodgers, RN (active 1935-1973), north and south wings were added to the original 1951 section, and the first of three floors of a professional office building for physicians' offices was built. Physical growth and renovation in 1993 nearly doubled the space to 110,000 square feet but maintained the total beds at 155. The emphasis has shifted to improved delivery of care and overall staff efficiency in an era in which inpatient stays are getting shorter and more and varied services are provided on an outpatient basis.

In 1984 the hospital added health services for homebound patients in the central Susquehanna Valley. The need and growth of such a program is reflected in the statistics; 70 employees now serve more than 10,000 patients annually, whereas six employees, consisting of a registered nurse, a home health aide, a medical social worker, and physical, occupational, and speech therapists, served 1,000 patients that first year. In 1986 a program called Continued Care, which provides in-home non-skilled services, was established; and Evangelical Hospice, a comprehensive program for terminally ill patients who want to die at home, along with their families, was added in 1989.

The large group practice of the Geisinger Medical Center, located in nearby Danville, came to Union County in 1991, when Geisinger established a clinic on West Market Street, Lewisburg; the clinic relocated in a large, newly constructed facility in Brook Park in 1993. Another Geisinger clinic was opened in Mifflinburg in 1995.

Many of the service agencies are multi-county programs. These include the Union/Snyder/Northumberland Foster Grandparent Program; Family Planning; the Union/Snyder Area Agency on Aging; and Union/Snyder/Columbia/Montour Mental Health and Mental Retardation. Private nonprofit organizations such as Snyder/Union/ Mifflin Head

Start; SUN Home Health; Big Brothers/Big Sisters; and Habitat for Humanity provide further cooperative services. Other multi-county programs include Green Thumb, Susquehanna Valley Legal Services, Aids Resources, Family Planning, and the Haven Ministries. The latter, located in Sunbury, operates the only homeless shelter available to residents of Union County.

One of the newer social service organizations is the Union/Snyder Habitat for Humanity, founded in 1991. A branch of the national organization, Habitat is administered by a local volunteer board of directors. After Habitat built its first home in Beaver Springs, Snyder County, the organization erected its second home in Glen Iron, Union County, in 1991. The goal is to construct one house a year, with donated materials and labor used to the greatest extent possible; and the home construction alternates between the neighboring counties. Partner families who will own these homes are solicited, selected, and nurtured in a variety of ways. Each family agrees to pay the mortgage, though it is interest-free.

Day care became a necessity for many families with two working parents. Nursery schools, which were few in 1970, proliferated — both privately run centers as well as institutionally affiliated ones. Bucknell University established its day care center, Sunflower, in 1978; it is open to all members of the community but was designed for university staff. Another, Union County's Community Child Care, now with eleven sites, grew from caring for 60 children in 1969 to 400 today.

The federal penitentiary in Lewisburg generated a different set of social service needs in the late 1960s. The Prison Visitors' Project was a loosely organized group of citizens formed at that time to help those arriving in Lewisburg by public transportation at 6:00 A.M. on Saturdays to visit inmates of the penitentiary. At that time in the morning, the visitors could not go to the penitentiary, nor were they able to get a breakfast in town. With an identified need for as many as several dozen women and children, group leaders met with local church officials to form a partnership whereby the churches provided the facilities and the volunteers provided the food and labor. For three or four years this effort continued, in addition to occasionally providing chartered buses from Washington, D.C., or Philadelphia, and soliciting books from publishers for the main prison library. When the New York bus changed its arrival time in Lewisburg to 8 A.M., the need to provide the breakfasts ended; and by 1973 the Prison Visitors' Service ceased. At the same time, the Lewisburg Prison Project was beginning.

The Lewisburg Prison Project (LPP) currently serves the federal prisons in Lewisburg and Allenwood, as well as eleven state and 32 county prisons in the middle judicial district of Pennsylvania. The prison project has a staff of two attorneys, an executive director, and paralegals. The organization was formed by a group of concerned citizens in 1973 with the idea of providing legal services and due process for prisoners, without a fee.[30] For four years after its incorporation, the group was denied access to inmates, until 1977, when Michael Quinlan, executive assistant to Norman Carlson, director of the Federal Bureau of Prisons, allowed paralegals to enter the Lewisburg facility. Over time there has developed a cordial working relationship that allows the LPP to counsel and assist, visit, litigate on behalf of prisoners, and prepare and distribute legal bulletins nationwide.

In 1977 A. Thomas Wilson, president judge for the 17th Judicial District (Union and Snyder Counties), recognized the need to establish a probation office that could provide him with information on juvenile and adult offenders appearing before him and could enforce his sentence orders. Eugene Curtis, a retired federal parole agent, was appointed the task of building the department; and by the time it was turned over to Dominic Herbst in 1979, the department had three probation officers and a clerical staff. From 1977 to 1980, the typical work load consisted of approximately 30 juvenile offenders and 90 adults for each county. From 1980 to 1988, the caseload grew, and the programs and services expanded. In 1988 President Judge James McClure separated the department into two single county agencies, with Scott Lizardi heading the department in Union County. The department continued to experience considerable growth and program development, and by 2000 the caseload in Union County had 100 juvenile and 325 adult offenders under supervision, with an additional 170 administrative cases. Probation/parole supervision, electronic monitoring, community service, drug screening, fines/cost collection, crisis intervention, and information/referral all come under this department's purview.

In late 1983, Herbst incorporated the Bethesda Day Treatment Center as a private nonprofit agency for troubled youth and court-referred juveniles. Located initially in Selinsgrove, the facility later relocated to Central Oaks Heights, just south of West Milton. Under the leadership of Herbst, now the president, and vice-president Jerilyn Keen, the agency has received national model status from the U.S. Department of Justice for three consecutive years beginning in 1991. In 1995 the Bethesda Family

Services Foundation was established to focus on national replication of Bethesda's relational healing model, which includes practical methods of parenting and family counseling both in private and in group instruction and seminars. Aspects of Bethesda's work have been featured on four national television shows since 1994; these include a one-hour special, hosted by George Foreman, called "Bad Dads," and "Victory Over Violence," narrated by Walter Cronkite. In seventeen years Bethesda has grown from one facility with a staff of four serving fifteen to twenty youths in Union and Snyder Counties to nine program centers with a staff of over 150 serving over 400 youths with a variety of program services throughout seven states. These youths are referred from juvenile probation departments as well as children and youth agencies in eleven counties in Pennsylvania, including Union County. Day treatment, alternative education programming, family-systems counseling, drug and alcohol outpatient counseling, and short term foster care are provided by Bethesda.

Helping others has extended to surplus food distribution through the Office of Human Resources, a program that was discontinued for a time. Private food banks were established by the First Baptist Church in Lewisburg and the Wesley United Methodist Church in Mifflinburg; on the government level, the Area Agency on Aging provides senior citizen meals, and the federal WIC (Women, Infants, and Children) program distributes vouchers for pregnant women and children. The Meals on Wheels Program operates out of the United Methodist Homes (now RiverWoods), and a consortium of Lewisburg churches runs a meal program one day each month.

Dramatic changes in the organization and delivery of emergency services and communications in the county began in 1978 when the Union County Department of Emergency Services was formed. The department combined the dispatching of fire and police departments from the sheriff's office with the county's civil defense efforts. This reorganization closely paralleled that of state and federal agencies which were making the transition from civil defense preparedness — designed in part to respond to Cold War threats — to emergency management of natural disasters like floods, blizzards, and tornadoes. Tom Hess became the full-time emergency management coordinator and director of emergency services in 1978; he is assisted by a clerk/typist and three full-time and five part-time dispatchers. The communications system in Union County, the first one in a SEDA-COG project in eleven Central Pennsylvania counties, became operational on September 11, 1978 .

At the beginning of 2000, Hess' staff consists of fifteen full-time people, eleven of whom are in the 911 Communications Center.[31] There is also a network of volunteers — rain-gauge observers and severe-weather reporters, as well as emergency squad members, some of whom are high school students. A typical week for Hess includes contacts with the Federal Bureau of Investigation, PennDOT, and the National Weather Service. Atypical weeks have included responding to major floods brought on by Hurricanes Agnes (1972), Eloise (1975), and Dennis (1999); blizzards (1993 and 1996, the latter of which was accompanied with fast-rising streams); the Three Mile Island nuclear plant disaster (1979); tornadoes in Gregg Township, which killed two area residents

A severe summer storm in 1983 caused damage in Buffalo Valley near the present Natural Foods Store and elsewhere along the Route 45 corridor. Courtesy of Union County Emergency Services.

Blizzard of '93

Snow accumulations in Pennsylvania

By The Associated Press

Storm snowfall totals, in inches, at selected locations in Pennsylvania, according to the National Weather Service:

Allentown-Easton, 18	Monroeton, 21
Altoona, 24	Montrose, 20
Bartonsville, 17	Muncy, 18
Bradford, 18	Myerstown, 11
Bushkill, 16	North Bend, 20
Clarence, 25	Philadelphia, 12
Corry, 12	Picture Rocks, 15
Danville, 16	Pine Grove, 16
Dewart, 20	Pittsburgh, 24
Dubois, 24	Poconos, 21
Edinboro, 9	Raven creek, 17
Elimsport, 9	Reading, 15
Erie, 12	Renovo, 15
Everson, 21	Ringtown, 18
Frackville, 17	Rushville, 17
Friedensburg, 19	Sabinsville, 27
Galeton, 21	Saladasburg, 17
Glennmoore, 10	Scranton, 20
Grove City, 16	Shoemakersville, 12
Harrisburg, 20	State College, 25
Hegins, 16	Stroud Township, 14
Irwin, 27	Tamaqua, 16
Jim Thorpe, 20	Tobyhanna, 22
Johnstown, 25	Towanda, 17
Junedale, 19	Trout Run, 18
Laporte, 30	Uniontown, 20
Larryville, 19	Washington County, 24
Lewisburg, 19	Watsontown, 19
Lock Haven, 25	Wellsboro, 17
McKeesport, 21	Wexford, 21
Millville, 16	Williamsport, 15
Milton, 18	

(1985); and the non-event of Y2K, for which preparation began a year and one-half ahead. Local preparedness for hazardous waste problems and for terrorist activities have been added to the department's list of responsibilities. As Union County begins the twenty-first century, Emergency Services, supported by a federally funded program, is creating a street address for every building in the county which will in turn be an integral part of a computer dispatching system. Vehicle locators are anticipated in the near future as well.

Planners grappled with the thorniest of issues and the stickiest of places. Planning came to Union County by way of Bucknell University in 1969. The Institute for Regional Affairs, supported by the university, was proposing regional approaches to solving problems in anticipation of projected growth and its attendant issues. George Fasic from the institute contracted with Union County for planning services. This contractual arrangement was supplanted by the creation of a Union County planning office in 1973 with John Trone as director. He was replaced by John Bevacqua in 1976, and in 1978 by Doug Hovey, who had worked with George Fasic from 1971 to 1975. When Fred Wilder became the new county planner in 1990 after working in Monroe County, Pennsylvania, the planning office, with a staff of three to four (mainly young) people, had already formulated its first comprehensive plan and its first historic preservation inventory. Wilder enlarged upon those early efforts with progressive planning through the 1990s.

Finding regional, broad-based solutions to local problems was not always easy to do. With fourteen separate governmental units in the eighth smallest but third fastest-growing county in Pennsylvania,[32] county planners had their work cut out for them. High school rivalries or personality conflicts could make or break the necessary cooperation. A regional police force, involving the neighboring communities of East Buffalo Township and the Borough of Lewisburg, is a good example of an issue brought to the table for serious and protracted discussion. Limestone Township still does not have a planning commission, and even the other townships and boroughs that do have them rely on the county planning staff to advise them and to move issues along. Many Union Countians are aware of planning issues such as the dangers of sprawl and the concept of urban growth boundaries that would confine development to existing or projected support systems. "Sustainable communities" and "urban growth boundaries" are buzz words at the turn of the century and the planning staff has done much to make this so. Providing regional solutions that can be accepted by so many different governmental units is the task facing the planners.

Organized downtown revitalization efforts started first in Mifflinburg in 1986, when a newly formed Mifflinburg Heritage and Revitalization Association (MHRA) hired a "main street manager," who would get businesses to refresh their appearance and to act cohesively. Empty store fronts from time to time often reflected personal business decisions to retire, move elsewhere, or start a different enterprise; but Union County's communities showed ongoing concern about too many vacancies. The expansion of the large malls that had been built in Lycoming and Snyder Counties in the early 1970s as well as the strip development on Route 15 were watched. Lewisburg, which in 1999 had more vacancies than seen in the previous 30 years, applied for a grant to initially support a main street effort similar to Mifflinburg's.

MHRA organized and sponsored May's annual Buggy Days, first held in 1986 and Christkindl Market in early December, which started in 1989. These community events combined history and commerce to become traditional events welcomed by local families as well as visitors from outside the region. New Berlin's Heritage Day, held on the fourth Saturday of August, began this type of event in 1971. Heritage Day started as a community-wide event to raise money to restore the 1814 former Union County courthouse, which was given to the New Berlin Heritage Association by the Union County Historical Society. Other institutionalized events became yearly celebrations, such as the Victorian Holiday Parade in Lewisburg (est. in 1981) with citizens like Russell (Buzz) Meachum and later Betty Cook and Jacquie Stiefel putting in long hours to make a nice event memorable, just as Rudi and Joannah Skucek and Carol Bohn have done with Mifflinburg's Christkindl Market. Attorney Graham Showalter organized a spectacular Fourth of July celebration in Lewisburg in 1995, which, in addition to the holiday, also celebrated the restoration of the 1901 Civil War Monument on University Avenue, which had been vandalized a couple of decades earlier. This old-time Fourth of July celebration has been repeated annually since and is emblematic of a town striving to retain the best of the past. The Harold Stiefel Memorial Show, featuring a classic movie at the Campus Theatre each fall to raise money for local nonprofit organizations, similarly has that special imprimatur imparted by the personality, the dream, and the energy to do something topnotch for the community.[33]

Over these years events which have become institutionalized have often been paired with certain names: Joel and Marsha Gori with the Summer Stacks and River Celebration;[34] Mary Jane Hyde, Owen Mahon, and Joan Wheatcroft with the Lewisburg Festival of the Arts; Bud Eaton, Joan Maurer, Gloria Maize, and Margaret Strome with New Berlin's Heritage Days; Kathy Ranney and Deb Johnson with Mifflinburg's Buggy Days; Paulene Poggi and

Elwood C. Hassinger with the West End Fair; Nelson Doebler with the New Columbia Apple Butter Boil; and more. These events, many of which have been ongoing for decades, represent both stability and innovation by natives and newcomers alike, and portray the county at its best.

In 2000 many of Union County's crossroad communities and larger villages and towns still retain a high percentage of their nineteenth-century structures. Lewisburg is often associated with its early-twentieth-century three-bulb cast iron light standard. Starting in 1977, a countywide historic structures survey was done by volunteers and lay historians like Charles M. Snyder, Lois Kalp, Elizabeth Hitchcock, and Nada Gray under auspices of the Union County Planning Commission. As a result, historic districts were proposed for the county's three largest towns: New Berlin, Lewisburg, and Mifflinburg. Mifflinburg's was approved by the state but never enacted by the town's borough council, while Lewisburg created its own Historic District along with supporting ordinances and architectural review board in 1985. These actions were taken in large part in response to several threats to historic properties. As a result, Lewisburg's Historic Architecture Review Board (HARB) is still in place as another governmental permitting agency, although its strictures and merits are debated at times.

New Berlin, the former county seat, has changed the least architecturally, in large part because since the mid-nineteenth century it has been literally "off the track" of either rail or road. In 1970 as well as 2000, the perception is that of a handsome but sleepy small town.[35] Even so, many changes have occurred in last 30 years. In the late 1990s Tara Lee Sportswear closed its doors while Playworld Systems moved to larger quarters in Lewisburg. However, new industries arrived: the New Berlin Plastics Company, QCast Aluminum, Sunset Restaurant, and Paper Magic; while QE Manufacturing, Snyder County Trust Bank, D.J. Mapes Garage, and SUN Area Vo-Tech School (now called SUN Area Career & Technology Center) have remained. The Second Evangelical Church is now the Union County Wrestling Academy. On the north side are several new housing developments; Teaberry Hill includes 40 homes built by the Spangler Brothers; Seminary Acres, on a small parcel of land near the site of the original Union Seminary, was built by Keister Construction as were the Rosedale Apartments on the former site of the Rosedale Dairy. Many service organizations are in the town; the Lions Club, American Legion, fire company, Heritage

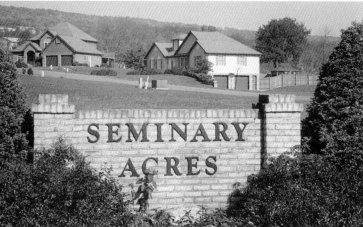

The Countryside and Seminary Acres are two of the newer subdivisions in East Buffalo Township and New Berlin, respectively. Photos by Jim Walter.

Association, Scouts, 4H, Youth and Recreations, and three churches all prosper. The Inn at Olde New Berlin and Gabriel's Gifts also welcome area residents and visitors. Started in the 1970s, the New Berlin Heritage Association acquired, researched, and executed the major preservation of the original Union County courthouse. The first floor of the restored building houses the U.S. post office, and the second floor is home to the association's collection of New Berlin artifacts. Recently, the association purchased a small building adjacent to the courthouse and uses it for office and storage space.

Visitors to Union County comment on the architectural homogeneity and preservation efforts both in the towns such as New Berlin and in the surrounding countryside. Tourism has been recognized as a major business, which in 1999 generated over $63 million

dollars in tourism spending, approximately 850 local jobs, and $3.8 million in local and state tax revenue.[36] Pamphlets detailing historic walking tours of the three main towns were produced in the early 1980s and are kept in print through the efforts of the Union County Historical Society, which in 1997 received statewide recognition for the series' excellence. The Oral Traditions Project of the Union County Historical Society has researched and showcased the rural skills and attitudes exemplified in the area's traditions, handed down from generation to generation by word of mouth. Started in 1973 as part of the Union County Bicentennial Commission, Oral Traditions for over 25 years secured grants to produce exhibitions, books, multimedia shows, record albums, and a movie based on the knowledge and talent of area residents considered treasures of information and insight: blacksmiths, fiddlers, millers, and pow wow practitioners. These efforts had a national as well as local audience, but, in particular, Oral Traditions heightened awareness and appreciation of rural traditions locally.

It is Union County's rural strength of character that is now being tested by the fast-moving modern age. There is a struggle between change and stability. Does an area such as Union County have an advantage in not being the first exposed to changes? Can it be able to pick and choose? This new century will tell more of Union County's story.

John Shively, basket maker, as well as Laurelton residents Harry and Dorothy Bingaman and Cora Boop participated in the film, *John Wesley Shively: Heritage*, produced in 1976 by the Oral Traditions Project. The movie was shown on WVIA-TV and supported by a National Endowment of the Arts grant. Photo by Jonathan Whitney, courtesy of the Oral Traditions Project.

ENDNOTES:

1 Several county-wide groups have won coveted state or national awards of recognition. For example, the Housing Authority of Union County, both in 1997 and 1998, won one of four national awards given by the National Association of Housing and Redevelopment Offices (NHRO) for its innovative programs; and the Union County Historical Society won the highest award given by the American Association of State and Local History (AASLH) in 1997 for its book, *Rural Delivery, Real Photo Postcards from Central Pennsylvania.*

2 In 1999 registration by party was Republican 2.1%, Democratic 27.8%, and all others 10.1%. In 1986 registration figures were 64.5%, 28.6%, and 6.9% respectively. When citizens cast their votes in the 1970 gubernatorial election, which was won by Milton Shapp, a Democrat, the percentages were not that different from these recent registration figures: the Republican candidate got 62%, the Democrat got 33.9%, and other was 4.1%. Likewise, when Nixon ran for reelection as president in 1972, he received 73.6% of the vote, his Democratic opposition got 24.3%, and other received 2.1 percent. These percentages show that those who register as "other" usually vote for one of the two main party candidates in a major election, thus widening the spread between Republicans and Democrats.

3 The Northeastern Federal Penitentiary — now called the U.S. Penitentiary at Lewisburg — has itself not seen a population increase with the number of inmates remaining at the 1,400-1,500 level over the last 68 years although it has gone from a medium- to a maximum-security institution with two different types of camps. Rather, it is the Allenwood site which has been transformed into a large complex, containing a low-security facility with 1,310 inmates and 219 staff, a medium-security facility with 1,191 inmates and 330 staff, and a high-security facility with 986 inmates and 391 staff; this represents a huge increase when compared to 1952, when there were about 100 housed at a camp.

4 Freight runs from Lewisburg to Mifflinburg or to Winfield.

5 The Rotary and Kiwanis in Lewisburg formed additional chapters which meet in the mornings in order to accommodate the needs of young working professionals.

6 Helen Strunk was also president of the Pennsylvania Bankers' Association from 1989 to 1990.

7 Martha Zeller became state president of AAUW from 1980 to 1982.

8 Nancy Neuman became state president (1975-1977) and then the national president of the League (1986-1990). Neuman has also received appointments to the Disciplinary Board of the Supreme Court of Pennsylvania, the Pennsylvania Housing Finance Agency Board, and the Federal Home Loan Bank of Pittsburgh.

9 Farida Zaid was a driving force in a number of community-based initiatives: the Union/Snyder Office of Human Resources, the conversion of the former North Ward School in Lewisburg into the main office of the Union/Snyder Area Agency for the Aging, the Lewisburg Senior Center, and the Lewisburg Community Child Care Center, as well as the Lewisburg Area Community Center (renamed the Donald Heiter Center). Zaid was initially hired as a rural planning specialist by George Fasic in 1971 under a federal demonstration grant from the Office of Economic Opportunity; her job was to work toward the integration of social concerns and physical planning as a staff member of the Regional

Planning Commission, which was a combined planning commission for Union and Snyder Counties.

10 The county plan was called *Vision 21*; a second citation received by the county planning commission was the Governor's Award for Environmental Excellence.

11 Although the county's statistics show that there were net gains of 454 people in 1970; 413 in 1980; and 1,689 in 1990, there are still many educated or highly skilled young people who left the area in order to find employment in their fields.

12 *Pennsylvania's Brain Drain Migration in the Mid-1990s* by Gordon F. De Jong and Pamela M. Klein of the Population Research Institute, Penn State University, July 1999.

13 The federal prison at Lewisburg over the years has housed famous prisoners such as Al Capone and Jimmy Hoffa, and more recently New York Mafia leader John Gotti and the Word Trade Center bombers.

14 Prentis-Hall, New York.

15 Instead, the fastest growing areas in the county were Buffalo, East Buffalo and White Deer Townships in the 1970s; East Buffalo Township in the 1980s; and Buffalo, West Buffalo, Lewis, and Limestone Townships in the 1990s. For example, when the red iron bridge in Lewis Township was replaced by a modern two-lane cement bridge in 1976, there was easier access to land contiguous to Penns Creek. This area of Lewis Township has witnessed growth in both new home construction and the conversion of summer and vacation cottages to year-round residences, causing the U.S. Postal Service to add a second rural route to the Millmont office. Some of these new residents are relocating from Centre County.

16 A group that is still Germanic has come to Union County: plain sect people — primarily "team Mennonites" from Lancaster County. Moving to Union County in significant numbers since in the late 1960s, they have helped to preserve rural farming traditions.

17 Federal population figures as presented by the Penn State Data Center's *Union County Data Book*, 1999, 14.

18 According to a survey made by the Harrisburg Diocese of the Roman Catholic Church.

19 Most of the Mennonites send their children to their own schools, and the more conservative members never send their children to local high schools.

20 U.S. Bureau of Commerce.

21 Information supplied by Bill Deitrick on October 21, 1999.

22 Giants in Jonathan Swift's *Gulliver's Travels*.

23 Statewide, Pennsylvanians have lost over a million acres of crop- and pasture-land from 1982 through 1992. From 1960 to 1990, Pennsylvania's ten largest metropolitan areas grew by only 13% while the land consumed for housing increased by 80%. From the *Report of the Pennsylvania 21st Century Environment Commission*, 1998.

24 Both groups have been in the forefront of local environmental education: the Audubon Society with programs and slide shows for the local schools, and the Sierra Club chapter with hikes and bicycle tours for its members and the general public.

25 *Environmental Protection Update*, Harrisburg, PA: DEP, 6:6, 31-32.

26 In 1982 a town/gown committee was formed in Lewisburg by Jeannette Lasansky, Owen Mahon, and others with the

cooperation of Dennis O'Brien, president of Bucknell. Goals of the group were to provide a forum for Bucknell and the residential/business communities and to anticipate areas of cooperation and compromise. Jacquie Stiefel continued this effort after 1989.

27 Some houses were as large as 4,000 square feet in areas like Gilead Heights in Union Township.

28 A more complete history of the authority was written in 2000 by director Jere Engle (1980-present); it is available at his office and in the reference area of the Union County Historical Society.

29 *Portrait of a Town* in April 1985 focused on Lewisburg, and *Decorated Furniture of the Mahantango Valley* featured the decorative arts of that area in lower Northumberland County, which is known for its regional furniture decoration. Two major exhibitions of central Pennsylvania quilts were held in 1985 and 1987 along with three-day symposia with nationally known speakers and attendees from across the nation.

30 At that time the prison was known as a "hell on earth," for within a relatively short time there were seven homicides.

31 The 911 Center was financially supported by the public safety telephone surcharge and paid for in five years (1993-1998).

32 1995 statistics.

33 Each year a classic movie is shown for a special one-evening event, complete with light refreshments, in support of an area nonprofit organization. In the 1990s Jacquie Stiefel began bringing first-run movies to the Campus Theatre. She also often had double features. There are no other movie theatres in the county.

34 These performance- and visually-rich events started in the early 1980s and are typical of the creative energies of the 1980s. Actor and recent arrival Joel Gori organized the creative force of others as well as himself every Wednesday evening during a six-week period of the summer. Originally held on the grounds of the Himmelreich Library on Market Street, Lewisburg, "Summer Stacks" after a couple years had outgrown the library site and moved a block east to the

park along the Susquehanna. At that point its name was changed to "River Celebration." Poetry, music, theater — much of it original — was supported by a large audience which passed the hat to cover the costs of the performances.

35 The 1990 census count was 899.

36 Information supplied by a piece written by Dan Baylor, former owner of the Country Cupboard, "In Recognition of Herbert R. Bendt," 1998.

Poster for Summer Stacks. Courtesy of Nancy Cleaver.

Community leaders Tom and Judy Mutchler decorate the Bicentennial Shop in Mifflinburg in 1976. From the collection of the Union County Historical Society.

GREAT ISSUES APPENDIX

by Charles M. Snyder

<u>1775-1800</u>

— Buffalo Valley's Role in the American Revolution
— The Local Response to Federalism
— Land: Who Got It and How?

<u>1800-1825</u>

— An Agricultural or Commercial Society?
— Personal Liberties and the Whiskey Tax
— Northumberland County Divided and Union County Formed

<u>1825-1850</u>

— Presidential Power vs. Congressional Leadership
— The Antimasonic Movement
— The Transportation Issue: Roads and Canals
— The Public School Issue

<u>1850-1875</u>

— Sectionalism vs. Nationalism: Response to the Civil War
— Free-Soil or the Extension of Slavery
— The Impact of the Railroads
— One County or Two? Readjustments to the Division of Union County into Snyder and Union Counties

<u>1875-1900</u>

— Free Enterprise vs. Regulation
— Bossism and the Local Response
— Agricultural Readjustments

<u>1900-1925</u>

— Nationalism vs. Internationalism
— World War I
— Adjustments to the Twentieth Century

<u>1925-1950</u>

— Depression and the New Deal
— World War II
— Economic Adjustments to Urbanization and Business
— Consolidation Efforts

<u>1950-1975</u>

— Rural Union County vs. Industrial Sprawl
— Big Government
— Local Governmental Institutions and a Planned Society
— National Outreach and Appeal
— Caring for the Environment and Thinking Ahead: Sustainable Communities
— Responding to Natural Disasters

<u>1975-2000</u>

— Bicentennial Celebrations/Preservation Efforts
— Demographic Changes and Responses - Social Services Growth
— Waste Issues: Recycling, Adaptive Use, Landfills, Waste Burner
— Transportation Artery - Routes I-80, 15, I-180, 45

GOVERNMENT APPENDIX

THE FORMATION OF UNION COUNTY TOWNSHIPS & BOROUGHS

1772 Buffalo	1824 Kelly	1823 Lewisburg
1776 White Deer	1836 East Buffalo	1827 Mifflinburg
1792 West Buffalo	1850 Limestone	1837 New Berlin
1811 Hartley	1857 Lewis	1858 Hartleton
1815 Union	1865 Gregg	

UNION COUNTY PRESIDENT JUDGES

1813-33—Seth Chapman; 1833-42—Ellis Lewis; 1842-61—Abraham S. Wilson; 1862-72—Samuel S. Woods; 1872-92—Joseph C. Bucher; 1892-1912—Harold M. McClure; 1912-22—Albert W. Johnson; 1922-32—Miles I. Potter; 1932-41—Curtis C. Lesher; 1941-42—Cloyd Steininger; 1942-52—A. Francis Gilbert; 1952-62—William L. Showers; 1962—Paul M. Showalter; 1962-74—Charles W. Kalp; 1974-84—A. Thomas Wilson; 1984-90—James F. McClure, Jr.; 1990-97—*Wayne A. Bromfield (J: 1986-90); 1997—*Harold F. Woelfel, Jr. (J: 1990-97); *Louise O. Knight (J: 1998-).

*In 1986, it became necessary to have two judges serve Union and Snyder Counties. New appointees are designated as Judges, while the senior judge is identified as the President Judge. Terms as Judge, prior to becoming President Judge, are shown above in parentheses.

UNION COUNTY ASSOCIATE JUDGES

1813-15—Hugh Wilson; 1815-20—John Bolender; 1820-40—Adam Light; 1840-41—George Schnabel; 1841-43—John Baskin; 1843-45—Joseph Stillwell; 1845-48—John Montelius; 1848-50—Jacob Wittenmyer; 1850-51—James Harrison; 1851—James Marshall; 1851-55—Jacob Wittenmyer; 1855-56—Philip Ruhl; 1856-60—John W. Simonton; 1860-61—John Walls; 1861-65—John W. Simonton; 1865-66—Martin Dreisbach; 1866-70—John W. Simonton; 1870-71—Jacob Hummel; 1871-75—Cyrus Hoffa; 1875-76—Jacob Hummel; 1876-80—William F. Wilson; 1880-81—George M. Royer; 1881-83—James Lepley; 1883-85—George M. Royer and James Lepley; 1886-90—Morris W. Cramer and Calvin M. Hayes; 1891-95—Jackson Gellinger and John W. Kauffman; 1896-1900—Daniel R. Harbeson and Samuel Keiser; 1901-05—William H. Blind and Henry Ernst; 1906-1911—George M. Englehart and W. W. Brown; 1912-18—A. K. Dieffenderfer and Gottlieb Rowe; 1918-21—Thomas M. Shively; 1918-24—A. K. Dieffenderfer; 1921-24—Ammon E. Reedy; 1924-30—David R. Pursley and Henry J. Yocum; 1930-36—Robert J. Smith and John T. Silverwood; 1936-42—Rev. William H. Clipman and Howard Leiser; 1942-48—Melvin R. Good; 1942-45—W. Clifford Reamer; 1945-47—Grant Myerly; 1948-50—John A. Arner and Harrison M. Hanselman; 1956-62—Fred C. Grenoble and George Grove; 1962-68—Fred C. Grenoble and John R. Middlesworth; 1968-69—Fred C. Grenoble; 1968-74—John R. Middlesworth.

The position of Associate Judge was abolished by state constitutional amendment adopted 8/23/68 and effective 1/1/69 when the Unified Judicial System was established. The act allowed existing officeholders to continue, thus John R. Middlesworth held the title until 1974.

MEMBERS OF THE STATE SENATE OF PENNSYLVANIA
REPRESENTING UNION COUNTY

1827-30—John Ray; 1835-39—Isaac Slenker; 1839-43—Robert P. Maclay; 1851-55—Eli Slifer; 1865-67—John Walls; 1871-77—Andrew H. Dill; 1878-88—S.P. Wolverton; 1889-92—Samuel D. Bates; 1893-96—William H. Hackenberg; 1897-1900—Edwin M. Hummel; 1901-04—Benjamin K. Focht; 1905-08—Frederic A. Godcharles; 1909-12—William C. McConnell; 1913-14—John T. Fisher; 1915-21—William C. McConnell; 1922-27—Charles Steele; 1928-31—Benjamin Apple; 1932-35—Charles E. Miller; 1936-44—George A. Dietrick; 1945-46—William I. Troutman; 1947-63—Samuel B. Wolfe; 1963-72—Preston B. Davis; 1973-80—Franklin Kury.

In 1982 Union County, which had previously been wholly in the 27th senatorial district, was split, with Gregg, Kelly, and White Deer Townships being placed in the 23rd senatorial district. Buffalo Township was later also added to the 23rd in the 1992 reapportionment.

Since 1981 the 27th was represented by Edward W. Helfrick, while Union County has been served by two senators in the 23rd: 1981-84—Henry G. Hager, and since 1984—Roger A. Madigan.

MEMBERS OF THE HOUSE OF REPRESENTATIVES OF PENNSYLVANIA REPRESENTING UNION COUNTY

1816-17—Jacob Brobst; 1817-18—Joseph Stillwell; 1818-19—John Ray; 1820-21—Daniel Caldwell; 1823-27—James Madden; 1829-32—Philip Ruhl; 1832-33—William L. Harris; 1833-34—Simon Shaffer; 1835-36—Robert P. Maclay; 1836-37—Henry Yearick; 1837-38—John Montelius; 1839-43—John A. VanValzah; 1849-50—Samuel Weirick; 1850-51—Eli Slifer; 1852-53—John W. Simonton; 1857-61—Thomas Hayes; 1863-64—Samuel H. Orwig; 1866-68—Charles D. Roush; 1869-70—Andrew H. Dill; 1870-71—William Young; 1872-76, 1878-82—Charles S. Wolfe; 1876-77, 1887-89—Alfred L. Hayes; 1881-82—S.H. Himmelreich; 1883-84—Albert Schooley; 1885-87—Horace P. Glover; 1890-91—James R. Ritter; 1892-98—Benjamin K. Focht; 1898-99—Francis E. Brown; 1900-02—Albert A Johnson; 1902-06—Dr. G. C. Mohn; 1906-08, 1910-12—Frank L. Dersham, 1908-10—J. Gundy Wolfe; 1912-20—Harry M. Showalter; 1920-22—Samuel B. Wolfe; 1922-24—John M. Gundy; 1924-26—James F. McClure; 1926-38—Francis T. Baker 1938-54—Charles R. Reagan; 1954-62—Louis A. Pursley; 1962-66—Karl A. Purnell; 1967-68—Harvey Murray, Jr.; 1969-80—Reno H. Thomas; 1981-88—John R. Showers; 1989—Russell H. Fairchild.

UNION COUNTY PROTHONOTARIES

1813-21—Simon Snyder, Jr.; 1821-24—Joseph Stillwell; 1824-30—Geoge A. Snyder; 1830-36—Joseph Stillwell; 1836-39—Robert P. Maclay; 1839—Samuel Roush 1839-40—Jacob H. Horning; 1840-41—John P. Gutelius; 1841-47—William Roshong; 1847-50—Jacob Haus; 1850-53—Joseph Eyster; 1853-62—Samuel Roush; 1862-65—James W. Sands; 1865-81—Willard O. Shaffer; 1881-85—C.H. Hassenplug; 1885-87—Willard O. Shaffer; 1888-89—D.U. Arird; 1889-1904—Willard O. Shaffer; 1904-11—T.E. Halfpenny; 1911-13—Ned F. Church; 1913-28—C. Dale Wolfe; 1928-55—Elwood M. Fetter; 1956-58—Mark C. Blank; 1958-81—Robert O. Brouse; 1981-87—Bertha W. Boyer; 1988—Dianne Lynch.

UNION COUNTY DISTRICT ATTORNEYS

1850-53—George Hill; 1853-56—William Van Gezer; 1856-59—James R. Hamlin; 1859-62—Joseph C. Bucher; 1862-76—Alfred Hayes; 1876-79—Andrew A. Leiser; 1879-82—D.H. Getz; 1882-91 John F. Duncan; 1892-95—D.H. Getz; 1895-1907—David L. Glover; 1908-09—James M. McKee; 1909-15—Cloyd N. Steininger; 1915-30—Curtis C. Lesher; 1930-51—William L. Showers; 1951-59—Paul M. Showalter; 1959-63—W. Roger Fetter; 1963-74—A. Thomas Wilson; 1974-75—James F. McClure, Jr.; 1975-95—Graham Showalter; 1996—D. Peter Johnson.

UNION COUNTY REGISTERS AND RECORDERS

1813-21—Simon Snyder, Jr.; 1821-24—Peter Hackenberg; 1824-30—John Maclay; 1830-36—Samuel Roush; 1836-39—George Aurand; 1839—Robert Forster; 1839-42—John Glover; 1842-45—Samuel Aurand; 1845—Henry Aurand, Jr.; 1845-51—Daniel Bellman; 1851-54—J.W. Pennington; 1854-57—George Merrill; 1863-69—Elisha K. Weikel; 1869-85—Reuben Kline; 1885-93—H.E. Gutelius; 1893-1902—William Shields; 1902-05—John F. Schrack; 1905-08—William E. Housel; 1908-15—Francis T. Baker; 1915-21—Ambrose B. Wagner; 1921-47—Warren S. Reed; 1947-75—J. Millard Wagner; 1976-79—Bessie K. Henry; 1980-95—Dorothy E. Dersham; 1996—Lorraine M. Lenhart.

UNION COUNTY SHERIFFS

1813-16—John Ray; 1816-19—Frederick Wise; 1816-19—Isaac Mertz; 1819-22—Jacob Rhoads; 1822-25—Philip Seebold; 1825-28—John Haas; 1828-31—John Cummings; 1831-34—John Cummings, Jr.; 1834-37—William Glover; 1837-40—Israel Gutelius; 1843-46—John M. Benfer; 1846-49—Henry S. Boyer; 1849-52—Archibald Thomas; 1852-55—John Kessler; 1855-61—Daniel D. Guldin; 1861-64—Lafayette Albright; 1864-67—Thomas Church; 1867-70—Lafayette Albright; 1870-73—Michael Kleckner; 1873-76—Lafayette Albright; 1876-79—Thomas P. Wagner; 1879-82—S.H. Himmelreich; 1882-86—C.A. Eaton; 1886-87—Peter W. Brown; 1888—R.A. Love; 1889-92—John Klingler; 1892-95—William B. Brown; 1895-97—David Gross; 1897-1900—Samuel H. Wagner; 1900-03—William W. Brown; 1903-06—Elmer E. Schoch; 1906-09—Harold W. Dieffenderfer; 1909-13—C. Furman Shaffer; 1913-17—John F. Hackenberg; 1917-21—Charles M. Renner; 1921-25—John F. Hackenberg; 1925-28—Harry S. Frock; 1928-29—Emily S. Frock; 1929-33—Lester M. Crabb; 1933-37—John F,. Hackenberg; 1937-41—Melvin R. Good; 1941-45—A. Paul Kline; 1945-61—John R. Middlesworth; 1961-77—William F. Haas; 1978-1997—Donald Everitt; 1998—John P. Schrawder.

UNION COUNTY COUNTY COMMISSIONERS

1814—Daniel Caldwell, Frederick Gutelius, Philip Moore; 1815—James Dale; 1816—John Bower; 1817—Henry Roush; 1818—Mishael Lincoln; 1819—Jacob German; 1820—William Kessler; 1821—Sebastian Witmer; 1822—Joseph Fuehrer; 1823—Christian Miller; 1824—Uriah Silby; 1825—George Weirick; 1826—Samuel Aurand; 1827—John Montelius; 1828—Thomas Youngman; 1829—John Ziegler; 1830—William Betz; 1831—Peter Hackenberg; 1832—Philip Frank 1833—J.F. Wilson; 1834—John Keller; 1835—James Harrison; 1836—Samuel Barber; 1837—John Snyder; 1838— Archibald Thomas; 1839—Jacob Hummel; 1840—Henry Hilbish; 1841—Samuel Boop; 1842—Jacob McCorley; 1843— Solomon Engle; 1844—Michael Clemens; 1845—H. Saunders, Jr.; 1846—Jacob Martin; 1847—R.H. Laird; 1848—Joseph Winters; 1849—James Barbin; 1850—John Wilt; 1851—George Heimbach; 1852—S.K. Herrold; 1853—Adam Sheckler; 1854—Samuel Leitzel; 1855—John D. Romig; 1856—R.V.B. Lincoln, Jacob Hummel, George Schoch; 1857—William Ruhl; 1858—R.V.B. Lincoln; 1859—James Pross; 1860—D.II. Kelly; 1861—F. Bolender; 1862—J.M. Walters; 1863—Robert Reed; 1864—Samuel Marshall; 1865—Michael Kleckner; 1866—Michael Brown; 1867—T.V. Harbeson; 1868—S.B. Hoffman; 1869—E.S. Gudykunst; 1870—T.V. Harbeson; 1871—S.B. Hoffman; 1872—William Steans; 1873—J.W. Kauffman; 1874—Joseph Boop; 1875—George Schoch; 1876-79—Joseph Boop, George Schoch, John Yarger; 1879-82— Joseph Boop, George Schoch, John Yarger; 1882-85—Joseph Musser, Samuel Marshal, J. Machamer; 18885-88—Jacob Spigelmeyer, Robert Brown, Thomas Reber; 1888-91—Charles Hendricks, Robert Brown, Michael Slear; 1891-94— Augustus A. Gemberling, Henry Ruhl, Frank L. Magee; 1894-97—Henry R. Hartman, Augustus A. Gemberling, S. Oliver Harbeson; 1897-1900—Augustus A. Gemberling, S. Oliver Harbeson, James Pursley; 1900-03—Augustus A. Gemberling, S. Oliver Harbeson, J.K. Berkheimer; 1903-06—S. Everitt Benner, William D. Williams, Amos Fauver; 1906- 09—S. Everitt Benner, John H. Hildebrand, George W. Walls; 1909-12—Joseph Spotts, Harry Walter, John Wingert; 1912- 16—James B. Chambers, Henry Ernst, David R. Pursley; 1916-20—J. William Ruhl, Henry A. Danowsky, B.O. Brown; 1920-24—J.William Ruhl, J Edward Hubler, W.H. Groover; 1924-27—George L. Schell; 1924-28—Frank D. Reigle, Thomas E. Spangler; 1927-28—Blaine O. Catherman; 1928-31—Harry W. Klose; 1928-32—Calvin F. Blouch, Samuel B. Miller; 1931-32—Harry Jamison; 1932-36—Archie R. Walter, W. Herman Sauers, Charles Zellers; 1936-40—Clyde G. Smith, Archie R. Walter, George W. Baker; 1940-44—Thomas Voneida, Millard G. Reedy, Andrew J. Kelly; 1944-46— Thomas Voneida; 1944-48—George H. Wagner, Andrew J. Kelly; 1946-48—Miles S. Wetezel; 1948-52—George H. Wagner, Miles S. Wetzel, George R. Hickernell; 1952-56—Eugene L. Boop, Miles S. Wetzel; 1952-55—George R. Hickernell; 1955-56—Frank Stoudt; 1956-60—Thelma J. Showalter, Anthony F. Flavio, David L. Martin; 1960-64— Thelma J. Showalter, Anthony F. Flavio, Franklin Benfer; 1964-68—L. Dice Miller, T. Ralph Shively, Frank Benfer; 1972- 76—L. Dice Miller, William Showers, Dale Spangler; 1976-79—W. Sherman Doebler, Thelma J. Showalter, John R. Showers; 1980-83—W. Sherman Doebler, John R. Showers, John R. Reichley; 1984-87—W. Sherman Doebler, John R. Reichley, Robert W. Donehower; 1988-91—W. Sherman Doebler, Ruth W. Zimmerman, Harry A. VanSickle; 1992-99— Ruth W. Zimmerman, Harry A. VanSickle, W. Max Bossert; 2000—Robert O. Brouse, Harry A. VanSickle, W. Max Bossert.

UNION COUNTY TREASURERS

1814-1855—Michael Schoch; Joseph Stillwell; Thomas Shipton; Christopher Seebold; William Kessler; Samuel Wilson; Samuel Aurand; Jacob Mauck; Isaac Peters; John P. Seebold; Michael Kleckner; Philip Gross; Archibald Thomas; Charles Seebold; Daniel Horlacher; Henry Solomon; 1856-57—Robert H. Laird; 1858-59—H.P. Sheller; 1860-61—Robert H. Laird; 1863-63—John A. Mertz; 1864-65—William Jones; 1866-67—John Hayes; 1868-69—William Jones; 1870-71—William Hauck; 1872-73—John Hertz; 1874-75—James Pross; 1876-79—Benjamin F. Eaton; 1879-82—Thomas Church; 1882-85— Weidler Rohland; 1885-88—J.P. Brooks; 1888-91—James Lepley; 1891-94—James K. Reish; 1894-97—D.P. Higgins; 1897- 1900—Daniel R. Smith; 1900-03—H.A. Taylor; 1903-06—Howard W. Dieffenderfer; 1906-09—W.L. Mertz; 1909-12— Ammon J. Steese; 1912-16—Gideon T. Biehl; 1916-20—M.D. Grove; 1920-24—Wilbur F. Bennage; 1924-28—Harry W. Klose; 1928-32—Oscar I. Liddick; 1932-36—Howard Leiser; 1936-40—J. Earl Miller; 1940-44—John R. Middlesworth; 1944-48—Charles R. Smith; 1948-52—Eugene L. Boop; 1952-56—Eleanor M. Bingaman; 1956-60—Warren Dieffenderfer; 1960-64—Robert Voneida; 1964-68—Warren Dieffenderfer; 1968-73—Josephine Good; 1973—Miriam Oberdorf; 1974- 75—Loretta Cromley; 1976-80—Miriam Oberdorf; 1981-99—Jean Derr; 2000—Diana Weikel.

ARCHITECTURAL APPENDIX

by Ted Strosser

This appendix is a brief, chronological listing of major architectural trends which appear in Union County, with corresponding examples. Building materials and technologies are discussed within 50-year increments leading up to the year 2000. All 100 buildings selected are still standing and were chosen as representative of each style. The names, locations, and dates were taken from the *1978 Historic Preservation Plan for Union County*. The numbers shown in parentheses ( ) correspond to the numbers from the 1978 survey. Buildings with NR behind them are listed on the National Register of Historic Places. When two dates are given for a building the first date indicates initial construction and the second indicates major renovation or redesign. This appendix is meant to be a point of departure for future, detailed studies of the incredible quality of architecture present in Union County. The illustrations of buildings which accompany this appendix were drawn by Jeanette Campbell.

PRE-1750

The land which now encompasses Union County was largely unexplored, even by frontiersmen, until after 1750. Native American settlements were primarily along major water routes, with Penns Creek and the Susquehanna River being the major "highways." No structures survive from this period.

1750-1800

LOG CONSTRUCTION

The first types of structures built by frontier settlers were small log cabins. Typically one or one-and-one-half stories high, they would have been erected very quickly, with no windows or openings beyond the one or two access doors. Each floor consists of one room. A rudimentary fireplace may or may not be present. A second-generation log cabin would be more properly called a log house. Hewn logs, windows, and more permanent fireplace/chimneys are the main differentiating features. Often log houses are a full two stories and may include two rooms per floor. Only a few of these second-generation log houses remain. Most that do survive have been encapsulated by, or attached to, later enlargements or "improvements."

Examples:
1) 34 Brown Street, Lewisburg, 1772 (39)
2) Kelly Homestead, Colonel Kelly Road, Kelly Twp., 1775 (58)
3) Packwood House, 8 Market Street, Lewisburg, 1795, 1866 (127) NR
4) Camp Ioka, Hartley Twp., early 1800s (116)

STONE HOUSES

The earliest homes in the county which remain largely unaltered are the stone houses. Built both in the towns and as farmsteads, a few very good examples survive. These houses are typically two-story structures with one of three plan types. The most simple are very small and have one room up and one down. They are essentially identical to the log houses, but built of more substantial materials. The side hall type typically has a long hall with two rooms to one side on each floor. The most elaborate and formal early stone houses feature a center hall with two rooms to each side of the main hall. The façade has five window "bays," and the front door is centered with some ornamental treatment.

Examples:
5) Lewis/Eberhart House, Quarry Road, Limestone Twp., 1760-80 (147)
6) Barber/Mensch/Purnell/Rippon House, Red Ridge Road, Limestone Twp., 1763-80 (143)
7) Peter Smith House, Leiser Road, White Deer Twp., 1772 (13)
8) Lee House, Route 304, Winfield, 1782 (197)
9) 137 S. Water Street, Lewisburg, 1786 (6)
10) Dale/Engle/Walker House, Strawbridge Road, Buffalo Twp., 1793 (63)

BRICK CONSTRUCTION

These have much the same types of floor plan as the stone houses discussed above. The brick would typically have been locally fired and the mortar made of local sand and burned lime. Since the brick was soft, painting and stucco were early treatments to protect and extend longevity.

Examples:
11) Gundy Homestead, Gundy Lane, East Buffalo Twp., 1775 (189)
12) 124 St. George Street, Lewisburg, 1788 (24)
13) 138 S. Front Street, Lewisburg, 1795 (14)

PLANK CONSTRUCTION

An early example of a not-so-common type of construction exists in Union County. Plank houses are typically two stories with planks placed vertically for the full two stories. They act as structure and sheathing all in one. Horizontal siding was often placed on the exterior to protect the planks from the weather.

Example:
14) Sierer/Heiser/Reigle House, Route 192 and Beaver Run Road, Buffalo Twp., 1770 (93)

(10)

(9)

(15)

MILLS

Two early mills survive from the eighteenth century in Union County. They show two different building techniques, one of timber frame and the other of masonry bearing walls.

Examples:

15) Groves Mill, Hoffa Mill Road, Kelly Twp., 1788 (61) brick

16) Mazeppa Mill, Johnson Mill Road, Buffalo Twp., 1789 (60) frame

1800-1850

LOG CONSTRUCTION

Log houses continued to be built throughout the early nineteenth century. Most are two stories and sheathed in wood siding on the exterior, with lath and plaster on the interior.

Example:

17) 432 Green Street, Mifflinburg, 1806 (102)

PLANK CONSTRUCTION

This type of construction was rarely used but continued through the early nineteenth century.

Example:

18) Killian House, White Deer, 1845-55 (272)

STONE CONSTRUCTION

Stone houses continued to be built in simple vernacular types, as well as with more formal designs.

Examples:

19) Spangler/Musser/Noll House, Violet Road, Limestone Twp., 1802 (283)

20) Barber/Wiand House, Red Ridge Road, Lewis Twp., 1811 (295)

21) 427-429 Market Street, New Berlin, 1817 (10)

BRICK CONSTRUCTION

The use of brick increased steadily throughout the nineteenth century. The first brick structures were public, commercial, and institutional in nature. Residential use of brick began to dominate after 1850, when industrial development allowed it, and eventually bricks came to be the material of choice. Some good religious structures also show some precursors of the Greek Revival Style.

Examples:

22) New Berlin Presbyterian Church, 318 Vine Street, New Berlin, 1843 (3) NR

23) Buffalo Crossroads Church, Meeting House Lane, Buffalo Twp., 1846 (81) NR

FRAME CONSTRUCTION

Wood frame techniques were increasingly used in residential construction in the mid-nineteenth century. Early in the century, however, frame construction was used for outbuildings, barns and mills.

Examples:

24) Herbster's Mill (Farm), Hartley Twp., 1839 (106)

25) Kline Octagonal Barn, Route 304, Limestone Twp., 1850s (252)

FEDERAL PERIOD

More a period than a style, Federal architecture came to Union County with the construction of the first county courthouse in 1815. Typically employing brick construction, these structures are more refined than earlier brick sructures, with particular attention paid to proportions and symmetry. Popular with private, public, and institutional construction, this period coincides with the rapid growth and advance of technologies.

Examples:

26) First Union County Courthouse, Route 304, New Berlin, 1815 (19) NR

27) Danowsky/Wagner House, Leiser Road, White Deer, 1821 (11)

28) Hummel/Borden House, Turkey Run Road, Limestone Twp., 1825-41 (157)

29) 124 Market Street, Lewisburg, 1830 (119)

30) 401 Market Street, Mifflinburg, 1845 (31)

1850-1900

This period saw an explosion of architectural styles as the Federal period faded away, and more ornamental Victorian styles came into fashion. In the more rural areas, vernacular construction still maintained a strong presence that continues through today.

FEDERAL PERIOD

This period configuration continued to be used later in Union County than in more urbanized areas. Two of the last and largest examples were built as urban townhouses. The raised basements, large windows, and nice proportions are typical of the period.

Examples:

31) 43-45 S. Second Street, Lewisburg, 1857 (25)

32) 415-419 Chestnut Street, Mifflinburg, 1861 (19)

(23)

(22)

(30)

(26)

(31)

(33)

VERNACULAR PUBLIC BUILDINGS

The 1870s saw a major building campaign of local, one-room schools. Most of these structures are nearly identical; approximately 24 ft. x 28 ft., they are built of brick with three large windows on each long side. A door flanked by two windows typically denotes the entrance end. Many still stand, but most of those have been converted into homes. Only a few retain their original form inside as well as outside.

Example:
33) Ramsey School, White Deer Twp., 1870s (190)

More elaborate schoolhouses were also built in this period.

Example:
34) Mazeppa School, Buffalo Twp., 1895 (56)

VERNACULAR VICTORIAN

Many local houses built in the last half of the nineteenth century cannot be attributed to any true Victorian style. Many are simply of vernacular construction, with some limited Victorian brackets, trim, and porches. Also, many early Federal period and vernacular homes were "improved" with the addition of Victorian bays, porches, and trim.

Examples:
35) NW corner of Main and Penn Streets, Hartleton, 1868 (277)
36) 1131 Market Street, East Buffalo Twp., 1873 (182)
37) Quarry Road, Limestone Twp., 1880s (284)

Commercial buildings began to look less like residential buildings as storefronts expanded and signage became more important. Wood construction began to fade in the more urbanized town centers, and brick became the predominant material of choice. In more rural areas, county stores were still more residential in nature and typically of wood frame construction.

Examples:
38) Hotel Hyman, Route 304, Winfield, 1868 (201)
39) 415-419 Chestnut Street, Mifflinburg, 1883 (11)
40) 326 Chestnut Street, Mifflinburg, 1883 (13)
41) drug store, Main Street, Hartleton, 1890s (279)

GREEK REVIVAL

This style, which drew inspiration from ancient Greek temples, and featured triangular pediments and simple, bold Doric columns, was well suited for churches, schools, government buildings, and houses. Lewisburg in particular has a good range of this style.

Examples:
42) 201 South Seventh Street, Lewisburg, 1849 (71)
43) North Ward School, 116 North Second Street, Lewisburg, 1855 (116)
44) Union County Courthouse, South Second and St. Louis Streets, Lewisburg, 1856 (23)
45) First Presbyterian Church, 18 Market Street, Lewisburg, 1856 (125)
46) 113-115 North Fourth Street, Lewisburg, prior to 1865 (183-4)

GOTHIC REVIVAL

This style followed close on the heels of the Greek Revival. Often associated with churches, it was also popular for residential construction. It marks one of the first styles popularized through pattern books. Steep roof lines, pointed arched windows, and vertical elements for emphasis are the major indicators of this style.

Examples:
47)   Bucknell President's House, 103 University Avenue, Lewisburg, 1855 (60)
48, 49) Twin Churches, White Deer Church Road, Kelly Twp., 1877-79 (43-44)
50)   Ray's Church, Route 45 West, Lewis Twp., 1883 (139)
51)   Lincoln Chapel, Lincoln Chapel Road, Hartley Twp., 1891 (118)

ITALIANATE

One of the many romantic styles popular in the latter part of the nineteenth century, this style is characterized by vertical proportions, flat roofs, arched windows (often paired), and large brackets at the cornice line.
Examples:
52) Slifer House, River Road, Kelly Twp., 1858 (73) NR
53) Ranck House, New Columbia, 1885 (275)
54) Griffey/Fairchild House, Route 44, Gregg Twp., 1886 (253) NR

ITALIAN VILLA

Sharing many of the same components of the Italianate style above, the Villa style is often more formal with towers and/or cupolas.

Examples:
55) 333 Chestnut Street, Mifflinburg, 1857 (55)
56) 60 South Second Street, Lewisburg, 1858 (140)

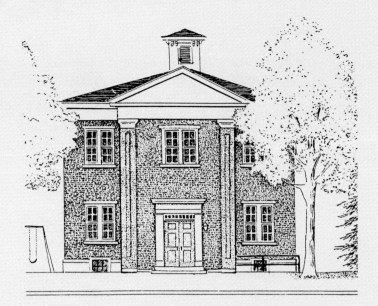

(43)

(46)

(52)

(57)

(59)

(69)

QUEEN ANNE

One of the most eclectic nineteenth-century styles, Queen Anne structures may often boast corner turrets; combinations of stone, brick, and terra cotta ornamentation; and wood siding and shakes. Bays, porches, and decorative patterns are also typical of the style.

Examples:

57) 201 Market Street, Lewisburg, 1880s-90s (26)

58) 40 South Second Street, Lewisburg, 1860 (136)

SHINGLE

This style is often associated with the grand mansions used as "summer homes," such as those in Newport, Rhode Island, and locally in Eagles Mere. The most obvious indicator of this style is the use of wood shingles on vertical wall surfaces, often with decorative inlays.

Examples:

59) 202 Market Street, Lewisburg, 1806-90 (113)

60) 108 North Second Street, Lewisburg, 1885 (117)

STICK

This style, also employed in summer homes, has western as well as eastern versions. Another popular use was in small railroad stations. The style employs smaller wood elements as brackets, exposed trusses, and trim elements.

Example:

61) White Deer Railroad Station, White Deer, 1871-73 (10)

ROMANESQUE REVIVAL

Sometimes more specifically referred to as Richardsonian Romanesque, this style typically employs rough stone with heavy round arches, dramatic roof lines, and projecting bays and porches.

Example:

62) 131 Market Street, Lewisburg, 1858 (140)

HIGH VICTORIAN GOTHIC

Polychrome brick or stone, marble columns (often with "incorrect" or squat proportions), and the use of multiple materials and forms exemplify this style. The style originated regionally with Philadelphia architect Frank Furness.

Examples:

63) Bucknell Hall, Loomis Street, Lewisburg, 1885

64) rear of Sovereign Bank, 16 South Third Street, Lewisburg, 1881 (28)

65) Beaver United Methodist Church, 40 South Third Street, Lewisburg, 1890 (30)

66) First Lutheran Church, 404 Market Street, Mifflinburg, 1898 (27)

SECOND EMPIRE

Another of the popular Victorian styles, this version is identified by the use of a mansard roof. Other typical elements include towers, paired windows, bays, and bracketed cornice lines.

Example:

67) 300 Market Street, New Berlin, 1846 (22)

BEAUX ARTS

This style is also sometimes referred to as Renaissance Revival. It employs classical forms in new compositions, and is often thought of as a continuation rather than a revival of the Renaissance. Pedimented temple fronts, three part compositions (base, middle, top) refer to the parts of a classical column (base, shaft, capital) and symmetrical compositions are common. This formal style expresses monumentality and is often used for banks, museums, theaters, schools, and governmental buildings.

Example:

68) 311 Market Street, Lewisburg, 1899 (50)

IRON FRONT COMMERCIAL

A building technology rather than an architectural style, this form employed iron in a new structural form which allowed large openings, principally along a street front. These structures were often loft buildings with ground floor commercial establishments and some type of light manufacturing on the upper floors.

Example:

69) 434 Market Street, Lewisburg, 1855 (64) NR

1900-1950

As the Victorian appeal for elaborate ornamentation began to fade, new technologies and building materials allowed for even more exploration of architectural styles. As with many trends and changes, most of the styles and technologies in building came later to Union County than to Philadelphia and more urbanized areas.

COLONIAL REVIVAL

Beginning at the end of the nineteenth century, and originally inspired by the nation's centennial, this style references much of the detailing used one hundred-plus years earlier. Overall building compositions rarely were truly "colonial" in nature. Dormers, columns, window and door surrounds and trim, and particularly interiors picked up on details from important landmarks such as Independence Hall and Mount Vernon.

Examples:

70) Rooke/Ross House, Route 304, Winfield, 1850, 1910 (198)

71) 600 Market Street, New Berlin, (13)

72) 18 Market Street, Mifflinburg, 1928 (25)

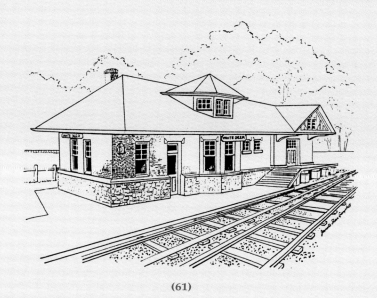

(61)

(76)

(73)

NEO-CLASSICAL

This style is an evolution of the Greek Revival since, many of the same elements are used, but at different scales and in combination with new elements. Many local examples are less detailed and use more contemporary technologies to deal with the increased size of the buildings. They do, however, use classical elements such as columns, base and cornice lines to the overall building, and proportions consistent with this style. The most detailed and well-proportioned example is the former Himmelreich Library. This building picks up on the neighboring Greek Revival Presbyterian Church and further develops details and elements in a more "Roman" style.

Examples:
73) 18 Market Street, Lewisburg, 1902 (124)
74) Laurelton Center, Route 45, Hartley Township 1917
75) Gamber House, RiverWoods, Kelly Twp., 1922 (72)
76) 301 Market Street, Lewisburg, 1932

ART DECO

New materials and technologies were used in new ways to "streamline" architecture. Glazed tiles, glass block, steel windows, aluminum, and neon lights combine to produce forms which often reflected the ideals of the building's inhabitants. This style was often associated with transportation, theaters, fast food restaurants, and skyscrapers. Union County is fortunate to have a very good example of this treasured style.

Example:
77) Campus Theater, 413 Market Street, Lewisburg, 1940 (144)

Less glamorous examples still contain many of the same basic elements.

Example:
78) Armory, Route 15 South, East Buffalo Twp., NR

REVIVALIST

Many of the Victorian styles were revived and/or continued through to the mid-1900s. Classical styles were still used for public buildings, Shingle style for mountain retreats, Queen Anne and others for streetcar suburbs, and Gothic and Romanesque for prisons.

Example:
79) Federal Penitentiary, Kelly Twp., 1932

BUNGALOW

More an arrangement of parts than a style, this form of construction was basically limited to residential buildings. Typically featuring a deep, full-width front porch with two large columns, this one-and-one-half story economical type of home fit well into the new suburban development that was economical for post-war, single-family homes. Many stylistic overtones could be applied such as Colonial Revival, Craftsmen, Shingle, etc.

Examples:
80) 202 St. Louis St., Lewisburg, 1905
81) 206 Market Street, Mifflinburg, 1914 (41)

AMERICAN FOURSQUARE

Like the Bungalow, the Foursquare is more an arrangement of parts than a style. Here, the two or two-and-one-half story home has a basically uniform layout. The proportions of width to height are basically square, as is the floor plan. Typically four rooms per floor also add to the "square" style. Like the Bungalow, different styles could be applied to this form. Many, however, were stripped-down versions with very little applied detail.

Examples:
82) 307 Chestnut Street, Mifflinburg, 1906 (18)
83) 203 Chestnut Street, Mifflinburg, 1909 (15)

COMMERCIAL

New technologies of steel frame construction and plate-glass curtain walls, and the increasing use of new materials such as reinforced concrete and aluminum transformed the look of the commercial districts in the early 1900s. Three- and four-story structures with large storefronts and flat roofs became more common. Masonry became the material of choice after several disastrous fires in larger cities.

Examples:
84) Laurelton High School, Laurelton, 1905 (110)
85) 224 St. Louis Street, Lewisburg, 1913 (145)
86) 343 Chestnut Street, Mifflinburg, 1914 (114)
87) 326 Market Street, Lewisburg, 1919

INTERNATIONAL STYLE

A lone example of this more "urbanized" style exists within Union County. This style emphasizes the machine age with horizontal long, clean, ribbon windows, and dynamically asymmetrical lines in a production, assembly-line approach to building.

Example:
88) 247 Stein Lane, Lewisburg, East Buffalo Twp., 1939 (184)

1950-2000

It is still too soon to tell what buildings built within the last 50 years will be looked at as important typical or atypical examples of architecture in Union County.

Many new manufactured building materials have been developed which imitate traditional materials with lower initial costs. Time will tell if vinyl siding, synthetic stucco, fiberglass shingles, and manufactured stone products will stand the test of time and one day be worthy of preservation. While still available, materials such as brick, wood siding, natural stone, and metal or slate roofing seem to be used in limited amounts or on rare upscale housing. It seems architecture is following society's desire for low-cost, quick-to-install, easy-to-maintain materials.

Rampant residential and commercial development threatens the rural agricultural landscapes which define much of Union County. One acre at a time, larger-scale developments such as Great Stream Commons and the proposed Mifflinburg by-pass further threaten to dilute the cultural landscape into faceless suburban sprawl. Much of this new direction in development patterns is the result of our automobile-oriented society.

Although it is still early to clearly categorize buildings of the recent past, several structures reflect trends and stylistic approaches of the past 50 years.

Examples:
89) Bertrand Library, quadrangle, Bucknell University, Lewisburg, 1951
90) 119 Market Street, lower facade, Lewisburg, 1952
91) Evangelical Community Hospital, Route 15 North, Lewisburg, 1953
92) Mifflinburg Bowling Lanes, Route 45, Mifflinburg, 1961
93) Langone Center, Bucknell University, Lewisburg, 1970
94) Mifflinburg Middle School, East Market Street, Mifflinburg, 1974
95) Computer Center, Bucknell University, Lewisburg , 1981
96) 545A Salem Church Rd., East Buffalo Twp., 1985
97) Weis Center for the Performing Arts, Bucknell University, Lewisburg , 1988
98) Lewisburg Medical Park, JPM Road, Kelly Township, c. 1988
99) Public Library for Union County, Reitz Boulevard, East Buffalo Township, 1989
100) JPM Corporate Headquarters, 155 North 15th Street, Lewisburg, 1997

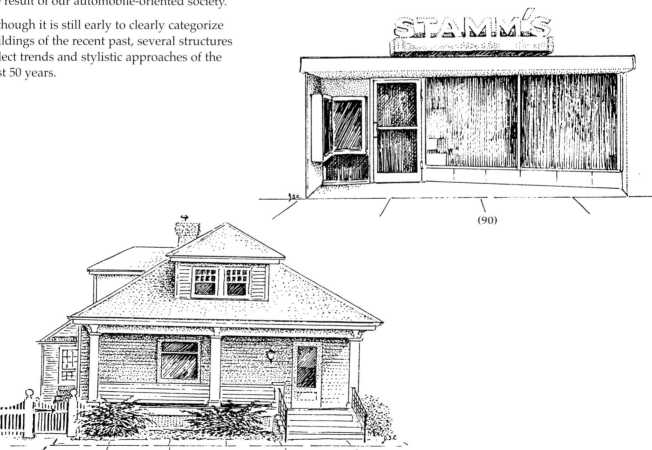

(90)

(81)

SELECT BIBLIOGRAPHY

BUCKNELL HISTORY:

Bucknell/Now and Then—A Sesquicentennial Miscellany. Lewisburg, PA: Bucknell University, 1996.

Oliphant, J. Orin. *The Rise of Bucknell University.* New York: Appleton-Century-Crofts, 1965.

Theiss, Lewis Edwin. *Centennial History of Bucknell University.* Williamsport, PA: Grit Publishing Co. Press, 1946.

CRAFT TRADITIONS:

Dunn, David. *Clocks of the Susquehanna Valley.* Lewisburg, PA: Packwood House Museum,1989.

Gray, Nada. *Holidays/Victorian Woman Celebrate in Pennsylvania.* Lewisburg, PA: Oral Traditions Project of Union County Historical Society, 1983.

Lasansky, Jeannette. *A Good Start/The Aussteier or Dowry.* Lewisburg, PA: Oral Traditions Project of Union County Historical Society, 1990.

_____. "Blacksmiths and Tinsmiths in Union County to 1880," *Heritage 1978.* Lewisburg, PA: Union County Historical Society, 1978.

_____. *In The Heart of Pennsylvania.* Lewisburg, PA: Oral Traditions Project of Union County Historical Society, 1985.

_____. *Redware Pottery of Central Pennsylvania.* Lewisburg, PA: Oral Traditions Project of Union County Historical Society, 1979.

_____. *To Cut, Piece and Solder.* Lewisburg, PA: Oral Traditions Project of Union County Historical Society, 1982.

_____. *To Draw, Upset and Weld.* Lewisburg, PA: Oral Traditions Project of Union County Historical Society, 1980.

_____. *Willow, Oak and Rye: Basket Traditions of Pennsylvania.* Lewisburg, PA: Oral Traditions Project of Union County Historical Society, 1978.

Musser, Marie Purnell. *Country Chairs of Pennsylvania.* Mifflinburg, PA: 1990.

Walker, Sandra Rambo. *Country Cloth to Coverlets.* Lewisburg, PA: Oral Traditions Project of Union County Historical Society, 1981.

GENERAL:

Beers, D.G. *Atlas of Union & Snyder Counties Pennsylvania.* Philadelphia: Pomeroy & Beers, 1868.

Blake, Jody and Jeannette Lasansky. *Rural Delivery/Real Photo Postcards from Central Pennsylvania 1905-1935.* Lewisburg, PA: Union County Historical Society, 1996.

Danowsky, Harold M. "Historical Tour of Union County," *Heritage 1978.* Union County Historical Society, Lewisburg, PA: 1978.

Finsterbush, Thomas. *A Guide to Union County Cemeteries.* Lewisburg, PA: Union County Historical Society, to be completed c. 2003.

Groover, Claire. *As It Used to Be.* Winfield, PA: 1976.

A Guide to Union County Churches. Lewisburg, PA: Union County Historical Society, c. 1990.

History of the Susquehanna and Juniata Valleys—Counties of Mifflin, Juniata, Perry, Union and Snyder, Vols. 1 & 2. Philadelphia: Everts, Peck & Richards, 1886.

Linn, John Blair. *Annals of Buffalo Valley, Pennsylvania, 1755-1855.* Harrisburg, PA: Lane S. Hart, 1877.

Lontz, Mary Belle. *History of the Schools of Union County.* Milton, PA: 1984.

_____. *Index to the Annals of Buffalo Valley.* Milton, PA: 1965.

_____. *Tombstone Inscriptions of Union County.* Milton, PA: 1967, 1992.

Zimmerman, Larry E. *Homeowners of 1868 in Union and Snyder Counties, Pennsylvania.* Chicago: Adams Press, 1989.

LEWISBURG:

Beckman, Robert E. *William Cameron Engine Company/100 Years of Service 1874-1974.* Lewisburg, PA: Wm. Cameron Engine Company, 1974.

Directory of Prominent Business Places in Lewisburg, PA and Calendar of 1880. 1880. Reprint, *Heritage 1980.* Union County Historical Society, Lewisburg, PA: 1980.

Hussey, John A. "New Light Upon Talbert H. Green [Paul Geddes of Lewisburg] as Revealed by His Own Letters and Other Sources," *California Historical Society Quarterly XVIII,* 1939, 32-63.

Kalp, Lois. *Town on the Susquehanna/1769-1975.* Lewisburg, PA: 1980.

Klingman, G. Howard. *Buffalo Valley Telephone Company 1904-1974.* Lewisburg, PA: Buffalo Valley Telephone Company, 1974.

Lasting Impressions/South Ward School, Lewisburg, Pennsylvania 1861-1995. Lewisburg, PA: South Ward School Parent Association, 1995.

Mauser, I.H. *Centennial History of Lewisburg.* 1886. Reprint, annotated by Charles McCool Snyder, John Zeller, Nada Gray, and Donald Baumgardner, *Heritage 1984-1986.* Union County Historical Society, Lewisburg, PA: 1986.

Nessel, Rev. William J., O.S.F.S. *Catholic Origins in Buffalo Valley and Chillisquaque Twp. of Central Pennsylvania.* De Sales Publishing, 1990.

One Hundred & Fifty Years of Church Life, 1833-1988. Lewisburg, PA: First Presbyterian Church of Lewisburg, 1983.

Sacred Heart Catholic Church, 50th Anniversary. Tappan, NY: Custombook, Inc., c. 1977.

Snyder, Charles McCool. *A History of Citizens' Electric Company, Lewisburg, Pennsylvania 1911-1986.* Lewisburg, PA: Citizens' Electric Company, 1986.

St. John's United Church of Christ, 150th Anniversary, 1824-1974. Lewisburg, PA: 1974.

West Branch Canal/How Lewisburg Became a Canal Port. Sunbury, PA: Northumberland County Historical Society, 1996.

MIFFLINBURG:

History of the First Lutheran Church 1798-1992. Mifflinburg, PA: Elias Bicentennial Historical Committee, 1991. Reprint, Charles M. Steese, 1931.

Lincoln, Richard Van Buskirk. *History of Mifflinburg.* 1900. Reprint, annotated by editor Joseph Foster, *Heritage 1992.* Union County Historical Society, Lewisburg, PA: 1992.

Snyder, Charles McCool. *Buggy Town. An Era in American Transportation.* Lewisburg, PA: Oral Traditions Project of Union County Historical Society, 1984.

_____. *Mifflinburg/A Bicentennial History.* Mifflinburg, PA: Mifflinburg Bicentennial Committee, 1992.

MILITARY:

Lontz, Mary Belle. *Revolutionary War Soldiers of Union County.* Lewisburg, PA: 1980.

Reagle, Kenn. "Theodore Sterner Christ: Civil War Surgeon from Union County," *Heritage 2000.* Lewisburg, PA: Union County Historical Society, 2000.

Sauers, Richard A. *Advance the Colors Vol. 1.* Harrisburg, PA: Capitol Preservation Committee, 1987.

_____. *Advance the Colors Vol. 2.* Harrisburg, PA: Capitol Preservation Committee, 1991.

OTHER:

Barsch, Vincent E. *New Berlin, PA 1792 - 1992, A Bicentennial History.* New Berlin, PA: New Berlin Heritage Association, 1992.

Baumgartner, Donald J. "Benjamin K. Focht, Defender of Rural Conservatism." *Heritage 1978.* Union County Historical Society, Lewisburg, PA: 1978.

Dershem, Arna. *The History of White Deer Township from Colonial Days to the Present.* New Columbia, PA: White Deer Twp. Bicentennial Commission, 1976.

Frey, S.G. "History of Cowan." *The Lewisburg Journal.* (1897).

Gray, Nada. "Translating the Spirit of '76 into Long Term Benefits," *Heritage 1978.* Union County Historical Society, Lewisburg, PA: 1978.

Johnson, Dorothy C. *The History of Mazeppa Union Church, 150th Anniversary, 1841 -1991.* Mazeppa, PA: 1991.

Lincoln, Richard Van Buskirk. *History of Union County: Townships of Hartley, Lewis and West Buffalo and the Borough of Hartleton. 1899-1900.* Reprint, *Heritage 1994.* Union County Historical Society, Lewisburg, PA: 1994.

_____. *History of Union County: New Berlin and the Townships of Limestone and Buffalo. 1899-1900.* Reprint, *Heritage 1996.* Union County Historical Society, Lewisburg, PA: 1996.

_____. *History of Union County: Kelly, White Deer, Gregg, East Buffalo and Union Twps. 1899-1900.* Reprint, *Heritage 1998.* Union County Historical Society, Lewisburg, PA:1998.

Lontz, Mary Belle. *Gregg Township and the Ordinance Land.* Milton, PA: 1997.

Nada Gray and Jeannette Lasansky, left and right, seated with examples of white oak splint baskets—one of the many area crafts studied by the Oral Traditions Project which Lasansky directed. The results of the project's work were reflected in sixteen books, two record albums, many multi-media shows, a 16mm movie, and hundreds of tape recordings produced starting in 1977. All this material is part of the collection of the Union County Historical Society. Photo by Marcia Milne. From the collection of the Union County Historical Society.

Old Buffalo Church, Presbyterian Church, Organized 1773. Mifflinburg, PA: 1773 Buffalo Church Association, 1998.

Scott, Louise Goehring. *Westfall: A Family History.* ms., c. 1996.

Snyder, Charles McCool. *200 Years of Witness and Service, Dreisbach's Ger. Reformed & Ev. Lutheran Church, 1788 -1988.* Mifflinburg, PA: 1988.

_____. "It Happened in Millmont," *Mifflinburg Telegraph* . (January 20 & 27, 1994).

_____. "New Beginnings in Swengel," *Mifflinburg Telegraph* . (March 24, 1994).

Vicksburg 125th Anniversary, 1865-1990. Vicksburg, PA: Vicksburg Anniversary Committee, 1990.

INDEX